IF FOUND, please notify and arrange return to owner. This text is an important study guide for the owner's career and/or exam preparation.

Name: _____

Address: _____

City, State, ZIP: _____

Telephone: (_____) _____ Email: _____

Gleim Publications, Inc., offers five university-level study systems:

Auditing & Systems Exam Questions and Explanations with Test Prep Software
Business Law/Legal Studies Exam Questions and Explanations with Test Prep Software
Federal Tax Exam Questions and Explanations with Test Prep Software
Financial Accounting Exam Questions and Explanations with Test Prep Software
Cost/Managerial Accounting Exam Questions and Explanations with Test Prep Software

The following is a list of Gleim examination review systems:

CIA Review: Part 1, The Internal Audit Activity's Role in Governance, Risk, and Control
CIA Review: Part 2, Conducting the Internal Audit Engagement
CIA Review: Part 3, Business Analysis and Information Technology
CIA Review: Part 4, Business Management Skills
CIA Review: A System for Success

CMA Review: Part 1, Financial Planning, Performance, and Control
CMA Review: Part 2, Financial Decision Making
CMA Review: A System for Success

CPA Review: Financial
CPA Review: Auditing
CPA Review: Business
CPA Review: Regulation
CPA Review: A System for Success

EA Review: Part 1, Individuals
EA Review: Part 2, Businesses
EA Review: Part 3, Representation, Practices, and Procedures
EA Review: A System for Success

An order form is provided at the back of this book or contact us at www.gleim.com or (800) 874-5346.

Groundwood Paper and Highlighters — All Gleim books are printed on high quality groundwood paper. We recommend you use a non-bleed-through (dry) highlighter (ask for it at your local office supply store) when highlighting items within these books.

REVIEWERS AND CONTRIBUTORS

Garrett W. Gleim, B.S., CPA (not in public practice), is a graduate of The Wharton School at the University of Pennsylvania. Mr. Gleim coordinated the production staff, reviewed the manuscript, and provided production assistance throughout the project.

Grady M. Irwin, J.D., is a graduate of the University of Florida College of Law and has taught in the University of Florida College of Business. Mr. Irwin provided substantial editorial assistance throughout the project.

John F. Rebstock, B.S.A., is a graduate of the Fisher School of Accounting at the University of Florida. He has passed the CIA and CPA exams. Mr. Rebstock reviewed portions of the manuscript.

Kristina M. Rivet, CPA, graduated *cum laude* from Florida International University. She has extensive public accounting experience in the areas of financial accounting, tax, and consulting. Ms. Rivet provided substantial editorial assistance throughout the project.

Stewart B. White, B.M., *cum laude*, University of Richmond, B.S., Virginia Commonwealth University, has passed the CPA, CIA, and CISA exams and has worked in the fields of retail management, financial audit, IT audit, COBOL programming, and data warehouse management. Mr. White provided substantial editorial assistance throughout the project.

A PERSONAL THANKS

This manual would not have been possible without the extraordinary effort and dedication of Jacob Brunny, Julie Cutlip, Kate Devine, Eileen Nickl, Teresa Soard, Joanne Strong, and Candace Van Doren, who typed the entire manuscript and all revisions, and drafted and laid out the diagrams and illustrations in this book.

The author also appreciates the production and editorial assistance of Katie Anderson, Ryan Cianciolo, Katie Larson, Cary Marcous, Jean Marzullo, Shane Rapp, Drew Sheppard, Katie Wassink, and Martha Willis.

The author also appreciates the critical reading assistance of Brett Babir, Ellen Buhl, Lauren Bull, Reed Daines, Lawrence Lipp, and Andrew Stargel.

Finally, we appreciate the encouragement, support, and tolerance of our families throughout this project.

SIXTEENTH EDITION

PART 3

BUSINESS ANALYSIS AND
INFORMATION TECHNOLOGY

by

Irvin N. Gleim, Ph.D., CPA, CIA, CMA, CFM

with the assistance of
Stewart B. White, CIA

ABOUT THE AUTHOR

Irvin N. Gleim is Professor Emeritus in the Fisher School of Accounting at the University of Florida and is a member of the American Accounting Association, Academy of Legal Studies in Business, American Institute of Certified Public Accountants, Association of Government Accountants, Florida Institute of Certified Public Accountants, The Institute of Internal Auditors, and the Institute of Management Accountants. He has had articles published in the *Journal of Accountancy, The Accounting Review,* and *The American Business Law Journal* and is author/coauthor of numerous accounting and aviation books and CPE courses.

Gleim Publications, Inc.
P.O. Box 12848
University Station
Gainesville, Florida 32604
(800) 87-GLEIM or (800) 874-5346
(352) 375-0772
Fax: (352) 375-6940
Internet: www.gleim.com
Email: admin@gleim.com

For updates to the first printing of the sixteenth edition
of *CIA Review: Part 3*

Go To: www.gleim.com/updates

Or: Scan code with your mobile device

Or: Email update@gleim.com with **CIA 3 16-1** in the subject line. You will receive our current update as a reply.

Updates are available until the next edition is published.

ISSN: 1547-8068

ISBN: 978-1-58194-020-6 *CIA Review: Part 1*
ISBN: 978-1-58194-021-3 *CIA Review: Part 2*
ISBN: 978-1-58194-022-0 *CIA Review: Part 3*
ISBN: 978-1-58194-023-7 *CIA Review: Part 4*
ISBN: 978-1-58194-041-1 *CIA Review: A System for Success*

ACKNOWLEDGMENTS FOR PART 3

The author is grateful for permission to reproduce the following materials copyrighted by The Institute of Internal Auditors: Certified Internal Auditor Examination Questions and Suggested Solutions (copyright © 1980 - 2008), excerpts from *The Practice of Modern Internal Auditing* (2nd ed.), excerpts from *Sawyer's Internal Auditing* (5th ed.), parts of the 2012 *Certification Candidate Handbook*, The IIA Code of Ethics, *International Standards for the Professional Practice of Internal Auditing*, Practice Advisories, and parts of Practice Guides.

This publication is designed to provide accurate and authoritative information with regard to the subject matter covered. It is sold with the understanding that the publisher is not engaged in rendering legal, accounting, or other professional service.

If legal advice or other expert assistance is required, the services of a competent professional person should be sought.

(From a declaration of principles jointly adopted by a Committee of the American Bar Association and a Committee of Publishers.)

TABLE OF CONTENTS

GLEIM® CIA Review System

PREFACE

The purpose of this book is to help **you** prepare to pass Part 3 of the CIA exam. Our overriding consideration is to provide an inexpensive, effective, and easy-to-use study program. This book

1. Explains how to optimize your grade by focusing on Part 3 of the CIA exam.

2. Defines the subject matter tested on Part 3 of the CIA exam.

3. Outlines all of the subject matter tested on Part 3 in 10 easy-to-use-and-complete study units, including all relevant authoritative pronouncements.

4. Presents multiple-choice questions from past CIA examinations to prepare you for questions in future CIA exams. Our answer explanations are presented to the immediate right of each question for your convenience. Use a piece of paper to cover our explanations as you study the questions.

5. Suggests exam-taking and question-answering techniques to help you maximize your exam score.

The outline format, the spacing, and the question-and-answer formats in this book are designed to facilitate readability, learning, understanding, and success on the CIA exam. Our most successful candidates use the Gleim CIA Review System*, which includes books, Test Prep Software Download, Audio Review, Gleim Online, FREE Practice Exams, and access to a Personal Counselor; or a group study CIA review program. (Check our website for live courses we recommend.) This review book and all Gleim *CIA Review* materials are compatible with other CIA review materials and courses that are based on The IIA's exam content outlines.

To maximize the efficiency and effectiveness of your CIA review program, augment your studying with *CIA Review: A System for Success*. This booklet has been carefully written and organized to provide important information to assist you in passing the CIA examination.

Thank you for your interest in our materials. We deeply appreciate the thousands of letters and suggestions we have received from CIA, CMA, CPA, and EA candidates and accounting students and faculty during the past 5 decades.

If you use Gleim materials, we want YOUR feedback immediately after the exam and as soon as you have received your grades. The CIA exam is NONDISCLOSED, and you must maintain the confidentiality and agree not to divulge the nature or content of any CIA question or answer under any circumstances. We ask only for information about our materials, i.e., the topics that need to be added, expanded, etc.

Please go to www.gleim.com/feedbackCIA3 to share your suggestions on how we can improve this edition.

Good Luck on the Exam,

Irvin N. Gleim

April 2012

PREPARING FOR AND TAKING THE CIA EXAM

Notice to CIA Candidates

In the fall of 2011, The IIA announced the following changes to the CIA exam, effective January 1, 2012:

1. The reduction of the amount of pretest questions for each part from 20 to 10 (which reduces the total amount of questions from 100 to 90)

2. The removal of the Pearson VUE tutorial from the beginning of the exam, and the subsequent availability of the tutorial on The IIA's website (www.globaliia.org/certification)

3. The reduction of total seat time for each part from 3 hours (2 hours and 45 minutes for 100 questions plus 15 minutes for tutorial and survey) to 2 hours and 30 minutes (2 hours and 25 minutes for 90 questions plus 5 minutes for survey)

NOTE: There is no change to the total number of scored questions per part (80), nor does the time allocable to each question change.

FOLLOW THESE STEPS TO PASS THE EXAM

1. Read this **Introduction** to familiarize yourself with the content and structure of Part 3 of the CIA exam. In the following pages, you will find

   a. An **overview of Part 3** and what it generally tests, including The IIA's abbreviated exam content outlines

   b. A detailed plan with **steps to obtain your CIA certification**, including

      1) The order in which you should apply, register, schedule your exam, and buy your study materials

      2) The studying tactics on which you should focus

      3) How to organize your study schedule to make the most out of each resource in the Gleim CIA Review System (i.e., books, Test Prep Software Download, Audio Review, Gleim Online, Diagnostic Quizzes, Practice Exams, etc.)

   c. Tactics for your **actual test day**, including

      1) Time budgeting, so you complete all questions with time to review

      2) Question-answering techniques to obtain every point you can

      3) An explanation of how to be in control of your CIA exam

2. Scan the Gleim *CIA Review: A System for Success* booklet and note where to revisit later in your studying process to obtain a deeper understanding of the CIA exam.

   a. *CIA Review: A System for Success* has six study units:

      Study Unit 1: The CIA Examination: An Overview and Preparation Introduction
      Study Unit 2: CIA Exam Content Outlines
      Study Unit 3: Content Preparation, Test Administration, and Performance Grading
      Study Unit 4: Multiple-Choice Questions
      Study Unit 5: Preparing to Pass the CIA Exam
      Study Unit 6: How to Take the CIA Exam

   b. If you feel that you need even more details on the test-taking experience, access Pearson VUE's **Testing Tutorial and Practice Exam** at www.vue.com/athena. You should also view The IIA's **CBT Exam Tutorial** at www.globaliia.org/certification. It is available in all languages in which the exam is offered.

      1) These tutorials are most useful to candidates who have little or no experience with computerized exams and have anxiety about performing well in unfamiliar circumstances.

3. BEFORE you begin studying, take a **Diagnostic Quiz** at www.gleim.com/ciadiagnosticquiz or use our **Gleim Diagnostic Quiz App** for iPhone, iPod Touch, and Android.

   a. The Diagnostic Quiz includes a representative sample of 40 multiple-choice questions and will determine your weakest areas in Part 3.

   b. When you are finished, one of our **Personal Counselors** will consult with you to better focus your review on any areas in which you have less confidence.

4. Follow the steps outlined on page 8, "How to Study a Study Unit Using the Gleim CIA Review System." This is the **study plan** that our most successful candidates adhere to. Study until you have reached your **desired proficiency level** (e.g., 75%) for each study unit in Part 3.

   a. As you proceed, be sure to check any **Updates** that may have been released.

      1) Gleim Online is updated automatically.

2) Test Prep Software is updated by the Online Library Updates system in the Tools menu of your Test Prep. You can (and should) set your Test Prep to automatically update at least once a month.

3) Book updates can be viewed at www.gleim.com/updates, or you can have them emailed to you. See the information box in the top right corner of page iv for details.

   b. **Review the *CIA Review: A System for Success* booklet** and become completely comfortable with what will be expected from you on test day.

5. Shortly before your test date, take a **Practice Exam** (FREE with the purchase of the complete Gleim CIA Review System!) at www.gleim.com/ciapracticeexam.

   a. This timed and scored exam emulates the actual CIA exam and tests you not only on the content you have studied, but also on the question-answering and time-management techniques you have learned throughout the Gleim study process.

   b. When you have completed the exam, study your results to discover where you should **focus your review during the final days before your exam**.

6. **Take and PASS** Part 3 of the CIA exam!

   a. When you have completed the exam, please contact Gleim with your **suggestions, comments, and corrections**. We want to know how well we prepared you for your testing experience.

INTRODUCTION TO CIA

CIA is the acronym for Certified Internal Auditor. The CIA designation is international, with the examination administered in numerous countries. The CIA exam has been administered by The Institute of Internal Auditors (The IIA) since 1974.

According to The IIA, the CIA is a "globally accepted certification for internal auditors" through which "individuals demonstrate their competency and professionalism in the internal auditing field." Successful candidates will have gained "educational experience, information, and business tools that can be applied immediately in any organization or business environment."

OVERVIEW OF THE CIA EXAMINATION

The total exam is 10 hours of testing (including 5 minutes per part for a survey). It is divided into four parts, as follows:

Part 1 – The Internal Audit Activity's Role in Governance, Risk, and Control
Part 2 – Conducting the Internal Audit Engagement
Part 3 – Business Analysis and Information Technology
Part 4 – Business Management Skills

Each part consists of 90 questions, and testing lasts 2 hours and 25 minutes plus 5 minutes for a survey. The exam is offered continually throughout the year.

The CIA exam is computerized to facilitate easier testing. Pearson VUE, the testing company that The IIA contracts to proctor the exams, has hundreds of testing centers worldwide. The Gleim Test Prep Software, Gleim Online, and Gleim CIA Practice Exams provide exact exam emulations of the Pearson VUE computer screens and procedures to prepare you to PASS.

SUBJECT MATTER FOR PART 3

Below, we have provided The IIA's abbreviated exam content outline for Part 3. The percentage coverage of each topic is indicated to its right. (Note that The IIA percentage coverage is given in ranges, e.g., 15-25%, as presented in Appendix A. Below, we present the midpoint of each range to simplify and provide more relevant information to CIA candidates, e.g., 20% instead of 15-25%. In other words, the percentages listed are plus or minus 5% of the percentage coverages you can expect to encounter during the actual exam.) We adjust the content of our materials to any changes in The IIA's content outlines.

Part 3: Business Analysis and Information Technology

A. Business Processes	20%
B. Financial Accounting and Finance	20%
C. Managerial Accounting	15%
D. Regulatory, Legal, and Economics	10%
E. Information Technology (IT)	35%

Appendix A contains the content outlines in their entirety as well as cross-references to the subunits in our text where topics are covered. Remember that we have studied and restudied the content outlines in developing our *CIA Review* materials. Accordingly, you do not need to spend time with Appendix A. Rather, it should give you confidence that Gleim *CIA Review* is the best review source available to help you PASS the CIA exam.

NONDISCLOSED EXAM

As part of The IIA's nondisclosure policy and to prove each candidate's willingness to adhere to this policy, a confidentiality and nondisclosure statement must be accepted by each candidate before each part is taken. This statement is reproduced here to remind all CIA candidates about The IIA's strict policy of nondisclosure, which Gleim consistently supports and upholds.

> *This exam is confidential and is protected by law. It is made available to you, the examinee, solely for the purpose of becoming certified. You are expressly prohibited from disclosing, publishing, reproducing, or transmitting this exam, in whole or in part, in any form or by any means, verbal or written, electronic or mechanical, for any purpose, without the prior written permission of The Institute of Internal Auditors (IIA).*
>
> *The IIA requires all exam candidates to read and accept the above Non-Disclosure Agreement and General Terms of Use for IIA exams prior to taking an IIA Exam.*
>
> *If you do not accept the exam non-disclosure agreement, your exam will be terminated. If this occurs, your registration will be voided, you will forfeit your exam registration fee, and you will be required to register and pay for that exam again in order to sit for it in the future.*

THE IIA'S REQUIREMENTS FOR CIA DESIGNATIONS

The CIA designation is granted only by The IIA. Candidates must complete the following steps to become a CIA:

1. Complete the appropriate certification application form online and register for the part(s) you are going to take. The *CIA Review: A System for Success* booklet contains concise instructions on the application and registration process and a useful worksheet to help you keep track of your process and organize what you need for exam day. Detailed instructions and screenshots for every step of the application and registration program can also be found at www.gleim.com/accounting/cia/steps.

2. Pass all four parts of the CIA exam or pass Parts 1, 2, and 3 and gain approval for Professional Recognition Credit for Part 4 (see *CIA Review: A System for Success*).

3. Fulfill or expect to fulfill the education and experience requirements (see *CIA Review: A System for Success*).

4. Provide a character reference proving you are of good moral character.

5. Comply with The IIA's Code of Ethics.

Credits can be retained as long as the requirements are fulfilled. Once a designation is earned, the CIA must comply with the program's CPE requirement (see "Maintaining Your CIA Designation" on page 6). Contact Gleim for all of your CPE needs.

CIA EXAM FEES

Fees	IIA Members	Nonmembers	Professors/ Full-Time Students
Exam Application (initial nonrefundable fee)	US $75	US $100	US $50
Exam Parts Registration (per part/per sitting)	US $150	US $200	US $105
Deferrals/Cancelations/Changes			
...at least 2 days prior to your appointment*	US $50	US $50	US $50

*If you have not made any necessary changes or cancelations at least 2 days prior to your appointment, you will forfeit your exam fee and must pay to register again.

SPECIAL PROFESSOR AND STUDENT EXAMINATION FEE

The exam application fee is the charge for enrolling candidates in the CIA program. The CIA examination is available to professors and full-time students at reduced fees. For them, the exam application fee is US $50 (instead of US $75), plus an exam registration fee of US $105 (instead of US $150) per part. Professors and students may sit for each part at this special rate one time only.

1. To be eligible for the reduced rate, a student must

    a. Be enrolled as a senior in an undergraduate program or as a graduate student

    b. Be a full-time student as defined by the institution in which the student is enrolled (a minimum of 12 semester hours or its equivalent for senior-level undergraduate students and 9 semester hours for graduate students)

    c. Register for and take the CIA exam while enrolled in school

2. To be eligible for the reduced rate, a professor must

    a. Work full-time or part-time as a professor with an accredited educational institution

    b. Provide a letter from the local IIA chapter verifying his/her eligibility for professor status for pricing

3. In addition to the above requirements, candidates must do the following:

    a. Submit a completed and signed Full-Time Student/Professor Status Form in CCMS or via fax

    b. Complete the CIA Application – Student/Professor Form in CCMS

    c. Provide a completed and signed Character Reference Form

    d. Pay the one-time US $50 exam application fee and then the US $105 exam registration fee for each part

MAINTAINING YOUR CIA DESIGNATION

After certification, CIAs are required to maintain and update their knowledge and skills. As of January 1, 2012, practicing CIAs must complete and report 40 hours of Continuing Professional Education (CPE) every year. The reporting deadline is December 31. See The IIA's website (www.globaliia.org/certification) or the 2012 *Certification Candidate Handbook* for information on how to report your CPE hours during the transition from pre-2012 reporting requirements. Complete your CPE Reporting Form through the online Certification Candidate Management System. Nonmembers must submit a US $100 processing fee with their report. Contact Gleim for all of your CPE needs.

ELIGIBILITY PERIOD

Candidates must complete the program certification process within 4 years of application approval. If a candidate has not completed the certification process within 4 years, all fees and exam parts will be forfeited.

STEPS TO BECOME A CIA

1. Become knowledgeable about the exam, and decide which part you will take first.

2. Purchase the Gleim CIA Review System (including books, Test Prep Software Download, Audio Review, Gleim Online, Practice Exams, and access to a Personal Counselor) to thoroughly prepare for the CIA exam. Commit to systematic preparation for the exam as described in our review materials, including *CIA Review: A System for Success*.

3. Communicate with your Personal Counselor to design a study plan that meets your needs. Call (800) 874-5346 or email CIA@gleim.com.

4. Apply for membership in The IIA (suggested but not required).

5. Register online to take the desired part of the exam. You will receive authorization to take the exam from The IIA and will then have 180 days to take that exam part.

6. Schedule your test with Pearson VUE (online or call center).

7. Work systematically through each study unit in the Gleim CIA Review System.

8. Sit for and PASS the CIA exam while you are in control, as described in Study Unit 6 of *CIA Review: A System for Success*. Gleim will make it easy.

9. Contact Gleim with your comments on our study materials and how well they prepared you for the exam.

10. Enjoy your career, pursue multiple certifications (CMA, CPA, EA, etc.), recommend Gleim to others who are also taking these exams, and stay up-to-date on your continuing professional education with Gleim CPE.

More specifically, you should focus on the following **system for success** on the CIA exam:

1. **Understand the exam, including its purpose, coverage, preparation, format, administration, grading, and pass rates.**

    a. The better you understand the examination process from beginning to end, the better you will perform.

    b. Study the Gleim *CIA Review: A System for Success*. Please be sure you have a copy of this useful booklet. (*CIA Review: A System for Success* is also available online at www.gleim.com/sfs.)

2. **Learn and understand the subject matter tested.** The IIA's exam content outlines for Part 3 are the basis for the study outlines that are presented in each of the 10 study units that make up this book.* You will also learn and understand the material tested on the CIA exam by answering numerous multiple-choice questions from previous CIA exams. Multiple-choice questions with the answer explanations to the immediate right of each question are a major component of each study unit.

3. **Practice answering past exam questions to perfect your question-answering techniques.** Answering past exam questions helps you understand the standards to which you will be held. This motivates you to learn and understand while studying (rather than reading) the outlines in each of the 10 study units.

    a. Question-answering techniques are suggested for multiple-choice questions in Study Unit 4 of *CIA Review: A System for Success*.

    b. Our **CIA Test Prep** Software contains thousands of additional multiple-choice questions that are not offered in our books. Additionally, CIA Test Prep Software has many useful features, including documentation of your performance and the ability to simulate the CIA exam environment.

    c. Our **CIA Gleim Online** is a powerful Internet-based program that allows CIA candidates to learn in an interactive environment and provides feedback to candidates to encourage learning. It includes multiple-choice questions in Pearson VUE's format. Each CIA Gleim Online candidate has access to a Personal Counselor, who helps organize study plans that work with busy schedules.

    d. Additionally, each candidate should view Pearson VUE's Testing Tutorial and Practice Exam at www.vue.com/athena and The IIA's CBT Exam Tutorial at www.globaliia.org/certification (where it is available in every language in which the CIA exam can be taken).

4. **Plan and practice exam execution.** Anticipate the exam environment and prepare yourself with a plan: When to arrive? How to dress? What exam supplies to bring? How many questions and what format? Order of answering questions? How much time to spend on each question? See Study Unit 6 in *CIA Review: A System for Success*.

    a. Expect the unexpected and adjust! Remember, your sole objective when taking an examination is to maximize your score. You must outperform your peers, and being as comfortable and relaxed as possible gives you an advantage!

5. **Be in control.** Develop confidence and ensure success with a controlled preparation program followed by confident execution during the examination.

PRELIMINARY TESTING: GLEIM CIA DIAGNOSTIC QUIZZES

The five Gleim CIA Diagnostic Quizzes provide a representative sample of 40 multiple-choice questions for each exam part to identify your preliminary strengths and any weaknesses before you start preparing in earnest for the CIA exam. They also provide you with the actual exam experience, i.e., what you will encounter when you take the CIA exam at Pearson VUE.

When you have completed each quiz, one of our Personal Counselors will consult with you to better focus your review on any areas in which you have less confidence. After your consultation, you will be able to access a Review Session, where you can study answer explanations for the correct and incorrect answer choices of the questions you answered incorrectly.

For smart phone users, there is also a Gleim Diagnostic Quiz App for iPhone, iPod Touch, and Android. See our website (www.gleim.com/ciadiagnosticquiz) for more information.

---

*Please fill out our online feedback form (www.gleim.com/feedbackCIA3) IMMEDIATELY after you take the CIA exam so we can adapt to changes in the exam. Our approach has been approved by The IIA.

HOW TO STUDY A STUDY UNIT USING THE GLEIM CIA REVIEW SYSTEM

To ensure that you are using your time effectively, we recommend that you follow the steps listed below when using all of the CIA Review System materials together (books, Test Prep Software Download, Audio Review, and Gleim Online):

1. (25 minutes, plus 10 minutes for review) In the CIA Gleim Online course, complete Multiple-Choice Quiz #1 in 25 minutes. It is expected that your scores will be lower on the first quiz in each study unit than on subsequent quizzes.

   a. Immediately following the quiz, you will be prompted to review the questions you flagged and/or answered incorrectly. For each question, analyze and understand why you were unsure or answered it incorrectly. This step is an essential learning activity.

2. (30 minutes) Use the online audiovisual presentation for an overview of the study unit. CIA Audio Review can be substituted for audiovisual presentations and can be used while driving to work, exercising, etc.

3. (45 minutes) Complete the 30-question True/False quiz. It is interactive and most effective if used prior to studying the Knowledge Transfer Outline.

4. (60 minutes) Study the Knowledge Transfer Outline, particularly the troublesome areas identified from the multiple-choice questions in the Gleim Online course. The Knowledge Transfer Outlines can be studied either online or from the books.

5. (25 minutes, plus 10 minutes for review) Complete Multiple-Choice Quiz #2 in the Gleim Online course.

   a. Immediately following the quiz, you will be prompted to review the questions you flagged and/or answered incorrectly. For each question, analyze and understand why you were unsure or answered it incorrectly. This step is an essential learning activity.

6. (50 minutes) Complete two 20-question quizzes while in Test Mode from the CIA Test Prep Software. Review as needed.

When following these steps, you will complete all 10 units in about 45 hours. Then spend about 5-10 hours using the CIA Test Prep Software to create customized tests for the problem areas you identified. When you are ready, create 20-question quizzes that draw questions from all 10 study units. Continue taking 20-question quizzes until you approach your desired proficiency level, e.g., 75%+.

The times mentioned above are recommendations based on prior candidate feedback and how long you will have to answer questions on the actual exam. Each candidate's time spent in any area will vary depending on proficiency and familiarity with the subject matter.

CIA GLEIM ONLINE

CIA Gleim Online is a versatile, interactive, self-study review program delivered via the Internet. It is divided into four courses (one for each part of the CIA exam) and emulates the CIA exam.

Each course is broken down into 10 individual, manageable study units. Completion time per study unit will be about 4 hours. Each study unit in the course contains an audiovisual presentation, 30 true/false study questions, a Knowledge Transfer Outline, and two 20-question multiple-choice quizzes.

CIA Gleim Online provides you with access to a Personal Counselor, a real person who will provide support to ensure your competitive edge. CIA Gleim Online is a great way to get confidence as you prepare with Gleim. This confidence will continue during and after the exam.

GLEIM BOOKS

This edition of the Gleim *CIA Review* books has the following features to make studying easier:

1. **Examples:** Illustrative examples, both hypothetical and those drawn from actual events, are set off in shaded, bordered boxes.

EXAMPLE

A manufacturer paid US $112,000 for a new machine that it estimates will produce 8,000 titanium rods before becoming obsolete. At the end of the 5-year useful life, the entity estimates that the machine can be sold for US $14,000.

Depreciable base = US $112,000 – $14,000 = US $98,000

---

2. **Gleim Success Tips:** These tips supplement the core exam material by suggesting how certain topics might be presented on the exam or how you should prepare for an issue.

Correct use of a forecasting method is worthless to an internal auditor if (s)he chooses the wrong method. Being able to determine when a method should be applied is crucial for CIA candidates.

---

3. **Memory Aids:** We offer mnemonic devices to help you remember important concepts.

Jane **P**ayne **U**pdated **A**n **A**nalysis of **F**ixed **C**osts, **P**roperty, and **R**evenues

CIA TEST PREP SOFTWARE

Twenty-question tests in the **CIA Test Prep** Software will help you focus on your weaker areas. Make it a game: How much can you improve?

Our CIA Test Prep (in test mode) forces you to commit to your answer choice before looking at answer explanations; thus, you are preparing under true exam conditions. It also keeps track of your time and performance history for each study unit, which is available in either a table or graphical format.

STUDYING WITH BOOKS AND SOFTWARE

Simplify the exam preparation process by following our suggested steps listed below. DO NOT omit the step in which you diagnose the reasons for answering questions incorrectly; i.e., learn from your mistakes while studying so you avoid making similar mistakes on the CIA exam.

1. In test mode, answer a 20-question diagnostic test before studying any other information.

2. Study the Knowledge Transfer Outline for the corresponding study unit in your Gleim book.

   a. Place special emphasis on the weaker areas that you identified with the initial diagnostic test in Step 1.

3. Take two or three 20-question tests in test mode after you have studied the Knowledge Transfer Outline.

4. Immediately following each test, you will be prompted to review the questions you flagged and/or answered incorrectly. For each question, analyze and understand why you answered it incorrectly. This step is an essential learning activity.

5. Continue this process until you approach a predetermined proficiency level, e.g., 75%+.

6. Modify this process to suit your individual learning process.

   a. Learning from questions you answer incorrectly is very important. Each question you answer incorrectly is an **opportunity** to avoid missing actual test questions on your CIA exam. Thus, you should carefully study the answer explanations provided to understand why you chose the incorrect answer so you can avoid similar errors on your exam. This study technique is clearly the difference between passing and failing for many CIA candidates.

   b. Also, you **must** determine why you answered questions incorrectly and learn how to avoid the same error in the future. Reasons for missing questions include

      1) Misreading the requirement (stem)
      2) Not understanding what is required
      3) Making a math error
      4) Applying the wrong rule or concept
      5) Being distracted by one or more of the answers
      6) Incorrectly eliminating answers from consideration
      7) Not having any knowledge of the topic tested
      8) Employing bad intuition when guessing

   c. It is also important to verify that you answered correctly for the right reasons (i.e., read the discussion provided for the correct answers). Otherwise, if the material is tested on the CIA exam in a different manner, you may not answer it correctly.

   d. It is imperative that you complete your predetermined number of study units per week so you can review your progress and realize how attainable a comprehensive CIA review program is when using the Gleim CIA Review System. Remember to meet or beat your schedule to give yourself confidence.

Avoid studying Gleim questions to learn the correct answers. Use Gleim questions to help you learn how to answer CIA questions under exam conditions. Expect the unexpected and be prepared to deal with it. Become an educated guesser when you encounter questions in doubt; you will outperform the inexperienced exam taker.

GLEIM AUDIO REVIEWS

Gleim **CIA Audio Reviews** provide an average of 30 minutes of quality review for each study unit. Each review provides an overview of the Knowledge Transfer Outline in the *CIA Review* book. The purpose is to get candidates "started" so they can relate to the questions they will answer before reading the study outlines in each study unit.

The audios get to the point, as does the entire Gleim System for Success. We are working to get you through the CIA exam with minimum time, cost, and frustration. You can listen to sample audio reviews on our website at www.gleim.com/accounting/demos.

FINAL REVIEW: GLEIM CIA PRACTICE EXAM

Take a CIA Practice Exam (FREE with your complete CIA Review System) shortly before you take the actual exam to gain experience in the computer-based exam environment. The Practice Exam is 2 hours and 25 minutes (145 minutes) long and contains 90 multiple-choice questions, just like the CIA exam. Therefore, it tests you not only on the content you have studied, but also on the question-answering and time-management techniques you have learned.

For the most realistic practice exam experience, we suggest you complete the entire exam in one sitting, just like the actual CIA exam. Once you have completed the Practice Exam and received your grade, you will be provided with a Review Session that shows which questions were answered incorrectly. Additionally, you will be able to study answer explanations to assist you in learning the topics.

TIME-BUDGETING AND QUESTION-ANSWERING TECHNIQUES FOR THE EXAM

The following suggestions are to assist you in maximizing your score on each part of the CIA exam. Remember, knowing how to take the exam and how to answer individual questions is as important as studying/reviewing the subject matter tested on the exam.

1. **Budget your time.**
    a. We make this point with emphasis. Just as you would fill up your gas tank prior to reaching empty, so too should you finish your exam before time expires.
    b. You have 145 minutes to answer 90 questions, i.e., 1.61 minutes per question. We suggest you attempt to answer eight questions every 10 minutes, which is 1.25 minutes per question. This would result in completing 90 questions in 112.5 minutes to give you just over 30 minutes to review questions that you have flagged.
    c. Use the wipeboard provided by Pearson VUE for your Gleim Time Management System at the exam. List the question numbers for every 15 questions (i.e., 1, 16, 31, etc.) in a column on the left side of the wipeboard. The right side of the wipeboard will have your start time at the top and will be used for you to fill in the time you have remaining at each question checkpoint. Stay consistent with 1.25 minutes per question.
2. **Answer the items in consecutive order.**
    a. Do **not** agonize over any one item. Stay within your time budget.
    b. Note any items you are unsure of by clicking the "Flag for Review" button in the upper-right corner of your screen, and return to them later if time allows. Plan on going back to all the questions you flagged.
    c. Never leave a question unanswered. Make your best guess in the time allowed. Your score is based on the number of correct responses out of the 80 total scored questions, and you will not be penalized for guessing incorrectly.

3. **For each multiple-choice question,**

    a. **Try to ignore the answer choices.** Do not allow the answer choices to affect your reading of the question.

        1) If four answer choices are presented, three of them are incorrect. These incorrect answers are called **distractors** for good reason. Often, distractors are written to appear correct at first glance until further analysis.

        2) In computational items, distractors are carefully calculated such that they are the result of making common mistakes. Be careful, and double-check your computations if time permits.

    b. **Read the question carefully** to determine the precise requirement.

        1) Focusing on what is required enables you to ignore extraneous information and to proceed directly to determining the correct answer.

            a) Be especially careful to note when the requirement is an **exception**; e.g., "Which of the following is **not** an indication of fraud?"

    c. **Determine the correct answer** before looking at the answer choices.

        1) However, some multiple-choice questions are structured so that the answer cannot be determined from the stem alone. See the stem in b.1)a) above.

    d. **Read the answer choices carefully.**

        1) Even if the first answer appears to be the correct choice, do not skip the remaining answer choices. Questions often ask for the "best" of the choices provided. Thus, each choice requires your consideration.

        2) Treat each answer choice as a true/false question as you analyze it.

    e. **Click on the best answer.**

        1) You have a 25% chance of answering the question correctly by blindly guessing.

        2) For many of the multiple-choice questions, two answer choices can be eliminated with minimal effort, thereby increasing your educated guess to a 50-50 proposition.

4. After you have answered all 90 questions, return to the questions that you flagged. Also, verify that all questions have been answered.

5. **If you don't know the answer:**

    a. Again, guess; but make it an educated guess, which means select the best possible answer. First, rule out answers that you think are incorrect. Second, speculate on what The IIA is looking for and/or the rationale behind the question. Third, select the best answer, or guess between equally appealing answers. Your first guess is usually the most intuitive. If you cannot make an educated guess, read the stem and each answer and pick the best or most intuitive answer. It's just a guess!

    b. Make sure you accomplish this step within your predetermined time budget per checkpoint.

IF YOU HAVE QUESTIONS ABOUT GLEIM MATERIALS

Content-specific questions about our materials will be answered most rapidly if they are sent to us via email to accounting@gleim.com. Our team of accounting experts will give your correspondence thorough consideration and a prompt response.

Questions regarding the information in this Introduction (study suggestions, studying plans, exam specifics) should be emailed to personalcounselor@gleim.com.

Questions concerning orders, prices, shipments, or payments should be sent via email to customerservice@gleim.com and will be promptly handled by our competent and courteous customer service staff.

For technical support, you may use our automated technical support service at www.gleim.com/support, email us at support@gleim.com, or call us at (800) 874-5346.

HOW TO BE IN CONTROL WHILE TAKING THE EXAM

You have to be in control to be successful during exam preparation and execution. Control can also contribute greatly to your personal and other professional goals. Control is a process whereby you

1. Develop expectations, standards, budgets, and plans
2. Undertake activity, production, study, and learning
3. Measure the activity, production, output, and knowledge
4. Compare actual activity with expected and budgeted activity
5. Modify the activity, behavior, or study to better achieve the desired outcome
6. Revise expectations and standards in light of actual experience
7. Continue the process or restart the process in the future

Exercising control will ultimately develop the confidence you need to outperform most other CIA candidates and PASS the CIA exam! Obtain our *CIA Review: A System for Success* booklet for a more detailed discussion of control and other exam tactics.

Success stories!

Thank you! I was very pleased with my experience with the Gleim CIA system. You gave me a great start by creating a personalized study plan for me and recommended the right materials for my learning style. One area that I feel sets Gleim apart is the excellent and thorough explanations of problem solutions provided. Thank you again for an awesome product - I passed on my first attempt!

- *Diane Peters, CIA, Internal Controls Manager*

STUDY UNIT ONE
BUSINESS PROCESSES

(33 pages of outline)

This study unit addresses the analysis of business processes. A basic consideration is the pursuit of **quality** in all aspects of the organization's activities. The importance of quality management has resulted in the issuance of quality assurance standards by the International Organization for Standardization (ISO). Also crucial to successful business performance is effective planning. The aspect of planning covered in this study unit is **forecasting**, including a variety of mostly quantitative forecasting models. The study unit continues with **project management**, a topic of growing importance to all organizations in a technology-based society. The last three subunits describe **business process analysis**, including bottleneck management and process reengineering.

1.1 OVERVIEW OF QUALITY

1. **Perspectives on Quality**

   a. The traditional quality control process consisted of the mass inspection of goods as they came off the assembly line.

      1) Those defective items that could be modified cost-effectively to reach salable condition were reworked and then placed in finished goods inventory.

      2) Items whose defective condition could not be cured by rework were scrapped and written off.

   b. The focus of modern quality management is on preventing defects, not detecting them after production is finished.

      1) Quality management improves every phase of an entity's operations.

   c. Process quality is the effectiveness and efficiency of the entity's internal operations. Product quality is the conformance of the entity's output with customer expectations.

      1) Although improving the quality of processes increases efficiency, the most important component of a quality control system is ensuring the quality of the product.

2. **Measures**

    a.   The ultimate goal of any for-profit entity is to increase the value of owners' interests. Improved quality is simply a means to this end.

        1)   Most measures of quality are nonfinancial. They do not directly measure revenues or costs but rather productivity.

    b.   The following are examples of nonfinancial quality measures in manufacturing:

        1)   Number of products shipped per day
        2)   Number of defective products per thousand
        3)   Defective output as a percentage of total output

    c.   The following are examples of nonfinancial quality measures in service industries:

        1)   Customer time spent waiting to be served
        2)   Percentage of customers needing repeat service calls
        3)   Customer perceptions of employee courtesy

3. **Benchmarking**

    a.   Benchmarking is the comparison of some aspect of an organization's performance with best-in-class performance.

        1)   The process should be continuous, and whether an operation is best-in-class should be constantly re-evaluated.

    b.   Benchmarking can be either internal (comparison with the performance of another area within the organization) or external (comparison with the performance of another entity).

    c.   The following are examples of quality benchmarks:

        1)   Internal

            a)   Average time from initiation of customer service request to final resolution of problem for division that reports highest overall customer satisfaction.

        2)   External

            a)   Biggest competitor's customer satisfaction as reported in a third-party consumer comparison survey.

    d.   Benchmarking can be carried out as a continuous process together with the plan-do-check-act (PDCA) cycle. PDCA is a "management by fact," or scientific-method, approach to continuous improvement.

        1)   PDCA creates a process-centered environment. It involves (a) studying the current process, (b) collecting and analyzing data to identify causes of problems, (c) planning for improvement, and (d) deciding how to measure improvement ("plan").
        2)   The plan is then implemented on a small scale, if possible ("do").
        3)   The next step is to determine what happened ("check").
        4)   If the experiment was successful, the plan is fully implemented ("act").
        5)   The cycle is then repeated using what was learned from the preceding cycle.

4. **Kaizen**

    a.   Kaizen is the Japanese word for the continuous pursuit of improvement in every aspect of organizational operations.

        1)   For example, a kaizen budget projects costs based on future improvements. The possibility of such improvements must be determined, and the cost of implementation and the savings must be estimated.

5. **Quality Circles**

    a. Often those closest to a process know best how to improve it.

        1) Quality circles are a means of obtaining ideas for improving quality. They tend to be unstructured gatherings meant to encourage brainstorming and candid discussion.

6. **Six Sigma**

    a. Six Sigma is a quality improvement methodology devised by Motorola. Six Sigma is meant to reduce the number of defects per million opportunities (DPMO) in a mass-production process to 3.4, a level of good output of 99.99966%.

        1) The name Six Sigma (sometimes written 6σ) is derived from statistics. In a normal distribution (a bell curve), 99.99966% of the items are within six standard deviations.

        2) Statistical analysis has a major role in any Six Sigma program. Accurate, verifiable data are a necessity.

    b. Specific individuals in the organization have the following roles:

        1) The executive level must demonstrate commitment to the Six Sigma program and empower those in the other roles with enough authority and resources to implement the program successfully.

        2) Champions are responsible for overseeing the implementation of the Six Sigma program across the organization.

        3) Master black belts assist the champions in implementing the program across the organization.

        4) Black belts, like champions and master black belts, devote all of their time to the Six Sigma program. They oversee particular Six Sigma projects.

        5) Green belts and yellow belts do Six Sigma work in addition to their regular duties. They are closest to the production processes being improved.

Stop and review! You have completed the outline for this subunit. Study multiple-choice questions 1 and 2 on page 48.

1.2 COSTS OF QUALITY

1. **Four Costs of Quality**

    a. **Prevention costs** are incurred to prevent defects. Prevention is ordinarily less costly than the combined costs of appraisal, internal failure, and external failure. The following are examples:

        1) Design and implementation of a quality control system
        2) Costs of high-quality raw materials
        3) Preventive maintenance expense
        4) Training

    b. **Appraisal costs** are incurred to detect defective output during and after production. These consist of expenditures for inspection and testing.

    c. **Internal failure costs** are those associated with defective output discovered before shipping. The following are examples:

        1) Costs of rework
        2) Losses to scrap
        3) Write-offs of bad raw materials
        4) Production line downtime

    d.   **External failure costs** are associated with defective output discovered after it has reached the customer. The following are examples:

        1)   Storage of returned goods
        2)   Repair costs
        3)   Legal costs

    e.   These costs may be summarized in a cost-of-quality report. An example is presented below:

Cost-of-Quality Report

Prevention costs	US $10,000
Appraisal costs	6,000
Internal failure costs	5,000
External failure costs	3,000
Total costs of quality	US $24,000

2.   **Quality Cost Index**

    a.   These amounts may be used to calculate quality cost indices. These state costs of quality as a ratio to some other cost, such as total direct labor.

$$Quality\ cost\ index = \frac{Total\ costs\ of\ quality}{Total\ direct\ labor\ costs} \times 100$$

        1)   If direct labor costs for the period were US $110,000, the quality cost index was 21.8 [(US $24,000 ÷ $110,000) × 100].

Stop and review! You have completed the outline for this subunit. Study multiple-choice questions 3 through 5 beginning on page 48.

1.3 TOOLS FOR ASSESSING QUALITY

1.   **Statistical Control Charts**

    a.   Statistical control charts are graphic aids for monitoring the variability of any process subject to random variations.

        1)   The chart consists of three horizontal lines with a time scale from left to right. The center line represents the target value for the process being controlled. The upper line is the upper control limit (UCL), and the lower line is the lower control limit (LCL).

        2)   The process is measured periodically, and results are plotted on the chart. If a result is outside the limits, the process is considered out of control and corrective action is taken.

        3)   Statistical control charts make trends and cycles visible.

b.   Below is a chart depicting 2 weeks of production by a manufacturer that produces one precision part each day. To be salable, the part can vary from the standard by no more than +/– 0.1 millimeter.

Statistical Control Chart

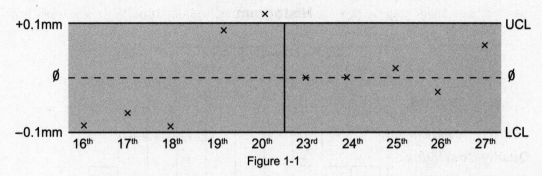

Figure 1-1

1) The part produced on the 20th had to be scrapped, and the equipment was adjusted to return the process to the controlled state for the following week's production.

2. **Pareto Diagrams**

a.   A Pareto diagram is a bar chart that assists managers in what is commonly called 80:20 analysis.

1) The 80:20 rule states that 80% of all effects are the result of only 20% of all causes. In the context of quality control, managers optimize their time by focusing their effort on the sources of most problems.

b.   The independent variable, plotted on the x axis, is the factor selected by the manager as the area of interest: department, time period, geographical location, etc. The frequency of occurrence of the defect (dependent variable) is plotted on the y axis.

1) The occurrences of the independent variable are ranked from highest to lowest, allowing the manager to see at a glance which areas are of most concern.

c.   Following is a Pareto diagram used by a chief administrative officer who wants to know which departments are generating the most travel vouchers that have been rejected because of incomplete documentation.

Pareto Diagram

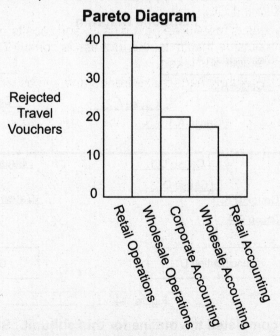

Figure 1-2

3.   **Histogram**

   a.   A histogram displays a continuous frequency distribution of the independent variable.

   b.   Below is a histogram showing the CAO the amount of travel reimbursement delayed by a typical returned travel voucher.

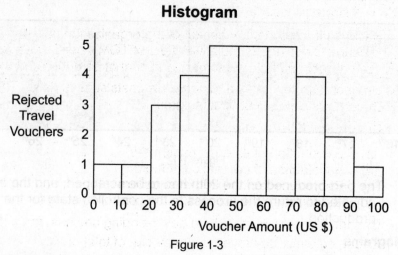

Figure 1-3

4.   **Fishbone Diagram**

   a.   A fishbone diagram (also called a cause-and-effect diagram or an Ishikawa diagram) is a total quality management process improvement technique.

      1)   It is useful in studying causation (why the actual and desired situations differ).

   b.   This format organizes the analysis of causation and helps to identify possible interactions among causes.

      1)   The head of the skeleton contains the statement of the problem.

      2)   The principal classifications of causes are represented by lines (bones) drawn diagonally from the heavy horizontal line (the spine).

      3)   Smaller horizontal lines are added in their order of probability in each classification.

   c.   Below is a generic fishbone diagram.

Fishbone Diagram

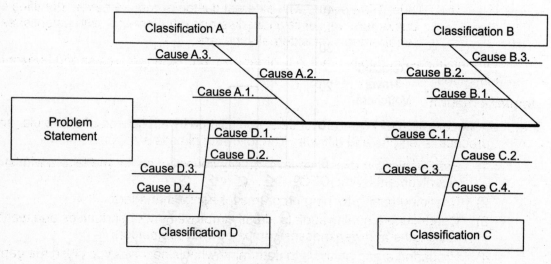

Figure 1-4

Stop and review! You have completed the outline for this subunit. Study multiple-choice questions 6 and 7 on page 50.

1.4 TOTAL QUALITY MANAGEMENT (TQM)

1. **Overview**

   a. TQM is a comprehensive approach. It treats the pursuit of quality as a basic organizational function that is as important as production or marketing. Accordingly, TQM is a strategic weapon.

      1) Because it affects every aspect of the organization, it is part of the organizational culture. Thus, the cumulative effect of TQM's continuous improvement process can attract and hold customers and cannot be duplicated by competitors.

   b. TQM can increase revenues and decrease costs substantially. The following are TQM's core principles or critical factors:

      1) Emphasis on the customer

         a) Satisfaction of external customers
         b) Satisfaction of internal customers
         c) Requirements for external suppliers
         d) Requirements for internal suppliers

      2) Continuous improvement as a never-ending process, not a destination

      3) Engaging every employee in the pursuit of total quality

         a) Avoidance of defects in products or services and satisfaction of external customers requires that all internal customers be satisfied.

2. **Definition**

   a. TQM is the continuous pursuit of quality in every aspect of organizational activities through

      1) A philosophy of doing it right the first time,
      2) Employee training and empowerment,
      3) Promotion of teamwork,
      4) Improvement of processes, and
      5) Attention to the satisfaction of internal and external customers.

         a) TQM emphasizes the supplier's relationship with the customer and identifies customer needs. It recognizes that everyone in a process is at some time a customer or supplier of someone else, either inside or outside of the organization.

         b) Thus, TQM begins with external customer requirements, identifies internal customer-supplier relationships and requirements, and establishes requirements for external suppliers.

   b. Organizations tend to be vertically organized, but TQM requires strong horizontal linkages.

3. **Implementation**

   a. Implementation of TQM cannot be accomplished by application of a formula, and the process is lengthy and difficult. The following phases are typical:

      1) Establishing an executive-level quality council of senior managers with strong involvement by the CEO

      2) Providing quality training programs for senior managers

      3) Conducting a quality audit to identify improvement opportunities and identify strengths and weaknesses compared with competitors

      4) Preparing a gap analysis to determine what is necessary to close the gap between the organization and the quality leaders in its industry and to establish a database for the development of the strategic quality improvement plan

    5) Developing strategic quality improvement plans for the short and long term
    6) Conducting employee communication and training programs
    7) Establishing quality teams to ensure that goods and services conform to specifications

       a) Hierarchal structure is replaced with teams of people from different specialties. This change follows from an emphasis on empowering employees and teamwork. Employees should

          i) Have proper training, necessary information, and the best tools;
          ii) Be fully engaged in the decision process; and
          iii) Receive fair compensation.

       b) If empowered employees with the required skills are assembled in teams, they will be more effective than if they work separately in a rigid structure.

          i) Moreover, a team is a way to share ideas, which results in process improvement.

    8) Creating a measurement system and setting goals
    9) Revising compensation, appraisal, and recognition systems
    10) Reviewing and revising the entire effort periodically

Stop and review! You have completed the outline for this subunit. Study multiple-choice questions 8 through 11 on page 51.

1.5 ISO FRAMEWORK

    1. **The International Organization for Standardization (ISO)**

       a. In 1987, the ISO introduced **ISO 9000**, a group of 11 voluntary standards and technical reports that provide guidance for establishing and maintaining a quality management system (QMS).

          1) The ISO's rules specify that its standards be revised every 5 years to reflect technical and market developments. (NOTE: ISO is not an acronym. It means equal, suggesting that entities certified under ISO 9000 have equal quality.)

          2) The current standards **(ISO 9001:2008)** were issued in November 2008. For specific and up-to-date information, see www.iso.org/iso/iso_9001_2008. The standards may be purchased from the ISO online store, www.iso.org/iso/store.htm.

       b. The intent of the standards is to ensure the quality of the process, not the product. The marketplace determines whether a product is good or bad.

          1) For this reason, the ISO deems it unacceptable for phrases referring to ISO certification to appear on individual products or packaging.

       c. ISO 9001:2008 is a generic standard that states requirements for a QMS. It applies when an entity needs to demonstrate its ability to (1) sell a product that meets customer and regulatory requirements and (2) increase customer satisfaction through improving the QMS and ensuring conformity with requirements.

    2. **Basic Requirements of an ISO QMS**

       a. Key Process Identification

          1) Key processes affecting quality must be identified and included.

          2) A process management approach must be used. It manages the entity as a set of linked processes that are controlled for continuous improvement.

    b.   General Requirements

        1)   The entity must have a quality policy and quality goals. It also must design a QMS to control process performance. Quality goals are measurable and specific.

        2)   The QMS is documented in the (a) quality policy, (b) quality manual, (c) procedures, (d) work instructions, and (e) records.

        3)   The entity also must demonstrate its ability to increase customer satisfaction through improving the QMS and ensuring conformity with requirements.

    c.   Management Responsibility

        1)   Management (a) reviews the quality policy, (b) analyzes data about QMS performance, and (c) assesses opportunities for improvement and the need for change.

        2)   Management ensures that systems exist to determine and satisfy customer requirements.

    d.   Resource Management

        1)   The resources needed to improve the QMS and satisfy customer requirements must be provided.

    e.   Product Realization

        1)   These processes result in products or services received by customers. They must be planned and controlled.

        2)   Issues are (a) means of control, (b) objectives, (c) documentation and records needed, and (d) acceptance criteria.

    f.   Measurement, Analysis, and Improvement

        1)   The entity must have processes for (a) inspection, (b) testing, (c) measurement, (d) analysis, and (e) improvement.

3.   **Aspects of ISO Certification**

    a.   Some entities are obtaining ISO certification because of concern that the European Union will require compliance with the standards in an attempt to restrict imports.

        1)   The standards are not yet mandatory. Exceptions are for certain regulated products (for which health and safety are concerns), such as medical devices, telecommunications equipment, and gas appliances.

        2)   Some customers demand that suppliers register.

        3)   ISO 9000 registration may be necessary to be competitive. It makes customers more comfortable with suppliers' products and services.

        4)   Many entities implementing the standards make internal process and quality improvements as a result. ISO 9000 forces them to share information and understand who internal customers and users are.

    b.   A registrar, or external auditor, must be selected. Registrars are usually specialists within certain Standard Industrial Classification (SIC) codes. Certification by a registrar avoids the need for each customer to audit a supplier.

        1)   Following an onsite visit, the registrar, if convinced that a quality system conforms to the selected standard, issues a certificate describing the scope of the registration. Registration is usually granted for a 3-year period.

        2)   All employees are subject to being audited. They must have the ability to "say what they do" and to demonstrate that they "do what they say."

4.   **Other Areas of Standardization**

    a.   The ISO also has issued ISO 14000, a set of environmental standards. These standards are comparable in purpose to ISO 9000 but concern environmental quality systems.

        1)   Although they have not been as widely adopted as the ISO 9000 standards, they may become necessary for conducting international business. Some European countries already have environmental systems standards in place, and the relationship of these single-country standards with ISO 14000 is not clear. However, individual countries' standards are typically more strict.

    b.   The scope of ISO 19011:2002 extends to (1) the principles of auditing, (2) managing audit programs, (3) conducting QMS audits and environmental management system (EMS) audits, and (4) the competence of QMS and EMS auditors.

        1)   It applies to all entities that must perform internal or external audits of QMSs or environmental management systems or manage an audit program.

        2)   ISO 19011 may apply to other types of audits if due consideration is given to identifying the competencies required of the auditors.

    c.   ISO 10012:2003 is a generic standard. It addresses the management of measurement processes and confirmation of measuring equipment used to support compliance with required measures.

        1)   It states quality management requirements of a measurement management system (MMS) that can be used as part of the overall management system.

        2)   It is not to be used as a requirement for demonstrating conformance with other standards. Interested parties may agree to use ISO 10012:2003 as an input for satisfying MMS requirements in certification activities.

            a)   However, other standards apply to specific elements affecting measurement results, e.g., details of measurement methods, competence of personnel, or comparisons among laboratories.

    d.   ISO 14063:2006 states principles, policies, strategies, and activities for environmental communications, whether external or internal. It addresses the unique circumstances of environmental communications and applies to every entity regardless of whether it has an EMS.

    e.   ISO Guide 64:2008 applies to environmental questions arising in the setting of product standards. Its purpose is to help standard setters to minimize negative environmental effects at each step in the product life cycle.

    f.   ISO 14050:2009 is a glossary of environmental management vocabulary.

Stop and review! You have completed the outline for this subunit. Study multiple-choice questions 12 and 13 on page 52.

1.6 REGRESSION AND CORRELATION

1. **Linear Regression**

    a.   Linear regression is the process of deriving the linear equation that describes the relationship between two variables.

        1)   Linear regression is performed using the least-squares method. This term describes the means by which calculus is used to find the straight line that minimizes the vertical distances between the individual data points and the regression line.

    b.   The **simple regression** equation is the algebraic formula for a straight line:

$$y = a + bx$$

   If: y = the dependent variable (the outcome)
        a = the y intercept
        b = the slope of the regression line (regression coefficient)
        x = the independent variable

        1)   The following is a business application:

EXAMPLE

A firm has collected observations on advertising expenditures and annual sales.

Advertising (US $000s)	Sales (US $000,000s)
71	26.3
31	13.9
50	19.8
60	22.9
35	15.1

Applying the least-squares method reveals that expected sales equal US $4.2 million plus 311.741 times the advertising expenditure.

$$y = US \$4,200,000 + 311.741x$$

The observations are graphed as follows:

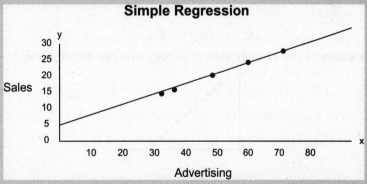

Figure 1-5

The firm can now project the amount it will have to spend on advertising to generate US $32,000,000 in sales.

$$y = US \$4,200,000 + 311.741x$$
$$US \$32,000,000 = US \$4,200,000 + 311.741x$$
$$311.741x = US \$27,800,000$$
$$x = US \$89,177$$

c.   Simple regression is only used when one independent variable is involved. **Multiple regression** is used when there is more than one independent variable.

1)   The example relating advertising to sales is unrealistic. Sales are dependent upon more than advertising.

2)   Multiple regression allows a firm to identify many factors (independent variables), and to weight each one according to its influence on the overall outcome.

$$y = a + b_1x_1 + b_2x_2 + b_3x_3 + b_4x_4 + etc.$$

d.   Assumptions of the linear regression model.

1)   The linear relationship established for x and y is only valid across the relevant range. The user must identify the relevant range and assure that (s)he does not project the relationship beyond it.

2)   Regression analysis establishes the linear relationship existing at a moment in time. Its use assumes that past relationships can be validly projected.

3)   The distribution of y around the regression line is constant for different values of x (constant variance). Thus, a limitation of the regression method is that it can only be used when cost patterns remain unchanged from prior periods.

e.   Cross-sectional regression permits the analysis of results for multiple groups of inputs (e.g., retail stores) at a moment in time rather than over a period of time.

2.   **Correlation Analysis**

a.   Regression analysis establishes the linear relationship between two variables, and **correlation analysis** is used to measure the strength of that relationship. The coefficient of correlation (r) has a range of –1 to +1.

b.   The various values of r can be depicted with scatter diagrams.

1)   A value of $r = 1$ indicates a perfect direct relationship.

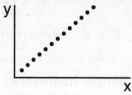

Figure 1-6

2)   A value of $r = -1$ indicates a perfect inverse relationship.

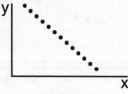

Figure 1-7

3)   A value of r between 0 and 1 indicates a direct relationship of varying degrees of strength.

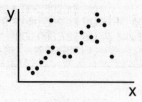

Figure 1-8

4) A value of $r = 0$ indicates no linear relationship.

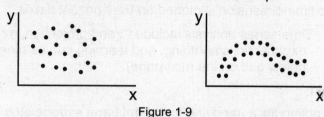

Figure 1-9

a) The right-hand graph above indicates that an r of zero does not mean the two variables have no relationship, only that any relationship they have cannot be expressed as a linear equation.

3. The **coefficient of determination (r^2)** is the coefficient of correlation squared. It indicates the proportion of the total variation in y that is explained by the variation in x. Its value has a range from 0 to 1.

    a. A value of $r = 1$ indicates that 100% of the variation in y is explained by the variation in x, i.e., all the data points lie along the regression line.

    b. The closer r^2 is to 0, the farther the data points lie from the regression line, i.e., the less explanatory power the correlation coefficient has.

        1) For example, if a linear relationship has a coefficient of correlation of –0.64, only 40.96% (-0.64^2) of the total variation in the outcome can be explained by the variation in the independent variable.

Stop and review! You have completed the outline for this subunit. Study multiple-choice questions 14 through 17 beginning on page 52.

1.7 FORECASTING -- TIME-SERIES MODELS

1. **Uses**

    a. **Forecasts** are the basis for business plans.

        1) Forecasts attempt to answer questions about the outcomes of events (e.g., the effect of a war involving a producer of oil on the oil market), the timing of events (e.g., when will unemployment fall), or the future value of a statistic (e.g., sales).

    b. Examples of forecasts include sales projections, inventory demand, cash flow, and future capital needs.

2. **Forecasting Methods**

    a. Qualitative (judgment) methods rely on experience and human intuition.

        1) The **Delphi method** summarizes the opinions of experts regarding a given problem.

        2) These summaries are then fed back to the experts without revealing the identities of the other participants. The process is repeated until the opinions converge on an optimal solution.

    b. Quantitative methods use mathematical models and graphs.

        1) **Causal relationship forecasting** quantifies the link between some factor in the organization's environment (the independent variable, plotted on the horizontal axis) and an outcome at a moment in time (the dependent variable, plotted on the vertical axis).

            a) The most common of these techniques is linear regression, discussed in Subunit 1.6.

2) **Time series analysis** relies on past experience to project future outcomes. The time dimension is plotted on the horizontal axis.

   a) Time series analysis includes trend projection, moving average, exponential smoothing, and learning curves (see items 3. through 6. below and on the next page).

3. **Trend Projection**

   a. Trend projection fits a trend line to the data and extrapolates it.

      1) The dependent variable (sales, profits, etc.) is regressed (i.e., plotted on the y axis) on time (the independent variable, plotted on the x axis).

   b. Changes in business activity over time may have several possible components:

      1) The secular trend is the long-term change that occurs despite variability.
      2) Seasonal variations are common in many businesses, most obviously retail, which experiences a large increase in activity during the winter holidays.
      3) Cyclical fluctuations are variations related to the level of aggregate economic activity (see Study Unit 7, Subunit 5).
      4) Irregular or random variables are the random happenings that affect business (weather, strikes, fires, etc.).

4. **Moving Average**

   a. A moving average is appropriate when the demand for a product is relatively stable and not subject to seasonal variations.

   b. Each period's average includes the newest observation and discards the oldest one, illustrated in the table below:

		Moving Average					
Month	Sales	January Forecast	February Forecast	March Forecast	April Forecast	May Forecast	June Forecast
September	US $6,200	US $ 6,200					
October	6,000	6,000	US $ 6,000				
November	5,800	5,800	5,800	US $ 5,800			
December	5,600	5,600	5,600	5,600	US $ 5,600		
January	5,400	US $23,600	5,400	5,400	5,400	US $ 5,400	
February	5,500	÷ 4	US $22,800	5,500	5,500	5,500	US $ 5,500
March	5,700	US $ 5,900	÷ 4	US $22,300	5,700	5,700	5,700
April	5,800		US $ 5,700	÷ 4	US $22,200	5,800	5,800
May	5,900			US $ 5,575	÷ 4	US $22,400	5,900
					US $ 5,550	÷ 4	US $22,900
						US $ 5,600	÷ 4
							US $ 5,725

5. **Exponential Smoothing**

   a. Exponential smoothing is useful when large amounts of data cannot be retained.

      1) Exponential means that greater weight is placed on the most recent data, with the weight assigned to older data falling off exponentially.

   b. The selection of the smoothing factor, called alpha (α), is important because a high alpha places more weight on recent data.

      1) The forecast for a period is the result for the previous period times the smoothing factor, plus the forecast for the previous period times 1 minus the smoothing factor.

6. **Learning Curves**

 a. A learning curve reflects the increased rate at which people perform tasks as they gain experience.

  1) The time required to perform a given task becomes progressively shorter during the early stages of production (see the following figure).

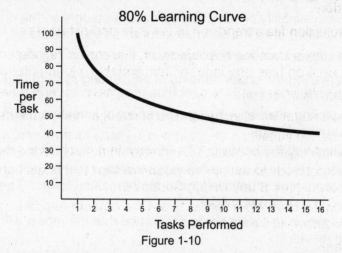

Figure 1-10

 b. The curve is usually expressed as a percentage of reduced time to complete a task for each doubling of cumulative production. The most common percentage used in practice is 80%.

  1) One common assumption made in a learning curve model is that the cumulative average time per unit is reduced by a certain percentage each time production doubles.

   a) The alternative assumption is that incremental unit time (time to produce the last unit) is reduced when production doubles.

 c. The following table assumes an 80% learning curve for a product whose first unit takes 100 minutes to produce:

Cumulative Units Produced	Cumulative Average Time per Unit or Incremental Unit Time	
1	100	
2	80	(100 × 80%)
4	64	(80 × 80%)
8	51.2	(64 × 80%)
16	40.96	(51.20 × 80%)

Stop and review! You have completed the outline for this subunit. Study multiple-choice questions 18 and 19 on page 54.

1.8 FORECASTING -- PROBABILISTIC MODELS

1. **Simulation**

   a. Simulation experiments with logical and mathematical models using a computer. Because of the behavior of the many variables involved and the complexity of their interactions, many problems cannot be solved by using simple algebraic formulas.

      1) The availability of computer spreadsheets makes the construction of simulation models a practical alternative for all sizes of entities.

   b. The first step is to define the objectives. Examples include

      1) Increasing the understanding of an existing system (e.g., an inventory system with rising costs),

      2) Exploring alternatives (e.g., the effect of investments on the firm's financial structure), and

      3) Estimating the behavior of a new system, such as a production line.

   c. The second step is to define the variables, their individual behavior, and their interrelationships in precise logical-mathematical terms. The variables then must be included in a coherent model.

   d. The third step is to obtain some assurance that the model will adequately predict the desired results.

      1) This can be accomplished by entering historical data into the model and comparing the output with actual results.

   e. The fourth step is to design the experiment. (Experimentation is sampling the operation of a system.) For example, if a change in a cost-flow assumption is simulated on an inventory model for 2 years, the results are a single sample.

      1) With replication, the sample size and the confidence level can be increased. The number of runs to be made, length of each run, measurements to be made, and methods for analyzing the results are part of the design of the experiment.

   f. The fifth and final step is to perform the simulation and analyze the results using appropriate statistical methods.

2. **Monte Carlo Simulation**

   a. Monte Carlo simulation uses a random number generator to produce individual values for a random variable.

      1) These numbers have a uniform probability distribution (equal likelihoods of occurrence). They are then transformed into values consistent with the desired distribution.

   b. The performance of a quantitative model may be investigated by randomly selecting values for each of the variables in the model (based on the probability distribution of each variable) and then calculating the value of the solution.

      1) If this process is performed many times, the distribution of results from the model will be obtained.

   c. For example, a new marketing model includes a factor for a competitor's introduction of a similar product any month within the next 3 years. Each month has an equal chance of being the month the competitor releases its product.

      1) The marketing department generates 1,000 random numbers between 1 and 36 to represent each of the months in the next 3 years.

      2) The simulation model is then run 1,000 times, each time using one of the generated random numbers to indicate which month the competitor's product hits the market. The results help the firm to choose its marketing strategy.

3. **Sensitivity Analysis**

   a. After a problem has been formulated into any mathematical model, it may be subjected to sensitivity analysis, which examines how the model's outcomes change as the parameters change. Examples include the following:

      1) Cost-volume-profit analysis can be used to determine how changes in the amounts of fixed costs and level of production will affect profitability.

      2) Capital budgeting can be used to determine how changes in assumptions about interest rates affect a project's profitability.

4. **Markov Process**

   a. A Markov process quantifies the likelihood of a future event based on the current state of the process.

      1) For example, a machine tool may be in one of two states, in adjustment or out of adjustment. Over time, the manufacturer can predict how likely the machine is to be in (out of) adjustment tomorrow based on its being in (out of) adjustment today.

   b. Another application is the aging of accounts receivable. An entity can predict how likely a 60-day-old receivable is to become a 90-day-old receivable, and how likely a 90-day-old receivable is to become delinquent.

      1) Such a series of successive probabilities is termed Markov chain analysis.

NOTE: Probabilistic models also are called stochastic, meaning that they contain both determinable and random elements.

5. **Game Theory**

   a. Game theory is a mathematical approach to decision making when confronted with an enemy or competitor. Games are classified according to the number of players and the algebraic sum of the payoffs.

      1) In a two-player game, if the payoff is given by the loser to the winner, the algebraic sum is zero, and the game is a zero-sum game. If it is possible for both players to profit, the game is a positive-sum game.

         a) A decision that results in neither player improving his/her position is a no-win strategy.

      2) In a cooperative game, the players are permitted to negotiate and form binding agreements prior to the selection of strategies. In these games, the sums of certain payoff combinations do not equal zero.

      3) The prisoner's dilemma is a special outcome of a partly competitive game in which each player has a strategy that dominates all other strategies. However, when each player chooses his/her dominant strategy, the outcome for both is less favorable than if one or both chooses some other strategy.

      4) Games against nature are formulations of problems in which only one player chooses a strategy, and the set of outcomes and payoffs is not influenced by the selection.

b.   Game theorists have developed various decision rules based on the level of risk the decision maker accepts.

1)   In this example, a small business wishes to open a new store in one of five locations. Market research provides the following payoff table:

Location:	A	B	C	D	E
Traffic Level: High	US $18	US $20	US $16	US $28	US $25
Medium	15	11	5	13	9
Low	(2)	5	2	(4)	(7)

2)   The maximax criterion is applied by risk-seeking, optimistic decision makers. They select the option with the highest potential payoff regardless of the state of nature. In the example, it is location D (US $28).

3)   The minimax criterion is applied by conservative (risk-averse) decision makers. They select the option with the lowest potential maximum loss. In the example, it is location B (US $5).

a)   The maximin criterion is applied by conservative players who wish to maximize the minimum payoff. In the example, it is also location B (US $5).

4)   The minimax regret criterion is applied by decision makers with moderate appetites for risk. This strategy seeks to minimize the effect of a bad decision in either direction (minimize opportunity loss).

a)   To determine the location meeting this criterion, an opportunity loss table must be prepared for each state of nature:

Opportunity Loss Tables

High traffic:	A	B	C	D	E
Highest profit of other locations	US $ 28	US $ 28	US $ 28		US $ 28
Profit	(18)	(20)	(16)		(25)
Opportunity loss	US $ 10	US $ 8	US $ 12		US $ 3

Medium traffic:	A	B	C	D	E
Highest profit of other locations		US $ 15	US $15	US $ 15	US $15
Profit		(11)	(5)	(13)	(9)
Opportunity loss		US $ 4	US $10	US $ 2	US $ 6

Low traffic:	A	B	C	D	E
Highest profit of other locations	US $5		US $ 5	US $5	US $ 5
Loss (profit)	2		(2)	4	7
Opportunity loss	US $7		US $ 3	US $9	US $12

b)   The decision maker next identifies the maximum regret (highest potential profit forgone) for each location:

Location:	A	B	C	D	E
Maximum regret	US $10	US $8	US $12	US $9	US $12

c)   The location with the lowest maximum regret is B (US $8).

5)   The insufficient reason (Laplace) criterion may be used by a risk-neutral player when probabilities cannot be assigned.

a)   The assumption is that, with no probability distribution, the probabilities must be equal, and the payoffs for the states of nature are simply added. The decision with the highest total is chosen.

6)   An expected value criterion may be used by a risk-neutral player, that is, one for whom the utility of a gain is the same as the disutility of an equal loss.

6.   **Expected Value**

   a.   When risk is quantifiable, expected value is a rational means of making the best decision (a choice among options).

   1)   The expected value of a decision is found by multiplying the probability of each state of nature by its payoff and adding the products. The best choice has the highest expected value.

   b.   In this example, a dealer in yachts may order zero, one, or two yachts for this season's inventory. The cost of carrying each excess yacht is US $50,000, and the profit on each yacht sold is US $200,000.

State of Nature = Actual Demand	Decision = Order 0	Decision = Order 1	Decision = Order 2
0 yachts	US $0	US $ (50,000)	US $(100,000)
1 yacht	0	200,000	150,000
2 yachts	0	200,000	400,000

   1)   The probabilities of the three states of nature are the following:

Demand	Pr
0	.10
1	.50
2	.40

   2)   The dealer may calculate the expected value of each decision as follows:

Order 0	Order 1	Order 2
US $0 × .1 = US $0	US $ (50,000) × .1 = US $ (5,000)	US $(100,000) × .1 = US $ (10,000)
0 × .5 = 0	200,000 × .5 = 100,000	150,000 × .5 = 75,000
0 × .4 = 0	200,000 × .4 = 80,000	400,000 × .4 = 160,000
EV(0) = US $0	EV(1) = US $175,000	EV(2) = US $225,000

   a)   The decision with the greatest expected value is to order two yachts.

Stop and review! You have completed the outline for this subunit. Study multiple-choice questions 20 through 23 beginning on page 54.

1.9 SELECTING THE FORECASTING METHOD

GLEIM
SUCCESS TIPS

Correct use of a forecasting method is worthless to an internal auditor if (s)he chooses the wrong method. Being able to determine when a method should be applied is crucial for CIA candidates.

Many forecasting questions ask for the correct method rather than the means of applying it. This subunit consists entirely of such questions. Please review Subunits 1.7 and 1.8, paying special attention to the nature and purpose of each forecasting method, before answering the questions.

Stop and review! You have completed the outline for this subunit. Study multiple-choice questions 24 through 29 beginning on page 55.

1.10 PROJECT MANAGEMENT

1. **Overview**

   a.   A project is a temporary undertaking with specified objectives that often involves a cross-functional team and working outside customary organizational lines. Hence, interpersonal skills are important in project management. A manager may not have line authority over some team members.

     1)   Examples include building construction, R&D projects, new product planning, feasibility studies, audit studies, movie production, and conversion to a new computer information system.

     2)   Project management techniques are designed to aid the planning and control of large-scale projects having many interrelated activities.

   b.   The following are three distinct roles for those involved in the project:

     1)   The project manager must have sufficient authority to direct projects across organizational boundaries. Most large- and medium-scale projects require the participation, or at least the cooperation, of employees from multiple departments and functions.

     2)   Project members often must continue performing their regular jobs while giving part of their time to the project. Obtaining acceptance from project members' immediate supervisors is therefore crucial.

     3)   The steering committee recommends projects to the executive level. Once a project is approved, the committee oversees the implementation of the project plan. The committee is composed of managers who have the authority to direct the commitment of resources.

   c.   A project manager must perform three principal tasks:

     1)   Planning -- determining goals and due dates and scheduling available resources

     2)   Implementation -- executing the plan and directing resources where needed

     3)   Monitoring -- correcting problems, meeting expectations, and finishing the project within the time and budgetary limits

   d.   The risk of an unsuccessful project can be analyzed in terms of four components:

     1)   Ensuring resources. Resources consist of personnel, equipment, computer processing time, and sometimes cash.

     2)   Maintaining scope. "Scope creep" often affects projects in organizations. The temptation is to continue adding functions to a new system or process. Keeping project members focused on the approved goals (and timetable) of the project is a role of the project manager.

     3)   Controlling cost. The cost of a project must be measured by the opportunity cost of resources used.

     4)   Providing deliverables. A deliverable may be as simple as a written report. Most large-scale projects have deliverables at the completion of each stage of the project to ensure that the project remains on schedule.

e.   Project management is the process of managing the trade-off between the two major inputs (time and cost) and the major output (quality). The project management triangle graphically depicts this relationship.

Project Management Triangle

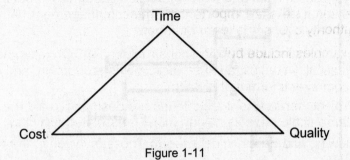

Figure 1-11

1)   The implication is that a high-quality deliverable can only be achieved either by devoting a large number of employee hours to a project or by spending a lot of money.

EXAMPLE

In the days before widespread computer use, old-fashioned job-order print shops used to display signs saying, "You Want It Fast -- Cheap -- Correct. Pick Two."

Designers of submarines often speak of their classic trade-off of depth, speed, and stealth. A vessel with sufficient shielding to be silent and to survive at great depths is too heavy to go very fast.

---

f.   Project management software is available. Among other things, it should

1)   Specify and schedule required activities
2)   Provide the ability to do sensitivity analysis of the effects of changes in plans
3)   Calculate a project's critical path
4)   Establish priorities
5)   Be able to modify or merge plans
6)   Manage all types of project resources
7)   Monitor progress, including adherence to time budgets for activities

g.   Common techniques for project management include Gantt charts, PERT, and CPM. They are suitable for any project having a target completion date and single start.

2. **Gantt Charts**

a.   Gantt charts are simple to construct and use. To develop a Gantt chart,

1)   Divide the project into logical subprojects called activities or tasks,
2)   Estimate the start and completion times for each activity, and
3)   Prepare a bar chart showing each activity as a horizontal bar along a time scale.

b.   Below is an example of a Gantt chart:

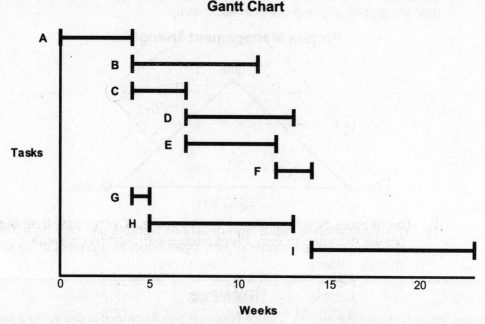

Figure 1-12

c.   Gantt charts show the projected start and finish times for each task as well as for the project as a whole.

1)   They also show, in a limited way, the interdependencies among tasks, i.e., which tasks can be performed simultaneously and which must be completed before other tasks can begin.

2)   In the example, tasks B, C, and G can begin as soon as task A is complete, but task I cannot begin until all others are complete.

d.   The major advantage of the Gantt chart is its simplicity: It requires no special tools or mathematics. It forces the planner to think ahead and define logical activities. As the project progresses, actual completion times can be compared with planned times.

e.   The major disadvantage of the Gantt chart is that it is unsuitable for a very large-scale project. The interdependencies among tasks become unmanageable and a more sophisticated tool is necessary.

3.   **Program Evaluation and Review Technique (PERT)**

a.   PERT was developed to control large-scale, complex projects. PERT diagrams are free-form networks showing each activity as a line between events. A sequence of lines shows interrelationships among activities.

1)   PERT diagrams are more complex than Gantt charts, but they have the advantages of incorporating probabilistic time estimates and identifying the critical path.

b.   A PERT network consists of two components:

1)   Events are moments in time representing the start or finish of an activity. They consume no resources and are depicted on a network diagram with circles (called nodes).

2)   Activities are tasks to be accomplished. They consume resources (including time) and have a duration over time. They are depicted as lines connecting nodes.

PERT Network

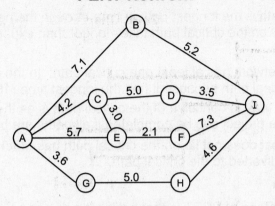

Figure 1-13

3) The network depicted above has five paths. To calculate their durations, the project manager makes a forward pass through the network.

Path	Time (days)	
A-B-I	7.1 + 5.2	= 12.3
A-C-D-I	4.2 + 5.0 + 3.5	= 12.7
A-C-E-F-I	4.2 + 3.0 + 2.1 + 7.3	= 16.6
A-E-F-I	5.7 + 2.1 + 7.3	= 15.1
A-G-H-I	3.6 + 5.0 + 4.6	= 13.2

   c. Some processes contain activities that are performed simultaneously because they have the same start node and end node. Concurrent activities cannot be depicted graphically on a PERT network. Every path between nodes must be unique. Thus, two paths cannot both be designated G-H.

Noncompliant PERT Network

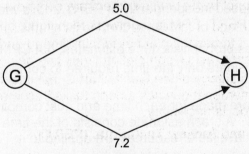

Figure 1-14

1) In such cases, a new destination node is created for the task that ends first. This node is connected to the other by a **dummy activity** that adds no time to the project. Its purpose is to establish the order of precedence.

Dummy Activity

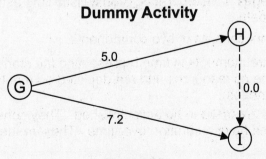

Figure 1-15

4.   **Calculating the Length of the Critical Paths**

   a.   The critical path is the longest path in time through the network. It is critical because, if any activity on the critical path takes longer than expected, the entire project will be delayed.

       1)   Every network has at least one critical path. In the example, path A-C-E-F-I is the critical path because it has the longest time (16.6 days).

       2)   Another way to conceive of the critical path is as the shortest amount of time in which a project can be completed if all paths are begun simultaneously.

   b.   Any activity that does not lie on the critical path has **slack time**, i.e., unused resources that can be diverted to the critical path.

5.   **Expected Duration**

   a.   A major advantage of PERT is that activity times can be expressed probabilistically.

       1)   Three estimates are made: optimistic, most likely, and pessimistic. The usual weighting of the three estimates is 1:4:1. (The most likely time for the duration of a task is the one indicated on the PERT diagram.)

       2)   In this example, the most likely duration of task B-I is 5.2 days. The organization estimates the optimistic time at 5.0 and the pessimistic time at 5.8. The expected duration of task B-I is calculated as follows:

	Estimates		Weights		
Optimistic	5.0	×	1	=	5.0
Most likely	5.2	×	4	=	20.8
Pessimistic	5.8	×	1	=	5.8
Totals			6		31.6

Expected duration: $31.6 \div 6 = 5.27$ days

6.   **Critical Path Method (CPM)**

   a.   CPM was developed independently of PERT and is widely used in the construction industry. Like PERT, CPM is a network technique, but it has two distinct differences:

       1)   PERT uses probabilistic time estimates, but CPM is a deterministic method.

       2)   PERT considers only the time required to complete a project. CPM incorporates cost amounts.

   b.   Two estimates are made for each time and cost combination: a normal estimate and a crash estimate. A crash estimate consists of the time and cost required to complete an activity if all available resources are applied to it.

       1)   Crashing a project applies all available resources to activities on the critical path (crashing a noncritical path activity is not cost-effective).

EXAMPLE

Figure 1-13 on page 37 can be converted to a CPM network with the addition of the following time and cost data for the critical path:

Critical Path Activity	Normal Time & Cost		Crash Time & Cost	
A-C	4.2	US $20,000	4.0	US $35,000
C-E	3.0	$10,000	2.0	$20,000
E-F	2.1	$18,000	2.0	$21,000
F-I	7.3	$60,000	6.5	$90,000

These amounts can be used to determine the costs and gains of crashing a given activity:

Critical Path Activity	Crash Cost Minus Normal Cost		Incremental Cost of Crashing	Normal Time Minus Crash Time		Time Gained
A-C	US $35,000 –	US $20,000 =	US $15,000	4.2 – 4.0	=	0.2
C-E	20,000 –	10,000 =	10,000	3.0 – 2.0	=	1.0
E-F	21,000 –	18,000 =	3,000	2.1 – 2.0	=	0.1
F-I	90,000 –	60,000 =	30,000	7.3 – 6.5	=	0.8

2) The most cost-effective activity to crash is determined with the following formula:

$$Time\text{-}cost\ tradeoff = \frac{Crash\ cost - Normal\ cost}{Normal\ time - Crash\ time}$$

EXAMPLE

The ratio of crash cost to time gained reveals the best activity for crashing:

Critical Path Activity	Incremental Cost of Crashing		Time Gained		Cost per Day to Crash
A-C	US $15,000	÷	0.2	=	US $75,000
C-E	10,000	÷	1.0	=	10,000
E-F	3,000	÷	0.1	=	30,000
F-I	30,000	÷	0.8	=	37,500

The most cost-effective activity to crash is C-E. Assuming this activity will be crashed, the network is recalculated to determine whether a new critical path will result. If so, the time-cost tradeoff of the activities on the new critical path are calculated and the process is repeated.

7. **Network Models**

   a. Network models are used to solve managerial problems pertaining to project scheduling, information systems design, and transportation systems design.

      1) Networks consisting of nodes and arcs may be created to represent in graphic form problems related to transportation, assignment, and transshipment.

   b. A shortest-route algorithm minimizes total travel time from one site to each of the other sites in a transportation system.

   c. The maximal flow algorithm maximizes throughput in networks with distinct entry (source node) and exit (sink node) points. Examples of applications are highway transportation systems and oil pipelines. Flows are limited by capacities of the arcs (e.g., highways or pipes).

   d. The minimal spanning tree algorithm identifies the set of connecting branches having the shortest combined length. A spanning tree is a group of branches (arcs) that connects each node in the network to every other node. An example problem is the determination of the shortest telecommunications linkage among users at remote sites and a central computer.

Stop and review! You have completed the outline for this subunit. Study multiple-choice questions 30 through 34 beginning on page 57.

1.11 BUSINESS PROCESS ANALYSIS -- EFFICIENCY AND WORKFLOW

1. **Overview**

   a. Process analysis studies the means of producing a product or service for the purpose of lowering costs and increasing effectiveness (accomplishment of objectives) and efficiency (economical, timely, and accurate accomplishment of objectives) while producing items of appropriate quality.

      1). It differs from traditional product (or service) quality control, which involves inspection during production to eliminate unacceptable results.

   b. Workflow is the sequence of steps needed to accomplish a task, including consideration of any necessary physical objects.

2. **Queuing Theory**

   a. Queuing theory is a form of workflow analysis. An organization can improve throughput by carefully designing the way inputs arrive at workstations and how they are processed upon arrival.

      1) Manufacturing production lines are examples of queuing systems. Examples from other industries include the following:

         a) Bank teller windows
         b) Retail checkout counters
         c) Highway toll booths
         d) Airport holding patterns

      2) The most significant aspects of queuing theory are the number of lines and the service facility structure.

         a) Single channel, single phase. All users form a single line and are served at one point. An automated teller machine (ATM) is an example.

ATM

Figure 1-16

         i) A slight variation is an airline check-in counter or the teller line at a bank. All users form a single line, but multiple service points perform the single phase of the process. This structure is treated as having a higher capacity single service point.

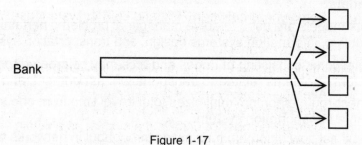

Bank

Figure 1-17

b)   Single channel, multiple phase. All users form a single line and must pass through more than one service point. A fast-food drive-through with sequential ordering microphone, payment station, and pickup window is an example.

Drive-through

Figure 1-18

c)   Multiple channel, single phase. This structure has many service points, each with its own line. The checkout area in a large retail store is an example.

Large store

Figure 1-19

d)   Multiple channel, multiple phase. Users form many lines, and each line has multiple, sequential service points. A hospital is an example. Each department (inpatient surgery, outpatient surgery, clinical diagnostics, emergency, etc.) has its own admissions process and performs significantly different services for each patient.

Hospital

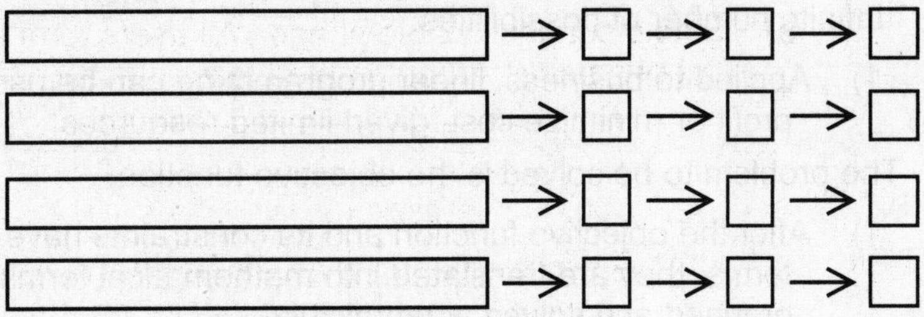

Figure 1-20

3)   As capacity use increases, so does customer waiting time.

a)   Somewhere between 75% and 85% of system use, most customers are not willing to wait. Thus, management must balance loss of customers and overcapacity.

4)   Mathematical models can be applied to derive the following information:

a)   Average capacity use of the system
b)   Average number of units in the queue
c)   Average number of units in the system as a whole
d)   Average time spent waiting in the queue
e)   Average time in the system as a whole

5)   Mathematical solutions are available for simple systems having unscheduled random arrivals. For other systems, simulation must be used to find a solution.

6) The arrivals in a queuing model occur in accordance with a Poisson process.

    a) The model has the following assumptions:

        i) The probability of occurrence of an event is constant,

        ii) The occurrence of an event is independent of any other,

        iii) The probability of an occurrence is proportional to the length of the interval, and,

        iv) If the interval is small enough, the probability of more than one occurrence approaches zero.

    b) The Poisson probability distribution is used to predict the probability of a specified number of occurrences of an event in a specified time interval, given the expected number of occurrences per time unit.

    c) The related exponential distribution is used to approximate service times. This distribution gives the probability of zero events in a given interval. Accordingly, it gives the probability that service time will not exceed a given length of time.

Stop and review! You have completed the outline for this subunit. Study multiple-choice questions 35 through 37 beginning on page 58.

1.12 BUSINESS PROCESS ANALYSIS -- MANAGING CONSTRAINTS

1. **Linear Programming**

    a. Linear programming optimizes a linear function subject to certain constraints. The objective of linear programming is to choose the best solution from a potentially infinite number of possibilities.

        1) Applied to business, linear programming can be used to maximize revenue or profit or minimize cost, given limited resources.

    b. The problem to be solved is the objective function.

        1) After the objective function and its constraints have been stated in business terms, they are translated into mathematical terms. The functions can then be graphed and solved algebraically.

EXAMPLE

A company produces products Grimthon and Jonquin and is seeking the most profitable output levels. The profits per unit sold of Grimthon and Jonquin are US $5,000 and US $4,000, respectively. The objective function is therefore

Maximize 5,000G + 4,000J

In business terms, the constraints are stated as follows:

- At least five total units must be produced to justify the setup costs.
- A study of market demand shows that only one unit of Grimthon can be sold for every three of Jonquin.
- The production line can produce two units of Grimthon for every three of Jonquin, up to a maximum of 30 units combined.
- Partial units but not negative units can be produced.

The company translates the constraints into mathematical relations, which are then restated as equations.

1. Minimum production: $G + J \geq 5$ ===> $G + J = 5$
2. Market balance: $G \leq 3J$ ===> $G = 3J$ ===> $G - 3J = 0$
3. Production capacity: $2G + 3J \leq 30$ ===> $2G + 3J = 30$
4. Nonnegativity: $G, J \geq 0$ ===> $G, J = 0$

c. The graphical method plots the linear functions represented by the constraint formulas.

1) The area enclosed by the graphed functions is the feasible region. The optimal solution is at the intersection of two or more constraint equations.

EXAMPLE

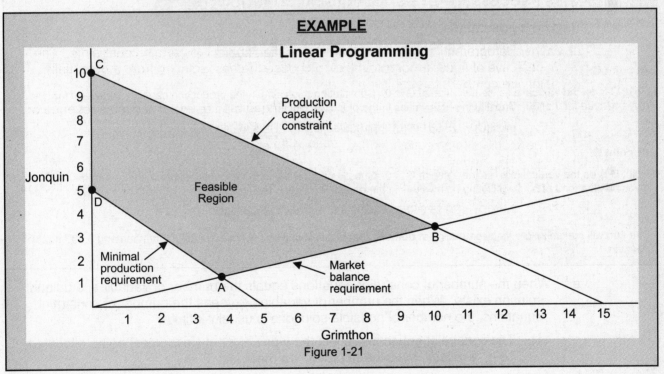

Figure 1-21

d. The algebraic method complements the graphical method. The combination of the two products that maximizes the objective function is at one of the corners of the feasible region.

1) Thus, the coordinates of these intersections may be determined by solving simultaneously the relevant **pairs of equations**.

EXAMPLE

At point A:

$$\begin{aligned}
\text{The minimal production requirement:} \quad & G + J = 5 \\
\text{The market balance requirement:} \quad & \underline{-G + 3J = 0} \\
& 4J = 5 \\
& J = 1.25
\end{aligned}$$

Substituting 1.25 for J in the minimal production requirement formula gives a value for G of 3.75. Substituting both values in the objective function results in the level of profit at point A:

$$\text{Profit(A)} = \text{US }\$5,000(3.75) + \$4,000(1.25) = \underline{\textbf{US \$23,750}}$$

At point B:

$$\begin{aligned}
\text{The market balance requirement:} \quad & G - 3J = 0 \\
\text{The production capacity constraint:} \quad & \underline{2G + 3J = 30} \\
& 3G = 30 \\
& G = 10
\end{aligned}$$

Substituting 10 for G in the market balance requirement formula gives a value for J of 3.333. Substituting both values in the objective function results in the level of profit at point B:

$$\text{Profit(B)} = \text{US }\$5,000(10) + \$4,000(3.333) = \underline{\textbf{US \$63,333}}$$

At point C:

Point C is on the vertical axis, so the value of G is 0. Substituting this value in the production capacity constraint formula gives a value for J of 10. Substituting both values in the objective function results in the level of profit at point C:

$$\text{Profit(C)} = \text{US }\$5,000(0) + \$4,000(10) = \underline{\textbf{US \$40,000}}$$

At point D:

Point D is on the vertical axis, so the value of G is 0. Substituting this value in the minimal production requirement formula gives a value for J of 5. Substituting both values in the objective function results in the level of profit at point D:

$$\text{Profit(D)} = \text{US }\$5,000(0) + \$4,000(5) = \underline{\textbf{US \$20,000}}$$

The firm will maximize profits by producing at **point B**, that is, at an output level of 10 units of Grimthon and 3.333 units of Jonquin.

---

e. When the number of constraint equations equals the number of variables, a unique solution exists. When the number of variables exceeds the number of constraint equations, the number of possible solutions is usually infinite.

1) The constraint equations reflect the types of input (resources) being allocated, e.g., available machine hours or raw materials.

f. A shadow price is the amount by which the value of the optimal solution of the objective function in a linear programming problem will change if a one-unit change is made in a binding constraint.

1) A nonbinding constraint has excess capacity, i.e., the optimal solution does not use all of the given resource. The shadow price for a nonbinding constraint is zero because a one-unit change will not affect the optimal solution when excess capacity exists.

2) The calculation of shadow prices is a simple example of sensitivity analysis, which is any procedure to test the responsiveness of the solution indicated by a model to changes in variables, alternative decisions, or errors.

g. The advantage of linear programming is its applicability to many types of problems and its usefulness for sensitivity analysis. A major disadvantage is the restrictiveness of its linear assumptions, for example, that all costs are variable or fixed.

2. **Theory of Constraints -- Overview**

   a. The theory of constraints (TOC) is a system to improve human thinking about problems. It has been greatly extended to include manufacturing operations.

   b. The basic premise of TOC as applied to business is that improving any process is best done not by trying to maximize efficiency in every part of the process but by focusing on the slowest part of the process, called the constraint.

      1) For example, during the early days of the American Civil War, several units calling themselves legions were formed, consisting of combined infantry, artillery, and cavalry. This arrangement did not last because the entire unit could only maneuver as fast as the slowest part. The artillery was the constraint.

      2) Increasing the efficiency of processes that are not constraints merely creates backup in the system.

   c. The steps in a TOC analysis are as follows:

      1) Identify the constraint.
      2) Determine the most profitable product mix given the constraint.
      3) Maximize the flow through the constraint.
      4) Increase capacity at the constraint.
      5) Redesign the manufacturing process for greater flexibility and speed.

3. **Detailed Steps in Performing a TOC Analysis**

   a. **Identify the constraint.**

      1) The bottleneck operation is usually where production delays are longest.

      2) A more sophisticated approach is to analyze available resources (number and skill level of employees, inventory levels, time spent in other phases of the process) and determine which phase has negative slack time, i.e., the phase without enough resources to keep pace with input.

      3) For example, a company makes three products: an airborne radar unit, a seagoing sonar unit, and a ground sonar unit. Under the current setup, the hours spent by each product in the two phases of the manufacturing process are as follows:

Product	Assembly	Testing
Airborne Radar	3	4
Seagoing Sonar	8	10
Ground Sonar	5	5

         a) The company has 150 hours available every month for testing. Under the current setup, therefore, the testing phase is the constraint.

   b. **Determine the most profitable product mix given the constraint.**

      1) In TOC analysis, short-term profit maximization requires maximizing the contribution margin through the constraint (the throughput margin or throughput contribution).

         a) The product to be produced is not necessarily the one with the highest contribution margin per unit, but the one with the highest throughput margin per unit. Thus, managers must make the most profitable use of the bottleneck operation.

      2) Throughput (supervariable) costing recognizes only direct materials costs as variable and thus relevant to throughput margin. All other manufacturing costs are ignored because they are considered fixed in the short run.

         Throughput margin = Sales − Direct materials

3) To determine the most profitable use of the bottleneck operation, a manager next calculates the throughput margin per unit of time spent in the constraint. Profitability is maximized by keeping the bottleneck operation busy with the product with the highest throughput margin per unit of time.

4) The company calculates the throughput margin on each product and divides by the hours spent in testing:

	Airborne Radar	Seagoing Sonar	Ground Sonar
Price	US $200,000	US $600,000	US $300,000
Minus: Materials costs	(100,000)	(400,000)	(250,000)
Throughput margin	US $100,000	US $200,000	US $ 50,000
Divided by: Constraint time	÷ 4	÷ 10	÷ 5
Throughput margin per hour	US $ 25,000	US $ 20,000	US $ 10,000

a) The crucial factor in determining the optimal product mix is not which product is most profitable in terms of total throughput margin (the seagoing sonar) but which one has the highest margin per time spent in the bottleneck operation (the airborne radar).

b) To derive the most profitable product mix given finite resources, customer demand must be considered. The company has determined that it can sell 12 units of radar, six units of seagoing sonar, and 22 units of ground sonar per month.

i) The available time in the bottleneck operation is first devoted to the product with the highest throughput margin (TM), then in descending order until the company is unable to meet demand.

ii) In the calculation below, the hours remaining after assignment to each product are the hours which can be devoted to the next product.

	Highest TM: Airborne Radar	2nd Highest TM: Seagoing Sonar	Lowest TM: Ground Sonar
Product:			
Demand in units	12	6	22
Hours per unit in bottleneck	× 4	× 10	× 5
Hours needed to fulfill demand	48	60	110
Hours available	150	102	42
Hours remaining	102	42	(68)

c) Applying the principles of TOC, the company will forgo some sales of the ground sonar in favor of products that are more profitable given the current constraint.

c. **Maximize the flow through the constraint.**

1) Production flow through a constraint is managed using the drum-buffer-rope (DBR) system.

a) The drum (i.e., the beat to which a production process marches) is the bottleneck operation (the constraint).

b) The buffer is a minimal amount of work-in-process input to the drum that is maintained to ensure that it is always in operation.

c) The rope is the sequence of activities preceding and including the bottleneck operation that must be coordinated to avoid inventory buildup.

d. **Increase capacity at the constraint.**

1) In the short-run, TOC encourages a manager to make the best use of the bottleneck operation. The intermediate step for improving the process is to increase the bottleneck operation's capacity.

e. **Redesign the manufacturing process for greater flexibility and speed.**

1) The long-term solution is to reengineer the entire process. The firm should take advantage of new technology, drop product lines requiring too much effort, and redesign remaining products to ease the manufacturing process.

a) Value engineering is useful for this purpose because it explicitly balances product cost and the needs of potential customers (product functions).

Stop and review! You have completed the outline for this subunit. Study multiple-choice question 38 on page 59.

1.13 BUSINESS PROCESS ANALYSIS -- REENGINEERING

1. **Overview**

a. One approach to business process analysis is business process reengineering. It involves process innovation and core process redesign. Instead of improving existing procedures, it finds new ways of doing things.

1) The emphasis is on simplification and elimination of nonvalue-adding activities. Thus, reengineering is not continuous improvement or simply downsizing or modifying an existing system. It should be reserved for the most important processes.

2) In the modern, highly competitive business environment, an organization may need to adapt quickly and radically to change. Accordingly, reengineering will usually be a cross-departmental process of innovation requiring substantial investment in information technology and retraining. Successful reengineering may bring dramatic improvements in customer service and the speed of new product introductions.

2. **Other Aspects**

a. A reengineered organization may use workflow process departmentation. Such a horizontal organization focuses on the flow of work between identifying and satisfying customer needs.

1) For example, sales, billing, and service might be combined in one account management process department.

b. Reengineering and TQM techniques eliminate many traditional controls. They exploit modern technology to improve productivity and decrease the number of clerical workers. Thus, controls should be automated and self-correcting and require minimal human intervention. Moreover, auditors must be prepared to encounter (and use) new technologies.

1) The emphasis therefore shifts to monitoring so management can determine when an operation may be out of control and corrective action is needed.

c. Monitoring is needed to assess the quality of internal control over time. Management considers whether internal control is properly designed and operating as intended and modifies it to reflect changing conditions. Monitoring may be in the form of separate, periodic evaluations or of ongoing monitoring.

1) Ongoing monitoring occurs as part of routine operations. It includes management and supervisory review, comparisons, reconciliations, and other actions by personnel as part of their regular activities.

d. Most reengineering and TQM methods also assume that humans will be motivated to work actively in improving operations when they are full participants in the process. However, these methods may be resisted by employees who are insecure because of lack of skills, fear of failure, breakup of work groups, and other factors.

Stop and review! You have completed the outline for this subunit. Study multiple-choice questions 39 and 40 on page 60.

QUESTIONS

1.1 Overview of Quality

1. A traditional quality control process in manufacturing consists of mass inspection of goods only at the end of a production process. A major deficiency of the traditional control process is that

A. It is expensive to do the inspections at the end of the process.

B. It is not possible to rework defective items.

C. It is not 100% effective.

D. It does not focus on improving the entire production process.

Answer (D) is correct. *(CIA, adapted)*
REQUIRED: The major deficiency of a traditional quality control process.
DISCUSSION: The process used to produce the goods is not thoroughly reviewed and evaluated for efficiency and effectiveness. Preventing defects and increasing efficiency by improving the production process raises quality standards and decreases costs.
Answer (A) is incorrect. Other quality control processes can also be expensive. Answer (B) is incorrect. Reworking defective items may be possible although costly. Answer (C) is incorrect. No quality control system will be 100% effective.

2. Which of the following criteria would be most useful to a sales department manager in evaluating the performance of the manager's customer-service group?

A. The customer is always right.

B. Customer complaints should be processed promptly.

C. Employees should maintain a positive attitude when dealing with customers.

D. All customer inquiries should be answered within 7 days of receipt.

Answer (D) is correct. *(CIA, adapted)*
REQUIRED: The criterion most useful for evaluating a customer-service group.
DISCUSSION: A criterion that requires all customer inquiries to be answered within 7 days of receipt permits accurate measurement of performance. The quantitative and specific nature of the appraisal using this standard avoids the vagueness, subjectivity, and personal bias that may afflict other forms of personnel evaluations.
Answer (A) is incorrect. Customer orientation is difficult to quantify. Answer (B) is incorrect. The standard specified is vague. Answer (C) is incorrect. No measure of a positive attitude has been specified for the employee.

1.2 Costs of Quality

3. The management and employees of a large household goods moving company believe that it if became nationally known as adhering to total quality management and continuous improvement, one result would be an increase in the company's profits and market share. What should the company focus on to achieve quality more economically?

A. Appraisal costs.

B. Prevention costs.

C. Internal failure costs.

D. External failure costs.

Answer (B) is correct. *(CIA, adapted)*
REQUIRED: The necessary focus for achieving quality more economically.
DISCUSSION: Prevention costs are incurred to prevent defects. Prevention is ordinarily less costly than the combined costs of appraisal, internal failure, and external failure.

4. Listed below are costs of quality that a manufacturing company has incurred throughout its operations.

Cost Items	Amount
Design reviews	US $275,000
Finished goods returned due to failure	55,000
Freight on replacement finished goods	27,000
Labor inspection during manufacturing	75,000
Labor inspection of raw materials	32,000
Manufacturing product-testing labor	63,000
Manufacturing rework labor and overhead	150,000
Materials used in warranty repairs	68,000
Process engineering	180,000
Product-liability claims	145,000
Product-testing equipment	35,000
Repairs to equipment due to breakdowns	22,000
Scheduled equipment maintenance	90,000
Scrap material	125,000
Training of manufacturing workers	156,000

The U.S. dollar amount of the costs of quality classified as prevention costs for the manufacturing firm would be

A. US $643,000

B. US $701,000

C. US $736,000

D. US $768,000

Answer (B) is correct. *(CIA, adapted)*
REQUIRED: The prevention costs.
DISCUSSION: Prevention costs are incurred to prevent defects. Examples are the costs of employee training, review of equipment design, preventive maintenance, and evaluation of suppliers. Accordingly, the prevention costs equal US $701,000 ($275,000 design reviews + $180,000 process engineering + $90,000 scheduled maintenance + $156,000 training).
Answer (A) is incorrect. US $643,000 omits scheduled equipment maintenance and includes labor inspection of raw materials (an appraisal cost). Answer (C) is incorrect. US $736,000 includes the cost of product testing equipment (an appraisal cost). Answer (D) is incorrect. US $768,000 includes the cost of product testing equipment and labor inspection of raw materials. Both costs are appraisal costs.

5. Quality cost indices are often used to measure and analyze the cost of maintaining a given level of quality. One example of a quality cost index, which uses a direct labor base, is computed as

$$Quality\ cost\ index = \frac{Total\ quality\ costs}{Total\ direct\ labor\ costs} \times 100$$

The following quality cost data were collected for May and June:

	May	June
Prevention costs	US $ 4,000	US $ 5,000
Appraisal costs	6,000	5,000
Internal failure costs	12,000	15,000
External failure costs	14,000	11,000
Direct labor costs	90,000	100,000

Based upon these cost data, the quality cost index

A. Decreased four points from May to June.

B. Was unchanged from May to June.

C. Increased 10 points from May to June.

D. Decreased 10 points from May to June.

Answer (A) is correct. *(CIA, adapted)*
REQUIRED: The change, if any, in the quality cost index.
DISCUSSION: The index for May was 40 [(US $4,000 + $6,000 + $12,000 + $14,000) ÷ $90,000], and the index for June was 36 [(US $5,000 + $5,000 + $15,000 + $11,000) ÷ $100,000].
Answer (B) is incorrect. The index decreased. Answer (C) is incorrect. The increase in prevention costs was 10% of the increase in labor costs. Answer (D) is incorrect. The decrease in appraisal costs was 10% of the increase in labor costs.

1.3 Tools for Assessing Quality

Questions 6 and 7 are based on the following information. An organization has collected data on the complaints made by personal computer users and has categorized the complaints.

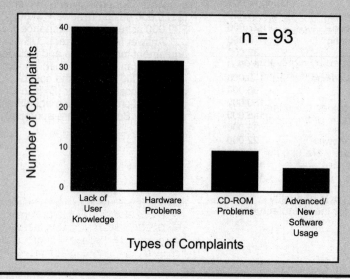

6. Using the information collected, the organization should focus on

   A. The total number of personal computer complaints that occurred.

   B. The number of computer complaints associated with CD-ROM problems and new software usage.

   C. The number of computer complaints associated with the lack of user knowledge and hardware problems.

   D. The cost to alleviate all computer complaints.

Answer (C) is correct. *(CIA, adapted)*
   REQUIRED: The organization's focus based on the data.
   DISCUSSION: Complaints based on lack of user knowledge and hardware problems are by far the most frequent according to this chart. Consequently, the company should devote its resources primarily to these issues.
   Answer (A) is incorrect. More detailed information is not available. The Pareto diagram does not focus on the total quantity of computer complaints. Answer (B) is incorrect. Complaints about CD-ROMs and software are infrequent. Answer (D) is incorrect. Cost information is not provided.

7. The chart displays the

   A. Arithmetic mean of each computer complaint.

   B. Relative frequency of each computer complaint.

   C. Median of each computer complaint.

   D. Absolute frequency of each computer complaint.

Answer (D) is correct. *(CIA, adapted)*
   REQUIRED: The information displayed.
   DISCUSSION: This Pareto diagram depicts the frequencies of complaints in absolute terms. It displays the actual number of each type of complaint. The chart does not display arithmetic means, relative frequencies, or medians of each type of complaint.

1.4 Total Quality Management (TQM)

8. Under a total quality management (TQM) approach,

- A. Measurement occurs throughout the process, and errors are caught and corrected at the source.
- B. Quality control is performed by highly trained inspectors at the end of the production process.
- C. Upper management assumes the primary responsibility for the quality of the products and services.
- D. A large number of suppliers are used in order to obtain the lowest possible prices.

Answer (A) is correct. *(CIA, adapted)*
REQUIRED: The true statement about total quality management.
DISCUSSION: TQM emphasizes quality as a basic organizational function. TQM is the continuous pursuit of quality in every aspect of organizational activities. One of the basic principles of TQM is doing it right the first time. Thus, errors should be caught and corrected at the source.
Answer (B) is incorrect. TQM emphasizes discovering errors throughout the process, not during inspection of finished goods. Answer (C) is incorrect. All members of the organization assume responsibility for quality of the products and services. Answer (D) is incorrect. The TQM philosophy recommends limiting the number of suppliers to create a strong relationship.

9. Which of the following is a characteristic of total quality management (TQM)?

- A. Management by objectives.
- B. On-the-job training by other workers.
- C. Quality by final inspection.
- D. Education and self-improvement.

Answer (D) is correct. *(CIA, adapted)*
REQUIRED: The characteristic of TQM.
DISCUSSION: TQM is the continuous pursuit of quality in every aspect of organizational activities. One of the means of achieving this is through employee training and empowerment.
Answer (A) is incorrect. MBO involves the aggressive pursuit of numerical quotas; any such mechanistic requirement runs counter to the pursuit of TQM. Answer (B) is incorrect. Informal learning from coworkers serves to entrench bad work habits. Answer (C) is incorrect. A goal of TQM is to prevent the generation of defective output.

10. In which of the following organizational structures does total quality management (TQM) work best?

- A. Hierarchal.
- B. Teams of people from the same specialty.
- C. Teams of people from different specialties.
- D. Specialists working individually.

Answer (C) is correct. *(CIA, adapted)*
REQUIRED: The structure in which TQM works best.
DISCUSSION: TQM advocates replacement of the traditional hierarchal structure with teams of people from different specialties. This change follows from TQM's emphasis on empowering employees and teamwork. Employees should (1) have proper training, necessary information, and the best tools; (2) be fully engaged in the decision process; and (3) receive fair compensation. If such empowered employees are assembled in teams of individuals with the required skills, TQM theorists believe they will be more effective than people performing their tasks separately in a rigid structure.
Answer (A) is incorrect. Hierarchal organization stifles TQM. Answer (B) is incorrect. TQM works best with teams of people from different specialties. Answer (D) is incorrect. Teamwork is essential for TQM.

11. Total quality management (TQM) in a manufacturing environment is best exemplified by

- A. Identifying and reworking production defects before sale.
- B. Designing the product to minimize defects.
- C. Performing inspections to isolate defects as early as possible.
- D. Making machine adjustments periodically to reduce defects.

Answer (B) is correct. *(CIA, adapted)*
REQUIRED: The activity characteristic of TQM.
DISCUSSION: TQM emphasizes quality as a basic organizational function. TQM is the continuous pursuit of quality in every aspect of organizational activities. One of the basic principles of TQM is doing it right the first time. Thus, errors should be caught and corrected at the source, and quality should be built in (designed in) from the start.

1.5 ISO Framework

12. Which of the following statements is **not** true regarding ISO 9000 standards?

A. Compliance with the standards is voluntary.

B. The ISO 9000 standards are revised every 5 years to account for technical and market developments.

C. The objective of ISO 9000 standards is to ensure high quality products and services.

D. ISO 9000 is a set of generic standards for establishing and maintaining a quality system within an entity.

Answer (C) is correct. *(Publisher, adapted)*
REQUIRED: The false statement regarding ISO 9000 standards.
DISCUSSION: The objective of ISO 9000 standards is to ensure consistent quality even if the quality is poor. The market determines the quality of the result.
Answer (A) is incorrect. Compliance is voluntary, but many entities are adopting the standards for competitive reasons or because of concern that the standards will be required in foreign markets. Answer (B) is incorrect. The ISO rules specify that standards are periodically revised every 5 years to reflect technical and market developments. Answer (D) is incorrect. ISO 9000 standards are generic and only ensure consistent quality in the product being produced.

13. Which of the following is a major element of the ISO 9000 quality management system standards?

A. The principle that improved employee satisfaction will lead to increased productivity.

B. The attitude and actions of the board and management regarding the significance of control within the organization.

C. The assessment of the risk that objectives are not achieved.

D. A requirement for organizations to monitor information on customer satisfaction as a measure of performance.

Answer (D) is correct. *(CIA, adapted)*
REQUIRED: The major element of QMS standards.
DISCUSSION: ISO 9000:2008 provides a model for quality assurance programs. It requires an entity to demonstrate its ability to increase customer satisfaction through improving the QMS and ensuring conformity with requirements.
Answer (A) is incorrect. The principle that improved employee satisfaction will lead to increased productivity is not an ISO 9000 standard. Following the eight management principles that underlie these standards should improve employee satisfaction. Answer (B) is incorrect. The control environment concept defined in the Glossary of The IIA's *Standards* is not reflected in the ISO 9000 standards. Answer (C) is incorrect. The ISO 9000 standards do not take a risk assessment approach. Risk assessment underlies internal auditing.

1.6 Regression and Correlation

14. A division uses a regression in which monthly advertising expenditures are used to predict monthly product sales (both in millions of US dollars). The results show a regression coefficient for the independent variable equal to 0.8. This coefficient value indicates that

A. The average monthly advertising expenditure in the sample is US $800,000.

B. When monthly advertising is at its average level, product sales will be US $800,000.

C. On average, every additional dollar of advertising results in US $.80 of additional sales.

D. Advertising is not a good predictor of sales because the coefficient is so small.

Answer (C) is correct. *(CIA, adapted)*
REQUIRED: The significance of the regression coefficient for the independent variable.
DISCUSSION: The regression coefficient represents the change in the dependent variable corresponding to a unit change in the independent variable. Thus, it is the slope of the regression line, represented by b in the linear equation $y = a + bx$.
Answer (A) is incorrect. A regression coefficient is unrelated to the means of the variables. Answer (B) is incorrect. To predict a specific value of sales, the value of the independent variable is multiplied by the coefficient. The product is then added to the y-intercept value. Answer (D) is incorrect. The absolute size of the coefficient bears no necessary relationship to the importance of the variable.

15. What coefficient of correlation results from the following data?

x	y
1	10
2	8
3	6
4	4
5	2

A. 0

B. –1

C. +1

D. Cannot be determined from the data given.

Answer (B) is correct. *(CIA, adapted)*

REQUIRED: The coefficient of correlation.

DISCUSSION: The coefficient of correlation (in standard notation, r) measures the strength of the linear relationship. The magnitude of r is independent of the scales of measurement of x and y. Its range is –1 to +1. A value of –1 indicates a perfectly inverse linear relationship between x and y. A value of zero indicates no linear relationship between x and y. A value of 1 indicates a perfectly direct relationship between x and y. As x increases by 1, y consistently decreases by 2. Hence, a perfectly inverse relationship exists, and r must be equal to –1.

Answer (A) is incorrect. A perfect negative correlation exists. Answer (C) is incorrect. An inverse, not a direct, relationship exists. Answer (D) is incorrect. A linear relationship exists between x and y.

16. The following data on variables x and y was collected from June to October:

	June	July	August	September	October
x	24	31	19	15	22
y	104	76	124	140	112

The correlation coefficient between variables x and y is nearest to

A. 1.0

B. –1.0

C. 0.5

D. 0.0

Answer (B) is correct. *(CIA, adapted)*

REQUIRED: The correlation coefficient.

DISCUSSION: The simplest way to solve this problem is to use a scatter diagram:

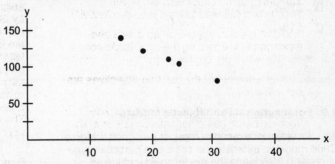

The data points appear to form a straight line with a negative slope. Thus, –1 is the best estimate of the coefficient of correlation.

Answer (A) is incorrect. A positive correlation coefficient implies that one variable increases (decreases) as the other increases (decreases). The data clearly do not support this conclusion. Answer (C) is incorrect. A positive correlation coefficient implies that one variable increases (decreases) as the other increases (decreases). The data clearly do not support this conclusion. Answer (D) is incorrect. A correlation coefficient of zero implies that the two variables are unrelated. The data clearly indicate that the two variables move in opposite directions.

17. The internal auditor of a bank has developed a multiple regression model that has been used for a number of years to estimate the amount of interest income from commercial loans. During the current year, the auditor applies the model and discovers that the r^2 value has decreased dramatically, but the model otherwise seems to be working. Which of the following conclusions is justified by the change?

A. Changing to a cross-sectional regression analysis should cause r^2 to increase.

B. Regression analysis is no longer an appropriate technique to estimate interest income.

C. Some new factors not included in the model are causing interest income to change.

D. A linear regression analysis would increase the model's reliability.

Answer (C) is correct. *(CIA, adapted)*

REQUIRED: The meaning of the decrease in r^2.

DISCUSSION: The coefficient of determination (r^2) is the amount of variation in the dependent variable (interest income) that is explained by the independent variables. In this case, less of the change in interest income is explained by the model. Thus, some other factor must be causing interest income to change. This change merits audit investigation.

Answer (A) is incorrect. Cross-sectional regression analysis is inappropriate. The auditor is trying to estimate changes in a single account balance over time. Answer (B) is incorrect. Regression analysis may still be the most appropriate methodology to estimate interest income, but the auditor should first understand the factors that may be causing r^2 to decrease. The reason may be a systematic error in the account balance. Answer (D) is incorrect. Linear regression models are simpler models, but the auditor should be searching for a systematic error in the account balance or applying a more complex model.

1.7 Forecasting -- Time-Series Models

18. To remove the effect of seasonal variation from a time series, original data should be

    A. Increased by the seasonal factor.

    B. Reduced by the seasonal factor.

    C. Multiplied by the seasonal factor.

    D. Divided by the seasonal factor.

Answer (D) is correct. *(CIA, adapted)*
    REQUIRED: Factoring out seasonal variation from a time series.
    DISCUSSION: Seasonal variations are common in many businesses. To remove the effect of seasonal variation from a time series, the original data (with the four trends) is divided by the seasonal norm.

19. A learning curve of 80% assumes that the incremental unit time is reduced by 20% for each doubling of output. Also, direct labor cost is proportionate to time worked. What is the incremental direct labor cost of the 16th unit produced as an approximate percentage of the first unit produced?

    A. 41%

    B. 31%

    C. 51%

    D. 64%

Answer (A) is correct. *(CIA, adapted)*
    REQUIRED: The cost of the last unit produced.
    DISCUSSION: The assumption is that the incremental unit time (time to produce the last unit) is reduced by 20% when production doubles. Thus, the labor cost of the sixteenth unit is 40.96% of that for the first unit (100% × 80% × 80% × 80% × 80%).
    Answer (B) is incorrect. This percentage is the average relative labor cost of the last eight units. It is based on the assumption that the cumulative average time per unit is reduced by 20% when production doubles. Answer (C) is incorrect. This percentage is the labor cost of the eighth unit relative to that of the first unit. Answer (D) is incorrect. This percentage is the labor cost of the fourth unit relative to that of the first unit.

1.8 Forecasting -- Probabilistic Models

20. An account executive has just designed a Monte Carlo model to estimate the costs of a particular type of project. Validating the model could include all **except**

    A. Checking for errors in the computer programming.

    B. Checking that assumed probability distributions are reasonable.

    C. Comparing test results with previously validated models.

    D. Applying the model.

Answer (D) is correct. *(CIA, adapted)*
    REQUIRED: The step not involved in validating a Monte Carlo model.
    DISCUSSION: The Monte Carlo technique is used in a simulation to generate the individual values for a random value. An essential step in the simulation procedure is to validate the mathematical model used. This process involves not only searching for errors but also verifying the assumptions. It also should provide some assurance that the results of the experiment will be realistic. This assurance is often obtained using historical data. If the model gives results equivalent to what actually happened, the model is historically valid. There is still some risk, however, that changes could make the model invalid for the future. The model should not be implemented until this validation process is complete.

21. The sales manager for a builder of custom yachts developed the following conditional table for annual production and sales

Demand	10	20	30	50
Probability	0.1	0.2	0.5	0.2

Yachts Built	Expected Profit			
10	US $10	US $10	US $10	US $10
20	0	20	20	20
30	(10)	10	30	30
50	(30)	(10)	10	50

According to the table, how many yachts should be built?

    A. 10

    B. 20

    C. 30

    D. 50

Answer (C) is correct. *(CIA, adapted)*
    REQUIRED: The number of units produced to yield maximum profit.
    DISCUSSION: To achieve the maximum expected profit, 30 yachts should be built. For each level of production, multiply the probability of demand by the expected profit. The computation for the maximum is:
0.1(–US $10) + 0.2($10) + 0.5($30) + 0.2($30) = US $22.
    Answer (A) is incorrect. Building 10 yachts only results in an expected profit of US $10. Answer (B) is incorrect. Building 20 yachts only results in an expected profit of US $18. Answer (D) is incorrect. Building 50 yachts only results in an expected profit of US $10.

22. Only two companies manufacture Product A. The finished product is identical regardless of which company manufactures it. The cost to manufacture Product A is US $1, and the selling price is US $2. One company considers reducing the price to achieve 100% market share but fears the other company will respond by further reducing the price. Such a scenario would involve a

A. No-win strategy.

B. Dual-win strategy.

C. One win-one lose strategy.

D. Neutral strategy.

Answer (A) is correct. *(CIA, adapted)*
REQUIRED: The effect of a price war.
DISCUSSION: If both firms reduce the selling price of Product A, neither will gain sales and the resultant price war will cause both firms to earn lower profits. This outcome is inevitable when reduced profit margins do not result in a significant increase in sales. This is classified as a no-win strategy.
Answer (B) is incorrect. Since both firms will experience lower profits, neither will win. Answer (C) is incorrect. Since both firms will experience lower profits, both will lose. Answer (D) is incorrect. Both firms will experience lower profits.

23. The decision rule that selects the strategy with the highest utility payoff if the worst state of nature occurs is the

A. Minimize regret rule.

B. Maximize utility rule.

C. Maximin rule.

D. Maximax rule.

Answer (C) is correct. *(CIA, adapted)*
REQUIRED: The rule that selects the strategy with the highest utility payoff if the worst state of nature occurs.
DISCUSSION: The maximin rule determines the minimum payoff for each decision and then chooses the decision with the maximum minimum payoff. It is a conservative criterion adopted by risk-averse players, that is, those for whom the disutility of a loss exceeds the utility of an equal gain.
Answer (A) is incorrect. The minimize regret rule selects the action that minimizes the maximum opportunity cost. Answer (B) is incorrect. The maximize utility rule is not a decision rule. Answer (D) is incorrect. The maximax rule selects the choice that provides the greatest payoff if the most favorable state of nature occurs.

1.9 Selecting the Forecasting Method

24. As part of a risk analysis, an auditor wishes to forecast the percentage growth in next month's sales for a particular plant using the past 30 months' sales results. Significant changes in the organization affecting sales volumes were made within the last 9 months. The most effective analysis technique to use would be

A. Unweighted moving average.

B. Exponential smoothing.

C. Queuing theory.

D. Linear regression analysis.

Answer (B) is correct. *(CIA, adapted)*
REQUIRED: The most effective analysis technique to forecast the percentage growth in next month's sales.
DISCUSSION: Under exponential smoothing, each forecast equals the sum of the last observation times the smoothing constant, plus the last forecast times one minus the constant. Thus, exponential means that greater weight is placed on the most recent data, with the weights of all data falling off exponentially as the data age. This feature is important because of the organizational changes that affected sales volume.
Answer (A) is incorrect. An unweighted average will not give more importance to more recent data. Answer (C) is incorrect. Queuing theory is used to minimize the cost of waiting lines. Answer (D) is incorrect. Linear regression analysis determines the equation for the relationship among variables. It does not give more importance to more recent data.

25. A firm is attempting to estimate its allowance for doubtful accounts. The probabilities of these doubtful accounts follow a transition process over time. They evolve from their starting value to a changed value. As such, the most effective technique to analyze the problem is

A. Markov chain analysis.

B. Econometric theory.

C. Monte Carlo analysis.

D. Dynamic programming.

Answer (A) is correct. *(CIA, adapted)*
REQUIRED: The most effective technique to analyze a problem involving changing probabilities.
DISCUSSION: A Markov chain is a series of events in which the probability of an event depends on the immediately preceding event. An example is the game of blackjack in which the probability of certain cards being dealt is dependent upon what cards have already been dealt. In the analysis of bad debts, preceding events, such as collections, credit policy changes, and writeoffs, affect the probabilities of future losses.
Answer (B) is incorrect. Econometrics forecasts the impact of different economic policies and conditions. Answer (C) is incorrect. Monte Carlo analysis is a simulation technique that uses random-number procedures to create values for probabilistic components. Answer (D) is incorrect. Dynamic programming is a problem-solving approach that breaks a large mathematical model into a number of smaller, manageable problems.

26. A chief executive officer (CEO) believes that a major competitor may be planning a new campaign. The CEO sends a questionnaire to key personnel asking for original thinking concerning what the new campaign may be. The CEO selects the best possibilities and then sends another questionnaire asking for the most likely option. The process employed by the CEO is called the

A. Least squares technique.

B. Delphi technique.

C. Maximum likelihood technique.

D. Optimizing of expected payoffs.

Answer (B) is correct. *(CIA, adapted)*
REQUIRED: The process employed by the CEO to encourage original thinking.
DISCUSSION: The Delphi technique is a forecasting or decision-making approach that attempts to avoid groupthink (the tendency of individuals to conform to what they perceive to be the consensus). The technique allows only written, anonymous communication among group members. Each member takes a position on the problem at hand. A summary of these positions is communicated to each member. The process is repeated for several iterations as the members move toward a consensus. Thus, the Delphi technique is a qualitative, not quantitative, technique.
Answer (A) is incorrect. Least squares refers to regression analysis and involves specified variables. Answer (C) is incorrect. The maximum likelihood technique is a complex alternative to least squares. Answer (D) is incorrect. Optimizing expected payoffs is used in the analysis of decision-making alternatives, which relies on historical information.

27. The marketing department of a company is deciding on the price to charge for a key product. In setting this price, marketing needs to consider the price that a major competitor will charge for a similar product because the competitor's price will affect the demand for the company's product. Similarly, in setting its price, the competitor will consider what the company will charge. What is an appropriate mathematical technique for analyzing such a decision?

A. Game theory.

B. Probability theory.

C. Linear programming.

D. Sensitivity analysis.

Answer (A) is correct. *(CIA, adapted)*
REQUIRED: The mathematical technique for analyzing the price to charge given the existence of competition.
DISCUSSION: Game (or decision) theory is a mathematical approach to decision making when confronted with an enemy or competitor. Games are classified according to the number of players and the algebraic sum of the payoffs. In a two-person game, if the payoff is given by the loser to the winner, the algebraic sum is zero and the game is called a zero-sum game. If it is possible for both players to profit, however, the game is a positive-sum game. Mathematical models have been developed to select optimal strategies for certain simple games.
Answer (B) is incorrect. Probability theory is a mathematical technique used to express quantitatively the likelihood of occurrence of an event. Answer (C) is incorrect. Linear programming is a mathematical technique for optimizing a given objective subject to certain constraints. Answer (D) is incorrect. Sensitivity analysis is a method for studying the effects of changes in one or more variables on the results of a decision model.

28. Because of the large number of factors that could affect the demand for its new product, interactions among these factors, and the probabilities associated with different values of these factors, the marketing department would like to develop a computerized model for projecting demand for this product. By using a random-number procedure to generate values for the different factors, it will be able to estimate the distribution of demand for this new product. This method of estimating the distribution of demand for the new product is called

A. Monte Carlo simulation.

B. Linear programming.

C. Correlation analysis.

D. Differential analysis.

Answer (A) is correct. *(CIA, adapted)*
REQUIRED: The method of estimating the distribution of demand for the new product.
DISCUSSION: Simulations that use a random-number procedure to generate values for the inputs are Monte Carlo simulations.
Answer (B) is incorrect. Linear programming is a mathematical technique for maximizing or minimizing a given objective subject to certain constraints. Answer (C) is incorrect. Correlation analysis is a statistical procedure for studying the relations among variables. Answer (D) is incorrect. Differential analysis is a method used for decision-making that compares differences in costs (and revenues) of two or more possibilities.

29. A company is deciding whether to purchase an automated machine to manufacture one of its products. Expected net cash flows from this decision depend on several factors, interactions among those factors, and the probabilities associated with different levels of those factors. The method that the company should use to evaluate the distribution of net cash flows from this decision and changes in net cash flows resulting from changes in levels of various factors is

- A. Simulation and sensitivity analysis.
- B. Linear programming.
- C. Correlation analysis.
- D. Differential analysis.

Answer (A) is correct. *(CIA, adapted)*
REQUIRED: The technique used to evaluate cash flows from the purchase of a machine.
DISCUSSION: Simulation is a technique for experimenting with logical and mathematical models using a computer. Sensitivity analysis examines how the model's outcomes change as the parameters change.
Answer (B) is incorrect. Linear programming is a mathematical technique for optimizing a given objective function subject to certain constraints. Answer (C) is incorrect. Correlation analysis is a statistical procedure for studying the relation between variables. Answer (D) is incorrect. Differential analysis is used for decision making that compares differences in costs (revenues) of two or more options.

1.10 Project Management

30. In the Gantt chart below, shaded bars represent completed portions of activities, bars depicted with broken lines represent uncompleted portions, and blank bars represent activities not yet begun.

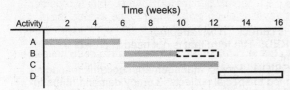

As of week 8, the Gantt chart shows that the project is

- A. Complete.
- B. Ahead of schedule.
- C. On schedule.
- D. Behind schedule.

Answer (C) is correct. *(CIA, adapted)*
REQUIRED: The status of a project according to the Gantt chart.
DISCUSSION: Activities B and C are the only activities that should be underway during week 8. Since both are underway and on schedule, the project is on schedule.
Answer (A) is incorrect. Activity B is incomplete, and activity D has not yet been started. Answer (B) is incorrect. As of week 8, activities B and C are underway, but neither is complete; thus, the project is not ahead of schedule. Answer (D) is incorrect. As of week 8, activities B and C are underway, but both are expected to finish on time.

31. The network below describes the interrelationships of several activities necessary to complete a project. The arrows represent the activities. The numbers between the arrows indicate the number of months to complete each activity.

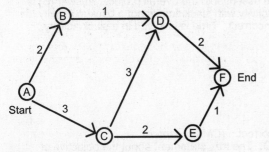

The shortest time to complete the project is

- A. 5 months.
- B. 6 months.
- C. 8 months.
- D. 14 months.

Answer (C) is correct. *(CIA, adapted)*
REQUIRED: The shortest time to complete the project.
DISCUSSION: The critical (longest) path through the network from node (A) to node (F) is path A-C-D-F. All other paths are shorter than path A-C-D-F, so the activities along those paths can be completed before the activities along path A-C-D-F. Thus, the shortest time to complete the project is 8 months (3 + 3 + 2).
Answer (A) is incorrect. The project cannot be completed in less than 8 months. Answer (B) is incorrect. The project cannot be completed in less than 8 months. Answer (D) is incorrect. No path through the network requires 14 months.

32. The following information and diagram apply to a project:

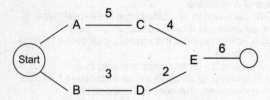

Activity	Time (days)	Immediate Predecessor
A	5	None
B	3	None
C	4	A
D	2	B
E	6	C, D

The earliest completion time for the project is

A. 11 days.

B. 14 days.

C. 15 days.

D. 20 days.

Answer (C) is correct. *(CIA, adapted)*
REQUIRED: The earliest completion time.
DISCUSSION: The two paths through the network are A-C-E (5 + 4 + 6 = 15 days) and B-D-E (3 + 2 + 6 = 11 days). The critical or longest path is thus A-C-E. Hence, the earliest completion time is 15 days.
Answer (A) is incorrect. The shortest, not the longest, path is 11 days. Answer (B) is incorrect. Neither of the paths through the network has a time of 14 days. Answer (D) is incorrect. The sum of all of the activity times is 20 days.

33. Which of the following terms is **not** used in project management?

A. Dummy activity.

B. Latest finish.

C. Optimistic time.

D. Lumpy demand.

Answer (D) is correct. *(CIA, adapted)*
REQUIRED: The term that is not used in project management.
DISCUSSION: Project management concerns managing teams assigned to special projects. Lumpy demand refers to periodic demand for a product or service that increases in large, lumpy increments.
Answer (A) is incorrect. A dummy activity allows concurrent activities on a PERT/CPM network to end on separate nodes. Answer (B) is incorrect. The latest finish is the latest that an activity can finish without causing delay in the completion of the project. Answer (C) is incorrect. Optimistic time is the time for completing a project if all goes well.

34. In a critical path analysis, if slack time in an activity exists, the activity

A. Is not essential to the overall project.

B. Is a backup activity to replace a main activity should it fail.

C. Could be delayed without delaying the overall project.

D. Involves essentially no time to complete.

Answer (C) is correct. *(CIA, adapted)*
REQUIRED: The implication of the existence of slack time.
DISCUSSION: Slack is the free time associated with activities not on the critical path. Slack represents unused resources that can be diverted to the critical path.
Answer (A) is incorrect. An activity with slack may nevertheless be essential to the overall project. Answer (B) is incorrect. An activity with slack time is not a backup activity. Answer (D) is incorrect. Time is involved in a slack activity.

1.11 Business Process Analysis -- Efficiency and Workflow

35. Queuing models are concerned with balancing the cost of waiting in the queue with the

A. Cost of providing service.

B. Number of customers in the queue.

C. Average waiting time in the queue.

D. Usage rate for the service being rendered.

Answer (A) is correct. *(CMA, adapted)*
REQUIRED: The true statement about the objective of queuing models.
DISCUSSION: Queuing (waiting-line) models minimize, for a given rate of arrivals, the sum of (1) the cost of providing service (including facility costs and operating costs) and (2) the cost of idle resources waiting in line. The latter may be a direct cost, if paid employees are waiting, or an opportunity cost in the case of waiting customers. This minimization occurs at the point where the cost of waiting is balanced by the cost of providing service.

36. The drive-through service at a fast-food restaurant consists of driving up to place an order, advancing to a window to pay for the order, and then advancing to another window to receive the items ordered. This type of waiting-line system is

A. Single channel, single phase.

B. Single channel, multiple phase.

C. Multiple channel, single phase.

D. Multiple channel, multiple phase.

Answer (B) is correct. *(CIA, adapted)*
REQUIRED: The type of waiting-line system described.
DISCUSSION: The drive-through represents a single queue (channel). Because this waiting line has three services in series, it may be said to be multiple phase. Another example is the typical factory assembly line. This terminology (channel, phase), however, is not used by all writers on queuing theory.
Answer (A) is incorrect. Service by one ticket-seller at a movie theater is an example of a single-channel, single-phase system. Answer (C) is incorrect. Supermarket checkout lines are a common example of multiple single-phase servers servicing multiple lines. Answer (D) is incorrect. An example of a multiple-channel, multiple-phase system is a set of supermarket checkout lines, each of which is served in sequence by a cashier and a person who packs grocery bags.

37. The arrival times in a waiting-line (queuing) model follow which probability distribution?

A. Binomial.

B. Chi-square.

C. Poisson.

D. Exponential.

Answer (C) is correct. *(CIA, adapted)*
REQUIRED: The distribution of the arrival time.
DISCUSSION: Queuing models assume that arrivals follow a Poisson process: The events (arrivals) are independent, any number of events must be possible in the interval of time, the probability of an event is proportional to the length of the interval, and the probability of more than one event is negligible if the interval is sufficiently small.
Answer (A) is incorrect. The binomial distribution is a discrete distribution in which each trial has just two outcomes. Answer (B) is incorrect. The chi-square distribution is a continuous distribution used to measure the fit between actual data and the theoretical distribution. Answer (D) is incorrect. Service time has an exponential distribution. This distribution gives the probability of zero events in a given interval, i.e., the probability of a specified time between arrivals.

1.12 Business Process Analysis -- Managing Constraints

38. Data regarding four different products manufactured by an organization are presented as follows. Direct material and direct labor are readily available from the respective resource markets. However, the manufacturer is limited to a maximum of 3,000 machine hours per month.

	Products			
	A	B	C	D
Unit price	US $15	US $18	US $20	US $25
Variable cost	7	11	10	16

Units Produced per
  Machine Hour:
    A: 3
    B: 4
    C: 2
    D: 3

The product that is the most profitable for the manufacturer in this situation is

A. Product A.

B. Product B.

C. Product C.

D. Product D.

Answer (B) is correct. *(CIA, adapted)*
REQUIRED: The product that is the most profitable for the manufacturer.
DISCUSSION: When resources are limited, maximum profits are achieved by maximizing the dollar contribution margin per limited or constraining factor. In this situation, machine hours are the constraining factor. Product B has a contribution margin per machine hour of US $28 [4 × (US $18 − 11)], which is greater than that of Product A [3 × (US $15 − $7) = US $24], Product C [2 × (US $20 − $10) = US $20], or Product D [3 × (US $25 − $16) = US $27].
Answer (A) is incorrect. Product A has the greatest contribution margin ratio (53%) but a lower CM per hour than B. Answer (C) is incorrect. Product C has a greater dollar unit contribution margin (US $10) but a lower CM per hour than B. Answer (D) is incorrect. Product D has the greatest selling price per unit (US $25) but a lower CM per hour than B.

1.13 Business Process Analysis -- Reengineering

39. A company has several departments that conduct technical studies and prepare reports for clients. Recently, there have been long delays in having these reports copied at the company's centralized copy center because of the dramatic increase in business. Management is considering decentralizing copy services to reduce the turnaround and provide clients with timely reports. An appropriate technique for minimizing turnaround time and the cost of providing copy services is

A. Queuing theory.

B. Linear programming.

C. Regression analysis.

D. Game theory.

Answer (A) is correct. *(CIA, adapted)*
REQUIRED: The appropriate method for minimizing turnaround time and the cost of providing copy services.
DISCUSSION: Two basic costs are involved in queuing (waiting-line) models: (1) the cost of providing service (including facility costs and operating costs) and (2) the cost of idle resources waiting in line. The latter may be a direct cost if paid employees are waiting, or an opportunity cost in the case of waiting customers. The objective of queuing theory is to minimize the total cost of the system, including both service and waiting costs, for a given rate of arrivals. This minimization occurs at the point at which cost of waiting is balanced by the cost of providing service. This company wishes to reduce the total of waiting costs (turnaround time) and the cost of copy services.
Answer (B) is incorrect. Linear programming is a mathematical technique for optimizing a given objective function subject to constraints. Answer (C) is incorrect. Regression analysis is a statistical procedure for estimating the relation between variables. Answer (D) is incorrect. Game theory is a mathematical approach to decision-making in which each decision-maker takes into account the courses of action of competitors.

40. An investment company is attempting to allocate its available funds between two investment alternatives, equities and bonds, which differ in terms of expected return and risk. The company would like to minimize its risk while earning an expected return of at least 10% and investing no more than 70% in either of the investment alternatives. An appropriate technique for allocating its funds between equities and bonds is

A. Linear programming.

B. Capital budgeting.

C. Differential analysis.

D. Queuing theory.

Answer (A) is correct. *(CIA, adapted)*
REQUIRED: The technique for allocating funds between equities and bonds.
DISCUSSION: Linear programming is a mathematical technique for planning resource allocation that optimizes a given objective function that is subject to certain constraints. In this case, the maximum investment is constrained by a 70% limit on either investment choice.
Answer (B) is incorrect. Capital budgeting is used to analyze and evaluate long-term capital investments. Answer (C) is incorrect. Differential analysis is used for decision making when differences in costs (revenues) for two or more options are compared. Answer (D) is incorrect. Queuing theory is used to minimize the sum of the costs of waiting lines and servicing waiting lines when items arrive randomly at a service point and are serviced sequentially.

Use the additional questions in Gleim *CIA Test Prep* Software to create Test Sessions that emulate Pearson VUE!

STUDY UNIT TWO
MANAGING BUSINESS RESOURCES

(21 pages of outline)

This study unit continues the treatment of business processes that began in the first study unit. The first two subunits concern the management of inventory, especially balancing the components of inventory cost. The third subunit addresses the objectives and factors that influence the pricing of the organization's products and services. Managing the entity's supply chain, the sources of its inputs and the handlers of its outputs, is the subject of the fourth subunit. The fifth subunit covers the management of human capital. The balanced scorecard, a tool to focus efforts on achieving organizational goals, is covered in the final subunit.

2.1 MANAGING INVENTORY COSTS AND QUANTITIES

 Managing inventory is different from accounting for inventory. Management of inventory usually applies to physical units rather than monetary amounts. The issue is efficient use of the entity's resources. Accounting for inventory, covered in Study Unit 3, is concerned with the measurement and reporting of inventory in terms of currency units. Candidates sitting for the CIA exam should read inventory questions carefully to determine which approach is tested.

1. **The Costs of Inventory**

   a. An entity carries inventories because of the difficulty in predicting the amount, timing, and location of supply and demand.

      1) Thus, one purpose of inventory control is to determine the optimal level of inventory necessary to minimize costs.

   b. The carrying costs (also called holding costs) of inventory include rent, insurance, taxes, security, depreciation, and opportunity cost (i.e., the pretax return forgone by investing capital in inventory rather than the best alternative).

      1) Carrying costs also may include a charge for shrinkage, e.g., from spoilage of perishable items, obsolescence, theft, or waste.

      2) The annual opportunity cost of carrying inventory equals the average inventory level, times the per-unit purchase price, times the cost of capital.

      3) Carrying costs are reduced by minimizing the amount of inventory. This practice risks stockouts, which result in lost contribution margin on sales and customer ill will.

         a) Safety stock is the amount of extra inventory that is kept to guard against stockouts.

    c.   Ordering costs are the fixed costs of placing an order with a vendor and receiving the goods, independent of the number of units ordered.

        1)   Frequent ordering of small quantities thus may not be cost-beneficial compared with the relevant carrying costs.

    d.   The challenge of inventory management is to minimize the total costs of inventory, i.e., the sum of carrying cost and ordering costs, as illustrated by this graph:

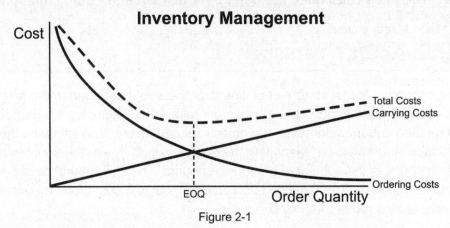

Figure 2-1

2. Economic Order Quantity (EOQ) Model

    a.   The EOQ results from using differential calculus to determine the minimum point on the total cost curve. It corresponds to the intersection of the carrying cost and ordering cost curves.

        1)   The basic formula is

$$EOQ = \sqrt{\frac{2aD}{k}}$$

            If: a = variable cost per order (or production setup)
                    D = periodic demand in units
                    k = unit periodic carrying cost

EXAMPLE

If periodic demand is uniform at 1,000 units, the cost to place an order is US \$4, and the cost to carry one unit in inventory for a period is US \$2, the EOQ is calculated as follows:

$$EOQ = \sqrt{\frac{2\,(US\ \$4)\,(1,000)}{US\ \$2}} = 63.25\ units\ per\ order$$

---

        a)   The formula shows that the EOQ varies directly with demand and order (setup) costs, but inversely with carrying costs.

        b)   The average level of inventory under this model is one-half of the EOQ.

        c)   The EOQ is a periodic model. The number of orders (production runs) per period is given by the periodic demand divided by the EOQ.

    b.   The limitations of the EOQ model are its restrictive assumptions.

        1)   The three variables in the formula (order placement or production setup cost, unit demand, per-unit carrying cost) remain constant throughout the period.

        2)   Full replenishment occurs instantly when the last item is used, stockout costs are zero, and no safety stock is held.

Stop and review! You have completed the outline for this subunit. Study multiple-choice questions 1 through 10 beginning on page 82.

2.2 INVENTORY MANAGEMENT METHODS

1.   **ABC Inventory Management**

    a.   The ABC system is a simple inventory management technique. It controls inventories by dividing items into three groups:

        1)   Group A consists of high-monetary-value items, which account for a small portion (perhaps 10%) of the total inventory usage.

        2)   Group B consists of medium-monetary-value items, which may account for perhaps 20% of the total inventory items.

        3)   Group C consists of low-monetary-value items, which account for the remaining 70% of sales or usage.

    b.   The ABC system permits managerial control over inventory to be exercised in the most cost-effective manner.

        1)   The stocking levels and activity of Group A items are reviewed on a regular basis.

        2)   Group B items may not need review as often as group A items, but they may need review more often than group C items.

        3)   For group C, extensive use of models and records is not cost effective. They are reviewed even less frequently.

2.   **Materials Requirements Planning (MRP)**

    a.   MRP is an integrated computer-based system designed to plan and control materials used in production.

        1)   MRP is a push system, that is, the demand for raw materials is driven by the forecast demand for the final product, which can be programmed into the computer.

b. The MRP system consults the **bill of materials (BOM)**, a record of which (and how many) subassemblies go into the finished product. The system then generates a complete list of every part and component needed.

EXAMPLE

A manufacturer has the following bill of materials for its product:

Subunit	Quantity
CM12	1
PR75	5

The bill of materials for the component subunits is as follows:

Subunit	Contains	Quantity
CM12	TT413	2
	XH511	3
PR75	LQ992	1

Current inventory quantities are as follows:

Subunit	On Hand
CM12	25
PR75	35
LQ992	50
TT413	30
XH511	40

The company has 20 units of the finished product in inventory and wishes to maintain this level throughout the year. Production of 40 units is scheduled for the upcoming month. The quantities of the principal subunits that must be produced are calculated below:

Subunit	Quantity per Finished Product		Production Run		Quantity Needed		Quantity On Hand		To Be Built
CM12	1	×	40	=	40	−	25	=	15
PR75	5	×	40	=	200	−	35	=	165

The parts that must be ordered from vendors can thus be calculated as follows:

Subunit	Components	Component Quantity		Subunits To Be Built		Quantity Needed		Quantity On Hand		To Be Purchased
CM12	TT413	2	×	15	=	30	−	30	=	0
	XH511	3	×	15	=	45	−	40	=	5
PR75	LQ992	1	×	165	=	165	−	50	=	115

---

c. MRP, in effect, creates schedules of when items of inventory will be needed in the production departments.

1) If parts are not in stock, the system automatically generates a purchase order on the proper date (considering lead times) so that deliveries will arrive on time. The timing of deliveries is vital to avoid both production delays and excessive inventory of raw materials.

3. **Just-in-Time (JIT)**

a. Modern inventory control favors the just-in-time model. Companies have traditionally built parts and components for subsequent operations on a preset schedule.

1) Such a schedule provides a cushion of inventory so that the next operation will always have parts to work with -- a just-in-case method.

b. In contrast, JIT limits output to the demand of the next operation. Reductions in inventory result in less money invested in idle assets; reduction of storage space requirements; and lower inventory taxes, pilferage, and obsolescence risks.

   1) High inventory often conceals production problems because defective parts can be overlooked when plenty of good parts are available. If only enough parts are made for the subsequent operation, however, any defects will immediately halt production.

   2) The focus of quality control under JIT shifts from the discovery of defective parts to the prevention of quality problems, so zero machine breakdowns (achieved through preventive maintenance) and zero defects are ultimate goals. Higher quality and lower inventory go together.

c. The ultimate objectives of JIT methods are increased competitiveness and higher profits through

   1) Higher productivity,
   2) Reduced order costs as well as carrying costs,
   3) Faster and cheaper setups,
   4) Shorter manufacturing cycle times,
   5) Better due date performance,
   6) Improved quality, and
   7) More flexible processes.

d. JIT systems are based on a manufacturing philosophy that combines purchasing, production, and inventory control. It also treats many inventory-related activities as nonvalue-added. Carrying inventory is regarded as indicating problems, such as poor quality, long cycle times, and lack of coordination with suppliers.

   1) A JIT system reduces carrying costs by eliminating inventories and increasing supplier deliveries. Ideally, shipments are received just in time to be part of the manufacturing process. This system increases the risk of stockout costs because inventory is reduced or eliminated.

e. However, JIT also reorganizes the production process to eliminate waste of resources. JIT is a pull system. Items are pulled through production by current demand, not pushed through by anticipated demand. Thus, one operation produces only what is needed by the next operation, and components and raw materials arrive just in time to be used.

   1) In a pull system, workers might often be idle if they were not multiskilled. Hence, (a) central support departments are reduced or eliminated, (b) space is saved, (c) fewer and smaller factories may be required, and (d) materials and tools are brought close to the point of use. Manufacturing cycle time and setup time are also reduced. As a result, on-time delivery performance and response to changes in markets are enhanced, and production of customized goods in small lots becomes feasible.

f. The lower inventory in a JIT system eliminates the need for some internal controls. Frequent receipt of deliveries from suppliers often means less need for a sophisticated inventory control system and for control personnel.

   1) JIT also may eliminate central receiving areas, hard copy receiving reports, and storage areas. A central warehouse is not needed because deliveries are made by suppliers directly to the area of production.

   2) The quality of parts provided by suppliers is verified by use of statistical controls rather than inspection of incoming goods. Storage, counting, and inspecting are eliminated in an effort to perform only value-adding work.

g. In a JIT system, the dependability of suppliers is crucial. Organizations that adopt JIT systems therefore have strategic teaming agreements with a few carefully chosen suppliers who are extensively involved in the buyer's processes.

1) Long-term contracts are typically negotiated to reduce order costs.

2) Buyer-supplier relationships are further facilitated by electronic data interchange (EDI), a technology that allows the supplier access to the buyer's online inventory management system. Thus, electronic messages replace paper documents (purchase orders and sales invoices), and the production schedules and deliveries of the parties can be more readily coordinated.

4. **Computer-Integrated Manufacturing (CIM)**

a. A CIM system involves (1) designing products using computer-aided design (CAD), (2) testing the design using computer-aided engineering (CAE), (3) manufacturing products using computer-aided manufacturing (CAM), and (4) integrating all components with a computerized information system.

1) CIM is a comprehensive approach to manufacturing in which design is translated into product by centralized processing and robotics. The concept also includes materials handling.

2) The advantages of CIM include increased productivity, flexibility, integration, synergism, and cost minimization because of decreased waste, scrap, rework, and spoilage.

b. Flexibility is a key advantage. A traditional manufacturing system might become disrupted from an emergency change, but CIM will reschedule everything in the plant when a priority requirement is inserted into the system. The areas of flexibility include the following:

1) Varying production volumes during a period
2) Handling new parts added to a product
3) Changing the proportion of parts being produced
4) Adjusting to engineering changes of a product
5) Adapting the sequence in which parts come to the machinery
6) Adapting to changes in materials

5. **Manufacturing Resource Planning**

a. Manufacturing resource planning (MRP-II) expands the scope of MRP to integrate all facets of a manufacturing business, including production, sales, inventories, schedules, and cash flows.

1) The same system is used for both financial reporting and management of operations (both use the same transactions and numbers).

2) MRP-II uses a master production schedule (MPS), which is a statement of the anticipated manufacturing schedule for selected items for selected periods.

a) MRP also uses the MPS. Thus, MRP is a component of an MRP-II system.

3) A further refinement in MRP-II is the inclusion of a feedback loop that makes possible the continuous revision of a production plan.

Stop and review! You have completed the outline for this subunit. Study multiple-choice questions 11 through 20 beginning on page 84.

2.3 PRICING

1. **Pricing Objectives**

   a. Profit maximization seeks the highest profit, even if it results in lost market share.

   b. Market share maximization seeks to capture market share from competitors, even if profits are lost.

   c. Image-oriented objectives seek to enhance the consumer's perception of the merchandise mix.

   d. Stabilization objectives seek to maintain a stable relationship between the prices of the entity and the industry leader.

2. **Price-Setting Factors -- Internal**

   a. Decisions regarding the marketing mix.

   b. Total costs (fixed and variable) in the value chain.

   c. Organizational location of pricing decisions.

   d. Level of productive capacity. Under peak-load pricing, prices vary directly with capacity usage. Thus, when demand falls and idle capacity is available, the price of a product or service tends to be lower.

3. **Price-Setting Factors -- External**

   a. Industry structure (monopoly, pure competition, monopolistic competition, oligopoly)

      1) For example, a monopolist is usually able to charge a higher price because it has no competitors. However, an entity selling a relatively undifferentiated product in a highly competitive market may have no control over price.

   b. Customer perceptions of price and value

   c. Supply and demand

      1) A normal good is one for which quantity demanded increases as the price decreases.

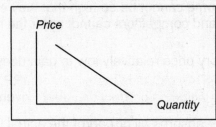

Figure 2-2

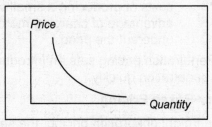

Figure 2-3

      2) Prestige goods have some intermediate range of prices over which the reaction to a price increase is an increase in the quantity demanded.

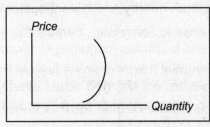

Figure 2-4

         a) Within this intermediate range, the demand curve is upward sloping. Consumers interpret the higher price to indicate a better or more desirable product. Above some price, the relation between price and quantity demanded will again be negatively sloped.

3)   If demand for a good is price elastic (inelastic), the ratio of the percentage change in quantity demanded to the percentage change in price is greater (less) than 1.0.

a)   For example, if customer demand is price elastic, a price increase results in the reduction of the seller's total revenue.

d.   Competitors' products, costs, prices, and amounts supplied

4.   **Cost-Based Pricing**

a.   A cost-based price recovers the value chain costs and provides the desired return on investment.

b.   A **cost-plus price** equals the cost plus a markup.

5.   **Market-Based Pricing**

a.   A market (buyer)-based price responds to the product's perceived value and competitors' actions rather than to the seller's cost.

1)   Nonprice variables in the marketing mix increase the perceived value. For example, a cup of coffee may have a higher price at an expensive restaurant than in a fast-food setting.

b.   Market-based pricing is typical given many competitors and an undifferentiated product, as in many commodities markets, e.g., agricultural products or natural gas.

6.   **Competition-Based Pricing**

a.   A going-rate price is based largely on competitors' prices.
b.   A sealed-bid price is based on an entity's perception of its competitors' prices.

7.   **New Product Pricing**

a.   Market (price) skimming introduces a new product at the highest possible price given the benefits of the product.

1)   For market skimming to work, the product must appear to be worth its price, the costs of producing a small volume cannot be so high that they eliminate the advantage of charging more, and competitors cannot enter the market and undercut the price.

b.   Penetration pricing sets an introductory price relatively low to gain deep market penetration quickly.

8.   **Delivery-Based Pricing**

a.   In freight absorption pricing, the seller absorbs all or part of the actual freight charges. Customers are not charged actual delivery costs.

b.   In uniform delivered pricing, the seller charges the same price, inclusive of shipping costs, to all customers, regardless of their location. This price is the average actual freight cost. Thus, both nearby and distant customers are charged the same amount.

1)   This policy is easy to administer, permits the entity to advertise one price nationwide, and facilitates marketing to faraway customers.

c.   In zone pricing, differential freight charges are set for customers on the basis of their location. Customers are not charged actual average freight costs.

d.   In FOB-origin pricing, each customer pays its actual freight costs.

9.   **Product-Mix Pricing**

a.   Product-line pricing sets price steps among the products in the line based on costs, consumer perceptions, and competitors' prices.

b.   Optional-product pricing requires the entity to choose which products to offer as accessories and which as standard features of a main product.

    c. Captive-product pricing involves products that must be used with a main product, such as razor blades with a razor. Often the main product is relatively cheap, but the captive products have high markups.

    d. By-product pricing usually sets prices at any amount in excess of storing and delivering by-products. Such prices allow the seller to reduce the costs and therefore the prices of the main products.

    e. Product-bundle pricing involves selling combinations of products at a price lower than the combined prices of the individual items. This strategy promotes sales of items consumers might not otherwise buy if the price is low enough. An example is season tickets for sports events.

10. Illegal Pricing

    a. Predatory pricing, the practice of pricing products below cost to destroy competitors, may be illegal.

    b. Price discrimination may be legal in some circumstances, e.g., senior citizen discounts.

    c. Collusive pricing results when conspirators restrict output and set artificially high prices, e.g., a cartel.

    d. Dumping is a trade practice that violates international agreements. It occurs when an entity charges a price (1) lower than that in its home market or (2) less than the cost of product. Dumping is done to penetrate a market or as a result of export subsidies.

11. Target Pricing

    a. A target price is the expected market price for a product or service, given the entity's knowledge of its customers and competitors. Hence, under target pricing, the sales price is known before the product is developed.

        1) Subtracting the unit target profit margin from the target price determines the long-term unit target cost. If cost-cutting measures do not permit the product to be made at or below the target cost, it will be abandoned.

    b. Value engineering is a means of achieving targeted cost levels. The purpose is to minimize costs without sacrificing customer satisfaction. It is a systematic approach to assessing all aspects of the value chain cost buildup for a product:

        1) R&D,
        2) Design of products,
        3) Design of processes,
        4) Production,
        5) Marketing,
        6) Distribution, and
        7) Customer service.

12. Product Life-Cycle Pricing -- Purpose

    a. Life-cycle costing is sometimes used as a basis for cost planning and product pricing. It estimates a product's revenues and expenses over its expected life cycle.

        1) The result is to highlight upstream and downstream costs in the cost planning process that often receive insufficient attention.

    b. Emphasis is on the need to price products to cover all costs, not just production costs.

13. **Product Life-Cycle Pricing -- Policies**

a. During precommercialization, the strategy is to innovate by conducting R&D, marketing research, and production tests. The entity has no sales and therefore no pricing policy, but it has high investment costs.

b. The introduction stage is characterized by slow sales growth and lack of profits because of the high expenses of promotion. Cost-plus prices are charged. They initially may be high to permit cost recovery when unit sales are low.

c. In the growth stage, sales and profits increase rapidly, cost per customer decreases, customers are early adopters, new competitors enter an expanding market, new product models and features are introduced, and promotion spending declines or remains stable. Prices are set to penetrate the market.

d. Some writers identify a separate stage between growth and maturity. During the shakeout period, the overall growth rate falls, price cutting occurs, industry profits decrease, and weaker competitors leave the market. The entity eliminates weak products and product lines, strengthens R&D and engineering efforts, and reduces prices through effective promotions.

e. In the maturity stage, sales peak but growth declines, competitors are most numerous but may begin to decline in number, and per-customer cost is low. Profits are high for large market-share entities. For others, profits may fall because of competitive price-cutting and increased R&D spending to develop improved versions of the product.

f. During the decline stage, sales and profits drop as prices are cut, and some competitors leave the market. Customers include late adopters, and per-customer cost is low. Weak products and unprofitable methods of distribution are eliminated, and advertising budgets are reduced to the level needed to retain the most loyal customers.

14. **Price Adjustments**

a. Encouraging or rewarding customers with price adjustments can be an important part of pricing strategy.

1) Cash discounts improve cash flow by encouraging prompt payment.

2) Quantity discounts encourage large-volume purchases.

3) Functional (trade) discounts are offered to other members of the marketing channel.

4) Seasonal discounts are offered for sales out of season. They help smooth production.

5) Trade-in and promotional allowances reduce list prices.

Stop and review! You have completed the outline for this subunit. Study multiple-choice questions 21 through 29 beginning on page 88.

2.4 SUPPLY CHAIN MANAGEMENT

1. **The Supply Chain**

a. The supply chain consists of flows from sources of (1) raw materials, (2) components, (3) finished goods, (4) services, or (5) information through intermediaries to ultimate consumers.

1) These flows and the related activities may occur across the functions in an organization's value chain (R&D, design, production, marketing, distribution, and customer service). These flows and the related activities also may occur across separate organizations.

2) The activities in the supply chain, wherever they occur, should be integrated and coordinated for optimal cost management.

Example of a Supply Chain

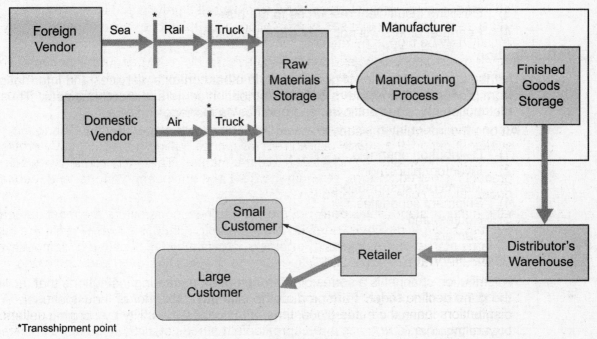

*Transshipment point

Figure 2-5

2. **Supply Chain Coordination**

a. Sharing of information and coordination among the organizations in the supply chain can avoid the bullwhip, or whiplash, effect on inventories. This phenomenon begins when retailers face uncertain demand from consumers caused by randomness in buying habits.

1) However, the variability of retailers' orders to manufacturers is affected by factors in addition to consumer demand. In turn, manufacturers' orders to suppliers may reflect a still greater variability because those orders depend on factors in addition to retailer demand.

2) This cascade of demand variability throughout the supply chain may be caused by

a) Difficulties of predicting demand and derived demand at each link in the supply chain

b) The need to purchase or manufacture goods in cost-efficient batches

c) Changes in price that may encourage purchases in anticipation of future increases

d) Shortages that may lead to rationing by suppliers or manufacturers and hoarding by manufacturers or retailers

b. Sharing of information about sales, inventory, pricing, advertising campaigns, and sales forecasts by all functions and organizations in the supply chain moderates demand uncertainty for all parties. The following are desired results:

1) Minimization of inventories held by suppliers, manufacturers, and retailers
2) Avoidance of stockouts
3) Fewer rush orders
4) Production as needed by retailers

c.   The following are examples of difficulties in supply-chain inventory management:

1)   Incompatibility of the information systems of the parties

2)   Refusal of some parties to share information, possibly because of security concerns

3)   Devoting insufficient resources to the task

4)   Fear that others will not meet their obligations

3.   **Distribution**

a.   Distribution is the transfer of goods (and, in other contexts, services and information) from producers to customers or from distribution centers to merchandisers. Thus, distribution manages outflows, and purchasing manages inflows.

b.   Among the interrelated issues involved in distribution are selection of

1)   Distribution channels,
2)   Inventory placement,
3)   Means of transportation,
4)   Shipment schedules,
5)   Routes, and
6)   Carriers.

4.   **Distribution Channel**

a.   A distribution channel is a series of interdependent marketing institutions that facilitate the transfer of a product from producer to ultimate consumer or industrial user. A distribution channel creates place, time, and possession utility by bringing sellers and buyers together.

b.   The following are intermediaries (also called middlemen) between sellers and buyers:

1)   Merchant middlemen buy the goods outright and necessarily take title to them. These include merchant wholesalers (often called distributors or jobbers) and most retailers.

2)   An agent represents a principal in negotiating purchases, sales, or both, but does not take title to the goods.

3)   A broker serves as a go-between. Unlike an agent, a broker ordinarily does not maintain a relationship with a particular buyer or seller. A broker also does not assume title risks. An example is a travel agency.

4)   A consignee merely sells the consignor's goods for a fee. Title remains with the consignor until the goods are sold and title passes to the buyer.

5)   Facilitating intermediaries are persons or entities outside the channel that perform some services (inventory control, financial services, risk management, information services, promotions) more effectively and efficiently than the channel members.

c.   The efficiencies gained by introducing intermediaries into a distribution channel can be calculated mathematically.

1)   For instance, if a certain channel has three producers that serve the same three customers, the number of contacts is nine (three producers × three customers). If a distributor begins serving this channel, the number of contacts is reduced to six (three products + three customers).

5. **Channel Structures**

   a. The channel structure describes the relationship between the entities that make up the distribution system.

      1) Conventional distribution systems consist of one or more independent producers, wholesalers, and retailers, each of which is a separate profit-maximizing business. The profit objective of each independent channel member may result in actions that are not profit maximizing for the system as a whole, and the system offers no means for defining roles and controlling channel conflict.

   b. In vertical distribution systems, producers, wholesalers, and retailers act as a unified system. Channel conflict is managed through common ownership, contractual relationships, or administration by one or a few dominant channel members.

      1) Conflict is between levels, e.g., when a manufacturer tries to enforce resale price agreements with dealers.

   c. Horizontal distribution systems consist of two or more entities at one level of the channel working together to exploit new opportunities, such as the introduction of ATMs in supermarkets. The joint nature of horizontal distribution efforts is the tool for managing channel conflict.

      1) Conflict occurs at the same level, e.g., when service standards vary.

   d. In a multichannel system, a single entity sets up two or more channels to reach one or more customer segments. Because such a system is managed by a single firm, channel conflicts can be evaluated and managed internally.

      1) Conflict is between channels, e.g., when the manufacturer's stores compete with other retailers.

6. **Inventory Placement**

   a. Forward placement puts inventory close to final customers at a distribution center (warehouse), wholesaler, or retailer. This option minimizes transportation costs and delivery times.

      1) Forward placement is typical for convenience goods. These are consumer goods and services that are usually low-priced and widely available. Consumers buy them often and with a minimum of comparison and effort. Examples are soap and newspapers. Producers of convenience goods ordinarily use intensive distribution to sell their products through a large number of retail or wholesale units.

   b. Backward placement involves keeping inventory at the factory or, in the extreme case, maintaining no inventory at all (i.e., building to order). This option is indicated when products are customized or when regional demand fluctuates unpredictably.

   c. Scheduling movements of freight balances purchasing, production, customer response times, shipping costs, and selection of routes and carriers.

Stop and review! You have completed the outline for this subunit. Study multiple-choice questions 30 through 33 beginning on page 91.

2.5 MANAGING HUMAN RESOURCES

1. **Overview**

   a. Managing human resources means acquiring, retaining, and developing employees. These functions should be consistent with the strategy and structure of the organization.

      1) The essential activities include the following:

         a) Developing a human resource strategy

            i) Such a strategy at its broadest is a systems approach that treats employees and future employees as **human capital**, that is, as intangible assets whose fullest potential should be developed.

         b) Recruitment and selection

         c) Evaluation of performance

         d) Training and development

   b. Research indicates that a people-centered human resource strategy improves employee retention and profits. Jeffrey Pfeffer (see Kreitner, *Management*, 9th ed., page 357) suggests the following practices:

      1) A job security policy
      2) Stringent hiring procedures
      3) Employee empowerment (e.g., use of self-managed teams)
      4) Basing compensation on performance
      5) Comprehensive training
      6) Reduction of status differences
      7) Information sharing

   c. Human resource planning consists of forecasting future employment requirements. It includes the hiring, training, and monitoring of employees.

      1) Planning includes scanning the external environment to understand the area's labor supply, workforce composition, and work patterns.

      2) Companies must forecast future employee needs to ensure adequate resources when needed. Labor resources are not always as mobile as raw materials.

      3) A human resource audit evaluates compliance with laws and regulations, determines whether operations are efficient, and considers the company's recruitment and salary and benefit programs.

      4) Human resource or human asset accounting attempts to measure the value, and the changes in value, of the organization's investment in human capital.

2. **Designing the Job**

   a. Job analysis is the first step. It involves interviewing superior employees about the way they accomplish their tasks, analyzing work flows, and studying the methods used to achieve work-unit objectives.

   b. A job description, based on job analysis, should list basic duties. For higher-level positions, reporting relationships may also be included.

      1) For example, for an accounting clerk, the job description may include

         a) Preparing payroll checks,
         b) Maintaining inventory ledgers, and
         c) Preparing invoices.

   c. Job specifications, based on the job description, should list the abilities needed by a person hired for that job.

3. **Recruitment**

    a.   Many countries have laws that prohibit employment discrimination with regard to any employment action, for example, hiring, training, compensation, retention, or promotion. Prohibited bases of discrimination may be race, color, religion, sex, national origin, age, or disability.

    b.   The law may prohibit doing the following in recruiting interviews:

        1)   Making notation of sex
        2)   Asking marital status (may ask after hiring for insurance purposes)
        3)   Asking for number of children (may ask after hiring for insurance purposes)
        4)   Asking for height and weight
        5)   Asking for criminal record (only for security clearance)
        6)   Asking type of military discharge
        7)   Asking age

    c.   Using temporary or part-time workers gives management the flexibility to adjust quickly to changing market conditions.

4. **Selection**

    a.   The criteria for employee selection should come from job specifications developed from each job description and include education, experience, physical characteristics, and personal characteristics.

        1)   All requirements, including selection tests, must be based on their relationship to the ability to perform successfully in a specific job category.

        2)   Employee information preferably should be verified.

    b.   According to Del J. Still (see Kreitner, pp. 359-360), the selection process involves

        1)   Preparation by developing job descriptions and job specifications and writing interview questions
        2)   Reviewing those questions for fairness and conformity with the law
        3)   Organizing by defining the roles and methods of interviewers
        4)   Collecting information from applicants
        5)   Evaluating
        6)   Meeting to discuss information about applicants
        7)   Deciding whether to offer employment

    c.   Interviewing is the most frequently used selection method. Because the unstructured interview is subject to cultural and other forms of bias, the structured interview is preferable.

        1)   It consists of written questions related to the job that have standard answers. The questions are created and scored by a committee so as to minimize bias.

    d.   Testing applicants for jobs with quantifiable output (e.g., jobs requiring clerical skills or manual dexterity) is easier than testing for positions with a less tangible work product (e.g., public relations director or human resource manager).

        1)   All tests must be validated in each organization and for minority and nonminority groups before they can be predictive of successful performance.

        2)   Tests must be given to all applicants for the same job category.

5.   **Training and Development**

   a.   Training consists of organizational programs to prepare employees to perform currently assigned tasks. Kreitner (p. 373) defines training broadly as "using guided experience to change employee behavior or attitude."

   1)   On-the-job or experiential training, for example, by job rotation, apprenticeships, and mentoring arrangements, is usually less costly than off-the-job training. However, it may disrupt the workplace and result in increased errors. It is suited to acquisition of technical skills.

   2)   Off-the-job training is provided, for example, in classroom lectures, film study, and simulations. It is well suited to development of problem solving and interpersonal abilities and to teaching of complex skills.

   3)   Computer-based training is expected to become more common.

   b.   Development includes programs to prepare people to perform future tasks and acquire new skills.

   1)   The focus is mostly on management and organizational development of human relations skills. Management coaching and mentoring enhance the development process.

   c.   The evaluation and appraisal process helps identify individual strengths and weaknesses as the basis for training and development opportunities. Also, jobs and markets change, leading to a need for workers with different skills. Organizations thrive when workers value lifelong learning.

   1)   Viewing performance evaluation as a training and developmental process can foster a culture in which evaluation is sought out.

   2)   A training needs assessment should be conducted to (a) determine what training is relevant to employees' jobs, (b) determine what training will improve performance, (c) determine whether training will make a difference, (d) distinguish training needs from organizational problems, and (e) link improved job performance with the organization's objectives and bottom line.

   3)   Self-assessment normally yields shorter-term training needs and often has more to do with employees' personal career goals than with strategic business needs. Thus, self-assessment often may be used only as a supplement to other approaches.

   d.   Training and development programs are successful when they achieve the greatest retention (learning) of skills and knowledge that are transferred to the job. The following is a model for the process of learning:

   1)   Establishing objectives
   2)   Modeling the skills or making a meaningful presentation of facts
   3)   Practicing the skills
   4)   Obtaining feedback

6.   **Performance Evaluation**

   a.   Reasons

   1)   Evaluations are important to employees, the employer, and the organization.

   2)   Evaluations provide an opportunity for growth and may prevent disputes.

   3)   Evaluations tend to focus on who did the job, how it was done, or what was done.

b. Types

1) Behavior-oriented evaluation rewards the behavior desired by management. Behavior control involves examining work processes rather than work output.

2) Goal-oriented evaluation measures how well the employee attained the objectives set by management.

3) Trait-oriented evaluation tends to reward what the supervisor thinks of the employee rather than the job the employee did.

4) Employee-oriented evaluation focuses on who did the job.

c. Purposes

1) Performance criteria identify necessary job-related abilities.

2) Performance objectives help employees direct their energies toward achieving the organization's objectives without constant supervision.

3) Performance outcomes promote employee satisfaction by acknowledging when jobs are completed and done well.

4) Evaluation distinguishes effective from ineffective job performance.

5) The employer and the organization develop employee strengths and identify weaknesses.

6) Evaluation sets compensation.

a) But separating performance evaluations from compensation decisions may be beneficial. An advantage is that more emphasis is placed on long-term objectives. It also emphasizes other rewards, such as feelings of achievement and the recognition of superiors.

b) Another advantage is that the employee's good performance can be separated from the overall company's bad financial performance.

c) A disadvantage is that the employee may not be motivated immediately by a good appraisal because of the delay in receipt of any monetary reward. The evaluation also may not be taken as seriously by the employee if compensation is not correlated with performance.

7) Evaluation identifies promotable employees.

a) Internal promotions motivate employees and are less difficult and expensive than external hiring.

b) Many firms look to external candidates for certain jobs because they bring a fresh perspective to the organization's problems and may have more up-to-date training or education.

7. **Problems of Evaluation**

a. Halo Effect

1) A manager's judgment on one positive trait affects ratings on other traits. In contrast, the horn effect allows one negative trait to influence the evaluation of other traits.

b. Centralizing Tendency

1) All personnel are rated within the same narrow range, e.g., "All my people are good." In a sense, all employees are rated average.

c. Recency Effect

1) The most recent behavior overshadows overall performance.

d. Differing Standards

1) Some managers have stricter standards than others, making cross-departmental comparisons difficult.

e.   Personal Bias

1)   Traits may not reflect actual job performance, so appraisal can be biased by the degree to which the manager likes the subordinate.

f.   Leniency Error

1)   This occurs when a manager fails to give a negative evaluation because of fear of damaging a good working relationship with a worker.

g.   Contrast Error

1)   This is the tendency to rate people relative to other people rather than performance standards. If most employees are mediocre, a person performing at an average level is rated as "outstanding." That same person might be rated as "poor" if most workers perform at an above-average level.

2)   Although such comparisons may be appropriate at times, the normal rating process should be based on job requirements.

h.   Once-a-Year Process

1)   The long time period involved tends to limit the usefulness and accuracy of any job-related information.

8.   **Major Types of Appraisals**

a.   Management by Objectives (MBO)

1)   This approach is a participative process in which supervisors and subordinates mutually establish objectives. A rating is based on achievement of the objectives.

b.   Behaviorally Anchored Rating Scales (BARS)

1)   BARS contain descriptions of good and bad performance. They are developed through job analysis for a number of specific job-related behaviors and then used for evaluation of employees.

c.   Check-the-Box

1)   This method provides a list of categories for rating performance for the supervisor to check off. Methods using check the box evaluations include

a)   Graphic scale, which provides a list of job duties and a scale to grade them, i.e., 1 = Excellent, etc.

b)   A checklist, which provides statements relating to job performance, and the evaluator checks the statements that apply.

c)   A method similar to the checklist method in that it provides statements for the evaluator to choose from but requires the evaluator to choose the one that most resembles the employee's performance and the one that least resembles the employee's performance, which is called forced choice.

d.   Comparative Methods

1)   These involve comparing an employee's performance to the work of others. Comparative methods include

a)   Ranking, which ranks all employees from highest to lowest. This method can lend itself to bias on the part of the evaluator.

b)   Pairing an employee with other employees and ranking him/her against the other employee(s), which is known as paired comparison.

c)   The forced normal distribution. This method distributes employees along a bell-shaped curve. It compels evaluators to rate some employees in the tails of the curve even though their performance levels are not normally distributed.

e. Narrative Method

    1) This technique includes essays and the critical incidents method, both of which consume large amounts of time and effort.

    2) Field reviews require human resources personnel to prepare the evaluation for each employee based on the supervisor's input.

        a) The supervisor has the ability to veto or modify.

f. 360° Performance Appraisal

    1) This method uses a multirater model for employee assessment. It provides anonymous feedback by peers, customers, supervisors, and subordinates.

    2) Appraisal is subjective and may be affected by popularity.

    3) Evaluations do not include copies of job descriptions or performance goals.

9. **Characteristics of Effective Evaluation Systems**

a. Relevant

    1) Criteria should be reliable and valid. They should relate to employee functions, that is, to activities over which the employees exert control.

b. Unbiased

    1) Systems should be based on performance, not on unrelated personal characteristics.

c. Significant

    1) The focus should be on the important part of the job, not what is convenient to evaluate.

d. Practical

    1) Systems should be as objective, easy to use, clearly understood, and efficient as possible.

10. **Safety**

a. Employers may have responsibilities to their employees under local and national law. Employers may have to comply with, among other things,

    1) Standards regulating the workplace environment and the safety of equipment

        a) Employers may have a general duty to provide a safe workplace for employees.

        b) Employers may be required to inform employees about legal requirements.

    2) Laws that may prohibit employers from discriminating on the basis of a disability

    3) Workers' compensation laws that provide payments to employees injured at work, including lost wages, medical expenses, and, in some cases, training for employment in a different field

Stop and review! You have completed the outline for this subunit. Study multiple-choice questions 34 through 37 beginning on page 92.

2.6 THE BALANCED SCORECARD

1. **CSFs and SWOT Analysis**

   a. The trend in managing implementation of the entity's strategy is the balanced scorecard approach. A balanced scorecard connects critical success factors (CSFs) with measures of performance.

   b. CSFs are financial and nonfinancial measures of the elements of performance vital to competitive advantage. SWOT analysis (strengths, weaknesses, opportunities, and threats) is used to identify CSFs.

2. **Four Categories of Measures**

   a. **Financial**

      1) The CSFs may be sales, fair value of the entity's shares, profits, and liquidity.

      2) Measures may include (a) sales, (b) projected sales, (c) accuracy of sales projections, (d) new product sales, (e) share prices, (f) operating earnings, (g) earnings trend, (h) revenue growth, (i) gross margin percentage, (j) cost reductions, (k) economic value added (EVA), (l) return on investment (or any of its variants), (m) cash flow coverage and trends, (n) turnover (assets, receivables, and inventory), and (o) interest coverage.

   b. **Customer**

      1) The CSFs may be (a) customer satisfaction, (b) customer retention rate, (c) dealer and distributor relationships, (d) marketing and selling performance, (e) prompt delivery, and (f) quality.

      2) Measures may include (a) returns, (b) complaints, (c) survey results, (d) coverage and strength of distribution channels, (e) market research results, (f) training of marketing people, (g) sales trends, (h) market share and its trend, (i) on-time delivery rate, (j) service response time and effectiveness, and (k) warranty expense.

   c. **Internal Business Processes**

      1) The CSFs may be (a) quality, (b) productivity (an input-output relationship), (c) flexibility of response to changing conditions, (d) operating readiness, and (e) safety.

      2) Measures may include (a) rate of defects, (b) amounts of scrap and rework, (c) returns, (d) survey results, (e) field service reports, (f) warranty costs, (g) vendor defect rate, (h) cycle (lead) time, (i) labor and machine efficiency, (j) setup time, (k) scheduling effectiveness, (l) downtime, (m) capacity usage, (n) maintenance, and (o) accidents and their results.

   d. **Learning, Growth, and Innovation**

      1) The CSFs may be (a) development of new products, (b) promptness of their introduction, (c) human resource development, (d) morale, and (e) competence of the workforce.

      2) Measures may include (a) new products marketed, (b) amount of design changes, (c) patents and copyrights registered, (d) R&D personnel qualifications, (e) actual versus planned shipping dates, (f) hours of training, (g) skill set levels attained, (h) personnel turnover, (i) personnel complaints and survey results, (j) financial and operating results, (k) technological capabilities, (l) organizational learning, and (m) industry leadership.

EXAMPLE

Each **objective** is associated with one or more **measures** that permit the organization to estimate progress toward the objective. Achievement of the objectives in each **perspective** makes it possible to achieve the organization's objectives.

Balanced Scorecard

Financial Perspective

    Objective: Increase shareholder value   **Measures:** Increase in ordinary (common) share price
                                                                          Reliability of dividend payment

Customer Perspective

    Objective: Increase customer satisfaction   **Measures:** Greater market share
                                                                            Higher customer retention rate
                                                                                 Positive responses to surveys

Internal Business Process Perspective

    Objective: Improve product quality   **Measures:** Achievement of zero defects

    Objective: Improve internal processes   **Measures:** Reduction in delivery cycle time
                                                                                Smaller cost variances

Learning, Growth, and Innovation Perspective

    Objective: Increase employee confidence   **Measures:** Number of suggestions to improve processes
                                                                                 Positive responses to surveys

    Objective: Increase employee competence   **Measures:** Attendance at internal and external training
                                                                                                   seminars

---

3.   **Problems in Implementation**

    a.   Using too many measures, with a consequent loss of focus on CSFs

    b.   Failing to evaluate personnel on nonfinancial as well as financial measures

    c.   Including measures that will not have long-term financial benefits

    d.   Not understanding that subjective measures (such as customer satisfaction) are imprecise

    e.   Trying to achieve improvements in all areas at all times

    f.   Not observing when current nonfinancial measures no longer relate to ultimate financial success

Stop and review! You have completed the outline for this subunit. Study multiple-choice questions 38 through 40 beginning on page 93.

QUESTIONS

2.1 Managing Inventory Costs and Quantities

1. With regard to inventory management, an increase in the frequency of ordering will normally

A. Reduce the total ordering costs.

B. Have no impact on total ordering costs.

C. Reduce total carrying costs.

D. Have no impact on total carrying costs.

Answer (C) is correct. *(CIA, adapted)*
REQUIRED: The effect of an increase in the frequency of ordering.
DISCUSSION: If orders are placed more frequently, fewer items are carried and carrying costs fall.

2. An entity sells 1,500 units of a particular item each year and orders the items in equal quantities of 500 units at a price of US $5 per unit. No safety stocks are held. If the entity has a cost of capital of 12%, its annual opportunity cost of carrying inventory is

A. US $150

B. US $180

C. US $300

D. US $900

Answer (A) is correct. *(CIA, adapted)*
REQUIRED: The annual cost of carrying inventory.
DISCUSSION: The annual opportunity cost of carrying inventory equals the average inventory level, times the per-unit purchase price, times the cost of capital. The average inventory level is the order quantity divided by 2. Thus, the annual opportunity cost of carrying inventory is US $150 [(500 units ÷ 2) × $5 × .12].
Answer (B) is incorrect. A US $180 cost is obtained by using the total annual quantity rather than the average inventory level and by not multiplying by the unit price. Answer (C) is incorrect. A US $300 cost is obtained by using the order size rather than the average inventory level. Answer (D) is incorrect. A US $900 cost is based on the total annual quantity rather than the average inventory level.

3. A company stocks, maintains, and distributes inventory. The company decides to add to the safety stock and expedite delivery for several product lines on a trial basis. For the selected product lines, the company will experience

A. An increase in some costs but no change in the service level.

B. A change in the service level.

C. An increase in ordering, carrying, and delivery costs.

D. A decrease in ordering, carrying, and delivery costs.

Answer (B) is correct. *(CIA, adapted)*
REQUIRED: The effect of increasing safety stock.
DISCUSSION: Safety stocks are amounts held in excess of forecast demand to avoid the losses associated with stockouts. Holding safety stocks improves the level of service to customers at the expense of increased holding costs.
Answer (A) is incorrect. Service will improve. Answer (C) is incorrect. Ordering costs will not increase. The fixed costs of the ordering department will be unaffected. Also, the department's variable costs should not change because the EOQ will be the same. However, in the first year, an additional order may be necessary to increase the safety stock. Answer (D) is incorrect. Delivery will increase under the new expedited delivery policy. Moreover, increasing the safety stock increases carrying costs.

4. An organization sells a product for which demand is uncertain. Management would like to ensure that there is sufficient inventory on hand during periods of high demand so that it does not lose sales (and customers). To do so, the organization should

A. Keep a safety stock.

B. Use a just-in-time inventory system.

C. Employ a materials requirements planning system.

D. Keep a master production schedule.

Answer (A) is correct. *(CIA, adapted)*
REQUIRED: The means of ensuring that sufficient inventory is on hand.
DISCUSSION: Safety stock is inventory maintained to reduce the number of stockouts resulting from higher-than-expected demand during lead time. Maintaining a safety stock avoids the costs of stockouts, e.g., lost sales and customer dissatisfaction.
Answer (B) is incorrect. The goal of a just-in-time inventory system is to reduce, not increase, inventory on hand. Answer (C) is incorrect. Materials requirements planning is a system for scheduling production and controlling the level of inventory for components with dependent demand. Answer (D) is incorrect. A master production schedule is a statement of the timing and amounts of individual items to be produced.

5. When the economic order quantity (EOQ) decision model is employed, the <List A> are being offset or balanced by the <List B>.

	List A	List B
A.	Ordering costs	Carrying costs
B.	Purchase costs	Carrying costs
C.	Purchase costs	Quality costs
D.	Ordering costs	Stockout costs

Answer (A) is correct. *(CIA, adapted)*
REQUIRED: The true statement about cost relationships in the EOQ.
DISCUSSION: The objective of the EOQ model is to find an optimal order quantity that balances carrying and ordering costs. Only variable costs should be considered. The EOQ is the point where the ordering cost and carrying cost curves intersect. It corresponds to the minimum point on the total inventory cost curve.
Answer (B) is incorrect. The price (purchase costs) is not directly incorporated into the EOQ model. Answer (C) is incorrect. Neither the price nor quality costs are incorporated into the EOQ model. Answer (D) is incorrect. Stockout costs are not directly incorporated into the EOQ model.

6. The purpose of the economic order quantity model is to

A. Minimize the safety stock.

B. Minimize the sum of the order costs and the holding costs.

C. Minimize the inventory quantities.

D. Minimize the sum of the demand costs and the backlog costs.

Answer (B) is correct. *(CIA, adapted)*
REQUIRED: The purpose of the economic order quantity model.
DISCUSSION: The purpose of the EOQ model is to minimize the sum of inventory order costs (or production setup) and holding (carrying) costs. The EOQ equals the square root of twice the annual demand multiplied by the variable cost per order, divided by the unit periodic holding cost.
Answer (A) is incorrect. The basic EOQ model does not include safety stock. Answer (C) is incorrect. In the EOQ model, costs, not quantities, are to be minimized. Answer (D) is incorrect. Quantity demanded is a variable in the model, but order costs, not demand costs, are relevant. Backlogs are customer orders that cannot be filled immediately because of stockouts. Backlog costs are not quantified in the model.

7. One of the elements included in the economic order quantity (EOQ) formula is

A. Safety stock.

B. Yearly demand.

C. Selling price of item.

D. Lead time for delivery.

Answer (B) is correct. *(CIA, adapted)*
REQUIRED: The element to include in the EOQ calculation.
DISCUSSION: The basic EOQ formula is used to minimize the total of inventory carrying and ordering costs. The basic EOQ equals the square root of a fraction consisting of a numerator equal to the product of twice the unit periodic demand and the variable cost per order and a denominator equal to the unit periodic carrying cost.
Answer (A) is incorrect. The safety stock is not included in the basic EOQ formula. Answer (C) is incorrect. The selling price of the item is not included in the basic EOQ formula. Answer (D) is incorrect. The lead time for delivery is not included in the basic EOQ formula.

8. The EOQ (economic order quantity) model calculates the cost-minimizing quantity of a product to order, based on a constant annual demand, carrying costs per unit per annum, and cost per order. For example, the EOQ is approximately 447 units if the annual demand is 10,000 units, carrying costs are US $1 per item per annum, and the cost of placing an order is US $10. What will the EOQ be if the demand falls to 5,000 units per annum and the carrying and ordering costs remain at US $1 and US $10, respectively?

A. 316

B. 447

C. 483

D. 500

Answer (A) is correct. *(CIA, adapted)*
REQUIRED: The EOQ given demand, carrying cost, and order cost.
DISCUSSION: The EOQ formula is

$$X = \sqrt{\frac{2aD}{k}}$$

If: a = variable cost per order (or production setup)
D = periodic demand in units
k = unit periodic carrying cost

$$\sqrt{\frac{2 \times US\ \$10 \times 5,000}{US\ \$1}} = 316.23$$

Answer (B) is incorrect. The EOQ is 447 when demand is 10,000 units per year. Answer (C) is incorrect. The EOQ of 483 results when annual demand is 11,664 units. Answer (D) is incorrect. The EOQ of 500 results when annual demand is 12,500 units.

Questions 9 and 10 are based on the following information. Using an EOQ analysis (assuming a constant demand), it is determined that the optimal order quantity is 2,500. The company desires a safety stock of 500 units. A 5-day lead time is needed for delivery. Annual inventory holding costs equal 25% of the average inventory level. It costs the company US $4 per unit to buy the product, which it sells for US $8. It costs the company US $150 to place a detailed order, and the monthly demand for the product is 4,000 units.

9. Annual inventory holding costs equal

   A. US $750

   B. US $1,250

   C. US $1,750

   D. US $2,250

Answer (C) is correct. *(CIA, adapted)*
   REQUIRED: The annual inventory holding costs using the EOQ technique.
   DISCUSSION: Given that demand is constant and the EOQ is 2,500 units, the average inventory level without regard to safety stock is 1,250 units (2,500 ÷ 2). Adding safety stock results in an average level of 1,750 units (1,250 + 500). Given also that annual holding costs are 25% of average inventory and that unit cost is US $4, total annual holding cost is US $1,750 [(1,750 units × US $4) × 25%].
   Answer (A) is incorrect. A US $750 cost results from subtracting instead of adding the cost of holding safety stock. Answer (B) is incorrect. A US $1,250 cost ignores safety stock. Answer (D) is incorrect. A US $2,250 cost results from double counting the cost of holding safety stock.

10. Total inventory ordering costs per year equal

   A. US $1,250

   B. US $2,400

   C. US $2,880

   D. US $3,600

Answer (C) is correct. *(CIA, adapted)*
   REQUIRED: The total inventory ordering costs using the EOQ technique.
   DISCUSSION: Total annual demand is 48,000 units (4,000 per month × 12). Hence, total annual ordering costs equal US $2,880 [US $150 cost per order × (48,000 units ÷ 2,500 EOQ)].
   Answer (A) is incorrect. A US $1,250 cost equals the annual holding cost of the average inventory excluding safety stock. Answer (B) is incorrect. A US $2,400 cost assumes an EOQ of 3,000 units. Answer (D) is incorrect. A US $3,600 cost assumes an EOQ of 2,000 units.

2.2 Inventory Management Methods

11. The company uses a planning system that focuses first on the amount and timing of finished goods demanded and then determines the derived demand for raw material, components, and subassemblies at each of the prior stages of production. This system is referred to as

   A. Economic order quantity.

   B. Materials requirements planning.

   C. Linear programming.

   D. Just-in-time purchasing.

Answer (B) is correct. *(CIA, adapted)*
   REQUIRED: The planning system that calculates derived demand for inventories.
   DISCUSSION: Materials requirements planning (MRP) is usually a computer-based information system designed to plan and control raw materials used in a production setting. It assumes that estimated demand for materials is reasonably accurate and that suppliers can deliver based upon this accurate schedule. It is crucial that delivery delays be avoided because, under MRP, production delays are almost unavoidable if the materials are not on hand. An MRP system uses a parts list, often called a bill of materials, and lead times for each type of material to obtain materials just as they are needed for planned production.
   Answer (A) is incorrect. The economic order quantity is a decision model that focuses on the trade-off between carrying and ordering costs. Answer (C) is incorrect. Linear programming is a decision model concerned with allocating scarce resources to maximize profit or minimize costs. Answer (D) is incorrect. Just-in-time purchasing involves the purchase of goods such that delivery immediately precedes demand or use.

12. Which of the following inventory items would be the most frequently reviewed in an ABC inventory control system?

A. Expensive, frequently used, high stockout cost items with short lead times.

B. Expensive, frequently used, low stockout cost items with long lead times.

C. Inexpensive, frequently used, high stockout cost items with long lead times.

D. Expensive, frequently used, high stockout cost items with long lead times.

Answer (D) is correct. *(CIA, adapted)*
REQUIRED: The most frequently reviewed items in an ABC inventory control system.
DISCUSSION: The ABC system is a method for controlling inventories that divides inventory items into three groups:

Group A -- high-monetary-value items, which account for a small portion (perhaps 10%) of the total inventory usage

Group B -- medium-monetary-value items, which may account for about 20% of the total inventory items

Group C -- low-monetary-value items, which account for the remaining 70% of sales or usage

The ABC system permits the proper degree of managerial control to be identified and exercised over each group. Group A items are reviewed on a regular basis. Group B items may not have to be reviewed as often as group A items, but more often than group C items. For group C, extensive use of models and records is not cost effective. It is cheaper to order large quantities infrequently. The ABC method therefore reduces the safety-stock investment because high-value items are frequently monitored and medium-value items are monitored more often than inexpensive items. Frequent review can prevent stockouts and decrease inventory levels, and the cost of such review is minimized if it is limited to high- or medium-value items.
Answer (A) is incorrect. Long, not short, lead times prompt a more frequent review. Answer (B) is incorrect. High, not low, stockout costs prompt a more frequent review. Answer (C) is incorrect. Expensive, not inexpensive, items prompt a more frequent review.

13. An advantage of using bar codes rather than other means of identification of parts used by a manufacturer is that

A. The movement of all parts is controlled.

B. The movement of parts is easily and quickly recorded.

C. Vendors can use the same part numbers.

D. Vendors use the same identification methods.

Answer (B) is correct. *(CIA, adapted)*
REQUIRED: The advantage of using bar codes to identify parts in a manufacturing setting.
DISCUSSION: A reason to use bar codes rather than other means of identification is to record the movement of parts with minimal labor costs.
Answer (A) is incorrect. The movement of parts can escape being recorded with any identification method. Answer (C) is incorrect. Each vendor has its own part-numbering scheme, which is unlikely to correspond to the buyer's scheme. Answer (D) is incorrect. Each vendor has its own identification method, although vendors in the same industry often cooperate to minimize the number of bar-code systems that they use.

14. An appropriate technique for planning and controlling manufacturing inventories, such as raw materials, components, and subassemblies whose demand depends on the level of production is

A. Materials requirements planning.

B. Regression analysis.

C. Capital budgeting.

D. Linear programming.

Answer (A) is correct. *(CIA, adapted)*
REQUIRED: The appropriate technique for planning and controlling manufacturing inventories whose demand depends on the level of production.
DISCUSSION: Materials requirements planning (MRP) is a system that translates a production schedule into requirements for each component needed to meet the schedule. It is usually implemented in the form of a computer-based information system designed to plan and control raw materials used in production. It assumes that forecast demand is reasonably accurate and that suppliers can deliver based upon this accurate schedule. MRP is a centralized push-through system; output based on forecasted demand is pushed through to the next department or to inventory.
Answer (B) is incorrect. Regression analysis is used to fit a linear trend line to a dependent variable based on one or more independent variables. Answer (C) is incorrect. Capital budgeting is the process of planning expenditures for long-lived assets. It involves choosing among investment proposals using a ranking procedure. Answer (D) is incorrect. Linear programming is a decision model concerned with allocating scarce resources to maximize profit or minimize costs.

15. A company manufactures banana hooks for retail sale. The bill of materials for this item and the parts inventory for each material required are as follows:

Bill of Materials

Raw Material	Quantity Required	On Hand
Wooden neck	1	0
Wooden base	1	0
Swag hook	1	300
Wood screws	2	400
Foot pads	4	1,000

An incoming order calls for delivery of 2,000 banana hooks in 2 weeks. The company has 200 finished banana hooks in current inventory. If no safety stocks are required for inventory, what are the company's net requirements for swag hooks and screws needed to fill this order?

	Swag Hooks	Wood Screws
A.	1,500	1,400
B.	1,500	3,200
C.	1,700	3,600
D.	1,800	3,600

Answer (B) is correct. *(CIA, adapted)*
REQUIRED: The company's net requirements for swag hooks and screws needed to fill an order.
DISCUSSION: The company needs 1,800 banana hooks (2,000 – 200) and therefore 1,800 swag hooks (1 × 1,800) and 3,600 wood screws (2 × 1,800). Given that 300 swag hooks and 400 wood screws are on hand, the company must obtain 1,500 swag hooks (1,800 – 300) and 3,200 wood screws (3,600 – 400).
Answer (A) is incorrect. A total of 1,400 wood screws assumes that one wood screw is used per banana hook. Answer (C) is incorrect. A total of 1,700 swag hooks and 3,600 wood screws would be needed if no banana hooks were in current inventory. Answer (D) is incorrect. A total of 1,800 swag hooks would be needed if no swag hooks were in current inventory. Also, 3,600 wood screws would be needed if no banana hooks were in current inventory.

16. The effect of just-in-time production approaches

A. Reduces the dependency on suppliers.

B. Reduces the cost of implementing strategies.

C. Decreases production facility flexibility.

D. Increases the need for a dependable workforce.

Answer (B) is correct. *(CIA, adapted)*
REQUIRED: The effect of just-in-time production approaches.
DISCUSSION: A just-in-time (JIT) inventory system can reduce the cost of production by lowering or eliminating inventory costs.
Answer (A) is incorrect. JIT production approaches increase the need for reliable suppliers. When inventories are at low or nonexistent levels, supplier performance is critical. Answer (C) is incorrect. JIT production increases flexibility. Production is pulled by demand. Answer (D) is incorrect. JIT requires workers to be multiskilled and independent. Such traits are needed in a pull system.

17. A manufacturing company is attempting to implement a just-in-time (JIT) purchase policy system by negotiating with its primary suppliers to accept long-term purchase orders which result in more frequent deliveries of smaller quantities of raw materials. If the JIT purchase policy is successful in reducing the total inventory costs of the manufacturing company, which of the following combinations of cost changes would be most likely to occur?

	Cost Category to Increase	Cost Category to Decrease
A.	Purchasing costs	Stockout costs
B.	Purchasing costs	Quality costs
C.	Quality costs	Ordering costs
D.	Stockout costs	Carrying costs

Answer (D) is correct. *(CIA, adapted)*
REQUIRED: The combination of cost changes.
DISCUSSION: The objective of a JIT system is to reduce carrying costs by eliminating inventories and increasing the deliveries made by suppliers. Ideally, shipments are received just in time to be incorporated into the manufacturing process. This system increases the risk of stockout costs because the inventory buffer is reduced or eliminated.
Answer (A) is incorrect. The supplier may seek a concession on the selling price that will raise purchasing costs, but the manufacturing company's stockout costs will increase. Answer (B) is incorrect. The cost of quality is not necessarily affected by a JIT system. Answer (C) is incorrect. Fewer purchase orders are processed by the manufacturer, so the ordering costs are likely to decrease. However, the cost of quality is not necessarily affected by a JIT system.

18. Just-in-time (JIT) inventory systems have been adopted by large manufacturers to minimize the carrying costs of inventories. Identify the primary vulnerability of JIT systems.

A. Computer resources.

B. Materials supply contracts.

C. Work stoppages.

D. Implementation time.

Answer (C) is correct. *(CIA, adapted)*
REQUIRED: The primary vulnerability of JIT systems.
DISCUSSION: JIT minimizes inventory by relying on coordination with suppliers to provide deliveries when they are needed for production. Consequently, work stoppages are more likely due to stockouts, because the inventory buffer is reduced or eliminated.
Answer (A) is incorrect. JIT systems can require significant computer resources, but they can also be maintained manually. Answer (B) is incorrect. Contracts may have to be renegotiated with strict delivery and quality specifications, but these changes usually occur over extended periods. Answer (D) is incorrect. JIT can be implemented over an extended period or a shorter time frame depending on the manufacturer's immediate needs.

19. An inventory planning method that minimizes inventories by arranging to have raw materials and subcomponents arrive immediately preceding their use is called

A. A safety stock planning system.

B. An economic order quantity model.

C. A just-in-time inventory system.

D. A master budgeting system.

Answer (C) is correct. *(CIA, adapted)*
REQUIRED: The inventory planning method that minimizes inventories by arranging to have raw materials and subcomponents arrive immediately preceding their use.
DISCUSSION: JIT is a manufacturing philosophy popularized by the Japanese that combines purchasing, production, and inventory control. As with MRP, minimization of inventory is a goal; however, JIT also encompasses changes in the production process itself. An emphasis on quality and a "pull" of materials related to demand are key differences between JIT and MRP. The factory is organized so as to bring materials and tools close to the point of use rather than keeping them in storage areas. A key element of the JIT system is reduction or elimination of waste of materials, labor, factory space, and machine usage. Minimizing inventory is the key to reducing waste. When a part is needed on the production line, it arrives just in time, not before. Daily deliveries from suppliers are the ultimate objective, and some Japanese users have been able to get twice-daily deliveries.
Answer (A) is incorrect. Safety stock is the inventory maintained in order to reduce the number of stockouts resulting from higher-than-expected demand during lead time. Answer (B) is incorrect. The economic order quantity is the order quantity that minimizes total inventory costs. Answer (D) is incorrect. The master budget is the detailed financial plan for the next period.

20. A major justification for investments in computer-integrated manufacturing (CIM) projects is

A. Reduction in the costs of spoilage, reworked units, and scrap.

B. Lower carrying amount and depreciation expense for factory equipment.

C. Increased working capital.

D. Stabilization of market share.

Answer (A) is correct. *(CIA, adapted)*
REQUIRED: The major justification for investments in CIM.
DISCUSSION: Automating and computerizing production processes requires a substantial investment in fixed assets and an increase in risk because of greater fixed costs. CIM also necessitates an increase in software costs and extensive worker retraining. However, the costs of spoilage, rework, and scrap are reduced along with labor costs. The qualitative advantages of CIM are increased flexibility, shorter manufacturing lead time, quicker development of new products, better product delivery and service, faster response to market changes, and improved competitiveness.
Answer (B) is incorrect. An increase in fixed assets results in a higher carrying amount and depreciation expense. Answer (C) is incorrect. Working capital normally is reduced as investments shift from current to fixed assets. Answer (D) is incorrect. CIM is not directly related to market share.

2.3 Pricing

21. Which one of the graphs depicts the demand curve for prestige goods?

A.
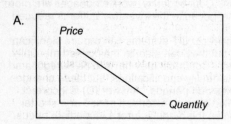

B.
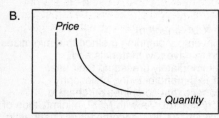

C.
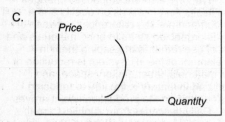

D.
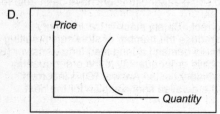

Answer (C) is correct.   *(CIA, adapted)*

REQUIRED: The graph depicting the demand curve for prestige goods.

DISCUSSION: Over some intermediate range of prices, the reaction to a price increase for prestige goods is an increase, not a decrease, in the quantity demanded. Within this intermediate range, the demand curve is upward sloping. The reason is that consumers interpret the higher price to indicate a better or more desirable product. Above some price level, the relation between price and quantity demanded will again become negatively sloped.

Answer (A) is incorrect. This graph describes the familiar, negatively sloped relation between price charged and the resulting demand level for normal goods. Answer (B) is incorrect. The demand curve for a normal good can be linear or curvilinear. Answer (D) is incorrect. This demand curve has the same basic shape as the demand curve for prestige goods, but it bends the wrong way. As prices increase, quantity demanded first falls and then rises in this graph.

22. Market-skimming pricing strategies could be appropriate when

A. No buyers want the product at a high price.

B. The costs of producing a small volume are low.

C. Competitors can easily enter the market.

D. The product is of poor quality.

Answer (B) is correct.   *(CIA, adapted)*

REQUIRED: The circumstances under which market-skimming pricing strategies are appropriate.

DISCUSSION: Market-skimming pricing is used when a new product is introduced at the highest price possible given the benefits of the product. For market skimming to work, the product must appear to be worth its price, the costs of producing a small volume cannot be so high that they eliminate the advantage of charging more, and competitors cannot enter the market and undercut the price.

Answer (A) is incorrect. If no buyers want the product at a high price, this marketing strategy is inappropriate. Answer (C) is incorrect. If competitors can easily enter the market, they can undercut the price. Answer (D) is incorrect. The product quality and image must support a high price.

23. Which of the following pricing policies involves the selling company setting freight charges to customers at the actual average freight cost?

A. Freight absorption pricing.

B. Uniform delivered pricing.

C. Zone pricing.

D. FOB-origin pricing.

Answer (B) is correct. *(CIA, adapted)*
    REQUIRED: The pricing policy that results in setting freight charges at actual average cost.
    DISCUSSION: In uniform delivered pricing, the company charges the same price, inclusive of shipping costs, to all customers, regardless of their location. This price is the company's average actual freight cost. Thus, both nearby and distant customers are charged the same amount. This policy is easy to administer, permits the company to advertise one price nationwide, and facilitates marketing to faraway customers.
    Answer (A) is incorrect. In freight absorption pricing, the selling company absorbs all or part of the actual freight charges. Customers are not charged actual delivery costs. Answer (C) is incorrect. In zone pricing, differential freight charges are set for customers on the basis of their location. Customers are not charged actual average freight costs. Answer (D) is incorrect. In FOB-origin pricing, each customer pays its actual freight costs.

24. In which product-mix pricing strategy is it appropriate for the seller to accept any price that exceeds the storage and delivery costs for the product?

A. By-product pricing.

B. Optional-product pricing.

C. Captive-product pricing.

D. Product-bundle pricing.

Answer (A) is correct. *(CIA, adapted)*
    REQUIRED: The pricing strategy that accepts any price greater than storage and delivery costs.
    DISCUSSION: A by-product is a product of relatively minor importance generated during the production of one or more other products. Its production entails no additional costs. Any amount received above the storage and delivery costs for a by-product allows the seller to reduce the main product's price to make it more competitive.
    Answer (B) is incorrect. Optional products are offered for sale along with the main product. They are unlikely to have a zero production cost, so the seller must receive a price above their storage and delivery costs. Answer (C) is incorrect. Captive products must be used along with the main product, such as film for use with a camera. Sellers often make their profits on the captive products rather than on the main product, which is sold at a low price. The captive products therefore will be priced well above the storage and delivery costs. Answer (D) is incorrect. Product bundles are combinations of products sold together at a reduced price, such as season tickets for a theater. Products are bundled to promote the sale of certain items that consumers might not otherwise purchase. The combined price of the bundle must be low enough to encourage consumers to buy the bundle but must recover production costs and provide some profit for the seller, so the price must exceed storage and delivery costs.

25. Buyer-based pricing involves

A. Adding a standard markup to the cost of the product.

B. Determining the price at which the product will earn a target profit.

C. Basing prices on the product's perceived value.

D. Basing prices on competitors' prices.

Answer (C) is correct. *(CIA, adapted)*
    REQUIRED: The definition of buyer-based pricing.
    DISCUSSION: Market-based pricing, also called buyer-based pricing, bases prices on the product's perceived value rather than on the seller's cost. Nonprice variables in the marketing mix augment the perceived value. For example, a cup of coffee may have a higher price at an expensive restaurant than at a fast-food outlet.
    Answer (A) is incorrect. Adding a standard markup to the cost of the product is cost-plus pricing. Answer (B) is incorrect. Determining the price at which the product will earn a target profit is target profit pricing. Answer (D) is incorrect. Basing prices on competitors' prices is going-rate pricing.

Questions 26 through 28 are based on the following information. While auditing a marketing department, the internal auditor discovered that the product life cycle model was used to structure the marketing mix.

26. Under such a philosophy, the price charged on a consistent basis for a specific product would probably be lowest during which life cycle stage?

    A. Introduction stage.

    B. Growth stage.

    C. Maturity stage.

    D. Decline stage.

Answer (C) is correct. *(CIA, adapted)*
    REQUIRED: The product life cycle stage during which the price charged on a consistent basis for a specific product is likely to be the lowest.
    DISCUSSION: During the maturity stage, competition is at its greatest. Thus, firms engage in competitive price-cutting measures, generally resulting in the lowest prices seen during a product's life cycle.
    Answer (A) is incorrect. During the introduction stage, per-unit costs of production are high and little competition exists. Hence, prices are at their highest. Answer (B) is incorrect. During the growth stage, prices will be lower than during the introduction stage, but not as low as during the maturity stage. In the growth stage, costs are dropping and competitors are being added, but costs are not at their minimum and competitors are not at their maximum. Answer (D) is incorrect. During the decline stage, price-cutting predominates as firms struggle to maintain sales volume in the face of a permanent decrease in demand. However, late in the decline stage, there are few competitors, so prices can be raised. In addition, per-unit costs are on the rise because volume is declining, resulting in higher prices.

27. Under such a philosophy, the opportunity for cost reductions would be greatest in which stage of the life cycle?

    A. Introduction stage.

    B. Growth stage.

    C. Maturity stage.

    D. Decline stage.

Answer (B) is correct. *(CIA, adapted)*
    REQUIRED: The product life cycle stage during which the opportunity for cost reductions is greatest.
    DISCUSSION: During the growth stage, the opportunity for cost reductions is at its maximum because production volume is increasing at a high rate. Thus, fixed costs are being spread over more units of production, and the benefits of the learning curve are being realized.
    Answer (A) is incorrect. Production volume is low during the introduction stage. Although costs are also high during this period, low volume reduces the opportunities for cost reductions. Answer (C) is incorrect. Production volume changes little during the maturity stage. The result is less opportunity for cost reductions. Answer (D) is incorrect. Costs per unit typically rise during the decline stage as production volume declines.

28. The manager has asked the auditor for advice about increasing advertising of various products. During which stage of the life cycle would it be appropriate to advertise that the company's product is the lowest price and best quality of all competitors?

    A. Introduction stage.

    B. Growth stage.

    C. Maturity stage.

    D. Decline stage.

Answer (C) is correct. *(CIA, adapted)*
    REQUIRED: The product life cycle stage during which it is appropriate to advertise that the firm's product is lower-priced and of better quality than competing products.
    DISCUSSION: The maturity stage is the ideal time for advertising lower prices and superior quality because this is the period during a product's life when competition is greatest. Due to the availability of many alternatives or substitutes, a firm has reasons to set itself apart. Because price and quality are both concerns of customers during the maturity stage, it is ideal for the firm to differentiate its product by advertising low prices and higher quality.
    Answer (A) is incorrect. Few competitors exist during the introduction stage, and quality is sometimes poor. Answer (B) is incorrect. Buyers are less concerned with price and quality during the growth stage than in the maturity stage. Answer (D) is incorrect. Few competitors exist during the decline stage. Moreover, prices may rise late in the decline stage for the remaining firms as per-unit costs increase.

29. Which of the following price adjustment strategies is designed to smooth production for the selling firm?

- A. Cash discounts.
- B. Quantity discounts.
- C. Functional discounts.
- D. Seasonal discounts.

Answer (D) is correct. *(CIA, adapted)*
REQUIRED: The price adjustment strategy intended to stabilize production.
DISCUSSION: Seasonal discounts are designed to smooth production by the selling firm. For example, a ski manufacturer offers seasonal discounts to retailers in the spring and summer to encourage early ordering.
Answer (A) is incorrect. Cash discounts encourage prompt payment. Answer (B) is incorrect. Quantity discounts encourage large volume purchases. Answer (C) is incorrect. Functional or trade discounts are provided to channel members in return for the performance of certain functions, such as selling, storing, and record keeping.

2.4 Supply Chain Management

30. An organization must manage its flows of raw materials, components, finished goods, services, or information through intermediaries to ultimate consumers. These flows may occur across the functions in an organization's

- A. Supply chain.
- B. Value chain.
- C. Full-function chain.
- D. Integrated chain.

Answer (B) is correct. *(Publisher, adapted)*
REQUIRED: The organizational arrangement in which flows of materials, components, goods, services, or information may occur.
DISCUSSION: The supply chain consists of flows from sources of (1) raw materials, (2) components, (3) finished goods, (4) services, or (5) information through intermediaries to ultimate consumers. These flows and the related activities may occur across the functions in an organization's value chain (R&D, design, production, marketing, distribution, and customer service). These flows and the related activities also may occur across separate organizations.
Answer (A) is incorrect. The supply chain consists of the flows that may occur across the functions in an organization's value chain or separate organizations. Answer (C) is incorrect. The phrase "full-function chain" is not a technical term. Answer (D) is incorrect. The phrase "integrated chain" is not a technical term.

31. The bullwhip, or whiplash, effect on inventories begins when retailers face uncertain demand from consumers caused by randomness in buying habits. It can be avoided by

- A. The need to purchase or manufacture goods in cost-efficient batches.
- B. Changes in price that may encourage purchases in anticipation of future increases.
- C. Shortages that may lead to rationing by suppliers or manufacturers and hoarding by manufacturers or retailers.
- D. Sharing of information and coordination among the organizations in the supply chain.

Answer (D) is correct. *(Publisher, adapted)*
REQUIRED: The means of preventing the bullwhip, or whiplash, effect.
DISCUSSION: Sharing information about sales, inventory, pricing, advertising campaigns, and sales forecasts by all functions and organizations in the supply chain moderates demand uncertainty for all parties. The desired results are (1) minimization of inventories held by suppliers, manufacturers, and retailers; (2) avoidance of stockouts; (3) fewer rush orders; and (4) production as needed by retailers.
Answer (A) is incorrect. The need to purchase or manufacture goods in cost-efficient batches is a cause of the bullwhip, or whiplash, effect. Answer (B) is incorrect. Purchases in anticipation of future price increases cause the bullwhip, or whiplash, effect. Answer (C) is incorrect. Rationing by suppliers or manufacturers and hoarding by manufacturers or retailers cause the bullwhip, or whiplash, effect.

32. The airlines have been leaders in the use of technology. Customers can make reservations either with an airline or through a travel agency. In this situation, a travel agency is classified as which type of distribution channel?

- A. An intermediary.
- B. A jobber.
- C. A distributor.
- D. A facilitating agent.

Answer (A) is correct. *(CIA, adapted)*
REQUIRED: The type of distribution channel of which a travel agency is an example.
DISCUSSION: Marketing intermediaries assist companies in promoting, selling, and distributing their goods and services to ultimate consumers. For example, travel agents access an airline's computerized reservation system and make reservations for their customers without ever taking title to the ticket.
Answer (B) is incorrect. Jobbers buy from manufacturers, then resell the products. Answer (C) is incorrect. Distributors, or wholesalers, usually have selective or exclusive distribution rights. Answer (D) is incorrect. Facilitating agents assist in functions other than buying, selling, or transferring title.

33. A distribution channel moves goods from producers to customers. Suppose a channel has four producers, each serving the same four customers, and no middlemen. If a distributor is introduced, the number of contacts (among producers, customers, and the distributor) in the channel will

    A. Be unaffected.

    B. Decrease from eight to four.

    C. Increase from eight to 16.

    D. Decrease from 16 to eight.

Answer (D) is correct. *(CIA, adapted)*
    REQUIRED: The effect on the number of contacts.
    DISCUSSION: The number of contacts without a distributor is 16 (four producers × four customers). The number with a distributor is eight (four producers + four customers). Thus, the effort required of producers and consumers is reduced by the distributor, thereby increasing marketing efficiency.
    Answer (A) is incorrect. The introduction of a distributor will affect the number of contacts in the marketing channel. Answer (B) is incorrect. The number of contacts declined from 16 to eight. Answer (C) is incorrect. The number of contacts decreased.

2.5 Managing Human Resources

34. A manager discovers by chance that a newly hired employee has strong beliefs that are very different from the manager's and from those of most of the other employees. The manager's best course of action would be to

    A. Facilitate the reassignment of the new hire as quickly as possible before this situation becomes disruptive.

    B. Ask the rest of the team for their reaction and act according to the group consensus.

    C. Take no action unless the new hire's behavior is likely to cause harm to the organization.

    D. Try to counsel the new hire into more reasonable beliefs.

Answer (C) is correct. *(CIA, adapted)*
    REQUIRED: The manager's best course of action when a new employee has strong beliefs that are very different from the manager's beliefs.
    DISCUSSION: The only legitimate grounds on which the supervisor may take action is the employee's behavior. Personal beliefs, such as those on religious and political matters, cannot be the basis of personnel actions. Discrimination on the basis of personal beliefs could expose the organization to legal action.

35. When faced with the problem of filling a newly created or recently vacated executive position, organizations must decide whether to promote from within or to hire an outsider. One of the disadvantages of promoting from within is that

    A. Internal promotions can have negative motivational effect on the employees of the firm.

    B. Internal promotions are more expensive to the organization than hiring an outsider.

    C. It is difficult to identify proven performers among internal candidates.

    D. Hiring an insider leads to the possibility of social inbreeding within the firm.

Answer (D) is correct. *(CIA, adapted)*
    REQUIRED: The disadvantage of promoting from within.
    DISCUSSION: Hiring an internal candidate can lead to social inbreeding. Many firms look to external candidates for certain jobs because they bring a fresh perspective to the organization's problems and may have more up-to-date training or education.
    Answer (A) is incorrect. Internal promotions usually lead to increased motivation among employees. Answer (B) is incorrect. Internal promotions are less expensive. The firm can avoid the expenses associated with an executive search and certain training costs. Answer (C) is incorrect. It is more difficult to identify proven performers from among outside candidates than internal candidates.

36. Performance appraisal systems might use any of three different approaches: (1) who did the job, (2) how the job was done, or (3) what was accomplished. Which approach is used by a system that places the focus on how the job was done?

    A. Behavior-oriented.

    B. Goal-oriented.

    C. Trait-oriented.

    D. Employee-oriented.

Answer (A) is correct. *(CIA, adapted)*
    REQUIRED: The approach used in a performance appraisal system that emphasizes how the job was done.
    DISCUSSION: Behavior-oriented performance evaluation rewards the behavior that is desired by management. Behavior control involves examining work processes rather than work output.
    Answer (B) is incorrect. The goal-oriented approach measures how well the employee attained the objectives or goals set by management. Answer (C) is incorrect. A trait-oriented approach tends to reward what the supervisor thinks of the employee rather than the job the employee did. Answer (D) is incorrect. An employee-oriented approach would focus on who did the job.

37. Which of the following hiring procedures provides the most control over the accuracy of information submitted on an employment application?

A. Applicants are required to submit unofficial copies of their transcripts along with the application as verification of their educational credentials.

B. The hiring organization calls the last place of employment for each finalist to verify the employment length and position held.

C. Letters of recommendation that attest to the applicant's character must be mailed directly to the hiring organization rather than being submitted by the applicant.

D. Applicants are required to sign a statement that the information on the application is true and correct as a confirmation of its truth.

Answer (B) is correct. *(CIA, adapted)*
REQUIRED: The hiring procedure that provides control over candidate application information.
DISCUSSION: Calling the last place of employment for candidates to verify information represents an independent verification of employment. The hiring organization is performing the verification process.
Answer (A) is incorrect. The applicant is providing the transcript, leading to a loss of independence. In addition, the transcript is unofficial, making it very easy to change the information and send a photocopy of the altered transcript. Answer (C) is incorrect. There is nothing to prevent the applicants from writing the letters themselves, putting fraudulent return address information on the letters, and mailing them. Answer (D) is incorrect. If an applicant is going to lie about information, there is no reason to believe that the applicant will not sign the applicant's own name to the fraudulent information. This is not an independent verification.

2.6 The Balanced Scorecard

38. Which one of the following is **not** a characteristic of an innovative manufacturing company?

A. Emphasis on continuous improvement.

B. Responsiveness to the changing manufacturing environment.

C. Emphasis on existing products.

D. Improved customer satisfaction through product quality.

Answer (C) is correct. *(CIA, adapted)*
REQUIRED: The item not a characteristic of an innovative manufacturing company.
DISCUSSION: Innovative companies are customer driven. Because customers demand ever better quality and competitors are attempting to provide that quality, continuous improvement (called kaizen by the Japanese) is essential for such companies. Thus, the flow of innovative products and services must be continuous. Simply emphasizing existing products is not an effective strategy for most organizations.
Answer (A) is incorrect. Continuous improvement is important for achieving and maintaining high levels of performance. Answer (B) is incorrect. More and more manufacturers are automating to achieve high quality, deliver customized products on time, minimize inventory, and increase flexibility. Answer (D) is incorrect. Customer satisfaction is the highest priority according to modern management practice.

39. A balanced scorecard is primarily concerned with

A. Staff.

B. Structure.

C. Strategy.

D. Systems.

Answer (C) is correct. *(CIA, adapted)*
REQUIRED: The focus of the balanced scorecard.
DISCUSSION: The scorecard is primarily a tool to assist the organization in describing and clarifying its strategy and then alignment of its performance measures to that strategy.
Answer (A) is incorrect. Although a balanced scorecard should be developed with staff in mind, the primary aim is the alignment of performance measures with strategy. Answer (B) is incorrect. Structure should be created after the scorecard has been developed to ensure that responsibilities, competencies and measures are appropriate to achieve the agreed-upon strategies. Answer (D) is incorrect. Systems are a means to achieving objectives that have been established after the development of the scorecard.

40. Which of the following is an example of an efficiency measure?

A. The rate of absenteeism.

B. The goal of becoming a leading manufacturer.

C. The number of insurance claims processed per day.

D. The goal of increasing market share.

Answer (C) is correct. *(CIA, adapted)*
REQUIRED: The example of an efficiency measure.
DISCUSSION: The number of insurance claims processed per day is a typical measure used in a balanced scorecard. It relates to the critical success factor of productivity. This factor is based on an input-output (efficiency) relationship. An organizational structure is efficient if it facilitates the accomplishment of organizational objectives with minimum resources and fewest unsought consequences. An efficient organizational structure maximizes output for a given amount of input. Thus, an efficiency measure compares input with output. Insurance claims processed per day relates output (claims processed) to input (a day's work).
Answer (A) is incorrect. The rate of absenteeism does not compare input and output. Answer (B) is incorrect. The goal of becoming a leading manufacturer concerns effectiveness, not efficiency. Answer (D) is incorrect. The goal of increasing market share concerns effectiveness, not efficiency.

Use the additional questions in Gleim *CIA Test Prep* Software to create Test Sessions that emulate Pearson VUE!

STUDY UNIT THREE
FINANCIAL ACCOUNTING -- BASIC

(35 pages of outline)

The first four subunits cover the fundamentals of accrual-basis accounting. Subunit 5 describes methods of recognizing revenue on the accrual basis. The next four subunits discuss measurement of current assets. Subunits 10 and 11 address external financial reporting. The final four subunits cover noncurrent assets.

Note on Accounting Principles

The CIA exam is an international exam. Thus, it does not test knowledge of any country's accounting rules. No candidate must know the differences between U.S. GAAP and IFRS.

3.1 THE ACCRUAL BASIS OF ACCOUNTING

1. **Cash Basis**

   a. Recognition is formally recording or incorporating items into an entity's financial statements. The timing of recognition is the major distinction between the cash basis (used, for example, to account for cash) and the accrual basis (used in general-use financial statements).

      1) Under the cash basis, revenues are recognized when cash is received, and expenses are recognized when cash is paid. Entities that receive cash at the time a sale is made, such as street vendors, operate on this basis.

      2) The financial operations of larger entities are based more on credit than on cash. The cash basis is inadequate for the fair presentation of such an entity's financial statements. Thus, they use the accrual basis.

2. **Accrual Basis**

    a. Accrual accounting records the financial effects of transactions and other events and circumstances when they occur rather than when their direct cash consequences occur.

        1) Use of credit means that the cash from a sale may not be received (and the cash for a purchase may not be paid) until a later accounting period.

        2) The amounts owed to and by the entity are recorded in receivables and payables accounts not needed under the cash basis. These balances are reduced when cash is received or paid.

3. **Accruals and Deferrals**

    a. Accrual-basis transactions and events are recognized in the accounting period when they occur rather than when the associated cash is paid or received. This requires accounts that record accruals and deferrals.

    b. **Accruals** anticipate future cash flows. They reflect the amounts of cash that must be paid or received at some later date for goods or services received or provided today.

        1) For example, an entity incurs an expense by having its carpets cleaned, with the price due within 10 days. The entity has incurred a liability (owes money) because it has already received the benefits of the service.

        2) The entity records an accrued expense to acknowledge that it must pay cash to compensate another party for a service already performed.

        Maintenance expense   US $800
            Accounts payable   US $800

        a) No cash has passed from the entity to the cleaner, but both the income statement and statement of financial position are affected. The debit to an expense reflects a current consumption of economic benefit, and the credit to a payable reflects the future cash outflow.

    c. **Deferrals** arise from past cash flows. They are amounts of cash paid or received today in anticipation of goods or services to be received or provided at some later date.

        1) For example, a magazine publisher has received cash from subscribers entitling them to receive the next 12 issues. The publisher must deliver a product over the next year, but it has already received the benefits of the cash.

        2) The publisher must record deferred revenue (a liability), also called unearned income, to acknowledge its obligation to other parties.

        Cash   US $24,000
            Unearned subscription revenue   US $24,000

        a) Cash has passed from the customers to the publisher, and the publisher must now provide a product. The debit to an asset reflects the cash inflow, and the credit to a liability reflects the outstanding obligation.

        3) Another common deferral is prepaid expense. It is a cash prepayment for goods or services to be received over a specified period. In this example, an entity pays 1 year of insurance premiums in advance.

        Prepaid insurance   US $100,000
            Cash   US $100,000

        a) Cash has passed from the entity to the insurer, which must now provide a service. The debit to an asset reflects the future benefit expected, and the credit to cash reflects the immediate cash payment.

    d.   Accruals and deferrals may be both current and noncurrent.

        1)   If the benefit is expected to be received within 1 year or the operating cycle (whichever is longer), the accrual or deferral is current. The prepaid insurance cited in c.3) on the previous page is an example.

        2)   If the amount the entity paid was for 5 years of insurance coverage, it would have recognized a current asset (US $100,000 ÷ 5 years = US $20,000) and a noncurrent asset (US $100,000 − $20,000 = US $80,000).

4.   Allocation

    a.   Allocation is the accrual-accounting process of distributing an amount according to a plan or formula. Assigning a total cost to the accounting periods expected to be benefited is a common allocation.

        1)   In the prepaid insurance example on the previous page, the entity received one-twelfth of the benefit during the first month after the prepayment. Thus, it allocates one-twelfth of the prepayment to expense (US $100,000 ÷ 12 = US $8,333).

Insurance expense	US $8,333
Prepaid insurance	US $8,333

        2)   Depreciation of capital assets and amortization of intangible assets (other than goodwill) over their estimated useful lives are also time-based allocations.

    b.   Assigning the total cost of a lump-sum purchase of assets to each of the assets acquired is an example of allocation not related to the passage of time.

EXAMPLE

Financial statement amounts can be calculated based on the relationship among receivables, payables, accruals, and deferrals.

On January 1 of the year just ended, an entity had the following balances:

Accounts receivable	US $15,000 Dr.
Unearned revenue	-0-

During the year, cash collections totaled US $40,000. At the close of business on December 31, the following are balances in the accounts:

Accounts receivable	US $25,000 Dr.
Unearned revenue	8,000 Cr.

From this information, earned revenue can be calculated by adjusting cash collected (US $40,000). The adjustments are for unearned and earned amounts. The increase in unearned revenue (US $8,000) is an unearned cash inflow not included in income. The increase in receivables (US $25,000 − $15,000 = US $10,000) is an earned amount with no cash inflow. Earned revenue for the year therefore can be calculated as follows:

Cash collections	US $40,000
Minus: increase in unearned revenue	(8,000)
Plus: increase in accounts receivable	10,000
Earned revenue for year	US $42,000

Stop and review! You have completed the outline for this subunit. Study multiple-choice questions 1 and 2 on page 130.

3.2 REVENUE RECOGNITION -- TIMING

1. **Revenue Recognition Principle**

   a. Accrual-basis accounting is necessary when the cash from a sale is not received (and the cash for a purchase is not paid) until an accounting period later than the one in which the transactions occurred.

   b. The proper accounting treatment of this delay between the earning of revenue and the receipt of cash is guided by the revenue recognition principle. Thus, an entity recognizes revenue when

      1) It is probable that future economic benefits will flow to the entity (because an earning process is substantially complete) and

      2) The benefits can be reliably measured.

2. **The Matching Principle**

   a. Expenses should be recognized in the same period as directly related revenues.

      1) For example, assume that customers prepay for 5 years of warranty coverage. If the seller believes that warranty costs will be incurred evenly over the period, it should recognize revenue from the contracts evenly over the same period.

Stop and review! You have completed the outline for this subunit. Study multiple-choice questions 3 through 5 on page 131.

3.3 THE ACCOUNTING CYCLE

The accounting cycle is the series of steps taken to maintain financial records in accordance with the accrual basis. After identification and measurement of items to be recorded, the steps in the accounting cycle are as follows:

Step 1: Journalize transactions
Step 2: Post journal entries to the ledgers
Step 3: Prepare an unadjusted trial balance
Step 4: Record entries to adjust accrued and deferred accounts
Step 5: Prepare an adjusted trial balance
Step 6: Prepare financial statements
Step 7: Record entries to close temporary (nominal) accounts
Step 8: Prepare a post-closing trial balance (optional)
Step 9: Record entries to reverse the accrual entries (optional)

Memory aid: **J**ane **P**ayne **U**pdated **A**n **A**nalysis of **F**ixed **C**osts, **P**roperty, and **R**evenues

1. **Journalization**

   a. The recording of transactions in journals occurs daily throughout the accounting period. Many entities use the calendar month as their accounting period.

2. **Posting**

   a. Journal entries may be posted to the appropriate ledgers either immediately (in real-time automated systems) or overnight (in batch systems).

3. **Unadjusted Trial Balance**

   a. The financial records must be closed at the end of each period before preparation of accrual-basis financial statements. The first step in the closing process is preparing an unadjusted trial balance.

      1) This step establishes that the sum of debit balances in the general ledger equals the sum of credit balances.

4. **Adjusting Entries**

   a. Accrued and deferred amounts must be adjusted to account for the passage of time or the delivery of goods and performance of services.

      1) In the publisher example on page 96, assume that a single issue of the magazine is delivered to the subscribers during each month. Because one-twelfth of the obligation has been performed, the publisher reclassifies a portion of unearned revenue as earned (US $24,000 ÷ 12 = US $2,000) at the end of each month.

Unearned subscription revenue	US $2,000	
Subscription revenue		US $2,000

      2) One common accrual is salaries expense.

         a) Because it is known that the entity has an obligation at the end of the current period for employee work performed during the period, an accrual is recorded.

Salaries expense	US $113,000	
Accrued wages payable		US $113,000

      3) Recognition of depreciation expense is another common adjusting entry.

5. **Adjusted Trial Balance**

   a. An adjusted trial balance is prepared to prove that total debits in the general ledger still equal total credits after the posting of adjusting entries.

6. **Financial Statements**

   a. The adjusted trial balance is used to prepare accrual-basis financial statements.

7. **Closing Entries**

   a. The temporary (nominal) accounts must now be closed (reduced to zero). Thus, no income or expense amounts carry over to the next accounting period. Their balances normally are transferred to an income summary account.

Net revenues	US $415,000	
Income summary		US $415,000
Income summary	US $375,000	
Expense accounts (salaries, utilities, etc.)		US $375,000

      1) For a for-profit entity, the balance in the income summary account is closed to retained earnings.

Income summary	US $40,000	
Retained earnings		US $40,000

8. **Post-Closing Trial Balance**

   a. A post-closing trial balance can be prepared to prove that total debits in the general ledger still equal total credits after closing the nominal accounts.

9.   **Reversing Entries**

   a.   Reversing entries simplify the bookkeeping process. Any accrual entry can be reversed.

   1)   In the accrued wages payable example on the previous page, the amount recognized (US $113,000) was not equal to the first cash outflow for payment of wages in the next period. The reason is that the accrual allocated the expense between the periods. By reversing the accrual at the start of the next period, the entity can debit expense for the full amount paid without regard to any allocation. Assuming that the amount owed on the first wages payment date in the next period is US $150,000, the following entries may be made:

Accrued wages payable	US $113,000	
Salaries expense		US $113,000
	(reversing entry)	
Salaries expense	US $150,000	
Accrued wages payable		US $150,000

   2)   Most computerized accounting systems permit certain entries to be designated as reversible. The software automatically reverses these entries on the first day of the next accounting period without intervention by the accounting staff.

Stop and review! You have completed the outline for this subunit. Study multiple-choice questions 6 and 7 on page 132.

3.4 CONCEPTS OF FINANCIAL ACCOUNTING

1.   **The Objective of General-Purpose Financial Reporting**

   a.   The objective is to report financial information that is **useful in making decisions** about providing resources to the reporting entity.

   b.   Primary users of financial information are current or prospective investors and creditors who cannot obtain it directly.

   1)   Their decisions depend on expected returns.

   a)   Accordingly, primary users need information that helps them to assess the potential for future net cash inflows.

   2)   Primary users cannot obtain all necessary information solely from general-purpose financial reports. These reports

   a)   Do not suffice to determine the value of the entity and

   b)   Are significantly based on estimates, judgments, and models.

   c.   The information reported relates to the entity's economic resources and claims to them (financial position) and to changes in those resources and claims.

   1)   Information about economic resources and claims helps to evaluate liquidity, solvency, financing needs, and the probability of obtaining financing.

   d.   Users need to differentiate between changes in economic resources and claims arising from (1) the entity's performance and (2) other events and transactions (e.g., issuing debt and equity). Information about financial performance is useful for

   1)   Understanding the return on economic resources, its variability, and its components;

   2)   Evaluating management; and

   3)   Predicting future returns.

    e.   The accrual basis of accounting is preferable to the cash basis for evaluating past performance and predicting future performance.

        1)   An entity should increase its economic resources other than by obtaining resources from investors and creditors.

            a)   Information about this performance is useful in evaluating potential operating net cash inflows.

        2)   Information about financial performance also is useful in determining how external factors (e.g., interest rate changes) affected economic resources and claims.

    f.   Information about cash flows is helpful in

        1)   Understanding operations;
        2)   Evaluating financing and investing activities, liquidity, and solvency;
        3)   Interpreting other financial information; and
        4)   Assessing the potential for net cash inflows.

2.   **Underlying Assumptions**

    a.   Certain assumptions underlie the environment in which the reporting entity operates. They have developed over time and are generally recognized by the accounting profession. The most basic assumption is that the **accrual basis** of accounting is used (see Subunit 3.1).

    b.   **Going-concern assumption.** It is assumed that the entity (1) will operate indefinitely and (2) has no need or intent to liquidate or materially reduce its operations.

        1)   Given this need or intent, another basis of accounting, e.g., liquidation value, must be used and disclosed.

    c.   **Economic-entity assumption.** The reporting entity is separately identified for the purpose of economic and financial accountability. Thus, the economic affairs of owners and managers are kept separate from those of the reporting entity.

        1)   The legal entity and the economic entity are not necessarily the same. For example, consolidated reporting is permitted, if not required, even though the parent and its subsidiaries are legally distinct entities.

    d.   **Monetary-unit (unit-of-money) assumption.** Accounting records are kept in terms of money. Using money as the unit of measure is the best way of providing economic information to users of financial statements.

        1)   Changes in the purchasing power of the monetary unit are assumed not to be significant.

    e.   **Periodicity (time period) assumption.** Even though the most accurate way to measure an entity's results of operations is to wait until it liquidates, this method is not followed. Instead, financial statements are prepared periodically throughout the life of an entity to ensure the timeliness of information.

        1)   The periodicity assumption requires reporting estimates in the financial statements. It sacrifices some degree of faithful representation of information for increased relevance.

3. **Fundamental Qualitative Characteristics of Useful Financial Information**

    a. **Relevance.** Relevant information is able to make a difference in user decisions. To do so, it must have predictive value, confirmatory value, or both.

        1) Something has predictive value if it can be used as an input in a predictive process.

        2) Something has confirmatory value with respect to prior evaluations if it provides feedback that confirms or changes (corrects) them.

        3) Predictive value and confirmatory value are interrelated. For example, current revenue may confirm a prior prediction and also be used to predict the next period's revenue.

        4) **Materiality.** Information is material if its omission or misstatement can influence user decisions based on a specific entity's financial information. Thus, it is an entity-specific aspect of relevance.

    b. **Faithful representation.** Useful information faithfully represents the economic phenomena that it purports to represent.

        1) A representation is perfectly faithful if it is complete (containing what is needed for user understanding), neutral (unbiased in its selection and presentation), and free from error (but not necessarily perfectly accurate).

    c. Useful information is relevant and faithfully represented. The process for applying these characteristics is to

        1) Identify a phenomenon that may be useful to users,
        2) Identify the relevant information, and
        3) Determine whether the information is available and can be faithfully represented.

4. **Enhancing Qualitative Characteristics of Useful Financial Information**

    a. **Comparability.** Information should be comparable with similar information for (1) other entities and (2) the same entity for another period or date. Thus, comparability allows users to understand similarities and differences.

        1) Consistency is a means of achieving comparability. It is the use of the same methods, for example, accounting principles, for the same items.

    b. **Verifiability.** Information is verifiable (directly or indirectly) if knowledgeable and independent observers can reach a consensus (but not necessarily unanimity) that it is faithfully represented.

    c. **Timeliness.** Information is timely when it is available in time to influence decisions.

    d. **Understandability.** Understandable information is clearly and concisely classified, characterized, and presented.

        1) Information should be readily understandable by reasonably knowledgeable and diligent users, but information should not be excluded because of its complexity.

5. **Cost Constraint**

    a. This pervasive constraint is that the costs of reporting should be justified by its benefits.

        1) Provider costs (collection, processing, verification, and distribution) ultimately are incurred by users as reduced returns.

        2) Other user costs include those to analyze and interpret the information provided or to obtain or estimate information not provided.

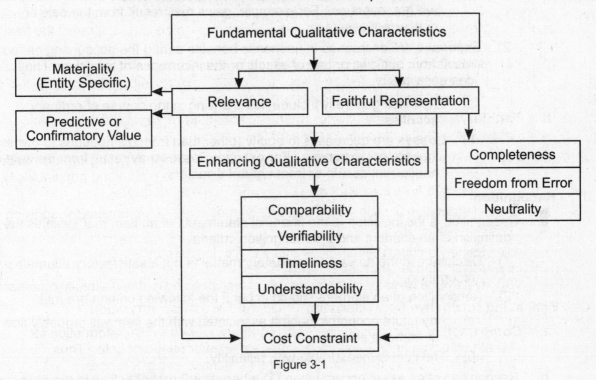

Figure 3-1

6. **Elements of Financial Statements**

    a. The elements are groups of transactions and other events classified based on their economic characteristics.

    b. The following directly relate to measurements reported in the statement of financial position:

        1) **Assets** are resources controlled by the entity as a result of past events. They represent probable future economic benefits to the entity.

        2) **Liabilities** are present obligations of the entity arising from past events. Their settlement is expected to result in an outflow from the entity of economic benefits.

        3) **Equity** is the residual interest in the assets of the entity after subtracting all its liabilities.

            a) It is affected not only by operations but also by transactions with owners, such as dividends and contributions.

    c.   The following directly relate to measuring performance in the income statement:

       1)   **Income** includes increases in economic benefits during the accounting period in the form of inflows or enhancements of assets or decreases of liabilities. They result in increases in equity other than those relating to contributions by owners.

          a)   **Revenues** are increases in equity (other than from owner contributions) that occur in ordinary activities.

          b)   **Gains** are increases in equity (other than from owner contributions) that are not revenues. For example, gains may result from the sale of noncurrent assets.

       2)   **Expenses** are decreases in economic benefits during the accounting period that result from outflows or use of assets or the incurrence of liabilities. They decrease equity.

          a)   Expenses generally include items arising in the course of ordinary activities.

          b)   **Losses** are decreases in equity (other than from distributions to owners) that are not expenses. For example, losses may result from the sale of noncurrent assets or from natural disasters.

7.   **Recognition**

    a.   Recognition is the inclusion in the financial statements of an item that satisfies the definition of an element and the recognition criteria.

       1)   Disclosure in the notes or explanatory matter is not a satisfactory alternative to recognition.

       2)   Recognition of an element should occur if the following criteria are met:

          a)   Any future economic benefit associated with the item will probably flow to or from the entity.

          b)   The item is measurable with reliability.

    b.   Recognition of an **asset** occurs when (1) a benefit will probably flow to the entity and (2) the item's cost or value is reliably measurable.

    c.   Recognition of a **liability** occurs when (1) a benefit will probably flow from the entity as a result of settling a present obligation and (2) the settlement amount is reliably measurable.

    d.   Recognition of **income** (revenues and gains) occurs at the same time as recognition of increases in assets or decreases in liabilities.

       1)   The usual procedures for income recognition, such as that revenue be earned, reflect the recognition criteria, that is, (a) reliable measurement and (b) a sufficient probability.

    e.   Recognition of **expenses** (and losses) occurs at the same time as recognition of increases in liabilities or decreases in assets.

       1)   Expenses are recognized if the costs are directly associated with the earning of particular income items. This process is often called matching (see Subunit 3.2).

       2)   Expenses also are recognized when they are broadly or indirectly associated with income. In these cases, a systematic and rational allocation procedure, such as depreciation or amortization, is used.

       3)   Immediate recognition of expenses is appropriate when an expenditure results in no future economic benefit.

8. **Measurement Attributes**

    a. Measurement is the determination of the amounts at which the elements are to be recognized. Different measurement attributes are used. The following are examples:

    b. **Historical Cost**

        1) This is the most common measurement attribute. Assets are recorded at the cash paid or the fair value of other assets given. Liabilities are recorded at the amount of proceeds received or, in some cases, at the amount of cash expected to be paid to satisfy the obligation.

            a) Examples are property, plant, and equipment and some inventories.

        2) The historical cost basis has the advantages of reliability and objectivity.

    c. **Realizable (Settlement) Value**

        1) Assets are recorded at the amount of cash currently obtainable by sale in an orderly disposal. Liabilities are recorded at the undiscounted amount of cash expected to be paid for settlement in the normal course of business. Examples are accounts receivable, some inventories, and trade payables.

    d. **Present Value**

        1) Assets (liabilities) are recorded at the discounted amount of the future net cash inflows (outflows) that are expected to be generated (required for settlement) in the normal course of business. Examples are bonds receivable or payable.

    e. **Current Cost**

        1) Assets are recorded at the amount of cash to be paid if the same or an equivalent asset were currently obtained. An example is a liability recorded at the undiscounted amount of cash needed for current settlement.

Stop and review! You have completed the outline for this subunit. Study multiple-choice questions 8 and 9 beginning on page 132.

3.5 REVENUE RECOGNITION -- METHODS

1. **Long-Term Construction Contracts -- Income Statement**

    a. When the outcome of a long-term construction contract can be reliably estimated, it must be accounted for using the **percentage-of-completion method**. Three methods are available to determine the stage of completion as of the reporting date:

        1) The ratio of contract costs incurred to date to estimated total contract costs,
        2) Surveys of the work performed to date, or
        3) The physical proportion of the contract work completed to date.

    b. The proportion-of-costs method is the most commonly used.

    c. The principal accounting issue is determining the revenue or gross profit to be recognized in a period. Assuming revenue is not separately recognized, the steps in this process are as follows:

        1) Add costs incurred to date and estimated costs to complete to arrive at estimated total costs.

        2) Subtract estimated total costs from the contract price to arrive at estimated total gross profit.

        3) Divide the costs incurred to date by the estimated total costs to arrive at the percentage of completion as of the reporting date.

4) Multiply the estimated gross profit by the reporting-date percentage of completion to arrive at the gross profit earned to date.

5) Subtract gross profit recognized in prior periods from gross profit earned to date to arrive at gross profit to be recognized in the current period.

EXAMPLE of Percentage-of-Completion Method

A contractor is constructing an office complex for a real estate developer. The contract price is US $75 million. The revenue and gross profit recognized to date are US $37,500,000 and US $6,000,000, respectively. As of the close of Year 4 of the project, the contractor has incurred US $44 million of costs. The best estimate of the costs to finish the project is US $19 million.

Contract price		US $75,000,000
Costs incurred to date	US $44,000,000	
Estimated costs to complete	19,000,000	
Estimated total costs		($63,000,000)
Estimated total gross profit		US $12,000,000

Thus, at the end of Year 4, the complex is 69.84% complete (US $44,000,000 ÷ $63,000,000). The revenue and gross profit recognized in Year 4 are calculated as follows:

	Revenue	Gross Profit
Estimated totals	US $75,000,000	US $12,000,000
Percentage of completion	× 69.84%	× 69.84%
Amounts earned to date	US $52,380,000	US $ 8,380,800
Amounts recognized in prior periods (given)	(37,500,000)	(6,000,000)
Amounts recognized in current period	US $14,880,000	US $ 2,380,800

---

    d.   If a loss [(costs to date + estimated costs to complete) > contract price] on the project is anticipated at the reporting date, the entire loss is recognized immediately.

2. **Long-Term Construction Contracts -- Statement of Financial Position**

    a.   Long-term construction contracts have effects on the statement of financial position as well as on the income statement. The contractor submits progress billings to the customer during the course of the contract, and the customer pays these invoices.

        1)   Neither transaction has an effect on revenue or gross profit, as shown below:

The customer is billed:

Accounts receivable	US $1,100,000	
Progress billings		US $1,100,000

The customer pays:

Cash	US $1,100,000	
Accounts receivable		US $1,100,000

    b.   If total costs and gross profit debited to construction in progress exceed (are less than) progress billings, the contractor recognizes a current asset (liability).

    c.   A variation on the entry in 1.c.5) is to credit periodic revenue for the gross amount. This practice requires a debit to a nominal account (a cost of revenue earned account similar to cost of goods sold) that equals the costs incurred in the current period. The periodic entry is

Construction in progress (gross profit)	US $XXX	
Construction expenses (a nominal account)	XXX	
Gross revenue		US $XXX

3. **Revenue Recognition after Delivery -- Installment Method**

    a. The installment method is used when collection is over an extended period, and no reasonable basis exists for estimating collectibility.

        1) If bad debts can be reasonably estimated, the full profit is recognized in the period of sale.

        2) A partial gross profit is recognized as each installment is collected. It equals cash collections times the applicable gross profit percentage.

        3) A different gross profit percentage is calculated for each accounting period during which installment sales are made. This percentage is applied to all future cash collections on sales from that period.

EXAMPLE of Installment Method

The following information is available about a retailer who sells goods on the installment basis and uses the installment method:

	Year 1	Year 2
Installment sales	US $100,000	US $150,000
Cost of installment sales	85,000	132,000
Cash collections on Year 1 sales	64,000	32,000
Cash collections on Year 2 sales	-0-	110,000

The gross profit percentage on installment sales is 15% for Year 1 [(US $100,000 – $85,000) ÷ $100,000] and 12% for Year 2 [(US $150,000 – $132,000) ÷ $150,000]. The following are the amounts of gross profit recognized and deferred for Year 1:

	Year 1 Sales
Cash collections	US $64,000
GP percentage on installment sales	× 15%
Gross profit recognized in Year 1	US $ 9,600

Remaining deferred gross profit on Year 1 sales: (US $100,000 – $85,000) – $9,600 = US $5,400

The following are the amounts of gross profit recognized and deferred for Year 2:

	Year 1 Sales	Year 2 Sales
Cash collections	US $32,000	US $110,000
GP percentage on installment sales	× 15%	× 12%
Gross profit recognized in Year 2	US $ 4,800	US $ 13,200

Remaining deferred gross profit on Year 1 sales: US $5,400 – $4,800 = US $600
Remaining deferred gross profit on Year 2 sales: (US $150,000 – $132,000) – $13,200 = US $4,800

4.   **Revenue Recognition after Delivery -- Cost-Recovery Method**

   a.   The cost-recovery method of accounting for installment sales is used when considerable doubt exists about collection.

   1)   Gross profit is not recognized until cash collections exceed cost of sales.

EXAMPLE of Cost-Recovery Method

In Year 1, a retailer that uses the cost-recovery method recorded a sale of goods as follows:

Installment receivable (selling price)	US $100,000	
Inventory (cost of sales)		US $70,000
Deferred gross profit (difference)		30,000

During the year, the customer made an installment payment. The retailer recognizes no revenue in Year 1 because cash collections have not exceeded cost of sales.

Cash	US $50,000	
Installment receivable		US $50,000

In Year 2, the customer made another installment payment.

Cash	US $25,000	
Installment receivable		US $25,000

After the Year 2 payment, cash collections (US $50,000 in Year 1 + $25,000 in Year 2) exceed cost of sales (US $70,000). Deferred gross profit equal to the excess is recognized.

Deferred gross profit (US $75,000 – $70,000)	US $5,000	
Realized gross profit		US $5,000

Also in Year 2, the retailer determined that US $10,000 of the receivable is uncollectible.

Deferred gross profit	US $10,000	
Installment receivable		US $10,000

---

5.   **Sales with High Rates of Returns**

   a.   Some industries, notably publishing, operate on the understanding that a substantial percentage of nondefective merchandise will be returned to the manufacturer or distributor.

   b.   In such circumstances, revenue recognition occurs when the amount of returns can be reasonably estimated.

6.   **Consignment Sales**

   a.   Under a consignment arrangement, the consignor ships goods to the consignee, who acts as a sales agent for the consignor. The goods are in the physical possession of the consignee but remain the property of the consignor and are included in its inventory.

   b.   Revenue and the related cost of goods sold (including freight costs) for consigned goods are recognized by the consignor only upon sale and delivery to a customer. Accordingly, revenue recognition occurs when notification is received that the consignee has sold the goods.

Stop and review! You have completed the outline for this subunit. Study multiple-choice questions 10 through 12 on page 133.

3.6 ACCOUNTS RECEIVABLE

1. **Definition**

    a. Accounts receivable, often called trade receivables, are the amounts owed to an entity by its customers. Because they involve the receipt of cash in the future, they should (technically) be measured with an interest component.

    b. In practice, the amount of interest involved does not justify the cost of the necessary record keeping.

2. **Initial Measurement**

    a. Sales (cash) discounts are offered for early payment. The entity accepts a lower amount to increase its cash flow.

        1) A common discount is 2% of the price if paid within 10 days, with the full amount due within 30 days. This is abbreviated 2/10, n/30.

    b. The entity may initially measure accounts receivable one of two ways:

        1) The **gross method** is used when customers are not expected to pay soon enough to take the discount. Receivables are recorded at their face amounts, and discounts taken are recognized as a contra revenue in the income statement.

        2) The **net method** is used when customers are expected to pay within the discount period. Receivables are recorded net of the cash discount, and discounts not taken are recognized as a revenue, such as sales discounts forfeited.

EXAMPLE of Recording Sales Discounts

	Gross Method		Net Method	
An item is sold with terms of 2/10, n/30:				
Accounts receivable	US $1,000		US $980	
Sales		US $1,000		US $980
Payment is received within the discount period:				
Cash	US $ 980		US $980	
Sales discounts	20			
Accounts receivable		US $1,000		US $980
Payment is received after the discount period:				
Cash	US $1,000		US $980	
Accounts receivable		US $1,000		US $980
Cash			US $ 20	
Sales discounts forfeited				US $ 20

---

3. **Subsequent Measurement**

    a. Because collection in full of all accounts receivable is unlikely, they are reported at net realizable value (NRV).

        1) Thus, an allowance contra to accounts receivable is established. This method attempts to match bad debt expense with the related revenue.

            a) Gross accounts receivable minus the allowance equals NRV.

        2) The common measures of the allowance are the percentage-of-sales (an income-statement approach) and the percentage-of-receivables (a statement-of-financial-position approach).

b. Under the **percentage-of-sales method**, bad debt expense is debited each period for an amount based on the estimated percentage of sales that is uncollectible. The entry is not affected by the amount of the allowance.

Bad debt expense (US $4,500,000 gross sales × 0.5%)	US $22,500	
Allowance for uncollectible accounts		US $22,500

c. Under the **percentage-of-receivables method**, the allowance is adjusted to equal the estimated amount that is uncollectible. Bad debt expense is the amount of the adjustment.

1) Entities usually prepare an aging schedule, in which receivables are grouped by the time that has passed since the sales transaction. A different percentage is applied to each group based on the entity's experience with bad debts.

EXAMPLE of an Aging Schedule

	Balance		Percentage Historically Uncollectible		Balance Needed in Allowance
31 - 60 days old	US $440,000	×	2%	=	US $ 8,800
61 - 90 days old	120,000	×	8%	=	9,600
91 - 120 days old	75,000	×	11%	=	8,250
Over 120 days old	13,000	×	16%	=	2,080
Totals	US $648,000				US $28,730

---

2) If the beginning balance was a credit of US $9,010, the entry is as follows:

Bad debt expense (US $28,730 – $9,010)	US $19,720	
Allowance for uncollectible accounts		US $19,720

4. Writing Off Specific Bad Debts

a. Some customers are unwilling or unable to satisfy their debts. A bad debt is recorded as follows:

Allowance for uncollectible accounts	US $XXX	
Accounts receivable		US $XXX

1) Bad debt expense is unaffected.

5. Collection of Account Previously Written Off

a. Occasionally, a payment is made on an account already written off. The first entry reestablishes the account for the amount the customer has agreed to pay (any deficiency under the original debt remains written off):

Accounts receivable	US $250	
Allowance for uncollectible accounts		US $250

b. The second entry records the receipt of cash:

Cash	US $250	
Accounts receivable		US $250

1) The net effect of these entries is to return the amount written off to the allowance to absorb future write-offs. The assumption is that the original write-off was in error and that some other account is uncollectible.

2) Bad debt expense is unaffected.

COMPREHENSIVE EXAMPLE of Accounts Receivable

A retailer had the following beginning account balances for the year just ended:

Cash	US $85,000 Dr.
Accounts receivable	66,000 Dr.
Allowance for doubtful accounts	3,000 Cr.

The retailer recorded the following transactions during the year:

Sales on credit:
(A) Accounts receivable .... US $520,000
    Sales .... US $520,000

Collections on credit sales:
(B) Cash .... US $495,000
    Accounts receivable .... US $495,000

Bad debt expense recognized:
(C) Bad debt expense (US $520,000 × 0.75%) .... US $3,900
    Allowance for uncollectible accounts .... US $3,900

Account previously written off collected:
(D1) Accounts receivable .... US $420
    Allowance for uncollectible accounts .... US $420

(D2) Cash .... US $420
    Accounts receivable .... US $420

Accounts considered uncollectible written off:
(E) Allowance for uncollectible accounts .... US $600
    Accounts receivable .... US $600

Permanent Accounts			Nominal Accounts	
Cash	**Accounts Receivable**	**Allowance for Uncoll. Accounts**	**Sales**	**Bad Debt Expense**
US $ 85,000	US $ 66,000		US $3,000	US $ -0- US $ -0-
(B) 495,000	(A) 520,000 US $495,000 (B)	3,900 (C)	520,000 (A) (C) 3,900
(D2) 420	(D1) 420 420 (D2) (E) US $600	420 (D1)	
	600 (E)	US $6,720	
	US $ 90,400		

The retailer reports net accounts receivable of US $83,680 (US $90,400 gross − $6,720 allowance).

---

6. **Transfers with Recourse**

    a. Even when a transfer of receivables with recourse qualifies as a sale, the transferor (seller) may be required to make payments to the transferee or to buy back the assets in specified circumstances.

        1) For example, the seller usually becomes liable for defaults up to a given percentage of the transferred receivables.

        2) Thus, the sale proceeds are reduced by the fair value of the recourse obligation.

    b. If the transfer with recourse does not qualify as a sale, the parties account for the transaction as a secured borrowing with a pledge of noncash collateral.

        1) In general, a transfer of receivables or other financial assets is treated as a sale if the transferor surrenders control and the risks and rewards of ownership.

        2) The terms of the transfer agreement therefore determine whether the transaction is a sale or borrowing.

Stop and review! You have completed the outline for this subunit. Study multiple-choice questions 13 through 15 beginning on page 134.

3.7 INVENTORY -- FUNDAMENTALS

1.   **Costs Included in Inventory**

   a.   The cost of inventory includes the purchase price (net of allowances and returns), shipping charges, and any other costs necessary to bring the inventory to a location and condition ready for use.

   1)   Goods shipped FOB shipping point are included in the buyer's inventory after they are shipped (while in transit).

   2)   Goods shipped FOB destination are included in the seller's inventory until they are delivered at their destination.

   3)   Goods on consignment are included in the seller's inventory.

2.   **Inventory Systems**

   a.   Perpetual vs. Periodic

   1)   A perpetual system is used by an entity that requires continuously accurate balances.

   2)   A periodic system is used by an entity with no need to monitor inventory on a continuous basis.

   b.   Purchases

   1)   In a perpetual system, acquisitions are added to inventory as they occur.

   2)   In a periodic system, the beginning balance is retained throughout the period. Acquisitions are debited to purchases.

   a)   Purchases is increased by shipping costs (transportation-in or freight) and decreased by discounts, allowances, and returns.

   c.   Sales

   1)   In a perpetual system, inventory and cost of goods sold are adjusted as sales occur.

   2)   In a periodic system, changes in inventory and cost of goods sold are recorded only at the end of the period.

   a)   Cost of goods sold equals goods available for sale (beginning inventory plus purchases) minus ending inventory.

   d.   Closing

   1)   In a perpetual system, a physical count is needed at least once a year to detect material misstatements in the perpetual records.

   a)   Inventory over-and-short is debited (credited) when the physical count is less (greater) than the balance in the perpetual records.

   b)   Inventory over-and-short is either closed to cost of goods sold or reported separately under other revenues or other expenses.

   2)   In a periodic system, the physical count must be taken at the end of each reporting period. It allows adjustment of the inventory balance to the physical count and calculation of cost of goods sold.

EXAMPLE of Inventory Purchasing

A retailer begins the month with an inventory of 1,000 units at a cost of US $10 each (US $10,000). A purchase of 200 additional units at US $10 each is made:

Perpetual system			Periodic system		
Inventory (200 × US $10)	US $2,000		Purchases	US $2,000	
Accounts payable		US $2,000	Accounts payable		US $2,000

A sale of 400 units at US $12 each is made:

Perpetual system			Periodic system		
Accounts receivable	US $4,800		Accounts receivable	US $4,800	
Sales (400 × US $12)		US $4,800	Sales		US $4,800
Cost of goods sold	US $4,000				
Inventory (400 × US $10)		US $4,000			

The retailer's physical count determines that 800 units are in ending inventory. Also, the retailer must update its periodic records and close the purchases account:

Perpetual system			Periodic system		
Balances are correct.			Inventory (physical count)	US $8,000	
			Cost of goods sold	4,000	
			Inventory (beginning balance)		US $10,000
			Purchases (balance)		2,000

If the difference is immaterial, it can be debited directly to cost of goods sold.

---

3. **Recording Purchase Discounts**

    a. When an entity's suppliers offer sales discounts, the same guidelines apply as when the entity itself offers discounts.

    1) The **gross method** is used when the entity does not expect to pay soon enough to take the discount. Payables are recorded at their face amounts, and discounts taken are credited to purchase discounts (an account contra to purchases).

    2) The **net method** is used when the entity expects to pay within the discount period. Payables are recorded net of the cash discount, and discounts not taken are recognized as an expense, such as purchase discounts forfeited.

    b. The following example illustrates the differences between the two methods under a periodic inventory system.

    1) In a perpetual system, the debits and credits to purchases, purchase discounts, and purchase discounts forfeited would be made directly to inventory.

EXAMPLE of Recording Purchase Discounts

	Gross Method		Net Method	
Inventory is purchased with terms of 2/10, n/30:				
Purchases	US $1,000		US $980	
Accounts payable		US $1,000		US $980
Payment is made within the discount period:				
Accounts payable	US $1,000		US $980	
Purchase discounts		US $ 20		
Cash		980		US $980
Payment is made after the discount period:				
Accounts payable	US $1,000		US $980	
Cash		US $1,000		US $980
Purchase discounts forfeited			US $ 20	
Cash				US $ 20

4.   **Ending Inventory and Cost of Goods Sold**

a.   Ending inventory affects both the statement of financial position and the income statement.

1)   For a retailer, cost of goods sold is calculated based on changes in inventory:

Retailer

Beginning inventory	US $ XXX,XXX
Plus: net purchases	XX,XXX
Plus: freight-in	X,XXX
Goods available for sale	US $ XXX,XXX
Minus: ending inventory	(XX,XXX)
Cost of goods sold	US $(XXX,XXX)

2)   For a manufacturer, cost of goods sold is calculated as follows:

Manufacturer

Beginning finished goods		US $XXX,XXX
Cost of goods produced:		
Beginning work-in-progress	US $XX,XXX	
Current costs:		
Direct materials	XX,XXX	
Direct labor	XX,XXX	
Overhead	XX,XXX	
Ending work-in-progress	(XX,XXX)	XXX,XXX
Ending finished goods		(XXX,XXX)
Cost of goods sold		US $ XXX,XXX

Stop and review! You have completed the outline for this subunit. Study multiple-choice questions 16 through 18 beginning on page 135.

3.8 INVENTORY -- COST FLOW METHODS

1.   **Five Methods**

a.   The inventory cost flow methods covered in this outline are specific identification, moving-average, weighted-average, FIFO, and LIFO.

2.   **Specific Identification**

a.   Specific identification is the most accurate (and record-intensive) method of tracking inventory. Every inventory item and its associated cost is entered in the entity's books.

b.   Formerly, this method was cost-beneficial only for low-volume, high-cost items, but advances in technology are making it more affordable for higher-volume, lower-cost items.

3. Moving-Average

a. This method is appropriate for use with a perpetual system because a new average is calculated each time inventory changes.

EXAMPLE of Moving-Average

	Units				Dollars		
	Units	Price	Additions	Reductions	Inventory Balance	Total Units	Revised Unit Cost
Mar. 31 inventory	1,000 ×	US $12.50 =	US $12,500		US $12,500 ÷	1,000 =	US $12.50
Apr. 14 purchase	2,000 ×	12.20 =	24,400		36,900 ÷	3,000 =	12.30
Apr. 20 sale	(1,800) ×	12.30 =		US $(22,140)	14,760 ÷	1,200 =	12.30
Apr. 24 purchase	3,200 ×	12.60 =	40,320		55,080 ÷	4,400 =	12.52
Apr. 28 sale	(800) ×	12.52 =		(10,015)	45,065 ÷	3,600 =	12.52
Total available			US $77,220				

Cost of goods sold is calculated as follows:

Goods available for sale	US $77,220
Minus: ending inventory	(45,065)
Cost of goods sold	**US $32,155**

---

4. Weighted-Average

a. This method is appropriate for use with a periodic system because a new average is calculated only at the end of the period.

EXAMPLE of Weighted-Average

	Units	Price	Extended
Mar. 31 inventory	1,000 ×	US $12.50 =	US $12,500
Apr. 14 purchase	2,000 ×	12.20 =	24,400
Apr. 24 purchase	3,200 ×	12.60 =	40,320
Total available	6,200		US $77,220
Apr. 20 sale	(1,800)		
Apr. 28 sale	(800)		
Ending inventory	3,600		

A single per-unit cost is calculated for the entire period.

Average per-unit cost = US $77,220 ÷ 6,200 = US $12.4548
Ending inventory = 3,600 units × US $12.4548 = US $ 44,837

Cost of goods sold can then be calculated.

Goods available for sale	US $77,220
Minus: ending inventory	(44,837)
Cost of goods sold	**US $32,383**

5. **First-In, First-Out (FIFO)**

   a. Under FIFO, the first goods acquired are considered the first sold. The advantage is that it states ending inventory approximately at current replacement cost.

   b. However, FIFO has the disadvantage of matching current revenues with older costs in a period of rising costs. The effect is to decrease cost of goods sold and increase profits and taxes. In a period of declining costs, FIFO has the opposite effects.

   c. The measurement is the same whether a perpetual or periodic system is used.

EXAMPLE of FIFO

Purchases					Inventory Consists of				
	Units	Price	Goods Available			Units	Per-Unit Cost		Balance
Mar. 31 inventory	1,000	× US $12.50 =	US $12,500	Beg. layer		1,000	× US $12.50 =		US $12,500
				Beg. layer		1,000	× US $12.50 =		US $12,500
Apr. 14 purchase	2,000	× US $12.20 =	24,400	Apr. 14 layer		2,000	× 12.20 =		24,400
				Inventory bal.		3,000			US $36,900
Apr. 20 sale	(1,800)								
From Mar. 31 layer	1,000			Beg. layer		0	× US $12.50 =	US $	0
From Apr. 14 layer	800			Apr. 14 layer		1,200	× 12.20 =		14,640
				Inventory bal.		1,200			US $14,640
				Apr. 14 layer		1,200	× US $12.20 =		US $14,640
Apr. 24 purchase	3,200	× US $12.60 =	40,320	Apr. 24 layer		3,200	× 12.60 =		40,320
Apr. 28 sale	(800)			Inventory bal.		4,400			US $54,960
From Apr. 14 layer	800			Apr. 14 layer		400	× US $12.20 =	US $	4,880
From Apr. 24 layer	0			Apr. 24 layer		3,200	× 12.60 =		40,320
Total available			US $77,220	Inventory bal.		3,600			US $45,200

Cost of goods sold is calculated as follows:

Goods available for sale	US $77,220
Minus: ending inventory	(45,200)
Cost of goods sold	**US $32,020**

---

6. **Comparison**

   a. Cost of goods sold, ending inventory, and income differ with the method used:

Comparison of the Three Methods

	Goods Available for Sale	Ending Inventory	Cost of Goods Sold
Weighted-average	US $77,220	US $(44,837)	US $32,383
Moving-average	77,220	(45,065)	32,155
FIFO	77,220	(45,200)	32,020

7. **Last-In, First-Out (LIFO)**

   a. Under LIFO, the last goods acquired are considered the first sold.

      1) In a period of rising costs, LIFO has the advantage of increasing cost of goods sold and decreasing profits and taxes.

      2) In a period of declining costs, LIFO has the opposite effects.

   b. One disadvantage of LIFO is possible liquidation of one or more layers of inventory. The result may be to match older and much lower costs with current revenues.

   c. LIFO is permissible under U.S. GAAP but not under IFRS.

Stop and review! You have completed the outline for this subunit. Study multiple-choice questions 19 and 20 beginning on page 136.

3.9 INVENTORY -- ESTIMATION AND ERRORS

1. **Purpose**

   a. An estimate of inventory may be needed when an exact count is not feasible, e.g., for interim reporting purposes or when inventory records have been destroyed.

      1) The gross profit method and the retail method are widely used for inventory estimation.

2. **Gross Profit Method**

   a. The gross profit method may be used to estimate the ending inventory if net sales, net purchases, and a reliable estimate of the gross profit percentage are known.

Gross Profit Method

Net sales		US $X,XXX,XXX
Beginning inventory	US $XXX,XXX	
Plus: net purchases	X,XXX	
Goods available for sale	US $XXX,XXX	
Minus: ending inventory	(XX,XXX)	
Cost of goods sold [net sales × (1.0 – GP%)]		(XXX,XXX)
Gross profit (net sales × GP%)		US $ XXX,XXX

EXAMPLE of Gross Profit Method

A retailer needs an estimate of ending inventory for quarterly reporting purposes. The firm's best estimate of the gross profit percentage is its historical rate of 25%. The following additional information is available:

Net sales	US $1,000,000
Net purchases	300,000
Beginning inventory	800,000

Goods available for sale equal US $1,100,000 ($800,000 + $300,000). Estimated cost of goods sold for the quarter is US $750,000 [$1,000,000 × (1.0 – .25)]. Estimated ending inventory is therefore US $350,000 ($1,100,000 – $750,000).

---

3. **Retail Method**

   a. Under the retail method, the estimate of ending inventory at cost is a percentage of the ending balance at retail.

   Estimated ending inventory at cost = Ending inventory at retail × Cost-retail ratio

      1) The following is the most common calculation:

Retail Method

	Cost	Retail
Beginning inventory	US $XXX,XXX	US $XXX,XXX
Plus: net purchases	XX,XXX	XX,XXX
Plus: net markups	--	X,XXX
Minus: abnormal shortage	(XXX)	(XXX)
Goods available for sale	US $XXX,XXX ÷	US $XXX,XXX = Cost-retail ratio
Minus: sales		(XXX,XXX)
Minus: net markdowns		(X,XXX)
Minus: normal shortage		(XXX)
Ending inventory at retail		US $XXX,XXX
Times: cost-retail ratio		× XX% ◄ - - - -
Ending inventory at cost		US $XXX,XXX

b.   The following are the components of the calculation:

1)   Both net markups and net markdowns adjust the balance at retail because they affect the retail price of a good. For the same reason, neither affects the cost calculation.

a)   The cost-retail ratio is lower because net markdowns are excluded from goods available for sale. The result is a more conservative inventory estimate.

2)   Abnormal shortage (spoilage, shrinkage, breakage, etc.) affects both the cost and retail calculations because these goods are not available for sale.

3)   Normal shortage is subtracted from the retail balance only because it is anticipated in the setting of retail prices.

EXAMPLE of Retail Method

A retailer decides to use the retail method for estimating ending inventory.

	Cost	Retail	Cost-Retail Ratio
Beginning inventory	US $ 90,000	US $100,000	
Plus: net purchases	40,000	50,000	
Plus: net markups	--	1,500	
Minus: abnormal shortage	(1,000)	(1,500)	
Goods available for sale	US $129,000 ÷	US $150,000 =	0.86
Minus: sales		(120,000)	
Minus: net markdowns		(4,000)	
Minus: normal shortage		(1,000)	
Ending inventory at retail		US $ 25,000	
Times: cost-retail ratio		× 0.86	
Ending inventory at cost		US $ 21,500	

---

4.   **Inventory Errors**

a.   An error in ending inventory causes the misstatement of certain financial statement line items. Overstatement and understatement errors reverse in the subsequent period.

1)   For example, an overstatement error in year-end inventory has the following effects in the first year:

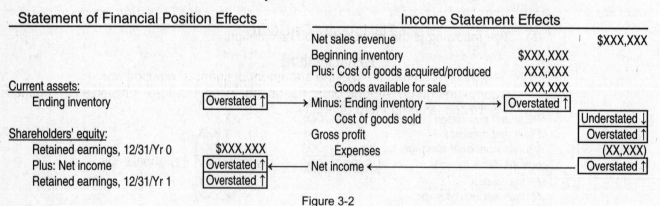

Figure 3-2

2)   At the end of the second year, retained earnings is correctly stated:

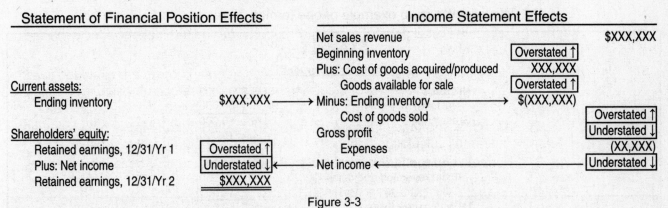

Figure 3-3

Stop and review! You have completed the outline for this subunit. Study multiple-choice question 21 on page 137.

3.10 FINANCIAL STATEMENTS

1.   **Statement of Financial Position**

a.   The statement of financial position, also called the balance sheet, reports the amounts in the accounting equation at a moment in time. The accounting equation may be stated in two ways:

The Accounting Equation

$$Assets = Liabilities + Equity$$

$$Assets - Liabilities = Equity$$

1)   The first version reports the entity's resources to the left and the sources of financing of those resources to the right.

2)   The second version reports equity as a residual amount, i.e., what remains for investors after creditors have been satisfied.

2.   **Income Statement**

a.   The income statement reports the results of an entity's operations over a period of time.

The Income Equation

$$Income\ (Loss) = Revenues + Gains - Expenses - Losses$$

1)   The income statement and the statement of financial position are complementary. Among other things, net income or loss is reported in retained earnings, a component of equity.

b.   No income statement format is required.

1)   The following is an example of one format:

EXAMPLE

Income Statement

Net sales	US $200,000
Cost of goods sold	(150,000)
Gross profit	US $ 50,000
Selling expenses	(6,000)
Administrative expenses	(5,000)
Income from operations	US $ 39,000
Other revenues and gains	3,500
Other expenses and losses	(2,500)
Income before taxes	US $ 40,000
Income taxes	(16,000)
Net income	US $ 24,000

---

2)   An example of a more detailed format can be found in Appendix C.

c.   A discontinued operation is a component of an entity that has been disposed of or meets the criteria for classification as held for sale.

1)   A single amount is disclosed on the face of the income statement equal to the sum of

a)   After-tax profit or loss of the discontinued operation

b)   After-tax gain or loss on

i)   Measurement at fair value minus costs to sell or

ii)   Disposal of the assets that constitute the discontinued operation.

2)   An analysis of the single amount is disclosed in the notes or on the face of the income statement.

3)   The following is an example of the presentation of a discontinued operation:

EXAMPLE

Discontinued Operation

Income from continuing operations before income taxes		US $ 555,000
Income taxes		(206,000)
Income from continuing operations		US $ 349,000
Discontinued operations		
Loss from operations of component unit -- X Division		
(including gain on disposal of $200,000)	US $ (340,000)	
Income tax benefit	56,000	
Loss on discontinued operations		(284,000)
Net income		US $ 65,000

---

3.   **Statement of Comprehensive Income**

a.   All nonowner changes in equity must be presented either in one continuous statement or in two separate but consecutive statements (an income statement and a statement of other comprehensive income).

1)   Comprehensive income for a period consists of (a) net income or loss (the bottom line of the income statement) and (b) other comprehensive income.

2) The following are examples of components of other comprehensive income:

  a) The effective portion of a gain or loss on a hedging instrument in a cash flow hedge

  b) A gain or loss on remeasurement of certain financial assets

  c) Translation gains and losses for financial statements of foreign operations

  d) Certain amounts associated with accounting for defined benefit postretirement plans

---

EXAMPLE

Statement of Other Comprehensive Income

Net income		US $24,000
Other comprehensive income (net of tax):		
Loss on defined benefit postretirement plans	US $(2,000)	
Gains on foreign currency translation	4,500	
Gains on remeasuring certain financial assets	1,100	
Effective portion of losses on cash flow hedges	(800)	(2,800)
Total comprehensive income		US $21,200

---

4. **Statement of Changes in Equity**

   a. Changes in equity resulting from transactions with owners must be presented separately from changes resulting from nonowner transactions.

   b. Each of the following components must be reported on the face of the statement:

      1) Total comprehensive income (net income + other comprehensive income)

      2) The effects of retrospective application of accounting policies or restatement of errors, with separate subtotals for each component of equity

      3) Contributions from and distributions to owners

      4) A reconciliation of the beginning balance for each component of equity to the ending balance that separately discloses each change

---

EXAMPLE

Statement of Changes in Equity

	Common Stock	Retained Earnings	Total Equity
Beginning balance	US $1,000,000	US $240,000	US $1,240,000
Comprehensive income	--	110,000	110,000
Changes in accounting policy	--	(25,000)	(25,000)
Dividends distributed	--	(180,000)	(180,000)
Shares issued	200,000	--	200,000
Ending balance	US $1,200,000	US $145,000	US $1,520,000

---

5. **Notes to the Financial Statements**

   a. Notes describe the basis of preparation and the significant policies applied, make required disclosures not presented on the face of the statements, and provide additional information needed for a fair presentation.

6. **Interim Financial Reporting**

   a. An interim period is shorter than a full year. An interim financial report contains either a complete set of financial statements or a set of condensed financial statements.

      1) The minimum content of an interim financial report includes condensed versions of the statement of financial position, income statement, statement of changes in equity, and cash flow statement. It also includes selected notes.

b.   If the interim report includes a complete set of statements, they should meet the requirements for annual statements.

   1)   Other line items or notes are included if necessary to prevent the interim report from being misleading.

   2)   Basic and diluted earnings per share (EPS) are presented on the face of the income statement in both annual and interim statements.

   3)   The interim report should contain various comparative and cumulative statements.

c.   Materiality is determined in relation to the interim data.

d.   If an estimate in an interim report changes significantly in the final interim period, but no interim report is published for that period, disclosures should be made in the notes to the annual statements.

e.   Accounting policies are generally the same in interim and annual statements.

   1)   Frequency of measurement should not affect annual results, so interim measurements are made on a year-to-date basis. Thus, if an item is recognized and measured in an earlier interim period and the estimate changes in a later interim period, the earlier estimate is adjusted in the later interim report.

f.   Revenues received and costs incurred unevenly over the year should not be anticipated or deferred at the end of an interim period unless such treatment is appropriate at year end.

g.   Interim reports ordinarily require a greater use of estimates than annual reports.

7.   **Financial Statement Relationships**

a.   Financial statements complement each other. They describe different aspects of the same transactions, and more than one statement is necessary to provide information for a specific economic decision.

   1)   Moreover, the components of one statement relate to those of other statements.

b.   Among the relationships are those listed below.

   1)   Accrual-basis net income or loss from the statement of income is reported in

      a)   A statement of cash flows prepared using the indirect method of presenting cash flows from operating activities

      b)   Retained earnings, a component of the statement of financial position

   2)   The components of cash and equivalents from the statement of financial position are reconciled with the corresponding items in the statement of cash flows.

   3)   Items of equity from the statement of financial position are reconciled with the beginning balances on the statement of changes in equity.

   4)   When an entity has material ending inventories, these amounts are reported in current assets on the statement of financial position and are reflected in the calculation of cost of goods sold on the statement of income.

   5)   Amortization and depreciation reported in the statement of income also are reflected in asset and liability balances in the statement of financial position.

   NOTE: See Appendix C for a complete set of financial statements. The complementary relationships among these statements are lettered.

Stop and review! You have completed the outline for this subunit. Study multiple-choice questions 22 through 25 beginning on page 137.

3.11 STATEMENT OF CASH FLOWS

1. **Purpose**

    a. A cash flow statement is presented for each period for which financial statements are presented. Users need to assess the entity's ability to generate cash and cash equivalents.

        1) Cash equivalents are short-term, highly liquid investments readily convertible to known amounts of cash. Their risk of changes in fair value is insignificant. Usually, only investments with short maturities, e.g., 3 months or less, qualify.

        2) Cash flows are classified and separately disclosed as from operating, investing, or financing activities.

2. **Operating Activities**

    a. These are the principal revenue-producing activities of the entity. They also include any other activities that are not investing or financing activities. In general, the effects of operating activities are recognized in income. Examples include

        1) Cash inflows from sales of goods and services, royalties, fees, commissions, and refunds of taxes.

            a) Securities and loans held for dealing or trading are similar to inventory. Thus, the related cash flows are deemed to be from operating activities.

        2) Cash outflows to suppliers, employees, and governments.

        3) Cash flows in the form of interest and dividends. However, depending on the accounting framework used, cash outflows (inflows) in the form of interest and dividends also may be classified as from financing (investing) activities.

3. **Investing Activities**

    a. These include acquiring, or disposing of, noncurrent assets and other investments that are not cash equivalents.

    b. In general, investing activities are associated with noncurrent assets. Examples include:

        1) Cash inflows from sales and cash outflows from purchases of (a) property, plant, and equipment; (b) intangible assets; (c) other noncurrent assets; and (d) equity or debt of other entities.

        2) Cash inflows from repayments of advances and loans made to others and from futures, forward, option, and swap contracts.

        3) Cash outflows from advances and loans made to others and from futures, forward, option, and swap contracts.

4. **Financing Activities**

    a. These include changes in contributed equity and borrowing.

    b. In general, financing activities are associated with noncurrent liabilities and equity items. Examples include the following:

        1) Cash inflows from issuing equity instruments and current or noncurrent debt

        2) Cash outflows from purchases and redemptions of the entity's own shares and from repayments of debt

5.   **Operating Activities -- Direct Method vs. Indirect Method**

   a.   The **direct method** discloses major classes of gross cash flows. It is the preferable (but not required) method because it provides more information than the indirect method. This information may be obtained from the accounting records or by adjusting sales, cost of sales, and other income statement items for

   1)   Changes in inventories and in operating receivables and payables,
   2)   Other noncash items, and
   3)   Investing or financing cash flows.

   b.   The **indirect method** adjusts income or loss for (1) noncash transactions, (2) deferrals or accruals of past or future operating cash flows, and (3) income or expense related to investing or financing cash flows. The result is net cash flow from (used by) operating activities.

   1)   The adjustments are similar to those for the direct method.

6.   **Noncash Investing and Financing Transactions**

   a.   Information about noncash investing and financing transactions is separately disclosed.

   b.   Examples are (1) the conversion of debt to equity, (2) acquiring assets by assuming liabilities or by capitalizing a lease, or (3) exchanging noncash items.

   NOTE: See Appendix C for a sample statement of cash flows.

Stop and review! You have completed the outline for this subunit. Study multiple-choice questions 26 through 28 beginning on page 139.

3.12 PROPERTY, PLANT, AND EQUIPMENT -- ACQUISITION AND MEASUREMENT

1.   **Definition**

   a.   Property, plant, and equipment (PPE), also called fixed assets, consist of tangible property expected to benefit the entity for more than 1 year that are held for the production or supply of goods or services, rental to others, or administrative purposes.

2.   **Initial Measurement**

   a.   PPE are measured initially at cost if the recognition criteria are met. Thus, (1) it must be probable that the entity will receive future economic benefits, and (2) the cost must be reliably measurable.

   b.   Initial cost includes

   1)   The net purchase price (minus trade discounts and rebates, plus purchase taxes and import duties).
   2)   The directly attributable costs of bringing the asset to the location and condition needed for its intended operation, such as architects' and engineers' fees, site preparation, delivery and handling, installation, assembly, and testing.
   3)   The estimated costs of eventual decommissioning of the asset, i.e., for removal and site restoration.

   c.   Costs excluded from the initial measurement of PPE include the following:

   1)   Administrative and other general overhead
   2)   Preproduction costs, e.g., those for opening a new plant, introducing a new product, or doing business in a new place
   3)   Interest not associated with a self-constructed asset

   d.   Interest (borrowing costs) directly attributable to the acquisition, construction, or production of a qualifying asset is included in its initial carrying amount.

3. **Subsequent Costs**

   a. These are incurred to add to, replace part of, or service an item of PPE. They are added to its carrying amount if the recognition criteria are met.

   b. Thus, day-to-day servicing costs are expensed, but costs of replacements and major inspections are included in the carrying amount.

4. **Donated Assets**

   a. In general, contributions received should be recognized as (1) revenues or gains in the period of receipt and (2) assets, decreases in liabilities, or expenses. They are measured at fair value.

   b. Contributions made are recognized as expenses and as increases of liabilities or decreases in assets. Contributions made also are measured at fair value.

Stop and review! You have completed the outline for this subunit. Study multiple-choice questions 29 through 31 beginning on page 140.

3.13 PROPERTY, PLANT, AND EQUIPMENT -- DEPRECIATION

1. **Depreciable Base**

   a. Depreciation is the process of systematically and rationally allocating the historical cost of a capital asset to the periods benefited. It is not a process of valuation.

      1) The debit is to depreciation expense, and the credit is to accumulated depreciation (a contra asset).

   b. The asset's depreciable base (i.e., the amount to be allocated) is calculated as follows:

   Depreciable base = Historical cost − Estimated salvage value (residual value)

EXAMPLE of Depreciable Base Calculation

A manufacturer paid US $112,000 for a new machine that it estimates will produce 8,000 titanium rods before becoming obsolete. At the end of the 5-year useful life, the entity estimates that the machine can be sold for US $14,000.

Depreciable base = US $112,000 − $14,000 = US $98,000

---

2. **Straight-Line Method**

   a. This method allocates an equal amount of the asset's depreciable base to each period of the asset's estimated useful life.

   $$Periodic\ expense = \frac{Depreciable\ base}{Estimated\ useful\ life}$$

EXAMPLE of Straight-Line Depreciation

The manufacturer applies straight-line depreciation:

Year	Straight-Line Formula	Depreciation Expense
1	US $98,000 ÷ 5	US $19,600
2	$98,000 ÷ 5	19,600
3	$98,000 ÷ 5	19,600
4	$98,000 ÷ 5	19,600
5	$98,000 ÷ 5	19,600
Total		US $98,000

3. Units-of-Production Method

a. This method allocates a proportional amount of the asset's cost based on its level of output.

$$Periodic\ expense\ =\ Depreciable\ base\ \times\ \frac{Units\ produced\ during\ current\ period}{Estimated\ total\ lifetime\ units}$$

EXAMPLE of Units-of-Production Depreciation

Over its 5-year life, the machine produces 2,310 rods, 1,900 rods, 1,740 rods, 1,350 rods, and 800 rods, respectively, for a total of 8,100. The total number of rods produced thus exceeded the original estimate (8,100 > 8,000). If the entity applied the units-of-production method in Year 5, the machine's carrying amount would fall below its estimated salvage value. Thus, Year 5 depreciation expense is simply the difference between carrying amount and salvage value.

Year	Units-of-Production Formula	Depreciation Expense
1	US $98,000 × (2,310 ÷ 8,000)	US $28,298
2	$98,000 × (1,900 ÷ 8,000)	23,275
3	$98,000 × (1,740 ÷ 8,000)	21,315
4	$98,000 × (1,350 ÷ 8,000)	16,538
5	Calculated directly	8,574
Total		US $98,000

---

4. Sum-of-the-Years'-Digits (SYD) Method

a. SYD is an accelerated method that multiplies the depreciable base (a constant) by a decreasing fraction.

1) Thus, higher amounts are charged to depreciation expense during the earlier (presumably more productive) years of the asset's life.

$$Periodic\ expense\ =\ Depreciable\ base\ \times\ \frac{Number\ of\ years\ remaining\ in\ useful\ life}{Sum\ of\ all\ years\ in\ useful\ life}$$

EXAMPLE of Sum-of-the-Years'-Digits Depreciation

The manufacturer applies sum-of-the-years'-digits depreciation. The denominator is 15 (5 + 4 + 3 + 2 + 1):

Year	Sum-of-the-Years'-Digits Formula	Depreciation Expense
1	US $98,000 × (5 ÷ 15)	US $32,667
2	$98,000 × (4 ÷ 15)	26,133
3	$98,000 × (3 ÷ 15)	19,600
4	$98,000 × (2 ÷ 15)	13,067
5	$98,000 × (1 ÷ 15)	6,533
Total		US $98,000

---

5. Declining-Balance Methods

a. These are also accelerated methods. The most common are 150% and 200% (often called double-declining-balance).

1) The depreciable base is not used. Instead, the asset's carrying amount is reduced annually by a constant percentage of the straight-line rate until it equals the estimated salvage value.

$$Periodic\ expense\ =\ Carrying\ amount\ \times\ \frac{Declining\-balance\ percentage}{Estimated\ useful\ life}$$

EXAMPLE of Declining-Balance Depreciation

The manufacturer has elected to apply double-declining-balance depreciation. The annual percentage will be 40% (200% ÷ 5 years).

Year	Beginning Carrying Amount		Annual Percentage		Depreciation Expense	Ending Carrying Amount
1	US $112,000	×	40%	=	US $44,800	US $67,200
2	67,200	×	40%	=	26,880	40,320
3	40,320	×	40%	=	16,128	24,192
4	24,192	×	40%	=	9,677	14,515
5	14,515	×	40%	=	515*	14,000**
Total					US $98,000	

* Calculated directly to reach salvage value
** Depreciation ceases when carrying amount equals salvage value

Stop and review! You have completed the outline for this subunit. Study multiple-choice questions 32 through 34 beginning on page 141.

3.14 PROPERTY, PLANT, AND EQUIPMENT -- DISPOSAL

1. **Journal Entry**

   a. Depreciation is recorded up to the date of disposal so that the asset's carrying amount is properly stated.

   b. The asset and its related accumulated depreciation are removed from the books.

   <u>Selling price greater than carrying amount:</u>

Cash	$xx,xxx	
Accumulated depreciation -- plant asset	x,xxx	
Plant asset		$xx,xxx
Gain on disposal of plant asset		x,xxx

   <u>Selling price less than carrying amount:</u>

Cash	$xx,xxx	
Accumulated depreciation -- plant asset	x,xxx	
Loss on disposal of plant asset	x,xxx	
Plant asset		$xx,xxx

2. **Nonmonetary Exchanges**

   a. Nonmonetary exchanges are reciprocal transactions primarily involving nonmonetary assets (such as PPE). They transfer the usual risks and rewards of ownership.

      1) The accounting for nonmonetary exchanges also applies when a transaction includes a small monetary consideration (boot).

   b. In general, the accounting for nonmonetary exchanges is based on **fair value**.

      1) The fair value of the asset given up is the cost of the asset acquired.

         a) If the fair value of the asset acquired is more clearly determinable, it is used to measure the transaction.

      2) Gain or loss is recognized on the exchange.

c. When certain exceptions apply, the accounting for a nonmonetary exchange is based on the **carrying amount** of the assets given up. Unless boot is received, no gain is recognized.

1) The following is the main exception:

a) The exchange lacks commercial substance because it is not expected to change the entity's cash flows significantly.

EXAMPLE

Jayhawk Co. and Wildcat Co. agree to exchange pieces of machinery lacking commercial substance in a transaction. The following information is relevant:

	Jayhawk Co.	Wildcat Corp.
Historical cost	US $ 280,000	US $ 300,000
Accumulated depreciation	(150,000)	(160,000)
Fair value	250,000	275,000

Jayhawk's entry

Machinery and equipment (carrying amount given up)	US $130,000	
Accumulated depreciation (balance in account)	150,000	
Machinery and equipment (historical cost of old machine)		US $280,000

Wildcat's entry

Machinery and equipment (carrying amount given up)	US $140,000	
Accumulated depreciation (balance in account)	160,000	
Machinery and equipment (historical cost of old machine)		US $300,000

---

2) Boot may be received in an exchange accounted for at carrying amount. The recipient recognizes a partial gain calculated as follows:

Total potential gain × Boot's proportion of assets received

3) If a loss is indicated in any nonmonetary exchange measured at the carrying amount of the assets given up, the entire loss is recognized.

4) Summary:

Measure of Exchange	Gain	Loss
Fair value	Full	Full
Carrying amount – no boot received	None	Full
Carrying amount – boot received	Partial	Full

Stop and review! You have completed the outline for this subunit. Study multiple-choice questions 35 and 36 beginning on page 142.

3.15 INTANGIBLE ASSETS

1. **Definition**

a. An intangible asset is an identifiable nonmonetary (nonfinancial) asset that lacks physical substance.

b. The following are examples of intangible assets:

1) Licenses

2) Patents (an exclusive legal right to use or sell an invention, such as a device or process)

3) Computer software not integral to the related hardware (but an operating system is an item of PPE)

4) Copyrights (legal protection for tangible expressions of ideas, e.g., novels, songs, and software)

5) Franchises
6) Customer lists obtained from others
7) Trademarks

2. **Initial Recognition**

   a. Initial recognition of an intangible asset is at cost. Recognition is permitted only when it is probable that the entity will receive the expected economic benefits, and the cost is reliably measurable.

   b. Cost includes the purchase price (including purchase taxes and import duties) and any directly attributable costs to prepare the asset for its intended use, such as legal fees.

      1) If an intangible asset is obtained in a business combination, its cost is its fair value at the date of acquisition.

   c. Internally generated goodwill is not an asset, but goodwill acquired in a business combination is an asset.

   d. Items expensed as incurred include expenditures for research and for

      1) Startup activities (unless included in an item of PPE),
      2) Training,
      3) Advertising and promotion, and
      4) Relocating or reorganizing part or all of an entity.

   e. Past expenses. Once expenditures for an intangible item have been expensed, they may not subsequently be capitalized.

3. **Measurement after Recognition**

   a. An intangible asset is carried at cost minus any accumulated amortization and impairment losses.

   b. The useful life of an intangible asset is finite or indefinite. If it is determined to be finite, the entity assesses the number of production (or similar) units in that life.

      1) An indefinite life has no foreseeable limit on the period during which the asset will produce net cash inflows.

4. **Amortization**

   a. Amortization of an intangible asset with a finite useful life begins when it is available for use. Its amortizable amount is systematically allocated over its useful life.

      1) Amortization is normally recognized in income or loss.
      2) The amortization method for an intangible asset should reflect the pattern of consumption of the economic benefits. But if a reliable determination cannot be made, the straight-line method is used.
      3) An intangible asset with an indefinite useful life is not amortized. Instead, it is tested for impairment at least annually.

5. **Research and Development**

   a. Research is original and planned investigation undertaken with the prospect of gaining new scientific or technical knowledge and understanding.

   b. Development is the application of research findings or other knowledge to a plan or design for the production of new or substantially improved materials, devices, products, processes, systems, or services prior to the commencement of commercial production for use.

   c. Most R&D costs are expensed as incurred.

Stop and review! You have completed the outline for this subunit. Study multiple-choice questions 37 and 38 on page 143.

QUESTIONS

3.1 The Accrual Basis of Accounting

1. A service entity keeps its accounting records on a cash basis. During the recent year, the entity collected US $600,000 from customers. The following information is also available:

	Beginning of Year	End of Year
Accounts receivable	US $120,000	US $180,000
Unearned revenue	0	15,000

What was the amount of service revenue for the year on an accrual basis?

A. US $525,000

B. US $555,000

C. US $645,000

D. US $675,000

Answer (C) is correct. *(CIA, adapted)*
REQUIRED: The amount of service revenue for the year on an accrual basis.
DISCUSSION: The amount of service revenue for the year on an accrual basis equals US $645,000 ($600,000 cash collected – $15,000 unearned revenue + $60,000 increase in accounts receivable).
Answer (A) is incorrect. US $525,000 results from subtracting rather than adding the US $60,000 increase in receivables. Answer (B) is incorrect. US $555,000 results from subtracting the increase in receivables and adding the increase in unearned revenue. Answer (D) is incorrect. US $675,000 results from adding the US $15,000 increase in unearned revenue.

Question 2 is based on the following information. Statements of financial position on December 31, Year 1, and December 31, Year 2, are presented below:

Assets:	Dec. 31, Year 1	Dec. 31, Year 2
Cash	US $ 50,000	US $ 60,000
Accounts receivable	95,000	89,000
Allowance for uncollectible accounts	(4,000)	(3,000)
Inventory	120,000	140,000
Property, plant, and equipment	295,000	340,000
Accumulated depreciation	(102,000)	(119,000)
Total Assets	US $ 454,000	US $ 507,000

Liabilities and equity:		
Trade accounts payable	US $ 62,000	US $ 49,000
Interest payable	8,000	11,000
Bonds payable	200,000	200,000
Unamortized bond discount	(15,000)	(10,000)
Equity	199,000	257,000
Total liabilities and equity	US $454,000	US $507,000

Additional information for Year 2:

1. Cash payments to suppliers of merchandise were US $180,000.
2. Sales revenue was US $338,000.
3. US $3,000 of accounts receivable was written off.
4. Equipment was acquired for US $65,000.
5. Depreciation expense was US $30,000.
6. Interest expense was US $20,000.

---

2. Cash interest payments in Year 2 were

A. US $8,000

B. US $12,000

C. US $20,000

D. US $25,000

Answer (B) is correct. *(CIA, adapted)*
REQUIRED: The cash interest payments.
DISCUSSION: The interest payable credited in Year 1 was US $15,000 ($20,000 interest expense – $5,000 amortized bond discount). Thus, the cash interest payment was US $12,000 ($8,000 beginning interest payable + $15,000 interest payable credited in Year 1 – $11,000 ending interest payable).
Answer (A) is incorrect. US $8,000 is the beginning interest payable. Answer (C) is incorrect. US $20,000 is the interest expense for Year 1. Answer (D) is incorrect. US $25,000 is the interest expense plus the amortized discount.

3.2 Revenue Recognition -- Timing

3. ABC operates a catering service that specializes in business luncheons for large corporations. ABC requires customers to place their orders 2 weeks in advance of the scheduled events. ABC bills its customers on the 10th day of the month following the date of service and requires that payment be made within 30 days of the billing date. Conceptually, ABC should recognize revenue from its catering services at the date when a

A. Customer places an order.

B. Luncheon is served.

C. Billing is mailed.

D. Customer's payment is received.

Answer (B) is correct. *(CIA, adapted)*
REQUIRED: The moment when revenue should be recognized.
DISCUSSION: Recognition of revenue occurs when (1) the flow of future economic benefits to the entity is probable and (2) the benefits can be reliably measured. The most common time at which these two conditions are met is when goods are delivered or services are rendered. Thus, ABC has substantially accomplished what it must do to be entitled to future economic benefits when it serves the luncheon. It should then accrue a receivable and revenue.
Answer (A) is incorrect. The certainty and measurability criteria are not met when the customer places an order. Answer (C) is incorrect. The date for billing is a matter of administrative procedure and convenience. The revenue should be recognized at the date the service was performed. Answer (D) is incorrect. The revenue should be recognized at the point of performance of the service. To wait until the receivable is collected is to ignore the accrual basis of accounting, which is identified in the Framework for the Preparation and Presentation of Financial Statements as an underlying assumption of financial accounting.

4. A company provides fertilization, insect control, and disease control services for a variety of trees, plants, and shrubs on a contract basis. For US $50 per month, the company will visit the subscriber's premises and apply appropriate mixtures. If the subscriber has any problems between the regularly scheduled application dates, the company's personnel will promptly make additional service calls to correct the situation. Some subscribers elect to pay for an entire year because the company offers an annual price of US $540 if paid in advance. For a subscriber who pays the annual fee in advance, the company should recognize the related revenue

A. When the cash is collected.

B. Evenly over the year as the services are performed.

C. At the end of the contract year after all of the services have been performed.

D. At the end of the fiscal year.

Answer (B) is correct. *(CIA, adapted)*
REQUIRED: The appropriate timing of revenue recognition.
DISCUSSION: Recognition of revenue occurs when (1) it is probable that future economic benefits will flow to the entity and (2) the benefits can be reliably measured. The most common time at which these two conditions are met is when goods are delivered or services are rendered. In the situation presented, the performance of the service (monthly spraying) is so significant to creating a sufficient probability of a flow of future economic benefits that it should be the triggering event for revenue recognition.
Answer (A) is incorrect. A liability is recognized when the cash is collected prior to the rendition of the service. Answer (C) is incorrect. Revenue from services rendered is recognized when the services have been performed. A portion of the services is performed monthly. Thus, a portion of the related revenue should be recognized monthly rather than waiting until the entire contract year is complete. Answer (D) is incorrect. A portion of the related revenue should be recognized monthly rather than waiting until the entire fiscal year is complete.

5. An entity sells a durable good to a customer on January 1, Year 1, and the customer is automatically given a 1-year warranty. The customer also buys an extended warranty package, extending the coverage for an additional 2 years to the end of Year 3. At the time of the original sale, the company expects warranty costs to be incurred evenly over the life of the warranty contracts. The customer has only one warranty claim during the 3-year period, and the claim occurs during Year 2. The company will recognize income from the sale of the extended warranty

A. On January 1, Year 1.

B. In Year 2 and Year 3.

C. At the time of the claim in Year 2.

D. December 31, Year 3, when the warranty expires.

Answer (B) is correct. *(CIA, adapted)*
REQUIRED: The recognition of revenue from the sale of an extended warranty.
DISCUSSION: Under the matching principle, expenses are recognized in the same period as the related revenues. Because warranty costs are expected to be incurred evenly over the life of the warranty contracts, the earning process (the provision of warranty coverage) also occurs evenly over the 2-year period. Thus, income should be recognized on the straight-line basis over the life of the extended warranty contract.
Answer (A) is incorrect. The recognition of income from the sale of the extended warranty is deferred until the extended warranty period begins. Answer (C) is incorrect. The income should be recognized evenly over the life of the contract. It is not related to the timing of the claims. Answer (D) is incorrect. Income is recognized over the life of the warranty, not at expiration.

3.3 The Accounting Cycle

6. The correct order of the following steps of the accounting cycle is

    A. Posting, closing, adjusting, reversing.

    B. Posting, adjusting, closing, reversing.

    C. Posting, reversing, adjusting, closing.

    D. Adjusting, posting, closing, reversing.

Answer (B) is correct. *(CIA, adapted)*
    REQUIRED: The proper sequence of steps in the accounting cycle.
    DISCUSSION: After identification and measurement of items to be recorded, the steps in the accounting cycle are, in order, (1) journalizing transactions, (2) posting journal entries to the ledgers, (3) preparing an unadjusted trial balance, (4) recording adjusting entries, (5) preparing an adjusted trial balance, (6) preparing financial statements, (7) closing temporary (nominal) accounts, (8) preparing a post-closing trial balance (optional), and (9) reversing the accrual entries (optional).
    Answer (A) is incorrect. Adjusting entries are made prior to closing. Answer (C) is incorrect. Reversing entries are made after adjustments and closing entries. Answer (D) is incorrect. Posting is done prior to adjusting.

7. Which of the following statements is the best description of reversing entries?

    A. The recording of reversing entries is a mandatory step in the accounting cycle.

    B. Reversing entries are made at the end of the next accounting period, after recording regular transactions of the period.

    C. Reversing entries are identical to the adjusting entries made in the previous period.

    D. Reversing entries are the exact opposite of the adjustments made in the previous period.

Answer (D) is correct. *(CIA, adapted)*
    REQUIRED: The best description of reversing entries.
    DISCUSSION: Reversing entries are made at the beginning of a period to reverse the effects of adjusting entries made at the end of the preceding period. They are optional entries made for the sake of convenience in recording the transactions of the period. In order for reversing entries to reverse the prior adjustments, they must be the exact opposite of the adjustments made in the previous period.
    Answer (A) is incorrect. Reversing entries are optional. Answer (B) is incorrect. Reversing entries are made at the beginning of the next accounting period. Answer (C) is incorrect. Reversing entries are the exact opposite of the adjustments made in the previous period.

3.4 Concepts of Financial Accounting

8. An entity with total assets of US $100,000,000 and profit of US $9,000,000 purchases staplers with an estimated life of 10 years for US $1,000. In connection with the purchase, the company debits miscellaneous expense. This scenario is most closely associated with which of the following concepts or principles?

    A. Materiality and going concern.

    B. Relevance and neutrality.

    C. Reliability and comparability.

    D. Materiality and the balance between cost and benefit.

Answer (D) is correct. *(CIA, adapted)*
    REQUIRED: The concepts or principles most closely associated with the choice of an accounting method.
    DISCUSSION: In principle, assets with a limited economic life should be capitalized and depreciated. However, the effect on the financial statements of expensing rather than capitalizing and depreciating the staplers is clearly not material given that they cost US $1,000 and the entity has total assets of US $100,000,000. The choice of treatment is not likely to influence the decisions of financial statement users. The balance between benefit and cost is a pervasive constraint. The benefits should exceed the cost of information. Specifically, the cost of producing the information about depreciation expense over 10 years for the staplers probably is higher than the benefits of the information for decision making. Thus, the expedient procedure of expensing the US $1,000 should be followed.
    Answer (A) is incorrect. The going-concern principle relates to circumstances in which there is doubt as to the viability of the entity. Materiality is an entity-specific aspect of relevance. Answer (B) is incorrect. Relevance is a fundamental qualitative characteristic of information in financial statements. Information is relevant if it makes a difference in user decisions. Thus, it permits users to predict the outcome of future events or confirm or correct their prior expectations. Answer (C) is incorrect. Comparability is an enhancing qualitative characteristic. Financial statements must be comparable for the same entity over time and also among different entities. Information is relevant if it makes a difference in user decisions. Thus, it permits users to predict the outcome of future events or confirm or correct their prior expectations.

9. The amortization of intangible assets with finite useful lives is justified by the

  A. Economic entity assumption.

  B. Going concern assumption.

  C. Monetary unit assumption.

  D. Historical cost assumption.

Answer (B) is correct. *(CIA, adapted)*
REQUIRED: The reason for amortizing intangible assets.
DISCUSSION: Every business is assumed to be a going concern that will continue operating indefinitely. Thus, liquidation values are not important. For example, if an entity is not a going concern, its intangible assets are reported at liquidation values, not at historical cost net of amortization.
Answer (A) is incorrect. The economic entity assumption is that every entity's affairs are separate from those of its owners. Answer (C) is incorrect. The monetary unit assumption provides that all transactions and events can be measured in terms of money. Answer (D) is incorrect. The historical cost principle deems cost to be the most objective and reliable measure.

3.5 Revenue Recognition -- Methods

10. A company uses the percentage-of-completion method and reports the following:

	Year 1	Year 2
Construction costs	US $100	US $200
Estimated cost to complete at year end	300	0

The contract price is US $1,000. What is the profit recognized in Year 2?

  A. US $150

  B. US $400

  C. US $550

  D. US $800

Answer (C) is correct. *(CIA, adapted)*
REQUIRED: The gross profit recognized under the percentage-of-completion method.
DISCUSSION: At the end of Year 1, estimated total costs were US $400 ($100 incurred to date + $300 estimated costs to complete), and estimated total profit was US $600 ($1,000 contract price – $400 estimated total costs). Hence, the amount of profit recognized in Year 1 was US $150 [$600 estimated total profit × ($100 cost incurred ÷ $400 estimated total cost)]. The project was completed in Year 2 at an additional cost of US $200. Actual profit was therefore US $700 ($1,000 contract price – $300 actual total cost). Profit recognized in Year 2 is US $550 ($700 actual total gross profit – $150 recognized in Year 1).
Answer (A) is incorrect. The profit recognized in Year 1 is US $150. Answer (B) is incorrect. The estimated total cost at the end of Year 2 is US $400. Answer (D) is incorrect. Improperly subtracting the costs incurred in Year 2 from the contract price results in US $800.

11. An entity has appropriately used the installment method of accounting since it began operations at the beginning of the current year. The following information pertains to its operations for this year:

Installment sales	US $1,200,000
Cost of installment sales	840,000
Collections on installment sales	480,000
General and administrative expenses	120,000

The amount of gross profit deferred at the end of the current year should be

  A. US $720,000

  B. US $288,000

  C. US $216,000

  D. US $144,000

Answer (C) is correct. *(CIA, adapted)*
REQUIRED: The amount of gross profit deferred at the end of the current year.
DISCUSSION: The gross profit on installment sales is US $360,000 ($1,200,000 installment sales – $840,000 cost of installment sales). Accordingly, the gross profit percentage is 30% (US $360,000 gross profit ÷ $1,200,000 installment sales), and the amount of gross profit deferred at the end of the current year is US $216,000 [($1,200,000 installment sales – $480,000 collections) × 30%]. General and administrative expenses have no effect on the computation of realized gross profit or deferred gross profit. They are to be classified as operating expenses on the income statement in the period in which they are incurred.
Answer (A) is incorrect. The year-end balance of installment accounts receivable is US $720,000. Answer (B) is incorrect. Improperly applying the gross profit percentage to the sum of cost of sales and general and administrative expenses results in US $288,000. Answer (D) is incorrect. Treating general and administrative expenses as costs of installment sales results in US $144,000.

12. DEF is the consignee for 1,000 units of product X for ABC Company. ABC should recognize the revenue from these 1,000 units when

  A. The agreement between DEF and ABC is signed.

  B. ABC ships the goods to DEF.

  C. DEF receives the goods from ABC.

  D. DEF sells the goods and informs ABC of the sale.

Answer (D) is correct. *(CIA, adapted)*
REQUIRED: The moment when the consignor should recognize revenue.
DISCUSSION: Under a consignment arrangement, the consignor ships goods to the consignee, who acts as sales agent for the consignor. The goods are in the physical possession of the consignee but remain the property of the consignor and are included in the consignor's inventory. Revenue and the related cost of goods sold from consigned goods are recognized by the consignor only when the merchandise is sold and delivered to the final customer. Accordingly, recognition occurs when notification is received that the consignee has sold the goods.

3.6 Accounts Receivable

13. An internal auditor is deriving cash flow data based on an incomplete set of facts. Bad debt expense was US $2,000. Additional data for this period follow:

Credit sales	US $100,000
Gross accounts receivable -- beginning balance	5,000
Allowance for bad debts -- beginning balance	(500)
Accounts receivable written off	1,000
Increase in net accounts receivable (after subtraction of allowance for bad debts)	30,000

How much cash was collected this period on credit sales?

A. US $64,000

B. US $68,000

C. US $68,500

D. US $70,000

Answer (B) is correct. *(CIA, adapted)*
REQUIRED: The cash collected on accounts receivable.
DISCUSSION: Beginning net A/R was US $4,500 ($5,000 beginning gross A/R – $500 beginning allowance), and ending net A/R was US $34,500 ($4,500 beginning net A/R + $30,000 increase). To determine ending gross A/R, the ending allowance must be calculated:

Beginning allowance for bad debts	US $ 500	Cr.
Bad debt expense	2,000	Cr.
A/R written off	1,000	Dr.
Ending allowance for bad debts	US $1,500	Cr.

Ending gross A/R was therefore US $36,000 ($34,500 net A/R + $1,500 allowance), allowing cash collected on credit sales to be calculated as follows:

Beginning gross A/R	US $ 5,000
Plus: credit sales	100,000
Minus: A/R written off	(1,000)
Minus: ending gross A/R	(36,000)
Cash collections on credit sales	US $ 68,000

Answer (A) is incorrect. US $64,000 equals credit sales minus the ending gross accounts receivable. Answer (C) is incorrect. US $68,500 equals credit sales, minus the increase in net accounts receivable, minus the ending allowance. Answer (D) is incorrect. US $70,000 equals credit sales minus the increase in net accounts receivable.

Question 14 is based on the following information. Statements of financial position on December 31, Year 1, and December 31, Year 2, are presented below:

	Dec. 31, Year 1	Dec. 31, Year 2
Assets:		
Cash	US $ 50,000	US $ 60,000
Accounts receivable	95,000	89,000
Allowance for uncollectible accounts	(4,000)	(3,000)
Inventory	120,000	140,000
Property, plant, and equipment	295,000	340,000
Accumulated depreciation	(102,000)	(119,000)
Total Assets	US $ 454,000	US $ 507,000

	Dec. 31, Year 1	Dec. 31, Year 2
Liabilities and equity:		
Trade accounts payable	US $ 62,000	US $ 49,000
Interest payable	8,000	11,000
Bonds payable	200,000	200,000
Unamortized bond discount	(15,000)	(10,000)
Equity	199,000	257,000
Total liabilities and equity	US $454,000	US $507,000

Additional information for Year 2:

1. Cash payments to suppliers of merchandise were US $180,000.
2. Sales revenue was US $338,000.
3. US $3,000 of accounts receivable was written off.
4. Equipment was acquired for US $65,000.
5. Depreciation expense was US $30,000.
6. Interest expense was US $20,000.

14. Cash collections from customers in Year 2 were

A. US $341,000

B. US $338,000

C. US $344,000

D. US $335,000

Answer (A) is correct. *(CIA, adapted)*
REQUIRED: The cash collections from customers.
DISCUSSION: Cash collections from customers equals beginning accounts receivable, plus sales revenue, minus accounts written off, minus ending accounts receivable. In Year 2, cash collections from customers were US $341,000 ($95,000 + $338,000 – $3,000 – $89,000).
Answer (B) is incorrect. US $338,000 is the sales revenue for the year. Answer (C) is incorrect. US $344,000 includes the US $3,000 of accounts written off. Answer (D) is incorrect. US $335,000 is sales revenue minus accounts written off.

15. At the end of September, an entity has outstanding accounts receivable of US $350 on third-quarter credit sales, composed as follows:

Month	Credit Sales	Still Outstanding at the End of September
July	US $600	US $100
August	900	170
September	500	80

The percentage of receivables in the 31-to-60-day age group at the end of September is

A. 22.86%

B. 28.57%

C. 48.57%

D. 71.43%

Answer (C) is correct. *(CIA, adapted)*
 REQUIRED: The percentage of receivables in the 31-to-60-day age group.
 DISCUSSION: Receivables from August sales still outstanding at the end of September are in the 31-to-60-day age group. This group represents 48.57% of total receivables [US $170 ÷ ($100 + $170 + $80)].
 Answer (A) is incorrect. This percentage is the proportion of receivables in the 0-to-30-day age group at the end of September. Answer (B) is incorrect. This percentage is the proportion of receivables in the 61-to-90-day age group at the end of September. Answer (D) is incorrect. This percentage is the proportion of outstanding receivables that are from 0 to 60 days old at the end of September.

3.7 Inventory -- Fundamentals

16. An entity had the following account balances in the pre-closing trial balance:

Opening inventory	US $100,000
Closing inventory	150,000
Purchases	400,000
Transportation-in	6,000
Purchase discounts	40,000
Purchase allowances	15,000
Returned purchases	5,000

The entity had net purchases for the period of

A. US $340,000

B. US $346,000

C. US $370,000

D. US $376,000

Answer (B) is correct. *(CIA, adapted)*
 REQUIRED: The net purchases.
 DISCUSSION: Purchase discounts, allowances, and returns are subtractions from purchases because they are reductions of cost. Transportation-in is an addition because it increases cost. Thus, net purchases equals US $346,000 ($400,000 + $6,000 – $40,000 – $15,000 – $5,000).
 Answer (A) is incorrect. Failing to include transportation-in in the calculation results in US $340,000. Answer (C) is incorrect. Improperly omitting transportation-in and adding, rather than subtracting, purchase allowances results in US $370,000. Answer (D) is incorrect. Improperly adding, rather than subtracting, purchase allowances results in US $376,000.

17. A physical inventory count showed an entity had inventory costing US $1,000,000 on hand at December 31, Year 1. Excluded from this amount were the following:

- Goods costing US $82,000, shipped to a customer free on board (FOB) shipping point on December 28, Year 1. They were expected to be received by the customer on January 4, Year 2.

- Goods costing US $122,000, shipped to a customer free on board (FOB) destination December 30, Year 1. They were expected to be received by the customer on January 5, Year 2.

Compute the correct ending inventory to be reported on the shipper's statement of financial position at December 31, Year 1.

A. US $1,000,000

B. US $1,082,000

C. US $1,122,000

D. US $1,204,000

Answer (C) is correct. *(CIA, adapted)*
 REQUIRED: The correct ending inventory balance.
 DISCUSSION: The goods shipped FOB shipping point should be counted in the buyer's, not the seller's, inventory because title and risk of loss pass at the time and place of shipment. These goods were properly excluded from ending inventory. The goods shipped FOB destination were improperly excluded from the seller's ending inventory. The title and risk of loss did not pass until the time and place where the goods reached their destination and were duly tendered. Thus, the correct ending inventory is US $1,122,000 ($1,000,000 beginning balance + $122,000 goods shipped FOB destination).
 Answer (A) is incorrect. US $1,000,000 results from excluding the goods shipped FOB destination. Answer (B) is incorrect. US $1,082,000 results from excluding the goods shipped FOB destination and from including the goods shipped FOB shipping point. Answer (D) is incorrect. US $1,204,000 results from including the goods shipped FOB shipping point.

Question 18 is based on the following information. Statements of financial position on December 31, Year 1, and December 31, Year 2, are presented below:

	Dec. 31, Year 1	Dec. 31, Year 2
Assets:		
Cash	US $ 50,000	US $ 60,000
Accounts receivable	95,000	89,000
Allowance for uncollectible accounts	(4,000)	(3,000)
Inventory	120,000	140,000
Property, plant, and equipment	295,000	340,000
Accumulated depreciation	(102,000)	(119,000)
Total Assets	US $ 454,000	US $ 507,000

Liabilities and equity:	Dec. 31, Year 1	Dec. 31, Year 2
Trade accounts payable	US $ 62,000	US $ 49,000
Interest payable	8,000	11,000
Bonds payable	200,000	200,000
Unamortized bond discount	(15,000)	(10,000)
Equity	199,000	257,000
Total liabilities and equity	US $454,000	US $507,000

Additional information for Year 2:

1. Cash payments to suppliers of merchandise were US $180,000.
2. Sales revenue was US $338,000.
3. US $3,000 of accounts receivable was written off.
4. Equipment was acquired for US $65,000.
5. Depreciation expense was US $30,000.
6. Interest expense was US $20,000.

18. Cost of goods sold in Year 2 was

A. US $147,000

B. US $160,000

C. US $167,000

D. US $180,000

Answer (A) is correct. *(CIA, adapted)*
REQUIRED: The cost of goods sold.
DISCUSSION: Cost of goods sold equals beginning inventory, plus purchases, minus ending inventory. To determine cost of goods sold, purchases must be calculated. Purchases equal US $167,000 ($49,000 ending accounts payable + $180,000 payments to suppliers – $62,000 beginning accounts payable). Thus, cost of goods sold equals US $147,000 ($120,000 beginning inventory + $167,000 purchases – $140,000 ending inventory).
Answer (B) is incorrect. US $160,000 results from assuming that US $180,000 of cash payments to suppliers equaled purchases. Answer (C) is incorrect. US $167,000 equals purchases. Answer (D) is incorrect. US $180,000 is the amount of cash payments to suppliers.

3.8 Inventory -- Cost Flow Methods

19. An entity started in Year 1 with 200 scented candles on hand at a cost of US $3.50 each. These candles sell for US $7.00 each. The following schedule represents the purchases and sales of candles during Year 1:

Transaction Number	Quantity Purchased	Unit Cost	Quantity Sold
1	---	---	150
2	250	US $3.30	---
3	---	---	100
4	200	3.10	---
5	---	---	200
6	350	3.00	---
7	---	---	300

If the entity uses periodic FIFO inventory pricing, the gross profit for Year 1 would be

A. US $2,755

B. US $2,805

C. US $2,854

D. US $2,920

Answer (B) is correct. *(CIA, adapted)*
REQUIRED: The gross profit using periodic FIFO inventory pricing.
DISCUSSION: The FIFO method assumes that the first goods purchased are the first goods sold and that ending inventory consists of the latest purchases. Moreover, whether the inventory system is periodic or perpetual does not affect FIFO measurement. The cost of goods sold is US $2,445 {beginning inventory (200 units × $3.50) + purchases [(250 units × $3.30) + (200 units × $3.10) + (350 units × $3.00)] – ending inventory (250 units × $3.00)}. Thus, the gross profit for Year 1 using FIFO is US $2,805 [sales (750 units × $7.00) – cost of goods sold of $2,445].
Answer (A) is incorrect. US $2,755 equals sales minus purchases. Answer (C) is incorrect. US $2,854 results from using a weighted-average ending inventory and part of the cost of goods sold calculation. Answer (D) is incorrect. US $2,920 results from using periodic LIFO inventory pricing.

20. The cost of materials has risen steadily over the year. Which of the following methods of estimating the ending balance of the materials inventory account will result in the highest profit, assuming all other variables remain constant?

A. Last-in, first-out (LIFO).

B. First-in, first-out (FIFO).

C. Weighted average.

D. Specific identification.

Answer (B) is correct. *(CIA, adapted)*
REQUIRED: The inventory flow assumption yielding the highest profit given rising prices.
DISCUSSION: Profit will be higher when cost of goods sold is lower, other factors held constant. Cost of goods sold equals beginning inventory, plus purchases, minus ending inventory. Accordingly, cost of goods sold will be lowest when the ending inventory is highest. In an inflationary environment, ending inventory is highest under FIFO because the older, less expensive items are deemed to have been sold, leaving the more expensive items in the ending inventory.
Answer (A) is incorrect. LIFO yields the lowest profit. Answer (C) is incorrect. In an inflationary environment, weighted average results in a lower profit than FIFO. Answer (D) is incorrect. Under specific identification, the newest (most expensive) items are not necessarily in the ending inventory. The result is a higher cost of goods sold and lower profit than under FIFO.

3.9 Inventory -- Estimation and Errors

21. The following data are available from the records of a department store for the year ended December 31, Year 1:

	At Cost	At Retail
Merchandise inventory, as of January 1, Year 1	US $ 9,000	US $13,000
Purchases	33,000	46,000
Markups (net)		1,000
Markdowns (net)		4,000
Sales		48,000

Using the retail method to approximate valuation at lower of average cost or market, the department store's merchandise inventory at December 31, Year 1, is

A. US $8,400

B. US $8,000

C. US $6,000

D. US $5,600

Answer (D) is correct. *(CIA, adapted)*
REQUIRED: The year-end inventory value using the retail method.
DISCUSSION: Under the retail method, the value of ending inventory at retail is multiplied by the cost-to-retail ratio. Both markups and markdowns affect the calculation of retail, but they do not affect historical cost. The store's December 31, Year 1 inventory at cost can be estimated as follows:

	Cost	Retail
Beginning inventory	US $ 9,000	US $ 13,000
Plus: Purchases	33,000	46,000
Plus: Markups, net	--	1,000
Goods available for sale	US $42,000	US $ 60,000
Minus: Sales		(48,000)
Minus: Markdowns, net		(4,000)
Ending inventory at retail		US $ 8,000
Times: Cost-retail ratio (US $42,000 ÷ $60,000)		× .70
Ending inventory at cost		US $ 5,600

Answer (A) is incorrect. Failing to subtract the net markdowns to compute the merchandise inventory at retail at December 31, Year 1, results in US $8,400. Answer (B) is incorrect. Inventory at retail at December 31, Year 1, is US $8,000. Answer (C) is incorrect. Improperly including the net markdowns in the cost-to-retail ratio results in US $6,000.

3.10 Financial Statements

22. At January 1, Year 1, a sole proprietorship's assets totaled US $210,000, and its liabilities amounted to US $120,000. During Year 1, owner investments amounted to US $72,000, and owner withdrawals totaled US $75,000. At December 31, Year 1, assets totaled US $270,000, and liabilities amounted to US $171,000. The amount of net income for Year 1 was

A. US $0

B. US $6,000

C. US $9,000

D. US $12,000

Answer (D) is correct. *(CIA, adapted)*
REQUIRED: The net income.
DISCUSSION: Net income may be derived using the extended accounting equation (assets = liabilities + equity + profit). Equity at 1/1/Yr 1 was US $90,000 ($210,000 of assets – $120,000 of liabilities). Equity at 12/31/Yr 1 was US $99,000 ($270,000 – $171,000). Because owner transactions decreased assets by US $3,000 ($72,000 investment – $75,000 withdrawals), net income must have been US $12,000 [$99,000 – ($90,000 – $3,000)].
Answer (A) is incorrect. The entity made a profit. Answer (B) is incorrect. US $6,000 results from reversing the addition and subtraction of investments and withdrawals. Answer (C) is incorrect. US $9,000 is the difference between beginning and ending equity without considering the capital transactions with, and distributions to, the owner.

23. Because of inexact estimates of the service life and the residual value of a plant asset, a fully depreciated asset was sold in the current year at a material gain. This gain most likely should be reported

    A. In the other revenues and gains section of the current income statement.

    B. As part of sales revenue on the current income statement.

    C. In the extraordinary item section of the current income statement.

    D. As an adjustment to prior periods' depreciation on the statement of changes in equity.

Answer (A) is correct. *(CIA, adapted)*
    REQUIRED: The reporting of a material gain.
    DISCUSSION: Revenues occur in the course of ordinary activities. Gains may or may not occur in the course of ordinary activities. For example, gains may occur from the sale of noncurrent assets. Thus, the gain on the sale of a plant asset is not an operating item and should be classified in an income statement with separate operating and nonoperating sections in the other revenues and gains section.
    Answer (B) is incorrect. The asset sold was not inventory. Answer (C) is incorrect. The item does not meet the criteria for reporting as extraordinary under U.S. GAAP (extraordinary items may be reported under U.S. GAAP but not IFRS). Answer (D) is incorrect. The transaction is not the correction of an error in the financial statements of a prior period.

24. An entity decided to sell a line of its business. The assets were sold for US $100,000 and had a net carrying amount of US $70,000. The applicable tax rate was 20%. The result of this transaction may appear on the

    A. Statement of financial position as a fundamental error.

    B. Income statement as an extraordinary item.

    C. Income statement as a single amount for a discontinued operation.

    D. Income statement as an accounting change.

Answer (C) is correct. *(CIA, adapted)*
    REQUIRED: The reporting of a sale of a line of business.
    DISCUSSION: A discontinued operation is a component of an entity that has been disposed of or meets the criteria for classification as held for sale. A single amount is disclosed on the face of the income statement equal to the sum of (1) after-tax profit (loss) on discontinued operations and (2) after-tax gain (loss) on (a) remeasurement of noncurrent assets (or disposal groups) classified as held for sale at fair value minus cost to sell or (b) disposal of the assets that constituted the discontinued operation.
    Answer (A) is incorrect. A "fundamental error" is not recognized. Answer (B) is incorrect. The disposal of a component of an entity is not an extraordinary event. Answer (D) is incorrect. Accounting changes are changes in accounting principles, changes in accounting estimates, and changes in the reporting entity.

25. A gain occurs in the second fiscal quarter. How should the gain be accounted for?

    A. Recognized in full in the second quarter.

    B. Recognized equally over the second, third, and fourth quarters.

    C. Recognized only in the annual financial statements.

    D. Recognized equally in each quarter, by restating the first quarter.

Answer (A) is correct. *(CIA, adapted)*
    REQUIRED: The accounting treatment in interim statements of an extraordinary gain.
    DISCUSSION: Gains and losses similar to those that would not be deferred at year end should not be deferred to later interim periods of the same year. Hence, the gain should not be prorated.

3.11 Statement of Cash Flows

26. The management of ABC Corporation is analyzing the financial statements of XYZ Corporation because ABC is strongly considering purchasing a block of XYZ ordinary shares that would give ABC significant influence over XYZ. Which financial statement should ABC primarily use to assess the amounts, timing, and certainty of future cash flows of XYZ Company?

A. Income statement.

B. Statement of changes in equity.

C. Statement of cash flows.

D. Statement of financial position.

Answer (C) is correct. *(CIA, adapted)*
REQUIRED: The financial statement used to assess the amounts, timing, and uncertainty of future cash flows.
DISCUSSION: A statement of cash flows provides information about the cash receipts and cash payments of an entity during a period. This information helps investors, creditors, and other users to assess the entity's ability to generate cash and cash equivalents and the needs of the entity to use those cash flows. Historical cash flow data indicate the amount, timing, and certainty of future cash flows. It is also a means of verifying past cash flow assessments and of determining the relationship between profits and net cash flows and the effects of changing prices.
Answer (A) is incorrect. The statement of income is prepared on an accrual basis and is not meant to report cash flows. Answer (B) is incorrect. The statement of changes in equity is prepared on the accrual basis. Answer (D) is incorrect. The statement of financial position reports on financial position at a moment in time.

27. The following data were extracted from the financial statements of a company for the year ended December 31.

Net income	US $70,000
Depreciation expense	14,000
Amortization of intangibles	1,000
Decrease in accounts receivable	2,000
Increase in inventories	9,000
Increase in accounts payable	4,000
Increase in plant assets	47,000
Increase in contributed capital	31,000
Decrease in short-term notes payable	55,000

There were no disposals of plant assets during the year. Based on the information above, a statement of cash flows will report a net increase in cash of

A. US $11,000

B. US $17,000

C. US $54,000

D. US $69,000

Answer (A) is correct. *(CIA, adapted)*
REQUIRED: The net increase in cash during the year as reported on the statement of cash flows.
DISCUSSION: Depreciation and amortization are noncash expenses and are added to net income. A decrease in receivables indicates that cash collections exceed sales on an accrual basis, so it is added to net income. To account for the difference between cost of goods sold (which reduces net income) and cash paid to suppliers, a two-step adjustment of net income is necessary. The difference between COGS and purchases is the change in inventory. The difference between purchases and the amount paid to suppliers is the change in accounts payable. Accordingly, the conversion of COGS to cash paid to suppliers requires subtracting the inventory increase and adding the accounts payable increase. An increase in plant assets indicates an acquisition of plant assets, causing a decrease in cash, so it is deducted. An increase in contributed capital represents a cash inflow and is added to net income. A decrease in short-term notes payable is deducted from net income because it reflects a cash outflow. Thus, cash increased by US $11,000 ($70,000 net income + $14,000 + $1,000 + $2,000 – $9,000 + $4,000 – $47,000 + $31,000 – $55,000).
Answer (B) is incorrect. US $17,000 results from subtracting the amortization and the decrease in receivables and adding the increase in inventories. Answer (C) is incorrect. US $54,000 results from adjusting net income for the increase in plant assets and the increase in contributed capital only. Answer (D) is incorrect. US $69,000 results from failing to make the adjustments for receivables, inventories, notes payable, and accounts payable.

28. The comparative statement of financial position for an entity that had net income of US $150,000 for the year ended December 31, Year 2, and paid US $125,000 of dividends during Year 2 is as follows:

	12/31/Yr 2	12/31/Yr 1
Cash	US $150,000	US $180,000
Accounts receivable	200,000	220,000
Total assets	US $350,000	US $400,000
Payables	US $ 80,000	US $160,000
Share capital	130,000	125,000
Retained earnings	140,000	115,000
Total liabilities and shareholders' equity	US $350,000	US $400,000

If dividends paid are treated as a cost of obtaining financial resources, the amount of net cash from operating activities during Year 2 was

- A. US $70,000
- B. US $90,000
- C. US $150,000
- D. US $210,000

Answer (B) is correct. *(CIA, adapted)*
REQUIRED: The amount of net cash from operating activities during Year 2.
DISCUSSION: Net income is adjusted to determine the net cash from operations. The payment of cash dividends is regarded as a cash flow from a financing activity. Hence, it is not a reconciling item. However, the decrease in accounts receivable (US $220,000 – $200,000 = US $20,000) during the period represents a cash inflow (collections of pre-Year 2 receivables) not reflected in Year 2 net income. Moreover, the decrease in payables (US $160,000 – $80,000 = US $80,000) indicates a cash outflow (payment of pre-Year 2 liabilities) that also is not reflected in Year 2 net income. Accordingly, net cash from operations was US $90,000 ($150,000 + $20,000 – $80,000).
Answer (A) is incorrect. US $70,000 results from failing to add the reduction in accounts receivable to net income. Answer (C) is incorrect. US $150,000 is net income. Answer (D) is incorrect. US $210,000 results from subtracting the reduction in receivables and adding the reduction in payables.

3.12 Property, Plant, and Equipment -- Acquisition and Measurement

29. Which of the following is **not** an appropriate basis for measuring the cost of property, plant, and equipment?

- A. The purchase price, freight costs, and installation costs of a productive asset should be included in the asset's cost.

- B. Proceeds obtained in the process of readying land for its intended purpose, such as from the sale of cleared timber, should be recognized immediately as income.

- C. The costs of improvements to equipment incurred after its acquisition should be added to the asset's cost if they increase future service potential.

- D. All costs incurred in the construction of a plant building, from excavation to completion, should be considered as part of the asset's cost.

Answer (B) is correct. *(CIA, adapted)*
REQUIRED: The basis that is inappropriate for measuring the cost of property, plant, and equipment.
DISCUSSION: Accordingly, items of property, plant, and equipment (PPE) that meet the recognition criterion are initially measured at cost. The cost includes the purchase price (minus trade discounts and rebates, plus purchase taxes) and the directly attributable costs of bringing the assets to working condition for their intended use. Directly attributable costs include site preparation, installation, initial delivery and handling, architect and equipment fees, costs of removing the assets and restoring the site, etc. Accordingly, the cost of land includes the cost of obtaining the land and readying it for its intended uses, but it is inappropriate to recognize the proceeds related to site preparation immediately in profit or loss. They should be treated as reductions in the price of the land.
Answer (A) is incorrect. The purchase price, freight costs, and installation costs of a productive asset are included in the asset's cost. Answer (C) is incorrect. Subsequent costs are added to the carrying amount of an item of PPE if it is probable that, as a result, future economic benefits will be received, and the costs are reliably measurable. Answer (D) is incorrect. All costs of construction should be included as a part of the asset's cost.

30. An entity installed an assembly line in Year 1. Four years later, US $100,000 was invested to automate the line. The automation increased the market value and productive capacity of the assembly line but did not affect its useful life. Proper accounting for the cost of the automation should be to

- A. Report it as an expense in Year 5.

- B. Establish a separate account for the US $100,000.

- C. Allocate the cost of automation between the asset and accumulated depreciation accounts.

- D. Debit the cost to the property, plant, and equipment account.

Answer (D) is correct. *(CIA, adapted)*
REQUIRED: The proper accounting for the cost of the automation.
DISCUSSION: Subsequent costs are added to the carrying amount of an item of PPE if it is probable that, as a result, future economic benefits will be received, and the costs are reliably measurable. An extended useful life, improved output quantity or quality, and reduced operating costs are all future economic benefits.
Answer (A) is incorrect. The cost should be capitalized. Answer (B) is incorrect. The same account should be used. Answer (C) is incorrect. Allocation is not an accepted procedure.

Question 31 is based on the following information. Statements of financial position on December 31, Year 1, and December 31, Year 2, are presented below:

	Dec. 31, Year 1	Dec. 31, Year 2
Assets:		
Cash	US $ 50,000	US $ 60,000
Accounts receivable	95,000	89,000
Allowance for uncollectible accounts	(4,000)	(3,000)
Inventory	120,000	140,000
Property, plant, and equipment	295,000	340,000
Accumulated depreciation	(102,000)	(119,000)
Total Assets	US $ 454,000	US $ 507,000

Liabilities and equity:		
Trade accounts payable	US $ 62,000	US $ 49,000
Interest payable	8,000	11,000
Bonds payable	200,000	200,000
Unamortized bond discount	(15,000)	(10,000)
Equity	199,000	257,000
Total liabilities and equity	US $454,000	US $507,000

Additional information for Year 2:

1. Cash payments to suppliers of merchandise were US $180,000.
2. Sales revenue was US $338,000.
3. US $3,000 of accounts receivable was written off.
4. Equipment was acquired for US $65,000.
5. Depreciation expense was US $30,000.
6. Interest expense was US $20,000.

31. The carrying amount (cost minus accumulated depreciation) of property, plant, and equipment disposed of in Year 2 was

A. US $7,000

B. US $17,000

C. US $20,000

D. US $32,000

Answer (A) is correct. *(CIA, adapted)*
REQUIRED: The carrying amount of property, plant, and equipment disposed of.
DISCUSSION: The cost of PPE disposed of is US $20,000 ($295,000 beginning PPE + $65,000 acquisitions – $340,000 ending PPE). The accumulated depreciation is US $13,000 ($102,000 beginning accumulated depreciation + $30,000 depreciation expense – $119,000 ending accumulated depreciation). Thus, the carrying amount of PPE disposed of is US $7,000 ($20,000 cost of PPE – $13,000 accumulated depreciation).
Answer (B) is incorrect. US $17,000 is the difference between ending and beginning accumulated depreciation. Answer (C) is incorrect. US $20,000 is the cost of the PPE disposed. Answer (D) is incorrect. US $32,000 results from using the change in the PPE account without acquisitions minus the accumulated depreciation.

3.13 Property, Plant, and Equipment -- Depreciation

32. A theme park purchased a new, exciting ride and financed it through the manufacturer. The following facts pertain:

Purchase price	US $800,000
Delivery cost	50,000
Installation cost	70,000
Cost of trial runs	40,000
Interest charges for first year	60,000

The straight-line method is to be used. Compute the depreciation on the equipment for the first year assuming an estimated service life of 5 years.

A. US $160,000

B. US $184,000

C. US $192,000

D. US $204,000

Answer (C) is correct. *(CIA, adapted)*
REQUIRED: The depreciation expense.
DISCUSSION: Under the straight-line method, the annual depreciation expense for an asset equals the asset's amount (cost – residual value) divided by the asset's estimated useful life. The cost of the asset includes its price and the directly attributable costs of bringing it to working condition for intended use. Thus, the depreciation expense is US $192,000 [($800,000 purchase price + $50,000 delivery cost + $70,000 installation cost + $40,000 trial-run cost) ÷ 5-year estimated service life]. Borrowing costs incurred after the asset is prepared for its intended use are expensed even if the allowed alternative treatment of such costs is followed, and the asset otherwise satisfies the criteria for capitalization of such expenses.
Answer (A) is incorrect. US $160,000 excludes the delivery, installation, and trial-run costs. Answer (B) is incorrect. US $184,000 excludes the trial-run cost. Answer (D) is incorrect. US $204,000 includes the borrowing costs.

33. On January 1 of Year 1, an entity purchased a piece of equipment for US $250,000 that was originally estimated to have a useful life of 10 years with no residual value. Depreciation has been recorded for 3 years on a straight-line basis.

On January 1 of Year 4, the estimated useful life was revised so that the equipment is considered to have a total life of 20 years. Assume that the depreciation method and the useful life for financial reporting and tax purposes are the same. The depreciation expense in Year 4 on this equipment would be

A. US $8,750

B. US $10,294

C. US $12,500

D. US $14,706

Answer (B) is correct. *(CIA, adapted)*
   REQUIRED: The depreciation expense in Year 4 after a change in estimate.
   DISCUSSION: In Year 4, the carrying amount at the start of the period will be amortized over the revised estimated years of useful life. The depreciation recognized during Year 1 through Year 3 was US $75,000 [($250,000 ÷ 10) × 3 years]. Thus, the carrying amount at the beginning of Year 4 was US $175,000, and Year 4 depreciation based on the revised estimated useful life is US $10,294 [$175,000 ÷ (20 – 3)].
   Answer (A) is incorrect. The result of depreciating the remaining carrying amount over 20 years rather than the remaining 17 years is US $8,750. Answer (C) is incorrect. Accounting for the change in estimate retroactively results in US $12,500. Answer (D) is incorrect. Depreciating the original carrying amount over the revised estimate of remaining useful life results in US $14,706.

34. A depreciable asset has an estimated 20% residual value. At the end of the asset's estimated useful life, the accumulated depreciation will equal the original cost of the asset under which of the following depreciation methods?

	Declining-Balance	Sum-of-the-Years'-Digits (SYD)
A.	Yes	Yes
B.	Yes	No
C.	No	Yes
D.	No	No

Answer (D) is correct. *(CIA, adapted)*
   REQUIRED: The depreciation method under which accumulated depreciation equals the original cost of the asset at the end of its estimated useful life.
   DISCUSSION: At the end of the estimated useful life of a depreciable asset, the balance in accumulated depreciation should equal the depreciable base (original cost – estimated residual value), regardless of the depreciation method used. Periodic declining-balance depreciation is calculated without regard to residual value, but the asset is not depreciated below its residual value. The SYD percentage is applied annually to the depreciable base.

3.14 Property, Plant, and Equipment -- Disposal

35. An entity purchased a machine for US $700,000. The machine was depreciated using the straight-line method and had a residual value of US $40,000. The machine was sold on December 31, Year 1. The accumulated depreciation related to the machine was US $495,000 on that date. The entity reported a gain on the sale of the machine of US $75,000 in its income statement for the fiscal year ending December 31, Year 1. The selling price of the machine was

A. US $280,000

B. US $240,000

C. US $205,000

D. US $115,000

Answer (A) is correct. *(CIA, adapted)*
   REQUIRED: The selling price of the machine.
   DISCUSSION: The selling price minus the carrying amount of the machine equals the gain or loss on disposal. The carrying amount equals US $205,000 ($700,000 historical cost – $495,000 accumulated depreciation). Thus, the selling price was US $280,000 ($205,000 + $75,000 gain).
   Answer (B) is incorrect. Carrying amount, plus gain, minus residual value equals US $240,000. Answer (C) is incorrect. The carrying amount is US $205,000. Answer (D) is incorrect. The gain plus the residual value equals US $115,000.

36. An entity purchased new equipment on July 1, Year 4, having a list price of US $52,500. The entity traded old equipment that was being depreciated using the straight-line method and paid US $35,000 in cash. The following information pertains to the old equipment:

Cost on January 1, Year 1	US $38,900
Estimated useful life	5 years
Residual value	US $ 2,900
Fair value on July 1, Year 4	US $16,000

If the old and new equipment are dissimilar, the entity will record the new equipment at

A. US $45,100

B. US $48,700

C. US $51,000

D. US $52,500

Answer (C) is correct. *(CIA, adapted)*
REQUIRED: The amount recorded for new equipment if it is dissimilar to the old equipment that was traded.
DISCUSSION: The cost of what is received in an exchange of similar or dissimilar items of PPE is recorded at fair value unless the exchange lacks economic substance or the fair value of what is given or received is not reliably measurable. Hence, the entity will record the new equipment at the fair value of the old asset plus cash paid, or US $51,000 ($16,000 + $35,000).
Answer (A) is incorrect. US $45,100 equals the carrying amount of the old equipment after being depreciated for 4 years plus the cash paid for the new equipment. Answer (B) is incorrect. US $48,700 equals the carrying amount of the old equipment after being depreciated for 3.5 years plus cash paid for the new equipment. Answer (D) is incorrect. US $52,500 is the list price of the new equipment.

3.15 Intangible Assets

37. The costs of start-up activities, including fees of attorneys, should be

A. Capitalized, but not amortized, because of the indefinite life of the business.

B. Capitalized and amortized.

C. Capitalized and deferred until liquidation of the business.

D. Expensed when incurred.

Answer (D) is correct. *(CIA, adapted)*
REQUIRED: The proper accounting treatment of the costs of start-up activities.
DISCUSSION: Expenditures on start-up activities are expensed when incurred unless they are included in the cost of an item of property, plant, and equipment. These expenditures include the costs of establishing a new legal entity, such as legal and secretarial costs; pre-opening costs of an entity's new business facility; and the pre-operating costs of new operations, products, or processes.

38. The restriction that manufacturers should **not** market a new product that is illegally similar to that of another company's product is due to which public policy instrument?

A. Copyright.

B. Minimum standards for product warranties.

C. Anti-merger laws.

D. Patent laws.

Answer (D) is correct. *(CIA, adapted)*
REQUIRED: The public policy instrument prohibiting sales of products illegally similar to those of other sellers.
DISCUSSION: A patent is the exclusive legal right to use or sell an invention, such as a device or process. A patent may be given to any new and useful process, machine, manufacture, or composition of matter, and any infringement of a patent is a basis for a lawsuit. Thus, patent laws require that entities not design new products that are illegally similar to those of other entities that enjoy patent protection.
Answer (A) is incorrect. A copyright provides legal protection for tangible expressions of ideas, e.g., novels, songs, and software. Answer (B) is incorrect. Laws establishing minimum warranty standards do not limit the similarity of product offerings. Answer (C) is incorrect. Anti-merger laws can affect the ability of one entity to acquire another entity producing similar products if the result will be to lessen competition, but they do not affect the design of new products.

Use the additional questions in Gleim *CIA Test Prep* Software to create Test Sessions that emulate Pearson VUE!

STUDY UNIT FOUR
FINANCIAL ACCOUNTING -- ADVANCED

(28 pages of outline)

Study Unit 4 is the second of two study units on financial accounting. It addresses topics listed or suggested in The IIA's syllabus that were not covered in the preceding study unit.

Note Concerning Accounting Principles

The CIA exam is an international exam. Thus, it does not test knowledge of any country's accounting rules. No candidate must know the differences between U.S. GAAP and IFRS.

The knowledge of the rules of external financial accounting required of an internal auditor is less comprehensive than that required of a financial accountant. For example, candidates must make some calculations on the CIA exam, but the emphasis is more on the effects of various reporting rules on the financial statements than on the detailed computations.

4.1 THE TIME VALUE OF MONEY

1. **Time Value and Interest**

   a. A quantity of money to be received or paid in the future ordinarily is worth less than the same amount now. The difference is measured in terms of interest calculated using the appropriate discount rate.

      1) Interest is paid by a borrower or investee to a lender or investor for the use of money. It is a percentage of the amount (the principal) borrowed or invested.

   b. Standard tables have been developed to facilitate the calculations. Each entry in a table is a factor corresponding to an amount or annuity of 1 for a given interest rate and number of compounding periods. The factor also varies depending on whether a present value or a future value is to be calculated.

2. **Uses**

   a. Time value of money concepts have many applications. For example, they affect the accounting for noncurrent receivables and payables (bonds and notes), leases, and certain employee benefits.

3.   The Present Value (PV) of an Amount

a.   The PV of an amount is the value today of some future payment. It equals the future payment times the present value of 1 (a factor found in a standard table) for the given number of periods and interest rate.

EXAMPLE of Factors for PV of an Amount

	Present Value		
No. of Periods	6%	8%	10%
1	0.943	0.926	0.909
2	0.890	0.857	0.826
3	0.840	0.794	0.751
4	0.792	0.735	0.683
5	0.747	0.681	0.621

The present value of US $1,000, to be received in 3 years and discounted at 8%, is US $794 ($1,000 × 0.794).

---

4.   The Future Value (FV) of an Amount

a.   The FV of an amount is the amount available at a specified time in the future based on a single investment (deposit) today.

1)   The FV equals the current payment times the future value of 1 (a factor found in a standard table) for the given number of periods and interest rate.

b.   The interest factor for the FV of a present amount equals the reciprocal of the interest factor for the PV of a future amount, assuming the same interest rate and number of periods.

1)   For example, the factor for the FV of an amount is 1.191 for three periods at 6%. Thus, the factor for the PV of an amount for three periods at 6% is .840 (1 ÷ 1.191).

EXAMPLE of Factors for FV of an Amount

	Future Value		
No. of Periods	6%	8%	10%
1	1.060	1.080	1.100
2	1.124	1.166	1.210
3	1.191	1.260	1.331
4	1.262	1.360	1.464
5	1.338	1.469	1.611

The future value of US $1,000 invested today for 4 years at 10% interest will be US $1,464 ($1,000 × 1.464).

---

5.   Annuities

a.   An annuity is usually a series of equal payments at equal intervals of time, e.g., US $1,000 at the end of every year for 10 years.

b.   An **ordinary annuity (annuity in arrears)** is a series of payments occurring at the end of each period. In an **annuity due (annuity in advance)**, the payments are made (received) at the beginning of each period.

1)   Present value. The first payment of an ordinary annuity is discounted. The first payment of an annuity due is not discounted.

2)   Future value. Interest is not earned for the first period of an ordinary annuity. Interest is earned on the first payment of an annuity due.

    c.   The PV of an annuity is the value today of a series of equal payments at equal intervals discounted at a given rate. The interest factor for the present value of an ordinary annuity may be determined directly from a standard table.

        1)   This table also may be used to determine the factor for an annuity due. Thus, the factor for an ordinary annuity for one less period (n – 1) is increased by 1.0 to include the initial payment (which is not discounted in an annuity due).

EXAMPLE of Factors for PV of an Annuity

No. of Periods	Present Value		
	6%	8%	10%
1	0.943	0.926	0.909
2	1.833	1.783	1.736
3	2.673	2.577	2.487
4	3.465	3.312	3.170
5	4.212	3.993	3.791

The present value of an ordinary annuity of four payments of US $1,000 each discounted at 10% equals US $1,000 times the appropriate factor (US $1,000 × 3.170 = US $3,170).

Using the same table, the present value of an annuity due of four payments of US $1,000 each also may be calculated. This value equals US $1,000 times the factor for one less period (4 – 1 = 3), increased by 1.0. Thus, the present value of the annuity due for four periods at 10% is US $3,487 [$1,000 × (2.487 + 1.0)].

The present value of the annuity due (US $3,487) is greater than the present value of the ordinary annuity (US $3,170) because the payments occur 1 year sooner.

---

    d.   The FV of an annuity is the value that a series of equal payments at equal intervals will have at a certain moment in the future if interest is earned at a given rate. The interest factor for the future value of an ordinary annuity may be determined directly from a standard table.

        1)   This table also may be used to determine the factor for an annuity due. The factor for an ordinary annuity for one more period (n + 1) is decreased by 1.0. The final payment for the ordinary annuity for one more period earns no interest.

            a)   This result also is obtained by multiplying the ordinary annuity factor for the same number of periods by 1.0 plus the interest rate.

EXAMPLE of Factors for FV of an Annuity

No. of Periods	Future Value		
	6%	8%	10%
1	1.000	1.000	1.000
2	2.060	2.080	2.100
3	3.184	3.246	3.310
4	4.375	4.506	4.641
5	5.637	5.867	6.105

The future value of an ordinary annuity of three payments of US $1,000 each at 6% interest equals US $1,000 times the appropriate factor (US $1,000 × 3.184 = US $3,184).

Using the same table, the future value of an annuity due of three payments of US $1,000 each also may be calculated. This value equals US $1,000 times the factor for one additional period (3 + 1 = 4), decreased by 1.0 (4.375 – 1.0 = 3.375). Thus, the future value of the annuity due for three periods at 6% is US $3,375 (US $1,000 × 3.375).

The future value of the annuity due (US $3,375) is greater than the future value of an ordinary annuity (US $3,184). The payments are made earlier.

Stop and review! You have completed the outline for this subunit. Study multiple-choice questions 1 and 2 on page 172.

4.2 BONDS

1. **Nature of Bonds**

    a. Bonds are debt instruments.

    b. The issue price of a bond is a function of the market interest rate and reflects the bond's fair value.

    1) The proceeds from the sale of a bond equal the sum of the present values of the face amount and the interest payments (if the bond is interest-bearing).

2. **Bond Issuance**

    a. When the proceeds differ from the face amount, the difference is a premium or discount.

    b. If the bonds' stated rate is greater than the current market rate, the cash proceeds are greater than the face amount, and the bonds are sold at a premium.

EXAMPLE of a Bond Sold at a Premium

An entity issues 200 8%, 5-year, US $5,000 bonds when the market interest rate is 6%. The total face amount of bonds issued is therefore US $1,000,000 ($5,000 face amount × 200 bonds). Annual cash interest payments of US $80,000 ($1,000,000 face amount × 8% stated rate) will be made at the end of each year. The present value of the cash flows associated with this bond issue, discounted at the market rate of 6%, is calculated as follows:

Present value of face amount (US $1,000,000 × 0.74726)	US $ 747,260
Present value of cash interest (US $80,000 × 4.21236)	336,987 (rounded)
Cash proceeds from bond issue	US $1,084,247

Because the bonds are issued at a premium, the cash proceeds exceed the face amount. The issuer records the following entry:

Cash (present value of cash flows)	US $1,084,247	
Bonds payable (face amount)		US $1,000,000
Premium on bonds payable (difference)		84,247

---

  c. If the bonds' stated rate is less than the current market rate, the cash proceeds are less than the face amount, and the bonds are sold at a discount.

EXAMPLE of a Bond Sold at a Discount

An entity issues 200 6%, 5-year, US $5,000 bonds when the market interest rate is 8%. The total face amount of bonds issued is therefore US $1,000,000 ($5,000 face amount × 200 bonds). Annual cash interest payments of US $60,000 ($1,000,000 face amount × 6% stated rate) will be made at the end of each year. The present value of the cash flows associated with this bond issue, discounted at the market rate of 8%, is calculated as follows:

Present value of face amount (US $1,000,000 × 0.68058)	US $680,580
Present value of cash interest (US $60,000 × 3.99271)	239,566 (rounded)
Cash proceeds from bond issue	US $920,146

Because the bonds are issued at a discount, the cash proceeds are less than the face amount. The issuer records the following entry:

Cash (present value of cash flows)	US $920,146	
Discount on bonds payable (difference)	79,854	
Bonds payable (face amount)		US $1,000,000

---

3. **Bonds Sold between Interest Dates**

    a. When bonds are issued between interest payment dates, the buyer includes accrued interest in the purchase price.

EXAMPLE of a Bond Sold between Interest Dates

An entity issues 15-year bonds with a face amount of US $10,000,000, dated July 1, Year 4, and bearing interest at an annual rate of 9% payable semiannually on July 1 and January 1. The full interest amount will be paid each due date. The market rate of interest on bonds of similar risk and maturity, with the same schedule of interest payments, is also 9%. If the bonds are issued on November 1, Year 4, the total accrued interest that the issuer will receive from the buyers is calculated as follows:

Face amount	US $10,000,000
Times: stated rate	× 0.09
Annual cash interest	US $ 900,000
Divided by: months in a year	÷ 12
Monthly cash interest	US $ 75,000
Times: months of accrual	× 4
Accrued interest received from buyers	US $ 300,000

The sale of the bonds will be recorded as follows:

Cash	US $10,300,000	
Bonds payable		US $10,000,000
Interest payable		300,000

---

4. **Amortization of Premium or Discount**

    a. Bond premium or discount must be amortized over the life of the bonds using the **effective-interest method** (also called the effective-rate method). Under this method, interest expense changes every period, but the interest rate is constant.

        Annual interest expense = Carrying amount × Effective interest rate

        1) The cash paid for periodic interest equals the face amount of the bonds times the stated rate. It remains constant over the life of the bonds.

    b. The difference between interest expense and cash interest paid is the discount or premium amortization.

        1) Premium amortized, total interest expense, and the carrying amount of the bonds decrease each period when amortizing a premium. The periodic entry is

Interest expense	US $XXX	
Premium on bonds payable	XXX	
Cash		US $XXX

        2) Discount amortized, total interest expense, and the carrying amount of the bonds increase each period when amortizing a discount. The periodic entry is

Interest expense	US $XXX	
Discount on bonds payable		US $XXX
Cash		XXX

c.   At the maturity date, the discount or premium is fully amortized, and the carrying
amount of the bonds equals the face amount.

EXAMPLE of Amortization of a Premium

The issuer in the example on page 148 that issued bonds at a premium has the following amortization schedule (amounts rounded):

Year	Carrying Amount		Effective Rate		Interest Expense		Cash Paid		Premium Amortized	Ending Carrying Amount
1	US $1,084,247	×	6%	=	US $65,055	–	US $80,000	=	US $(14,945)	US $1,069,302
2	1,069,302	×	6%	=	64,158	–	80,000	=	(15,842)	1,053,460
3	1,053,460	×	6%	=	63,208	–	80,000	=	(16,792)	1,036,668
4	1,036,668	×	6%	=	62,200	–	80,000	=	(17,800)	1,018,868
5	1,018,868	×	6%	=	61,132	–	80,000	=	(18,868)	1,000,000
									US $(84,247)	

EXAMPLE of Amortization of a Discount

The issuer in the example on page 148 that issued bonds at a discount has the following amortization schedule (amounts rounded):

Year	Carrying Amount		Effective Rate		Interest Expense		Cash Paid		Discount Amortized	Ending Carrying Amount
1	US $920,146	×	8%	=	US $73,612	–	US $60,000	=	US $13,612	US $ 933,758
2	933,758	×	8%	=	74,701	–	60,000	=	14,701	948,459
3	948,459	×	8%	=	75,877	–	60,000	=	15,877	964,336
4	964,336	×	8%	=	77,147	–	60,000	=	17,147	981,483
5	981,483	×	8%	=	78,519	–	60,000	=	18,519	1,000,000
									US $79,854	

---

d.   Premium or discount can be amortized on a straight-line basis if the resulting periodic
interest expense is not materially different from that calculated under the effective-
rate method.

**Stop and review! You have completed the outline for this subunit. Study multiple-choice
questions 3 through 6 beginning on page 173.**

4.3 LEASES AND PENSIONS

1.   **Definition of a Lease**

a.   A lease is a long-term contract in which the owner of property (the lessor) allows
another party (the lessee) to use the property for a stated period in exchange for a
stated payment.

1)   The primary issue is whether the lease is a purchase-and-financing arrangement
(a capitalized lease, sometimes called a finance lease) or a long-term rental
contract (an operating lease).

2.   **Lease Capitalization Test**

a.   A lessor prefers to capitalize leases so they can be reported as noncurrent
receivables.

b.   A lessee prefers not to capitalize leases to avoid reporting debt on the statement of
financial position.

1)   The test for capitalization of a lease is whether it transfers substantially all of the
benefits and risks of ownership to the lessee.

3. **Lease Accounting**

    a. Capitalized Leases

        1) The lessor derecognizes the leased asset and records a noncurrent receivable.

            a) The receivable is amortized over the term of the lease as cash payments are received. Interest revenue also is recognized.

        2) The lessee recognizes the leased asset and records a noncurrent liability.

            a) The liability is amortized over the term of the lease as cash payments are made. Interest expense also is recognized.

            b) The lessee depreciates the leased asset according to its normal procedures.

    b. Operating Leases

        1) Leases that do not meet the test for capitalization are operating leases. The lessor retains substantially all the benefits and risks of ownership.

            a) The lessee reports periodic rental expense but no liability.

            b) The lessor reports periodic rental revenue but continues to recognize and depreciate an asset. Moreover, the lessor recognizes no gain or loss on sale.

                i) Thus, an operating lease is a form of off-balance-sheet financing.

        2) Rent is reported as an expense or revenue by the lessee or lessor, respectively, on a straight-line basis.

4. **Two Basic Types of Pensions**

    a. A defined contribution plan is the simpler of the two.

        1) The employer's only obligation is to deposit periodically a certain amount in the pension fund. The employee's eventual cash receipts depend upon the investment choices made.

    b. A defined benefit plan is far more complex.

        1) The employer is obligated to pay the employee periodically an agreed-upon amount during retirement, regardless of market conditions over the period of the pension fund's investments. Thus, the employer bears all investment risk.

        2) Estimation of the employer's total liability relies on a complex formula involving years of employment service, employee life expectancy, and compensation levels.

5. **Pension Terminology**

    a. Vesting occurs when an employee becomes entitled to receive pension benefits, usually after a certain number of years of employment.

    b. The employer's projected (defined) benefit obligation equals the present value of the amounts required to settle the obligation arising from services performed by employees in the current and prior periods.

    c. Prior service cost is the increase in the present value of the projected benefit obligation related to prior employee service that arises in the current period from the introduction of, or an amendment to, pension benefits.

6.   **Pension Accounting -- Defined Contribution Plans**

   a.   Income statement. The employer recognizes periodic pension expense based on services performed by eligible employees in the current period.

   b.   Statement of financial position. The employer recognizes a noncurrent liability for the contribution payable in exchange for an employee's services performed during the period. The amount is determined after subtracting any contribution already made.

      1)   If the contribution made exceeds the amount due, the excess is treated as a prepaid expense (an asset).

7.   **Pension Accounting -- Defined Benefit Plans**

   a.   Income statement. The employer recognizes periodic pension expense based on many factors. These include employee service performed in the current period, interest on the benefit obligation, the return on the investments of the pension fund, etc.

   b.   Statement of financial position. The employer recognizes a noncurrent liability or asset depending on whether the projected benefit obligation is underfunded or overfunded, respectively.

Stop and review! You have completed the outline for this subunit. Study multiple-choice questions 7 through 10 beginning on page 174.

4.4 DEFERRED TAXES

1.   **Definitions**

   a.   Income reported in the income statement (accrual basis) differs from income reported for tax purposes (modified cash basis).

      1)   The asset-and-liability method is used to account for the differences between accrual-basis income and tax-basis income. Thus, future income statement (and tax) consequences arise from statement of financial position measurements.

   b.   A **temporary difference (TD)** results when the financial accounting basis and the tax basis of an asset or liability differ. The effect is that a taxable or deductible amount will occur in future years when the asset is recovered or the liability is settled.

   c.   A **permanent difference** is an event that is recognized either in pretax financial income or in taxable income but never in both. It does not result in a deferred tax asset or liability.

   d.   Temporary differences have deferred tax consequences. Permanent differences do not.

2.   **Temporary Differences**

   a.   **Deferred tax liabilities (DTLs)** arise when TDs result in future taxable amounts. Taxable TDs occur when

      1)   Revenues or gains are included in taxable income after they are recognized in the financial statements.

         a)   An example is sales revenue accrued for financial reporting and recognized on the installment basis for tax purposes.

      2)   Expenses or losses are deductible for tax purposes before they are recognized in the financial statements.

         a)   An example is accelerated tax depreciation of property.

   b. **Deferred tax assets (DTAs)** arise when TDs will result in future deductible amounts. Deductible TDs occur when

   1) Revenues or gains are included in taxable income before they are recognized in the financial statements.

   a) An example is subscription revenue received in advance.

   2) Expenses or losses are deductible for tax purposes after they are recognized in the financial statements.

   a) Examples include bad debt expense recognized under the allowance method and warranty costs.

   c. TDs reverse in future periods.

   1) One example is the use of accelerated depreciation for tax purposes and straight-line depreciation for financial statement purposes. This results in an excess of tax deductions over financial statement expense in the early periods of the asset's life.

   a) However, financial statement expense exceeds tax deductions in the later periods. Thus, the initial tax benefits are reversed.

3. **Permanent Differences**

   a. Permanent differences between tax- and accrual-based income arise from events that are recognized under one accounting system and never under the other.

   1) Permanent differences do not result in a deferred tax asset or liability. Thus, they have no deferred tax consequences.

   b. One category of permanent differences consists of items included in income for financial reporting purposes but not for tax purposes.

   1) For example, interest on bonds issued by a government might not be taxable.

   c. Another category of permanent differences consists of items subtracted from income for financial reporting purposes but not deducted for tax purposes.

   1) For example, a fine resulting from a violation of law is not deductible.

   d. The third category of permanent differences consists of items deducted from income for tax purposes but not for financial reporting purposes.

   1) For example, certain dividends received may be deductible but must be included in income for financial reporting purposes.

4. **Applicable Tax Rates**

   a. A deferred tax liability or asset is measured using the tax rate(s) expected to apply when the liability or asset is expected to be settled or realized.

5. **The Basic Entry**

   a. The basic entry to record taxes in accordance with the asset and liability method is

Income tax expense (or benefit)	debit (or credit)
Income tax payable (or refundable)	credit (or debit)
Deferred income tax liability (or asset)	credit (or debit)

6. **Calculating Tax Expense (Benefit)**

   a. **Income tax expense or benefit** reported on the income statement is the sum of the following:

   1) **Current tax expense or benefit** is the amount of taxes paid or payable (or refundable) for the year based on the enacted tax law.

Current tax expense (benefit) = Taxable income (excess of deductions over revenue)
× Enacted rate

   2)   **Deferred tax expense or benefit** is the net change during the year in an entity's deferred tax amounts.

   Deferred tax expense (benefit) = Changes in DTL balances ± Changes in DTA balances

If the DTL balance increased during the year:		
Income tax expense	$xx,xxx	
Deferred tax liability		$x,xxx
Income tax payable		x,xxx

If the DTA balance increased during the year:		
Income tax expense	$x,xxx	
Deferred tax asset	x,xxx	
Income tax payable		$xx,xxx

If the DTL balance decreased during the year:		
Income tax expense	$x,xxx	
Deferred tax liability	x,xxx	
Income tax payable		$xx,xxx

If the DTA balance decreased during the year:		
Income tax expense	$xx,xxx	
Deferred tax asset		$x,xxx
Income tax payable		x,xxx

Stop and review! You have completed the outline for this subunit. Study multiple-choice questions 11 and 12 on page 175.

4.5 OTHER LIABILITIES

   1.   **Financial Liabilities**

      a.   A financial liability is a contractual obligation to (1) deliver cash or another financial asset to another entity or (2) exchange financial assets or financial liabilities with another entity under conditions that are potentially unfavorable.

         1)   Noncontractual liabilities are not financial liabilities. An example is income taxes payable.

         2)   Typical financial liabilities include trade accounts payable, notes payable, loans payable, and bonds payable.

      b.   A debtor derecognizes a liability only if it has been extinguished.

         1)   Extinguishment results only if the debtor

            a)   Pays the creditor and is relieved of its obligation with respect to the liability or

            b)   Is legally released from being the primary obligor, either judicially or by the creditor.

         2)   The difference between the carrying amount of a financial liability extinguished or transferred and the consideration paid is recognized in income or loss.

      c.   Current liabilities are obligations that ordinarily are (1) expected to be settled within the normal operating cycle, (2) held to be traded, or (3) due to be settled within 12 months after the reporting period.

         1)   Any other liability is noncurrent.

         2)   Current liabilities not settled within the normal operating cycle include the current part of interest-bearing debt, income taxes, and declared dividends.

   2.   **Accrued Expenses**

      a.   Ordinarily, accrued expenses (debit expense, credit a liability) meet recognition criteria in the current period but have not been paid as of year end. They are accounted for using basic accrual entries (see item 3. in Study Unit 3, Subunit 1).

   3.   **Effects of Nonaccrual**

      a.   If an entity fails to accrue expenses, income is overstated in that period and understated in the next period (when they are paid and presumably expensed).

         1)   Moreover, expenses incurred but unpaid and not recorded result in understated accrued liabilities and possibly understated assets (for example, if the amounts should be inventoried). In addition, working capital (current assets – current liabilities) will be overstated, but cash flows will not be affected.

EXAMPLE of Accrued Expenses

Windy Co. must determine the December 31, Year 2, year-end accruals for advertising and rent expenses. A US $500 invoice for advertising expense was received January 7, Year 3. It related to costs of US $375 for advertisements in December Year 2 and US $125 for advertisements in January Year 3. A lease, effective December 16, Year 1, calls for fixed rent of US $1,200 per month, payable beginning 1 month from the effective date. In addition, rent equal to 5% of net sales over US $300,000 per calendar year is payable on January 31 of the following year. Net sales for Year 2 were US $550,000.

- The US $375 of advertising expense should be accrued in Year 2. This amount can be directly related to events in that period. The US $125 amount is related to events in Year 3 and should not be accrued in Year 2.

- The fixed rental is due at mid-month. Thus, the fixed rental for the last half month of Year 2 (US $1,200 ÷ 2 = US $600) and the rental based on annual sales [(US $550,000 – $300,000) × 5% = US $12,500] also should be accrued.

In its December 31, Year 2, statement of financial position, Windy should report accrued liabilities of US $13,475 ($375 + $600 + $12,500).

---

4. **Deferred Revenues**

    a.   If the recognition criteria are not met, advance receipts (e.g., for rent, deposits, or subscriptions) are treated as liabilities (deferred revenues). Recognition is deferred until the obligation is partly or wholly satisfied, that is, when the increase in future economic benefits becomes reliably measurable.

        1)   When the recognition criteria are met, revenue is recognized by a debit to deferred revenue and a credit to revenue.

EXAMPLE of Deferred Revenues

The musical group Widget Express is going on a worldwide tour. Its advance ticket sales are US $10,000,000. The journal entry to recognize this deferred revenue as a liability is

Cash	US $10,000,000	
Advance ticket sales		US $10,000,000

After the first concert, Widget Express recognizes revenue:

Advance ticket sales	US $1,000,000	
Revenue		US $1,000,000

Stop and review! You have completed the outline for this subunit. Study multiple-choice questions 13 and 14 on page 176.

4.6 CONTINGENCIES AND WARRANTIES

1. **Contingencies**

    a.   A contingency is an existing condition, situation, or set of circumstances involving uncertainty as to possible gain (a gain contingency) or loss (a loss contingency). It ultimately will be resolved when one or more future events occur or do not occur.

        1)   An estimate is not a contingency. For example, the estimated depreciation for the period is not a contingency because it is certain that the economic benefits of a depreciable asset will be consumed.

    b.   The following are examples of loss contingencies:

        1)   Pending or threatened litigation
        2)   Obligation for product defects and warranties
        3)   Uncollectibility of receivables or a transfer of receivables with recourse
        4)   Guarantees, e.g., of the residual value of a leased asset of the debt of another
        5)   Coupons (premiums) offered to customers

    c.   A contingency may be

       1)   Probable. Future events are likely to occur.

       2)   Reasonably possible. The chance of occurrence is more than remote but less than probable.

       3)   Remote. The chance of occurrence is slight.

    d.   A material contingent loss must be accrued (debit loss, credit liability) when the following conditions are met:

       1)   It is probable that, at the end of the period, an asset has been impaired or a liability has been incurred.

       2)   The amount of the loss can be reasonably estimated.

    e.   If one or both conditions are not met but the probability of the loss is at least reasonably possible, the nature of the contingency must be described.

       1)   Also, an estimate of the amount or range of loss must be disclosed, or a statement must be included indicating that an estimate cannot be made.

    f.   Remote loss contingencies ordinarily are not disclosed.

       1)   However, a guarantee (e.g., of the indebtedness of another or to repurchase receivables) must be disclosed and recognized at fair value even if the probability of loss is remote.

    g.   No accrual is permitted for general or unspecified business risks, for example, those related to national and international economic conditions. No disclosure is required.

    h.   Gain contingencies are recognized only when realized. For example, an award of damages in a lawsuit is not realized if it is being appealed.

       1)   A gain contingency must be adequately disclosed, but misleading implications about realization must be avoided.

2. Warranties

    a.   A warranty is a written guarantee of a product or service. The seller agrees to repair or replace a product, refund all or part of the price, or provide additional service.

       1)   A warranty is customarily offered for a limited time, such as 90 days.

       2)   It may or may not be separable from the product or service.

    b.   A warranty creates a loss contingency. Thus, if incurrence of expense is probable, the amount can be reasonably estimated, and the amount is material, accrual accounting should be used. A contingent liability is recognized.

       1)   If these criteria are not met, warranty expense should be recorded as incurred, that is, on the cash basis.

    c.   The following are accrual-basis entries for warranty expense estimated as a percentage of sales when the warranty is not separable (an expense warranty):

       1)   To record a sale of product

Cash or accounts receivable	US $XXX
Sales revenue	US $XXX

       2)   To record related warranty expense accrued and incurred for the current period

Warranty expense	US $XXX
Estimated liability	US $XXX
Cash, inventory, wages payable, etc.	XXX

       3)   To record the costs incurred for prior period sales

Estimated liability	US $XXX
Cash, inventory, wages payable, etc.	US $XXX

d. The warranty or product maintenance contract may be separable (a sales warranty).

    1) Revenue on the warranty is deferred and is ordinarily recognized on the straight-line basis over the term of the contract.

        a) Costs are deferred and amortized only when they are directly related to, and vary with, the sale of the warranty. The primary example is a commission.

            i) Furthermore, if service costs are not incurred on a straight-line basis, revenue recognition over the contract's term should be proportionate to the estimated service costs.

3. Coupons and Premiums

a. Many sellers give buyers stamps, coupons, special labels, etc., that can be redeemed for premiums (cash or goods).

    1) In accordance with the matching principle, the expense associated with premium offers is recognized in the same period as the related revenue.

b. The following are typical entries to account for an offer to provide a toy in exchange for a sum of cash and a label from a box of the seller's primary product:

    1) To record inventory

Inventory of toys	US $XXX	
Cash or accounts payable		US $XXX

    2) To record sales of the primary product

Cash	US $XXX	
Sales		US $XXX

    3) To record redemptions when cash is received

Cash	US $XXX	
Premium expense	XXX	
Inventory of toys		US $XXX

    4) To record the estimated liability at the end of the period

Premium expense	US $XXX	
Estimated liability		US $XXX

Stop and review! You have completed the outline for this subunit. Study multiple-choice questions 15 through 20 beginning on page 176.

4.7 EQUITY

1. **Elements of Equity**

    a. Equity consists of (1) the par or stated value of shares (capital stock), (2) additional paid-in capital, (3) retained earnings, (4) accumulated other comprehensive income, and (5) treasury stock (if any). The usual classes of stock are common and preferred.

EXAMPLE of an Equity Section

Capital stock:

Preferred stock, US $50 par value, 6% cumulative, 10,000 shares authorized, issued, and outstanding	US $ 500,000	
Preferred stock, US $40 par value, 7% cumulative, 5,000 shares authorized, issued, and outstanding, each convertible to one no-par ordinary share	200,000	
Common stock, no par, stated value US $1 per share, 50,000 shares authorized, 45,000 issued and outstanding	50,000	
Common stock subscribed, 10,000 shares	10,000	
Common stock dividend distributable, 4,500 shares	4,500	
Stock warrants outstanding	1,500	
Total capital stock		US $ 766,000

Additional paid-in capital:

Excess over par -- preferred	US $ 464,000	
Excess over par -- common	800,000	1,264,000
Total paid-in capital		US $2,030,000

Retained earnings:

Retained earnings -- unappropriated	US $5,800,000	
Retained earnings -- appropriated for expansion	1,520,000	
Total retained earnings		7,320,000

Total paid-in capital and retained earnings	US $9,350,000
Accumulated other comprehensive income	611,000
Minus: receivable from stock subscription	(84,000)
Minus: cost of treasury stock (5,000 ordinary)	(100,000)
Total shareholders' equity	US $9,777,000

---

2. **Capital Stock**

    a. Issued (contributed) capital represents investments by owners in exchange for shares.

        1) One capital account shows the par or stated value of all shares outstanding (if shares have no par or stated value, the amount received is given).

            a) Amounts for each class of capital stock, such as common and preferred stock, are usually separately listed.

        2) Additional paid-in capital consists of the sources of issued capital in excess of par or stated value.

        3) Direct transaction costs are subtracted from equity.

        4) The number of shares authorized, issued, and outstanding must be disclosed, either on the face of the statement of financial position or in the notes.

3. **Retained Earnings**

   a. This amount is accumulated net income or loss. It is increased by net income and decreased by net loss, dividends, and certain transactions in treasury stock.

      1) An entity may appropriate retained earnings to, for example, comply with a bond indenture, retain assets, anticipate losses, or meet legal restrictions.

         a) The appropriation limits dividends but does not set aside assets. Moreover, any such transfer is excluded from the determination of net income or loss.

4. **Common and Preferred Stock**

   a. The **common shareholders** are the owners of the entity. They have voting rights, but holders of preferred stock do not.

      1) In liquidation, common shareholders receive residual distributions after all other claims have been satisfied, including those of preferred shareholders.

      2) Common shareholders may receive dividends at the discretion of the board of directors, subject to regulations of the jurisdiction of incorporation. For instance, laws may allow only entities that report a profit to pay dividends.

         a) Preferred shareholders must be paid dividends before common shareholders.

   b. **Preferred stock** may have any or all of the following characteristics:

      1) Callable shares may be redeemed at the option of the issuer. Thus, the issuer may require the holders to sell such shares back to the issuer.

      2) Cumulative shares accumulate dividends (dividends in arrears) that were not paid out in prior years (see item 9.b. on page 161).

      3) Participating shares participate in dividend distribution with common shareholders in a stated proportion.

      4) Convertible shares may be exchanged for shares of another class (usually common) at a predetermined ratio.

   c. Issuance of Shares

      1) Cash is debited, the appropriate class of capital stock is credited for the total par value, and additional paid-in capital is credited for the difference.

EXAMPLE of Stock Issuance

Parvenu Corp. issued 50,000 no-par common shares with a stated value of US $1. The market price was US $17 per share on the day of issue.

Cash (50,000 shares × US $17 market price)	US $850,000	
Common shares (50,000 shares × US $1 stated value)		US $ 50,000
Additional paid-in capital -- common (difference)		800,000

Parvenu also issued 10,000 US $50 par value, 6% preference shares. The market price at the time was US $62 per share.

Cash (10,000 shares × US $62 market price)	US $620,000	
6% preferred shares (10,000 shares × US $50 par value)		US $500,000
Additional paid-in capital -- preferred (difference)		120,000

---

      2) Requiring no-par shares to have a stated value prevents a corporation from crediting the entire proceeds of an issuance to additional paid-in capital (par value is usually unavailable for the payment of dividends).

5. **Treasury Stock**

    a. Treasury stock consists of the entity's own equity instruments reacquired for various purposes, e.g., mergers, exercise of options, or distribution of stock dividends.

       1) After treasury shares are reacquired, they are legally available to be reissued even if the intention is to cancel them.

       2) The acquisition of treasury shares results in a direct change in equity. This acquisition reduces the shares outstanding but not the shares authorized.

          a) Treasury shares are not assets, and dividends are not paid on them.

6. **Treasury Stock -- Acquisition**

    a. Cost Method vs. Par-Value Method

       1) Under the cost method, the entry is a debit to treasury stock and a credit to cash.

          a) In the statement of financial position, treasury stock is an unallocated reduction of the sum of the equity balances.

       2) Under the par-value method, the acquisition is treated as a constructive retirement. All related amounts are removed from the accounts.

          a) Because the cost method is much more commonly used, it is the only method used in this text.

7. **Treasury Stock -- Reissue**

    a. Reissue Price > Cost

       1) The excess is credited to additional paid-in capital from treasury stock transactions.

EXAMPLE of Reissue Price > Cost

Parvenu reissued 1,000 treasury shares that had been acquired for US $20 per share. At the time of reissue, the market price was US $22 per share.

Cost Method:

Cash (1,000 shares × US $22 market price)	US $22,000	
Treasury stock (1,000 shares × US $20 cost)		US $20,000
Additional paid-in capital from treasury stock transactions (difference)		2,000

---

    b. Reissue Price < Cost

       1) Under the cost method, the difference is debited to additional paid-in capital from treasury stock transactions. Once the balance in that account is eliminated, any remaining deficiency is debited to retained earnings.

EXAMPLE of Reissue Price < Cost

Parvenu reissued 1,000 treasury shares that had been acquired for US $20 per share. At the time of reissue, the market price was US $18 per share.

Cost Method:

Cash (1,000 shares × US $18 market price)	US $18,000	
Additional paid-in capital from treasury stock transactions (difference)	2,000	
Treasury stock (1,000 shares × US $20 cost)		US $20,000

---

8. **Retirement**

    a. When shares are retired, treasury stock is credited. The appropriate class of capital stock is debited for any par or stated value.

        1) Additional paid-in capital is debited to the extent it exists from the original issuance. Any remainder is debited to retained earnings or credited to additional paid-in capital from share retirement.

9. **Cash Dividends**

    a. Cash dividends cannot be rescinded. The following are the entries:

        Declaration
        Retained earnings   US $XXX
            Dividends payable   US $XXX

        Payment
        Dividends payable   US $XXX
            Cash   US $XXX

    b. If dividends on preferred shares are cumulative, dividends in arrears and the preferred dividends for the current period must be paid before common shareholders may receive dividends.

        1) Dividends in arrears are not a liability until they are declared and are not recognized in the financial statements.

    c. Preferred shares also may be participating.

        1) For example, they may share equally in a cash dividend after a basic return has been paid to holders of common and preferred shares.

10. **Stock Dividends and Splits**

    a. A stock dividend involves no distribution of cash or other property. Stock dividends are accounted for as a reclassification of equity, not as liabilities.

        1) The recipient does not recognize income. It has the same proportionate interest in the entity and the same total carrying amount as before the stock dividend.

    b. Stock splits are issuances of shares that do not affect any aggregate par or stated value of shares issued and outstanding or total equity.

        1) No entry is made, and no transfer from retained earnings occurs.

11. **Rights**

    a. In a rights offering, each shareholder is issued a certificate or warrant that is a call option to buy a certain number of shares at a fixed price. If the rights are exercised, the issuer accounts for the proceeds as an increase in capital stock at par value or stated value, if any, with any remainder credited to additional paid-in capital.

        1) However, if rights issued without consideration expire, capital stock is unaffected.

        2) The recipient allocates the carrying amount of the shares owned between those shares and the rights based on relative fair values. The portion of the price allocated to the rights increases (decreases) the discount (premium) on the investment.

        3) Transaction costs of redeeming share rights reduce equity.

Stop and review! You have completed the outline for this subunit. Study multiple-choice questions 21 through 24 beginning on page 178.

4.8 ACCOUNTING CHANGES

1. **Definition**

   a. Accounting changes include changes in principles and estimates.

   b. To facilitate comparison, the same accounting policies ordinarily should be followed consistently.

2. **Changes in Accounting Principle**

   a. A change in accounting principle is allowed if it can be justified as preferable or is required.

      1) A change in principle does not occur when the principle is chosen for events or transactions differing in substance or transactions or that have not previously occurred or that are not material.

   b. Changes in accounting principle normally are accounted for by retrospective application.

      1) The opening balances of all equity accounts for the first period presented are adjusted.

      2) All other amounts are adjusted as if the new policy had always been in effect.

      3) A new principle is not retrospectively applied to the extent it is impracticable to determine period-specific effects or the cumulative effect.

         a) Impracticable means that the entity cannot apply a requirement after making every reasonable effort.

3. **Changes in Accounting Estimate**

   a. A change in accounting estimate results from reassessing the status and expected benefits and obligations related to assets and liabilities.

   b. A change in estimate is based on new information and is not an error correction.

      1) Its effect is accounted for prospectively, that is, in the period of change (if the change affects that period only) or in the period of change and in future periods (if the change affects both).

      2) Examples of estimates are (a) uncollectible receivables, (b) inventory obsolescence, (c) service lives and residual values of depreciable assets, (d) warranty costs, (e) the pattern of consumption of the economic benefits of depreciable or amortizable assets, (f) periods benefited by a deferred cost, and (g) recoverable mineral reserves.

      3) If distinguishing between a change in estimate and a change in accounting principle is difficult, the change is accounted for as a change in estimate.

         a) An example is a change in the method of depreciating or amortizing long-lived assets.

Stop and review! You have completed the outline for this subunit. Study multiple-choice questions 25 through 28 beginning on page 180.

4.9 ACCOUNTING ERRORS

1.   **Correction of Errors**

     a.   All material prior-period errors must be corrected retrospectively in the first set of financial statements issued after their discovery. This is done by restating the comparative amounts for the prior periods when the error occurred.

          1)   If the error occurred prior to the first period presented, the opening balances for the first period presented are restated.

          2)   A material error is one that could, individually or collectively, affect the decisions of users of the financial statements.

          3)   Typical errors are mistakes in mathematical calculations, in the application of accounting policies, or in factual interpretation. Other examples are fraud or simple oversight.

          4)   Comparative information should be restated if practicable.

2.   **Error Analysis**

     a.   An accounting error affecting prior-period statements may or may not affect income or loss. For example, misclassifying an item as a gain rather than a revenue does not affect income or loss and is readily correctable. No adjustment is required.

     b.   An error that affects prior-period income or loss is counterbalancing if it self-corrects over two periods.

          1)   For example, understating ending inventory for one period (and the beginning inventory of the next period) understates the income and retained earnings of the first period but overstates the income of the next period by the same amount (assuming no tax changes). Ending retained earnings for the second period is not misstated.

               a)   Despite the self-correction, the financial statements remain misstated. They should be restated if presented comparatively in a later period.

EXAMPLE of a Self-Correcting Error

Year 1			Year 2	
Beginning inventory			Beginning inventory	U
+ Purchases			+ Purchases	
− Ending inventory	(U)		− Ending inventory	
= Cost of goods sold	(O)		= Cost of goods sold	(U)
Income	(U)		Income	(O)
Retained earnings	(U)		Retained earnings	

---

          2)   An example of a noncounterbalancing error is a misstatement of depreciation. Such an error does not self-correct over two periods. Thus, an adjustment will be necessary.

Stop and review! You have completed the outline for this subunit. Study multiple-choice questions 29 through 32 beginning on page 181.

4.10 EXCHANGE RATES

1. **Definitions**

    a. A functional currency is the currency of an entity's primary economic environment.

    b. A foreign currency is any currency that is not the functional currency.

    c. A foreign currency transaction is fixed, or requires settlement, in a foreign currency.

    d. A foreign operation has activities not in the reporting entity's currency or country.

    e. The reporting currency is the currency in which the statements are reported.

    f. The spot rate is the current exchange rate. It is not a future (or forward) rate.

2. **Reporting Transactions in the Functional Currency**

    a. A foreign currency transaction is initially recognized in the functional currency at the spot rate between the functional and foreign currencies at the transaction date.

    b. If the monetary aspect of the transaction has not yet occurred at the end of the period, monetary items are translated at the spot rate at the end of the period.

    1) Nonmonetary items measured at historical cost are not retranslated at the end of the period. They remain translated at the rate on the transaction date.

    2) Nonmonetary items measured at fair value are not retranslated at the reporting date. They remain translated at the rates when the fair values were measured.

    c. An exchange difference arises when a given amount of one currency is translated into another currency at different exchange rates at different times. This can happen at initial recognition, at the end of the period, or upon settlement of monetary items.

    1) These exchange differences ordinarily are recognized in the income statement when they arise.

EXAMPLE of a Foreign Currency Transaction

JRF Corporation, a U.S. entity, purchases and receives radios from Tokyo Corporation, a Japanese entity, on December 15, Year 1. The transaction is fixed in yen and calls for JRF to pay Tokyo 1.5 million yen on January 15, Year 2. The spot rate for yen is US $.01015 at the time of the transaction. The spot rate is US $.01010 on December 31, Year 1, and US $.01020 on January 15, Year 2. JRF records the transaction as follows:

12/15/Year 1:

Inventory	US $15,225	
Accounts payable (yen) (1,500,000 × US $0.01015 spot rate)		US $15,225

12/31/Year 1:

Accounts payable (yen)	75	
Transaction gain [US $15,225 – (1,500,000 × $.01010) = US $75 gain]		75

1/15/Year 2:

Accounts payable (yen)	15,150	
Transaction loss [(1,500,000 × US $.01020) – $15,150 = US $150 loss]	150	
Cash		15,300

---

2) If the books of an entity are kept in a currency not its functional currency, all amounts must be remeasured as described above in items 2.a. through c.

3) An exchange difference with respect to a monetary item that is part of a net investment in a foreign entity (a share of its net assets) is recorded in other comprehensive income in the consolidated statements until disposal of the investment.

3. **Reporting Currency not the Functional Currency**

    a. Translation from the functional currency to a different reporting currency is done as follows:

    1) Assets and liabilities for each statement of financial position presented are translated at the spot rate at the end of the period.

    2) Revenues, expenses, gains, and losses for each income statement presented are translated at the exchange rates at the transaction dates (but an average rate may be used).

b.   Such exchange differences are recognized in other comprehensive income.

EXAMPLE of Foreign Currency Translation

A U.S.-based conglomerate has a subsidiary in Norway that keeps its books using the krone (kr) (its local currency), but the subsidiary's primary operations involve entities whose functional currency is the euro. Accordingly, to prepare the consolidated financial statements, the parent first must remeasure all unsettled transactions of the subsidiary from kroner to euros. It then must translate those remeasured amounts into U.S. dollars ($).

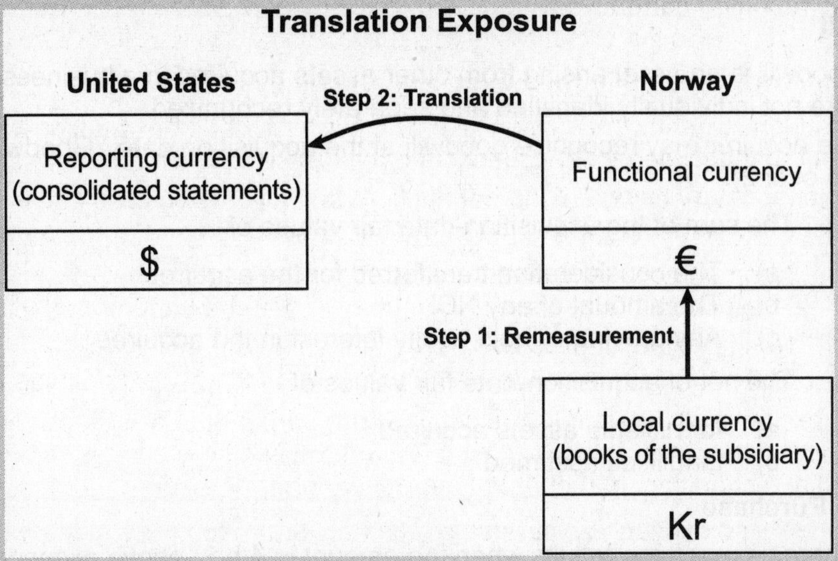

Translation Exposure

Figure 4-1

Stop and review! You have completed the outline for this subunit. Study multiple-choice question 33 on page 183.

4.11 BUSINESS COMBINATIONS

1.   **Definitions**

   a.   A business combination is a transaction or event in which an acquirer obtains control of one or more businesses.

      1)   The acquirer must be identified in every combination. It is the combining entity that controls one or more businesses. The acquisition date is when the acquirer gains control.

      2)   An entity is presumed to have control when it acquires more than 50% of the voting power of a second entity.

2.   **Acquisition Method**

   a.   This method is used for all business combinations. The acquisition method involves the following:

      1)   Identifying the acquirer

      2)   Determining when the acquirer obtained control of the acquiree (the acquisition date)

      3)   Recognition and measurement of

         a)   Identifiable assets acquired
         b)   Liabilities assumed
         c)   Any noncontrolling interest (NCI)

      4)   Recognition and measurement of

         a)   Goodwill or
         b)   Gain from a bargain purchase

3.   **Measurement**

   a.   Measurement of assets acquired and liabilities assumed is customarily at acquisition-date fair value.

      1)   Intangible assets acquired must be recognized and measured even if they were not recognized by the acquiree.

   b.   An NCI is measured at fair value.

4.   **Goodwill**

   a.   Goodwill is an asset arising from other assets acquired in a business combination that are not individually identified and separately recognized.

   b.   The acquirer may recognize goodwill at the acquisition date. Goodwill is the excess of 1) over 2):

      1)   The sum of the acquisition-date fair values of

         a)   The consideration transferred for the acquiree
         b)   The amount of any NCI
         c)   Any previously held equity interest in the acquiree

      2)   The net of acquisition-date fair values of

         a)   Identifiable assets acquired
         b)   Liabilities assumed

5.   **Bargain Purchase**

   a.   A bargain purchase results when the amount in 4.b.2) above exceeds that in 4.b.1). The excess is recognized as a gain in the income statement.

EXAMPLE

Acquirer (AR) obtained 75% of the equity interests of Acquiree (AE) in a forced sale. AR had no prior equity interest in AE. AR determined that the following are appropriate fair value measures to be used in accounting for this combination:

Consideration (US $300,000 of cash and US $250,000 of other assets) transferred by AR	US $ 550,000
AE's identifiable assets acquired	1,000,000
AE's liabilities assumed	200,000
NCI in AE	210,000

The gain is US $40,000 [($1,000,000 assets − $200,000 liabilities) − $550,000 consideration − $210,000 NCI]

AR records the following entry in the consolidated statements:

Identifiable assets	US $1,000,000	
Cash		US $300,000
Other assets		250,000
Liabilities		200,000
Equity -- NCI (AE)		210,000
Gain -- bargain purchase		40,000

If AR had instead transferred US $400,000 in cash, it would have debited goodwill for US $60,000 ($650,000 consideration + $210,000 NCI − $1,000,000 assets + $200,000 liabilities).

Stop and review! You have completed the outline for this subunit. Study multiple-choice question 34 on page 183.

4.12 THE EQUITY METHOD AND CONSOLIDATED REPORTING

1. **Thresholds**

   a. The process for choosing the accounting method to be used by an investor begins with an assumption about the influence conferred by the percentage of the investee's voting power held by the investor. The diagram below depicts the possibilities:

% Voting Power	Presumed Influence	Accounting Method
100%		
	Control	Consolidation
50%		
	Significant	Equity Method
20%		
	Little or none	Fair Value or Other Method
0%		

2. **Equity Method**

   a. An entity should account for an investment using the equity method when it has significant influence over the investee.

   1) Significant influence is presumed when the investor holds at least 20% of the voting power of the investee.

   b. The equity method involves recognizing both distributed and undistributed amounts arising from an investment over which the entity has significant influence.

   1) The investment is initially recorded at cost and subsequently adjusted for the investor's undistributed share of the investee's income or loss.

   2) The investor's share of the investee's income or loss is reported in the investor's income statement. Distributions from the investee reduce the investment balance.

3. **Consolidation**

   a. A parent entity should present consolidated financial statements. These present the parent and all of its subsidiaries as if they were a single economic entity (the economic entity approach).

   1) A parent is an entity with one or more subsidiaries.

   2) A subsidiary is an entity that is controlled by another entity.

   3) An entity is presumed to have control when it acquires more than 50% of the voting power of a second entity.

   b. Consolidation procedures consist of

   1) Combining like items

   2) Eliminating the investment in each subsidiary and the parent's share of each subsidiary's equity

   3) Identifying noncontrolling interests (NCIs) in the income statement and net assets (equity) of consolidated subsidiaries in the statement of financial position

   4) Eliminating intragroup balances, transactions, income, and expenses in full

   c. NCIs are separately presented in equity in the consolidated statement of financial position. NCIs in profit or loss also are separately reported.

EXAMPLE

Consolidated Income Statement

Revenues	US $ XXX,XXX
Expenses	(XXX,XXX)
Pretax income from continuing operations	US $ XX,XXX
Income tax expense	(XX,XXX)
After-tax income from continuing operations	US $ XX,XXX
Discontinued operations (after tax)	(X,XXX)
Net income or loss	US $ XX,XXX
Minus: Profit or loss – NCI	(X,XXX)
Net income or loss – parent	US $ XX,XXX

EXAMPLE

Consolidated Equity

Equity:	
Parent equity:	
Common stock, par value	US $XXX,XXX
Additional paid-in capital	XX,XXX
Retained earnings	XXX,XXX
Accumulated other comprehensive income	XX,XXX
Total parent equity	US $XXX,XXX
NCI	XX,XXX
Total equity	US $XXX,XXX

Stop and review! You have completed the outline for this subunit. Study multiple-choice question 35 on page 183.

4.13 PARTNERSHIPS

1. **Partnerships Defined**

   a. A partnership is an association of two or more persons to carry on, as co-owners, a business for profit.

2. **Partnership Formation**

   a. Partners **contribute cash and other property** as the basis of their equity in a partnership. Cash is recorded at its nominal amount and property at its **fair value**.

EXAMPLE of Partnership Formation

Gilda Rosecrans, Bill Bragg, and Tim Thomas agree to form Chickamauga Partners. Besides cash, each partner contributes tangible property consisting of a building, inventory, and equipment, respectively. Rosecrans's building is subject to a $45,000 mortgage. The values of the contributions on the date of formation are as follows:

Partner	Cash	Property at Carrying Amount	Property at Fair Value
Rosecrans	US $20,000	US $80,000	US $110,000
Bragg	55,000	18,000	15,000
Thomas	40,000	30,000	20,000

The journal entry to record the formation of the partnership is

Cash (US $20,000 + $55,000 + $40,000)	US $115,000	
Inventory	15,000	
Equipment	20,000	
Building	110,000	
Mortgage payable		US $45,000
Bragg, capital (US $55,000 + $15,000)		70,000
Rosecrans, capital (US $20,000 + $110,000 – $45,000)		85,000
Thomas, capital (US $40,000 + $20,000)		60,000

   b.   Equity includes only the partners' capital accounts.

   c.   The partners may decide that a partner's contribution exceeds the fair value of cash and tangible property contributed, e.g., because (s)he has special expertise. Two accounting methods may be used.

        1)   Under the **bonus method**, only the fair values of cash and tangible property contributed are recorded. The partners then allocate the capital accounts to reflect a partner's special contribution.

EXAMPLE of Bonus Method

Dick McPherson and Josh Logan contribute US $90,000 and US $10,000, respectively, to their new partnership. The usual journal entry is

Cash	US $100,000	
McPherson, capital		US $90,000
Logan, capital		10,000

However, the two partners agree that Logan's special expertise is worth more than the cash he contributed. Their agreement results in a 60:40 allocation.

Cash	US $100,000	
McPherson, capital		US $60,000
Logan, capital		40,000

        2)   Under the **goodwill method**, the partners record an asset for the fair value of the intangible benefit contributed by a given partner.

EXAMPLE of Goodwill Method

McPherson and Logan acknowledge the worth of Logan's expertise by recognizing goodwill. The entry for their 60:40 allocation of equity is

Cash	US $100,000	
Goodwill	30,000	
McPherson, capital		US $78,000
Logan, capital		52,000

3.   **Additions and Withdrawals of Capital**

a.   Existing partners may make **additional contributions** to the partnership.

1)   The appropriate asset is debited for the nominal amount of cash or fair value of property, and that partner's capital account is credited. No reapportionment of equity among the partners is performed.

b.   Partners' withdrawals are recorded in **distribution accounts**.

EXAMPLE of Partner Withdrawals

Rosecrans and Thomas withdraw cash from Chickamauga Partners:

Rosecrans, distributions	US $10,000	
Thomas, distributions	5,000	
Cash		US $15,000

Distribution accounts are nominal accounts that are closed to partnership capital at the end of each period.

Rosecrans, capital	US $10,000	
Thomas, capital	5,000	
Rosecrans, distributions		US $10,000
Thomas, distributions		5,000

---

4.   **Partnership Income and Loss**

a.   Profit and loss are distributed equally among partners unless the partnership agreement provides otherwise.

1)   The equal distribution is based on the number of partners, not capital balances.

2)   If the partnership agreement specifies how profits are to be shared but is silent with respect to losses, losses are divided in the same manner as profits.

EXAMPLE of Partnership Income Allocation

Chickamauga Partners' agreement is that net income will be distributed 50% to Rosecrans and 25% each to Bragg and Thomas. The partnership's net income for the period is US $60,000.

Income summary	US $60,000	
Bragg, capital		US $15,000
Rosecrans, capital		30,000
Thomas, capital		15,000

The distribution of profit and loss is not based on the relative proportions of the partners' capital balances, but only on the contractual agreement entered into by the partners at the time of formation. Had Chickamauga Partners lacked such an agreement, profits and losses would have been distributed equally. Given three partners, each would have received 33 1/3% of the net income.

The statement of partners' capital can be prepared once the books are closed:

	Bragg	Rosecrans	Thomas	Totals
Capital balances, beginning of year	US $70,000	US $ 85,000	US $60,000	US $215,000
Add: Allocation of net income	15,000	30,000	15,000	60,000
Minus: Distributions	0	(10,000)	(5,000)	(15,000)
Capital balances, end of year	US $85,000	US $105,000	US $70,000	US $260,000

5. **Sale of a Partnership Interest**

    a. When an existing partner sells his/her interest in a partnership to an outside party, the new partner is entitled to share in the partnership's profits and losses. However, (s)he is not allowed to participate in management unless the remaining partners admit the new partner to the partnership.

    ### EXAMPLE of Sale of a Partnership Interest

    Bill Bragg sells his interest in Chickamauga Partners to Jenna Longstreet for US $100,000, an amount greater than Bragg's capital balance.

Bragg, capital	US $85,000	
Longstreet, capital		US $85,000

    (The cash exchanged between Bragg and Longstreet is irrelevant to the partnership accounting.) Longstreet now shares in the partnership's profits and losses. She owns Bragg's partnership interest but may not participate in management.

    ---

6. **Addition of a New Partner**

    a. New partners may contribute cash, property, or services. A partner's tangible and intangible contributions may be recognized using one of four accounting methods.

        1) **Bonus Credited to the Original Partners**

            a) If the fair value of the new partner's contribution exceeds the credit to his/her capital account, the excess is a bonus to the existing partners.

        2) **Goodwill Credited to the Original Partners**

            a) If the original partners wish to recognize an increase in total partnership capital in excess of the new partner's contribution, the excess is debited to goodwill.

        3) **Revaluation of Current Assets**

            a) The existing partners may recognize changes in the fair values of the partnership assets and any increase as a bonus in their respective capital accounts.

        4) **Bonus or Goodwill Credited to the New Partner**

            a) The existing partners acknowledge an intangible benefit brought to the partnership in addition to cash or property.

7. **Withdrawal of a Partner**

    a. When a partner withdraws, the transaction is in essence a buy-out by the remaining partners. An appraisal determines the fair values of the partnership assets, and the withdrawing partner receives cash or other property equal to his/her capital balance after the appraisal. One of three accounting methods may be used.

        1) **Bonus Method**

            a) The results of the appraisal are not formally recognized.

        2) **Goodwill Method**

            a) Tangible assets are formally remeasured, and any goodwill is recognized.

        3) **Hybrid Method**

            a) Tangible assets are formally remeasured, but goodwill is not recognized.

8.   **Liquidation of a Partnership – Process**

a.   When the partners dissolve their partnership, the process of liquidating noncash assets and settling liabilities begins. The liquidation process has **four steps**:

1)   First, any gain or loss realized from the actual sale of assets is allocated to the partners' capital accounts in accordance with the profit-and-loss ratio.

2)   Second, remaining noncash assets are assumed to have a fair value of zero, resulting in an **assumed loss** equal to their carrying amounts. This amount is allocated to the partners' accounts in accordance with the profit-and-loss ratio.

3)   Third, if at least one of the partners' capital accounts has a deficit balance, the deficit is allocated to the remaining partners' accounts.

4)   Fourth, the final balances in the partnership accounts equal the amounts of cash, if any, that may be distributed to the partners.

Stop and review! You have completed the outline for this subunit. Study multiple-choice questions 36 through 40 beginning on page 184.

QUESTIONS

4.1 The Time Value of Money

1. The relationship between the present value of a future sum and the future value of a present sum can be expressed in terms of their respective interest factors. If the present value of US $200,000 due at the end of 8 years, at 10%, is US $93,300, what is the approximate future value of US $200,000 invested for the same length of time and at the same rate?

A. US $93,300

B. US $200,000

C. US $293,300

D. US $428,724

Answer (D) is correct. *(CIA, adapted)*
   REQUIRED: The approximate future value of an amount.
   DISCUSSION: The interest factor for the future value of a present sum is equal to the reciprocal of the interest factor for the present value of a future sum. Thus, the future value is US $428,724 [($200,000 ÷ $93,300) × $200,000].
   Answer (A) is incorrect. US $93,300 is the present value of US $200,000 to be received in 8 years. Answer (B) is incorrect. US $200,000 is the present value, not the future value, of US $200,000 invested today. Answer (C) is incorrect. The addition of the present and future values has no accounting meaning.

2. If the amount to be received in 4 years is US $137,350, and given the correct factor from the 10% time-value-of-money table below, what is the current investment?

Interest Factors for 10%

Periods	FV	PV	FV of Ordinary Annuity	PV of Ordinary Annuity
1	1.1000	.9091	1.0000	.9091
2	1.2100	.8264	2.1000	1.7355
3	1.3310	.7513	3.3100	2.4869
4	1.4641	.6830	4.6410	3.1699
5	1.6105	.6029	6.1051	3.7908

A. US $30,034.33

B. US $43,329.44

C. US $93,810.05

D. US $201,094.14

Answer (C) is correct. *(CIA, adapted)*
   REQUIRED: The current investment required to receive a future amount of money at a given interest rate.
   DISCUSSION: The current investment is the present value of the given future amount. It equals the future amount multiplied by the factor for the present value of US $1 for four periods at 10%. Accordingly, the current investment is US $93,810.05 ($137,350 × .6830).
   Answer (A) is incorrect. US $30,034.33 cannot be derived from any of the time value factors given. Answer (B) is incorrect. US $43,329.44 results from incorrectly dividing by the factor for the present value of an ordinary annuity for four periods. Answer (D) is incorrect. US $201,094.14 results from incorrectly using the factor for the future value of US $1 for four periods.

4.2 Bonds

3. On January 1, an entity issued a 10-year US $500,000 bond at 96% of its face amount. The bond bears interest at 12%, payable on January 1 and July 1. The entry to record the issuance of the bond on January 1 is

A. Cash   US $480,000
    Bonds payable   US $480,000

B. Cash   US $500,000
    Bonds payable   US $500,000

C. Cash   US $480,000
    Discount on bonds payable   20,000
    Bonds payable   US $500,000

D. Cash   US $500,000
    Premium on bonds payable   US $ 20,000
    Bonds payable   480,000

Answer (C) is correct. *(CIA, adapted)*
REQUIRED: The entry to record the issuance of the bond.
DISCUSSION: The entity received US $480,000 cash on the issuance of the bond. Its face amount is US $500,000, the amount to be paid at maturity. Hence, the credit to bonds payable is US $500,000. The US $20,000 difference is recorded as a discount on bonds payable (a debit) and is amortized over the life of the issue.
Answer (A) is incorrect. The entry to bonds payable is based on the face, or maturity, amount of the bond issued. The difference between the amount received on issuance and the face amount is recorded as a premium or discount on bonds payable. Answer (B) is incorrect. The discount should be recognized. Answer (D) is incorrect. The debit to cash is US $480,000, a US $20,000 discount should be debited, and the credit to bonds payable is US $500,000.

4. On May 1, Year 1, an entity issued, at 103 plus accrued interest, 500 of its 12%, US $1,000 bonds. The bonds are dated January 1, Year 1, and mature on January 1, Year 6. Interest is payable semiannually on January 1 and July 1. The journal entry to record the issuance of the bonds and the receipt of the cash proceeds is

A. Cash   US $515,000
    Interest payable   20,000
    Bonds payable   US $500,000
    Premium on bonds payable   35,000

B. Cash   US $525,000
    Bonds payable   US $500,000
    Premium on bonds payable   15,000
    Interest payable   10,000

C. Cash   US $535,000
    Bonds payable   US $500,000
    Premium on bonds payable   15,000
    Interest payable   20,000

D. Cash   US $535,000
    Bonds payable   US $500,000
    Premium on bonds payable   35,000

Answer (C) is correct. *(CIA, adapted)*
REQUIRED: The journal entry to record the issuance of a bond at a premium plus accrued interest.
DISCUSSION: The face amount of the 500 bonds is equal to US $500,000 (500 × $1,000). The cash proceeds excluding interest from the issuance of the bonds are US $515,000 ($500,000 × 103%). The US $15,000 premium is the difference between the cash issuance proceeds and the face amount of the bonds. Because the bonds were issued between interest payment dates, the issuer also is entitled to receive accrued interest for the 4 months between the prior interest date and the issuance date. The accrued interest is US $20,000 [500 bonds × $1,000 face value × 12% stated rate × (4 ÷ 12)]. The issuing entity will therefore receive US $535,000 in cash ($515,000 + $20,000). The resulting journal entry includes a US $535,000 debit to cash, a US $500,000 credit to bonds payable, a US $15,000 credit to premium, and a US $20,000 credit to either interest payable or interest expense.
Answer (A) is incorrect. The bond premium is US $15,000 ($500,000 × .03), and interest payable should be credited. Answer (B) is incorrect. Interest payable should be US $20,000 [$500,000 × .12 × (4 ÷ 12)]. Answer (D) is incorrect. The premium on bonds payable should not include interest payable.

5. The effective-interest method and the straight-line method of amortizing a bond discount differ in that the effective-interest method results in

A. Higher total interest expense over the term of the bonds.

B. Escalating annual interest expense over the term of the bonds.

C. Shrinking annual interest expense over the term of the bonds.

D. Constant annual interest expense over the term of the bonds.

Answer (B) is correct. *(CIA, adapted)*
REQUIRED: The difference between the effective-interest method and the straight-line method of amortizing a bond discount.
DISCUSSION: Under the effective-interest method, interest expense for each period equals the effective interest rate times the carrying amount of the bond issue. As the discount is amortized, the carrying value rises and interest expense increases.
Answer (A) is incorrect. The two methods of amortization result in the same total interest expense over the term of the bonds. Answer (C) is incorrect. Annual interest expense would decrease if a premium were being amortized. Answer (D) is incorrect. The straight-line method results in constant annual interest expense.

6. If bonds are initially sold at a discount and the effective-interest method of amortization is used, interest expense

- A. In the earlier periods will be less than interest expense in the later periods.
- B. In the earlier periods will be greater than interest expense in the later periods.
- C. Will equal the cash interest payment each period.
- D. Will be less than the cash interest payment each period.

Answer (A) is correct. *(CIA, adapted)*
REQUIRED: The effect on interest expense if bonds are initially sold at a discount and the effective-interest method of amortization is used.
DISCUSSION: Interest expense equals the carrying amount of the liability at the beginning of the period times the effective interest rate. The carrying amount of the liability equals the face amount of the bond minus the discount. As the discount is amortized over the life of the bond, the carrying amount increases. Consequently, the interest expense increases over the term of the bond.
Answer (B) is incorrect. Interest expense will increase over the term of the bonds. Answer (C) is incorrect. Interest expense exceeds the cash interest payment when bonds are issued at a discount. The reason is that the effective rate is higher than the nominal rate. The excess of interest expense over the cash payment is the amount of discount amortized each period. Answer (D) is incorrect. Interest expense exceeds the cash interest payment when bonds are issued at a discount. The reason is that the effective rate is higher than the nominal rate. The excess of interest expense over the cash payment is the amount of discount amortized each period.

4.3 Leases and Pensions

7. Capital and operating leases differ in that the lessor

- A. Obtains use of the asset only under a capital lease.
- B. Is using the lease as a source of financing only under an operating lease.
- C. Makes rent payments that are actually installment payments constituting a payment of both principal and interest only under a capital lease.
- D. Finances the transaction through the leased asset only under a capital lease.

Answer (D) is correct. *(CIA, adapted)*
REQUIRED: The difference between capital and operating leases.
DISCUSSION: A lease is either a rental or an installment purchase arrangement between a lessor (the owner or seller of the property) and a lessee (the renter or purchaser). The issue in all leases is whether substantially all of the benefits and risks of ownership have been transferred from the lessor to the lessee. If so, the lease should be capitalized because it is a purchase-and-financing arrangement. If they have not transferred, the lease is a rental arrangement (an operating lease).
Answer (A) is incorrect. The lessee obtains use of the asset under both types of leases. Answer (B) is incorrect. The lessee uses the lease as a source of financing under a capital lease, not an operating lease. Answer (C) is incorrect. The lessee makes payments to the lessor under both types of leases.

8. Which of the following statements about a capital lease is **false**?

- A. The lessor capitalizes the net investment in the lease.
- B. The lessor records the leased item as an asset.
- C. The lessee records depreciation or capital cost allowance on the leased asset.
- D. The lease arrangement represents a form of financing.

Answer (B) is correct. *(CIA, adapted)*
REQUIRED: The false statement about a capital lease.
DISCUSSION: When a lease is capitalized, the lessor derecognizes the leased item and records lease payments receivable. The lessee records and depreciates the leased item.
Answer (A) is incorrect. If a lease is capitalized, the lessor recognizes a net receivable equal to the net investment in the lease: gross investment (minimum lease payments from the lessor's perspective plus unguaranteed residual value) discounted at the interest rate implicit in the lease. Answer (C) is incorrect. The lessee records depreciation on the leased asset under a capitalized lease. This process is separate from the accounting for the lease obligation. Answer (D) is incorrect. A capitalized lease is, in essence, a purchase-and-financing arrangement.

9. An employee's right to obtain pension benefits regardless of whether (s)he remains employed is known as his/her

    A. Prior service cost.

    B. Defined benefit plan.

    C. Vested interest.

    D. Minimum liability.

Answer (C) is correct. *(CIA, adapted)*
    REQUIRED: The term for the right to obtain pension benefits regardless of future employment.
    DISCUSSION: Vested benefits are those to which employees are entitled. Vesting generally takes place upon completion of a certain number of years of employment.
    Answer (A) is incorrect. Prior service cost relates to benefits for employee service provided prior to the adoption or amendment of a defined benefit plan. Answer (B) is incorrect. A defined benefit plan provides a defined benefit based on one or more factors, such as level of compensation, years of service, or age. Answer (D) is incorrect. Minimum liability is an obsolete term.

10. The projected (defined) pension obligation of a company includes benefit obligations to <List A> employees at <List B> salary levels.

	List A	List B
A.	Vested	Current
B.	Vested	Future
C.	Vested and nonvested	Current
D.	Vested and nonvested	Future

Answer (D) is correct. *(CIA, adapted)*
    REQUIRED: The nature of the defined postemployment benefit.
    DISCUSSION: The measurement of a projected (defined) benefit pension obligation includes estimates of future salary increases and the benefits defined in the plan.
    Answer (A) is incorrect. The projected (defined) benefit pension obligation includes both vested and nonvested benefits and is calculated at future levels. Answer (B) is incorrect. The projected (defined) benefit pension obligation includes both vested and nonvested benefits. Answer (C) is incorrect. The projected (defined) benefit pension obligation is calculated at future levels.

4.4 Deferred Taxes

> Questions 11 and 12 are based on the following information. An entity has purchased an asset with a 10-year useful life. It will use an accelerated depreciation method for tax purposes. For reporting purposes, it will use straight-line depreciation because it is believed to better reflect the usage of the asset over its useful life.

11. During the 10-year life of the asset, the entity will report as deferred tax an amount that

    A. Increases steadily for the 10 years.

    B. Is constant.

    C. Increases and then decreases.

    D. Decreases and then increases.

Answer (C) is correct. *(CIA, adapted)*
    REQUIRED: The deferred tax amount reported.
    DISCUSSION: The cumulative deferred tax increases, peaks, and then decreases to zero over the life of the asset. In the early years, the asset is depreciated more quickly for tax purposes than for financial reporting purposes. This temporary difference reverses in later years. Hence, in the early years, actual taxes payable will be less than tax expense reported in the financial statements, and a deferred tax liability will be recognized. By the end of the asset's useful life, cumulative actual taxes paid will equal cumulative reported tax expense, so the deferred tax balance will be zero.

12. When calculating cash flows accruing to the entity, using financial statements prepared for tax purposes will result in

    A. No effect on cash flow amounts.

    B. An overstatement of cash flows throughout the economic life of the asset.

    C. An understatement of cash flows throughout the economic life of the asset.

    D. An overstatement of cash flows in the early years and then an understatement of cash flows in the later years of the economic life of the asset.

Answer (A) is correct. *(CIA, adapted)*
    REQUIRED: The effect on cash flows of using financial statements prepared for tax purposes.
    DISCUSSION: Cash flows are not affected by the basis of accounting used to prepare the financial statements. Accordingly, whether the financial statements are prepared based on the tax basis, the cash basis, or accounting principles generally accepted in a given country, cash flows should be the same. For example, the cash inflow or outflow resulting from using an accelerated depreciation method to determine actual tax expense or benefit (the amount paid to or refunded by the taxing authority) is completely unaffected by the depreciation method used in the financial statements. However, if cash flows are derived indirectly by adjusting profit or loss reported in the financial statements, different adjustments are necessary to arrive at the same cash flow amounts if different bases of accounting are used in the preparation of the financial statements.

4.5 Other Liabilities

13. The publisher of a popular magazine offers a special discounted price for a 3-year subscription. At the end of the reporting period, the amount that has already been collected but pertains to future periods is best referred to as

A. Accrued subscriptions revenue (an asset account).

B. Deferred subscriptions revenue (a liability account).

C. Earned subscriptions revenue (a revenue account).

D. Precollected subscriptions receivable (a deferred asset account).

Answer (B) is correct. *(CIA, adapted)*
REQUIRED: The best description of revenue that has already been collected but pertains to future periods.
DISCUSSION: Revenue is recognized in the period in which the recognition criteria are met. Thus, when it is received in advance, the amount applicable to future periods is deferred. This deferral arises because the entity still must satisfy an obligation to perform in the future before it is entitled to the future economic benefits. The amount received in advance is considered a liability because it represents a present obligation arising from a past event. Accordingly, deferred or unearned revenue is an amount that has been received but that has not met the recognition criteria for revenue.
Answer (A) is incorrect. An accrued revenue is revenue that has met the recognition criteria but has not been received. Answer (C) is incorrect. The revenue will be recognized in future periods when forthcoming issues of the magazine are published and distributed to the subscribers. Answer (D) is incorrect. "Precollected receivable" is not a standard accounting term.

14. In performing an audit, you encounter an adjusting journal entry recorded at year end that contains a debit to rental revenue and a credit to unearned rental revenue. The purpose of this journal entry is to record

A. Accrued revenue.

B. Unexpired cost.

C. Expired cost.

D. Deferred revenues.

Answer (D) is correct. *(CIA, adapted)*
REQUIRED: The purpose of an adjusting entry debiting rental revenue and crediting deferred revenue rental.
DISCUSSION: A deferred revenue is a revenue item that has been received but has not met the recognition criteria. The journal entry described in the question is an adjusting entry to transfer an amount from the revenue account to a liability (deferred revenue) account. The initial collection of cash in advance from the tenant was apparently recorded by a credit to revenue. An adjusting entry is therefore required at year end to transfer any remaining amount that does not qualify for revenue recognition.
Answer (A) is incorrect. An accrued revenue has met the recognition criteria but has not yet been received. The journal entry described indicates that collection has been made. Answer (B) is incorrect. The entry concerns a revenue rather than an expense transaction. Answer (C) is incorrect. The entry concerns a revenue rather than an expense transaction.

4.6 Contingencies and Warranties

15. Because of a defect discovered in its seat belts in December Year 1, an automobile manufacturer believes it is probable that it will be required to recall its products. The final decision on the recall is expected to be made in March Year 2 and is estimated to be US $2.5 million. How should this information be reported in the December 31, Year 1, financial statements?

A. As a loss of US $2.5 million and a liability of US $2.5 million.

B. As a prior-period adjustment of US $2.5 million.

C. As an appropriation of retained earnings of US $2.5 million.

D. It should not be disclosed because it has not yet happened.

Answer (A) is correct. *(CIA, adapted)*
REQUIRED: The reporting of a probable loss from a product recall.
DISCUSSION: Because the contingent loss is probable and presumably can be reasonably estimated, the entity must recognize a loss and a liability for US $2.5 million.
Answer (B) is incorrect. A prior period adjustment is used to account for errors, not loss contingencies. Answer (C) is incorrect. The entity must recognize a loss and a liability. Answer (D) is incorrect. If the loss is probable and can be reasonably (reliably) estimated, it should be recognized by a debit to income.

16. An entity has been sued for US $100 million for producing and selling an unsafe product. Attorneys for the entity cannot reliably predict the outcome of the litigation. In its financial statements, the entity should

A. Make the following journal entry and disclose the existence of the lawsuit in a note.

Estimated loss from litigation	US $100,000,000	
Estimated liability for litigation loss		US $100,000,000

B. Disclose the existence of the lawsuit in a note without making a journal entry.

C. Neither make a journal entry nor disclose the lawsuits in a note because bad publicity will hurt the entity.

D. Make the following journal entry and disclose the existence of the lawsuit in a note.

Cost of goods sold	US $100,000,000	
Estimated liability for litigation loss		US $100,000,000

Answer (B) is correct. *(CIA, adapted)*
REQUIRED: The financial statement treatment of a loss from pending litigation.
DISCUSSION: The inability to determine whether a loss is probable and to make a reasonable estimate of the loss prevents loss recognition but requires disclosure if the loss is reasonably possible (possible).
Answer (A) is incorrect. A journal entry is made when the outflow in settlement is probable and can be reasonably (reliably) estimated. Answer (C) is incorrect. A disclosure must be made. Answer (D) is incorrect. A journal entry is made when the outflow in settlement is probable and can be reasonably estimated.

17. An entity allows customers to redeem 20 coupons for a toy (cost US $3). Estimates are that 40% of coupons distributed will result in redemption. Since beginning the promotion this year, 4 million coupons were distributed and 1 million coupons redeemed. The adjusting entry to accrue for unredeemed coupons at year end is

A.
Premium expense	US $90,000	
Estimated liability for premiums		US $90,000

B.
Sales	US $90,000	
Estimated liability for premiums		US $90,000

C.
Premium expense	US $1,800,000	
Estimated liability for premiums		US $1,800,000

D.
Sales	US $1,800,000	
Estimated liability for premiums		US $1,800,000

Answer (A) is correct. *(CIA, adapted)*
REQUIRED: The adjusting entry to accrue for unredeemed coupons at year end.
DISCUSSION: An expense and a liability should be accrued for the coupons still outstanding that are expected to be redeemed. Of the 4 million coupons distributed, 40%, or 1.6 million, are estimated to be redeemable. Of those, 1 million have already been redeemed, and 600,000 more are expected to be redeemed. The promotion requires 20 coupons to receive one toy, so 30,000 (600,000 ÷ 20) more toys will be required. Each toy costs US $3, creating a liability of US $90,000 (30,000 × $3).
Answer (B) is incorrect. The debit should be to an expense. Answer (C) is incorrect. Although an expense should be accrued, the amount is incorrect. Answer (D) is incorrect. The debit should be to an expense, and the amount is incorrect.

18. An entity introduced a new product that carries a 2-year warranty against defects. It estimates that warranty costs will be 2% of sales in the year of sale and 3% of sales in the year following the year of sale. Sales in Year 1 and Year 2 were US $5 million and US $7 million, respectively. Actual costs of servicing the warranty in Year 1 and Year 2 were US $110,000 and US $260,000, respectively. What amount of warranty expense must the entity recognize in Year 2?

A. US $260,000

B. US $290,000

C. US $350,000

D. US $370,000

Answer (C) is correct. *(CIA, adapted)*
REQUIRED: The warranty expense.
DISCUSSION: The warranty expense must be matched with revenue in the year of sale. Thus, the expense related to Year 2 sales must be recognized in Year 2 even if actual expenditures will not occur until Year 3. The expense related to Year 2 sales equals US $350,000 [$7,000,000 × (2% for the year of sale + 3% for the year after the year of sale)].
Answer (A) is incorrect. US $260,000 is the actual cost of servicing the warranty in Year 2. Answer (B) is incorrect. US $290,000 equals the sum of 2% of Year 2 sales and 3% of Year 1 sales. Answer (D) is incorrect. US $370,000 equals the actual cost of servicing the warranty in Year 1 and Year 2.

19. Which of the following is an example of a contingent liability?

A. A retail store in a shopping mall pays the lessor a minimum monthly rent plus an agreed-upon percentage of sales.

B. An entity is refusing to pay the invoice for the annual audit because it seems higher than the amount agreed upon with the public accounting entity's partner.

C. An entity accrues income tax payable in its interim financial statements.

D. A lessee agrees to reimburse a lessor for a shortfall in the residual value of an asset under lease.

Answer (D) is correct. *(CIA, adapted)*
REQUIRED: The example of a contingent liability.
DISCUSSION: The liability resulting from a guarantee is contingent on the lessor's not receiving the full residual value from a third party. A liability is recognized for a guarantee even if the probability of loss is remote.
Answer (A) is incorrect. The amount of rent is not uncertain. Rent expense can be accrued as sales occur. Answer (B) is incorrect. A service was received and the entity owes an amount. The amount is not contingent on a future event. The entity can accrue the amount that it expected the invoice to show. Answer (C) is incorrect. As of the date of the interim financial statements, the income tax is payable because earnings have occurred. The amount or the timing of the payment as of the date of the statements is not uncertain.

20. The selling price of a new entity's units is US $10,000 each. The buyers are provided with a 2-year warranty that is expected to cost the entity US $250 per unit in the year of the sale and US $750 per unit in the year following the sale. The entity sold 80 units in the first year of operation and 100 units in the second year. Actual payments for warranty claims were US $10,000 and US $65,000 in Years 1 and 2, respectively. The amount charged to warranty expense during the second year of operation is

A. US $25,000

B. US $65,000

C. US $85,000

D. US $100,000

Answer (D) is correct. *(CIA, adapted)*
REQUIRED: The amount charged to warranty expense during the second year of operation.
DISCUSSION: Under the accrual method, the total estimated warranty costs are charged to operating expense in the year of sale. The total estimated warranty cost per unit is US $1,000 ($250 + $750). In Year 2, 100 units were sold, so the warranty expense recognized is US $100,000.
Answer (A) is incorrect. US $25,000 is the expected amount of warranty claims for the first year of second-year sales. Answer (B) is incorrect. US $65,000 is the actual amount of claims in the second year. Answer (C) is incorrect. US $85,000 is the expected amount of warranty claims in the second year.

4.7 Equity

21. At December 31, Year 1, an entity had the following equity accounts:

Common stock, US $10 par, 100,000 shares authorized, 40,000 shares issued and outstanding	US $ 400,000
Additional paid-in capital from issuance of common stock	640,000
Retained earnings	1,000,000
Total equity	US $2,040,000

Each of the 40,000 common shares outstanding was issued at a price of US $26. On January 2, Year 2, 2,000 shares were reacquired for US $30 per share. The cost method is used in accounting for treasury stock. Which of the following correctly describes the effect of the acquisition of the treasury stock?

A. Common stock is reduced by US $20,000.

B. Additional paid-in capital from issuance of common stock is reduced by US $32,000.

C. The retained earnings account balance is reduced by US $8,000.

D. Total equity is reduced by US $60,000.

Answer (D) is correct. *(CIA, adapted)*
REQUIRED: The effect of the acquisition of the treasury shares under the cost method.
DISCUSSION: Using the cost method, the journal entry to record the acquisition of treasury stock includes a debit to treasury stock for US $60,000. The balance of treasury stock is classified as a contra equity item. Thus, the acquisition of treasury stock reduces total equity by US $60,000 (2,000 shares × $30).
Answer (A) is incorrect. The common stock balance is not affected when treasury stock is acquired. Answer (B) is incorrect. Additional paid-in capital is not affected when treasury stock is acquired and accounted for by the cost method. Answer (C) is incorrect. Retained earnings is not affected by treasury stock acquisitions when the cost method is used.

22. An entity had the following account balances at December 31 of Year 1:

Common stock, US $10 par,
  100,000 shares authorized,
    80,000 shares issued and outstanding   US $800,000
Additional paid-in capital   400,000
Retained earnings   500,000

All shares outstanding were issued in a prior period for US $15 per share. On January 5 of Year 2, 1,000 shares were purchased for the treasury for US $17 per share. These treasury shares were sold on February 6 of Year 2, for US $18 per share. The effect of the purchase and sale of the 1,000 treasury stock was to

A. Increase equity by US $1,000.

B. Increase equity by US $2,000.

C. Increase equity by US $3,000.

D. Not change equity.

Questions 23 and 24 are based on the following information. An entity has issued 1,000 common shares with a par value of US $10, and its credit balance in retained earnings is US $5,000. Two proposals are under consideration. The first is a stock split giving each shareholder two new shares for each share formerly held. The second is to declare and distribute a 10% stock dividend.

---

23. The stock split proposal will <List A> earnings per share by <List B> than will the stock dividend proposal.

	List A	List B
A.	Increase	More
B.	Increase	Less
C.	Decrease	More
D.	Decrease	Less

24. Under the stock <List A>, the par value per outstanding share will <List B>.

	List A	List B
A.	Dividend	Increase
B.	Split	Increase
C.	Dividend	Decrease
D.	Split	Decrease

Answer (A) is correct. *(CIA, adapted)*
   REQUIRED: The effect on shareholders' equity of the purchase and sale of treasury stock.
   DISCUSSION: Assuming the cost method is used, the journal entry to record the purchase of treasury stock is

Treasury stock   US $17,000
   Cash   US $17,000

The journal entry to record the sale is

Cash   US $18,000
   Treasury stock   US $17,000
   Additional paid-in capital from treasury stock   1,000

Consequently, the net effect is to increase equity by US $1,000.

Answer (C) is correct. *(CIA, adapted)*
   REQUIRED: The effect of a stock split and a stock dividend on earnings per share.
   DISCUSSION: The stock split will double the number of shares outstanding to 2,000. The 10% stock dividend will increase the number of outstanding shares to 1,100. The higher number of shares in the split will result in a lower earnings per share than will result from the stock dividend.

Answer (D) is correct. *(CIA, adapted)*
   REQUIRED: The effect of a stock split and a stock dividend on par value.
   DISCUSSION: A stock split results in a lower par value per share because the total number of shares increases but the total par value of outstanding shares does not change.
   Answer (A) is incorrect. Par value per share does not change following a stock dividend. Answer (B) is incorrect. Par value per share decreases following a stock split. Answer (C) is incorrect. Par value per share does not change following a stock dividend.

4.8 Accounting Changes

25. On January 1, Year 1, an entity purchased a machine for US $10,000. The estimated useful life was 10 years, with no residual value. The entity depreciates its property, plant, and equipment using the straight-line method. On January 1, Year 5, it was estimated that the machine had a remaining useful life of 3 years. Compute the entity's Year 5 depreciation expense for the machine.

A. US $1,000

B. US $2,000

C. US $3,000

D. US $6,000

Answer (B) is correct. *(CIA, adapted)*
REQUIRED: The depreciation expense.
DISCUSSION: The machine's net carrying amount at January 1, Year 5, is US $6,000 ($10,000 cost – $4,000 accumulated depreciation for 4 years). A change in accounting estimate is applied prospectively. Thus, depreciation expense is US $2,000 per year for the next 3 years.
Answer (A) is incorrect. The amount of US $1,000 is based on the assumption of no change in estimate. Answer (C) is incorrect. The amount of US $3,000 is based on the assumption of a 2-year remaining useful life. Answer (D) is incorrect. The amount of US $6,000 is the carrying amount at January 1, Year 5.

26. The following financial statement notes are extracts from the audited financial statements of public entities. Which note describes a change in accounting estimate **not** involving a change in principle?

A. The entity changed its depreciation of capital assets based on a reassessment of the useful lives of the assets. Accordingly, the entity changed its rate of amortization from 5% and 6% to 8% and 10%, for machinery and equipment.

B. Prior to Year 5, plant and equipment (other than customer service replacement parts) were depreciated using the declining-balance method. Plant and equipment are now depreciated on a straight-line basis.

C. During the year, the entity changed its method of accounting for noninterest-bearing, nonrecourse loans due from employees, pursuant to a change in generally accepted accounting principles.

D. Effective January 1, Year 5, the entity changed to the weighted-average method of inventory valuation. Prior to Year 5, the FIFO method was used.

Answer (A) is correct. *(CIA, adapted)*
REQUIRED: The note describing a change in accounting estimate not involving a change in principle.
DISCUSSION: Accounting estimates, e.g., service lives, residual values, warranty costs, uncollectible accounts, and inventory obsolescence, are a necessary part of preparing financial statements. However, they inevitably change as new events occur and as additional experience and information are obtained. When altered conditions require a change in estimate, it is accounted for prospectively. Thus, a change in the estimate of the service lives of depreciable assets is a change in accounting estimate not involving a change in principle.
Answer (B) is incorrect. A change from declining-balance depreciation to straight-line depreciation is a change in an accounting estimate inseparable from (effected by) a change in principle. In theory, this change reflects a change in the expected pattern of consumption of the future economic benefits of the asset (a change in estimate). But the change is implemented using a change in an accounting principle (the change to the straight-line method). Answer (C) is incorrect. A change in an accounting principle has occurred. It is appropriate when it is required by the applicable standards. Answer (D) is incorrect. A change in the method of accounting for inventory is a change in accounting principle.

27. An entity changes its method of accounting for inventory during the current year because it believes that the result will be improved reporting. In its financial statements for the year, how should the entity report the adjustment resulting from the change if the practicability criterion is met?

A. Not disclosed in the financial statements.

B. Reported as an adjustment to beginning retained earnings of the earliest period presented.

C. Disclosed as a separate inventory balance for the current year.

D. Included in the income statement for the current period as a cumulative effect adjustment.

Answer (B) is correct. *(CIA, adapted)*
REQUIRED: The treatment of a change in inventory methods.
DISCUSSION: A voluntary change in accounting principle should be applied retrospectively unless any resulting adjustment that relates to prior periods is impracticable. Impracticable means that the entity cannot apply the principle after making every reasonable effort to do so. Thus, if it is not impracticable to apply the new policy retrospectively, it should be applied to comparative information as far back as practicable. Thus, the opening balances of retained earnings and other components of equity for the earliest period presented must be adjusted. The opening balances of assets and liabilities for the same period also are adjusted.
Answer (A) is incorrect. The effects of changes in accounting principles must be reported in the financial statements for the period. Answer (C) is incorrect. The new policy should be retrospectively applied if practicable. Answer (D) is incorrect. Retrospective application is required to the extent practicable. Recognition of the cumulative effect of the change as an item in the income statement is not permitted.

28. Because changes in accounting estimates relate to changes in circumstances in the <List A> period, they should be reported <List B>.

	List A	List B
A.	Current	Not at all
B.	Current	Prospectively
C.	Prior	Retroactively
D.	Prior	Not at all

Answer (B) is correct. *(CIA, adapted)*
REQUIRED: The reporting of accounting estimates.
DISCUSSION: Changes in accounting estimates arise as new events occur, as more experience is obtained, or as additional evidence is acquired. A change should be reported in the period in which it occurs and in future periods if they are affected. Retrospective reporting is not feasible because it would result in continual adjustments of prior years' financial statements.
Answer (A) is incorrect. Changes in accounting estimates should be reported. Answer (C) is incorrect. Changes in accounting estimates arise from changes in current, not prior, circumstances. Answer (D) is incorrect. Changes in accounting estimates arise from changes in current, not prior, circumstances.

4.9 Accounting Errors

29. Which of the following errors is **not** self-correcting over two accounting periods?

A. Failure to record accrued wages.

B. Failure to record depreciation.

C. Overstatement of inventory.

D. Failure to record prepaid expenses.

Answer (B) is correct. *(CIA, adapted)*
REQUIRED: The error not self-correcting over two accounting periods.
DISCUSSION: A failure to record depreciation must be corrected because the effects of the error do not automatically reverse in future periods. Expenses are understated in the year of the error, but no corresponding overstatement of expenses occurs in later years.
Answer (A) is incorrect. Understatement of accrued wages is a self-correcting error. Future wage expense will be overstated, and future liabilities will be understated, respectively. Answer (C) is incorrect. Overstatement of inventory and the consequent understatement of cost of goods sold is a self-correcting error. Future cost of goods sold will be overstated, and future expenses will be understated, respectively. Answer (D) is incorrect. Understatement of prepaid expenses (overstatement of expenses) is a self-correcting error. Future assets will be understated, and future expenses will be understated, respectively.

30. How are material prior-period errors in financial statements accounted for when comparative statements are issued?

A. They are included in the determination of profit or loss for the current period.

B. Prior-period financial statements are adjusted and reissued.

C. They are corrected by restating comparative amounts for years when errors occurred.

D. They are charged or credited directly to the closing balance of current-year retained earnings.

Answer (C) is correct. *(CIA, adapted)*
REQUIRED: The accounting for prior period adjustments.
DISCUSSION: All material prior-period errors must be corrected retrospectively in the first set of financial statements issued after their discovery. This may be done by restating the comparative amounts for the prior periods when the error occurred. If the error occurred prior to the first period presented, the opening balances for the first period presented are restated. A material error is one that could, individually or collectively, affect the decisions of users of the financial statements. However, comparative information should be restated only if practicable.
Answer (A) is incorrect. Errors are excluded from the determination of current period income or loss. Answer (B) is incorrect. Prior-period financial statements need not be reissued. However, if comparative statements are presented, the prior-period statements must be restated if it is practicable to do so. Answer (D) is incorrect. Errors are adjustments of the current year's opening balance of retained earnings and other relevant balances.

Questions 31 and 32 are based on the following information. An audit of an entity has revealed the following four errors that have occurred but have not been corrected:

1. Inventory at December 31, Year 3: US $40,000, understated

2. Inventory at December 31, Year 4: US $15,000, overstated

3. Depreciation for Year 3: US $7,000, understated

4. Accrued expenses at December 31, Year 4: US $10,000, understated

31. The errors cause the reported net income for the year ending December 31, Year 4, to be

A. Overstated by US $72,000.

B. Overstated by US $65,000.

C. Understated by US $25,000.

D. Understated by US $50,000.

Answer (B) is correct. *(CIA, adapted)*
REQUIRED: The effect of the errors on reported net income for the year ending December 31, Year 4.
DISCUSSION: The effect of the understatement of the Year 3 year-end inventory (beginning inventory for Year 4) was to overstate Year 4 profit by US $40,000. The reason is that beginning inventory is a component of cost of sales. The overstatement of the December 31, Year 4, inventory overstated Year 4 net income by US $15,000 because the amounts in ending inventory are excluded from cost of sales. The understatement of Year 3 depreciation expense (a nominal account) has no effect on Year 4 net income. Finally, the failure to accrue US $10,000 of expenses for Year 4 overstated Year 4 net income. The net effect of these errors was a US $65,000 ($40,000 + $15,000 + $0 + $10,000) overstatement.
Answer (A) is incorrect. The understatement of Year 3 depreciation expense (a nominal account) has no effect on Year 4 net income. Answer (C) is incorrect. The understatement of Year 4 beginning inventory also understated net income. Answer (D) is incorrect. The understatement of accrued expenses also overstated net income.

32. The errors cause the reported retained earnings at December 31, Year 4, to be

A. Overstated by US $65,000.

B. Overstated by US $32,000.

C. Overstated by US $25,000.

D. Understated by US $18,000.

Answer (B) is correct. *(CIA, adapted)*
REQUIRED: The effect of the errors on the reported retained earnings at December 31, Year 4.
DISCUSSION: The Year 3 inventory error reversed in Year 4 (excluding tax considerations) and therefore had no effect on reported retained earnings at December 31, Year 4. The US $15,000 inventory error at year end of Year 4 and the failure to accrue US $10,000 of expenses for Year 4 both overstated retained earnings as well as Year 4 profit. The omission of US $7,000 of depreciation overstated Year 3 net income and Year 3 and Year 4 retained earnings. Hence, the net effect of the errors on December 31, Year 4, retained earnings was a US $32,000 ($0 + $15,000 + $7,000 + $10,000) overstatement.
Answer (A) is incorrect. The net effect of the errors on Year 4 net income was US $65,000. Answer (C) is incorrect. The understatement of depreciation also affected retained earnings. Answer (D) is incorrect. This amount (US $18,000) is based on the assumption that depreciation was overstated by US $7,000.

4.10 Exchange Rates

33. A U.S. company and a European company purchased the same shares on a European exchange and held the shares for 1 year. If the value of the euro weakened against the U.S. dollar during the period, in comparison with the European company's return, the U.S. company's return will be

A. Lower.

B. Higher.

C. The same.

D. Indeterminate from the information provided.

Answer (A) is correct. *(CIA, adapted)*
   REQUIRED: The effect of the decline in value of one currency in relation to another.
   DISCUSSION: The U.S. company presumably used U.S. dollars to purchase euros that in turn were used for the share purchase. The European company presumably made a direct share purchase with euros. Given that the euro weakened against the U.S. dollar, at the end of the period the exchange rate in terms of euros per U.S. dollar was lower than when the share purchases were made. In other words, a given amount of euros would purchase fewer U.S. dollars at the end of the period. Accordingly, the U.S. company's rate of return (euros to be exchanged for U.S. dollars ÷ U.S. dollars invested) is lower than the European company's return (euros ÷ euros invested). The reason is that the unfavorable exchange rate movement does not adversely affect the European company's rate of return.
   Answer (B) is incorrect. The return to the U.S. company is adversely affected by the exchange rate movement. Answer (C) is incorrect. The return to the U.S. company is directly affected by the exchange rate movement, while the return to the European company is not. Answer (D) is incorrect. The return to the U.S. company is adversely affected, and the return to the European company is unaffected.

4.11 Business Combinations

34. Entity A acquires all of the voting shares of Entity B for US $1,000,000. At the time of the acquisition, the net fair value of the identifiable assets acquired and liabilities assumed had a carrying amount of US $900,000 and a fair value of US $800,000. The amount of goodwill Entity A will record on the acquisition date is

A. US $0

B. US $100,000

C. US $200,000

D. US $300,000

Answer (C) is correct. *(CIA, adapted)*
   REQUIRED: The goodwill recorded.
   DISCUSSION: Given no prior equity interest or noncontrolling interest, goodwill equals the excess of the fair value of the consideration transferred over the fair value of the net of the identifiable assets acquired and liabilities assumed. Consequently, goodwill is US $200,000 ($1,000,000 – $800,000).
   Answer (A) is incorrect. Goodwill must be recorded. Answer (B) is incorrect. The amount of US $100,000 is the excess of the acquisition cost over the carrying amount. Answer (D) is incorrect. The amount of US $300,000 equals goodwill plus the excess of the carrying amount over fair value.

4.12 The Equity Method and Consolidated Reporting

35. When the equity method is used to account for the investment in an investee over which significant influence is exercised, the recording of the receipt of a cash dividend from the investee will result in

A. The recognition of investment income.

B. A reduction in the investment balance.

C. An increase in a liability account.

D. An increase in a special equity account.

Answer (B) is correct. *(CIA, adapted)*
   REQUIRED: The effect under the equity method of the receipt of a cash distribution.
   DISCUSSION: When the equity method is used, the investment is initially recorded at cost on the entity's books. The carrying amount is subsequently adjusted to recognize the income or loss of the investee after the date of acquisition. Dividends received from an investee reduce the carrying amount.
   Answer (A) is incorrect. When the equity method is used, investment income (loss) is recognized for the investee's share of the income or loss of the investee. Dividends received from the investee are recorded as a reduction of the investment account. Answer (C) is incorrect. The investment account is credited. Answer (D) is incorrect. The investment account is credited.

4.13 Partnerships

36. Pilates and Wesson drafted a partnership agreement that lists the following assets contributed at the partnership's formation:

	Contributed by	
	Pilates	Wesson
Cash	US $40,000	US $60,000
Inventory	--	30,000
Building	--	80,000
Furniture and equipment	30,000	--

The building is subject to a mortgage of US $20,000, which the partnership has assumed. The partnership agreement also specifies that profits and losses are to be distributed evenly. What amounts should be recorded as capital for Pilates and Wesson at the formation of the partnership?

	Pilates	Wesson
A.	US $70,000	US $170,000
B.	US $70,000	US $150,000
C.	US $110,000	US $110,000
D.	US $120,000	US $120,000

Answer (B) is correct. *(CPA, adapted)*
REQUIRED: The capital balances of partners at the formation of the partnership.
DISCUSSION: The balances should reflect the fair values of the assets contributed. The building should be valued net of the mortgage. Hence, the capital balances for Pilates and Wesson are US $70,000 ($40,000 + $30,000) and US $150,000 ($60,000 + $30,000 + $80,000 – $20,000), respectively.
Answer (A) is incorrect. The building should be included net of the mortgage. Answer (C) is incorrect. The partners did not agree to divide capital equally. Answer (D) is incorrect. The partners did not agree to divide capital equally, and the building should be included net of the mortgage.

37. Byrd and Katt formed a partnership and agreed to divide initial capital equally, even though Byrd contributed US $200,000 and Katt contributed US $168,000 in identifiable assets. Under the bonus approach to adjust the capital accounts, Katt's unidentifiable asset should be debited for

A. US $92,000

B. US $32,000

C. US $16,000

D. US $0

Answer (D) is correct. *(CPA, adapted)*
REQUIRED: The unidentifiable asset debited under the bonus approach.
DISCUSSION: The goodwill and the bonus methods are two means of adjusting for differences between the carrying amount and the fair value of partnership net assets. Under the goodwill method, assets are revalued. Under the bonus method, assets are not revalued. Instead, adjustments are made to partnership capital accounts. Consequently, total partnership capital differs between the two methods, and an unidentifiable asset may be debited under the goodwill but not the bonus method.
Answer (A) is incorrect. The amount of US $92,000 is 50% of the balance in each partner's capital account under the bonus method. Answer (B) is incorrect. The unidentifiable asset recognized under the goodwill method is US $32,000. Answer (C) is incorrect. The amount transferred from Byrd's capital account to Katt's capital account under the bonus method is US $16,000.

38. Redd and White are partners with capital account balances of US $60,000 and US $90,000, respectively. They agree to admit Blue as a partner with a one-third interest in capital and profits, for an investment of US $100,000, after revaluing the assets of Redd and White. Goodwill to the original partners should be

A. US $0

B. US $33,333

C. US $50,000

D. US $66,667

Answer (C) is correct. *(CPA, adapted)*
REQUIRED: The goodwill to the original partners.
DISCUSSION: If a one-third interest is worth an investment of US $100,000, the value of the partnership must be US $300,000 ($100,000 ÷ 33 1/3%). The total of the existing capital balances and Blue's investment is US $250,000 ($60,000 + $90,000 + $100,000). Thus, goodwill is US $50,000 ($300,000 – $250,000). The entry will be to debit cash (or property at fair value) for US $100,000 and goodwill for US $50,000, and to credit Blue's capital balance for US $100,000 and the capital balances of Redd and White for a total of US $50,000.
Answer (A) is incorrect. Goodwill should be recognized and credited to the capital balances of Redd and White. Answer (B) is incorrect. The amount of US $33,333 is one-third of the new partner's investment. Answer (D) is incorrect. The amount of US $66,667 is two-thirds of the new partner's investment.

39. Hi Shade, a partner in an accounting firm, decided to withdraw from the partnership. Shade's share of the partnership profits and losses was 20%. Upon withdrawing from the partnership, he was paid US $74,000 in final settlement of his interest. The total of the partners' capital accounts before recognition of partnership goodwill prior to Shade's withdrawal was US $210,000. After his withdrawal, the remaining partners' capital accounts, excluding their share of goodwill, totaled US $160,000. The total agreed upon goodwill of the firm was

A. US $120,000

B. US $160,000

C. US $210,000

D. US $250,000

Answer (A) is correct. *(CPA, adapted)*
REQUIRED: The amount of goodwill agreed upon prior to Shade's withdrawal.
DISCUSSION: The balance in Shade's account prior to recognition of goodwill was US $50,000 ($210,000 − $160,000). Given that he was paid US $74,000 upon withdrawing, Shade's account must have been credited with US $24,000 in goodwill. If his share of partnership profits and losses was 20%, the total agreed upon goodwill equals US $120,000 ($24,000 ÷ 20%).
Answer (B) is incorrect. The amount of US $160,000 was the sum of the remaining partners' capital balances exclusive of goodwill. Answer (C) is incorrect. The amount of US $210,000 was the sum of the partners' capital balances prior to Shade's withdrawal. Answer (D) is incorrect. The amount of US $250,000 assumes that Shade was assigned US $50,000 of goodwill.

40. When Brown retired from the partnership of Brown, Dart, and Prince, the final settlement of Brown's interest exceeded Brown's capital balance. Under the bonus method, the excess

A. Was recorded as goodwill.

B. Was recorded as an expense.

C. Reduced the capital balances of Dart and Prince.

D. Had no effect on the capital balances of Dart and Prince.

Answer (C) is correct. *(CPA, adapted)*
REQUIRED: The treatment of the excess of the settlement of a partner's interest over the capital balance.
DISCUSSION: The bonus method reduces the capital accounts of the other partners because the bonus, that is, the excess of settlement value over the retiring partner's capital balance, is deemed to be paid to the withdrawing partner by the remaining partners.
Answer (A) is incorrect. Goodwill is not recorded under the bonus method. Answer (B) is incorrect. The excess is not an expense. Answer (D) is incorrect. The excess reduces the capital accounts.

Use the additional questions in Gleim *CIA Test Prep* Software to create Test Sessions that emulate Pearson VUE!

STUDY UNIT FIVE
FINANCE

(37 pages of outline)

The emphasis of this study unit is on the financing of corporations. It begins with financial statement analysis. The essence of financial statement analysis is the calculation of financial ratios. These ratios establish relationships among financial statement amounts at a moment in time or for a given accounting period. Ratios also may be evaluated by comparison with those for other entities or with industry averages. Sources of funds may be internal or external, short-term or long-term, and debt or equity. Selecting the appropriate types and amounts of available financing sources is necessary to minimize the entity's cost of capital and maximize shareholder value.

5.1 FINANCIAL STATEMENT ANALYSIS -- LIQUIDITY RATIOS

1.   **Use**

   a.   Liquidity is an entity's ability to pay its current obligations as they come due and remain in business in the short run.

   b.   Liquidity depends on the ease with which current assets can be converted to cash. Liquidity ratios measure this ability by relating an entity's liquid assets to its current liabilities at a moment in time.

EXAMPLE of a Statement of Financial Position

RESOURCES	Current Year End	Prior Year End	FINANCING	Current Year End	Prior Year End
CURRENT ASSETS:			**CURRENT LIABILITIES:**		
Cash and equivalents	US $ 325,000	US $ 275,000	Accounts payable	US $ 150,000	US $ 75,000
Available-for-sale securities	165,000	145,000	Notes payable	50,000	50,000
Accounts receivable (net)	120,000	115,000	Accrued interest on note	5,000	5,000
Notes receivable	55,000	40,000	Current maturities of L.T. debt	100,000	100,000
Inventories	85,000	55,000	Accrued salaries and wages	15,000	10,000
Prepaid expenses	10,000	5,000	Income taxes payable	70,000	35,000
Total current assets	US $ 760,000	US $ 635,000	Total current liabilities	US $ 390,000	US $ 275,000
NONCURRENT ASSETS:			**NONCURRENT LIABILITIES:**		
Equity-method investments	US $ 120,000	US $ 115,000	Bonds payable	US $ 500,000	US $ 600,000
Property, plant, and equipment	1,000,000	900,000	Long-term notes payable	90,000	60,000
Minus: accum. depreciation	(85,000)	(55,000)	Employee-related obligations	15,000	10,000
Goodwill	5,000	5,000	Deferred income taxes	5,000	5,000
Total noncurrent assets	US $1,040,000	US $ 965,000	Total noncurrent liabilities	US $ 610,000	US $ 675,000
			Total liabilities	US $1,000,000	US $ 950,000
			EQUITY:		
			Preference shares, US $50 par	US $ 120,000	US $ 0
			Share premium on P.S.	10,000	0
			Ordinary shares, US $1 par	500,000	500,000
			Share premium on O.S.	100,000	100,000
			Retained earnings	70,000	50,000
			Total equity	US $ 800,000	US $ 650,000
Total assets	US $1,800,000	US $1,600,000	**Total liabilities and equity**	US $1,800,000	US $1,600,000

2.   **Working Capital**

   a.   Net working capital consists of the resources the company would have to continue operating in the short run if it had to settle all of its current liabilities at once.

   Current assets – Current liabilities

EXAMPLE

Current year: US $760,000 – $390,000 = US $370,000
Prior year: US $635,000 – $275,000 = US $360,000

Although the company's current liabilities increased, its current assets increased by US $10,000 more. The company has less working capital.

3.   **Current Ratio**

   a.   The current ratio, also called the working capital ratio, is the most common measure of liquidity.

   $$\frac{Current\ assets}{Current\ liabilities}$$

> ### EXAMPLE
>
> Current year: US $760,000 ÷ $390,000 = 1.95
> Prior year: US $635,000 ÷ $275,000 = 2.31
>
> Although working capital increased in absolute terms (US $10,000), current assets now provide less proportional coverage of current liabilities than in the prior year.

      1)   A low current ratio indicates a possible liquidity problem. An overly high ratio indicates that management may not be investing idle assets productively.

4.   **Quick (Acid-Test) Ratio**

    a.   The quick (acid-test) ratio excludes inventories and prepayments from the numerator because they are difficult to liquidate at their stated amounts. The quick ratio is therefore a more conservative measure than the basic current ratio.

$$\frac{Cash\ and\ equivalents\ +\ Marketable\ securities\ +\ Net\ receivables}{Current\ liabilities}$$

> ### EXAMPLE
>
> Current year: (US $325,000 + $165,000 + $120,000 + $55,000) ÷ $390,000 = 1.71
> Prior year: (US $275,000 + $145,000 + $115,000 + $40,000) ÷ $275,000 = 2.09
>
> Despite its increase in total working capital, the company's position in its most liquid assets declined.

      1)   This ratio measures the firm's ability to easily pay its short-term debts while avoiding the problem of inventory valuation.

Stop and review! You have completed the outline for this subunit. Study multiple-choice questions 1 through 4 beginning on page 223.

5.2 FINANCIAL STATEMENT ANALYSIS -- ACTIVITY RATIOS

1.   **Use**

    a.   Activity ratios reflect how quickly major noncash assets are converted to cash.

      1)   These ratios measure results for an accounting period. Thus, they relate information from the statement of financial position to information from the income statement.

> ### EXAMPLE of an Income Statement
>
> | | Current Year | Prior Year |
> |---|---|---|
> | **Net sales** | US $ 1,800,000 | US $ 1,400,000 |
> | Cost of goods sold | (1,450,000) | (1,170,000) |
> | Gross profit | US $ 350,000 | US $ 230,000 |
> | SG&A expenses | (200,000) | (160,000) |
> | **Operating income** | US $ 150,000 | US $ 70,000 |
> | Other income and expenses | (65,000) | (25,000) |
> | Income before interest and taxes | US $ 85,000 | US $ 45,000 |
> | Interest expense | (15,000) | (10,000) |
> | Income before taxes | US $ 70,000 | US $ 35,000 |
> | Income taxes (40%) | (28,000) | (14,000) |
> | **Net income** | **US $ 42,000** | **US $ 21,000** |

2.   **Receivables Activity Formulas**

a.   The accounts receivable turnover ratio is the number of times in a year the total balance of receivables is converted to cash.

$$\textit{Accounts receivable turnover} = \frac{\textit{Net credit sales}}{\textit{Average balance in receivables}}$$

1)   The ratio can be improved by increasing sales, speeding up collections, or both.
2)   A low turnover rate may indicate the presence of uncollectible balances.

EXAMPLE

All of the company's sales are on credit. Net trade receivables at the reporting date of the second prior year were US $105,000.

Current year: US $1,800,000 ÷ [($120,000 + $115,000) ÷ 2] = 15.3 times
Prior year: US $1,400,000 ÷ [($115,000 + $105,000) ÷ 2] = 12.7 times

The company turned over its trade receivables balance 2.6 more times during the current year, even as receivables were growing in absolute terms. Thus, the company's effectiveness at collecting accounts receivable has improved.

---

b.   The average collection period, also called the days' sales in receivables, measures the average number of days between the time of sale and receipt of payment.

$$\textit{Days' sales in receivables} = \frac{\textit{Days in year}}{\textit{Accounts receivable turnover ratio}}$$

EXAMPLE

Current year: 365 days ÷ 15.3 times = 23.9 days
Prior year: 365 days ÷ 12.7 times = 28.7 days

The denominator (calculated in the example above) increased, and the numerator is a constant. Accordingly, days' sales must decrease. In addition to improving its collection practices, the company also may have become better at assessing the creditworthiness of its customers.

---

3.   **Inventory Activity Ratios**

a.   Two ratios report the efficiency of inventory management.

b.   Inventory turnover measures the number of times in a year the total balance of inventory is converted to cash or receivables.

$$\textit{Inventory turnover} = \frac{\textit{Cost of goods sold}}{\textit{Average balance in inventory}}$$

1)   The ratio can be improved by increasing sales, reducing inventory levels, or both.
2)   A low turnover rate may indicate the presence of obsolete inventory.

EXAMPLE

The balance in inventories at the balance sheet date of the second prior year was US $45,000.

Current year: US $1,650,000 ÷ [($85,000 + $55,000) ÷ 2] = 23.6 times
Prior year: US $1,330,000 ÷ [($55,000 + $45,000) ÷ 2] = 26.6 times

The company did not turn over its inventory as often during the current year as in the prior year. A lower turnover is expected during a period of growing sales (and increasing inventory). It is not necessarily a sign of poor inventory management.

---

c. Days' sales in inventory measures the average number of days between the acquisition of inventory and its sale.

$$\text{Days' sales in inventory} = \frac{\text{Days in year}}{\text{Inventory turnover ratio}}$$

EXAMPLE

Current year: 365 days ÷ 23.6 times = 15.5 days
Prior year: 365 days ÷ 26.6 times = 13.7 days

Because the numerator is a constant, the decreased turnover means that days' sales in inventory increased. This is common during a period of increasing sales.

---

4. **Other Turnover Ratios**

   a. The total assets turnover and fixed assets turnover are broader-based ratios that measure the efficiency with which assets are used to generate revenue.

      1) Both cash and credit sales are included in the numerator.

$$\text{Total assets turnover} = \frac{\text{Net total sales}}{\text{Average total assets}}$$

$$\text{Fixed assets turnover} = \frac{\text{Net total sales}}{\text{Average net fixed assets}}$$

5. **Cash Conversion Cycle**

   a. The cash conversion cycle is the period during which cash is invested in inventory or receivables. It has three components:

      1) The inventory conversion period is the time from the purchase of materials to the sale of finished goods.

      2) The average collection period (see 2.b. on the previous page) is the time from the sale of finished goods to the collection of cash.

         a) The sum of these periods is the operating cycle.

Operating cycle = Days' sales in inventory + Days' sales in receivables

---

EXAMPLE

Current year: 15.5 days + 23.9 days = 39.4 days
Prior year: 13.7 days + 28.7 days = 42.4 days

The entity has slightly reduced its operating cycle while increasing sales and inventory.

---

      3) The payables deferral period is the time from the receipt of materials to payment of cash.

Cash conversion cycle = Operating cycle – Payables deferral period

---

EXAMPLE

The company's payables deferral period was 20.4 days for the current year and 17.7 days for the prior year.

Current year: 39.4 days – 20.4 days = 19.0 days
Prior year: 42.4 days – 17.7 days = 24.7 days

Stop and review! You have completed the outline for this subunit. Study multiple-choice questions 5 through 7 beginning on page 225.

5.3 FINANCIAL STATEMENT ANALYSIS -- SOLVENCY RATIOS

1. **Use**

   a. Solvency is an entity's ability to pay its noncurrent obligations as they come due and remain in business in the long run. The key ingredients of solvency are the entity's capital structure and degree of leverage.

      1) By contrast, liquidity relates to the ability to remain in business for the short run.

2. **Total Debt to Total Assets Ratio**

   a. The debt to total assets ratio (also called the debt ratio) reports the entity's debt burden per monetary unit of assets.

$$Debt\ ratio = \frac{Total\ liabilities}{Total\ assets}$$

EXAMPLE

Current Year: US $1,000,000 ÷ $1,800,000   = 0.556
Prior Year: US $950,000 ÷ $1,600,000   = 0.594

Although total liabilities increased in absolute terms, this ratio improved because total assets increased even more.

---

3. **Earnings Coverage**

   a. Earnings coverage is a creditor's best measure of an entity's ongoing ability to generate the earnings that will allow it to satisfy its long-term debts and remain solvent.

   b. The times-interest-earned ratio is an income statement approach to evaluating the ongoing ability to meet interest payments on debt obligations.

$$Times\text{-}interest\text{-}earned = \frac{Earnings\ before\ interest\ and\ taxes}{Interest\ expense}$$

   1) For the ratio to be meaningful, profit cannot be used in the numerator. What is being measured is the ability to pay interest. Thus, earnings before interest and taxes (EBIT) is appropriate.

EXAMPLE

Current Year: US $85,000 ÷ $15,000 = 5.67
Prior Year: US $45,000 ÷ $10,000 = 4.50

The entity has improved its ability to pay interest expense. In the prior year, EBIT was only four-and-a-half times interest expense, but in the current year, it is more than five-and-a-half times.

---

4. **Financial Leverage**

   a. Leverage is the degree of fixed (not variable) costs incurred. Leverage increases the entity's potential return on investment. However, it also increases risk because fixed costs must be covered regardless of the level of earnings.

      1) Although leverage arises from items on the statement of financial position, it is measured by examining its effects on the income statement.

         a) A general statement of leverage is

$$Degree\ of\ leverage = \frac{Pre\text{-}fixed\text{-}cost\ income\ amount}{Post\text{-}fixed\text{-}cost\ income\ amount}$$

         b) The higher the ratio, the greater the risk.

b. Financial leverage derives from the use of debt in the firm's financing structure. The greater the financial leverage, the greater the interest paid. (The related concept of operating leverage is discussed in Study Unit 6, Subunit 8.)

   1) Because scheduled principal and interest payments must be made regardless of the level of revenues, excess financial leverage can lead to insolvency if operating income is not sufficient to service debt.

   2) But if sales are high, profits are proportionally higher because debt service is constant regardless of the level of sales.

c. The degree of financial leverage (DFL) is a precise measure because it isolates interest as the only fixed financing cost:

   Monetary version:

   $$\textit{Degree of financial leverage} = \frac{EBIT}{\textit{Earnings before taxes}}$$

   1) The DFL for the entity whose income statement is presented on page 189 is 1.21 (US $85,000 ÷ $70,000).

d. Because interest expense is fixed, every monetary unit change in EBIT results in an equal monetary unit change in earnings before taxes.

   1) For example, if the entity's EBIT increases to US $95,000, earnings before taxes increases to US $80,000, a dollar-for-dollar change.

   2) This relationship allows DFL to be restated in percentage form and used to predict the effect a given change in EBIT will have on earnings before taxes.

   Percentage version:

   $$\textit{Degree of financial leverage} = \frac{\%\Delta \textit{ in earnings before taxes}}{\%\Delta \textit{ in EBIT}}$$

   a) For example, given a DFL of 1.21, every 1% change in EBIT changes earnings before taxes by 1.21%.

   b) Note that the numerator and denominator are switched from the monetary version.

Stop and review! You have completed the outline for this subunit. Study multiple-choice questions 8 through 10 beginning on page 227.

5.4 FINANCIAL STATEMENT ANALYSIS -- ROI AND PROFITABILITY

1.   **Return on Invested Capital**

    a.   Return on investment, or ROI (also called return on invested capital), is a broad concept for measures that reflect how efficiently an entity is using the resources contributed by its shareholders to generate a profit.

    b.   ROI is the most effective measure of corporate performance because it relates the income statement to the statement of financial position. All forms of ROI are some variation on this general ratio:

$$Return\ on\ investment\ (ROI) = \frac{Measure\ of\ profit}{Measure\ of\ capital}$$

        1)   Besides reflecting the effectiveness of management decision making and overall entity profitability, ROI also aids in forecasting earnings, planning, budgeting, and control. Each profit center, product line, etc., can be assessed on the basis of ROI.

    c.   Inconsistent definitions. The variety of definitions in use for the terms return and investment creates difficulties in comparability.

        1)   The numerator (return) may be adjusted by

            a)   Subtracting preferred dividends to leave only income available to common shareholders.

            b)   Adding back the noncontrolling interest in the income of a consolidated subsidiary (when invested capital is defined to include the noncontrolling interest).

            c)   Adding back interest expense.

            d)   Adding back both interest expense and taxes so that the numerator is earnings before interest and taxes (EBIT).

                i)   The result is the basic earning power ratio. It enhances comparability of entities with different capital structures and tax planning strategies.

        2)   The denominator (investment) may be adjusted by

            a)   Excluding nonoperating assets, such as investments, intangible assets, and the other asset category.

            b)   Excluding unproductive assets, such as idle plant, intangible assets, and obsolete inventories.

            c)   Excluding current liabilities to emphasize long-term capital.

            d)   Excluding debt and preferred shares to arrive at equity capital.

            e)   Stating invested capital at fair value.

NOTE: The examples below and on the next page use the financial statement excerpts presented on pages 188 and 189.

2. **Return on Assets**

   a. Return on assets, or ROA (also called return on total assets, or ROTA), is the most basic form of the ROI ratio.

   $$Return\ on\ assets\ (ROA)\ =\ \frac{Net\ income}{Average\ total\ assets}$$

   1) The entity's net income was US $42,000. The average total asset balance was US $1,700,000 [($1,800,000 + $1,600,000) ÷ 2]. ROA was therefore 2.47% (US $42,000 ÷ $1,700,000).

3. **DuPont Model**

   a. The original DuPont model treats ROA as the product of two components:

   $$Return\ on\ assets\ =\ Profitability\ \times\ Asset\ turnover$$

   $$\frac{Net\ income}{Average\ total\ assets}\ =\ \frac{Net\ income}{Net\ sales}\ \times\ \frac{Net\ sales}{Average\ total\ assets}$$

   1) The entity's profitability is 2.333% (US $42,000 net income ÷ $1,800,000 net sales), and the asset turnover is 1.06 times (US $1,800,000 net sales ÷ $1,700,000 average total assets). ROA can be confirmed by multiplying the two (2.333% × 1.06 = 2.47%).

   2) The advantage of this analysis is that it examines both the results of operations and the efficiency of asset usage in generating sales.

   3) One component has sales in the denominator and the other has sales in the numerator. Thus, they are both affected by changes in sales, but inversely.

4. **Return on Equity**

   a. Return on equity (ROE) is the second version of the ROI ratio. It is a less conservative measure than ROA because equity is a smaller base than total assets.

   $$Return\ on\ equity\ (ROE)\ =\ \frac{Net\ income}{Average\ total\ equity}$$

   1) This ratio measures the return available to all shareholders.

   2) The entity's net income was US $42,000, and average total equity was US $725,000 [($800,000 + $650,000) ÷ 2]. The ROE was therefore 5.79% (US $42,000 ÷ $725,000).

5. **Three-Component ROE**

   a. The DuPont model has been adapted and expanded. One widely used variation treats ROE as the product of three components:

   $$ROE\ =\ Profitability\ \times\ Turnover\ \times\ Equity\ multiplier$$

   $$ROE\ =\ \frac{Profit}{Net\ sales}\ \times\ \frac{Net\ sales}{Average\ total\ assets}\ \times\ \frac{Average\ total\ assets}{Average\ total\ equity}$$

   1) The first component (profitability) is from the income statement only. The second component (asset turnover) is from the income statement and statement of financial position. The third component (the equity multiplier) is from the statement of financial position only.

   2) The entity's profitability and asset turnover were determined in item 3.a.1) above to be 2.333% and 1.06 times, respectively. The equity multiplier is 2.34 (US $1,700,000 average assets ÷ $725,000 average equity). The product of all three components (2.333% × 1.06 × 2.34) is 5.79%, the same ROE calculated in item 4.a.2) above.

3) The equity multiplier reports the monetary amount of assets supported by each monetary unit of equity. Entities that are highly leveraged, that is, with a high proportion of debt, have a higher equity multiplier.

6. **Dividend Payout Ratio**

   a. Increasing shareholder wealth is the fundamental goal of any business. The dividend payout ratio measures the portion of available earnings the entity actually distributed to shareholders.

$$\text{Dividend payout ratio} = \frac{\text{Dividends paid to common shareholders}}{\text{Net income} - \text{Preferred dividends}}$$

   1) Growing entities tend to have a low payout. They prefer to use earnings for expansion.

7. **Profitability Ratios**

   a. Three common percentages measure profitability directly from the income statement:

   1) Gross profit is the percentage of gross revenues remaining after the entity pays for goods sold.

   2) Operating income is the percentage remaining after selling and general and administrative expenses have been paid.

   3) Net income is the percentage remaining after adjustments for other gains and losses, interest expense, and income taxes.

EXAMPLE		
	Current Year	Prior Year
Net sales	100.0%	100.0%
Cost of goods sold	(80.6%)	(83.6%)
Gross profit	**19.4%**	**16.4%**
SG&A expenses	(11.1%)	(11.4%)
Operating income	**8.3%**	**5.0%**
Other income and expense	(3.6%)	(1.8%)
Income before interest and taxes	4.7%	3.2%
Interest expense	(0.8%)	(0.7%)
Income before taxes	3.9%	2.5%
Income taxes (40%)	(1.6%)	(1.0%)
Net income	**2.3%**	**1.5%**

   b. The income statements above are presented in the **common-size** format. Line items on common-size statements are expressed as percentages of net sales (on the income statement) or total assets (on the statement of financial position).

   1) Thus, on a common-size income statement, net sales is 100%, and all other amounts are a percentage of net sales. On the statement of financial position, total assets and the total of liabilities and equity are each 100%.

   2) Each line item can be interpreted in terms of its proportion of the baseline amount. This process is **vertical analysis**.

   c. An alternative is **horizontal analysis**. It compares a single entity's ratios over time.

   1) One period is designated the base period, in which each line item is measured at 100%. The same line items of the other periods are stated as a percentage of the base-year line item.

Stop and review! You have completed the outline for this subunit. Study multiple-choice questions 11 through 14 beginning on page 229.

5.5 FINANCIAL STATEMENT ANALYSIS -- CORPORATE VALUATION

1. **Earnings per Share (EPS)**

   a. EPS is the most common performance measure used by investors. EPS states the amount of current-period earnings that can be associated with a single common share.

      1) Preferred shareholders have a superior claim to earnings. Thus, amounts associated with preferred stock must be removed during the calculation of EPS.

   b. Basic Earnings per Share (BEPS)

   $$\frac{Income\ or\ loss\ attributable\ to\ common\ equity\ holders}{Weighted\text{-}average\ outstanding\ ordinary\ shares}$$

      1) A BEPS amount also is calculated with a numerator equal to income or loss from continuing operations (if presented) attributable to common equity holders.

      2) The numerator is adjusted for after-tax preferred dividends and other effects of preferred stock treated as equity.

      3) The denominator includes shares from the time consideration is receivable, e.g., when cash is receivable or interest on convertible debt no longer accrues.

         a) Adjustments are made for events (other than conversion of potential common stock) that change common stock outstanding without an increase in resources, e.g., a stock split or a capitalization or bonus issue (a stock dividend).

   c. Diluted Earnings per Share (DEPS)

      1) Calculation of DEPS amounts requires adjustments of the BEPS numerator and denominator for the effects of dilutive potential common stock.

         a) A potential common share is a contract that may entitle holders to common stock.

            i) It is dilutive if it reduces (increases) EPS (loss per share) as a result of assuming the conversion of convertible instruments, exercise of options or warrants, or issue of common stock when conditions are satisfied.

      2) The BEPS numerators are adjusted for after-tax effects of

         a) Dividends or other items associated with dilutive potential common stock that was subtracted in arriving at the BEPS numerator,

         b) Recognized interest on dilutive potential common stock, and

         c) Other changes in income or expense associated with conversion of potential common stock.

      3) The BEPS denominator is adjusted for the weighted-average number of common stock assumed to have been issued upon conversion of all dilutive potential common stock.

         a) Conversion is assumed to have occurred at the earlier of the beginning of the period or issue date of the potential common stock.

2.   **Book Value per Share**

   a.   Book value per share equals the amount of net assets available to the shareholders of a given type of shares divided by the number of those shares outstanding.

$$\text{Book value per share} = \frac{\text{Total equity} - \text{Liquidation value of preferred stock}}{\text{Common stock outstanding}}$$

   1)   When preferred stock is cumulative and in arrears or participating, liquidation value exceeds its carrying amount. Book value per share is ordinarily based on historical cost expressed in nominal units of money.

   2)   Accordingly, it may be misleading because book values ordinarily differ materially from fair values. Fair value usually is what shares sell for on the open market. Book value may be materially higher or lower.

3.   **Price-Earnings (P-E) Ratio**

   a.   A high P-E ratio reflects the equity market's positive assessment of the entity's earnings quality and the likelihood that its earnings trend is favorable. It measures how much an investor must spend to acquire a unit of earnings.

$$\text{Price-earnings ratio} = \frac{\text{Market price per share}}{\text{Diluted earnings per share}}$$

4.   **Dividend Growth Model**

   a.   The dividend growth model is a popular tool for valuing shares.

$$\text{Expected share price} = \frac{\text{Next dividend*}}{\text{Required rate of return} - \text{Dividend growth rate}}$$

   * Next dividend = Current dividend × (1 + Dividend growth rate)

EXAMPLE

A corporation currently pays a dividend of US $4 per share that is expected to grow at a constant 2% annual rate. The price an investor with a required rate of return of 8% would be willing to pay for the share is calculated as follows:

   Expected share price = Next dividend ÷ (Required rate of return − Dividend growth rate)
   = [US $4 × (1.0 + .02)] ÷ (.08 − .02)
   = (US $4 × 1.02) ÷ .06
   = US $4.08 ÷ .06
   = US $68.00

---

   b.   The economic value of an entity for a period of time is the present value of its expected net future cash flows discounted at the cost of capital.

Stop and review! You have completed the outline for this subunit. Study multiple-choice questions 15 through 17 beginning on page 231.

5.6 FINANCIAL STATEMENT ANALYSIS -- COMPREHENSIVE

Candidates for the CIA exam often see questions involving multiple ratios. This subunit consists entirely of such questions. Please review Subunits 5.1 through 5.5 before attempting to answer the questions in this subunit.

Stop and review! You have completed the outline for this subunit. Study multiple-choice question 18 on page 232.

5.7 INVESTMENTS -- RISK AND RETURN

1. **Rate of Return**

   a. A return is the amount received by an investor as compensation for taking on the risk of the investment.

   $$Return\ on\ investment\ =\ Amount\ received\ -\ Amount\ invested$$

   ### EXAMPLE

   An investor paid US $100,000 for an investment that returned US $112,000. The investor's return is US $12,000 ($112,000 – $100,000).

   ---

   b. The rate of return is the return stated as a percentage of the amount invested.

   $$Rate\ of\ return\ =\ \frac{Return\ on\ investment}{Amount\ invested}$$

   ### EXAMPLE

   The investor's rate of return is 12% (US $12,000 ÷ $100,000).

   ---

2. **Two Basic Types of Investment Risk**

   a. Systematic risk, also called market risk, is the risk faced by all entities. Changes in the economy as a whole, such as the business cycle, affect all players in the market.

      1) For this reason, systematic risk is sometimes referred to as undiversifiable risk. Because all investment securities are affected, this risk cannot be offset through portfolio diversification.

   b. Unsystematic risk, also called company risk, is the risk inherent in a particular investment security. This type of risk is determined by the issuer's industry, products, customer loyalty, degree of leverage, management competence, etc.

      1) For this reason, unsystematic risk is sometimes referred to as diversifiable risk. Because individual securities are affected differently by economic conditions, this risk can be offset through portfolio diversification (see item 6. on page 201).

3. **Other Types of Investment Risk**

   a. Credit risk (or default risk) is the risk that the issuer of a debt security will default. This risk can be assessed by the use of credit-rating agencies.

   b. Foreign exchange risk (or exchange rate risk) is the risk that a foreign currency transaction will be affected by fluctuations in exchange rates.

   c. Interest rate risk is the risk that an investment security will fluctuate in value due to changes in interest rates. In general, the longer the time until maturity, the greater the degree of interest rate risk.

   d. Industry risk is the risk that a change will affect securities issued by entities in a particular industry. For example, an increase in fuel prices will negatively affect the airline industry.

   e. Political risk is the probability of loss from actions of governments, such as from changes in tax laws or environmental regulations or from expropriation of assets.

   f. Liquidity risk is the risk that a security cannot be sold on short notice for its market value.

   g. Business risk (or operations risk) is the risk of fluctuations in earnings before interest and taxes or in operating income when the entity uses no debt. It is the risk inherent in its operations that excludes financial risk, which is the risk to the shareholders from the use of financial leverage. Business risk depends on factors such as demand variability, sales price variability, input price variability, and amount of operating leverage.

4. **Relationship between Risk and Return**

    a. Whether the expected return on an investment is sufficient to induce an investor depends on its risk, the risks and returns of alternative investments, and the investor's attitude toward risk.

        1) Most investors (and people in general) are risk averse. They have a diminishing marginal utility for wealth. In other words, the utility of additional increments of wealth decreases. The utility of a gain does not outweigh the disutility of a potential loss of the same amount.

            a) This can be illustrated with the actions of people in a casino. Many people are willing to bet US $1 on one of the numbers on a roulette table because the chance of a gain of multiple dollars versus the loss of US $1 is acceptable. However, as the minimum amount of a bet increases (from US $1 to US $100 to US $1,000), the number of willing casual gamblers decreases because the chance for earning hundreds or thousands of dollars versus the probability of losing US $100 or US $1,000 is not acceptable.

            b) Because of risk aversion, risky securities must have higher expected returns. These higher expected returns induce investors to take on the additional risk. In a) above, if a casino were to provide better odds (i.e., a higher expected return) for higher bet amounts, more casual gamblers may be induced to play with higher minimum bets.

        2) A risk-neutral investor adopts an expected value approach. (S)he regards the utility of a gain as equal to the disutility of a loss of the same amount. Thus, a risk-neutral investor has a purely rational attitude toward risk.

            a) In the case of a roulette gambler, a risk-neutral person would be as willing to gamble if the table minimum were US $1, US $100, or US $1,000. If the individual is comfortable with the risk, it does not matter what amount the wager is.

        3) A risk-seeking investor has an optimistic attitude toward risk. (S)he regards the utility of a gain as exceeding the disutility of a loss of the same amount.

            a) In the case of a roulette gambler, a risk-seeking person would be more willing to gamble if the table minimum were higher. In fact, if the odds decreased, the gambler may be more willing to place a bet.

5. **Investment Securities**

    a. Financial managers may select from many financial instruments in which to invest and with which to raise money.

    b. An inverse relationship exists between the safety of an investment and its potential return. The following is a short list of widely available investment securities:

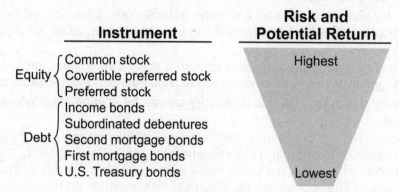

Instrument	Risk and Potential Return
Equity { Common stock / Covertible preferred stock / Preferred stock	Highest
Debt { Income bonds / Subordinated debentures / Second mortgage bonds / First mortgage bonds / U.S. Treasury bonds	Lowest

Figure 5-1

c. The reasons for the varying risk and potential return of these securities can be summarized as follows:

1) Equity securities are necessarily more risky than debt because a return (a profit) is not legally guaranteed.

    a) Preferred shareholders have priority over common shareholders in case of liquidation, but their potential returns are limited by the board of directors.

    b) Common shareholders are the residual owners of a corporation. They are last in priority during liquidation, but they have the right to receive excess profits.

2) U.S. Treasury bonds, mortgage bonds, debentures, and income bonds are all debt securities, meaning the issuer is legally obligated to redeem them. Because these returns are guaranteed, they are lower than those for equity investments.

    a) U.S. Treasury bonds are backed by the full faith and credit of the United States.

    b) Mortgage bonds are secured by real property.

    c) Debentures are unsecured.

    d) Income bonds pay a return only if the issuer is profitable.

6. **Diversification**

a. As described in the beginning of this subunit, specific risk (also called diversifiable risk, unsystematic risk, residual risk, and unique risk) is the risk associated with a single investment security. Specific risk is the risk that can be potentially eliminated by diversification.

1) Diversification reduces aggregate volatility.

    a) Some securities move in the same direction as other securities in the portfolio but by a smaller amount. Some securities move in the opposite direction as other securities.

    b) Thus, by combining imperfectly correlated securities into a portfolio, the risk of the group as a whole is less than the average of their standard deviations.

    c) However, the benefits of diversification become extremely small when more than about 20 to 30 different securities are held. Moreover, commissions and other transaction costs increase with greater diversification.

b. Market risk, also called undiversifiable risk and systematic risk, is the risk of the securities market as a whole. In theory, this is the only risk associated with a well-diversified portfolio.

7. **Beta**

a. The effect of an individual security on the volatility of a portfolio is measured by its sensitivity to movements by the overall market. This sensitivity is stated in terms of a security's beta coefficient (β).

b. The word beta is derived from the regression equation for regressing the return of an individual security (the dependent variable) to the overall market return. The beta coefficient is the slope of the regression line.

1) An average-risk security has a beta of 1.0 because its returns are perfectly positively correlated with those of the market. For example, if the market return increases by 20%, the return on the security increases by 20%.

2) A beta of less than 1.0 means that the security is less volatile than the market. For example, if the market return increases by 20% and the security's return increases only 10%, the security has a beta of .5.

3) A beta over 1.0 indicates a volatile security; e.g., if the return increases 30% when the market return increases by 15%, the security has a beta of 2.0.

4) A negative beta implies a negative correlation with the market.

8.   **Asset Valuation -- CAPM**

a.   The capital asset pricing model (CAPM) quantifies the expected return on an equity security by relating the security's level of risk to the average return available in the market.

b.   The CAPM formula is the sum of two components, the risk-free rate of return and the expected premium provided by the share.

1) The risk-free rate (R_F) is the return currently provided by the safest investments, i.e., government securities.

2) The market risk premium ($R_M - R_F$) is the excess of the average return on the market over the risk-free rate.

a)   In the CAPM, the market risk premium is weighted by the share's beta coefficient to arrive at the share's risk premium, i.e., the return that compensates an investor for the risk assumed.

Capital asset pricing model (CAPM):

$$Expected\ rate\ of\ return = R_F + \beta\,(R_M - R_F)$$

EXAMPLE

An investor is considering the purchase of a share with a beta value of 1.2. Treasury bills are currently paying 8.6%, and the average return on the market is 10.1%. U.S. Treasuries are considered the closest thing to a risk-free investment, so the market risk premium is 1.5% (10.1% − 8.6%). Thus, to buy the share, the investor must expect a rate of return of 10.4% [8.6% + (1.2 × 1.5%)].

---

c.   The CAPM can be graphically depicted as follows:

Capital Asset Pricing Model (CAPM)

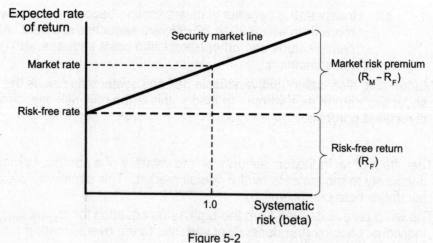

Figure 5-2

9. **Efficient Markets Hypothesis**

   a. The efficient markets hypothesis states that current share prices immediately and fully reflect all relevant information. Hence, the market is continuously adjusting to new information and acting to correct pricing errors.

   b. In other words, securities prices are always in equilibrium. The reason is that securities are subject to intense analysis by many thousands of highly trained individuals. These analysts work for well-capitalized institutions with the resources to take very rapid action when new information is available.

      1) The efficient markets hypothesis states that it is impossible to obtain abnormal returns consistently.

   c. Under the efficient markets hypothesis, the expected return of each security is equal to the return required by the marginal investor given the risk of the security. Moreover, the price equals its fair value as perceived by investors. The efficient markets hypothesis has three forms (versions).

      1) Strong form

         a) All public and private information is instantaneously reflected in securities' prices. Thus, insider trading is assumed not to result in abnormal returns.

      2) Semistrong form

         a) All publicly available data are reflected in security prices, but private or insider data are not immediately reflected. Accordingly, insider trading can result in abnormal returns.

      3) Weak form

         a) Current securities prices reflect all recent past price movement data, so technical analysis will not provide a basis for abnormal returns in securities trading.

   d. Empirical data have refuted the strong form of the efficient markets hypothesis but not the weak and semistrong forms.

Stop and review! You have completed the outline for this subunit. Study multiple-choice questions 19 through 21 on page 233.

5.8 INVESTMENTS -- DERIVATIVES

1. **Overview**

   a. A derivative instrument is an investment transaction in which gain or loss is derived from some other economic event, for example, the price of a given share, a foreign currency exchange rate, or the price of a certain commodity.

      1) Derivatives are used to speculate (incur risk) or to hedge (avoid risk).

   b. Derivatives are a type of financial instrument, along with cash, accounts receivable, notes receivable, bonds, preferred stock, common stock, etc. Derivatives are not, however, claims on business assets, such as those represented by equity securities.

2. **Hedging**

   a. Hedging is the process of using offsetting commitments to minimize or avoid the effects of adverse price movements.

   b. An entity has a long position in an asset whenever the entity owns the asset. An entity with a long position therefore benefits from an increase in the asset's value.

EXAMPLE

An investor buys 100 shares of Collerup Corporation. The investor now has a long position in Collerup Corporation. In financial market terminology, this is referred to as being "long Collerup."

c.   An entity has a short position in an asset when the entity sells an asset that it does not own at the time of the sale. Entities take short positions when they believe the value of the asset will decrease.

1)   Typically, the entity with the short position must borrow the asset from an entity that owns it before the short sale takes place.

EXAMPLE

Money Management Fund A believes that the share price of Collerup Corporation will decrease (perhaps due to a future poor earnings announcement). Fund A borrows Collerup shares from Fund B. Fund A then sells on the appropriate exchange. Fund A is selling short because the fund is selling shares it does not actually own.

- If the price of Collerup decreases, Fund A repurchases the shares at the lower price and returns them to Fund B, thereby making a profit.
- If the price of Collerup remains the same or increases, Fund A must purchase the shares on the exchange (at the higher price), thereby incurring a loss.

---

d.   Hedging is a trade that attempts to offset any fluctuation in value of the asset underlying an existing long or short position. To hedge the investment, the entity takes a position in a financial instrument that is almost perfectly correlated with the original asset but in the opposite direction.

1)   An entity with a long position in an asset profits when the asset's value increases and incurs a loss when the asset's value decreases.

a)   The entity would thus like to reduce the risk of a decrease in value. The entity therefore takes a short position in a financial instrument that is almost perfectly correlated with the original asset but in the opposite direction.

EXAMPLE

The owner of a small gold mine knows it has 1 ton of ore that can be extracted over the next year. Currently, the price of gold is high, so the owner wants to lock in the current gold price, i.e., guarantee that the gold currently owned can be sold in the future at the high price. To do this, the owner sells short gold futures.

- If gold decreases in value, the owner loses money on the gold in the mine but profits from the short position in gold futures.
- If gold increases in value, the owner loses money on the short position in gold futures but profits from the gold in the mine.

---

2)   An entity with a short position in an asset incurs a loss when the asset's value increases and profits when the asset's value decreases.

a)   The entity would thus like to reduce the risk of an increase in value. The entity therefore takes a long position in a financial instrument that is almost perfectly correlated with the original asset but in the opposite direction.

EXAMPLE

Coffee Primero, LLC, is a coffee roasting company. It purchases and imports green coffee from equatorial countries and then roasts and sells the coffee to restaurants and individuals.

Coffee Primero enters into a long-term contract to sell coffee to a restaurant at a fixed price. This is a short position in coffee because the company has obligated itself to supply a customer with coffee that it does not yet own. Furthermore, if the price of coffee changes, Coffee Primero could gain or lose money because of the fluctuation in the value of coffee. To hedge the risk of this short position, Coffee Primero can purchase a derivative such as coffee futures from a commodity exchange.

---

3)   The examples above and on the previous page illustrate the basic principle that once a hedge is initiated, the total value of the hedger's portfolio remains the same because of the offsetting of the two positions.

3. Options

    a.   A party who buys an option has bought the right to demand that the counterparty (the seller or writer of the option) buy or sell an underlying asset on or before a specified future date. The buyer holds all of the rights and the seller has all of the obligations. The buyer pays a fee to be able to dictate – in the future – whether the seller buys or sells the underlying asset from the buyer.

> Many CIA candidates become intimidated when studying options. An option is merely a very standardized legal contract that requires two parties to comply with its terms. These contracts are really no more complicated than the legal contract a person has with his/her cell phone carrier. Individuals pay the cellular phone company money, and in return the cell phone provider is obligated to supply the individual with telephone service when the individual wants to place a phone call. Furthermore, some cell phone carriers charge on the basis of pay-as-you-go while others charge a fixed amount for a fixed amount of minutes. There are many terms associated with cell phone providers, and, similar to cell phones, options have their own terminology. The terms below and on the next page are useful for people in finance because they indicate how a contract is standardized, allowing people to communicate quickly and concisely when discussing options.

        1)   A call option gives the buyer (holder) the right to purchase (i.e., the right to call for) the underlying asset (shares, currency, commodity, etc.) at a fixed price.

        2)   A put option gives the buyer (holder) the right to sell (i.e., the right to put onto the market) the underlying asset (shares, currency, commodity, etc.) at a fixed price.

        3)   The asset that is subject to being bought or sold under the terms of the option is the underlying.

        4)   The party buying an option is the holder. The seller is the writer.

        5)   The exercise of an option is always at the discretion of the option holder (the buyer) who has, in effect, bought the right to exercise the option or not. The seller of an option has no choice; (s)he must perform if the holder chooses to exercise the option.

    b.   An option has an expiration date after which it can no longer be exercised.

        1)   An option that can be exercised only on its expiration date is a European option.

        2)   An option that grants the buyer the right to exercise anytime on or before expiration is an American option.

EXAMPLE

A June US $85 Lando call means that (1) the underlying is Lando Corp. shares, (2) the exercise price is US $85, and (3) the call expires in June.

---

    c.   Determining the correct price for an option is a complex calculation, discussed later in this subunit.

        1)   The exercise price (or strike price) is the price at which the owner can purchase (in the case of a call) or sell (in the case of a put) the asset underlying the option contract.

        2)   The option price, also called option premium, is the amount the buyer pays to the seller to acquire an option.

d.   An option can be covered or uncovered.

1)   A covered option is one in which the seller (writer) is hedging an already existing position. This existing position could be a long or short position.

a)   A party selling a covered option is not speculating but rather is writing the option as a vehicle to insure his/her existing position.

EXAMPLE

An investor holds 100 shares of Lando Corp. and sells call options. If the buyer (holder) of the options decides to exercise them, the investor will not have to purchase the shares at the time of exercise; (s)he can simply sell the shares (s)he has to the option holder.

---

2)   An uncovered (naked) option is a speculative instrument. Because the writer does not have an existing position in the underlying, (s)he may have to acquire it at an unknown price in the future to satisfy his/her obligations under the option contract.

e.   Options can be classified by their underlying assets.

1)   A share option is an option whose underlying asset is a traded equity security.

2)   An index option is an option whose underlying asset is a market index. If exercised, settlement is made by cash because delivery of the underlying is impossible.

3)   Long-term equity anticipation securities (LEAPS) are examples of long-term share options or index options, with expiration dates up to 3 years away.

4)   Foreign currency options give the holder the right to buy a specific foreign currency at a designated exchange rate.

4.   **Valuing an Option**

a.   The price of an option (the option premium) consists of two components, intrinsic value and the time premium, also called extrinsic value (option premium = intrinsic value + time premium).

1)   The intrinsic value of a call option is the amount by which the exercise price is less than the current price of the underlying.

a)   If an option has a positive intrinsic value, it is said to be in-the-money.

EXAMPLE

An investor holds call options for 200 shares of Locksley Corporation with a strike price of US $48 per share. Locksley is currently trading at US $50 per share. The investor's options have an intrinsic value of US $2 each ($50 – $48).

---

b)   If the exercise price of a call option is greater than the current price of the underlying, exercising the option gives the holder no advantage over acquiring the underlying at the market price, and the options have no intrinsic value (the intrinsic value of an option can never fall below US $0).

i)   If an option has an intrinsic value of US $0, it is said to be out-of-the-money.

EXAMPLE

An investor holds call options for 200 shares of Locksley Corporation with a strike price of US $48 per share. Locksley is currently trading at US $45 per share. The investor's options are out-of-the-money (they have no intrinsic value).

---

2) The intrinsic value of a put option is the amount by which the exercise price is greater than the current price of the underlying.

a) If an option has a positive intrinsic value, it is said to be in-the-money.

EXAMPLE

An investor holds put options for 200 shares of Locksley Corporation with a strike price of US $48 per share. Locksley is currently trading at US $45 per share. The investor's options have an intrinsic value of US $3 ($48 – $45).

---

b) If the exercise price of a put option is less than the current price of the underlying, exercising the option gives the holder no advantage over selling the underlying at the market price, and the options have no intrinsic value (the intrinsic value of an option can never fall below US $0).

i) If an option has an intrinsic value of US $0, it is said to be out-of-the-money.

EXAMPLE

An investor holds put options for 200 shares of Locksley Corporation with a strike price of US $48 per share. Locksley is currently trading at US $50 per share. The investor's options are out-of-the-money (they have no intrinsic value).

---

3) The time premium (extrinsic value) of an option is the extra amount investors are willing to pay for the added protection provided by an option over a straightforward long or short position in the underlying.

a) The size of the time premium is in direct proportion to the length of time remaining until exercise. As the exercise date approaches, uncertainty diminishes, and the time premium decreases.

b) If an option has no time premium, its price consists entirely of its intrinsic value. Such an option is said to be trading at parity. If an option is out-of-the-money, its price consists entirely of its time premium.

b. Usually the market value of an option is more than its intrinsic value. The two best-known models for valuing options are the Black-Scholes formula for call options and the binomial method. The equations themselves are complex and beyond the scope of an internal auditing text, but some general statements can be made about the factors that affect the outcomes.

1) Exercise price

a) In general, the buyer of a call option benefits from a low exercise price. Likewise, the buyer of a put option generally benefits from a high exercise price.

b) Thus, an increase in the exercise price of an option results in a decrease in the value of a call option and an increase in the value of a put option.

2) Price of underlying

a) As the price of the underlying increases, the value of a call option also will increase. The exercise price is more of a bargain with each increase in the price of the underlying.

b) The value of a put option will decrease as the price of the underlying increases because selling at a lower-than-market price has no benefit.

3) Interest rates

    a) Buying a call option is like buying the underlying on credit. The purchase of the option is a form of down payment. If the option is exercised in a period of rising interest rates, the exercise price is paid in inflated currency, making it more attractive for the option holder.

    b) A rise in interest rates will therefore result in a rise in the value of a call option and a fall in the value of a put option.

4) Length of the contract

    a) The more time between origination and the expiration date, the more volatile any investment is.

    b) Thus, an increase in the term of an option (both calls and puts) increases its value (i.e., price) of the option.

5) Volatility of the price of the underlying

    a) The more volatile the price of the underlying, the more likely it is to rise above (fall below) the strike price of a call (put), making the option a worthwhile investment.

    b) An increase in the volatility of the price of the underlying will result in an increase in the value of the option (both calls and puts).

c. These factors and their effects can be summarized as follows:

Increase in	Value of call option will	Value of put option will
Exercise price of option	Decrease	Increase
Price of underlying	Increase	Decrease
Interest rates	Increase	Decrease
Length of the contract	Increase	Increase
Volatility of price of underlying	Increase	Increase

5. Forward Contracts

a. One method of reducing risk is the simple forward contract. The two parties agree that, at a set future date, one of them will perform and the other will pay a specified amount for the performance.

    1) A common example is that of a retailer and a wholesaler who agree in September on the prices and quantities of goods that will be shipped to the retailer's stores in time for the winter holiday season. The retailer has locked in a price and a source of supply, and the wholesaler has locked in a price and a customer.

b. The party that has contracted to buy the underlying at a future date has taken a long position, and the party that has contracted to deliver the underlying has taken a short position. The payoff structure is similar to that for options:

    1) If the market price of the underlying on the delivery date is higher than the contractual price, the party that has taken the long position benefits. (S)he will pay a lower-than-market price.

    2) If the market price of the underlying on the delivery date is lower than the contractual price, the party that has taken the short position benefits. (S)he will receive a higher-than-market price.

c. Note the significant difference between a forward contract and an option: In a contract, both parties must meet their contractual obligations, i.e., to deliver goods and to pay. Neither has the option of nonperformance.

    1) Forward contracts are heavily used on foreign currency exchanges.

6. **Futures Contracts**

    a.   A forward contract like the one described in item 5. is appropriate for a retailer and a wholesaler, who are exchanging very specific goods and can take the time to address all the facets of the contract.

        1)   Traders in undifferentiated commodities, such as grains, metals, fossil fuels, and foreign currencies, often do not have this luxury. The trading process of these products is eased by the use of futures contracts.

        2)   A futures contract is a commitment to buy or sell an asset at a fixed price during a specific future month to an unknown counterparty.

    b.   Futures contracts are actively traded on futures exchanges.

        1)   The clearinghouse randomly matches sellers who will deliver during a given month with buyers who are seeking delivery during the same month.

    c.   Because futures contracts are actively traded, the result is a liquid market in futures that permits buyers and sellers to net out their positions.

        1)   For example, a party who has sold a contract can net out his/her position by buying a futures contract. In contrast, a person holding a forward contract does not enjoy this liquidity, partly because forward contracts are not standardized.

    d.   Another distinguishing feature of futures contracts is that their prices are marked to market every day at the close of the day to each person's account. Thus, the market price is posted and netted to the account.

        1)   A mark-to-market provision minimizes a futures contract's chance of default because profits and losses on the contracts must be received or paid each day through a clearinghouse.

        2)   This requirement of daily settlement minimizes default and is necessary because futures contracts are sold on margin (i.e., they are highly leveraged).

    e.   Another difference is that the parties to a forward contract typically expect actual delivery of the subject matter to take place.

        1)   Futures contracts, on the other hand, are generally used as financial tools to offset the risks of changing economic conditions. Thus, the two parties simply exchange the difference between the contracted price and the market price prior to the expiration date.

    f.   Interest rate futures contracts involve risk-free securities such as Treasury bonds, T-bills, and money-market certificates.

        1)   The quantity traded is either US $100,000 or US $1,000,000, depending on which market is used.

EXAMPLE

If a corporation wants to borrow money in 6 months for a major project, but the lender refuses to commit itself to an interest rate, the interest rate futures market can be used to hedge the risk that interest rates might increase in the interim. The company agrees to sell Treasury bonds in 6 months. If interest rates do increase over the period, the value of the Treasury bonds will decline. The company can buy Treasury bonds in 6 months and use them to cover the delivery that it had promised in the futures contract. Because the price of Treasury bonds has declined over the period, the company will make a profit on their delivery. The interest rates that the company will have to pay on the upcoming loan will be higher, however. It has cost the company money to wait 6 months for the loan. The profit from the futures contract should approximately offset the loss resulting from the higher interest loan. If interest rates had declined, the company would have had the benefit of a lower interest loan but would have lost money on the Treasury bonds. The goal of any such hedging operation is to break even on the change in interest rates.

By hedging, the financial manager need not worry about fluctuations in interest rates but can concentrate instead on the day-to-day operations of the company.

7. **Swaps**

    a. Swaps are contracts by which the parties exchange cash flows. A swap is in effect a series of forward contracts. Three types are common:

        1) Interest rate swaps are agreements to exchange interest payments based on one interest structure for payments based on another structure.

            a) For example, an entity that has fixed debt service charges may enter into a swap with a counterparty that agrees to supply the first party with interest payments based on a variable rate that more closely tracks the first party's revenues.

            b) These agreements are highly customized.

        2) Currency swaps are agreements to exchange cash flows fixed in one currency for cash flows fixed in another.

            a) For example, a U.S. entity with revenues in euros has to pay suppliers and workers in dollars, not euros. To minimize exchange-rate risk, it might agree to exchange euros for dollars held by an entity that needs euros.

            b) The exchange rate will be an average of the rates expected over the life of the agreement.

        3) Credit default swaps are agreements by which one of the parties insures the other against default by a third party.

            a) For example, a large bank may agree to pay a constant stream of cash to another bank as long as one of the first bank's major debtors remains current on its loans. If the customer defaults, the second bank covers the first bank's loss. The second bank is, in effect, providing loan default insurance to the first bank.

            b) Unlike interest rate swaps, these agreements are usually bundled into large portfolios.

8. **Duration Hedging**

    a. Duration hedging involves hedging interest-rate risk. Duration is the weighted average of the periods of time to interest and principal payments. If duration increases, the volatility of the price of the debt instrument increases.

    b. Duration is lower if the nominal rate on the instrument is higher because more of the return is received earlier.

    c. The goal of duration hedging is not to equate the duration of assets and the duration of liabilities but for the following relationship to apply:

    (Value of assets) × (Duration of assets) = (Value of liabilities) × (Duration of liabilities)

        1) The entity is immunized against interest-rate risk when the total price change for assets equals the total price change for liabilities.

    d. Assets have positive duration numbers and liabilities have negative numbers. If the duration is positive, the exposure is to rising interest rates. Likewise, if the duration is negative, the exposure is to falling interest rates.

    e. Duration hedging does not provide a perfect hedge.

EXAMPLE

Gator Company has US $4,000,000 of net assets with a net duration of 4 years. This can be hedged by raising the duration of liabilities in any combination to achieve a duration match, such as US $4,000,000 of 4-year net duration liabilities, US $8,000,000 of 2-year net duration liabilities, or US $2,000,000 of 8-year net duration liabilities.

9. **Maturity Matching**

    a.   Maturity matching equalizes the life of an acquired asset with the debt instrument used to finance it. It is a hedging approach to financing because it reduces financial risk.

         1)   For instance, a debt due in 30 days should be paid off with funds that are currently invested in a 30-day marketable security, not with proceeds from a 10-year bond issue.

         2)   Moreover, long-term debt should not be paid with funds needed for day-to-day operations. Careful planning is needed to ensure that dedicated resources are available to retire long-term debt as it matures.

Stop and review! You have completed the outline for this subunit. Study multiple-choice questions 22 through 24 on page 234.

5.9 CORPORATE CAPITAL STRUCTURE -- DEBT FINANCING

1. **Debt vs. Equity**

    a.   An entity may have long-term funding requirements that it cannot, or does not want to, meet using retained earnings. It must therefore issue equity or debt securities. Certain hybrid forms also are used for long-term financing, e.g., convertible securities.

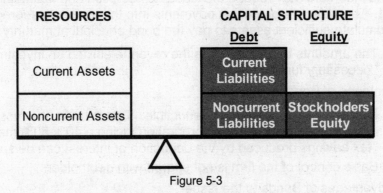

Figure 5-3

         1)   The principal considerations when reviewing financing choices are cost, risk, and the lender's (the investor's) view of the financing device.

2. **Aspects of Bonds**

    a.   Bonds are the principal form of long-term debt financing for corporations and governmental entities.

         1)   A bond is a formal contractual obligation to pay an amount of money (called the par value, maturity amount, or face amount) to the holder at a certain date, plus, in most cases, a series of cash interest payments based on a specified percentage (called the stated rate or coupon rate) of the face amount at specified intervals.

         2)   All of the terms of the agreement are stated in a document called an indenture.

b. Bringing a bond issue to market requires extensive legal and accounting work. The expense of this process is rarely worthwhile for bonds with maturities of less than 5 years.

   1) In general, the longer the term of a bond, the higher will be the return (yield) demanded by investors to compensate for increased risk. This relationship is depicted graphically by the yield curve.

Positive (Normal) Yield Curve

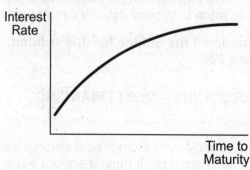

Figure 5-4

c. A bond indenture may require the issuer to establish and maintain a bond sinking fund. The objective of making payments into the fund is to segregate and accumulate sufficient assets to pay the bond principal at maturity.

   1) The amounts transferred plus the revenue earned on investments provide the necessary funds.

d. Advantages of Bonds to the Issuer

   1) Interest paid on debt is tax deductible. This is by far the most significant advantage of debt. For a corporation facing a 40%-50% marginal tax rate, the tax savings produced by the deduction of interest can be substantial.

   2) Basic control of the firm is not shared with debtholders.

e. Disadvantages of Bonds to the Issuer

   1) Unlike returns on equity investments, the payment of interest and principal on debt is a legal obligation. If cash flow is insufficient to service debt, the firm could become insolvent.

   2) The legal requirement to pay debt service raises a firm's risk level. Shareholders will consequently demand higher capitalization rates on retained earnings, which may result in a decline in the market price of the stock.

   3) Bonds may require some collateral that restricts the entity's assets.

   4) The amount of debt financing available to the individual firm is limited. Generally accepted standards of the investment community will usually dictate a certain debt-equity ratio for an individual firm. Beyond this limit, the cost of debt may rise rapidly, or debt may not be available.

3. **Types of Bonds**

a. Maturity Pattern

   1) A term bond has a single maturity date at the end of its term.
   2) A serial bond matures in stated amounts at regular intervals.

    b.   Valuation

        1)   Variable (or floating) rate bonds pay interest that is dependent on market conditions.

        2)   Zero-coupon or deep-discount bonds bear no stated rate of interest and thus involve no periodic cash payments; the interest component consists entirely of the bond's discount.

        3)   Commodity-backed bonds are payable at prices related to a commodity such as gold.

    c.   Redemption Provisions

        1)   Callable bonds may be repurchased by the issuer at a specified price before maturity. During a period of falling interest rates, this allows the issuer to replace old high-interest debt with new low-interest debt.

        2)   Convertible bonds may be converted into equity securities of the issuer at the option of the holder under certain conditions. The ability to become equity holders is an inducement to potential investors, allowing the issuer to offer a lower coupon rate.

    d.   Securitization

        1)   Mortgage bonds are backed by specific assets, usually real estate.

        2)   Debentures are backed by the borrower's general credit but not by specific collateral.

    e.   Ownership

        1)   Registered bonds are issued in the name of the holder. Only the registered holder may receive interest and principal payments.

        2)   Bearer bonds are not individually registered. Interest and principal are paid to whomever presents the bond.

    f.   Priority

        1)   Subordinated debentures and second mortgage bonds are junior securities with claims inferior to those of senior bonds.

    g.   Repayment Provisions

        1)   Income bonds pay interest contingent on the issuer's profitability.

        2)   Revenue bonds are issued by governmental units and are payable from specific revenue sources.

4.   **Bond Ratings**

    a.   Investors can judge the creditworthiness of a bond issue by consulting the rating assigned by a credit-rating agency. The higher the rating, the more likely the firm is to make good its commitment to pay the interest and principal.

    b.   This field is dominated by the three largest firms: Moody's, Standard & Poor's, and Fitch.

        1)   Investment-grade bonds are considered safe investments and thus have the lowest yields. The highest rating assigned is "triple-A." Some fiduciary organizations (such as banks and insurance companies) are only allowed to invest in investment-grade bonds.

        2)   Non-investment grade bonds, also called speculative-grade bonds, high-yield bonds, or junk bonds, carry high risk.

Stop and review! You have completed the outline for this subunit. Study multiple-choice questions 25 through 27 on page 235.

5.10 CORPORATE CAPITAL STRUCTURE -- EQUITY FINANCING

1. **Common Stock**

   a. The shareholders are the owners of a corporation, and their rights as owners, although reasonably uniform, depend on the laws where it is incorporated.

      1) Equity ownership involves risk because holders of shares are not guaranteed a return and are last in priority in a liquidation.

      2) Equity provides a source of funds for creditors if any losses occur on liquidation.

   b. Advantages to the Issuer

      1) Dividends are not fixed. They are paid from profits when available.

      2) They have no fixed maturity date for repayment of the capital.

      3) The sale of common shares increases the creditworthiness of the entity by providing more equity.

      4) Common shares are frequently more attractive to investors than debt because they increase in value with the success of the entity.

         a) The higher the common share value, the greater the advantage of equity financing over debt financing.

   c. Disadvantages to the Issuer

      1) Control (voting rights) of existing common shareholders may be diluted as more shares are sold.

      2) New common shares dilute earnings available to existing shareholders because of the greater number of shares outstanding.

      3) Underwriting costs (i.e., costs of issuing common shares) are typically higher for shares than other forms of financing.

      4) Too much equity may raise the average cost of capital of the entity above its optimal level.

      5) Common share cash dividends may not be tax deductible as an expense. They are after-tax reductions of cash.

   d. Common shareholders may have preemptive rights.

      1) Preemptive rights give common shareholders the right to purchase any additional issuances in proportion to their current ownership. Thus, they can maintain their ownership percentages.

2. **Preferred Stock**

   a. Preferred stock has features of debt and equity. It has a fixed charge and increases leverage, but payment of dividends is not a legal obligation. It is less risky for investors than common stock but more risky than bonds.

      1) Debt holders have priority over preferred shareholders in liquidation.

   b. Advantages to the Issuer

      1) Preferred stock is a form of equity and therefore increases the creditworthiness of the entity.

      2) Control is still held by common shareholders.

      3) Superior earnings are usually still reserved for the common shareholders.

    c.   Disadvantages to the Issuer

       1)   Cash dividends paid are not tax deductible in most countries. The result is a substantially greater cost relative to bonds.

       2)   In periods of economic difficulty, cumulative (past) dividends may create major managerial and financial problems.

    d.   Typical Provisions of Preferred Stock Issues

       1)   Par value. Par value is the liquidation value, and a percentage of par equals the preferred dividend.

       2)   Priority in assets and earnings. If the entity goes bankrupt, the preferred shareholders have priority over common shareholders.

       3)   Accumulation of dividends. If preferred dividends in arrears are cumulative, they must be paid before any common dividends can be paid.

       4)   Convertibility. Preferred share issues may be convertible into common shares at the option of the shareholder.

       5)   Participation. Preferred shares may participate with common shares in excess earnings. For example, 8% participating preferred shares might pay a dividend each year greater than 8% when the entity is extremely profitable. But nonparticipating preferred shares will receive no more than is stated on the face of the share.

       6)   Redeemability. Some preferred shares may be redeemed at a given time at the option of the holder, or otherwise at a time not controlled by the entity.

       7)   Voting rights. These may be conferred if preferred dividends are in arrears for a stated period.

       8)   Callability. The issuer may have the right to repurchase the shares.

       9)   Maturity. Preferred shares may have a sinking fund that allows for the purchase of the outstanding shares.

    e.   Advantages and Disadvantages to the Holder

       1)   Holding preferred shares rather than bonds may provide a tax advantage. A portion of dividends received from preferred shares may be tax deductible, but all bond interest received normally is taxable.

       2)   Among the rights typically associated with preferred shares are receipt of

           a)   Dividends at a specified rate before common shareholders and

           b)   Distributions before common shareholders (but after creditors) upon liquidation or bankruptcy.

       3)   However, preferred shareholders tend not to have voting rights or receive the same capital gains as common shareholders when the entity is successful.

Stop and review! You have completed the outline for this subunit. Study multiple-choice questions 28 through 30 on page 236.

5.11 CORPORATE CAPITAL STRUCTURE -- COST OF CAPITAL

1.   **Overview**

   a.   An entity's cost of capital is the rate of return it must pay to attract investors.

   1)   Because debt and equity attract investors for different reasons, each form of capital has its own cost.

   b.   Providers of equity capital are exposed to more risk than are lenders because (1) the entity is not legally obligated to pay them a return and (2) in case of liquidation, equity investors trail creditors in priority.

   1)   To compensate for this higher level of risk, equity investors demand a higher return, making equity financing more expensive than debt.

   c.   An entity's weighted-average cost of capital (WACC) is a single, composite rate of return on its combined components of capital.

2.   **Optimal Capital Structure**

   a.   Standard financial theory provides a model for the optimal capital structure of every entity.

   1)   This model holds that shareholder wealth-maximization results from minimizing the weighted-average cost of capital. Thus, the focus of management should not be on maximizing earnings per share (EPS can be increased by taking on more debt, but debt increases risk).

   2)   The relevant relationships are depicted below:

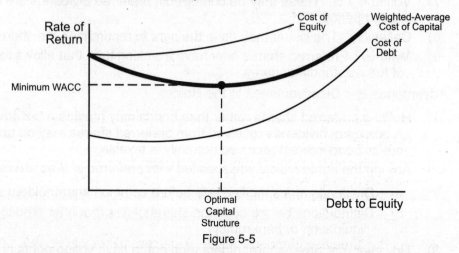

Figure 5-5

   b.   Ordinarily, entities cannot identify this optimal point precisely. Thus, they should attempt to find an optimal range for the capital structure.

   1)   An entity's management usually designates a target capital structure for the entity, i.e., the proportions of the components of capital. An example might be 30% long-term debt and 70% equity.

3. **Marginal Cost of Capital**

    a. While internally generated capital is the least expensive form of capital, an entity cannot rely solely on retained earnings to fund new projects. Retained earnings alone are rarely sufficient to fund all of a corporation's long-term needs.

        1) Also, maintaining the entity's optimal capital structure requires the issuance of new securities at some point.

    b. The marginal cost of capital is the cost to the entity of the next monetary unit of new capital raised after existing internal sources are exhausted. Each additional monetary unit raised becomes increasingly expensive as investors demand higher returns to compensate for increased risk.

EXAMPLE

A company has determined that it requires US $4,000,000 of new funding to fulfill its plans. Retained earnings are insufficient, and the entity wants to maintain its capital structure of 30% long-term debt and 70% equity. The cost of raising the US $2,800,000 shortfall between retained earnings and funding needs will be at some rate above the current WACC.

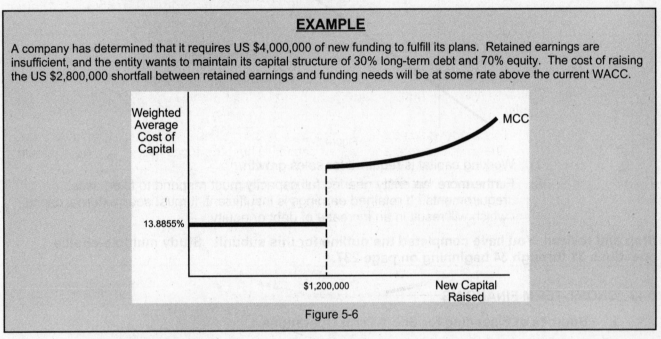

Figure 5-6

---

4. **Cost of New Capital**

    a. Because of interest rate fluctuations, the cost of new debt will rarely be the historical, or embedded, rate. Also, if the entity's debt load is already considerable, new debtholders will demand a higher interest rate to compensate for the increased risk.

        Interest rate on new debt – (Interest rate × Marginal tax rate)

        1) As tax rates rise, the deductibility of interest makes debt a more attractive financing option.

    b. The calculation of the per-share cost of new equity uses a form of the dividend growth model.

        1) This model assumes that shareholders will demand increasing dividends over time and the dividend payout ratio will remain constant.

        (Next dividend ÷ Net issue proceeds) + Dividend growth rate

    c. The use of internally generated capital (i.e., retained earnings) involves a lower cost than either debt or equity because the entity incurs no cost of registering and issuing securities.

        1) The cost of retained earnings is the rate of return shareholders require on equity capital. This is an opportunity cost.

5. **Funds Needed Line**

    a. To ensure short-term and long-term survival, entities use budgeting and financial forecasts. Additional funds needed must be calculated to avoid shortages of working capital and provide for capital expansion.

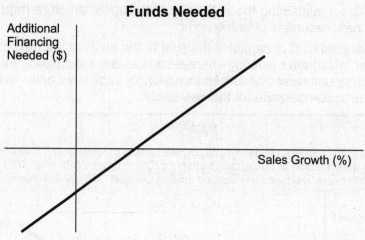

Funds Needed

Figure 5-7

    1) Working capital is required for sales growth.

    2) Furthermore, an entity nearing full capacity must respond to fixed asset requirements. If retained earnings is insufficient, it must seek external capital, which will result in an increase of debt or equity.

Stop and review! You have completed the outline for this subunit. Study multiple-choice questions 31 through 34 beginning on page 237.

5.12 SHORT-TERM FINANCING

1. **Sources of Financing for Short-Term Operations**

    a. Spontaneous sources (those that arise in the normal course of business)
    b. Commercial banks
    c. Market-traded instruments

2. **Spontaneous Forms of Financing**

    a. Trade credit arises when a company is offered credit terms by its suppliers as described in item 3. in Study Unit 3, Subunit 7.

        1) For example, a vendor has delivered goods for US $160,000 on terms of net 30. The entity has effectively gotten a 30-day interest-free US $160,000 loan.

    b. Accrued expenses, such as salaries, wages, interest, dividends, and taxes payable, are another source of (interest-free) spontaneous financing.

        1) For instance, employees work 5, 6, or 7 days a week but are only paid every 2 weeks. An entity carries on operations constantly but must only remit federal income taxes every quarter.

        2) Accruals have the additional advantage of fluctuating directly with operating activity, satisfying the matching principle.

   c.   **Check float.** The float period is the time between when a check is written and when it clears the payor's checking account. Check float results in an interest-free loan to the payor because of the delay between payment by check and its subtraction from the bank account.

      1)   For example, assume that (a) the total of checks written by an entity equals the total of checks received and (b) checks written require 1 more day to clear than checks received. The net float is therefore positive. In the situation, it equals 1 day's receipts.

3.   **Cost of Not Taking a Discount**

   a.   If an early payment discount is offered, it is usually to the entity's advantage to take the discount. The annualized cost of not taking a discount can be calculated with the following formula:

$$\frac{Discount\ \%}{100\% - Discount\ \%} \times \frac{Days\ in\ year}{Total\ payment\ period - Discount\ period}$$

EXAMPLE

A vendor has delivered goods on terms of 2/10, net 30. The entity has chosen to pay on day 30. The effective rate the entity paid by forgoing the discount is calculated as follows (using a 360-day year):

Cost of not taking discount = [2% ÷ (100% − 2%)] × [360 days ÷ (30 days − 10 days)]
                              = (2% ÷ 98%) × (360 days ÷ 20 days)
                              = 2.0408% × 18
                              = 36.73%

The entity chose to finance US $160,000 for 20 days (30 − 10) rather than pay US $156,800 ($160,000 × 98%) after 10 days. In effect, the entity paid US $3,200 ($160,000 − $156,800) to delay payment for 20 days.

---

      1)   Only entities in dire cash flow situations would incur a 36.73% cost of funds.

4.   **Formal Financing Arrangements**

   a.   Commercial banks offer short-term financing in the form of term loans and lines of credit.

      1)   A term loan is one that must be repaid by a date certain, such as a note.

      2)   A line of credit allows an entity to continuously reborrow amounts up to a certain ceiling, as long as certain minimum payments are made each month (similar to a consumer's credit card).

5.   **Simple Interest Loans**

   a.   A simple interest loan is one in which the interest is paid at the end of the loan term. The effective rate on the loan is the same as the nominal (stated) rate. The relevant formulas are presented here:

Amount needed = Invoice amount × (1.0 − Discount %)

Interest expense = Amount needed × Stated rate

EXAMPLE

An entity has received an invoice for US $120,000 with terms of 2/10, net 30. It wishes to take the discount but does not have sufficient cash. However, the entity's bank will lend it the necessary amount for 30 days at a nominal annual rate of 6%, due at the end of the loan term.

      Amount needed = Invoice amount × (1.0 − Discount %)
                     = US $120,000 × (100% − 2%)
                     = US $120,000 × 98%
                     = US $117,600

   Interest expense (annualized) = Amount needed × Stated rate
                              = US $117,600 × 6%
                              = US $7,056

6. **Effective Interest Rate on a Loan**

   a. The effective rate on any financing arrangement is the ratio of the amount the entity must pay to the amount it receives. The most basic statement of this ratio uses the dollar amounts generated by the equations illustrated in the previous example.

$$Effective\ interest\ rate = \frac{Net\ interest\ expense}{Usable\ funds}$$

   b. As mentioned above, the effective rate and the nominal rate on a simple interest loan are the same.

EXAMPLE

The entity calculates the effective rate on this loan as follows:

Effective rate = Net interest expense (annualized) ÷ Usable funds
= US $7,056 ÷ $117,600
= 6.0%

---

7. **Discounted Loans**

   a. A discounted loan is one in which the interest is paid at the beginning of the loan term.

$$Total\ borrowings = \frac{Amount\ needed}{(1.0 - Stated\ rate)}$$

EXAMPLE

A company needs to pay a US $90,000 invoice. Its bank has offered to extend this amount at an 8% nominal rate on a discounted basis.

Total borrowings = Amount needed ÷ (1.0 – Stated rate)
= US $90,000 ÷ (100% – 8%)
= US $90,000 ÷ 92%
= US $97,826

Effective rate = Net interest expense (annualized) ÷ Usable funds
= (US $97,826 × 8%) ÷ $90,000
= US $7,826 ÷ $90,000
= 8.696%

---

   1) Because the borrower gets the use of a smaller amount, the effective rate on a discounted loan is higher than its nominal rate.

   b. As with all financing arrangements, the effective rate can be calculated without reference to monetary amounts:

$$Effective\ rate\ on\ discounted\ loan = \frac{Stated\ rate}{(1.0 - Stated\ rate)}$$

EXAMPLE

The entity calculates the effective rate on this loan without using monetary amounts:

Effective rate = Stated rate ÷ (1.0 – Stated rate)
= 8% ÷ (100% – 8%)
= 8% ÷ 92%
= 8.696%

---

8. **Loans with Compensating Balances**

   a. Rather than charge cash interest, banks will sometimes require borrowers to maintain a compensating balance during the term of a financing arrangement.

$$Total\ borrowings = \frac{Amount\ needed}{(1.0 - Compensating\ balance\ \%)}$$

EXAMPLE

A company has received an invoice for US $120,000 with terms of 2/10, net 30. It wishes to take the discount but does not have sufficient cash. However, the entity's bank will lend it the necessary amount for 30 days at a nominal annual rate of 6% with a compensating balance of 10%.

Total borrowings = Amount needed ÷ (1.0 − Compensated balance %)
= (US $120,000 × 98%) ÷ (100% − 10%)
= US $117,600 ÷ 90%
= US $130,667

Effective rate = Net interest expense (annualized) ÷ Usable funds
= (US $130,667 × 6%) ÷ $117,600
= US $7,840 ÷ $117,600
= 6.667%

---

1) As with a discounted loan, the borrower has access to a smaller amount than the face amount of the loan and so pays an effective rate higher than the nominal rate.

b. Once again, the monetary amounts involved are not needed to determine the effective rate.

$$Effective\ rate\ with\ comp.\ balance = \frac{Stated\ rate}{(1.0 - Compensating\ balance\ \%)}$$

EXAMPLE

Effective rate = Standard rate ÷ (1.0 − Compensating balance %)
= 6% ÷ (100% − 10%)
= 6% ÷ 90%
= 6.667%

---

9. **Market-Based Instruments**

a. Bankers' acceptances are drafts drawn by a nonfinancial entity on deposits at a bank.

1) The acceptance by the bank is a guarantee of payment at maturity. The payee can thus rely on the creditworthiness of the bank rather than on that of the (presumably riskier) drawer.

2) Because they are backed by the prestige of a large bank, these instruments are highly marketable once they have been accepted.

b. Commercial paper consists of short-term, unsecured notes payable issued in large denominations (US $100,000 or more) by large corporations with high credit ratings to other corporations and institutional investors, such as pension funds, banks, and insurance companies.

1) Maturities of commercial paper are at most 270 days. No general secondary market exists for commercial paper. Commercial paper is a lower-cost source of funds than bank loans. It is usually issued at below the prime rate.

2) The advantages of commercial paper are that it (a) provides broad and efficient distribution, (b) provides a great amount of funds (at a given cost), and (c) avoids costly financing arrangements.

3) The disadvantages are that (a) dealings in the market are less personal than relationships with banks and (b) the funds available are limited to the excess liquidity of big corporations.

10. **Secured Financing**

    a.   Loans can be secured by pledging receivables, i.e., committing the proceeds of the receivables to paying off the loan. A bank will often lend up to 80% of outstanding receivables, depending upon the average age of the accounts and the assessed likelihood of their collectibility.

    b.   Warehouse financing uses inventory as security for the loan.

        1)   A third party, such as a public warehouse, holds the collateral and serves as the creditor's agent, and the creditor receives the terminal warehouse receipts as evidence of its rights in the collateral.

        2)   A field warehouse is established when the warehouser takes possession of the inventory on the debtor's property. The inventory is released (often from a fenced-in area) as needed for sale. Warehouse receipts may be negotiable or nonnegotiable.

11. **Factoring Receivables**

    a.   When an entity pledges receivables, the entity retains ownership of the accounts and simply commits to sending the proceeds to a creditor. Under a factoring arrangement, the entity sells the accounts receivable outright. The financing cost is usually high.

        1)   However, an entity that uses a factor can eliminate its credit department and accounts receivable staff. Also, bad debts are eliminated from the statement of financial position. These reductions in costs can more than offset the fee charged by the factor. The factor can often operate more efficiently than its clients because of the specialized nature of its service.

    b.   Before the advent of computers, factoring was often considered a last-resort source of financing, used only when bankruptcy was imminent. However, the factor's computerization of receivables means it can operate a receivables department more economically than most small entities. Factoring is no longer viewed as an undesirable source of financing.

Stop and review! You have completed the outline for this subunit. Study multiple-choice questions 35 through 39 beginning on page 238.

5.13 BUSINESS DEVELOPMENT LIFE CYCLES

1. **Business Development Life Cycles**

    a.   The business life cycle interacts with product life cycles and the overall economic cycle. For example, successful new product introductions may increase sales and profits during a recession.

    b.   In the formative stage, the emerging entity most likely relies on the personal resources of its owners, assistance from governmental agencies, and trade credit for its financing needs.

    c.   If the entity is successful and enters the stage of rapid growth, internal financing becomes feasible, and trade credit continues to be used. Moreover, the entity's performance may enable it to secure bank credit to meet seasonal needs and intermediate-term loans. Such an entity also may attract equity financing from venture capitalists.

        1)   If the entity is extremely successful, it may be able to issue securities that are publicly traded. Thus, the entity may enter the formal capital and money markets. These markets provide financing at lower cost than venture capitalists.

d.   The entity must consider the limitations of the product life cycle. Absent the development of new products, growth will not continue, and the entity will enter the product maturity and decline stage. The financing pattern at this stage usually includes internal financing, diversification, share repurchases, and mergers.

e.   Another perspective on life cycles compares the entity's growth rate with the economy's.

   1)   Thus, during the early stages of the cycle, the entity's rate is much greater than that of the economy. Later, the rates tend to be about the same. In the decline stage, the entity's growth rate is lower than the economy's.

   2)   Accordingly, its earnings, dividends, and share price fall. Entities with growth rates that do not approximate the economy's growth rate are nonconstant growth entities. Calculations using the dividend growth model are more complicated for such entities.

Stop and review! You have completed the outline for this subunit. Study multiple-choice question 40 on page 239.

QUESTIONS

5.1   Financial Statement Analysis -- Liquidity Ratios

1. The following are the January 1 and June 30 statements of financial position of an entity (in millions):

	Jan. 1	June 30
Cash	US $ 3	US $ 4
Accounts receivable	5	4
Inventories	8	10
Fixed assets	10	11
Total assets	US $26	US $29
Accounts payable	US $ 2	US $ 3
Notes payable	4	3
Accrued wages	1	2
Long-term debt	9	11
Equity	10	10
Total liabilities and equity	US $26	US $29

From January 1 to June 30, the net working capital

A. Decreased by US $1 million.

B. Stayed the same.

C. Increased by US $1 million.

D. Increased by US $2 million.

Answer (C) is correct. *(CIA, adapted)*
   REQUIRED: The behavior of the net working capital.
   DISCUSSION: Net working capital equals current assets (for this entity, cash, accounts receivable, and inventories) minus current liabilities (accounts payable, notes payable, accrued wages). From January 1 to June 30, the net working capital increased by US $1,000,000 {[($4 + $4 + $10) − ($3 + $3 + $2)] − [($3 + $5 + $8) − ($2 + $4 + $1)]}.
   Answer (A) is incorrect. A decrease of US $1,000,000 results from omitting inventories. Answer (B) is incorrect. The difference between all assets and all liabilities stayed the same. Answer (D) is incorrect. An increase of US $2,000,000 results from omitting accrued wages.

Questions 2 through 4 are based on the following information.

RST Corporation's Statements of Financial Position
End of Year 5 and Year 6

Assets	Year 6	Year 5
Current assets:		
Cash	US $ 5,000	US $ 4,000
Marketable securities	3,000	2,000
Accounts receivable (net)	16,000	14,000
Inventory	30,000	20,000
Total current assets	$ 54,000	$ 40,000
Noncurrent assets:		
Long-term investments	11,000	11,000
PP&E	80,000	70,000
Intangibles	3,000	4,000
Total assets	US $148,000	US $125,000
Liabilities and Equity		
Current liabilities:		
Accounts payable	US $ 11,000	US $ 7,000
Accrued payables	1,000	1,000
Total current liabilities	$ 12,000	$ 8,000
Bonds payable, 10%, due Year 12	30,000	30,000
Total liabilities	US $ 42,000	US $ 38,000
Equity:		
Common stock,		
2,400 shares, US $10 par	US $ 24,000	US $ 24,000
Retained earnings	82,000	63,000
Total equity	$106,000	$ 87,000
Total liabilities and equity	US $148,000	US $125,000

The market value of RST's ordinary shares at the end of Year 6 was US $100 per share.

2. What is RST's current ratio at the end of Year 6?

A. 4.5 to 1.

B. 2.4 to 1.

C. 2.0 to 1.

D. 1.5 to 1.

Answer (A) is correct. *(CIA, adapted)*
REQUIRED: The current ratio at the end of Year 6.
DISCUSSION: The current ratio equals current assets divided by current liabilities. At the end of Year 6, it was 4.5 to 1 (US $54,000 ÷ $12,000).
Answer (B) is incorrect. A ratio of 2.4 to 1 results from dividing current liabilities by the amount of cash, which is not a meaningful ratio. Answer (C) is incorrect. A ratio of 2.0 to 1 is the quick (acid-test) ratio (cash, marketable securities, and net receivables divided by total current liabilities). Answer (D) is incorrect. A ratio of 1.5 to 1 results from dividing total current liabilities by the sum of cash and marketable securities, which is not a meaningful ratio.

3. What is RST's acid-test (or quick) ratio at the end of Year 6?

A. 2.40 to 1.

B. 2.18 to 1.

C. 2.00 to 1.

D. 1.50 to 1.

Answer (C) is correct. *(CIA, adapted)*
REQUIRED: The acid-test ratio at the end of Year 6.
DISCUSSION: The acid-test or quick ratio equals the sum of the quick assets (net accounts receivable, marketable securities, and cash) divided by current liabilities. This ratio at the end of Year 6 is 2.0 to 1 [(US $5,000 + $3,000 + $16,000) ÷ $12,000].
Answer (A) is incorrect. A ratio of 2.4 to 1 results from dividing total current liabilities (US $12,000) by the amount of cash (US $5,000), which is not a meaningful ratio. Answer (B) is incorrect. A ratio of 2.18 to 1 results from dividing quick assets (US $5,000 + $3,000 + $16,000) by accounts payable (US $11,000) results in 2.18. The denominator should include all current liabilities other than accounts payable. Answer (D) is incorrect. A ratio of 1.5 to 1 results from dividing total current liabilities (US $12,000) by the sum of cash (US $5,000) and marketable securities (US $3,000), which is not a meaningful ratio.

4. Based on a comparison of RST's quick ratios in Year 5 and Year 6, what is a likely conclusion?

A. RST has improved its management of long-term investments in Year 6.

B. RST has written off obsolete inventory in Year 6.

C. RST's ability to meet short-term financing needs has declined since Year 5.

D. RST's ability to meet short-term financing needs has improved since Year 5.

Answer (C) is correct. *(CIA, adapted)*
REQUIRED: The likely conclusion based on a comparison of consecutive-year quick ratios.
DISCUSSION: RST's quick ratio decreased from 2.5 in Year 5 [(US $4,000 cash + $2,000 marketable securities + $14,000 net A/R) ÷ $8,000] to 2.0 in Year 6 [(US $5,000 + $3,000 + $16,000) ÷ $12,000]. RST has fewer assets that are easily convertible to cash available to meet current liabilities. Thus, its ability to meet short-term financing needs (i.e., liquidity) has declined.
Answer (A) is incorrect. The quick ratio compares the quick assets (current assets minus inventory) with current liabilities; it does not provide a basis for conclusions about long-term investments. Answer (B) is incorrect. The quick ratio does not consider inventory. Answer (D) is incorrect. RST is less liquid in Year 6.

5.2 Financial Statement Analysis -- Activity Ratios

Question 5 is based on the following information. Presented below are partial year-end financial statement data for entities A and B.

	A	B
Cash	US $100	US $200
Accounts receivable	unknown	100
Inventories	unknown	100
Net fixed assets	200	100
Accounts payable	100	50
Long-term debt	200	50
Common stock	100	200
Retained earnings	150	100

	A	B
Sales	US $600	US $5,800
Cost of goods sold	300	5,000
Administrative expenses	100	500
Depreciation expense	100	100
Interest expense	20	10
Income tax expense	40	95
Net income	40	95

5. Based on 365 days per year, B has days' sales outstanding to the nearest full day of

A. 0 days.

B. 3 days.

C. 6 days.

D. 7 days.

Answer (C) is correct. *(CIA, adapted)*
REQUIRED: The days' sales outstanding for Company B.
DISCUSSION: Days' sales in receivables (the average collection period) equals the days in the year divided by the receivables turnover ratio (net credit sales ÷ average accounts receivable). Assuming sales are net credit sales and that ending accounts receivable equals average accounts receivable, the turnover ratio is 58 (US $5,800 ÷ $100), and the days' sales in receivables equals 6 days (365 ÷ 58) (rounded).
Answer (A) is incorrect. Accounts receivable divided by sales equals 0 days. Answer (B) is incorrect. If accounts payable is used rather than accounts receivable, the result is 3 days. Answer (D) is incorrect. If average cost of goods sold per day is used rather than sales, the result is 7 days.

Question 6 is based on the following information.

UVW Corporation's Income Statement for Year 5 and Year 6

	Year 6	Year 5
Sales (all are credit)	US $285,000	US $200,000
Cost of goods sold	150,000	120,000
Gross profit	$135,000	$ 80,000
S and A expense	65,000	36,000
Income bef. int. & inc. tax	$ 70,000	$ 44,000
Interest expense	3,000	3,000
Income before income tax	$ 67,000	$ 41,000
Income tax expense	27,000	16,000
Net income	US $ 40,000	US $ 25,000

UVW Corporation's Statements of Financial Position
End of Year 5 and Year 6

Assets	Year 6	Year 5
Current assets:		
Cash	US $ 5,000	US $ 4,000
Marketable securities	3,000	2,000
Accounts receivable (net)	16,000	14,000
Inventory	30,000	20,000
Total current assets	$ 54,000	$ 40,000
Noncurrent assets:		
Long-term investments	11,000	11,000
PP&E	80,000	70,000
Intangibles	3,000	4,000
Total assets	US $148,000	US $125,000

Liabilities and Equity		
Current liabilities:		
Accounts payable	US $ 11,000	US $ 7,000
Accrued payables	1,000	1,000
Total current liabilities	$ 12,000	$ 8,000
Bonds payable, 10%, due Year 12	30,000	30,000
Total liabilities	US $ 42,000	US $ 38,000
Equity:		
Common stock,		
2,400 shares, US $10 par	US $ 24,000	US $ 24,000
Retained earnings	82,000	63,000
Total equity	$106,000	$ 87,000
Total liabilities and equity	US $148,000	US $125,000

The market value of UVW's common stock at the end of Year 6 was US $100 per share.

6. What is UVW's accounts receivable turnover for Year 6?

A. 19 times.

B. 16 times.

C. 10 times.

D. 6 times.

Answer (A) is correct. *(CIA, adapted)*
REQUIRED: The accounts receivable turnover for Year 6.
DISCUSSION: The accounts receivable turnover equals net credit sales divided by average trade receivables (net). In Year 6, the accounts receivable turned over 19 times {US $285,000 ÷ [($16,000 ending A/R + $14,000 beginning A/R) ÷ 2]}.

Answer (B) is incorrect. It was incorrectly derived by dividing average sales of Years 5 and 6 [(US $285,000 + $200,000) ÷ 2] by average receivables (US $15,000), which produces no meaningful ratio. Answer (C) is incorrect. It was incorrectly derived by dividing cost of goods sold (US $150,000) for Year 6 by average accounts receivable (US $15,000), which produces no meaningful ratio. Answer (D) is incorrect. It is the inventory turnover ratio, which equals the cost of goods sold for Year 6 (US $150,000) divided by average inventory (US $25,000).

Question 7 is based on the following information. An entity had the following opening and closing inventory balances during the current year:

	1/1	12/31
Finished goods	US $ 90,000	US $260,000
Raw materials	105,000	130,000
Work-in-progress	220,000	175,000

The following transactions and events occurred during the current year:

- US $300,000 of raw materials were purchased, of which US $20,000 were returned because of defects.

- US $600,000 of direct labor costs were incurred.

- US $750,000 of production overhead costs were incurred.

7. Assume that cost of goods sold for the current year ended December 31 is US $2,000,000. Inventory turnover on total inventory for the entity would be

A. 2.04 times.

B. 3.54 times.

C. 4.08 times.

D. 4.82 times.

Answer (C) is correct. *(CIA, adapted)*
 REQUIRED: The inventory turnover on total inventory.
 DISCUSSION: Inventory turnover is the ratio of cost of goods sold to the average inventory balance. The total average inventory is US $490,000 [($90,000 BFG + $105,000 BRM + $220,000 BWIP + $260,000 EFG + $130,000 ERM + $175,000 EWIP) ÷ 2]. Hence, total inventory turnover is 4.08 times (US $2,000,000 COGS ÷ $490,000 average total inventory).
 Answer (A) is incorrect. A turnover of 2.04 times results from adding all inventory balances, opening and closing, to obtain the denominator of the turnover ratio. Answer (B) is incorrect. A turnover of 3.54 times results from using the year-end inventory balances only. Answer (D) is incorrect. A turnover of 4.82 times results from using the opening inventory balances only.

5.3 Financial Statement Analysis -- Solvency Ratios

8. An entity purchased a new machine for US $500,000 by borrowing the required funds from a bank for 180 days. What will be the direct impact of this transaction?

A. Decrease the current ratio and increase the debt ratio.

B. Increase the current ratio and decrease the debt ratio.

C. Increase the current ratio and increase the debt ratio.

D. Decrease the current ratio and decrease the debt ratio.

Answer (A) is correct. *(CIA, adapted)*
 REQUIRED: The direct effect of purchasing a new machine on the current and the debt ratios.
 DISCUSSION: The borrowing of funds for 180 days constitutes short-term borrowing. The new machine is a fixed asset. Current liabilities have increased, and current assets have remained constant. Consequently, the current ratio (current assets ÷ current liabilities) has decreased. Total debt and total assets increased by the same absolute amount, and the debt ratio (total debt ÷ total assets) should have increased, assuming total debt is less than total assets.

Question 9 is based on the following information.

UVW Corporation's Income Statement for Year 5 and Year 6

	Year 6	Year 5
Sales (all are credit)	US $285,000	US $200,000
Cost of goods sold	150,000	120,000
Gross profit	$135,000	$ 80,000
S and A expense	65,000	36,000
Income bef. int. & inc. tax	$ 70,000	$ 44,000
Interest expense	3,000	3,000
Income before income tax	$ 67,000	$ 41,000
Income tax expense	27,000	16,000
Net income	US $ 40,000	US $ 25,000

UVW Corporation's Statements of Financial Position
End of Year 5 and Year 6

Assets	Year 6	Year 5
Current assets:		
Cash	US $ 5,000	US $ 4,000
Marketable securities	3,000	2,000
Accounts receivable (net)	16,000	14,000
Inventory	30,000	20,000
Total current assets	$ 54,000	$ 40,000
Noncurrent assets:		
Long-term investments	11,000	11,000
PP&E	80,000	70,000
Intangibles	3,000	4,000
Total assets	US $148,000	US $125,000
Liabilities and Equity		
Current liabilities:		
Accounts payable	US $ 11,000	US $ 7,000
Accrued payables	1,000	1,000
Total current liabilities	$ 12,000	$ 8,000
Bonds payable, 10%, due Year 12	30,000	30,000
Total liabilities	US $ 42,000	US $ 38,000
Equity:		
Common stock,		
2,400 shares, US $10 par	US $ 24,000	US $ 24,000
Retained earnings	82,000	63,000
Total equity	$106,000	$ 87,000
Total liabilities and equity	US $148,000	US $125,000

The market value of UVW's common stock at the end of Year 6 was US $100 per share.

9. Based on a comparison of UVW's times-interest-earned ratios in Year 5 and Year 6, what is a likely conclusion?

A. UVW's long-run solvency has declined.

B. UVW's long-run solvency has improved.

C. UVW's liquidity has improved.

D. UVW's liquidity has declined.

Answer (B) is correct. *(CIA, adapted)*
REQUIRED: The likely conclusion based on a comparison of times-interest-earned ratios in Year 5 and Year 6.
DISCUSSION: The times-interest-earned ratio increased from 14.67 times in Year 5 (44,000 ÷ 3,000) to 23.33 times in Year 6 (70,000 ÷ 3,000). This increase signifies that UVW has more profit available to meet the interest payments on its debt and that long-run solvency has improved. Consequently, creditors will view UVW's obligations as less risky.
Answer (A) is incorrect. Long-run solvency has improved. Answer (C) is incorrect. Liquidity is an entity's short-term solvency, that is, its ability to meet current liabilities with current assets by converting assets to cash. It is not related to the times-interest-earned ratio, which compares profit before interest and taxes with interest expense associated with long-term investments. Answer (D) is incorrect. The times-interest-earned ratio is not a liquidity measure.

Question 10 is based on the following information. Presented below are partial year-end financial statement data for entities A and B.

	A	B
Cash	US $100	US $200
Accounts receivable	unknown	100
Inventories	unknown	100
Net fixed assets	200	100
Accounts payable	100	50
Long-term debt	200	50
Common stock	100	200
Retained earnings	150	100

	A	B
Sales	US $600	US $5,800
Cost of goods sold	300	5,000
Administrative expenses	100	500
Depreciation expense	100	100
Interest expense	20	10
Income tax expense	40	95
Net income	40	95

10. The degree of financial leverage (DFL) of B, to two decimal places, is

A. 1.03

B. 1.05

C. 1.12

D. 1.25

Answer (B) is correct. *(CIA, adapted)*
REQUIRED: The degree of financial leverage for B.
DISCUSSION: The degree of financial leverage equals profit before interest and taxes divided by profit before taxes. Profit before interest and taxes for B is US $200 ($95 profit + $10 interest + $95 tax expense). Thus, the DFL is 1.05 [$200 ÷ ($200 − $10)].

Answer (A) is incorrect. This ratio would be the result if depreciation expense were omitted from the calculation of profit before interest and tax. Answer (C) is incorrect. This ratio would be the result if profit were used instead of profit before interest and taxes for B. Answer (D) is incorrect. This ratio is the degree of financial leverage for A.

5.4 Financial Statement Analysis -- ROI and Profitability

11. Return on investment (ROI) is a very popular measure employed to evaluate the performance of corporate segments because it incorporates all of the major ingredients of profitability (revenue, cost, investment) into a single measure. Under which one of the following combination of actions regarding a segment's revenues, costs, and investment would a segment's ROI always increase?

	Revenues	Costs	Investment
A.	Increase	Decrease	Increase
B.	Decrease	Decrease	Decrease
C.	Increase	Increase	Increase
D.	Increase	Decrease	Decrease

Answer (D) is correct. *(CIA, adapted)*
REQUIRED: The circumstances in which ROI always increases.
DISCUSSION: An increase in revenue and a decrease in costs will increase the ROI numerator. A decrease in investment will decrease the denominator. The ROI must increase in this situation.

Answer (A) is incorrect. ROI is not certain to increase if investment increases. Answer (B) is incorrect. ROI is not certain to increase if revenue, costs, and investment decrease. Answer (C) is incorrect. ROI is not certain to increase if costs and investment increase.

Question 12 is based on the following information.
An entity reports the following account balances at year end:

Account	Balance
Long-term debt	US $200,000
Cash	50,000
Net sales	600,000
Fixed assets (net)	320,000
Tax expense	67,500
Inventory	25,000
Common stock	100,000
Interest expense	20,000
Administrative expense	35,000
Retained earnings	150,000
Accounts payable	65,000
Accounts receivable	120,000
Cost of goods sold	400,000
Depreciation expense	10,000

Additional Information:

The opening balance of common stock was US $100,000.

The opening balance of retained earnings was US $82,500.

The entity had 10,000 common stock outstanding all year.

No dividends were paid during the year.

12. For the year just ended, the entity had a rate of return on equity, rounded to two decimals, of

A. 31.21%

B. 58.06%

C. 67.50%

D. 71.68%

Answer (A) is correct. *(CIA, adapted)*
REQUIRED: The rate of return on equity for the year just ended.
DISCUSSION: Rate of return on equity, a profitability ratio, measures the rate of return on investment. The ratio equals profit (minus any preferred dividends) divided by average ordinary equity.

$$\frac{Sales - COGS - Adm.\ Exp. - Deprec. - Interest - Tax}{(Beginning\ Ordinary\ Equity + Ending\ Ordinary\ Equity) \div 2}$$

$$= \frac{US\ \$600,000 - \$400,000 - \$35,000 - \$10,000 - \$20,000 - \$67,500}{(US\ \$182,500 + \$250,000) \div 2}$$

$$= \frac{US\ \$67,500}{US\ \$216,250}$$

$$= 31.21\%$$

Answer (B) is incorrect. Excluding common stock from the denominator results in 58.06%. Answer (C) is incorrect. Excluding retained earnings from the denominator results in 67.50%. Answer (D) is incorrect. Excluding interest expense and tax expense from the numerator results in 71.68%.

13. Which of the following financial statement analyses is most useful in determining whether the various expenses of a given entity are higher or lower than industry averages?

A. Horizontal.

B. Vertical.

C. Activity ratio.

D. Defensive-interval ratio.

Answer (B) is correct. *(CIA, adapted)*
REQUIRED: The analysis most useful in determining whether various expenses of an entity are higher or lower than industry averages.
DISCUSSION: Vertical analysis is the expression of each item on a financial statement in a given period in relation to a base figure. On the income statement, each item is stated as a percentage of sales. Thus, the percentages for the entity in question can be compared with industry norms.
Answer (A) is incorrect. A horizontal analysis indicates the proportionate change over a period of time and is useful in trend analysis of an individual entity. Answer (C) is incorrect. Activity ratio analysis includes the preparation of turnover ratios such as those for receivables, inventory, and total assets. Answer (D) is incorrect. The defensive-interval ratio is part of a liquidity analysis.

Question 14 is based on the following information. An entity's financial statements for the current year are presented below:

Statement of Financial Position	
Cash	US $100
Accounts receivable	200
Inventory	50
Net fixed assets	600
Total assets	US $950
Accounts payable	US $140
Long-term debt	300
Share capital	260
Retained earnings	250
Total liabilities and equity	US $950

Statement of Income and Retained Earnings	
Sales	US $3,000
Cost of goods sold	1,600
Gross profit	$1,400
Operations expenses	970
Operating income	$ 430
Interest expense	30
Income before tax	$ 400
Income tax	200
Net income	$ 200
Plus Jan. 1 retained earnings	150
Minus dividends	100
Dec. 31 retained earnings	US $ 250

14. The entity has a dividend-payout ratio of

A. 19.6%

B. 28.6%

C. 40.0%

D. 50.0%

Answer (D) is correct. *(CIA, adapted)*
REQUIRED: The dividend-payout ratio.
DISCUSSION: The dividend-payout ratio is the ratio of dividends paid to profit for the period. Hence, it equals 50.0% (US $100 dividends ÷ $200 profit).
Answer (A) is incorrect. The ratio of dividends paid to the December 31 carrying amount of ordinary equity is 19.6%. Answer (B) is incorrect. The ratio of dividends paid to the sum of beginning retained earnings and profit is 28.6%. Answer (C) is incorrect. The ratio of dividends paid to the December 31 retained earnings is 40.0%.

5.5 Financial Statement Analysis -- Corporate Valuation

15. Entity A has 50,000 common shares and 10,000 preferred shares outstanding at the start of the year on January 1. The preferred shares are entitled to a US $2 per share annual cash dividend, payable on December 31. The entity had net income of US $150,000 for the year. On April 1, the entity issued 15,000 additional common shares for cash.

Entity B is identical to entity A in all respects except that it had 75,000 common shares outstanding for the entire year.

Basic earnings per share for entity B is approximately

A. US $1.73

B. US $1.87

C. US $2.00

D. US $2.27

Answer (A) is correct. *(CIA, adapted)*
REQUIRED: The BEPS for Company B.
DISCUSSION: BEPS equals profit minus preferred dividends, divided by common shares outstanding. Thus, BEPS equals US $1.73 {[$150,000 – (10,000 preferred shares × $2)] ÷ 75,000 common shares}.
Answer (B) is incorrect. Improperly assuming the preferred dividend is US $1 results in US $1.87. Answer (C) is incorrect. Failing to subtract preferred dividends from net income results in US $2.00. Answer (D) is incorrect. Adding the preferred dividends to net income results in US $2.27.

16. In calculating diluted earnings per share when an entity has convertible bonds outstanding, the weighted-average number of common shares outstanding must be <List A> to adjust for the conversion feature of the bonds, and the net income attributable to common shareholders must be <List B> by the amount of interest expense on the bonds, net of tax.

	List A	List B
A.	Increased	Increased
B.	Increased	Decreased
C.	Decreased	Increased
D.	Decreased	Decreased

Answer (A) is correct. *(CIA, adapted)*
REQUIRED: The appropriate calculation of DEPS.
DISCUSSION: The weighted-average number of common shares outstanding must be increased to reflect the shares into which the bonds could be converted. Also, the effect of the bond interest on profit attributable to common shareholders (net income after subtracting preferred dividends) must be eliminated. In this way, diluted earnings per share is calculated as if the bonds had been converted into common shares as of the start of the year.
Answer (B) is incorrect. The net income attributable to common shareholders must be increased. Answer (C) is incorrect. The weighted-average number of common shares outstanding must be increased. Answer (D) is incorrect. Both the weighted-average number of common shares outstanding and the net income attributable to common shareholders must be increased.

Question 17 is based on the following information. An entity reports the following account balances at year end:

Account	Balance
Long-term debt	US $200,000
Cash	50,000
Net sales	600,000
Fixed assets (net)	320,000
Tax expense	67,500
Inventory	25,000
Common stock	100,000
Interest expense	20,000
Administrative expense	35,000
Retained earnings	150,000
Accounts payable	65,000
Accounts receivable	120,000
Cost of goods sold	400,000
Depreciation expense	10,000

Additional Information:

The opening balance of common stock was US $100,000.

The opening balance of retained earnings was US $82,500.

The entity had 10,000 common stock outstanding all year.

No dividends were paid during the year.

17. At year end, the entity has a book value per share of

A. US $10.00

B. US $15.00

C. US $21.63

D. US $25.00

Answer (D) is correct. *(CIA, adapted)*
REQUIRED: The carrying amount per share at year end.
DISCUSSION: Book value per share, based on amounts drawn from the statement of financial position, measures the per share amount that would be received if the entity were liquidated. The book value per share for this entity at year end is US $25 [($100,000 ordinary equity + $150,000 retained earnings) ÷ 10,000 ordinary shares outstanding at year end].
Answer (A) is incorrect. Excluding retained earnings from the numerator results in US $10.00. Answer (B) is incorrect. Excluding ordinary shares from the numerator results in US $15.00. Answer (C) is incorrect. Using average equity results in US $21.63.

5.6 Financial Statement Analysis -- Comprehensive

18. All else being equal, an entity with a higher dividend-payout ratio will have a <List A> debt-to-assets ratio and a <List B> current ratio.

	List A	List B
A.	Higher	Higher
B.	Higher	Lower
C.	Lower	Higher
D.	Lower	Lower

Answer (B) is correct. *(CIA, adapted)*
REQUIRED: The implications of a higher dividend-payout ratio.
DISCUSSION: An entity with a higher dividend-payout ratio is distributing more of its earnings as dividends to ordinary shareholders. It will have less cash and less total assets than a comparable entity with a lower payout ratio. The debt-to-assets ratio will be higher because total assets are lower, and the current ratio will be lower because cash is lower.
Answer (A) is incorrect. The current ratio will be lower. Answer (C) is incorrect. The debt-to-assets ratio will be higher, and the current ratio will be lower. Answer (D) is incorrect. The debt-to-assets ratio will be higher.

5.7 Investments -- Risk and Return

19. Which of the following classes of securities are listed in order from lowest risk/opportunity for return to highest risk/opportunity for return?

A. Corporate first mortgage bonds; corporate income bonds; preferred shares.

B. Corporate income bonds; corporate mortgage bonds; subordinated debentures.

C. Common shares; corporate first mortgage bonds; corporate second mortgage bonds.

D. Preferred shares; ordinary shares; corporate debentures.

Answer (A) is correct. *(CIA, adapted)*
REQUIRED: The correct listing of classes of securities from lowest to highest risk/opportunity for return.
DISCUSSION: The general principle is that risk and return are directly correlated. Corporate first mortgage bonds are less risky than income bonds or shares because they are secured by specific property. In the event of default, the bondholders can have the property sold to satisfy their claims. Holders of first mortgages have rights paramount to those of any other parties, such as holders of second mortgages. Income bonds pay interest only in the event the corporation earns income. Thus, holders of income bonds have less risk than shareholders because meeting the condition makes payment of interest mandatory. Preferred shareholders receive dividends only if they are declared, and the directors usually have complete discretion in this matter. Also, shareholders have claims junior to those of debtholders if the entity is liquidated.
Answer (B) is incorrect. The proper listing is mortgage bonds, subordinated debentures, and income bonds. Debentures are unsecured debt instruments. Their holders have enforceable claims against the issuer even if no income is earned or dividends declared. Answer (C) is incorrect. The proper listing is first mortgage bonds, second mortgage bonds, and ordinary shares. The second mortgage bonds are secured, albeit junior, claims. Answer (D) is incorrect. The proper listing is debentures, preferred shares, and ordinary shares. Holders of ordinary shares cannot receive dividends unless the holders of preferred shares receive the stipulated periodic percentage return, in addition to any arrearages if the preferred shares are cumulative.

20. The risk that securities cannot be sold at a reasonable price on short notice is called

A. Default risk.

B. Interest-rate risk.

C. Purchasing-power risk.

D. Liquidity risk.

Answer (D) is correct. *(CIA, adapted)*
REQUIRED: The term for the risk that securities cannot be sold at a reasonable price on short notice.
DISCUSSION: An asset is liquid if it can be converted to cash on short notice. Liquidity (marketability) risk is the risk that assets cannot be sold at a reasonable price on short notice. If an asset is not liquid, investors will require a higher return than for a liquid asset. The difference is the liquidity premium.
Answer (A) is incorrect. Default risk is the risk that a borrower will not pay the interest or principal on a loan. Answer (B) is incorrect. Interest-rate risk is the risk to which investors are exposed because of changing interest rates. Answer (C) is incorrect. Purchasing-power risk is the risk that inflation will reduce the purchasing power of a given sum of money.

21. The difference between the required rate of return on a given risky investment and that of a risk-free investment with the same expected return is the

A. Risk premium.

B. Coefficient of variation.

C. Standard error of measurement.

D. Beta coefficient.

Answer (A) is correct. *(CIA, adapted)*
REQUIRED: The amount above the risk-free rate that represents the difference between the required rate of return on a risky investment and that of a risk-free investment with the same expected return.
DISCUSSION: The market risk premium is the amount above the risk-free rate required to include average investors to enter the market. The risk premium is the portion of expected return attributed to the increased risk.
Answer (B) is incorrect. The coefficient of variation represents the standard deviation of an investment's returns divided by the mean returns. Answer (C) is incorrect. The standard error represents a measure of variability in the investment's returns. Answer (D) is incorrect. The beta coefficient represents the sensitivity of the investment's returns to the market returns.

5.8 Investments -- Derivatives

22. An entity has recently purchased some shares of a competitor as part of a long-term plan to acquire the competitor. However, it is somewhat concerned that the market price of these shares could decrease over the short run. The entity could hedge against the possible decline in the shares' market price by

    A. Purchasing a call option on those shares.

    B. Purchasing a put option on those shares.

    C. Selling a put option on those shares.

    D. Obtaining a warrant option on those shares.

Answer (B) is correct. *(CIA, adapted)*
    REQUIRED: The means of hedging against the possible decline in the shares' market price.
    DISCUSSION: A put option is the right to sell shares at a given price within a certain period. If the market price falls, the put option may allow the sale of shares at a price above market, and the profit of the option holder will be the difference between the price stated in the put option and the market price, minus the cost of the option, commissions, and taxes. The entity that issues the shares has nothing to do with put (and call) options.
    Answer (A) is incorrect. A call option is the right to purchase shares at a given price within a specified period. Answer (C) is incorrect. Selling a put option could force the entity to purchase additional shares if the option is exercised. Answer (D) is incorrect. A warrant gives the holder a right to purchase shares from the issuer at a given price (it is usually distributed along with debt).

23. The activity of trading futures with the objective of reducing or controlling risk is called

    A. Insuring.

    B. Hedging.

    C. Short-selling.

    D. Factoring.

Answer (B) is correct. *(CIA, adapted)*
    REQUIRED: The name for the activity of trading futures with the objective of reducing or controlling risk.
    DISCUSSION: Hedging is the use of offsetting commitments to minimize the effect of adverse future price movements. Thus, a financial manager may limit many risk exposures by trading in futures markets.
    Answer (A) is incorrect. Insurance is a contract in which the insurer undertakes to guarantee the insured against loss from specified contingencies or perils up to a specified amount. Answer (C) is incorrect. Short-selling is the sale of commodities or shares that are not owned in anticipation of a price decline. Answer (D) is incorrect. Factoring is the sale of accounts receivable.

24. A call option on an ordinary share is more valuable when there is a lower

    A. Market value of the underlying share.

    B. Exercise price on the option.

    C. Time to maturity on the option.

    D. Variability of market price on the underlying share.

Answer (B) is correct. *(CIA, adapted)*
    REQUIRED: The circumstance under which a call option is more valuable.
    DISCUSSION: The lower the exercise price, the more valuable the call option. The exercise price is the price at which the call holder has the right to purchase the underlying share.
    Answer (A) is incorrect. A call option is the right to purchase an ordinary share at a set price for a set time period. If the underlying share has a lower market value, the call option is less, not more, valuable. Answer (C) is incorrect. A call option is less, not more, valuable given less time to maturity. When the option has less time to maturity, the chance that the share price will rise is smaller. Answer (D) is incorrect. A call option is less, not more, valuable if the price of the underlying share is less variable. Less variability means a lower probability of a price increase.

5.9 Corporate Capital Structure -- Debt Financing

25.

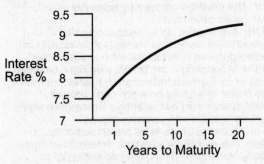

The yield curve shown implies that the

A. Credit risk premium of corporate bonds has increased.

B. Credit risk premium of municipal bonds has increased.

C. Long-term interest rates have a higher annualized yield than short-term rates.

D. Short-term interest rates have a higher annualized yield than long-term rates.

Answer (C) is correct. *(CIA, adapted)*
    REQUIRED: The implication of the yield curve.
    DISCUSSION: The term structure of interest rates is the relationship between yield to maturity and time to maturity. This relationship is depicted by a yield curve. Assuming the long-term interest rate is an average of expected future short-term rates, the curve will be upward sloping when future short-term interest rates are expected to rise. Furthermore, the normal expectation is for long-term investments to pay higher rates because of their higher risk. Thus, long-term interest rates have a higher annualized yield than short-term rates.
    Answer (A) is incorrect. The yield curve does not reflect the credit risk premium of bonds. Answer (B) is incorrect. The yield curve does not reflect the credit risk premium of bonds. Answer (D) is incorrect. Long-term interest rates should be higher than short-term rates.

26. Convertible bonds and bonds issued with warrants differ in that

A. Convertible bonds have lower coupon rates than straight bonds, while bonds issued with warrants have higher coupon rates than straight bonds.

B. Convertible bonds have higher coupon rates than straight bonds, while bonds issued with warrants have lower coupon rates than straight bonds.

C. Convertible bonds remain outstanding after the bondholder exercises the right to become a common shareholder, while bonds that are issued with warrants do not.

D. Bonds that are issued with warrants remain outstanding after the bondholder exercises the right to become a common shareholder, while convertible bonds do not.

Answer (D) is correct. *(CIA, adapted)*
    REQUIRED: The difference between convertible bonds and bonds issued with warrants.
    DISCUSSION: Warrants are usually detachable. They are options to purchase equity securities. The bonds remain outstanding if the warrants are exercised. Convertible bonds must be surrendered when the conversion privilege is exercised.
    Answer (A) is incorrect. Bonds issued with warrants and convertible bonds have lower coupon rates than conventional bonds. Answer (B) is incorrect. Bonds issued with warrants and convertible bonds have lower coupon rates than conventional bonds. Answer (C) is incorrect. Convertible bonds do not remain outstanding.

27. Zero-coupon bonds

A. Sell for a small fraction of their face value because their yield is much lower than the market rate.

B. Increase in value each year as they approach maturity, providing the owner with the total payoff at maturity.

C. Are redeemable in measures of a commodity such as barrels of oil, tons of coal, or ounces of rare metal (e.g., silver).

D. Are high-interest-rate, high-risk, unsecured bonds that have been used extensively to finance leveraged buyouts.

Answer (B) is correct. *(CIA, adapted)*
    REQUIRED: The feature of zero-coupon bonds.
    DISCUSSION: Zero-coupon bonds sell at a deep discount and increase in value each year until maturity. These bonds are not interest-bearing.
    Answer (A) is incorrect. Deep discount bonds pay interest significantly below the market rate, and zero-coupon bonds are not interest-bearing. Answer (C) is incorrect. Commodity-backed bonds are redeemable in measures of a commodity. Answer (D) is incorrect. Junk bonds are high-interest-rate, high-risk, unsecured bonds.

5.10 Corporate Capital Structure -- Equity Financing

28. Common shareholders with preemptive rights are entitled to

A. Vote first at annual meetings.

B. Purchase any additional bonds sold by the entity.

C. Purchase any additional shares sold by the entity.

D. Gain control of the entity in a proxy fight.

Answer (C) is correct. *(CIA, adapted)*
REQUIRED: The privilege enjoyed by common shareholders with preemptive rights.
DISCUSSION: Preemptive rights protect common shareholders' proportional ownership interests from dilution in value. A secondary purpose is to maintain the shareholders' control of the entity. Accordingly, the preemptive right, whether granted by statute or by the corporate charter, grants common shareholders the power to acquire on a pro rata basis any additional common shares sold by the entity. Preemptive rights also apply to debt convertible into common shares.
Answer (A) is incorrect. There is no prescribed order of shareholder voting. Answer (B) is incorrect. Preemptive rights concern only equity ownership. Thus, they do not apply to nonconvertible debt. Answer (D) is incorrect. A proxy fight is an attempt to gain control of an entity by persuading shareholders to grant their voting rights to others.

29. Preferred shares are securities with characteristics of both common shares and bonds. Preferred shares have <List A> like common shares and <List B> like bonds.

	List A	List B
A.	A maturity date	A fixed periodic payment
B.	No maturity date	No fixed periodic payment
C.	A maturity date	No fixed periodic payment
D.	No maturity date	A fixed periodic payment

Answer (D) is correct. *(CIA, adapted)*
REQUIRED: The characteristics of preferred shares.
DISCUSSION: Like common shares (but unlike bonds), preferred shares have no maturity date, although certain preferred shares (transient preferred shares) must be redeemed within a short time (e.g., 5 to 10 years). Like bonds (but unlike common shares), preferred shares have a fixed periodic payment. The fixed payment is in the form of a stated dividend in the case of the preferred shares and interest payments in the case of bonds. However, preferred dividends, unlike interest, do not become an obligation unless declared.
Answer (A) is incorrect. Preferred shares do not have a maturity date. Answer (B) is incorrect. Preferred shares have fixed periodic dividend payments. Answer (C) is incorrect. Preferred shares do not have a maturity date but do have fixed periodic dividend payments.

30. An entity must select from among several methods of financing arrangements when meeting its capital requirements. To acquire additional growth capital while attempting to maximize earnings per share, an entity should normally

A. Attempt to increase both debt and equity in equal proportions, which preserves a stable capital structure and maintains investor confidence.

B. Select debt over equity initially, even though increased debt is accompanied by interest costs and a degree of risk.

C. Select equity over debt initially, which minimizes risk and avoids interest costs.

D. Discontinue dividends and use current cash flow, which avoids the cost and risk of increased debt and the dilution of EPS through increased equity.

Answer (B) is correct. *(CIA, adapted)*
REQUIRED: The financing arrangement that should be selected to acquire additional growth capital while attempting to maximize earnings per share.
DISCUSSION: Earnings per share will ordinarily be higher if debt is used to raise capital instead of equity, provided that the entity is not over-leveraged. The reason is that the cost of debt is lower than the cost of equity because interest is tax deductible. However, the prospect of higher EPS is accompanied by greater risk to the entity resulting from required interest costs, creditors' liens on the entity's assets, and the possibility of a proportionately lower EPS if sales volume fails to meet projections.
Answer (A) is incorrect. EPS is not a function of investor confidence and is not maximized by concurrent proportional increases in both debt and equity. EPS are usually higher if debt is used instead of equity to raise capital, at least initially. Answer (C) is incorrect. Equity capital is initially more costly than debt. Answer (D) is incorrect. Using only current cash flow to raise capital is usually too conservative an approach for a growth-oriented entity. Management is expected to be willing to take acceptable risks to be competitive and attain an acceptable rate of growth.

5.11 Corporate Capital Structure -- Cost of Capital

31. The marginal cost of debt for an entity is defined as the interest rate on <List A> debt minus the <List B>.

	List A	List B
A.	New	Entity's marginal tax rate
B.	Outstanding	Entity's marginal tax rate
C.	New	Interest rate times the entity's marginal tax rate
D.	Outstanding	Interest rate times the entity's marginal tax rate

Answer (C) is correct. *(CIA, adapted)*
REQUIRED: The definition of the marginal cost of debt.
DISCUSSION: The marginal, or incremental, cost of debt is the interest rate on new debt minus the entity's marginal tax rate multiplied by the interest rate.
Answer (A) is incorrect. The relevant interest rate is the one for new debt minus the entity's marginal tax rate multiplied by the interest rate. Answer (B) is incorrect. The marginal cost of debt financing is the interest rate on new debt minus the entity's marginal tax rate multiplied by the interest rate. Moreover, the marginal or incremental cost of debt to the entity is based on the cost of newly issued debt, not on the cost of outstanding debt. Answer (D) is incorrect. The marginal, or incremental, cost of debt is based on the cost of newly issued debt, not the cost of outstanding debt.

32. The marginal cost of capital (MCC) curve for an entity rises twice, first when the entity has raised US $75 million and again when US $175 million of new funds has been raised. These increases in the MCC are caused by

A. Increases in the returns on the additional investments undertaken.

B. Decreases in the returns on the additional investments undertaken.

C. Decreases in the cost of at least one of the financing sources.

D. Increases in the cost of at least one of the financing sources.

Answer (D) is correct. *(CIA, adapted)*
REQUIRED: The reason for the increases in the MCC.
DISCUSSION: The MCC is a weighted average of the costs of various new financing sources. If the cost of any source of new financing increases, the MCC curve will rise. The curve shifts upward with each incremental increase in financing cost because the lowest-cost sources are assumed to be used first.
Answer (A) is incorrect. Financing costs do not directly depend on rates of return on investment. Answer (B) is incorrect. Financing costs do not directly depend on rates of return on investment. Answer (C) is incorrect. As additional funds are raised, an increase in the cost of a source of financing, not a decrease, will result in an increase in the MCC.

33. A firm seeking to optimize its capital budget has calculated its marginal cost of capital and projected rates of return on several potential projects. The optimal capital budget is determined by

A. Calculating the point at which marginal cost of capital meets the projected rate of return, assuming that the most profitable projects are accepted first.

B. Calculating the point at which average marginal cost meets average projected rate of return, assuming the largest projects are accepted first.

C. Accepting all potential projects with projected rates of return exceeding the lowest marginal cost of capital.

D. Accepting all potential projects with projected rates of return lower than the highest marginal cost of capital.

Answer (A) is correct. *(CIA, adapted)*
REQUIRED: The determinant of the optimal capital budget.
DISCUSSION: In economics, a basic principle is that a firm should increase output until marginal cost equals marginal revenue. Similarly, the optimal capital budget is determined by calculating the point at which marginal cost of capital (which increases as capital requirements increase) and marginal efficiency of investment (which decreases if the most profitable projects are accepted first) intersect.
Answer (B) is incorrect. The intersection of average marginal cost with average projected rates of return when the largest (not most profitable) projects are accepted first offers no meaningful capital budgeting conclusion. Answer (C) is incorrect. The optimal capital budget may exclude profitable projects as lower-cost capital goes first to projects with higher rates of return. Answer (D) is incorrect. Accepting projects with rates of return lower than the cost of capital is not rational.

34. When calculating the cost of capital, the cost assigned to retained earnings should be

A. Zero.

B. Lower than the cost of external common equity.

C. Equal to the cost of external common equity.

D. Higher than the cost of external common equity.

Answer (B) is correct. *(CIA, adapted)*
REQUIRED: The cost assigned to retained earnings when calculating cost of capital.
DISCUSSION: Newly issued (i.e., external) common equity is more costly than retained earnings. The company incurs issuance costs when raising new, outside funds.
Answer (A) is incorrect. The cost of retained earnings is the rate of return shareholders require on equity capital the firm obtains by retaining earnings. The opportunity cost of retained funds will be positive. Answer (C) is incorrect. Retained earnings will always be less costly than external equity financing. Earnings retention does not require the payment of issuance costs. Answer (D) is incorrect. Retained earnings will always be less costly than external equity financing. Earnings retention does not require the payment of issuance costs.

5.12 Short-Term Financing

35. The correct equation for calculating the approximate percentage cost, on an annual basis, of not taking trade discounts is

A. $\dfrac{Discount\ \%}{100 - Discount\ \%} \times \dfrac{360}{[Days\ credit\ is\ outstanding - Discount\ period]}$

B. $\dfrac{Discount\ \%}{100} \times \dfrac{360}{[Days\ credit\ is\ outstanding - Discount\ period]}$

C. $\dfrac{100 - Discount\ \%}{Discount\ \%} \times \dfrac{360}{[Days\ credit\ is\ outstanding - Discount\ period]}$

D. $\dfrac{Discount\ \%}{100 - Discount\ \%} \times \dfrac{[Days\ credit\ is\ outstanding - Discount\ period]}{360}$

Answer (A) is correct. *(CIA, adapted)*
REQUIRED: The equation for calculating the percentage cost of not taking trade discounts.
DISCUSSION: The first term of the formula is the periodic cost of the trade discount, calculated as the cost per unit of trade credit (discount %) divided by the funds made available by not taking the discount (100% – discount %). The second term represents the number of times per year this cost is incurred. The multiple of these terms is the approximate annual percentage cost of not taking the trade discount. A precise formula would incorporate the effects of compounding when calculating the annual cost.
Answer (B) is incorrect. The denominator of the first term should represent the funds made available by not taking the discount (100% – discount %). Answer (C) is incorrect. The first term is the reciprocal of the correct term. Answer (D) is incorrect. The second term is the reciprocal of the correct term.

36. An entity has accounts payable of US $5 million with terms of 2% discount within 15 days, net 30 days (2/15, net 30). It can borrow funds from a bank at an annual rate of 12%, or it can wait until the 30th day when it will receive revenues to cover the payment. If it borrows funds on the last day of the discount period in order to obtain the discount, its total cost will be

A. US $51,000 less.

B. US $75,500 less.

C. US $100,000 less.

D. US $24,500 more.

Answer (B) is correct. *(CIA, adapted)*
REQUIRED: The effect on total cost of taking a cash discount.
DISCUSSION: To take advantage of the 2% discount, the entity will need to borrow US $4,900,000 ($5,000,000 × 98%). The interest on this amount for the 15 days until revenues are received to repay it amounts to US $24,500 [$4,900,000 principal × 12% annual interest rate × (15 ÷ 360) duration of loan], and the total cost will be US $4,924,500. The total cost if the discount is not taken will be US $5,000,000, resulting in a savings of US $75,500 by taking out the loan.
Answer (A) is incorrect. US $51,000 less is based on a 30-day borrowing period. Answer (C) is incorrect. US $100,000 less does not consider the interest paid. Answer (D) is incorrect. US $24,500 more reflects interest paid but ignores the discounted price.

37. Why would an entity maintain a compensating cash balance?

A. To make routine payments and collections.

B. To pay for banking services.

C. To provide a reserve in case of unforeseen fluctuations in cash flows.

D. To take advantage of bargain purchase opportunities that may arise.

Answer (B) is correct. *(CIA, adapted)*
REQUIRED: The use of a compensating cash balance.
DISCUSSION: The compensating cash balance is the money left in a checking account in the bank in order to compensate the bank for services it provides.
Answer (A) is incorrect. The cash balance maintained for making routine payments and collections is called the transactions balance. Answer (C) is incorrect. The cash balance maintained as a reserve for unforeseen cash flow fluctuations is called the precautionary balance. Answer (D) is incorrect. It is the speculative cash balance that is maintained in order to enable the entity to take advantage of any bargain purchase opportunities that may arise.

38. An example of secured short-term financing is

A. Commercial paper.

B. A warehouse receipt.

C. A revolving credit agreement.

D. Trade credit.

Answer (B) is correct. *(CIA, adapted)*
    REQUIRED: The example of secured short-term financing.
    DISCUSSION: A warehouse receipt is one of the two major types of documents of title; the other is the bills of lading. A warehouse receipt is issued by a person engaged in the business of storing goods for hire. Security for short-term inventory financing can be arranged if the debtor places its inventory under the control of the lender or its agent (e.g., a public warehouse), and the lender holds the warehouse receipts.
    Answer (A) is incorrect. Commercial paper is a type of unsecured, short-term promissory note issued by large entities to other entities, insurance companies, mutual funds, etc.
Answer (C) is incorrect. A revolving credit agreement is a formal line of credit, usually with a bank, that large entities often use.
Answer (D) is incorrect. Accounts payable, or trade credit, is the most common source of unsecured short-term financing.

39. Factoring is the

A. Selling of accounts receivable by one entity to another.

B. Selling of inventory by one entity to another.

C. Conversion of accounts receivable to bad debt on financial statements for accounts that are long overdue.

D. Adjustment of inventories on financial statements for supplies that have become obsolete.

Answer (A) is correct. *(CIA, adapted)*
    REQUIRED: The definition of factoring.
    DISCUSSION: A factor purchases an entity's accounts receivable and assumes the risk of collection. The seller receives money immediately to reinvest in new inventories. The financing cost is usually high: about 2 points or more above prime, plus a fee for collection. Factoring has been traditional in the textile industry for years, and recently companies in many industries have found it an efficient means of operation. An entity that uses a factor can eliminate its credit department, accounts receivable staff, and bad debts. These reductions in costs can more than offset the fee charged by the factor, which can often operate more efficiently than its clients because of the specialized nature of its service.

5.13 Business Development Life Cycles

40. In which stage of an entity's development is it most likely to seek and obtain external equity financing in the form of venture capital?

A. Formation.

B. Rapid growth.

C. Growth to maturity.

D. Maturity and industry decline.

Answer (B) is correct. *(CIA, adapted)*
    REQUIRED: The stage of development in which venture capital is sought.
    DISCUSSION: At the rapid growth stage, if an entity is reasonably profitable, it will experience financing needs in excess of funds available either internally or from trade credit or bank credit. Additional debt financing often results in an unreasonable amount of financial leverage at this stage, and public equity financing ordinarily is not yet available. Hence, a rapidly growing entity is most likely to seek and obtain venture capital financing.
    Answer (A) is incorrect. During the formation stage, personal savings, trade credit, and government agencies are the main sources of financing. Prior to demonstrating initial success, an entity is not likely to attract venture capital financing easily. Answer (C) is incorrect. In the growth to maturity stage of development, the entity is able to access formal markets for debt and equity. It has a record of success and a better balance between cash inflows and outflows than in the rapid growth stage. Formal capital markets provide financing at lower cost than venture capitalists, so venture capital is not likely to be sought at this stage. Answer (D) is incorrect. The decline phase is characterized by more than adequate cash flows, relative to available investment opportunities, so venture capital is not likely to be sought at this stage of development.

STUDY UNIT SIX
MANAGERIAL ACCOUNTING

(39 pages of outline)

Study Unit 6 covers basic concepts of managerial accounting. One basic concept is **cost behavior**, that is, whether costs are fixed, variable, or some combination. Cost behavior must be understood to plan for entity profitability. This study unit also addresses **cost allocation methods**. These methods are used to assign indirect costs to cost objects. Other subunits apply to costing systems, budgeting, marginal analysis, transfer pricing, and responsibility systems.

6.1 COST MANAGEMENT TERMINOLOGY

1. **Basic Definitions**

   a. A cost is the measure of a resource used up for some purpose.

      1) For financial reporting, a cost can either be capitalized as an asset or expensed.

   b. A cost object is any entity to which costs can be attached.

      1) Examples are products, processes, employees, departments, and facilities.

   c. A cost driver is the basis used to assign costs to a cost object.

      1) A cost driver is an activity measure, such as direct labor hours or machine hours, that is a factor in causing the incurrence of cost.

2. **Manufacturing vs. Nonmanufacturing**

   a. The costs of manufacturing a product can be classified as one of three types:

      1) **Direct materials** are those tangible inputs to the manufacturing process that can feasibly be traced to the product, e.g., sheet metal welded together for a piece of heavy equipment.

         a) All costs of bringing materials to the production line, e.g., transportation-in, are included in the cost of direct materials.

      2) **Direct labor** is the cost of human labor that can feasibly be traced to the product, e.g., the wages of the welder. But an overtime premium is usually treated as overhead.

      3) **Manufacturing overhead** consists of all costs of manufacturing that are not direct materials or direct labor.

         a) Indirect materials are tangible inputs to the manufacturing process that cannot feasibly be traced to the product, e.g., the welding compound used to put together a piece of heavy equipment.

      b)   Indirect labor is the cost of human labor connected with the manufacturing process that cannot feasibly be traced to the product, e.g., the wages of assembly line supervisors and janitorial staff.

      c)   Factory operating costs include utilities, real estate taxes, insurance, depreciation on factory equipment, etc.

b.   Manufacturing costs are often grouped into the following classifications:

    1)   Prime cost equals direct materials plus direct labor, i.e., those costs directly attributable to a product.

    2)   Conversion cost equals direct labor plus manufacturing overhead, i.e., the costs of converting raw materials into the finished product.

c.   The following are nonmanufacturing costs:

    1)   Selling (marketing) costs are incurred in getting the product from the factory to the consumer, e.g., sales personnel salaries and product transportation.

    2)   Administrative expenses are incurred by a company not directly related to producing or marketing the product, e.g., executive salaries and depreciation on the headquarters building.

3.   **Product vs. Period**

a.   One of the most important classifications in managerial accounting is whether to capitalize a cost as part of finished goods inventory or to expense it as incurred.

    1)   **Product costs** (inventoriable costs) are capitalized as part of finished goods inventory. They eventually become a component of cost of goods sold.

    2)   **Period costs** are expensed as incurred. They are not capitalized in finished goods inventory and are thus excluded from cost of goods sold.

b.   This distinction is crucial because of the required treatment of manufacturing costs for external financial reporting purposes.

    1)   All manufacturing costs (direct materials, direct labor, variable overhead, and fixed overhead) must be treated as product costs, and all selling and administrative (S&A) costs must be treated as period costs.

      a)   This approach is called **absorption costing** (full costing).

    2)   For internal reporting, a more useful accounting treatment is often to capitalize only variable manufacturing costs as product costs. All other costs (variable S&A and the fixed portion of both production and S&A expenses) are period costs.

      a)   This approach is called **variable costing** (direct costing).

    3)   The following table summarizes these two approaches:

	Absorption Costing (For external reporting)	Variable Costing (For internal reporting only)
Product Costs (Included in Cost of Goods Sold)	Variable production costs	
	Fixed production costs	
Period Costs		Fixed production costs
	Variable S&A expenses	
(Excluded from Cost of Goods Sold)	Fixed S&A expenses	

      a)   These treatments are explained more fully in Subunit 6.3.

4. **Direct vs. Indirect**

    a. **Direct costs** are associated with a particular cost object in an economically feasible way. They can be traced to that object.

        1) Examples are the direct materials and direct labor inputs to a manufacturing process discussed in item 2.a.

    b. **Indirect costs** cannot be associated with a particular cost object in an economically feasible way and must be allocated to that object.

        1) Examples are the indirect materials and indirect labor inputs to a manufacturing process discussed in item 2.a.3).

        2) To simplify the allocation process, indirect costs are often collected in cost pools.

            a) A cost pool is an account into which similar cost elements with a common cause are accumulated.

            b) Manufacturing overhead is a commonly used cost pool into which various untraceable costs of the manufacturing process are accumulated.

    c. Common costs are indirect costs shared by two or more users.

        1) Because common costs cannot be directly traced to the users that generate the costs, they must be allocated on a systematic and rational basis.

        2) An example is depreciation on the headquarters building. This is a direct cost when accounting for the building as a whole. However, it is a common cost of the departments located in the building and must be allocated to them.

Stop and review! You have completed the outline for this subunit. Study multiple-choice questions 1 through 3 on page 280.

6.2 COST BEHAVIOR AND RELEVANT RANGE

1. **Variable Costs**

    a. Variable cost per unit remains constant in the short run regardless of the level of production.

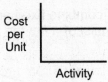

Figure 6-1

However, variable costs in total vary directly and proportionally with changes in volume.

Figure 6-2

EXAMPLE of a Variable Cost

An entity requires one unit of direct material to be used in each finished good it produces.

Number of Outputs Produced	Input Cost per Unit	Total Cost of Inputs
0	US $10	US $ 0
100	10	1,000
1,000	10	10,000
5,000	10	50,000
10,000	10	100,000

2.   Fixed Costs

a.   Fixed costs in total remain unchanged in the short run regardless of production level. For example, the amount paid for an assembly line is the same even if production is halted entirely.

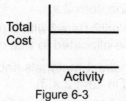

Figure 6-3

b.   However, fixed cost per unit varies indirectly with the activity level.

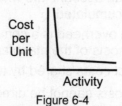

Figure 6-4

EXAMPLE of a Fixed Cost

The historical cost of the assembly line is fixed, but its cost per unit decreases as production increases.

Number of Outputs Produced	Cost of Assembly Line	Per Unit Cost of Assembly Line
100	US $1,000,000	US $10,000
1,000	1,000,000	1,000
5,000	1,000,000	200
10,000	1,000,000	100

3.   Other Cost Behaviors

a.   Mixed (semivariable) costs combine fixed and variable elements. For example, rental expense on a car may consist of a flat fee per month plus an additional fee for each mile driven.

Figure 6-5

EXAMPLE of a Mixed Cost

The entity rents a piece of machinery to make its production line more efficient. The rental is US $150,000 per year plus US $1 for every unit produced.

Number of Outputs Produced	Fixed Cost of Extra Machine	Variable Cost of Extra Machine	Total Cost of Extra Machine
0	US $150,000	US $ 0	US $150,000
100	150,000	100	150,100
1,000	150,000	1,000	151,000
5,000	150,000	5,000	155,000
10,000	150,000	10,000	160,000

b. Sometimes the fixed and variable portions of a mixed cost are not set by contract as in the previous example and thus must be estimated. Two methods of estimating mixed costs are in general use:

1) The high-low method is the less accurate but the easier of the two methods.

a) The difference in cost between the highest and lowest levels of activity (not output) is divided by the difference in the activity level to arrive at the variable portion of the cost.

EXAMPLE of the High-Low Method

An entity has the following cost data:

Month	Machine Hours	Maintenance Costs
April	1,000	US $2,275
May	1,600	3,400
June	1,200	2,650
July	800	1,900
August	1,200	2,650
September	1,000	2,275

The numerator can be derived by subtracting the cost at the lowest level (July) from the cost at the highest level (May) [US $3,400 – $1,900 = US $1,500].

The denominator can be derived by subtracting the lowest level of activity (July) from the highest level (May) [1,600 – 800 = 800].

The variable portion of the cost is therefore US $1.875 per machine hour (US $1,500 ÷ 800).

The fixed portion can be calculated by inserting the appropriate values for either the high or low month in the range:

Fixed portion = Total cost – Variable portion
= US $1,900 – ($1.875 × 800 hours)
= US $1,900 – $1,500
= US $400

---

2) The regression (scattergraph) method is more complex. It determines the average rate of variability of a mixed cost rather than the variability between the high and low points in the range.

4. Linear vs. Nonlinear Cost Functions

a. Four of the five costs described so far in this subunit are linear-cost functions. Thus, they change at a constant rate (or remain unchanged) over the short run.

b. But fixed cost per unit is a nonlinear-cost function.

1) Fixed cost per unit approaches the x axis while never intersecting it. It intersects the y axis at the zero level of activity. The function shows a high degree of variability over its range as a whole (see item 2.b.).

2) Another nonlinear-cost function is a step-cost. It is constant over small ranges of output but increases by steps (discrete amounts) as levels of activity increase.

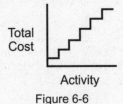

Figure 6-6

a) Both fixed and variable costs can display step-cost characteristics. If the steps are relatively narrow, these costs are usually treated as variable. If the steps are wide, they relate more to fixed costs.

5.   **Relevant Range and Marginal Cost**

a.   The **relevant range** defines the normal limits within which per-unit variable costs remain constant and fixed costs are not changeable. It is valid for a specified time span.

1)   The relevant range is established by such factors as the efficiency of an entity's current manufacturing plant and its agreements with labor unions and suppliers.

b.   Relevant range and marginal cost are related concepts.

1)   Marginal cost is incurred by a one-unit increase in the activity level of a particular cost driver. Accordingly, marginal cost remains constant across the relevant range.

a)   However, the relevant range exists only for a specified time span. Thus, all costs are variable in the long run.

2)   Investment in new, more productive equipment results in higher total fixed costs but may result in lower total and per-unit variable costs.

Stop and review! You have completed the outline for this subunit. Study multiple-choice questions 4 and 5 on page 281.

6.3 ABSORPTION (FULL) VS. VARIABLE (DIRECT) COSTING

1.   **Overview**

a.   Under **absorption costing** (sometimes called full or full absorption costing), the fixed portion of manufacturing overhead is included in the cost of each product.

1)   Product cost thus includes all manufacturing costs, both fixed and variable.

2)   Absorption-basis cost of goods sold is subtracted from sales to arrive at gross margin.

3)   Total selling and administrative (S&A) expenses (i.e., both fixed and variable) are then subtracted from gross margin to arrive at operating income.

4)   For external reporting purposes, product cost should include all manufacturing costs.

b.   **Variable costing** (direct costing) is more appropriate for internal reporting.

1)   Product cost includes only variable manufacturing costs.

2)   Variable cost of goods sold and variable S&A expenses are subtracted from sales to arrive at the contribution margin.

a)   This element (sales – total variable costs) of the variable costing income statement is the amount available for covering fixed costs (both manufacturing and S&A).

b)   For this reason, some accountants call the method contribution margin reporting.

EXAMPLE of Absorption vs. Variable Costing

An entity, during its first month in business, produced 100 units and sold 80 while incurring the following costs:

Direct materials	US $1,000
Direct labor	2,000
Variable overhead	1,500
Manufacturing costs -- variable costing	**US $4,500**
Fixed overhead	3,000
Manufacturing costs -- absorption costing	**US $7,500**

The difference between the two methods is illustrated below:

	Manufacturing Costs	Divided by: Units Produced	Equals: Per-Unit Cost	Times: Units in Ending Inventory	Equals: Cost of Ending Inventory
Absorption costing	US $7,500	100	US $75	20	US $1,500
Variable costing	4,500	100	45	20	900

The per-unit selling price of the finished goods was US $100, and the company incurred US $200 of variable S&A expenses and US $600 of fixed S&A expenses.

The following are partial income statements prepared using the two methods:

		Absorption Costing (External reporting)	Variable Costing (For internal reporting only)
	Sales	**US $ 8,000**	**US $ 8,000**
	Beginning finished goods inventory	US $ 0	US $ 0
Product Costs	Plus: variable production costs	4,500 (a)	4,500 (a)
	Plus: fixed production costs	3,000 (b)	
	Goods available for sale	US $7,500	US $4,500
	Minus: ending finished goods inventory	(1,500)	(900)
	Cost of goods sold	**US $(6,000)**	**US $(3,600)**
	Minus: variable S&A expenses		(200) (c)
	Gross margin (abs.) / Contribution margin (var.)	**US $ 2,000**	**US $ 4,200**
Period Costs	Minus: fixed production costs		(3,000) (b)
	Minus: variable S&A expenses	(200) (c)	
	Minus: fixed S&A expenses	(600) (d)	(600) (d)
	Operating income	**US $ 1,200**	**US $ 600**

The US $600 difference in operating income (US $1,200 – $600) is the **difference between the two ending inventory amounts** (US $1,500 – $900).

Absorption costing reports 20% of fixed overhead costs (US $3,000 × 20% = US $600) in inventory because 20% of the month's production (100 available – 80 sold = 20 on hand) was not sold.

2. **Income Effects**

    a. As production and sales change, the two methods have varying effects on operating income.

        1) When everything produced during a period is sold that period, the two methods report the same operating income. Both recognize total budgeted fixed costs.

b.   When production and sales are not equal, the two methods report different operating income.

1)   ILLUSTRATION:

When production △△△△△△△ **exceeds sales,** △△△	**When production** △'△ △ **is less than sales,** △△△△△△△
ending inventory increases. ↑↑↑↑↑↑↑↑↑↑↑↑↑↑↑	**ending inventory decreases.** ↓↓↓↓↓↓
Under absorption costing, some fixed costs are still in ending inventory.	**Under absorption costing,** fixed costs in beginning inventory are expensed.
Under variable costing, all fixed costs have been expensed.	**Under variable costing,** only the current period's fixed costs are expensed.
Operating income is higher under <u>absorbtion</u> costing.	**Operating income is higher under <u>variable</u> costing.**

Figure 6-7

c.   The diagram above explains why many entities prefer variable costing for internal reporting.

1)   Under absorption costing, operating income increases whenever production exceeds sales.

2)   Thus, a production manager can increase absorption-basis operating income merely by increasing production, regardless of customer demand for the product.

   a)   The carrying costs of inventory also increase.

3)   This practice can be discouraged by using variable costing for performance reporting.

Stop and review! You have completed the outline for this subunit. Study multiple-choice questions 6 through 9 beginning on page 282.

6.4 CAPITAL BUDGETING

1.   **Overview**

a.   Capital budgeting is the process of planning and controlling investments for long-term projects.

1)   A capital project should only be undertaken if management expects it will increase shareholder value. Thus, the adequate measurement of a potential project's future net cash flows is crucial to the proper investment decision.

b.   A capital project's relevant cash flows can be divided into three categories:

1)   The net initial investment consists of the cash outlays the entity must make to undertake the project.

2)   The after-tax net cash inflows from operations consist of the excess of yearly cash collections from the project over required ongoing expenditures for the project.

3) The depreciation tax shield is the increase in cash inflows resulting from the tax benefit of additional depreciation charges.

EXAMPLE of Capital Project Cash Flows

An entity is considering a 5-year capital project that will require the purchase of new plant and equipment costing US $90,000. The project will increase annual cash sales by US $60,000 and annual expenses by US $45,000, of which US $15,000 is additional depreciation expense. The entity's tax rate is 40%.

1)	Net initial investment		US $90,000
2)	After-tax net cash inflows from operations:		
	Additional cash sales	US $60,000	
	Additional nondepreciation expenses	(30,000)	
	Additional cash inflow from operations	US $30,000	
	Minus: income tax expense (US $30,000 × .40)	(12,000)	18,000
3)	Depreciation tax shield:		
	Annual depreciation expense	US $15,000	
	Times: tax rate	× .40	6,000

---

c. The following are three common methods for assessing the desirability of a capital project: net present value, internal rate of return, and payback period.

2. Net Present Value (NPV)

a. The NPV method expresses a project's estimated monetary return. The relevant cash flows (after-tax) are discounted using the entity's hurdle rate (most often the cost of capital) to arrive at an NPV for the project as a whole.

1) Present value tables are not necessary to calculate a project's NPV. The following formula can be used:

$$NPV = \frac{Cash\ Flow_0}{(1 + r)^0} + \frac{Cash\ Flow_1}{(1 + r)^1} + \frac{Cash\ Flow_2}{(1 + r)^2} + \frac{Cash\ Flow_3}{(1 + r)^3} + etc.$$

2) The subscripts and exponents represent the discount periods. The variable r is the discount rate.

b. If the NPV is positive, the project will add to shareholder value and should be undertaken.

EXAMPLE of Net Present Value

The entity's hurdle rate is 8%.

After-tax net cash inflows from operations	US $18,000	
Depreciation tax shield	6,000	
Total annual cash inflows	US $24,000	
Times: PV factor for 5-period ordinary annuity	× 3.993	
Present value of annual cash inflows		US $95,832
Net initial investment	US $90,000	
Times: PV factor for money spent today	× 1.000	
Present value of net initial investment		(90,000)
Net present value of proposed project		US $ 5,832

If sufficient funds are available, the entity should undertake this project.

---

3.   **Internal Rate of Return (IRR)**

a.   The IRR method expresses a project's estimated return in percentage terms.

1)   A project's IRR is the discount rate at which NPV is zero. Managers compare the IRR with the entity's hurdle rate. If the IRR of the project is higher, it is undertaken.

2)   The calculation involves determining the NPVs for successively higher discount rates until NPV equals zero.

b.   This method is often considered a less satisfactory approach than NPV because it can cause an entity to reject projects that will increase shareholder value simply because their IRRs do not exceed the hurdle rate.

EXAMPLE of Internal Rate of Return

The net present value of the project is recalculated with a discount rate of 10% (using a higher hurdle rate causes the NPV to decrease).

After-tax net cash inflows from operations	US $18,000	
Depreciation tax shield	6,000	
Total annual cash inflows	US $24,000	
Times: PV factor for 5-period ordinary annuity	× 3.791	
Present value of annual cash inflows		US $90,984
Net initial investment		(90,000)
Net present value of proposed project		US $ 984

Raising the discount percentage a small amount reduces the NPV to zero. The project's IRR is thus slightly greater than 10%. Because the entity's hurdle rate is 6%, the project is considered suitable using the IRR method.

---

4.   **Payback Period**

a.   The payback period method is even less satisfactory. It consists of calculating the time it will take for the undiscounted cash inflows to equal the net initial investment.

1)   If the project pays for itself within a specified (often arbitrary) time period, it is considered acceptable.

2)   This method is widespread because of its simplicity, but it has two significant weaknesses: It ignores all cash inflows after the cutoff date, and it disregards the time value of money.

5.   **Comparing NPV and IRR**

a.   The NPV and IRR methods give the same accept/reject decision if projects are independent.

1)   Independent projects have unrelated cash flows. Hence, all acceptable independent projects can be undertaken. However, if projects are mutually exclusive, the NPV and IRR methods may rank them differently.

b.   If one of two or more mutually exclusive projects is accepted, the others must be rejected. For example, the decision to build a shopping mall on a piece of land eliminates placing an office building on the same land.

1)   When choosing between mutually exclusive projects, the ranking differences between NPV and IRR become very important. In the example on the next page, an entity using IRR would accept S and reject T. An entity using NPV would make the opposite choice.

EXAMPLE of NPV vs. IRR

Below are the cash flows for two potential capital projects.

	Initial	Period 1	IRR
Project S	US $(178,571)	US $200,000	12%
Project T	(300,000)	330,000	10%

If capital is available for only one project, using IRR alone suggests that Project S be selected.

Discounting both projects' net cash flows at the entity's hurdle rate (6%) suggests a different decision.

Project S	Project T
US $(178,571) × 1.000 = US $(178,571)	US $(300,000) × 1.000 = US $(300,000)
200,000 × 0.943 = 188,679	330,000 × 0.943 = 311,321
NPV **US $ 10,108**	NPV **US $ 11,321**

Project S has a higher internal rate of return, but Project T is preferable because it adds more shareholder value.

6. **Investment Opportunity Schedule (IOS)**

   a. An IOS is a graph useful in determining the optimal capital budgets. In the example below, the IOS depicts the internal rate of return (y axis) and the new capital required (x axis) for each of four projects.

EXAMPLE of an Investment Opportunity Schedule

An entity is considering the following four capital projects. Sufficient funds are available for all four.

	Project A	Project B	Project C	Project D
New capital	US $2,000,000	US $1,500,000	US $2,500,000	US $2,000,000
Internal rate of return	12.0%	8.0%	10.5%	11.0%

The projects are arranged in descending order by IRR.

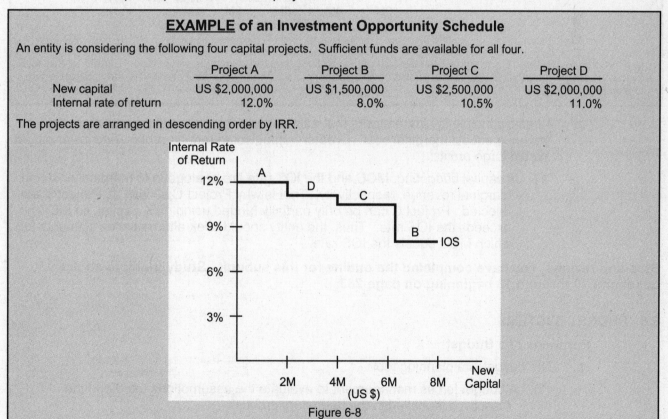

Figure 6-8

b.   The marginal cost of capital (MCC) function can be combined with the IOS to identify the projects to be accepted.

EXAMPLE of Capital Rationing

The entity can raise US $5.5 million of new capital at a cost of 10%. Any additional capital will cost 11.5%.

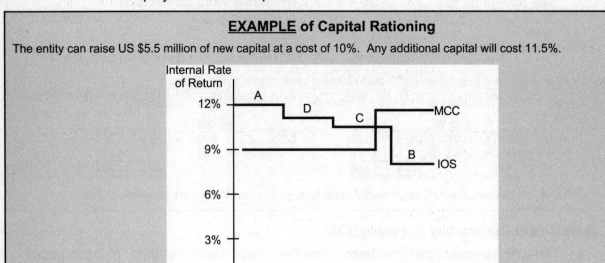

Figure 6-9

The IRRs of Projects A and D are higher than the cost of the required capital and should be accepted. The IRR of Project B is below the cost of the required capital and should be rejected. Project C cannot be entirely funded at the acceptable rate and also is rejected.

---

c.   A basic principle in economics is that a firm should increase output until marginal revenue equals marginal cost. Greater output would reduce profits, and lower output would forgo profits.

   1)   In capital budgeting, MCC and the IOS rate are analogous to marginal cost and marginal revenue, respectively. That is why Project C as well as Project B are rejected. Project C can be only partially funded using 10% capital, so MCC exceeds the IOS rate. Thus, the entity should seek alternative investments for which MCC equals the IOS rate.

Stop and review! You have completed the outline for this subunit. Study multiple-choice questions 10 through 13 beginning on page 283.

6.5 BUDGET SYSTEMS

1.   **Purposes of a Budget**

   a.   The budget is a planning tool.

      1)   A budget forces management to evaluate the assumptions used and the objectives identified in the budgetary process.

   b.   The budget is a control tool.

      1)   A budget helps control costs by setting guidelines and provides a framework for manager performance evaluations.

   c.   The budget is a motivational tool.

      1)   A budget helps to motivate employees. Employees are particularly motivated if they help prepare the budget.

   d.   The budget is a means of communication and coordination.

      1)   A budget states the entity's objectives in numerical terms. It thus requires segments of the entity to communicate and cooperate.

2. **The Master Budget**

    a.   The master budget, also called the comprehensive budget or annual profit plan, consists of the organization's operating and financial plans for a specified period (ordinarily a year or single operating cycle).

        1)   Carefully drafting the budget calendar is important. Lower-level budgets are inputs to higher-level budgets.

    b.   In the **operating budget**, the emphasis is on obtaining and using current resources.

        1)   Sales budget
        2)   Production budget
        3)   Direct materials budget
        4)   Direct labor budget
        5)   Manufacturing overhead budget
        6)   Ending finished goods inventory budget
        7)   Cost of goods sold budget
        8)   Nonmanufacturing budget

            a)   R&D budget
            b)   Design budget
            c)   Marketing budget
            d)   Distribution budget
            e)   Customer service budget
            f)   Administrative budget

        9)   Pro forma income statement

    c.   In the **financial budget**, the emphasis is on obtaining the funds needed to purchase operating assets. It contains the following:

        1)   Capital budget (completed before the operating budget is begun)
        2)   Projected cash payment schedule
        3)   Projected cash collection schedule
        4)   Cash budget
        5)   Pro forma statement of financial position
        6)   Pro forma statement of cash flows

3. **Project Budgets**

    a.   A project budget consists of all the costs expected to attach to a particular project, such as the design of a new airliner or the building of a single ship.

        1)   The costs and profits associated with it are significant enough to be tracked separately.

    b.   A project will typically use resources from many parts of the organization, e.g., design, engineering, production, marketing, accounting, and human resources.

        1)   All of these aspects of the project budget must align with those of the entity's master budget.

EXAMPLE of a Project Budget

Function	1st Quarter	2nd Quarter	3rd Quarter	4th Quarter	Totals
Design	US $ 800,000	US $ 200,000	US $ --	US $ --	US $1,000,000
Engineering	500,000	1,200,000	400,000	--	2,100,000
Production	--	2,100,000	1,500,000	1,500,000	5,100,000
Marketing	--	100,000	200,000	200,000	500,000
Accounting	100,000	100,000	100,000	100,000	400,000
Human Resources	20,000	20,000	20,000	20,000	80,000
Totals	**US $1,420,000**	**US $3,720,000**	**US $2,220,000**	**US $1,820,000**	**US $9,180,000**

4. **Activity-Based Budgeting (ABB)**

    a. ABB applies activity-based costing principles (see Subunit 6.12) to budgeting. It focuses on the numerous activities necessary to produce and market goods and services and requires analysis of cost drivers.

        1) Budget line items are related to activities performed.

        2) This approach contrasts with the traditional emphasis on functions or spending categories. The costs of non-value-added activities are quantified.

    b. Activity-based budgeting provides greater detail than traditional, especially regarding indirect costs, because it permits the isolation of numerous cost drivers.

        1) A cost pool is established for each activity, and a cost driver is identified for each pool.

        2) The budgeted cost for each pool is determined by multiplying the demand for the activity by the estimated cost of a unit of the activity.

5. **Zero-Based Budgeting (ZBB)**

    a. ZBB is a budget and planning process in which each manager must justify his/her department's entire budget every budget cycle.

        1) ZBB differs from the traditional concept of incremental budgeting, in which the current year's budget is simply adjusted to allow for changes planned for the coming year.

        2) The managerial advantage of incremental budgeting is that the manager has to make less effort to justify changes in the budget.

    b. Under ZBB, a manager must begin the budget process every year from a base of zero. All expenditures must be justified regardless of variance from previous years.

        1) The objective is to encourage periodic reexamination of all costs in the hope that some can be reduced or eliminated.

    c. ZBB begins with the lowest-level budgetary units of the entity.

        1) It requires determination of objectives, operations, and costs for each activity and the alternative means of carrying out that activity.

        2) Different levels of service (work effort) are evaluated for each activity, measures of work and performance are established, and activities are ranked according to their importance to the entity.

        3) For each budgetary unit, a decision package is prepared that describes various levels of service that may be provided, including at least one level of service lower than the current one.

            a) Accordingly, ZBB requires managers to justify each expenditure for each budget period and to review each cost component from a cost-benefit perspective.

    d. The major limitation of ZBB is that it requires more time and effort to prepare than a traditional budget.

6. **Continuous (Rolling) Budgeting**

    a. A continuous (rolling) budget is revised on a regular (continuous) basis. Typically, such a budget is continuously extended for an additional month or quarter in accordance with new data as the current month or quarter ends.

        1) For example, if the budget cycle is 1 year, a budget for the next 12 months will be available continuously as each month ends.

    b. The principal advantage of a rolling budget is that it requires managers always to be thinking ahead.

        1) The disadvantage is the amount of time managers must constantly spend on budget preparation.

7. **Kaizen Budgeting**

    a. The Japanese term kaizen means continuous improvement, and kaizen budgeting assumes the continuous improvement of products and processes. It requires estimates of the effects of improvements and the costs of their implementation.

        1) Accordingly, kaizen budgeting is based not on the existing system but on changes yet to be made.

        2) Budget targets, for example, target costs, cannot be reached unless those improvements occur.

8. **Static and Flexible Budgeting**

    a. A static budget is based on only one level of sales or production.

EXAMPLE of a Static Budget

A company has the following static budget for the upcoming month based on production and sales of 1,000 units:

Sales revenue (US $400 per unit)	US $400,000
Minus: variable costs (US $160 per unit)	(160,000)
Contribution margin	US $240,000
Minus: fixed costs	(200,000)
Operating income	US $ 40,000

---

    b. A flexible budget is a series of budgets prepared for various levels of activity within the relevant range.

EXAMPLE of a Flexible Budget

A company has the following flexible budget for the upcoming month based on production and sales of 800 units, 1,000 units, and 1,200 units.

	800 Units	1,000 Units	1,200 Units
Sales revenue (US $400 per unit)	US $320,000	US $400,000	US $480,000
Minus: variable costs (US $160 per unit)	(128,000)	(160,000)	(192,000)
Contribution margin	US $192,000	US $240,000	US $288,000
Minus: fixed costs	(200,000)	(200,000)	(200,000)
Operating income	US $ (8,000)	US $ 40,000	US $ 88,000

It is clear that operating income is highly sensitive to the activity level.

Stop and review! You have completed the outline for this subunit. Study multiple-choice questions 14 through 16 beginning on page 285.

6.6 OPERATING BUDGET COMPONENTS

1. **Example Budgets**

    a. This subunit consists of a series of interrelated example budgets. Key numbers in these examples are identified using the following acronyms:

Sales budget	SB 1-2
Production budget	PB
Direct materials budget	DMB 1-8
Direct labor budget	DLB 1-5
Manufacturing overhead budget	MOB 1-4
Ending finished goods inventory budget	EFGIB
Cost of goods sold budget	CGSB
Nonmanufacturing costs budget	NCB

    b. The source column for each budget (other than the sales budget) contains the references to numbers developed in prior example budgets. This labeling procedure demonstrates the connections among the phases of the budgetary process.

2.   **Sales Budget as Starting Point**

    a.   The sales budget is based on the sales forecast. The sales forecast in turn is based on recent sales trends, conditions in the economy and industry, market research, activities of competitors, and credit and pricing policies.

    b.   The sales budget must specify both projected unit sales and revenues.

EXAMPLE of a Sales Budget

The price cut in the third month is expected to increase sales.

	April	May	June	2nd Quarter Totals	Ref.
Projected sales in units	1,000	1,200	1,800	4,000	SB1
Selling price	× US $400	× US $400	× US $380		
Projected total sales	US $400,000	US $480,000	US $684,000	US $1,564,000	SB2

---

3.   **Production Budget**

    a.   The production budget follows directly from the sales budget. The production budget is concerned with units only.

    b.   To minimize finished goods carrying costs and obsolescence, the levels of production are dependent upon the projections in the sales budget.

EXAMPLE of a Production Budget

	Source	April	May	June	2nd Quarter Totals	Ref.
Projected sales in units	SB1	1,000	1,200	1,800	4,000	
Add: desired ending inventory (10% of next month's sales)		120	180	200		
Total needed		1,120	1,380	2,000	4,500	
Minus: beginning inventory		(100)	(120)	(180)		
Units to be produced		1,020	1,260	1,820	4,100	PB

---

4.   **Direct Materials and Direct Labor Budgets**

    a.   The direct materials budget is concerned with both units and input prices.

EXAMPLES of Two Direct Materials Budgets

In June, use of Raw Material A is expected to become more efficient. Raw Material B is expected to be less costly.

Raw Material A	Source	April	May	June	2nd Quarter Totals	Ref.
Units to be produced	PB	1,020	1,260	1,820		
Raw material per finished product		× 4	× 4	× 3		DMB1
Total units needed for production		4,080	5,040	5,460		
Raw material cost per unit		× US $12	× US $12	× US $12		DMB2
Cost of units used in production		US $48,960	US $60,480	US $65,520	US $174,960	DMB3
Add: desired units in ending inventory (20% of next month's need)		1,008	1,092	1,600		
Total needs		5,088	6,132	7,060		
Minus: beginning inventory		(400)	(1,008)	(1,092)		
Raw material to be purchased		4,688	5,124	5,968		
Raw material cost per unit		× US $12	× US $12	× US $12		
Cost of raw material to be purchased		US $56,256	US $61,488	US $71,616		DMB4

-- Continued on next page --

EXAMPLE -- continued

Raw Material B	Source	April	May	June	2nd Quarter Totals	Ref.
Units to be produced	PB	1,020	1,260	1,820		
Raw material per finished product		× 2	× 2	× 2		DMB5
Total units needed for production		2,040	2,520	3,640		
Raw material cost per unit		× US $10	× US $10	× US $ 8		DMB6
Cost of units used in production		US $20,400	US $25,200	US $29,120	US $74,720	DMB7
Add: desired units in ending inventory (20% of next month's need)		504	728	900		
Total needs		2,544	3,248	4,540		
Minus: beginning inventory		(200)	(504)	(728)		
Raw material to be purchased		2,344	2,744	3,812		
Raw material cost per unit		× US $10	× US $10	× US $ 8		
Cost of raw material to be purchased		**US $23,440**	**US $27,440**	**US $30,496**		DMB8

b. The direct labor budget depends on wage rates, amounts and types of production, numbers and skill levels of employees, fringe benefits, etc.

EXAMPLE of a Direct Labor Budget

No new efficiencies are expected, and the wage rate is set by contract with the union.

	Source	April	May	June	2nd Quarter Totals	Ref.
Units to be produced	PB	1,020	1,260	1,820	4,100	
Direct labor hours per unit		× 2	× 2	× 2		DLB1
Projected total direct labor hours		2,040	2,520	3,640	8,200	DLB2
Direct labor cost per hour		× US $18.641	× US $18.641	× US $18.641		
Total projected direct labor cost		**US $38,027**	**US $46,975**	**US $67,852**	**US $152,854**	DLB3

5. Cost of Fringe Benefits

EXAMPLE of an Employee Fringe Benefit Projection

	Source	April	May	June	2nd Quarter Totals	Ref.
Projected direct labor wages	DLB3	US $38,027	US $46,975	US $67,852	US $152,854	
Employer taxes (7.65%)		2,909	3,594	5,191	11,693	
Health insurance (12.1%)		4,601	5,684	8,210	18,495	
Life insurance (5%)		1,901	2,349	3,393	7,643	
Pension matching (4%)		1,521	1,879	2,714	6,114	
Total projected direct labor cost		**US $48,960**	**US $60,480**	**US $87,360**	**US $196,800**	DLB4

The **full per-hour cost of labor** can now be determined. This will be used in determining the costs of units remaining in ending finished goods inventory.

Assume first-in, first-out (FIFO) is used for all inventories and that ending inventory for June consists only of units produced in June. Thus, the calculation uses only June's data.

Total Projected Direct Labor Cost	÷	Total Projected Direct Labor Hours	=	Full Direct Labor Cost per Hour	Ref.
US $87,360	÷	3,640	=	**US $24**	**DLB5**

Employee fringe benefits may be included in direct labor costs or overhead. The **effect on cost of goods sold is the same** because both are variable manufacturing costs.

6.   Manufacturing Overhead Budget

a.   The manufacturing overhead budget has a variable component and a fixed component (for a more thorough discussion of mixed costs, see Subunit 6.2).

1)   **Variable overhead** costs vary with the level of production.

a)   Indirect materials
b)   Some indirect labor
c)   Variable factory operating costs (e.g., electricity)

EXAMPLE of a Variable Overhead Budget

Variable overhead is applied to finished goods on the basis of direct labor hours.

Variable overhead	Source	April	May	June	2nd Quarter Totals	Ref.
Projected total direct labor hours	DLB2	2,040	2,520	3,640	8,200	
Variable OH rate per direct labor hour		× US $2	× US $2	× US $2		MOB1
Projected variable overhead		**US $4,080**	**US $5,040**	**US $7,280**	**US $16,400**	**MOB2**

---

2)   **Fixed overhead** costs remain the same regardless of the level of production.

a)   Real estate taxes
b)   Insurance
c)   Depreciation

EXAMPLE of a Fixed Overhead Budget

Fixed overhead is applied based on the number of units produced.

Fixed overhead	Source	April	May	June	2nd Quarter Totals	Ref.
Projected fixed overhead		**US $9,000**	**US $9,000**	**US $9,000**	**US $27,000**	**MOB3**
Divided by: projected output	SB1	÷ 1,000	÷ 1,200	÷ 1,800		
Equals: Fixed OH applied per unit		US $ 9.00	US $ 7.50	US $ 5.00		MOB4

---

7.   Ending Finished Goods Inventory Budget

a.   The ending finished goods inventory budget is prepared once the components of finished goods cost have been projected. The result directly affects the assets presented in the pro forma income statement.

1)   Financial statements are pro forma when they reflect projected, not actual, results.

EXAMPLE of a Unit-Cost Calculation

Assume first-in, first-out (FIFO) is used for all inventories and that ending inventory for June consists only of units produced in June. Thus, the calculation uses only June's data.

	Source	Qty.	Source	Input Cost	Cost per Finished Unit
Production costs in ending inventory:					
Direct materials – raw material A	DMB1	3	DMB2	US $12.00	US $ 36.00
Direct materials – raw material B	DMB5	2	DMB6	8.00	16.00
Direct labor	DLB1	2	DLB5	24.00	48.00
Variable overhead	DLB1	2	MOB1	2.00	4.00
Fixed overhead	--	1	MOB4	5.00	5.00
Finished goods cost					US $109.00

Thus, the cost of ending inventory is $21,800.

Total FIFO Cost per Finished Unit		Budgeted Units at June 30		Budgeted Ending Inventory	Ref.
US $109.00	×	200	=	**US $21,800**	**EFGIB**

8. **Cost of Goods Sold Budget**

    a. The cost of goods sold budget combines the projections for materials, labor, and overhead. The result directly affects the pro forma income statement.

EXAMPLE of a Cost of Goods Sold Budget for the Quarter

	Source			Ref.
Beginning finished goods inventory			US $ 16,200	
Manufacturing costs:				
Direct materials used – A	DMB3	US $174,960		
Direct materials used – B	DMB7	74,720		
Direct labor employed	DLB4	196,800		
Variable overhead	MOB2	16,400		
Fixed overhead	MOB3	27,000		
Cost of goods manufactured			489,880	
Cost of goods available for sale			US $506,080	
Ending finished goods inventory	EFGIB		(21,800)	
Cost of goods sold			**US $484,280**	**CGSB**

---

    b. The example above was prepared using absorption costing. Thus, it includes all manufacturing costs, both variable and fixed, in cost of goods sold. This will be used to arrive at gross margin on the pro forma income statement.

9. **Nonmanufacturing Budget**

    a. The nonmanufacturing budget consists of the individual budgets for R&D, design, marketing, distribution, customer service, and administrative costs.

        1) The development of separate budgets reflects a value chain approach.

            a) An alternative is to prepare a single S&A budget for nonproduction costs.

        2) The variable and fixed portions of costs must be treated separately.

            a) Some S&A costs vary directly with sales. Sales efforts must increase to sell more products.

            b) Other S&A expenses, such as sales support staff, are fixed. They must be paid for any level of sales.

            c) As the variable portion of S&A costs increases, contribution margin is decreased.

EXAMPLE of a Nonmanufacturing Costs Budget

Variable and fixed costs are presented separately.

	Source	April	May	June	2nd Quarter Totals	Ref.
Variable nonmanufacturing costs:						
Projected sales in units	SB1	1,000	1,200	1,800	4,000	
Variable S&A expenses		× US $3	× US $3	× US $3		
Total variable nonmanufacturing costs		US $ 3,000	US $ 3,600	US $ 5,400	US $ 12,000	
Fixed nonmanufacturing costs:						
Research and development		US $ 8,000	US $ 8,000	US $ 8,000	US $ 24,000	
Design		4,000	4,000	4,000	12,000	
Marketing		7,000	7,000	7,000	21,000	
Distribution		10,000	10,000	10,000	30,000	
Customer service		11,000	11,000	11,000	33,000	
Administrative		50,000	50,000	50,000	150,000	
Total fixed nonmanufacturing costs		US $90,000	US $90,000	US $90,000	US $270,000	
Total nonmanufacturing costs		**US $93,000**	**US $93,600**	**US $95,400**	**US $282,000**	**NCB**

3) Tradeoffs among elements of S&A expenses may affect contribution margin.

   a) For example, fixed advertising expense increases contribution margin, but the same sales level may be reached using variable sales commissions, a method that reduces contribution margin.

10. **Pro Forma Income Statement**

   a. The pro forma budgeted income statement is the result of the operating budget process.

      1) It is used to decide whether the budgeted activities will result in a loss or an unacceptable level of income.

EXAMPLE of a Pro Forma Income Statement

	Source	
Sales	SB2	US $1,564,000
Cost of goods sold	CGSB	(484,280)
Gross margin		1,079,720
Nonmanufacturing costs	NCB	(282,000)
Operating income		**US $ 797,720**

Stop and review! You have completed the outline for this subunit. Study multiple-choice questions 17 through 19 beginning on page 286.

6.7 TRANSFER PRICING

1. **Overview**

   a. Transfer prices are charged by one segment of an organization for goods and services it provides to another segment of the same organization.

      1) Transfer pricing is used by profit and investment centers (a cost center's costs are allocated to producing departments).

   b. Upper management's challenge is to set transfer pricing policy such that segment managers achieve overall entity goals by pursuing their segment goals.

   c. Thus, transfer pricing should motivate managers by encouraging goal congruence and managerial effort.

      1) Goal congruence is alignment of a manager's individual goals with those of the organization.

      2) Managerial effort is the extent to which a manager attempts to accomplish a goal.

2. **Three Basic Methods for Determining Transfer Prices**

   a. Cost plus pricing sets price at the selling segment's full cost of production plus a reasonable markup.

   b. Market pricing uses the price the selling segment could obtain on the open market.

   c. Negotiated pricing gives the segments the freedom to bargain among themselves to agree on a price.

<u>EXAMPLE</u> of Transfer Price Calculation

A conglomerate refines nitrogen and manufactures fertilizer. Upper management is considering the factors involved in setting transfer pricing policy. External markets exist for both products. The Fertilizer Division would like to pay only the Nitrogen Division's cost plus 10%. The Nitrogen Division wants to sell at the market price. When forced to compromise, management of the two divisions settled on an average of the two prices. The Nitrogen Division's results under the three alternatives are calculated as follows:

Nitrogen Division	Full Cost Plus 10%	Market Price	Negotiated Price
Revenues:			
Revenue per cubic foot	US $ 3.30	US $ 4.00	US $ 3.65
Times: cubic feet	× 10,000	× 10,000	× 10,000
Total division revenue	**US $ 33,000**	**US $ 40,000**	**US $ 36,500**
Costs (for all three prices):			
Purchase cost per cubic foot	US $ 2.00		
Division variable costs	0.25		
Division fixed costs	0.75		
Per-cubic foot division costs	US $ 3.00		
Times: cubic feet	× 10,000		
Total division costs	**US $ 30,000**		
Operating income:			
Total division revenue	US $ 33,000	US $ 40,000	US $ 36,500
Total division costs	(30,000)	(30,000)	(30,000)
Division operating income	**US $ 3,000**	**US $ 10,000**	**US $ 6,500**

The Fertilizer Division's results under the three alternatives are calculated as follows:

Fertilizer Division		
Revenues:		
Revenue per pound	US $ 14.00	
Times: pounds	× 5,000	
Total division revenue	**US $ 70,000**	
Costs:		
Division variable costs	US $ 4.00	
Division fixed costs	0.50	
Per-pound division costs	US $ 4.50	
Times: pounds	× 5,000	
Total division costs	**US $ 22,500**	

	Full Cost Plus 10%	Market Price	Negotiated Price
Operating income:			
Total division revenue	US $ 70,000	US $ 70,000	US $ 70,000
Transferred-in costs	(33,000)	(40,000)	(36,500)
Total division costs	(22,500)	(22,500)	(22,500)
Division operating income	**US $ 14,500**	**US $ 7,500**	**US $ 11,000**

The motive of each manager to set a different price is clear. However, the following calculation shows that the choice among the three methods is irrelevant to the organization as a whole. Motivating management is the main concern of transfer pricing.

	Full Cost Plus 10%	Market Price	Negotiated Price
Nitrogen Division operating income	US $ 3,000	US $10,000	US $ 6,500
Fertilizer Division operating income	14,500	7,500	11,000
Combined operating incomes	**US $17,500**	**US $17,500**	**US $17,500**

3. **Minimum Transfer Price**

   a.   The minimum price that a seller is willing to accept is calculated as follows:

$$\begin{matrix} \text{Minimum} \\ \text{transfer} \\ \text{price} \end{matrix} = \begin{matrix} \text{Incremental} \\ \text{cost} \\ \text{to date} \end{matrix} + \begin{matrix} \text{Opportunity} \\ \text{cost of} \\ \text{selling internally} \end{matrix}$$

       1)   The opportunity cost of selling internally varies depending on two factors: the existence of an external market for the product and whether the seller has excess capacity.

4. **Choice of Transfer Price**

   a.   Scenario 1 -- External market exists and seller has no excess capacity.

       1)   The opportunity cost to sell internally is the contribution margin the seller would have received selling on the external market.

       2)   The seller can sell everything it produces on the open market, so this margin must be included in the transfer price to make selling internally worthwhile.

   b.   Scenario 2 -- External market exists and seller has excess capacity

       1)   Both segments benefit from any price between the floor of the incremental cost to date and a ceiling of the market price.

       2)   The seller cannot demand the full contribution margin because the open market may not purchase its full output.

   c.   Scenario 3 -- No external market exists

       1)   The seller cannot demand anything above its incremental cost to date.

5. **Multinational Considerations**

   a.   When segments are located in different countries, taxes and tariffs may override any other considerations when setting transfer prices.

EXAMPLE of Multinational Pricing

The Nitrogen Division is located in Canada, which imposes a combined tax and tariff burden of 45%, while the Fertilizer Division located in the U.S. is subject only to a 20% income tax.

	Full Cost Plus 10%	Market Price	Negotiated Price
Nitrogen Division operating income	US $ 3,000	US $10,000	US $ 6,500
Fertilizer Division operating income	14,500	7,500	11,000
Combined operating incomes	**US $17,500**	**US $17,500**	**US $17,500**
Canadian taxes and tariffs (45%)	US $ 1,350	US $ 4,500	US $ 2,925
U.S. income tax (20%)	2,900	1,500	2,200
Combined tax liability	**US $ 4,250**	**US $ 6,000**	**US $ 5,125**

If tax minimization is the entity's overall goal, upper management is no longer unconcerned about which transfer pricing policy to select.

---

   b.   Exchange rate fluctuations, threats of expropriation, and limits on transfers of profits outside the host country are additional concerns.

       1)   Thus, because the best transfer price may be a low one because of the existence of tariffs or a high one because of the existence of foreign exchange controls, the effect may be to skew the performance statistics of management.

2) The high transfer price may result in foreign management appearing to show a lower return on investment than domestic management, but the ratio differences may be negated by the fact that a different transfer pricing formula is used.

Stop and review! You have completed the outline for this subunit. Study multiple-choice questions 20 and 21 on page 287.

6.8 COST-VOLUME-PROFIT (CVP) ANALYSIS

1. **Use Cost-Volume-Profit Analysis**

    a. CVP analysis (breakeven analysis) is a tool for understanding the interaction of revenues with fixed and variable costs.

       1) Changes in assumptions about cost behavior and the relevant ranges in which those assumptions are valid may affect the relationships among revenues, variable costs, and fixed costs at various production levels.

       2) Thus, CVP analysis allows management to discern the probable effects of changes in sales volume, sales price, product mix, etc.

2. **Breakeven Point**

    a. The breakeven point is the level of production at which all fixed costs and cumulative variable costs have been covered.

       1) Each additional unit produced above the breakeven point generates profit.

    b. Calculating breakeven in terms of units provides useful information for the production function.

$$Breakeven\ point\ in\ units\ = \frac{Fixed\ costs}{Unit\ contribution\ margin\ (UCM)}$$

EXAMPLE of a Breakeven Point in Units

A manufacturer sells its product for US $.60 per unit. It incurs a unit variable cost of US $.20 and has fixed costs of US $10,000. The breakeven point in units can be calculated as follows:

Breakeven point in units = Fixed costs ÷ UCM
= US $10,000 ÷ ($.60 selling price − $.20 variable cost)
= US $10,000 ÷ $.40
= 25,000 units

---

  c. Breakeven also can be calculated in terms of monetary units to facilitate profit planning.

$$Breakeven\ point\ in\ monetary\ units\ = \frac{Fixed\ costs}{Contribution\ margin\ ratio\ (CMR)}$$

EXAMPLE of a Monetary Breakeven Point

The manufacturer's contribution margin ratio is 66.667% (US $.40 UCM ÷ $.60 selling price). The breakeven point in dollars can be calculated as follows:

Breakeven point in dollars = Fixed costs ÷ CMR
= US $10,000 ÷ 66.667%
= US $15,000

---

d.   The results of breakeven analysis can be depicted graphically with units on the horizontal axis and monetary units on the vertical axis.

CVP (Breakeven) Analysis

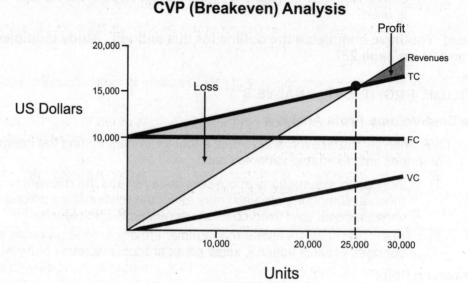

Figure 6-10

3.   **Calculating Target Sales Volume**

a.   The basic breakeven formula can be adapted to determine the level of production necessary to achieve a certain level of profitability.

b.   At breakeven, pretax operating income (PTOI) equals zero. This relationship can be used to calculate the unit sales necessary to achieve a certain target PTOI.

$$Sales \quad - \quad Variable\ costs \quad - \quad Fixed\ costs \quad = \quad PTOI$$
$$(Q \times Selling\ price) - (Q \times Unit\ var.\ cost) - Fixed\ costs = PTOI$$

EXAMPLE of Target Operating Income

A manufacturer sells its product at US $6.00 each with variable costs of US $2.00 each. Fixed costs are US $37,500. How many units (Q) must be sold to realize a pretax operating income of 15%?

Sales – Variable costs – Fixed costs = Target operating income
(Q × Selling price) – (Q × Unit var. cost) – Fixed costs = Q × Selling price × .15
(Q × US $6.00) – (Q × $2.00) – $37,500 = Q × US $6.00 × .15
Q × US $4.00 = (Q × US $.90) + $37,500
Q × US $3.10 = US $37,500
Q = 12,097

---

c.   This analysis can be extended to net income.

$$PTOI \times (1 - Tax\ rate) = Target\ net\ income$$

EXAMPLE of Target Net Income

A manufacturer has a selling price of US $2.00 each, a unit variable cost of US $1.20, fixed costs of US $10,000, and an effective tax rate of 40%. How many units (Q) must be sold to achieve a US $60,000 net income?

(Sales – Variable costs – Fixed costs) × (1 – Tax rate) = Target net income
(Q × Selling price) – (Q × Unit var. cost) – Fixed costs = US $60,000 ÷ (1.0 – 4.0)
(Q × US $2.00) – (Q × $1.20) – $10,000 = US $60,000 ÷ .60
(Q × US $.80) – $10,000 = US $100,000
Q × US $.80 = US $110,000
Q = 137,500 units

---

4. Operating Leverage

a. Closely related to breakeven analysis is the concept of operating leverage. (For an explanation of leverage, see Study Unit 5, Subunit 3.)

1) Operating leverage results from the use of productive assets in the firm's operations. They require the incurrence of fixed costs for depreciation, property taxes, etc.

b. A high productive plant capacity allows the entity to expand output quickly in times of growth.

1) If sales are high, pretax operating income is proportionally higher than for an entity with low operating leverage (i.e., one with a higher reliance on variable manufacturing costs).

2) On the other hand, if sales are low, high fixed operating costs reduce pretax operating income substantially.

c. The degree of operating leverage (DOL) is a precise measure because it isolates the effect of fixed manufacturing costs.

1) The calculation of the DOL requires data from an income statement prepared on the variable costing basis. Thus, DOL cannot be derived using an entity's external financial statements.

Monetary version:

$$\text{Degree of operating leverage} = \frac{\text{Contribution margin}}{\text{Pretax operating income}}$$

2) The DOL for the manufacturer whose variable costing income statement is presented on page 247 is 7.00 (US $4,200 contribution margin ÷ $600 operating income).

d. The only difference between contribution margin and pretax operating income is fixed costs. Thus, every monetary unit change in contribution margin has an equal effect on pretax operating income.

1) For example, if the entity's contribution margin increases to US $5,200, pretax operating income increases to US $1,600, a dollar-for-dollar change.

2) This relationship allows DOL to be restated in percentage form and used to predict the effect of a given change in contribution margin on pretax operating income.

Percentage version:

$$\text{Degree of operating leverage} = \frac{\%\Delta \text{ in pretax operating income}}{\%\Delta \text{ in contribution margin}}$$

a) For example, a DOL of 7.00 means that every 1% change in contribution margin results in a 7% change in pretax operating income.

b) The numerator and denominator of the monetary version are reversed in the percentage version.

Stop and review! You have completed the outline for this subunit. Study multiple-choice questions 22 through 29 beginning on page 288.

6.9 RELEVANT COSTS

1. **Overview**

   a. The typical problem for which marginal (differential or incremental) analysis can be used involves choices among courses of action.

      1) Quantitative analysis emphasizes the ways in which revenues and costs vary with the option chosen. Thus, the focus is on incremental revenues and costs, not the totals of all revenues and costs for the given option.

EXAMPLE of a Special Order Decision

An entity produces a product for which it incurs the following unit costs:

Direct materials	US $2.00
Direct labor	3.00
Variable overhead	.50
Fixed overhead	.50
Total cost	US $6.00

The product normally sells for US $10 per unit. An application of marginal analysis is necessary if a foreign buyer, who has never before been a customer, offers to pay US $5.60 per unit for a special order of the entity's product.

- The immediate reaction might be to refuse the offer because the selling price is less than the average cost of production.

However, marginal analysis results in a different decision. Assuming that the entity has idle capacity, only the marginal costs should be considered.

- In this example, the only marginal costs are for direct materials, direct labor, and variable overhead. No additional fixed overhead costs would be incurred.
- Because marginal revenue (the US $5.60 selling price) exceeds marginal costs (US $2 materials + $3 labor + $.50 variable OH = US $5.50 per unit), accepting the special order will be profitable.

If a competitor bids US $5.80 per unit, the entity can still profitably accept the special order while underbidding the competitor by setting a price below US $5.80 per unit but above US $5.50 per unit.

---

   b. Applying marginal analysis requires caution because of the many qualitative factors involved.

   c. Qualitative factors include the following:

      1) Special price concessions may violate laws prohibiting price discrimination.
      2) Government contract pricing regulations may apply.
      3) Sales to a special customer may affect sales in the entity's regular market.
      4) Regular customers may learn of a special price and demand equal terms.
      5) Disinvestment, such as by discontinuing a product line, may reduce sales in other product lines.

         a) For example, the discontinued line may have been an unintended loss leader. The lower prices on these items may have increased sales of other items as a result of greater customer traffic in a department store or supermarket.

      6) An outsourced product's quality should be acceptable and the supplier reliable.
      7) Employee morale may be affected. If employees are laid off or asked to work too few or too many hours, morale may be affected favorably or unfavorably.

2. **Make-or-Buy Decisions (Insourcing vs. Outsourcing)**

   a. The entity should use available resources as efficiently as possible before outsourcing. Often, an array of products can be produced efficiently if production capacity is available.

      1) If not enough capacity is available to produce all products, those that are produced least efficiently should be outsourced (or capacity should be expanded).

      2) Support services, such as computer processing, legal work, accounting, and training, also may be outsourced.

      3) Moreover, both products and services may be outsourced nationally or internationally. Thus, computer programming, information processing, customer service via telephone, etc., as well as manufacturing tasks, may be not only outsourced but outsourced offshore.

   b. In a make-or-buy decision, the manager considers only the costs relevant to the investment decision. If the total relevant costs of production are less than the cost to buy the item, it should be insourced.

      1) The key variable is total relevant costs, not total costs.

      2) Sunk costs are irrelevant. For example, a production plant's cost of repairs last year is irrelevant to this year's make-or-buy decision. The carrying amount of old equipment is another example.

      3) Costs that do not differ between two alternatives should be ignored because they are not relevant to the decision being made.

      4) Opportunity costs must be considered when idle capacity is not available. They are of primary importance because they represent the forgone opportunities of the entity.

EXAMPLE of a Make-or-Buy Decision

Should an entity make or buy an item?

	Make	Buy
Total variable cost	US $10	
Allocation of fixed cost	5	
Total unit costs	US $15	US $13

If the plant has excess capacity, the decision should be to produce the item. Total variable cost (US $10) is less than the purchase price.

- However, if the plant is operating at capacity, the opportunity cost of displaced production becomes a relevant cost that might alter the decision in favor of purchasing the item from a supplier.

---

3. **Capacity Constraints and Product Mix**

   a. Marginal analysis also applies to decisions about which products and services to sell and in what quantities given the known demand and resource limitations.

      1) For example, if the entity can sell as much as it can produce and has a single resource constraint, the decision rule is to maximize the contribution margin per unit of the constrained resource.

         a) However, given multiple constraints, the decision is more difficult. In that case, sophisticated techniques like linear programming must be used.

4. **Disinvestment**

   a. Disinvestment decisions are to terminate an operation, product or product line, business segment, branch, or relationship with a major customer.

      1) In general, if the marginal cost of a project exceeds the marginal revenue, the entity should disinvest.

   b. Four steps should be taken in making a disinvestment decision:

      1) Identify fixed costs that will be eliminated by the disinvestment decision, e.g., insurance on equipment used.

      2) Determine the revenue needed to justify continuing operations. In the short run, this amount should at least equal the variable cost of production or continued service.

      3) Establish the opportunity cost of resources currently committed to the operation, product, etc.

      4) Determine whether the carrying amount of the assets is equal to their economic value. If not, reevaluate the decision using current fair value rather than the carrying amount.

   c. When an entity disinvests, excess capacity exists unless another project uses this capacity immediately. The cost of idle capacity should be treated as a relevant cost.

5. **Sell-or-Process-Further Decisions**

   a. In determining whether to sell a product at the split-off point or process the item further at additional cost, the joint cost of the product is irrelevant because it is a sunk cost.

   b. The sell-or-process-further decision should be based on the relationship between the incremental costs (the cost of additional processing) and the incremental revenues (the benefits received).

Stop and review! You have completed the outline for this subunit. Study multiple-choice questions 30 through 34 beginning on page 291.

6.10 COST ACCUMULATION SYSTEMS

1. **Actual, Normal, and Standard Costing**

   a. Actual costing is the most accurate method of accumulating costs. However, it is also the least timely and most volatile method.

      1) After the end of the production period, all actual costs incurred for a cost object are totaled, and indirect costs are allocated.

      2) Because per-unit costs depend on the level of production, large fluctuations may arise from period to period. This volatility can lead to the reporting of misleading financial information.

   b. Normal costing charges actual direct materials and direct labor to a cost object but applies overhead on the basis of budgeted (normalized) rates. This compensates for the fluctuations in unit cost inherent in actual costing.

      1) Extended normal costing extends the use of normalized rates to direct materials and direct labor, so that all three major input categories use normalized rates.

   c. Standard costing is a system designed to alert management when the actual costs of production differ significantly from target costs.

      1) Standard costs are predetermined, attainable unit costs. A standard cost is not just an average of past costs, but an objectively determined estimate of what a cost should be.

      2) Standard costs can be used with both job-order and process-costing systems.

2.   **Cost Accumulation Systems**

    a.   Job-order costing is appropriate when producing products with individual characteristics or when identifiable groupings are possible.

        1)   Costs are attached to specific jobs. Each job will result in a single, identifiable end product.

        2)   Examples are any industry that generates custom-built products, such as shipbuilding.

    b.   Process costing is used when similar products are mass produced on a continuous basis.

        1)   For a thorough explanation, see Subunit 6.11.

    c.   Operation costing is a hybrid of job-order and process costing and is used by entities whose manufacturing processes involve some similar and some dissimilar operations.

        1)   Direct materials costs are charged to specific products (as in job-order systems).

        2)   Conversion costs are accumulated and a unit conversion cost for each operation is derived (as in process costing).

    d.   Activity-based costing (ABC) attaches costs to activities rather than to physical goods.

        1)   For a thorough explanation, see Subunit 6.12.

    e.   Life-cycle costing emphasizes the need to price products to cover all the costs incurred over the life of a product, not just the costs of production.

        1)   Costs incurred before production, such as R&D and product design, are upstream costs.

        2)   Costs incurred after production, such as marketing and customer service, are downstream costs.

    f.   Backflush costing delays the assignment of costs until the goods are finished.

        1)   After production is finished for the period, standard costs are flushed backward through the system to assign costs to products. The result is that detailed tracking of costs is eliminated.

        2)   Backflush costing is best suited to companies that maintain low inventories because costs can flow directly to cost of goods sold. It is often used with just-in-time (JIT) inventory, one of the goals of which is the maintenance of low inventory levels.

            a)   Backflush costing complements JIT because it simplifies costing.

Stop and review! You have completed the outline for this subunit. Study multiple-choice questions 35 and 36 beginning on page 293.

6.11 PROCESS COSTING

1. **Overview**

   a. Process costing assigns costs to similar products or service units that are mass produced on a continuous basis (e.g., petroleum products, thread, computer monitors).

   b. Process costing is an averaging process that calculates the average cost of all units.

      1) Costs are accumulated for a cost object that consists of a large number of similar units.

      2) Work-in-process is stated in terms of equivalent units.

      3) Unit costs are established.

2. **Quantity Schedule**

   a. Some units are incomplete at the end of each accounting period. Thus, accumulated costs should be assigned proportionally to all units worked on during the period (completed and incomplete).

      1) For this purpose, equivalent units of production (EUP) are calculated.

   b. The preparation of a quantity schedule aids in this process. The quantity schedule is based on this fundamental relationship:

   Beginning WIP + Units started = Units transferred out + Ending WIP

EXAMPLE of a Process Costing Quantity Schedule

Department A of a manufacturer prepared the following quantity schedule for the month just ended:

Inputs	Physical Units
Beginning WIP (80% complete for direct materials, 40% complete for conversion costs)	2,000
Started during month	8,000
Units to account for	10,000

Outputs	Physical Units
Transferred to Department B	9,000
Ending WIP (90% complete for direct materials, 70% complete for conversion costs)	1,000
Units accounted for	10,000

---

   c. By adjusting the quantities in the various categories by their completion percentages, EUP for direct materials and conversion costs can be determined. They are used to allocate the costs of production.

EXAMPLE of Manufacturing Costs

The following costs were reported for Department A for the month:

	Direct Materials	Conversion Costs
Beginning work-in-process	US $ 11,000	US $ 3,000
Added during month	120,000	79,000

---

   d. The calculation of unit costs depends on whether the weighted-average or first-in, first-out (FIFO) cost-flow method is used.

3. **Unit-Cost Calculation under Weighted-Average**

a. Under the weighted-average method, prior-period work done and costs incurred related to BWIP are included in the calculation of EUP and unit costs. (See the bottom half of the quantity schedule.)

EXAMPLE of Weighted-Average EUP

	Physical Units		Completion Percentage		Equivalent Units Direct Materials		Equivalent Units Conversion Costs	
Transferred-out	9,000 (a)	×	100%	=	9,000		9,000	
Ending work-in-process:	1,000							
Direct materials		×	90%	=	900	(b)		
Conversion costs		×	70%	=			700	(c)
Weighted-average EUP					9,900	(d)	9,700	(e)

The relevant costs are allocated using the EUP amounts above. Just as all units worked on are included in the denominator of the unit-cost calculation, all costs incurred in prior periods and in the current period are included in the numerator.

	Unit Cost
Direct materials [(US $11,000 BWIP + $120,000 added) ÷ (d) 9,900 EUP]	US $13.2323
Conversion costs [(US $3,000 BWIP + $79,000 added) ÷ (e) 9,700 EUP]	8.4536
Unit cost for weighted-average	US $21.6859

The two groups of product (transfers out and EWIP) can now be appropriately costed:

Transferred to Department B [(a) 9,000 units × US $21.6859]		US $195,173
Ending WIP -- direct materials [(b) 900 EUP × US $13.2323]	US $11,909	
Ending WIP -- conversion costs [(c) 700 EUP × US $8.4536]	5,918	17,827
Total costs under weighted-average		US $213,000

The costs allocated under weighted-average reconcile with the costs to be accounted for (costs in BWIP + costs added during the month).

	Direct Materials	Conversion Costs	Totals
Beginning work-in-process	US $ 11,000	US $ 3,000	US $ 14,000
Added during month	120,000	79,000	199,000
Total costs to account for			US $213,000

4.   **Unit-Cost Calculation under First-In, First-Out (FIFO)**

    a.   Under the FIFO method, only current work done and costs incurred are considered in the calculation of EUP and unit costs.

EXAMPLE of FIFO EUP

	Physical Units		Completion Percentage		Equivalent Units Direct Materials		Conversion Costs	
Transferred-out	9,000 (a)	×	100%	=	9,000		9,000	
Ending work-in-process:	1,000							
Direct materials		×	90%	=	900	(b)		
Conversion costs		×	70%	=			700	(c)
Weighted-average EUP					9,900	(d)	9,700	(e)
Beginning work-in-process:	(2,000)							
Direct materials		×	80%	=	(1,600)	(f)		
Conversion costs		×	40%	=			(800)	(g)
FIFO EUP					8,300	(h)	8,900	(i)

To determine FIFO EUP, the calculation above eliminates from weighted-average EUP the work done on beginning work-in-process in the prior period.

	Unit Cost
Direct materials [US $120,000 added ÷ (h) 8,300 EUP]	US $14.4578
Conversion costs [US $79,000 added ÷ (i) 8,900 EUP]	8.8764
Unit cost for FIFO	US $23.3342

The two groups of product (transfers out and EWIP) can now be appropriately costed.

Transferred to Department B		
Beginning WIP (US $11,000 + $3,000)	US $ 14,000	
Costs to complete		
Direct materials [(2,000 – 1,600) EUP × US $14.4578]	5,783.12	
Conversion costs [(2,000 – 800) EUP × US $8.8764]	10,651.68	
	US $30,434.80	
Costs of units started and completed		
[(9,000 units transferred out – 2,000 units in BWIP) EUP × US $23.3342]	163,339.40	US $193,774.20
Ending WIP		
Direct materials (900 EUP × US $14.4578)	US $13,012.02	
Conversion costs (700 EUP × US $8.8764)	6,213.48	19,225.50
Total costs to account for		US $212,999.70

---

5.   **Weighted-Average vs. FIFO**

    a.   These formulas summarize the differences between the two methods of calculating EUP and unit costs:

        1)   Weighted-average includes prior-period work done and costs incurred related to BWIP in the calculation of EUP and unit costs.

Weighted-average

$$\frac{Costs}{EUP} = \frac{Costs\ in\ BWIP + Current\ costs\ added}{Physical\ units\ completed + EUP\ in\ EWIP}$$

---

        2)   FIFO calculates EUP and unit costs based only on work done and costs incurred during the current period.

FIFO

$$\frac{Costs}{EUP} = \frac{Current\ costs\ added}{EUP\ to\ complete\ BWIP + Physical\ units\ started\ and\ completed + EUP\ in\ EWIP}$$

6. **Spoilage**

    a. Abnormal spoilage exceeds the amount expected to occur under normal, efficient operating conditions. Because it arises from conditions outside the expected tolerances for production, abnormal spoilage is typically debited directly to a loss account and credited to work-in-process.

    b. Normal spoilage occurs under normal operating conditions. Because it is expected under efficient operations, it is a product cost and included in the cost of good output.

        1) In most departments, units are inspected at the end of the department's process. Thus, spoiled units are included in the EUP calculations using the completion percentages of transferred-out units.

Stop and review! You have completed the outline for this subunit. Study multiple-choice questions 37 through 39 beginning on page 294.

6.12 ACTIVITY-BASED COSTING

1. **Definition**

    a. Activity-based costing (ABC) is a response to the significant increase in the incurrence of indirect costs resulting from the rapid advance of technology. ABC is a refinement of an existing costing system (job-order or process).

        1) Under a traditional (volume-based) costing system, overhead is simply accumulated in a single cost pool and spread evenly across all end products.

        2) Under ABC, indirect costs are attached to activities that are then rationally allocated to end products.

    b. ABC may be used by manufacturing, service, or retailing entities.

2. **Problems of Volume-Based Costing**

    a. Volume-based costing inaccurately averages or spreads indirect costs over products or service units that use different amounts of resources.

        1) The result is product-cost cross-subsidization, the condition in which the miscosting of one product causes the miscosting of other products.

    b. The effect of using a traditional (volume-based) costing system can be summarized as follows:

        1) Direct labor and direct materials are traced to products or service units.

        2) A single pool of indirect costs (overhead) is accumulated for a given organizational unit.

        3) Indirect costs from the pool are assigned using an allocative (rather than a tracing) procedure, such as using a single overhead rate for an entire department, e.g., US $3 of overhead for every direct labor hour.

           a) The effect is an averaging of costs that may result in significant inaccuracy when products or service units do not use similar amounts of resources.

EXAMPLE of Volume-Based vs. Activity-Based Costing

The effect of volume-based costing can be illustrated as follows:

A company produces two similar products. Both products require one unit of raw material and 1 hour of direct labor. Raw materials costs are US $14 per unit, and direct labor is US $70 per hour.

During the month just ended, the company produced 1,000 units of Product A and 100 units of Product B. Manufacturing overhead for the month totaled US $20,000.

Using direct labor hours as the overhead allocation base, per-unit costs and profits are calculated as follows:

	Product A	Product B	Total
Raw materials	US $ 14,000	US $ 1,400	
Direct labor	70,000	7,000	
Overhead {US $20,000 × [$70,000 ÷ ($70,000 + $7,000)]}	18,182		
Overhead {US $20,000 × [$7,000 ÷ ($70,000 + $7,000)]}		1,818	
Total costs	**US $102,182**	**US $ 10,218**	**US $112,400**
Selling price	US $ 119.99	US $ 119.99	
Cost per unit	(102.18)	(102.18)	
Profit per unit	**US $ 17.81**	**US $ 17.81**	

The company's management accountants have determined that overhead consists almost entirely of production line setup costs, and that the two products require equal setup times. Allocating overhead on this basis yields vastly different results.

	Product A	Product B	Total
Raw materials	US $14,000	US $ 1,400	
Direct labor	70,000	7,000	
Overhead (US $20,000 × 50%)	10,000		
Overhead (US $20,000 × 50%)		10,000	
Total costs	**US $94,000**	**US $18,400**	**US $112,400**
Selling price	US $119.99	US $119.99	
Cost per unit	(94.00)	(184.00)	
Profit per unit	**US $ 25.99**	**US $ (64.01)**	

The high-volume Product A has been heavily subsidizing the setup costs for the low-volume Product B.

c.   The previous example assumed a single component of overhead for clarity. In reality, overhead has many components.

1)   The effect of traditional overhead allocation is illustrated in the following diagram. U.S. dollars are used here, but any currency can be substituted.

Overhead Allocation in a Traditional (Volume-Based) Cost Accumulation System

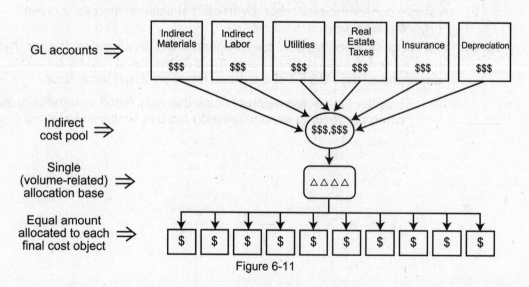

Figure 6-11

3. **Volume-Based vs. Activity-Based**

    a.   Volume-based systems were appropriate when direct costs were a high percentage of manufacturing costs.

        1)   With increasing automation, however, overhead became an ever greater percentage of the total. ABC was developed to address the increasing complexity of overhead costs.

    b.   A volume-based system, as illustrated on the previous page,

        1)   Accumulates costs in general ledger accounts (utilities, taxes, etc.),
        2)   Uses a single cost pool to combine the costs in all the related accounts,
        3)   Selects a single driver to use for the entire indirect cost pool, and
        4)   Allocates the indirect cost pool to final cost objects.

    c.   An activity-based system, by contrast,

        1)   Identifies organizational activities that constitute overhead,
        2)   Assigns the costs of resources consumed by the activities, and
        3)   Assigns the costs of the activities to final cost objects.

4. **ABC Step 1 – Activity Analysis**

    a.   An activity is a set of work actions undertaken within the entity, and a cost pool is established for each activity.

    b.   Activities are classified in a hierarchy according to the level of the production process at which they take place.

        1)   Unit-level activities are performed for each unit of output produced. Examples are using direct materials and direct labor.

        2)   Batch-level activities occur for each group of outputs produced. Examples are materials ordering, materials handling, and production line setup.

        3)   Product-sustaining (or service-sustaining) **activities** support the production of a particular product (or service), irrespective of the level of production. Examples are product design, engineering changes, and testing.

        4)   Facility-sustaining activities concern overall operations and therefore cannot be traced to products at any point in the production process. Examples are accounting, human resources, maintenance of physical plant, and safety/security arrangements.

EXAMPLE of an Activity Analysis

Fabulous Foundry formerly used a traditional job-order system to accumulate costs for the custom pipe fittings of all sizes that it produces. With increasing reliance on robots in the production process and computers for monitoring and control, overhead is now a greater percentage of the total while direct labor costs have shrunk. To obtain better data about product costs, Fabulous has decided to refine its job-order costing system by switching to ABC for the allocation of overhead.

The foundry's management accountants conducted extensive interviews with production and sales personnel to determine how the incurrence of indirect costs can be viewed as activities that consume resources. The accountants identified five activities and created a cost pool for each to capture the incurrence of indirect costs:

Activity	Hierarchy
Product design	Product-sustaining
Production setup	Batch-level
Machining	Unit-level
Inspection & testing	Unit-level
Customer maintenance	Facility-sustaining

5.   **ABC Step 2 – Assign Resource Costs to Activities**

a.   Once activities are designated, the next step in an ABC system is to assign the costs of resources to the activities. This is first-stage allocation.

b.   Identifying resource costs is not as simple as in a volume-based overhead allocation that combines certain accounts in one cost pool.

1)   A separate accounting system may be necessary to track resource costs separately from the general ledger.

c.   Once resources have been identified, resource drivers are designated to allocate resource costs to the activity cost pools.

1)   Resource drivers are measures of the resources consumed by an activity.

EXAMPLE of Resource Driver Assignment

Fabulous Foundry's management accountants identified the following resources used by its indirect cost processes:

Resource	Driver
Computer processing	CPU cycles
Production line	Machine hours
Materials management	Hours worked
Accounting	Hours worked
Sales & marketing	Number of orders

---

6.   **ABC Step 3 – Allocate Activity Cost Pools to Final Cost Objects**

a.   The final step in an ABC system is allocating the activity cost pools to final cost objects. This is second-stage allocation.

b.   Costs are reassigned to final-stage (or, if intermediate cost objects are used, next-stage) cost objects on the basis of activity drivers.

1)   Activity drivers are measures of the demands made on an activity by next-stage cost objects, such as the number of parts in a product used to measure an assembly activity.

EXAMPLE of Activity Driver Assignment

Fabulous Foundry's management accountants have designated these drivers to associate with their corresponding activities:

Activity	Driver
Product design	Number of products
Production setup	Number of setups
Machining	Number of units produced
Inspection & testing	Number of units produced
Customer maintenance	Number of orders

7. **Graphical Depiction**

Indirect Cost Assignment in an Activity-Based Costing System

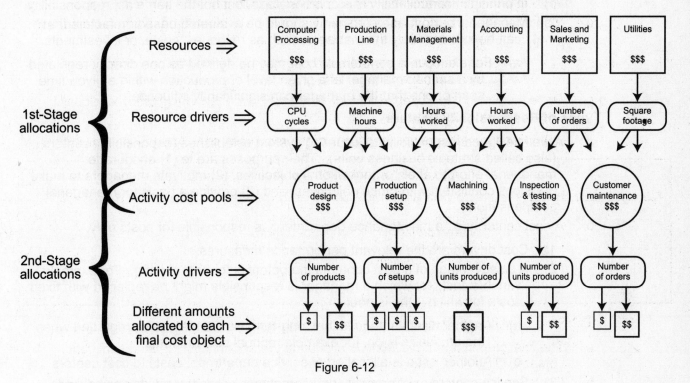

Figure 6-12

8. **Drivers**

a. Drivers (both resource and activity) must be chosen on the basis of a cause-and-effect relationship with the resource or activity cost being allocated, not simply a high positive correlation.

   1) A cost object may be a job, product, process, activity, service, or anything else for which a cost measure is desired.

   2) Intermediate cost objects receive temporary accumulations of costs as the cost pools move from their originating points to the final cost objects.

      a) For example, work-in-process is an intermediate cost object, and finished salable goods are final cost objects.

Stop and review! You have completed the outline for this subunit. Study multiple-choice questions 40 through 42 beginning on page 295.

6.13 RESPONSIBILITY ACCOUNTING

1. **Overview**

a. The primary distinction between centralized and decentralized organizations is in the degree of freedom of decision making by managers at many levels. Centralization assumes decision making must be consolidated so that activities throughout the organization may be more effectively coordinated.

   1) In decentralization, decision making occurs at as low a level as possible. The premise is that the local manager can make better decisions than a centralized manager.

   2) Decentralization typically reflects larger companies that are divided into multiple segments.

   3) In most organizations, a mixture of these approaches is used.

b.   Controllability is the extent to which a manager can influence activities and related revenues, costs, or other items.

1)   In principle, controllability is proportionate to, but not the same as, responsibility.

2)   Managerial performance ordinarily should be evaluated based on factors that can be influenced by the manager, such as revenues, costs, or investments.

a)   For example, a controllable cost may be defined as one directly regulated by a specific manager at a given level of production within a given time span or one that the manager can significantly influence.

2.   **Types of Responsibility Centers**

a.   A well-designed responsibility accounting system establishes responsibility centers (also called strategic business units). Their purposes are to (1) encourage managerial effort to attain organizational objectives, (2) motivate managers to make decisions consistent with those objectives, and (3) provide a basis for managerial compensation.

b.   A cost center, e.g., a maintenance department, is responsible for costs only.

1)   Cost drivers are the relevant performance measures.

2)   A disadvantage of a cost center is the potential for cost shifting. For example, variable costs for which a manager is responsible might be replaced with fixed costs for which (s)he is not.

a)   Another disadvantage is that long-term issues may be disregarded when the emphasis is on, for example, annual cost amounts.

b)   Another issue is allocation of service department costs to cost centers.

3)   Service centers exist primarily and sometimes solely to provide specialized support to other organizational subunits. They are usually operated as cost centers.

c.   A revenue center, e.g., a sales department, is responsible for revenues only.

1)   Revenue drivers are the relevant performance measures. They are factors that influence unit sales, such as changes in prices and products, customer service, marketing efforts, and delivery terms.

d.   A profit center, e.g., an appliance department in a retail store, is responsible for revenues and expenses.

e.   An investment center, e.g., a branch office, is responsible for revenues, expenses, and invested capital.

1)   The performance of investment centers can be evaluated on a return on investment basis, i.e., on the effectiveness of asset use.

3.   **Considerations**

a.   Controllability is not the only basis for responsibility.

1)   More than one manager may influence a cost, and responsibility may be assigned based on knowledge about its incurrence rather than ability to control it directly.

2)   Accordingly, a successful system is dependent upon the proper delegation of responsibility and authority.

b.   The purpose of a responsibility system is to motivate management performance that is consistent with overall company objectives (goal congruence).

1)   Goal congruence is promoted by encouraging cooperation among organizational functions (production, marketing, and support). Managers should be influenced to think of their products or services as salable outside the entity and to find new methods of earning profits.

    2) Suboptimization occurs when one segment of an entity takes action that is in its own best interests but is detrimental to the entity as a whole.

4. **Return on Investment (ROI)**

  a. ROI (also called return on invested capital) is a broad term for measures that reflect how efficiently a company is using the funds contributed by its shareholders to generate a profit

    1) ROI is the most effective measure of corporate performance because it relates the income statement to the statement of financial position. All forms of ROI are some variation on this general ratio:

$$Return\ on\ investment\ (ROI)\ =\ \frac{Measure\ of\ income}{Measure\ of\ capital}$$

    2) ROI reflects the effectiveness of management and overall entity profitability. It also aids in forecasting earnings, planning, budgeting, and control. Each profit center, etc., can be assessed on the basis of ROI.

  b. Return and investment may be defined in many ways. Thus, ROI measures may not be comparable.

    1) The following are examples of adjustments of the numerator (return):

      a) Subtracting preferred dividends to leave only income available to common shareholders

      b) Adding back the noncontrolling interest in the income of a consolidated subsidiary (when invested capital is defined to include the noncontrolling interest)

      c) Adding back interest expense

      d) Adding back both interest expense and taxes so that the numerator is earnings before interest and taxes (EBIT). The result is the basic earning power ratio. It enhances comparability of entities with different capital structures and tax planning strategies.

    2) The following are examples of adjustments of the denominator (investment):

      a) Excluding nonoperating assets, such as investments, intangible assets, and the other asset category

      b) Excluding unproductive assets, such as idle plant, intangible assets, and obsolete inventories

      c) Excluding current liabilities to emphasize long-term capital

      d) Excluding debt and preferred shares to arrive at equity capital

      e) Stating invested capital at market value

5. **Residual Income**

  a. Residual income is the excess of the return on an investment over a targeted amount equal to an imputed interest charge on invested capital.

    1) The rate is ordinarily the weighted-average cost of capital, but it may be an arbitrary hurdle rate.

  b. Projects with a positive residual income should be accepted, and projects with a negative residual income should be rejected.

  c. Residual income is often considered to be superior to ROI. It may be more consistent with maximizing profits.

Stop and review! You have completed the outline for this subunit. Study multiple-choice questions 43 through 45 on page 297.

QUESTIONS

6.1 Cost Management Terminology

1. Using absorption costing, fixed manufacturing overhead costs are best described as

A. Direct period costs.

B. Indirect period costs.

C. Direct product costs.

D. Indirect product costs.

Answer (D) is correct.   *(CIA, adapted)*
    REQUIRED: The manufacturing overhead costs under absorption costing.
    DISCUSSION: Using absorption costing, fixed manufacturing overhead is included in inventoriable (product) costs. Fixed manufacturing overhead costs are indirect costs because they cannot be directly traced to specific units produced.
    Answer (A) is incorrect. Fixed manufacturing overhead costs are neither direct nor period costs. Answer (B) is incorrect. Fixed manufacturing overhead costs are not period costs. Answer (C) is incorrect. Fixed manufacturing overhead costs are not direct costs.

2. A company experienced a machinery breakdown on one of its production lines. As a consequence of the breakdown, manufacturing fell behind schedule, and a decision was made to schedule overtime to return manufacturing to schedule. Which one of the following methods is the proper way to account for the overtime paid to the direct laborers?

A. The overtime hours times the sum of the straight-time wages and overtime premium would be charged entirely to manufacturing overhead.

B. The overtime hours times the sum of the straight-time wages and overtime premium would be treated as direct labor.

C. The overtime hours times the overtime premium would be charged to repair and maintenance expense, and the overtime hours times the straight-time wages would be treated as direct labor.

D. The overtime hours times the overtime premium would be charged to manufacturing overhead, and the overtime hours times the straight-time wages would be treated as direct labor.

Answer (D) is correct.   *(CIA, adapted)*
    REQUIRED: The proper way to account for the overtime paid to the direct laborers.
    DISCUSSION: Direct labor costs are wages paid to labor that can feasibly be specifically identified with the production of finished goods. Factory overhead consists of all costs, other than direct materials and direct labor, that are associated with the manufacturing process. Thus, straight-time wages would be treated as direct labor; however, because the overtime premium cost is a cost that should be borne by all production, the overtime hours times the overtime premium should be charged to manufacturing overhead.
    Answer (A) is incorrect. The straight-time wages times the overtime hours should still be treated as direct labor. Answer (B) is incorrect. Only the straight-time wages times the overtime hours is charged to direct labor. Answer (C) is incorrect. Labor costs are not related to repairs and maintenance expense.

3. The allocation of general overhead costs to operating departments can be **least** justified in determining

A. Income of a product or functional unit.

B. Costs for making management's decisions.

C. Costs for the federal government's cost-plus contracts.

D. Income tax payable.

Answer (B) is correct.   *(CIA, adapted)*
    REQUIRED: The least justified allocation of cost data to operating departments.
    DISCUSSION: In the short run, management decisions are made in reference to incremental costs without regard to fixed overhead costs because fixed overhead cannot be changed in the short run. Thus, the emphasis in the short run should be on controllable costs. For example, service department costs allocated as a part of overhead may not be controllable in the short run.
    Answer (A) is incorrect. Determining the income of a product or functional unit requires absorption (full-cost) data. Answer (C) is incorrect. Determining the costs for the federal government's cost-plus contracts requires absorption (full-cost) data. Answer (D) is incorrect. Absorption costing (full-costing) is currently required for tax purposes.

6.2 Cost Behavior and Relevant Range

4. An assembly plant accumulates its variable and fixed manufacturing overhead costs in a single cost pool, which is then applied to work in process using a single application base. The assembly plant management wants to estimate the magnitude of the total manufacturing overhead costs for different volume levels of the application activity base using a flexible budget formula. If there is an increase in the application activity base that is within the relevant range of activity for the assembly plant, which one of the following relationships regarding variable and fixed costs is true?

A. The variable cost per unit is constant, and the total fixed costs decrease.

B. The variable cost per unit is constant, and the total fixed costs increase.

C. The variable cost per unit and the total fixed costs remain constant.

D. The variable cost per unit increases, and the total fixed costs remain constant.

Answer (C) is correct. *(CIA, adapted)*
    REQUIRED: The effect on variable and fixed costs of a change in activity within the relevant range.
    DISCUSSION: Total variable cost changes when changes in the activity level occur within the relevant range. The cost per unit for a variable cost is constant for all activity levels within the relevant range. Thus, if the activity volume increases within the relevant range, total variable costs will increase. A fixed cost does not change when volume changes occur in the activity level within the relevant range. If the activity volume increases within the relevant range, total fixed costs will remain unchanged.

5. A company is attempting to determine if there is a cause-and-effect relationship between scrap value and output produced. The following exhibit presents the company's scrap data for the last fiscal year:

Scrap as a Percent of Standard Monetary Value of Output Produced

Month	Standard Monetary Value of Output	Percent Scrap (%)
Nov Year 7	US $1,500,000	4.5
Dec Year 7	1,650,000	2.5
Jan Year 8	1,600,000	3.0
Feb Year 8	1,550,000	2.5
Mar Year 8	1,650,000	1.5
Apr Year 8	1,500,000	4.0
May Year 8	1,400,000	2.5
Jun Year 8	1,300,000	3.5
Jul Year 8	1,650,000	5.5
Aug Year 8	1,000,000	4.5
Sep Year 8	1,400,000	3.5
Oct Year 8	1,600,000	2.5

The company's scrap value in relation to the standard monetary value of output produced appears to be

A. A variable cost.

B. A fixed cost.

C. A semi-fixed cost.

D. Unrelated to the standard monetary value of output.

Answer (D) is correct. *(CIA, adapted)*
    REQUIRED: The scrap value in relation to the standard dollar value of output.
    DISCUSSION: There is no systematic relationship between standard monetary units shipped and the percentage of scrap.
    Answer (A) is incorrect. A variable cost would remain a constant percentage of standard monetary units shipped. Answer (B) is incorrect. A fixed cost would be a lower percentage when standard monetary units shipped were high than when they were low. Answer (C) is incorrect. A semi-fixed cost as a percentage would move up and down with standard monetary units shipped, with a base level higher than zero percent.

6.3 Absorption (Full) vs. Variable (Direct) Costing

Questions 6 and 7 are based on the following information. A company manufactures and sells a single product. Planned and actual production in its first year of operation was 100,000 units. Planned and actual costs for that year were as follows:

	Manufacturing	Nonmanufacturing
Variable	US $600,000	US $500,000
Fixed	400,000	300,000

The company sold 85,000 units of product at a selling price of US $30 per unit.

6. Using absorption costing, the company's operating profit was

A. US $750,000

B. US $900,000

C. US $975,000

D. US $1,020,000

Answer (B) is correct. *(CIA, adapted)*
REQUIRED: The absorption-costing operating profit.
DISCUSSION: Under absorption costing, product costs include fixed and variable manufacturing costs. The unit product cost under absorption costing is US $10 [($600,000 + $400,000) ÷ 100,000 units produced]. All nonmanufacturing costs are expensed in the period incurred. Thus, operating profit is US $900,000.

Revenue (85,000 units × US $30)	US $2,550,000
Cost of goods sold (85,000 units × US $10)	(850,000)
Nonmanufacturing costs	
(US $500,000 + $300,000)	(800,000)
Operating profit	US $ 900,000

Answer (A) is incorrect. US $750,000 equals absorption costing profit minus ending inventory (15,000 units × US $10). Answer (C) is incorrect. US $975,000 treats the variable nonmanufacturing costs as manufacturing costs. Answer (D) is incorrect. US $1,020,000 assumes that all costs are manufacturing costs.

7. Using variable costing, the company's operating profit was

A. US $750,000

B. US $840,000

C. US $915,000

D. US $975,000

Answer (B) is correct. *(CIA, adapted)*
REQUIRED: The variable-costing operating profit.
DISCUSSION: Under variable costing, the product cost includes only variable manufacturing costs. All fixed costs are expensed in the period incurred. Unit product cost under variable costing is US $6 ($600,000 ÷ 100,000 units produced).

Revenue (85,000 units × US $30)	US $2,550,000
Variable cost of goods sold	
(85,000 units × US $6)	(510,000)
Variable nonmanufacturing costs	(500,000)
Contribution margin	US $1,540,000
Fixed costs	(700,000)
Operating profit	US $ 840,000

Answer (A) is incorrect. US $750,000 equals variable costing profit minus ending inventory (15,000 units × US $6). Answer (C) is incorrect. US $915,000 treats all variable costs as manufacturing costs. Answer (D) is incorrect. US $975,000 treats all variable costs and fixed manufacturing costs as product costs.

8. In a company, products pass through some or all of the production departments during manufacturing, depending upon the product being manufactured. Direct material and direct labor costs are traced directly to the products as they flow through each production department. Manufacturing overhead is assigned in each department using separate departmental manufacturing overhead rates. The inventory costing method that the manufacturing company is using in this situation is

A. Absorption costing.

B. Activity-based costing.

C. Backflush costing.

D. Variable costing.

Answer (A) is correct. *(CIA, adapted)*
REQUIRED: The appropriate inventory costing method.
DISCUSSION: Under absorption costing, inventories include all direct manufacturing costs and both variable and fixed manufacturing overhead (indirect) costs.
Answer (B) is incorrect. Activity-based costing develops cost pools for activities and then allocates those costs to cost objects based on the drivers of the activities. Answer (C) is incorrect. A backflush costing system applies costs based on output. Answer (D) is incorrect. Variable costing excludes fixed manufacturing overhead costs from inventoriable costs and treats them as period costs.

9. During its first year of operations, a company produced 275,000 units and sold 250,000 units. The following costs were incurred during the year:

Variable costs per unit:
Direct materials	US $15.00
Direct labor	10.00
Manufacturing overhead	12.50
Selling and administrative	2.50

Total fixed costs:
Manufacturing overhead	US $2,200,000
Selling and administrative	US $1,375,000

The difference between operating profit calculated on the absorption-costing basis and on the variable-costing basis is that absorption-costing operating profit is

A. US $200,000 greater.

B. US $220,000 greater.

C. US $325,000 greater.

D. US $62,500 less.

Answer (A) is correct. *(CIA, adapted)*
REQUIRED: The difference between absorption-costing and variable-costing operating profit.
DISCUSSION: Absorption-costing operating profit will exceed variable-costing operating income because production exceeds sales, resulting in a deferral of fixed manufacturing overhead in the inventory calculated using the absorption method. The difference of US $200,000 is equal to the fixed manufacturing overhead per unit (US $2,200,000 ÷ 275,000 = US $8.00) times the difference between production and sales (275,000 − 250,000 = 25,000, which is the inventory change in units).
Answer (B) is incorrect. Units produced, not units sold, should be used as the denominator to calculate the fixed manufacturing cost per unit. Answer (C) is incorrect. Fixed selling and administrative costs are not properly inventoriable under absorption costing. Answer (D) is incorrect. Variable selling and administrative costs are period costs under both variable- and absorption-cost systems in the determination of operating profit.

6.4 Capital Budgeting

10. A project is expected to result in the following adjustments over the next year:

● Cash sales increase by US $400,000.
● Expenses (except depreciation) increase by US $180,000.
● Depreciation increases by US $80,000.

Assume the corporate tax rate is 34%. The total relevant net cash flows during that year are

A. US $92,400

B. US $140,000

C. US $172,400

D. US $220,000

Answer (C) is correct. *(CIA, adapted)*
REQUIRED: The total relevant net cash flows.
DISCUSSION: The total relevant net cash flows for this project for the next year can be calculated as follows:

Additional cash sales	US $400,000	
Additional nondepreciation expenses	(180,000)	
Additional cash inflow from operations	US $220,000	
Minus: income tax expense		
(US $220,000 × .34)	(74,800)	
After-tax cash inflow from operations		US $145,200
Annual depreciation expense	US $ 80,000	
Times: tax rate	× .34	
Depreciation tax shield		27,200
Total relevant net cash flows		US $172,400

Answer (A) is incorrect. The increase in after-tax income is US $92,400. Answer (B) is incorrect. The increase in pre-tax income is US $140,000. Answer (D) is incorrect. Cash sales minus expenses other than depreciation equals US $220,000.

Questions 11 and 12 are based on the following information. A firm with an 18% desired rate of return is considering the following projects (on January 1, Year 1):

	January 1, Year 1 Cash Outflow (000's Omitted)	December 31, Year 5 Cash Inflow (000's Omitted)	Project Internal Rate of Return
Project A	US $3,500	US $7,400	16%
Project B	4,000	9,950	?

Present Value of $1 Due at the End of N Periods

N	12%	14%	15%	16%	18%	20%	22%
4	.6355	.5921	.5718	.5523	.5158	.4823	.4230
5	.5674	.5194	.4972	.4761	.4371	.4019	.3411
6	.5066	.4556	.4323	.4104	.3704	.3349	.2751

11. Using the net present value method, Project A's net present value is

A. US $(316,920)

B. US $(265,460)

C. US $0

D. US $316,920

Answer (B) is correct. *(CIA, adapted)*
REQUIRED: The net present value of Project A.
DISCUSSION: The cash flow at December 31 of Year 5 is 5 years from today, and the net present value method uses the firm's cost of capital of 18%. The present value factor for 18% for 5 years is .4371, and US $7,400,000 multiplied by .4371 equals US $3,234,540, which is US $265,460 less than the present cash outflow of US $3,500,000.
Answer (A) is incorrect. This answer discounts the cash inflow at the correct discount rate (18%), but for 4 years instead of 5, and also subtracts the cash inflow from the cash outflow, instead of vice versa. Answer (C) is incorrect. This answer cannot be computed using the table values and monetary amounts given. Answer (D) is incorrect. This answer discounts the cash inflow at the correct discount rate (18%), but for 4 years instead of 5.

12. Project B's internal rate of return is closest to

A. 15%

B. 18%

C. 20%

D. 22%

Answer (C) is correct. *(CIA, adapted)*
REQUIRED: The closest percentage to the internal rate of return for Project B.
DISCUSSION: The internal rate of return of a project is the discount rate at which the difference between the present value of the cash outflows and the present value of the cash inflows (the project's net present value) equals zero. When the cash flows and a set of discount rates are provided, the problem can be solved by calculating the NPV for each discount rate. The IRR is the discount rate with the result closest to zero. This is achieved by multiplying the cash inflow amount by each of the four relevant PV factors and subtracting the initial outflow. The present value of the cash outflow is US $4,000,000 no matter which rate is applied because US $1 today is worth US $1 at any discount rate:

Discount Rate	Cash Inflow	Present Value Factor	PV of Cash Inflow	PV of Cash Outflow	Net Present Value
15%	US $9,950,000 ×	0.4972 =	US $4,947,140 −	US $4,000,000 =	US $947,140
18%	9,950,000 ×	0.4371 =	4,349,145 −	4,000,000 =	349,145
20%	9,950,000 ×	0.4019 =	3,998,905 −	4,000,000 =	(1,095)
22%	9,950,000 ×	0.3411 =	3,393,945 −	4,000,000 =	(606,055)

The net present value of Project B at a discount rate of 20% is a loss of US $1,095, the closest of the four net present values to US $0.
Answer (A) is incorrect. The NPV at 15% is US $947,140. Discounting at 20% gets much closer to zero. Answer (B) is incorrect. The NPV at 18% is US $349,145. Discounting at 20% gets much closer to zero. Answer (D) is incorrect. The NPV at 22% is a loss of US $606,055. Discounting at 20% gets much closer to zero.

13. Everything else being equal, the internal rate of return (IRR) of an investment project will be lower if

A. The investment cost is lower.

B. Cash inflows are received later in the life of the project.

C. Cash inflows are larger.

D. The project has a shorter payback period.

Answer (B) is correct. *(CIA, adapted)*
REQUIRED: The true statement about the IRR.
DISCUSSION: The IRR is the discount rate at which the net present value of a capital project is zero. Because the present value of a dollar is higher the sooner it is received, projects with later cash flows will have lower net present values for any given discount rate than will projects with earlier cash flows, if other factors are constant. Hence, projects with later cash flows will have a lower IRR.
Answer (A) is incorrect. The present value of the cash inflows is inversely related to the discount rate; that is, if the discount rate is higher, the present value of the cash inflows is lower. If the investment cost is lower, a higher discount rate (the IRR) will be required to set the net present value equal to zero. Answer (C) is incorrect. The larger the cash inflows, the higher the IRR will be. Higher cash inflows have a higher present value at any given discount rate. A higher discount rate will be required to set the net present value equal to zero. Answer (D) is incorrect. Projects with shorter payback periods have higher cash inflows early in the life of the project. Projects with earlier cash inflows have higher IRRs.

6.5 Budget Systems

14. The major objectives of any budget system are to

A. Define responsibility centers, provide a framework for performance evaluation, and promote communication and coordination among organization segments.

B. Define responsibility centers, facilitate the fixing of blame for missed budget predictions, and ensure goal congruence between superiors and subordinates.

C. Foster the planning of operations, provide a framework for performance evaluation, and promote communication and coordination among organization segments.

D. Foster the planning of operations, facilitate the fixing of blame for missed budget predictions, and ensure goal congruence between superiors and subordinates.

Answer (C) is correct. *(CIA, adapted)*
REQUIRED: The major objectives of any budget system.
DISCUSSION: A budget is a realistic plan for the future expressed in quantitative terms. The process of budgeting forces a company to establish goals, determine the resources necessary to achieve those goals, and anticipate future difficulties in their achievement. A budget is also a control tool because it establishes standards and facilitates comparison of actual and budgeted performance. Because a budget establishes standards and accountability, it motivates good performance by highlighting the work of effective managers. Moreover, the nature of the budgeting process fosters communication of goals to company subunits and coordination of their efforts. Budgeting activities by entities within the company must be coordinated because they are interdependent. Thus, the sales budget is a necessary input to the formulation of the production budget. In turn, production requirements must be known before purchases and expense budgets can be developed, and all other budgets must be completed before preparation of the cash budget.
Answer (A) is incorrect. Responsibility centers are determined prior to budgeting. Answer (B) is incorrect. Responsibility centers are determined prior to budgeting, budgets do not fix blame but rather measure performance, and goal congruence is promoted but not ensured by budgets. Answer (D) is incorrect. Budgets do not fix blame but rather measure performance, and goal congruence is promoted but not ensured by budgets.

15. The major appeal of zero-based budgeting is that it

A. Solves the problem of measuring program effectiveness.

B. Relates performance to resource inputs by an integrated planning and resource-allocation process.

C. Reduces significantly the time required to review a budget.

D. Deals with some of the problems of the incremental approach to budgeting.

Answer (D) is correct. *(CIA, adapted)*
REQUIRED: The major appeal of zero-based budgeting.
DISCUSSION: The traditional approach to budgeting is to merely increase last year's amounts by a given percentage or increment. Zero-based budgeting divides programs into packages of goals, activities, and required resources. The cost of each package is then recalculated, without regard to previous performance.
Answer (A) is incorrect. Zero-based budgeting is not primarily a measurement tool for program effectiveness. Answer (B) is incorrect. The relationship of performance to resource inputs by integrated planning and resource allocation is part of the PPBS, or planning-programming-budgeting system. Answer (C) is incorrect. Zero-based budgeting generally increases the time required to review a budget rather than reduces it; i.e., it consists of a determination of resources needed rather than an extrapolation of resources used in prior periods.

16. A company prepares a flexible budget each month for manufacturing costs. Formulas have been developed for all costs within a relevant range of 5,000 to 15,000 units per month. The budget for electricity (a semivariable cost) is US $19,800 at 9,000 units per month, and US $21,000 at 10,000 units per month. How much should be budgeted for electricity for the coming month if 12,000 units are to be produced?

    A. US $26,400

    B. US $25,200

    C. US $23,400

    D. US $22,200

Answer (C) is correct. *(CIA, adapted)*
    REQUIRED: The amount that should be budgeted for electricity given desired units of production.
    DISCUSSION: A flexible budget consists of a fixed cost component and a variable cost component. The fixed cost component can be expected to remain constant throughout the budget's relevant range. The variable cost component, however, will change at a constant rate within the budget's range. The increase in budgeted cost of US $1,200 ($21,000 – $19,800) per 1,000 units of production can therefore be calculated as the variable cost per unit of US $1.20 [($21,000 – $19,800) ÷ 1,000] and the total fixed costs of US $9,000 [$21,000 – (10,000 × $1.20)]. These costs can then be used to determine the total cost of using 12,000 units of electricity [US $9,000 FC + (12,000 × $1.20)].
    Answer (A) is incorrect. The flexible budget for 12,000 units should be computed by determining the variable cost per unit of US $1.20 [($21,000 – $19,800) ÷ 1,000] and the total fixed costs of US $9,000 [$21,000 – (10,000 × $1.20)]. These costs can then be used to determine the total cost of using 12,000 units of electricity [US $9,000 FC + (12,000 × $1.20)]. Answer (B) is incorrect. The flexible budget for 12,000 units should be computed by determining the variable cost per unit of US $1.20 [($21,000 – $19,800) ÷ 1,000] and the total fixed costs of US $9,000 [$21,000 – (10,000 × $1.20)]. These costs can then be used to determine the total cost of using 12,000 units of electricity [US $9,000 FC + (12,000 × $1.20)]. Answer (D) is incorrect. US $22,200 is arrived at by subtracting the increase in budgeted cost of US $1,200.

6.6 Operating Budget Components

17. A company has budgeted sales of 24,000 finished units for the forthcoming 6-month period. It takes 4 pounds of direct materials to make one finished unit. Given the following:

	Finished units	Direct materials (pounds)
Beginning inventory	14,000	44,000
Target ending inventory	12,000	48,000

How many pounds of direct materials should be budgeted for purchase during the 6-month period?

    A. 48,000

    B. 88,000

    C. 92,000

    D. 96,000

Answer (C) is correct. *(CIA, adapted)*
    REQUIRED: The pounds of direct materials budgeted for purchase during the period.
    DISCUSSION: Required production of finished units is 22,000 units (target ending inventory of 12,000 + sales of 24,000 – beginning inventory of 14,000 lb.). Thus, 88,000 pounds of direct materials (22,000 × 4 lb. per unit) must be available. Required purchases of direct materials equal 92,000 pounds (target ending inventory of 48,000 + usage of 88,000 – beginning inventory of 44,000).
    Answer (A) is incorrect. The target ending inventory is 48,000. Answer (B) is incorrect. The amount that must be available for production is 88,000 pounds of direct material. The desired 4,000-lb. increase in direct materials inventory must also be added. Answer (D) is incorrect. The changes in finished goods and direct materials inventories were not considered.

18. Individual budget schedules are prepared to develop an annual comprehensive or master budget. The budget schedule that provides the necessary input data for the direct labor budget is the

    A. Sales forecast.

    B. Raw materials purchases budget.

    C. Schedule of cash receipts and disbursements.

    D. Production budget.

Answer (D) is correct. *(CMA, adapted)*
    REQUIRED: The budget schedule that provides the input data for the direct labor budget.
    DISCUSSION: A master budget typically begins with the preparation of a sales budget. The next step is to prepare a production budget. Once the production budget has been completed, the next step is to prepare the direct labor, raw material, and overhead budgets. Thus, the production budget provides the input necessary for the completion of the direct labor budget.
    Answer (A) is incorrect. The sales forecast is insufficient for completion of the direct labor budget. Answer (B) is incorrect. The raw material purchases budget is not needed to prepare a direct labor budget. Answer (C) is incorrect. The schedule of cash receipts and disbursements cannot be prepared until after the direct labor budget has been completed.

19. A company's budget for next year contains the following information:

	Units
Beginning finished goods inventory	85
Beginning work-in-process in equivalent units	10
Desired ending finished goods inventory	100
Desired ending work-in-process in equivalent units	40
Projected sales for next year	1,800

How many equivalent units should the company plan to produce next year?

A. 1,800

B. 1,565

C. 1,815

D. 1,845

Answer (D) is correct. *(CMA, adapted)*
REQUIRED: The equivalent units to produce in the coming year.
DISCUSSION: The finished units needed equal 1,815:

Needed for sales	1,800
Needed for ending inventory	100
Total finished units needed	1,900
Minus: beginning inventory	85
Finished units needed	1,815

The units to be produced equal 1,845:

Finished units needed	1,815
Needed for ending inventory	40
Total units in process	1,855
Minus: beginning WIP inventory	10
Units to be produced	1,845

Answer (A) is incorrect. Projected unit sales equals 1,800. Answer (B) is incorrect. Units needed for sales minus all inventory amounts equals 1,565. Answer (C) is incorrect. Finished units needed equals 1,815.

6.7 Transfer Pricing

20. A limitation of transfer prices based on actual cost is that they

A. Charge inefficiencies to the department that is transferring the goods.

B. Can lead to suboptimal decisions for the company as a whole.

C. Must be adjusted by some markup.

D. Lack clarity and administrative convenience.

Answer (B) is correct. *(CIA, adapted)*
REQUIRED: The limitation of transfer prices based on actual cost.
DISCUSSION: The optimal transfer price of a selling division should be set at a point that will have the most desirable economic effect on the firm as a whole while at the same time continuing to motivate the management of every division to perform efficiently. Setting the transfer price based on actual costs rather than standard costs would give the selling division little incentive to control costs.
Answer (A) is incorrect. Inefficiencies are charged to the buying department. Answer (C) is incorrect. By definition, cost-based transfer prices are not adjusted by some markup. Answer (D) is incorrect. Cost-based transfer prices provide the advantages of clarity and administrative convenience.

21. Division Z of a company produces a component that it currently sells to outside customers for US $20 per unit. At its current level of production, which is 60% of capacity, Division Z's fixed cost of producing this component is US $5 per unit and its variable cost is US $12 per unit. Division Y of the same company would like to purchase this component from Division Z for US $10. Division Z has enough excess capacity to fill Division Y's requirements. The managers of both divisions are compensated based upon reported profits. Which of the following transfer prices will maximize total company profits and be most equitable to the managers of Division Y and Division Z?

A. US $12 per unit.

B. US $18 per unit.

C. US $20 per unit.

D. US $22 per unit.

Answer (B) is correct. *(CIA, adapted)*
REQUIRED: The transfer price that will maximize total company profits and be most equitable to the managers of the divisions.
DISCUSSION: A unit price of US $18 is less than Division Y's cost of purchase from an outside supplier but exceeds Division Z's production cost. Accordingly, both Y and Z benefit.
Answer (A) is incorrect. US $12 per unit merely allows Division Z to recover its unit variable cost. Answer (C) is incorrect. At US $20 per unit, Division Y may be indifferent as to whether it purchases internally or externally. Buying from an outside source for US $20 per unit is contrary to the company's interests given idle capacity available for the component's manufacture and an incremental unit cost of US $20. Answer (D) is incorrect. At US $22 per unit, Division Y would have incentive to purchase from an external supplier (i.e., market price is US $20).

6.8 Cost-Volume-Profit (CVP) Analysis

Questions 22 through 26 are based on the following information. Data regarding Year 1 operations for a manufacturer that had no beginning or ending inventories are as follows:

Sales (150,000 units)	US $9,000,000
Variable costs:	
Direct materials	US $1,800,000
Direct labor	720,000
Manufacturing overhead	1,080,000
Selling expenses	450,000
Fixed costs:	
Manufacturing overhead	US $ 600,000
Administrative expenses	567,840
Selling expenses	352,800
Income tax rate	40%

22. The total contribution margin for Year 1 is

A. US $2,970,000

B. US $4,950,000

C. US $5,400,000

D. US $6,030,000

Answer (B) is correct. *(CIA, adapted)*
REQUIRED: The total contribution margin.
DISCUSSION: The total contribution margin can be calculated as follows:

Sales (150,000 units)		US $9,000,000
Variable costs:		
Direct materials	US $1,800,000	
Direct labor	720,000	
Manufacturing overhead	1,080,000	
Selling expenses	450,000	(4,050,000)
Contribution margin		US $4,950,000

Answer (A) is incorrect. US $2,970,000 results from subtracting income tax. Answer (C) is incorrect. US $5,400,000 omits variable selling costs from the calculation. Answer (D) is incorrect. US $6,030,000 omits variable overhead from the calculation.

23. The gross margin for Year 1 is

A. US $3,429,360

B. US $4,232,160

C. US $4,350,000

D. US $4,800,000

Answer (D) is correct. *(CIA, adapted)*
REQUIRED: The gross margin.
DISCUSSION: The gross margin can be calculated as follows:

Sales (150,000 units)		US $9,000,000
Manufacturing costs:		
Direct materials	US $1,800,000	
Direct labor	720,000	
Variable overhead	1,080,000	
Fixed overhead	600,000	(4,200,000)
Gross margin		US $4,800,000

This computation would have been far more complex had there been beginning or ending finished goods or work-in-process inventories.
Answer (A) is incorrect. US $3,429,360 equals pretax operating income (revenue minus total costs). Answer (B) is incorrect. US $4,232,160 equals the gross margin minus fixed administrative expenses. Answer (C) is incorrect. US $4,350,000 equals the gross margin minus the variable selling expenses.

24. The breakeven point in unit sales for Year 1 is

  A. 36,495 units.

  B. 42,240 units.

  C. 46,080 units.

  D. 56,320 units.

Answer (C) is correct. *(CIA, adapted)*
    REQUIRED: The breakeven point in unit sales.
    DISCUSSION: The breakeven point in unit sales equals total fixed costs divided by the unit contribution margin (UCM). These amounts can be obtained from the calculation of pretax operating profit:

Sales (150,000 units)		US $9,000,000
Variable costs:		
Direct materials	US $1,800,000	
Direct labor	720,000	
Manufacturing overhead	1,080,000	
Selling expenses	450,000	(4,050,000)
Contribution margin		US $4,950,000
Fixed costs:		
Manufacturing overhead	US $ 600,000	
Administrative expenses	567,840	
Selling expenses	352,800	(1,520,640)
Pretax operating profit		US $3,429,360

The UCM is thus US $33 ($4,950,000 total contribution margin ÷ 150,000 units sold), and the breakeven point in unit sales is 46,080 (US $1,520,640 fixed costs ÷ $33 UCM).
    Answer (A) is incorrect. It includes fixed manufacturing overhead and excludes variable selling expenses from the UCM calculation. It also excludes fixed selling expenses from the total fixed costs. Answer (B) is incorrect. It excludes variable selling expenses from the UCM calculation. Answer (D) is incorrect. It results from dividing total fixed costs by the total unit variable cost.

25. The manufacturer estimates that next year direct materials costs will increase by 10% and direct labor costs will increase by US $0.60 per unit to US $5.40 per unit. In addition, fixed selling expenses will increase by US $29,520. All other costs will be incurred at the same rates or amounts as the current year. What dollar sales volume, to the nearest dollar, would be required in Year 2 to earn the same net income as in Year 1?

  A. US $6,938,031

  B. US $8,736,000

  C. US $9,576,000

  D. US $10,374,000

Answer (C) is correct. *(CIA, adapted)*
    REQUIRED: The dollar sales required to earn the same net income in Year 2 as in Year 1.
    DISCUSSION: To achieve the manufacturer's goal of the same net income in Year 2 as in Year 1, the same pretax operating profit must be achieved. Achieving the same pretax operating profit will require contribution margin to increase to cover the additional fixed selling expenses, calculated as follows:

Sales (150,000 units)		US $9,000,000
Variable costs:		
Direct materials	US $1,800,000	
Direct labor	720,000	
Manufacturing overhead	1,080,000	
Selling expenses	450,000	(4,050,000)
Year 1 contribution margin		US $4,950,000
Additional fixed costs for Year 2		29,520
Year 2 target contribution margin		US $4,979,520

This target contribution margin can be divided by the contribution margin ratio (unit contribution margin ÷ unit selling price) to arrive at the target level of sales. Year 1 per-unit amounts are calculated as follows:

	Year 1 Total		Year 1 Units		Year 1 per Unit
Selling price	US $9,000,000	÷	150,000	=	US $60.00
Direct materials	1,800,000	÷	150,000	=	12.00
Direct labor					5.40
Variable overhead	1,080,000	÷	150,000	=	7.20
Variable selling					
expenses	450,000	÷	150,000	=	3.00

Year 2 target unit contribution margin is thus US $31.20 [$60.00 selling price − ($12.00 × 1.1 direct materials) − $5.40 direct labor − $7.20 variable overhead − $3.00 variable selling expenses]. The Year 2 target contribution margin ratio is 52% (US $31.20 ÷ $60.00), and the Year 2 target sales volume is US $9,576,000 ($4,979,520 fixed costs ÷ .52 CMR).
    Answer (A) is incorrect. US $6,938,031 includes net income instead of pretax operating income in the calculation. Answer (B) is incorrect. US $8,736,000 omits the unit variable selling expense from the calculation of the total unit variable cost. Answer (D) is incorrect. US $10,374,000 uses the variable cost ratio instead of the CMR.

26. Refer to the information on the preceding page(s). The manufacturer estimates that next year direct materials costs will increase by 10% and direct labor costs will increase by US $0.60 per unit to US $5.40 per unit. In addition, fixed selling expenses will increase by US $29,520. All other costs will be incurred at the same rates or amounts as the current year. What selling price would the company have to charge for its product in Year 2 to maintain the same contribution margin ratio as in Year 1?

A. US $61.80

B. US $64.00

C. US $64.50

D. US $72.00

Answer (B) is correct. *(CIA, adapted)*
REQUIRED: The current-year selling price necessary to maintain the same contribution margin ratio (CMR).
DISCUSSION: To achieve the manufacturer's goal of the same contribution margin ratio in Year 2 as in Year 1, the Year 1 per-unit contribution margin must first be calculated:

	Year 1 Total		Year 1 Units		Year 1 per Unit
Selling price	US $9,000,000	÷	150,000	=	US $60.00
Direct materials	1,800,000	÷	150,000	= US $12.00	
Direct labor	720,000	÷	150,000	=	4.80
Variable overhead	1,080,000	÷	150,000	=	7.20
Variable selling expenses	450,000	÷	150,000	=	3.00
Total variable costs					(27.00)
Contribution margin					US $33.00

Based on this data, Year 2 target per-unit variable cost will be US $28.80 [($12.00 × 1.1 direct materials) – $5.40 direct labor – $7.20 variable overhead – $3.00 variable selling expenses]. The target contribution margin ratio for Year 2 is the Year 1 contribution margin divided by the Year 1 selling price (US $33.00 ÷ $60.00 = 55%). The new selling price can now be calculated using the formula for the contribution margin ratio:

Contribution margin ratio = Contribution margin ÷
    Year 2 selling price
.55 = (Year 2 selling price – US $28.80) ÷
    Year 2 selling price
Year 2 selling price × .55 = Year 2 selling price – US $28.80
Year 2 selling price × .45 = US $28.80
Year 2 selling price = US $64.00

Answer (A) is incorrect. US $61.80 equals the original unit selling price plus the increase in the unit variable costs. Answer (C) is incorrect. US $64.50 omits the unit variable selling costs from all calculations. Answer (D) is incorrect. US $72.00 omits the unit variable selling costs from the calculation of the original unit variable cost.

27. Presented below is a cost-volume-profit chart for a firm. Various reference points are marked on the chart with letters.

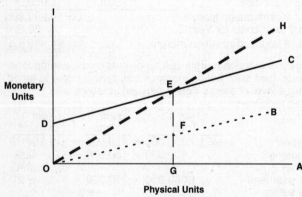

Physical Units

The letters CEH on the chart represent the

A. Total sales.

B. Total expenses.

C. Area of the chart where total sales exceed total expenses.

D. Area of the chart where total expenses exceed total sales.

Answer (C) is correct. *(CIA, adapted)*
REQUIRED: The meaning of the letters CEH on the chart.
DISCUSSION: A cost-volume-profit chart contains elements (lines, points, axes) that identify variable cost, fixed cost, the breakeven point, total revenue, profit, and volume in units. When the total sales revenue line (OH) rises above the total expense line (DC), a company will have positive net income.
Answer (A) is incorrect. Line HEO represents total sales. Answer (B) is incorrect. Line CED represents total expenses. Answer (D) is incorrect. The loss area, i.e., the area of the chart where total expenses exceed sales, is represented by the area OED.

28. A retail company determines its selling price by marking up variable costs 60%. In addition, the company uses frequent selling price markdowns to stimulate sales. If the markdowns average 10%, what is the company's contribution margin ratio?

    A. 27.5%

    B. 30.6%

    C. 37.5%

    D. 41.7%

Answer (B) is correct. *(CIA, adapted)*
    REQUIRED: The contribution margin ratio.
    DISCUSSION: The company's selling price can be stated in terms of the unit variable cost (UVC):

  Selling price = UVC × 1.6 markup × .90 markdown
             = UVC × 1.44

This can be substituted in the formula for contribution margin ratio (CMR) and solved as follows:

  CMR = UCM ÷ Selling price
       = (Selling price – UVC) ÷ Selling price
       = [(UVC × 1.44) – UVC] ÷ (UVC × 1.44)
       = (UVC × .44) ÷ (UVC × 1.44)
       = 30.56%

    Answer (A) is incorrect. Improperly omitting markdowns from the denominator results in 27.5%. Answer (C) is incorrect. Improperly omitting markdowns results in 37.5%. Answer (D) is incorrect. Improperly omitting markdowns from the numerator results in 41.7%.

29. If a high percentage of an entity's total costs is fixed, the entity's operating leverage will be

    A. High.

    B. Low.

    C. Unchanged.

    D. Unable to be determined.

Answer (A) is correct. *(CIA, adapted)*
    REQUIRED: The operating leverage when a large percentage of total cost is fixed.
    DISCUSSION: In business terminology, a high degree of operating leverage, other things held constant, means that a relatively small change in sales will result in a large change in operating income. Therefore, if a high percentage of an entity's total cost is fixed, the entity is said to have a high degree of operating leverage.
    Answer (B) is incorrect. The opposite is true. Answer (C) is incorrect. The entity has a high degree of operating leverage. Answer (D) is incorrect. The entity has a high degree of operating leverage.

6.9 Relevant Costs

30. A company manufactures a product that is sold for US $37.95. It uses an absorption-cost system. Plant capacity is 750,000 units annually, but normal volume is 500,000 units. Costs at normal volume are given below.

	Unit Cost	Total Cost
Direct materials	US $ 9.80	US $ 4,900,000
Direct labor	4.50	2,250,000
Manufacturing overhead	12.00	6,000,000
Selling and administrative:		
Variable	2.50	1,250,000
Fixed	4.20	2,100,000
Total cost	US $33.00	US $16,500,000

Fixed manufacturing overhead is budgeted at US $4.5 million. A customer has offered to purchase 100,000 units at US $25.00 each to be packaged in large cartons, not the normal individual containers. It will pick up the units in its own trucks. Thus, variable selling and administrative expenses will decrease by 60%. The company should compare the total revenue to be derived from this order with the total relevant costs of

    A. US $1,830,000

    B. US $1,880,000

    C. US $2,930,000

    D. US $3,150,000

Answer (A) is correct. *(CIA, adapted)*
    REQUIRED: The total relevant costs of the special order.
    DISCUSSION: The necessary assumptions are that all fixed costs and the unit variable costs of direct materials, direct labor, and variable manufacturing overhead are not affected by the special order. Hence, the fixed costs are not relevant. The unit costs of direct materials and direct labor are given as US $9.80 and US $4.50, respectively. The unit variable manufacturing overhead cost is US $3.00 [($6,000,000 total manufacturing overhead – $4,500,000 total fixed manufacturing overhead) ÷ 500,000 units normal volume]. The unit variable selling and administrative cost is US $1.00 [$2.50 × (1.0 – .60)]. Consequently, the total relevant cost of the special order is US $1,830,000 [($9.80 + $4.50 + $3.00 + $1.00) × 100,000 units].
    Answer (B) is incorrect. Variable manufacturing per unit is determined by using normal volume, not plant capacity, as the denominator level. Answer (C) is incorrect. The total relevant cost of the special order is US $1,830,000 [($9.80 + $4.50 + $3.00 + $1.00) × 100,000 units]. Answer (D) is incorrect. Fixed selling and administrative expenses of US $4.20 per unit should not be included. Furthermore, variable manufacturing of US $3 per unit, not total manufacturing overhead of US $12 per unit, should be used in the calculation of relevant costs.

Questions 31 and 32 are based on the following information. A company manufactures and sells a single product. It takes 2 machine hours to produce one unit. Annual sales are expected to be 75,000 units. Annual production capacity is 200,000 machine hours. Expected selling price is US $10 per unit. Cost data for manufacturing and selling the product are as follows:

Variable costs (per unit)	
Direct materials	US $3.00
Direct labor	1.00
Variable manufacturing overhead	0.80
Variable selling	2.00
Fixed costs (per year)	
Fixed manufacturing overhead	US $90,000
Fixed selling	60,000

31. The company receives a special order for 10,000 units at US $7.60. Variable selling cost for each of these 10,000 units will be US $1.20 instead of the normal US $2.00. This special order will not affect regular sales of 75,000 units. If the company accepts this special order, its profit will

A. Increase by US $8,000.

B. Increase by US $16,000.

C. Decrease by US $4,000.

D. Decrease by US $12,000.

Answer (B) is correct. *(CIA, adapted)*
REQUIRED: The change in profit resulting from a special order.
DISCUSSION: If the company accepts the special order, its revenue will increase by US $76,000 (10,000 units × $7.60). However, its incremental cost will include only the variable costs because fixed manufacturing and selling costs will be unchanged. The increase in cost from accepting the special order is US $60,000 [10,000 units × ($3.00 + $1.00 + $0.80 + $1.20)]. Thus, acceptance of the special order will increase profits by US $16,000 ($76,000 – $60,000).
Answer (A) is incorrect. An increase of US $8,000 assumes unit variable selling cost is US $2.00. Answer (C) is incorrect. Profit will increase. Answer (D) is incorrect. Profit will increase.

32. The company estimates that by reducing its selling price to US $9.30 per unit, it can increase sales to 90,000 units annually. Fixed costs per year and unit variable costs will remain unchanged. If the company reduces its selling price to US $9.30 per unit, its profit will

A. Decrease by US $5,000.

B. Decrease by US $15,000.

C. Decrease by US $45,000.

D. Increase by US $15,000.

Answer (B) is correct. *(CIA, adapted)*
REQUIRED: The effect on profit if selling price is reduced.
DISCUSSION: Because total fixed costs are unaffected, the change in profit is the change in the contribution margin. The contribution margin at the current selling price is US $240,000 [75,000 units × ($10 – $3 – $1 – $0.80 – $2)]. The contribution margin at the US $9.30 selling price is US $225,000 [90,000 units × ($9.30 – $3 – $1 – $0.80 – $2)]. Hence, profit will be reduced by US $15,000 ($240,000 – $225,000) if the selling price is lowered to US $9.30.

33. When applying the cost-benefit approach to a decision, the primary criterion is how well management goals will be achieved in relation to costs. Costs include all expected

A. Variable costs for the courses of action but not expected fixed costs because only the expected variable costs are relevant.

B. Incremental out-of-pocket costs as well as all expected continuing costs that are common to all the alternative courses of action.

C. Future costs that differ among the alternative courses of action plus all qualitative factors that cannot be measured in numerical terms.

D. Historical and future costs relative to the courses of action including all qualitative factors that cannot be measured in numerical terms.

Answer (C) is correct. *(CIA, adapted)*
REQUIRED: The costs included in the cost-benefit approach.
DISCUSSION: Marginal analysis is based on relevant costs. If costs do not vary with the option chosen, they are irrelevant. Moreover, the decision may be based on nonquantitative factors, for example, the desire to maintain a relationship with a vendor or to assume control over development of a product.
Answer (A) is incorrect. Variable and fixed costs may be relevant or irrelevant. Answer (B) is incorrect. Expected incremental out-of-pocket expenses should be considered, but common costs should not. Answer (D) is incorrect. Historical costs are not relevant to cost-benefit analysis because they are sunk costs.

34. A manufacturer has been approached by a new customer who wants to place a one-time order for a component similar to one that the manufacturer makes for another customer. Existing sales will not be affected by acceptance of this order. The manufacturer has a policy of setting its targeted selling price at 60% over full manufacturing cost. The manufacturing costs and the targeted selling price for the existing product are presented below.

Direct materials	US $ 2.30
Direct labor	3.60
Variable manufacturing overhead (applied at 75% of direct labor cost)	2.70
Fixed manufacturing overhead (applied at 150% of direct labor cost)	5.40
Total manufacturing cost	US $14.00
Markup (60% of full manufacturing cost)	8.40
Targeted selling price	US $22.40

The manufacturer has excess capacity to produce the quantity of the component desired by the new customer. The direct materials used in the component for the new customer would cost the manufacturer US $0.25 less than the component currently being made. The variable selling expenses (packaging and shipping) would be the same, or US $0.90 per unit.

Under these circumstances, the minimum unit price at which the manufacturer would accept the special order is one exceeding

- A. US $8.35
- B. US $9.25
- C. US $14.00
- D. US $14.80

Answer (B) is correct. *(CIA, adapted)*
REQUIRED: The minimum unit price at which the manufacturer would accept the special order.
DISCUSSION: Because the manufacturer has excess capacity and existing sales will be unaffected, the minimum price the manufacturer should be willing to accept is anything above the total variable cost of the unit (US $2.05 + $3.60 + $2.70 + $0.90 = US $9.25), an amount that includes the variable manufacturing cost and the variable selling expenses. The fixed costs are not relevant.
Answer (A) is incorrect. US $8.35 does not consider the variable selling expenses. Answer (C) is incorrect. US $14.00 includes the fixed manufacturing overhead, which will be incurred whether the order is accepted or not. Additional fixed manufacturing overhead costs will not be incurred because the manufacturer is below full capacity. The fixed manufacturing overhead is a sunk cost that is not relevant to this decision. Answer (D) is incorrect. US $14.80 does not consider that the manufacturer is below full capacity and that the customer is placing a one-time order. Under these circumstances, the manufacturer would not use its targeted selling price formula.

6.10 Cost Accumulation Systems

35. A new advertising agency serves a wide range of clients including manufacturers, restaurants, service businesses, department stores, and other retail establishments. The accounting system the advertising agency has most likely adopted for its record keeping in accumulating costs is

- A. Job-order costing.
- B. Operation costing.
- C. Relevant costing.
- D. Process costing.

Answer (A) is correct. *(CIA, adapted)*
REQUIRED: The most likely accounting system adopted by a company with a wide range of clients.
DISCUSSION: Job-order costing is used by organizations whose products or services are readily identified by individual units or batches. The advertising agency accumulates its costs by client. Job-order costing is the most appropriate system for this type of nonmanufacturing firm.
Answer (B) is incorrect. Operation costing would most likely be employed by a manufacturer producing goods that have common characteristics plus some individual characteristics. This would not be an appropriate system for an advertising agency with such a diverse client base. Answer (C) is incorrect. Relevant costing refers to expected future costs that are considered in decision making. Answer (D) is incorrect. Process costing is employed when a company mass produces a homogeneous product in a continuous fashion through a series of production steps.

36. Three commonly employed systems for product costing are termed job-order costing, operations costing, and process costing. Match the type of production environment with the costing method used.

	Job-Order Costing	Operations Costing	Process Costing
A.	Auto repair	Clothing manufacturer	Oil refining
B.	Loan processing	Drug manufacturing	Custom printing
C.	Custom printing	Paint manufacturing	Paper manufacturing
D.	Engineering design	Auto assembly	Motion picture production

Answer (A) is correct. *(CIA, adapted)*
REQUIRED: The match of the types of production environments with the costing methods.
DISCUSSION: Job-order costing is appropriate when producing products with individual characteristics and/or when identifiable groupings are possible. Process costing should be used to assign costs to similar products that are mass produced on a continuous basis. Operations costing is a hybrid of job order and process costing systems. It is used by companies that manufacture goods that undergo some similar and some dissimilar processes. Thus, job-order costing would be appropriate for auto repair, operations costing for clothing manufacturing, and process costing for oil refining.
    Answer (B) is incorrect. Custom printing would use job-order costing. Answer (C) is incorrect. Paint manufacturing would use process costing. Answer (D) is incorrect. Motion picture production would use job-order costing.

6.11 Process Costing

Questions 37 and 38 are based on the following information. A manufacturing company employs a process cost system. The company's product passes through both Department 1 and Department 2 in order to be completed. Conversion costs are incurred uniformly throughout the process in Department 2. The direct material is added in Department 2 when conversion is 80% complete. This direct material is a preservative that does not change the volume. Spoiled units are discovered at the final inspection and are recognized then for costing purposes. The physical flow of units for the current month is presented below.

Beginning work-in-process in Department 2	
(90% complete with respect to conversion costs)	14,000
Transferred in from Department 1	76,000
Completed and transferred to finished goods	80,000
Spoiled units – all normal	1,500
Ending work-in-process in Department 2	
(60% complete with respect to conversion costs)	8,500

37. If the manufacturing company uses the weighted-average method, the equivalent units for direct materials in Department 2 for the current month would be

A. 67,500

B. 80,000

C. 81,500

D. 90,000

Answer (C) is correct. *(CIA, adapted)*
REQUIRED: The equivalent units for direct materials based on the weighted-average method.
DISCUSSION: The weighted-average method does not distinguish between work done currently and in the prior period. Given that (1) materials are added when units are 80% complete and (2) ending work-in-process is 60% complete, the number of equivalent units for direct materials in ending work-in-process is zero. Assuming equivalent units are calculated for normal spoilage but inspection occurs when units are complete, the total weighted-average equivalent units for direct materials equals 81,500 (80,000 units transferred + 1,500 normally spoiled units).
    Answer (A) is incorrect. Improperly using the FIFO method to calculate equivalent units results in 67,500. Answer (B) is incorrect. The equivalent units for direct materials was 80,000. Answer (D) is incorrect. The number of physical, not equivalent, units was 90,000.

38. If the manufacturing company uses the FIFO (first-in, first-out) method, the equivalent units for conversion costs in Department 2 for the current month would be

A. 72,500

B. 74,000

C. 85,200

D. 86,600

Answer (B) is correct. *(CIA, adapted)*
REQUIRED: The equivalent units for conversion costs based on the FIFO method.
DISCUSSION: The FIFO method distinguishes between work done in the prior period and work done currently. The total FIFO equivalent units equals the work done currently on beginning work-in-process, plus the work done on ending work-in-process, plus all units started and completed currently. Hence, total FIFO equivalent units equals 74,000 {(10% × 14,000 units in BWIP) + (60% × 8,500 units in EWIP) + [100% × (81,500 spoiled and transferred – 14,000 units in BWIP)]}.
    Answer (A) is incorrect. Failing to account for spoilage results in 72,500 units. Answer (C) is incorrect. Improperly including only 90% of beginning work-in-process results in 85,200 units. Answer (D) is incorrect. Improperly using the weighted-average method to calculate equivalent units results in 86,600.

39. In a process-costing system, the cost of abnormal spoilage should be

A. Prorated between units transferred out and ending inventory.

B. Included in the cost of units transferred out.

C. Treated as a loss in the period incurred.

D. Ignored.

Answer (C) is correct. *(CIA, adapted)*
REQUIRED: The best accounting treatment for abnormal spoilage.
DISCUSSION: Abnormal spoilage is spoilage that is not expected to occur under normal, efficient operating conditions. Because of its unusual nature, abnormal spoilage is typically treated as a loss in the period in which it is incurred.
    Answer (A) is incorrect. Abnormal spoilage costs are not considered a component of the cost of good units produced. Answer (B) is incorrect. Abnormal spoilage costs are not considered a component of the cost of good units produced. Answer (D) is incorrect. Abnormal spoilage costs must be taken out of the manufacturing account.

6.12 Activity-Based Costing

40. Which of the following would be a reasonable basis for allocating the material handling costs to the units produced in an activity-based costing system?

A. Number of production runs per year.

B. Number of components per completed unit.

C. Amount of time required to produce one unit.

D. Amount of overhead applied to each completed unit.

Answer (B) is correct. *(CIA, adapted)*
REQUIRED: Identify a reasonable basis for allocating cost in an activity-based costing system.
DISCUSSION: An essential element of activity-based costing (ABC) is driver analysis, which identifies the cause-and-effect relationship between an activity and its consumption of resources and for an activity and the demands made on it by a cost object. There is a direct causal relationship between the number of components in a finished product and the amount of material handling cost incurred
    Answer (A) is incorrect. This allocation basis is related to batch costs and not to individual unit costs. Answer (C) is incorrect. This allocation basis is the traditional basis for allocating overhead costs to the units produced when the production process is labor-intensive. Answer (D) is incorrect. This is not an allocation basis but rather the result of the allocation process when determining product costs.

Questions 41 and 42 are based on the following information. Believing that its traditional cost system may be providing misleading information, an organization is considering an activity-based costing (ABC) approach. It now employs a full cost system and has been applying its manufacturing overhead on the basis of machine hours.

The organization plans on using 50,000 direct labor hours and 30,000 machine hours in the coming year. The following data show the manufacturing overhead that is budgeted.

Activity	Cost Driver	Budgeted Activity	Budgeted Cost
Material handling	No. of parts handled	6,000,000	US $ 720,000
Setup costs	No. of setups	750	315,000
Machining costs	Machine hours	30,000	540,000
Quality control	No. of batches	500	225,000
	Total manufacturing overhead cost:		US $1,800,000

Cost, sales, and production data for one of the organization's products for the coming year are as follows:

Prime costs:

Direct material cost per unit	US $4.40
Direct labor cost per unit (.05 DLH @ US $15.00/DLH)	.75
Total prime cost	US $5.15

Sales and production data:

Expected sales	20,000 units
Batch size	5,000 units
Setups	2 per batch
Total parts per finished unit	5 parts
Machine hours required	80 MH per batch

41. If the organization uses the traditional full cost system, the cost per unit for this product for the coming year will be

A. US $5.39

B. US $5.44

C. US $6.11

D. US $6.95

Answer (C) is correct. *(CIA, adapted)*
REQUIRED: The unit cost under traditional full costing.
DISCUSSION: Given that manufacturing overhead is applied on the basis of machine hours, the overhead rate is US $60 per hour ($1,800,000 ÷ 30,000) or US $.96 per unit [(80 machine hours per batch × $60) ÷ 5,000 units per batch]. Accordingly, the unit full cost is US $6.11 ($5.15 unit price cost + $.96).
Answer (A) is incorrect. US $5.39 assumes that 80 machine hours are required for the total production of 20,000 units. Answer (B) is incorrect. US $5.44 is based on the machining overhead rate (US $18). Answer (D) is incorrect. US $6.95 is based on the direct labor hour manufacturing overhead rate.

42. If the organization employs an activity-based costing system, the cost per unit for the product described for the coming year will be

A. US $6.00

B. US $6.08

C. US $6.21

D. US $6.30

Answer (D) is correct. *(CIA, adapted)*
REQUIRED: The unit cost under the ABC system.
DISCUSSION: Materials handling cost per part is US $.12 ($720,000 ÷ 6,000,000), cost per setup is US $420 ($315,000 ÷ 750), machining cost per hour is US $18 ($540,000 ÷ 30,000), and quality cost per batch is US $450 ($225,000 ÷ 500). Hence, total manufacturing overhead applied is US $22,920 [(5 parts per unit) × 20,000 units × $.12) + (4 batches × 2 setups per batch × $420) + (4 batches × 80 machine hours per batch × $18) + (4 batches × $450)]. The total unit cost is US $6.296 [$5.15 prime cost + ($22,920 ÷ 20,000 units) overhead].
Answer (A) is incorrect. US $6.00 assumes one setup per batch and 80 total machine hours. Answer (B) is incorrect. US $6.08 assumes that only 80 machine hours were used. Answer (C) is incorrect. US $6.21 assumes one setup per batch.

6.13 Responsibility Accounting

43. Which of the following techniques would be best for evaluating the management performance of a department that is operated as a cost center?

A. Return on assets ratio.

B. Return on investment ratio.

C. Payback method.

D. Variance analysis.

Answer (D) is correct. *(CIA, adapted)*
REQUIRED: The best method for evaluating a cost center.
DISCUSSION: A cost center is a responsibility center that is responsible for costs only. Of the alternatives given, variance analysis is the only one that can be used in a cost center. Variance analysis involves comparing actual costs with predicted or standard costs.
Answer (A) is incorrect. Return on assets cannot be computed for a cost center. The manager is not responsible for revenue (return) or the assets available. Answer (B) is incorrect. Return on investments cannot be computed for a cost center. The manager is not responsible for revenue (return) or the assets available. Answer (C) is incorrect. The payback method is a means of evaluating alternative investment proposals.

44. Residual income is often preferred over return on investment (ROI) as a performance evaluation because

A. Residual income is a measure over time while ROI represents the results for a single time period.

B. Residual income concentrates on maximizing absolute amounts of income rather than a percentage return as with ROI.

C. The imputed interest rate used in calculating residual income is more easily derived than the target rate that is compared to the calculated ROI.

D. Average investment is employed with residual income while year-end investment is employed with ROI.

Answer (B) is correct. *(CIA, adapted)*
REQUIRED: The reason residual income is often preferred to ROI for performance evaluation.
DISCUSSION: Residual income concentrates on earnings in excess of the minimum desired return. With ROI, a segment may reject a project that exceeds the minimum return if the project will decrease the segment's overall ROI. For example, a project that earns an ROI of 22%, which is greater than the target rate of 20%, might be rejected if the segment is currently earning 25%, because the project will decrease the segment's ROI. This would not occur if performance was measured using residual income.
Answer (A) is incorrect. Both measures represent the results for a single time period. Answer (C) is incorrect. The target rate for ROI is the same as the imputed interest rate used in the residual income calculation. Answer (D) is incorrect. Average investment should be employed in both methods. At any rate, the investment base employed for both methods would be the same.

45. A company plans to implement a bonus plan based on segment performance. In addition, the company plans to convert to a responsibility accounting system for segment reporting. The following costs, which have been included in the segment performance reports that have been prepared under the current system, are being reviewed to determine if they should be included in the responsibility accounting segment reports:

I. Corporate administrative costs allocated on the basis of net segment sales.

II. Personnel costs assigned on the basis of the number of employees in each segment.

III. Fixed computer facility costs divided equally among each segment.

IV. Variable computer operational costs charged to each segment based on actual hours used times a predetermined standard rate; any variable cost efficiency or inefficiency remains in the computer department.

Of these four cost items, the only item that could logically be included in the segment performance reports prepared on a responsibility accounting basis would be the

A. Corporate administrative costs.

B. Personnel costs.

C. Fixed computer facility costs.

D. Variable computer operational costs.

Answer (D) is correct. *(CIA, adapted)*
REQUIRED: The item included in the segment performance reports prepared on a responsibility accounting basis.
DISCUSSION: The variable computer cost can be included. The segments are charged for actual usage, which is under each segment's control. The predetermined standard rate is set at the beginning of the year and is known by the segment managers. Moreover, the efficiencies and inefficiencies of the computer department are not passed on to the segments. Both procedures promote a degree of control by the segments.
Answer (A) is incorrect. Corporate administrative costs should be excluded from the performance report. The segments have no control over their incurrence or the allocation basis. The allocation depends upon the segment sales (controllable) as well as the sales of other segments (uncontrollable). Answer (B) is incorrect. The segments have no control over the incurrence of personnel costs or the method of assignment, which depends upon the number of employees in the segment (controllable) in proportion to the total number of employees in all segments (not controllable). Answer (C) is incorrect. The segments have no control over fixed computer facility costs, and the equal assignment is arbitrary and bears no relation to usage.

STUDY UNIT SEVEN
REGULATORY, LEGAL, AND ECONOMIC ISSUES

(21 pages of outline)

This study unit addresses the effects of government regulation and the economic environment on business. The first subunit concerns such matters as environmental law, consumer protection, securities regulation, antitrust law, the money supply and interest rates, and criminal law. The second subunit covers international trade issues, such as comparative advantage and trade barriers. The third subunit addresses currency exchange rates, supply and demand, and market interactions. The fourth subunit discusses various tax structures and their effects on business. The fifth subunit describes key economic indicators, such as the gross domestic product and other national income concepts, inflation indexes, and the balance of payments. The sixth subunit outlines the legal rules of evidence. The final subunit addresses the nature and essential elements of contracts.

A topic tested at the awareness level is the impact of government legislation and regulation on business (Content Outline, Part 3). To address this broad subject, Subunit 7.1 provides an overview of some of the major areas of governmental activity.

7.1 REGULATION OF BUSINESS

1. **Agencies and Commissions**

    a. An administrative agency is any public officer or body that makes rules and renders decisions.

       1) An agency or commission may regulate a specific industry or one area affecting all industries.

       2) Agencies and commissions may have the functions of investigation, enforcement, rule making, and adjudication. They do not impose criminal sanctions.

       3) They must act within the authority granted by the enabling statutes.

       4) Administrative agency rules and regulations

          a) Should not go beyond the scope of the delegated authority of its enabling statutes

          b) May be issued under a general grant of authority to an agency to regulate an industry

          c) May be issued under a specific grant of authority to an agency to make detailed rules carrying out objectives of a statute

       5) Courts interpret statutes, regulations, and the actions of agencies when a dispute develops and one or both parties wish a judicial determination.

       6) Some rules and regulations, agencies, and legislation have sunset provisions that require periodic review and reenactment. Otherwise, they terminate.

2.   **Economic Regulation**

    a.   Such regulation usually affects prices and service to the public and is ordinarily industry specific.

3.   **Social Regulation**

    a.   This type of regulation has broader objectives and more extensive effects. It addresses quality of life issues that are difficult for market forces to remedy, such as workplace and product safety, pollution, and fair employment practices. It applies to most industries.

        1)   Social regulation has been criticized on the grounds that it (a) is costly; (b) contributes to overregulation; (c) may inhibit innovation; (d) increases inflation; and (e) may place a disproportionate burden on small entities, thereby having an anticompetitive effect.

        2)   Another criticism is that regulators are perceived to have little concern for the relation of marginal benefits and marginal costs.

4.   **Securities Law**

    a.   One purpose is to provide complete and fair disclosure to potential investors in an initial issuance of securities.

        1)   Disclosure is through a filing with a government agency. Potential investors may be required to receive a disclosure document, the contents of which may be highly regulated.

        2)   Exemptions. Certain securities and transactions may be exempt, for example, transactions by a person not an issuer, underwriter, or a dealer. Other exemptions also may be available.

        3)   Civil liability may be imposed on parties associated with a filing that contains a misstatement or omission of a material fact.

            a)   Liability also may be imposed for (1) failing to make a required filing or to deliver a required disclosure document to investors or (2) making a sale prior to a required filing.

        4)   Antifraud liability may be imposed on sellers in an initial issuance of securities. Liability also may result from selling a security using a communication containing an untrue statement, or an omission, of a material fact.

    b.   Other purposes are to regulate trading of securities after initial issuance, provide adequate information to investors, and prevent insiders from unfairly using nonpublic information.

        1)   Registration may be necessary for (a) securities exchanges, (b) brokers and dealers, (c) securities traded on exchanges, and (d) high-volume securities traded over the counter. Moreover, issuers may be required to file reports.

        2)   Insiders (officers, directors, and certain shareholders) may be required to surrender to the entity any short-swing profits earned on purchases and sales. They also may be prohibited from buying or selling shares based on inside information not available to the public.

            a)   Insider trading is buying or selling securities of an entity by any individuals who are aware of material nonpublic information not available to the general public. These individuals have a fiduciary obligation to shareholders or potential shareholders.

            b)   Civil and criminal penalties for insider trading may be imposed.

        3)   Antifraud provisions related to subsequent trading may make unlawful any fraudulent scheme.

4) In some countries, legislation prohibits secret payments to persons in foreign countries for purposes contrary to public policy. Examples are corrupt payments to foreign officials, political parties, or candidates for office for the purpose of obtaining or retaining business.

5. **Antitrust Law**

   a. Competition controls private economic power, increases output, and lowers prices. It promotes the following:

      1) Efficient allocation of resources (resulting in lower prices)
      2) Greater choice by consumers
      3) Greater business opportunities
      4) Fairness in economic behavior
      5) Avoidance of concentrated political power resulting from economic power

   b. Restraints of trade in domestic or foreign commerce may be prohibited.

      1) But only unreasonable restraints may be illegal.
      2) Some restraints may be automatically treated as violations.

         a) Price fixing is usually the most prosecuted violation.

   c. Other antitrust laws may prohibit the acquisition of shares or assets of another entity if the effect may be to lessen competition substantially or tend to create a monopoly.

      1) The following are other actions that may be prohibited by antitrust laws:

         a) Tying or tie-in sales (sales in which a buyer must take other products to buy the first product)

         b) Exclusive dealing (a requirement by the seller that a buyer not deal with the seller's competitors)

         c) Price discrimination

            i) Sellers may not be allowed to grant, and buyers may not induce, unfair discounts and other preferences. However, price discrimination may be justified by cost savings or the need to meet competition.

      2) Interlocking directorates also could be prohibited even if the entities ceased to be competitors.

   d. Unfair methods of competition and unfair or deceptive acts in commerce, including false or misleading advertising, are antitrust violations in some countries.

6. **Consumer Protection**

   a. A government agency may help to maintain the safety of drugs, food, cosmetics, etc., and also may enforce laws requiring the labeling of hazardous substances.

      1) New drugs may be required to be thoroughly tested before they are marketed. But the premarket review is usually based upon research supplied by the manufacturers.

   b. Other consumer protection laws may

      1) Prohibit deceptive packaging and labeling.
      2) Give consumers the right to obtain the information reported by credit agencies.
      3) Protect the public from unreasonable risk of injury from consumer products. They may emphasize safety standards for new products.

4) Prohibit discrimination in providing credit and

    a) Provide consumers with rights in contesting billing errors,

    b) Prohibit mailing of unsolicited credit cards, or

    c) Limit a consumer's liability for unauthorized use of lost or stolen credits cards.

5) Regulate written warranties on consumer products.

6) Prohibit abuses of consumers' rights by collection agencies.

7) Require disclosure of the terms and conditions of consumer credit.

7.   Environmental Protection

a. An agency may be created to centralize environmental control functions of the national government.

b. A national environmental policy may be established, and the consideration of environmental issues by government agencies may be promoted.

    1) Thus, agencies may be required to consider the adverse environmental effects of their actions, proposals, legislation, and regulations.

c. Air quality standards may be established for listed pollutants. The law may determine emission standards for stationary and mobile sources of pollution.

d. The law also may establish national water quality standards and pollution standards for each industry.

    1) It also may provide for a discharge permit program and grants and loans for publicly owned treatment plants.

    2) Additional provisions may apply to oil spills and toxic chemicals.

e. Still other laws may be designed to control hazardous waste.

    1) Management requirements may be imposed on generators, transporters, and owners of hazardous waste and on operators of treatment, storage, and disposal facilities.

8.   Money Supply and Interest Rates

a. The central bank (a group of regional banks) controls the money supply. Any policy designed to affect the money supply, and thus the economy, is monetary policy.

    1) Control of the growth of the money supply is essential to control spending, inflation, and the availability of credit. One reason is that the economic health of the nation requires the money supply to grow at the same rate as the economy.

b. The functions of a central bank include the following:

    1) Control of the money supply
    2) Check collection
    3) Serving as the fiscal agent of the government
    4) Supervision of the entire banking system
    5) Holding deposits (reserves) for member institutions

c. A commercial bank usually must have on reserve a certain percentage of its total deposits. These fractional reserve requirements may be required by law to

    1) Ensure that money will be available to carry out transactions
    2) Control the total supply of money

d. If a bank's actual reserves exceed the reserves required by law, it has excess reserves with which it can (and will, if it is a profit-maximizing bank) extend loans.

    1) An individual bank creates money equal to a multiple of its excess reserves when it lends the excess reserves rather than investing in securities.

2) Money multiplier. For the banking system as a whole, assuming no leakage (that is, assuming that all the money in the economy is in banks), money creation is measured by a multiple of excess reserves, as follows:

$$D = 1 \div r$$

If: D = the money multiplier
r = the legal reserve requirement

EXAMPLE

Assume the banking system's excess reserves increase by US $100. Using the formula above (and assuming the reserve requirement is 20%), the money supply is multiplied by 5.

$$D = 1 \div .2 = 5$$
$$(US \$100 \times 5) = US \$500$$

---

3) A market exists for the lending by member banks of their reserves to each other. Member banks are affiliated with the central bank. (But the distinction between member and nonmember banks may not be meaningful because the central bank may regulate the whole banking system.)

   a) Thus, if one bank has excess reserves, it can earn additional interest by lending to another member bank that needs additional reserves. These are very short-term loans.

e. A central bank uses monetary policy tools.

   1) Open-market operations. Purchase and sale of government securities is a primary mechanism of monetary control.

      a) Purchases are expansionary. They increase bank reserves and the money supply.

      b) Sales are contractional. Paying money into the central bank takes the money out of circulation, reduces bank reserves, and contracts the money supply.

      c) Interest rate changes may be used. Changes in the target for the rate charged by member banks for short-term loans to each other is one tool of monetary policy.

         i) For example, to lower the rate, the central bank buys government securities, putting more reserves into the system and exerting downward pressure on the rate. This process has the same effect as changing the money supply.

   2) Reserves. A legal reserve requirement is the percentage of deposits that must be kept on hand.

      a) Lowering the percentage is expansionary (allowing banks to put more of their excess reserves into circulation through loans).

      b) Raising the percentage has the opposite effect.

      c) This tool is not often used because of its powerful effects.

   3) Changing the rate at which member banks may borrow from the central bank.

      a) Lowering the rate encourages borrowing and increases the money supply.

      b) Raising the rate discourages borrowing, increases saving, and decreases the money supply.

Stop and review! You have completed the outline for this subunit. Study multiple-choice questions 1 through 5 beginning on page 320.

7.2 INTERNATIONAL TRADE

1.   **Comparative Advantage**

   a.   The laws of supply and demand affect imports and exports in the same way that they affect domestic goods. For example, a decrease in oil production in a single country can raise the world price of oil.

   1)   Net exports is the amount of a country's exports minus its imports. A nation has net imports if its imports exceed its exports.

   b.   The exchange ratio (terms of trade) is the ratio of a country's export price index to its import price index, multiplied by 100.

EXAMPLE

Country A's entire exports for the year consist of US $800,000 worth of coffee to Country B. Country B's entire exports consist of US $1,000,000 worth of concrete to Country A.

Country A's terms of trade are thus 80 [(US $800,000 ÷ $1,000,000) × 100]. Country B's terms of trade are 125 [(US $1,000,000 ÷ $800,000) × 100].

---

   1)   When the ratio falls, a country is said to have deteriorating terms of trade. When the ratio is less than 100, the country is an overall loser in terms of world trade.

   c.   Countries vary greatly in their efficiency in producing certain goods because of differences in such factors as the following:

   1)   Climatic and geographical conditions
   2)   Human capacities
   3)   Supply and type of capital accumulation
   4)   Proportions of resources
   5)   Political and social climates

   d.   Given these differences, countries can mutually benefit from trade.

   1)   The greatest advantage from trade is obtained when each nation specializes in producing what it can produce most efficiently or, more precisely, least inefficiently.

   a)   If nations specialize and then exchange with others, more is produced and consumed than if each nation tries to be self-sufficient.

   2)   Specialization of labor is beneficial for individuals. The same principle applies to nations.

   3)   The reason for this phenomenon is comparative advantage.

   a)   Comparative advantage is based on the principle of relative opportunity costs.

   b)   A country has a comparative advantage in the production of a good when it has a lower opportunity cost than another producer. That is, it has to sacrifice fewer units of another good to generate an additional unit of the first good.

EXAMPLE

Stellonia and Lumpen can produce the following output with 1 year of labor. Labor is the only input:

	Stellonia	Lumpen
Food (tons)	100	40
Cars	100	90

Stellonia has an absolute advantage regarding both products. It is a more efficient producer of food and cars because its output of each is greater with the same input.

However, Lumpen has a comparative advantage in production of one product.

- Stellonia is 2.5 times as efficient at producing food (100 ÷ 40), but only 1.1 times as efficient at producing cars (100 ÷ 90).
- If Lumpen devoted a year of labor to food, the world output of food would only increase by 40 tons. But if it devoted that same year of labor to cars, world car output would increase by 90.
- Stellonia gains one car by forgoing 1.0 ton of food (100 ÷ 100). However, Lumpen gains one car by forgoing just .44 ton of food (40 ÷ 90). Thus, Lumpen's comparative advantage arises because its opportunity cost is lower than that of Stellonia for cars with respect to food.

If the two countries specialize and engage in trade, the world has more of both food and cars. Thus, specialization and trade enhance world output without changing total input. Moreover, the greater abundance of affordable goods means that workers in both countries experience higher real wages.

---

     c)   A nation theoretically exports goods in which it has a comparative advantage and imports goods in which it has a comparative disadvantage.

2.   **Trade Barriers**

    a.   Even though individuals (as a whole) are best off under free trade, governments often establish policies designed to interfere in the workings of the marketplace.

    b.   Protectionism is any measure taken by a government to protect domestic producers. Protectionism takes many forms.

        1)   Tariffs are consumption taxes designed to restrict imports, e.g., a tax on German beer. Governments raise tariffs to discourage consumption of imported products. Domestic producers are not subject to the tariff and will therefore have a price advantage over their foreign competitors. However, absent such competition, the domestic price of the item will be higher. Domestic producers will sell more at a higher price, and domestic consumers will consume less following the price increase.

            a)   Revenue tariffs are usually applied to products that are not produced domestically. Their purpose is to provide the government with tax revenue.

        2)   Import quotas set fixed limits on different products, e.g., French wine.

            a)   In the short run, import quotas will help a country's balance of payments position by increasing domestic employment, but the prices of the products produced also will increase.

            b)   An embargo is a total ban on some kinds of imports. It is an extreme form of the import quota.

        3)   Domestic content rules require that at least a portion of any imported product be constructed from parts manufactured in the importing nation.

            a)   This rule is sometimes used by capital-intensive nations. Parts can be produced using idle capacity and then sent to a labor-intensive country for final assembly.

4) Voluntary export restrictions are agreements entered into by exporters to reduce the number of products made available in a foreign country in an attempt to avoid official sanctions.

    a) These restrictions can harm consumers. Because the supply of the product desired by consumers in the importing country is held artificially low, the exporter sometimes can charge a price high enough to earn abnormal profits.

5) A trigger price mechanism automatically imposes a tariff barrier against unfairly cheap imports by levying a duty (tariff) on all imports below a particular price (the price that activates the tariff).

6) Antidumping rules prevent foreign producers from selling excess goods on the domestic market at less than cost to eliminate competitors and gain control of the market.

7) Exchange controls limit foreign currency transactions and set exchange rates. The purpose is to limit the ability of a seller to remove (repatriate) its earnings from the country.

8) Export subsidies are payments by the government to producers in certain industries in an attempt to increase exports.

    a) A government may impose countervailing duties on imported goods if those goods were produced in a foreign country with the aid of a governmental subsidy.

9) Special tax benefits to exporters are an indirect form of export subsidy. However, the WTO has ruled some of these tax benefits to be illegal.

10) Certain exports may require licenses. For example, sales of technology with military applications are limited by western nations that are members of the Coordinating Committee for Multilateral Export Controls.

11) An extreme form of protectionism is expropriation of the assets of a foreign entity. It is also the greatest political risk of doing business abroad.

c. The economic effects of tariffs and quotas can be summarized as follows:

1) Workers are shifted from relatively efficient export industries into less efficient protected industries. Real wages decline as a result, as does total world output.

2) Under a tariff, the excess paid by the customer for an imported good goes into the government treasury where it can be spent for any purpose.

    a) Under a quota, prices also are driven up (by the induced shortage), but the excess goes to the exporter in the foreign country.

3) A tariff is imposed on all importers equally. Thus, the more efficient ones will still be able to set their prices lower than the less efficient ones.

    a) An import quota, on the other hand, does not affect foreign importers equally. Import licenses may be assigned as much for political favoritism as on any other grounds.

d. Advocates of trade barriers advance three basic arguments in favor of protectionism:

1) Reducing imports protects domestic jobs.
2) Certain industries are essential to national security.
3) Industries need protection in the early stages of development.

e. Some special-interest groups are strong and well-organized. They lobby effectively to pass legislation that restricts free trade.

Stop and review! You have completed the outline for this subunit. Study multiple-choice questions 6 through 10 beginning on page 321.

7.3 CURRENCY EXCHANGE RATES AND MARKETS

1. **Buying in a Foreign Market**

   a. When a person buys something from a seller in a foreign country, whether goods, a capital asset, or a financial instrument, the seller wishes to be paid in its domestic currency.

      1) For the buyer and seller to execute this transaction efficiently, the two currencies must be convertible to one another in an exchange market at an easily determinable rate.

2. **Fixed Exchange Rates**

   a. One unit of a currency is set equal to a given number of units of another currency by law.

EXAMPLE

In July 1986, the Saudi riyal was fixed at a ratio of 3.75 riyals to 1 U.S. dollar. Because the U.S. buys a large quantity of oil from Saudi Arabia, this fixed rate has the advantage of adding stability to the U.S. oil market.

---

3. **Floating Exchange Rates**

   a. The market is allowed to determine the exchange rate of two currencies.

      1) Thus, supply and demand functions exist for currencies.

      2) The rate at which the supply and demand for a currency in terms of another currency are equal is the equilibrium exchange rate.

EXAMPLE

Given the supply and demand curves below, domestic parties can exchange 20 local currency units (LCUs) for one foreign currency unit (FCU).

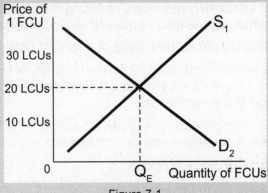

Figure 7-1

b.   A seller normally wants to be paid in its own currency. Thus, when the demand for a foreign country's products rises, demand for its currency also rises.

EXAMPLE

Assuming a fixed supply of FCUs, the equilibrium price of FCUs increases. This relationship is depicted by the rightward shift of the demand curve below:

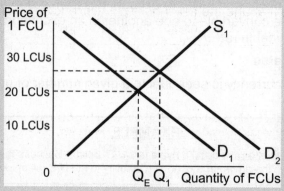

Figure 7-2

If a domestic buyer wants one FCU, it must pay 27.5 LCUs. Thus, LCUs have lost purchasing power (depreciated), and FCUs have gained purchasing power (appreciated).

---

1)   In general, the purchasing power of a currency moves in the same direction as demand for that country's output.

c.   Domestic incomes also affect the demand for a foreign currency.

1)   When incomes rise, buyers demand more goods and services, including those originating in other countries.

2)   The result is depreciation of the local currency. Incomes have risen, so the supply of LCUs also has risen, reducing their value. Moreover, the foreign currency has appreciated relative to the local currency.

d.   Relative interest rates affect the supply of a foreign currency.

1)   When the real interest rate in a foreign country is higher than that in the domestic economy, investors will tend to demand more of that foreign currency to take advantage of the higher rate.

a)   This principle does not apply, however, if the high interest rate in the foreign country is due to high inflation.

4.   **Interaction in Foreign Currency Markets**

a.   Exchange rates are set in the spot market and the forward market. The relevant market depends on when the transaction will be settled.

1)   The relevant exchange rates are the spot rate and the forward rate.

a)   The spot rate is the exchange rate in effect today to settle a transaction today.

b)   The forward rate is the exchange rate in effect today for a transaction that will be settled in the future.

2)   A rate can be locked in by purchasing a contract in the forward market at a definite rate.

a)   The spot and forward rates are calculated using the ratio of foreign currency units to a local currency unit (FCUs to one LCU). The ratio states how many FCUs can be purchased for one LCU.

b)   Discount or premium is determined by the following:

	LCU	FCU
Forward rate > spot rate	Premium	Discount
Spot rate > forward rate	Discount	Premium

b.   An entity can manage the risk inherent in currency exchange rates by hedging, that is, by purchasing or selling foreign currency futures.

EXAMPLE

Robespierre Gauge and Meter (RGM), a French corporation, has sold sophisticated electronic scales to a Japanese pharmaceutical business.

The sales price is fixed at ¥130,000,000 due in 90 days. The entity holding the receivable (RGM) wants to hedge the risk that the foreign currency (yen) will lose purchasing power against the domestic currency (euro).

Based on the spot rate in effect on the day of the sale, RGM buys a futures contract on the open market for ¥130,000,000 to be received in 90 days.

In 90 days, the yen has depreciated slightly against the euro, so the ¥130,000,000 RGM receives from the Japanese entity is worth fewer euros than RGM expected.

RGM sends a wire transfer to exchange the ¥130,000,000 for euros, receiving fewer than originally expected. RGM also sells the futures contract it had purchased 90 days earlier.

The loss in purchasing power of the yen and the gain in the value of the futures contract offset each other. Accordingly, the value of the hedged transaction in euros is approximately the same as on the day of the sale.

Stop and review! You have completed the outline for this subunit. Study multiple-choice questions 11 through 13 beginning on page 322.

7.4 METHODS OF TAXATION

1.   **Tax Uses**

   a.   Government, at all levels, finances its expenditures by taxation. Thus, taxes generate government revenues. National governments also use taxation as a means of implementing fiscal policy regarding inflation, full employment, economic growth, etc.

   b.   One reason for taxation is that individuals should pay tax based on the benefits received from the services (e.g., paying for the use of a public park or swimming pool). Another view is that consumers should pay taxes based on their ability to pay (e.g., taxes on income and wealth).

2.   **Tax Rate Structures**

   a.   Progressive. Higher income persons pay a higher percentage of their income in taxes.

   1)   Indexing is a means of avoiding the unfairness that results when inflation increases nominal but not real taxable income, subjecting it to higher tax rates. Adjusting tax bracket, deduction, and exemption amounts by reference to some index of inflation avoids this problem.

   b.   Proportional. At all levels of income, the percentage paid in taxes is constant (e.g., a flat tax on income).

c.   Regressive. As income increases, the percentage paid in taxes decreases (e.g., sales, payroll, property, or excise taxes). For example, an excise tax is regressive because its burden falls disproportionately on lower-income persons. As personal income increases, the percentage of income paid declines because an excise tax is a flat amount per quantity of the good or service purchased.

   1)   An excise tax increases the selling price of the product. This price increase will have a less negative effect on sales volume for products with less elastic demand. Examples of products with low elasticity of demand include gasoline, tobacco, and alcohol. The tax revenue generated by an increase in excise taxes is therefore higher if the tax is levied on products with less elastic demand.

      a)   Demand is price elastic if a given percentage change in price results in a greater percentage change in revenues in the opposite direction.

3. **Tax Rates**

   a.   The marginal tax rate is the rate applied to the last unit of taxable income.

      1)   The average tax rate is the total tax liability divided by the amount of taxable income.

      2)   The effective tax rate is the total tax liability divided by total economic income (includes amounts that do not have tax consequences).

4. **Direct vs. Indirect**

   a.   Direct taxes are imposed upon the taxpayer and paid directly to the government, e.g., the personal income tax.

      1)   Indirect taxes are levied against others and therefore only indirectly on the individual taxpayer, e.g., corporate income taxes.

5. **Tax Credits**

   a.   Tax credits, e.g., the investment tax credit, are deductions on the income tax return that lower investment cost and increase a project's net present value.

6. **Incidence of Taxation**

   a.   Who actually bears a particular tax is not always obvious. Accordingly, the person who actually bears an indirect tax may not be the one who pays the tax to the government.

   b.   The incidence of taxation is important when a government wants to change the tax structure. Because taxation is a form of fiscal policy, the government needs to know who will actually bear the burden of a tax, not just who will statutorily pay it.

   c.   Taxes such as the corporate income tax and corporate property and excise taxes are often shifted to customers in the form of higher prices.

      1)   However, sellers ordinarily must bear part of the burden. Passing on the entire tax might reduce unit sales unacceptably by raising the price too high. Thus, the effect of the tax is to reduce supply (because suppliers' costs increase) and quantity demanded by buyers (because the price increases). The combined loss of sellers and buyers is called the deadweight loss or excess burden of taxation.

   d.   Taxes such as windfall profits taxes are not shifted to customers via higher prices. This type of one-time-only tax levied on part of the output produced does not increase the equilibrium price of the taxed good.

e. Supply-side economists use the Laffer Curve to attempt to explain how people react to varying rates of income taxation. For example, if the income tax rate is 0%, zero revenue will be raised. Similarly, if the tax rate is 100%, income tax revenue will probably be zero because an earner who faces a tax rate of 100% will not work.

1) The optimal income tax rate will bring in the most revenue possible. A rate that is either too high or too low will generate less than optimal tax revenues.

2) Supply-side economists do not state that lowering income tax rates will produce more revenue. Instead, they claim that, if the rates are too high, lowering rates will produce more revenue because output and national income will increase. This result, in theory, should follow because of increased incentives to work, invest, and save.

3) However, economic policy should not be confused with political considerations. There are obvious political reasons for having higher or lower tax rates on certain income levels. Thus, the theory underlying the Laffer Curve does not address questions of redistributionist politics.

4) A criticism of the Laffer Curve is that it does not prescribe the optimal tax rate. The only way to know whether the current tax rates are too high or too low is to change them and see whether revenues increase.

a) Critics also have observed that the incentives provided by tax cuts may have relatively small supply-side effects and that those effects may be felt only in the very long run.

b) Still another potential problem is that cutting taxes in an expanding economy may overstimulate demand, thereby increasing inflation.

7. International Tax Considerations

a. Multinational corporations frequently derive income from several countries. The government of each country in which a corporation does business may enact statutes imposing one or more types of tax on the corporation.

b. Treaties. To avoid double taxation, two or more countries may adopt treaties to coordinate or synchronize the effects of their taxing statutes.

1) Treaties also are used to integrate other governmental goals, e.g., providing incentives for desired investment.

2) A treaty might modify the rules in a country's statutes that designate the source country of income or the domicile of an entity.

c. Multinational Corporations

1) Most countries tax only the income sourced to that country.

2) But some countries tax worldwide income (from whatever source derived) of a domestic corporation. Double taxation is avoided by allowing a credit for income tax paid to foreign countries or by treaty provisions.

3) In the case of foreign corporations, a country may tax only income sourced to it. Ordinarily, such income is effectively connected with engaging in a trade or business of the country. Certain source income, e.g., gain on the sale of most shares, may not be taxed.

8. **Value-Added Tax (VAT)**

    a.   Many major industrial nations have adopted a value-added tax (VAT).

        1)   The tax is levied on the value added to goods by each business unit in the production and distribution chain. The amount of value added is the difference between sales and purchases. Each entity in the chain collects the tax on its sales, takes a credit for taxes paid on purchases, and remits the difference to the government.

        2)   The consumer ultimately bears the tax through higher prices.

        3)   A VAT encourages consumer savings because taxes are paid only on consumption, not on savings. Because the VAT is based on consumption, people in the lower income groups spend a greater proportion of their income on this type of tax. Thus, the VAT is regressive.

        4)   Only those businesses that make a profit have to pay income taxes. The VAT, however, requires all businesses to pay taxes, regardless of income.

        5)   The VAT tax is not a useful tool for fiscal policy purposes.

Stop and review! You have completed the outline for this subunit. Study multiple-choice questions 14 through 17 beginning on page 323.

7.5 ECONOMIC INDICATORS

1. **Economic Indicators**

    a.   Economists use economic indicators to forecast changes in economic activity (measured as a change in GDP, discussed in item 2.a.).

        1)   Economic indicators are variables that in the past have had a high correlation with aggregate economic activity. Indicators may lead, lag, or coincide with economic activity. A leading indicator is a forecast of future economic trends, and a lagging indicator changes after the change in economic activity has occurred.

    b.   The best known indicators are the composite indexes calculated by The Conference Board, a private research group with many corporate and other members worldwide.

        1)   The following are leading indicators:

            a)   Average workweek for production workers
            b)   Prices of the ordinary shares of 500 companies
            c)   Average weekly initial unemployment insurance claims
            d)   New orders for consumer goods and materials
            e)   New orders for nondefense capital goods
            f)   Building permits for homes
            g)   Vendor performance (slower deliveries signal stronger demand)
            h)   Money supply
            i)   Index of consumer expectations
            j)   Interest rate spread

        2)   The following are lagging indicators:

            a)   Average duration of unemployment in weeks
            b)   Change in index of labor cost per unit of output
            c)   Average prime rate charged by banks
            d)   Ratio of manufacturing and trade inventories to sales
            e)   Commercial and industrial loans outstanding
            f)   Ratio of consumer installment credit outstanding to personal income
            g)   Change in consumer price index for services

3) The following are coincident indicators:

    a) Employees on nonagricultural payrolls
    b) Personal income minus transfer payments
    c) Industrial production (based on value added and physical output)
    d) Manufacturing and trade sales

2. **National Income Accounting**

  a. National income accounting measures the output and performance of the economy. The gross domestic product (GDP) is the principal measure. It is the total market value of all final goods and services produced within the boundaries of a country, whether by domestic or foreign-owned sources, during a specified period of time (usually a year).

  b. GDP is calculated without regard to the ownership of productive resources. Thus, the value of the output of a factory abroad is excluded regardless of its ownership, but the output of a foreign-owned factory is included in the host country's GDP.

  c. Income (resource cost) approach. GDP equals the sum of the items below.

    1) Employee compensation, interest, and rents
    2) Self-employment income
    3) Depreciation (consumption of fixed capital)
    4) Indirect business taxes (e.g., sales taxes)
    5) Rents, interest income, and corporate profits
    6) Net income of foreigners (a positive number if the amount earned domestically by foreigners exceeds the amount earned abroad by citizens)

  d. Expenditure approach. GDP is also the sum of

    1) Personal consumption expenditures
    2) Gross private domestic investment
    3) Government purchases
    4) Net exports

  e. To avoid double counting, the value added to each good or service at each stage of production over the period must be summed. Alternatively, the total market value of all final goods and services may be added.

  f. GDP is not an ideal measure of economic well-being.

    1) GDP is a monetary measure. Accordingly, comparing GDP over a period of time requires adjustment for changes in the price level. The GDP deflator is a price index used to convert nominal GDP to real GDP.

    2) Increases in GDP often involve environmental damage, such as noise, extreme population density in cities, or pollution.

    3) GDP is not adjusted for changes in the population (which changes per capita income).

    4) Changes in the value of leisure time are not considered.

    5) Some nonmarket transactions are excluded, e.g., the value of homemakers' work.

    6) Military expenditures are included at cost, not incremental total value.

  g. Other National Income Concepts

    1) The gross national product (GNP) measures the output of a country's production, including factors of production located outside the boundaries of the country. The GNP differs from the GDP because GNP includes the output of a country's workers located in another country. It also equals GDP minus net income of foreigners (a positive or negative amount).

2) Net domestic product (NDP) = GDP – depreciation.

3) National income (NI) = NDP + net income earned abroad – indirect business taxes (e.g., sales taxes).

    a) NI is the income earned by a nation's resources, whether located at home or abroad.

    b) NI plus depreciation and indirect business taxes equals GNP.

4) Personal income (PI) = NI – corporate income taxes and undistributed profits – required contributions to governmental Social Security programs + transfer payments (public and private).

5) Disposable income = PI – personal income taxes.

h. Real per capita output is GDP divided by population, adjusted for inflation. It is used as a measure of the standard of living.

3. **Measuring Inflation**

a. One type of index measures inflation at the consumer level in a country by a monthly pricing of items on a theoretical household shopping list.

1) The current index uses a base year as a reference point. The price in the current year of a specified group of goods and services is determined relative to the same items for the base year:

$$\frac{Price\ of\ specified\ items\ in\ a\ given\ year}{Price\ of\ the\ same\ items\ in\ the\ base\ year} \times 100$$

2) Another type of index measures increases in prices at the wholesale level. It is often accepted as a substitute for future inflation.

b. The GDP deflator is a price index that includes every item produced in the economy at the price at which it entered the GDP account. Nominal GDP is stated at the actual prices at time of measurement. Real GDP, after application of the deflator, is stated in base-year amounts.

1) Real GDP increases when resource inputs and their productivity increase. For example, to the extent that real GDP depends on labor inputs, real GDP equals total worker hours (labor input) times labor productivity (real output per worker per hour).

c. The distinction between nominal income and real income is crucial for understanding the effects of inflation.

1) Nominal income is the amount in money received by a consumer as wages, interest, rent, and profits.

2) Real income is the purchasing power of the income received. Purchasing power relates directly to the consumer's standard of living.

    a) Real income decreases when the rate of increase in nominal income does not at least equal the rate of inflation.

4. **Unemployment**

a. Frictional unemployment is the amount of unemployment caused by the normal operation of the labor market.

1) Frictionally unemployed people include those moving to another place, those ceasing work temporarily to pursue further education and training, and those who are simply between jobs.

2) This definition acknowledges that a certain amount of unemployment exists at any given time.

    b.   Structural unemployment results when the composition of the workforce does not match the need. It is the result of changes in consumer demand, technology, and geographical location.

        1)   As consumers' desires shift, certain skills become obsolete.

        2)   For example, the computer revolution has drastically changed the skills required for many jobs and completely eliminated others.

    c.   Cyclical unemployment is directly related to the level of an economy's output. For this reason, it is sometimes called deficient-demand unemployment.

        1)   As consumers slow their spending, entities cut back production and lay off workers.

    d.   Full Employment

        1)   The natural rate of unemployment consists of the sum of frictional and structural unemployment.

            a)   Economists consider the economy to be at full employment when all unemployed workers are in these categories.

            b)   The rate varies over time because of demographic and institutional changes in the economy.

        2)   The economy's potential output is the real (inflation-adjusted) domestic output that could be achieved if the economy sustained full employment.

            a)   This concept illustrates the importance of providing all interested workers with productive jobs.

Stop and review! You have completed the outline for this subunit. Study multiple-choice questions 18 through 20 on page 324.

7.6 LEGAL RULES OF EVIDENCE

    1.   **Sources**

        a.   The legal rules of evidence are found in statutes, case law, and constitutions. Their essential purpose is to govern the admissibility of evidence in legal proceedings, but they are drafted to protect the parties as well as to determine the truth.

           1)   Exclusionary rules prevent the admission of evidence whose value as proof is offset by its possible prejudicial effect. An internal auditor, however, need not be limited by the legal and constitutional safeguards imposed in court.

               a)   The internal auditor may examine and evaluate any information until, in his/her professional judgment, sufficient, reliable, relevant, and useful information has been collected.

               b)   In this text, the word "evidence" is used strictly in the legal context. The word "information" is used to signify the support for the internal auditor's observations, conclusions, and recommendations.

    2.   **Internal Audit**

        a.   Nevertheless, legal and internal auditing concepts have much in common. Information in the internal auditing context and evidence in the legal context are intended to provide a basis for belief, to prove or disprove something.

        b.   The legal rules of evidence may be most obviously relevant to internal auditors when they participate in fraud investigations or provide litigation-support services, but such knowledge also may be beneficial in ordinary engagement work.

3.   **Types of Evidence**

    a.   Best evidence or primary evidence is the most satisfactory and reliable method of proof.

        1)   The most frequent application of the best evidence rule is to documentary evidence.

        2)   To prove the content of a writing, the original contract, deed, business record, or other document must be produced if it is available.

            a)   The purpose of preventing the admission of testimonial evidence to prove the content of a writing is to avoid misinterpretation.

                i)   However, oral evidence may be admissible to explain the terms of a writing when it is subject to more than one reasonable interpretation.

    b.   Secondary evidence is less reliable than primary evidence because it may consist of copies of original documents or oral evidence regarding their content.

        1)   Nevertheless, copies may be admissible when the originals

            a)   Have been lost or destroyed without wrongful intent by the party offering the copies

            b)   Cannot be obtained through legal or other reasonable means by the party offering the copies

            c)   Are within the control of a public entity

        2)   Copies are preferable to written summaries of, or oral testimony about, original writings. However, these types of evidence may be admitted when the originals

            a)   Are too numerous to be processed feasibly
            b)   Cannot be considered by the court within a reasonable time
            c)   Are available to be produced for inspection at the court's discretion

        3)   Secondary evidence also may be admitted when production of the originals, such as the accounting records of a business, and their possession by the court for a long time might cause undue hardship on a party.

    c.   Direct evidence is proof without presumption or inference.

        1)   Examples are original documents and testimony about what a witness him/herself did, saw, or heard.

    d.   Circumstantial evidence is indirect evidence. It proves intermediate facts from which a primary fact that is material to the matter in dispute may be inferred.

        1)   For example, an alteration of online accounting data protected by password access is circumstantial evidence that an authorized person was responsible. However, this inference may be unsound if an unauthorized person has been able to obtain the necessary password.

    e.   Conclusive evidence is so powerful that it permits only one reasonable conclusion and needs no additional corroboration.

    f.   Corroborative evidence supports other evidence.

        1)   For example, the testimony of a second eyewitness to an event may confirm the account of the first witness.

g. Opinion evidence is usually excluded because of its potentially prejudicial effect.

1) Witnesses ordinarily are allowed to testify only as to factual matters within their direct experience.

2) An exception is made for expert opinion. Such testimony is allowed when it

a) Concerns matters beyond the knowledge of nonexperts

b) Is offered by someone whose special knowledge and objectivity will assist the court and the jury in determining the truth

h. Hearsay evidence is a statement other than one made by the declarant while testifying at the trial or hearing, offered in evidence to prove the truth of the matter asserted.

1) For example, if Employee A states that Employee B said that she saw Employee C steal from petty cash, Employee A's statement, if offered to prove that Employee C stole from petty cash, is hearsay.

2) Hearsay is normally inadmissible because it cannot be tested by cross-examination. Thus, if Employee A's knowledge of the matter is limited only to Employee B's statement, questions cannot be asked testing its truth.

3) Various exceptions to the hearsay rule exist based on circumstances promoting the reliability of the assertions.

a) For example, many business documents effectively are hearsay, but those created in the ordinary course of business (e.g., purchase orders and sales invoices) are admissible if properly authenticated.

Stop and review! You have completed the outline for this subunit. Study multiple-choice questions 21 through 23 on page 325.

7.7 CONTRACTS

1. **Contract Law**

a. No part of commercial law is more important than contract law. Billions of contract-based agreements to transfer property and services are negotiated daily by individuals, businesses, and governments.

b. Promise keeping is essential for planning in a modern complex society. Without a legal system committed to enforcement of private contracts, everyday transactions in a free-enterprise economy would be impossible.

1) Contract law allows parties to enter into private agreements with assurance that they are enforceable against a party that fails to perform.

c. A contract is a promise or an agreement that the law recognizes as establishing a duty of performance. It is enforceable by applying a remedy for its breach.

2. **Agreement**

a. The most basic element of a contract is a voluntary agreement by the parties. Agreement requires the mutual assent of the contracting parties reached through an offer by the offeror and acceptance by the offeree.

b. An offer is a statement or other communication that, if not terminated, confers upon the offeree the power of acceptance. An offer need not be in any particular form to be valid. It must

1) Be communicated to an offeree,

2) Indicate an intent to enter into a contract, and

3) Be sufficiently definite and certain.

    c.   Communication of an offer may be done in various ways and may occur over time. However, at some moment in the formation of a contract, each party expresses an intent to enter into a legally binding and enforceable agreement.

        1)   Whether an offer has been made is determined by an objective standard that uses the following test: Would a reasonable person assume that the power of acceptance had been conferred upon him/her?

            a)   An offer must be made with serious intent, not in anger, great excitement, or jest.

        2)   Language constituting an offer should be distinguished from that merely soliciting or inviting offers. Communications between parties may simply be preliminary negotiations concerning a possible contract. A party may initiate negotiations by suggesting the general nature of a possible contract.

    d.   An offer also must be definite and certain. If an offer is indefinite or vague or lacking an essential provision, no agreement arises from an attempt to accept it because the courts cannot tell what the parties are bound to do.

        1)   However, minor details left for future determination do not make an agreement too vague to be an offer.

    e.   An offer does not remain effective forever. The offer will terminate under any of the following circumstances:

        1)   Revocation by the offeror,
        2)   Rejection or counteroffer by the offeree,
        3)   Death or incompetency of either the offeror or offeree,
        4)   Destruction of the specific subject matter to which the offer relates,
        5)   Subsequent illegality of the offer, or
        6)   Lapse of a specified or reasonable time.

    f.   Acceptance of an offer is essential to the formation of a contract. An agreement consists of an offer and an acceptance.

        1)   To be effective, an acceptance must relate to the terms of the offer. The acceptance must be positive, unequivocal, and unconditional. It may not change, subtract from, add to, or qualify in any way the terms of the offer.

3. Consideration

    a.   Consideration is the primary basis for the enforcement of agreements in contract law. It is what is given to make a promise enforceable. Ordinarily, if a promise is not supported by consideration, it is not enforceable.

    b.   One requirement of consideration is mutuality of obligation. Both parties must give consideration. Consequently, something of legal value must be given in a bargained-for exchange when the parties intend an exchange.

    c.   The second required element of consideration is legal sufficiency (something of legal value). Consideration is legally sufficient to render a promise enforceable if the promisor receives a legal benefit or the promisee incurs a legal detriment.

        1)   To incur a legal detriment, the promisee must do (or promise to do) something that (s)he is not legally obligated to do. A legal detriment also consists of not doing (or promising not to do) something (s)he is legally entitled to do.

            a)   A cause-and-effect relationship must exist between the promise made by one party and the detriment incurred by the other.

4. **Capacity**

    a.   Parties to a contract must possess legal capacity. Capacity is the mental ability to make a rational decision, which includes the ability to perceive and appreciate all relevant facts. Three classes of parties are legally limited in their capacity to contract: minors (also known as infants), mentally incompetent persons, and intoxicated parties.

         1)   For public policy reasons, parties in these three groups are protected from the enforcement of most contracts against them.

5. **Legality**

    a.   Legality is an essential requirement for an agreement to be valid and enforceable. Formation or performance of an agreement may violate a criminal law, constitute a civil wrong upon which a suit may be filed, or be determined by a court to be contrary to public policy. In these instances, the agreement is illegal and unenforceable.

    b.   An agreement that is contrary to public policy has a negative effect on society that outweighs the interests of the parties. This principle reflects a balancing by the courts of freedom of contract and the public interest. Examples of agreements that may violate public policy are

         1)   Agreements to unduly restrain competition;
         2)   Clauses that excuse one of the parties from any liability;
         3)   Contracts calling for immoral acts; and
         4)   Agreements found to be unfair, oppressive, or unconscionable.

6. **Written Contracts**

    a.   An oral contract is as enforceable as a written contract. However, a statute may require that some contracts be in writing to be enforceable. For example, statutes may require the following to be in writing:

         1)   Contracts involving an interest in land

         2)   Contracts that by their terms cannot possibly be performed within 1 year (e.g., some employment contracts)

         3)   Collateral promises by which a person promises to answer for the debt or duty of another (e.g., a guarantee)

         4)   Contracts for the sale of goods for more than a stated amount

Stop and review! You have completed the outline for this subunit. Study multiple-choice questions 24 through 27 beginning on page 325.

QUESTIONS

7.1 Regulation of Business

1. Regulatory agencies usually do **not** have power to

A. Impose agency taxes on private industry.

B. Issue rules and regulations.

C. Investigate violations of statutes and rules.

D. Conduct hearings and decide whether violations have occurred.

Answer (A) is correct. *(CMA, adapted)*
REQUIRED: The true statement about the powers that regulatory agencies do not have.
DISCUSSION: A regulatory agency may regulate some aspect of all industries or may regulate a specific industry in accordance with power delegated by the enabling legislation. Agency functions include executive, adjudicatory, and rule-making activities. Such agencies, however, may not impose taxes.
Answer (B) is incorrect. Regulatory agencies have the power to issue rules and regulations. Answer (C) is incorrect. Regulatory agencies have the power to investigate violations of statutes and rules. Answer (D) is incorrect. Regulatory agencies have the power to conduct hearings and decide whether violations have occurred.

2. The basic purpose of most national securities laws is to regulate the issue of investment securities by

A. Providing a regulatory framework for those local governments that do not have their own securities laws.

B. Requiring disclosure of all relevant facts so that investors can make informed decisions.

C. Prohibiting the issuance of securities that the government determines are not of investment grade.

D. Channeling investment funds into uses that are economically most important.

Answer (B) is correct. *(CMA, adapted)*
REQUIRED: The means of regulating the issue of investment securities.
DISCUSSION: The basic purpose of the securities laws is to provide disclosure of adequate information so that investors can evaluate investments. This is accomplished through reporting requirements concerning the issuance and subsequent trading of securities. However, the government does not assess the merits of these securities.
Answer (A) is incorrect. National law applies in all parts of a country. Answer (C) is incorrect. The government does not determine the merits of securities. It evaluates whether sufficient information is provided. Answer (D) is incorrect. The securities laws generally are not intended to influence the investment of capital in more socially or economically beneficial ways.

3. An antifraud law that prohibits trading on the basis of inside information about a business corporation's shares most likely applies to

A. Officers and directors.

B. All officers, directors, and shareholders.

C. Officers, directors, and holders of a large amount of the corporation's shares.

D. Anyone who bases his/her trading activities on the inside information.

Answer (D) is correct. *(CMA, adapted)*
REQUIRED: The person(s) most likely prohibited from trading securities based on inside information.
DISCUSSION: Such antifraud provisions typically prohibit any person from engaging in manipulative or deceptive acts in the purchase or sale of any security. It prohibits trading on the basis of inside information and applies to anyone who has not made a full disclosure of the inside information. It may apply not only to officers, directors, and shareholders, but also to tippees, i.e., those who receive inside information from insiders.

4. Antitrust laws are intended to

A. Establish set profit percentages for entities in regulated industries.

B. Prohibit entities in the same industry from engaging in joint ventures.

C. Require entities in regulated industries to share any patent rights with other entities in that industry.

D. Ensure a free and competitive market in which consumer demand dictates prices.

Answer (D) is correct. *(Publisher, adapted)*
REQUIRED: The intent of antitrust laws.
DISCUSSION: Antitrust laws are designed to promote more efficient allocation of resources, greater choice for consumers, greater business opportunities, fairness in economic behavior, and avoidance of concentrated political power resulting from economic power. Competition results in greater output and lower prices than other market structures.
Answer (A) is incorrect. Profit percentages are not set by antitrust laws other than to the extent that price discrimination is prohibited. Answer (B) is incorrect. Entities may enter into joint ventures. Answer (C) is incorrect. Patents confer a monopoly for a statutory period.

5. Which one of the following examples of corporate behavior would most clearly represent a violation of antitrust law?

    A. A retailer offers quantity discounts to large institutional buyers.

    B. The members of a labor union meet and agree not to work for a specific entity unless the starting wage is at least a specified amount per hour.

    C. Two entities that are in different, unrelated industries merge.

    D. Two entities in the same industry agree in a telephone conversation to submit identical bids on a government contract.

Answer (D) is correct. *(CMA, adapted)*
    REQUIRED: The item that would most clearly represent a violation of antitrust law.
    DISCUSSION: Antitrust law addresses restraints of trade. Some types of arrangements are considered automatic violations. These violations may include price fixing, division of markets, group boycotts, and resale price maintenance. Agreeing to submit identical bids on a government contract is a form of price fixing.
    Answer (A) is incorrect. Quantity discounts are not prohibited. Answer (B) is incorrect. Antitrust laws usually do not apply to labor unions. Answer (C) is incorrect. Only mergers that could lead to restraint of trade are outlawed.

7.2 International Trade

6. The total exports of Vietnam are US $20,000,000 worth of rice to Greece, and the total exports of Greece are US $18,000,000 worth of olives to Vietnam. The terms of trade are

	Greece	Vietnam
A.	90	111
B.	120	180
C.	111	90
D.	97	103

Answer (A) is correct. *(CIA, adapted)*
    REQUIRED: The terms of trade given the value of two countries' exports.
    DISCUSSION: A country's terms of trade are calculated by dividing its export price index by its import price index and multiplying by 100. Greece's total exports (US $18,000,000) divided by its total imports (US $20,000,000) equals 0.9 × 100 = 90. Vietnam's total exports (US $20,000,000) divided by its total imports (US $18,000,000) equals 1.11 × 100 = 111.

7. The economic reasoning dictating that each nation specialize in the production of goods that it produces relatively more efficiently than other nations and import those goods that are produced relatively more efficiently by other nations is called the doctrine of

    A. Efficient trade.

    B. Diminishing returns.

    C. Relative competition.

    D. Comparative advantage.

Answer (D) is correct. *(CMA, adapted)*
    REQUIRED: The reason each nation should specialize in those goods it produces relatively more efficiently than other nations.
    DISCUSSION: The doctrine of comparative advantage relates to comparative costs within one country. It holds that a country should produce those products in which it has a comparative advantage, not necessarily those products in which it has an absolute advantage. The doctrine suggests that a country should produce those products for which the greatest efficiencies are attainable even if it could also produce other goods more efficiently than another nation. In the long run, importing a product in which a country has an absolute advantage but not a comparative advantage will result in an overall increase in global production.
    Answer (A) is incorrect. Efficient trade is not meaningful in this context. Answer (B) is incorrect. Diminishing returns is not meaningful in this context. Answer (C) is incorrect. Relative competition is not meaningful in this context.

8. Which of the following is a tariff?

    A. Licensing requirements.

    B. Consumption taxes on imported goods.

    C. Unreasonable standards pertaining to product quality and safety.

    D. Domestic content rules.

Answer (B) is correct. *(CIA, adapted)*
    REQUIRED: The example of a tariff.
    DISCUSSION: Tariffs are excise taxes on imported goods imposed either to generate revenue or protect domestic producers. Thus, consumption taxes on imported goods are tariffs.
    Answer (A) is incorrect. Licensing requirements limit exports, e.g., of militarily sensitive technology. Answer (C) is incorrect. Unreasonable standards pertaining to product quality and safety are nontariff trade barriers. Answer (D) is incorrect. Domestic content rules require that a portion of an imported good be made in the importing country.

9. Which of the following is an economic rationale for government intervention in trade?

    A. Maintaining spheres of influence.

    B. Protecting infant industries.

    C. Preserving national identity.

    D. Dealing with friendly countries.

Answer (B) is correct. *(Publisher, adapted)*
    REQUIRED: The best economic rationale for government intervention in trade.
    DISCUSSION: The infant-industry argument contends that protective tariffs are needed to allow new domestic industries to become established. Once such industries reach a maturity stage in their life cycles, the tariffs can supposedly be removed.

10. Governments most likely restrict trade in the long run to

  I.   Help foster new industries.
  II. Protect declining industries.
  III. Increase tax revenues.
  IV. Foster national security.

    A. I only.

    B. I and II only.

    C. II and III only.

    D. I, II, and IV only.

Answer (B) is correct. *(CIA, adapted)*
    REQUIRED: The reason(s) governments restrict trade in the long run.
    DISCUSSION: Governmental limitations on global competition are generally imposed for the announced purpose of protecting local entities and jobs and developing new industries. They also may have the effect of raising revenue in the short run. In the long run, tax revenues will decline because of reduced trade. Examples of governmental limitations are (1) tariffs; (2) duties; (3) quotas; (4) domestic content rules; (5) preferences for local entities regarding procurement, taxes, R&D, labor regulations, and other operating rules; and (6) other laws (e.g., antibribery or tax) enacted by a national government that restrict international trade. These limitations are most likely when industries are viewed as crucial.
    Answer (A) is incorrect. Governments often impose limitations on global competition to protect declining industries. Answer (C) is incorrect. Restrictions on global trade, e.g., tariffs, may increase tax revenues in the short run. However, in the long run, the effect of reduced trade is to decrease tax revenues. Answer (D) is incorrect. Restricting trade for national security reasons is often not necessary in the long run. For example, a ban on export of sensitive technology is no longer needed when it becomes obsolete.

7.3 Currency Exchange Rates and Markets

11. If the value of the U.S. dollar in foreign currency markets changes from US $1 = .95 euros to US $1 = .90 euros,

    A. The euro has depreciated against the dollar.

    B. Products imported from Europe to the U.S. will become more expensive.

    C. U.S. tourists in Europe will find their dollars will buy more European products.

    D. U.S. exports to Europe should decrease.

Answer (B) is correct. *(CMA, adapted)*
    REQUIRED: The effect of a depreciation in the value of the dollar.
    DISCUSSION: The dollar has declined in value relative to the euro. If an American had previously wished to purchase a European product that was priced at 10 euros, the price would have been about US $10.53. After the dollar's decline in value, the price of the item has increased to about US $11.11. Hence, imports from Europe should decrease and exports increase.
    Answer (A) is incorrect. The euro has appreciated (increased in value) relative to the dollar. Answer (C) is incorrect. Dollars will buy fewer European products. Answer (D) is incorrect. U.S. exports should increase.

12. Two countries have flexible exchange rate systems and an active trading relationship. If incomes <List A> in country 1, everything else being equal, then the currency of country 1 will tend to <List B> relative to the currency of country 2.

	List A	List B
A.	Rise	Remain constant
B.	Fall	Depreciate
C.	Rise	Depreciate
D.	Remain constant	Appreciate

Answer (C) is correct. *(CIA, adapted)*
    REQUIRED: The effect of a change in incomes in one nation on its currency.
    DISCUSSION: If incomes in country 1 rise, consumers in country 1 will increase their imports from country 2. The resulting increase in the supply of country 1's currency will result in a tendency for it to depreciate relative to the currency of country 2.
    Answer (A) is incorrect. If incomes in country 1 rise, the result will be a tendency for it to devalue relative to the currency of country 2. Answer (B) is incorrect. If incomes in country 1 fall, consumers in country 1 will reduce their imports. The resulting decrease in the supply of country 1's currency will result in a tendency for it to appreciate relative to the currency of country 2. Answer (D) is incorrect. If incomes in country 1 remain constant, the currency of country 1 will not tend to appreciate or depreciate relative to the currency of country 2.

13. An entity has a foreign-currency-denominated trade payable, due in 60 days. To eliminate the foreign currency exchange-rate risk associated with the payable, the entity could

A. Sell foreign currency forward today.

B. Wait 60 days and pay the invoice by purchasing foreign currency in the spot market at that time.

C. Buy foreign currency forward today.

D. Borrow foreign currency today, convert it to domestic currency on the spot market, and invest the funds in a domestic bank deposit until the invoice payment date.

Answer (C) is correct. *(CIA, adapted)*
  REQUIRED: The means of eliminating exchange-rate risk.
  DISCUSSION: The entity can arrange to purchase the foreign currency today rather than in 60 days by buying the currency in the forward market. This hedging transaction will eliminate the exchange-rate risk associated with the trade payable.
  Answer (A) is incorrect. A forward market sale of foreign currency is appropriate to hedge a receivable denominated in a foreign currency. Answer (B) is incorrect. Waiting to buy the currency in 60 days does not eliminate the risk of an adverse exchange-rate movement. Answer (D) is incorrect. This strategy would be comparable to a future sale of the foreign currency at a rate known today, which would not provide the currency needed to pay the invoice. However, the opposite strategy would be an effective money market hedge. If the entity converted domestic currency to foreign currency in the spot market today and invested in a foreign bank deposit or treasury bill, it could then use the proceeds from the foreign investment to pay the invoice in 60 days.

7.4 Methods of Taxation

14. An individual had taxable income of US $23,000 per year and paid US $8,000 in income tax. The individual's taxable income then increased to US $30,000 per year resulting in a US $10,000 income tax liability. The personal tax system being applied to this individual is

A. Progressive.

B. Regressive.

C. Marginal.

D. Proportional.

Answer (B) is correct. *(CIA, adapted)*
  REQUIRED: The nature of the personal tax system.
  DISCUSSION: The average tax rate of the individual has decreased from 34.8% (US $8,000 ÷ $23,000) to 33.3% (US $10,000 ÷ $30,000). Under a regressive tax system, the average tax rate falls as income rises, although the amount of tax paid may rise.
  Answer (A) is incorrect. Under a progressive tax system, both the amount of tax and the percentage of income paid in tax (the average tax rate) rise as income increases. In the case described, the individual pays a higher amount of tax but a lower percentage of income in tax. Answer (C) is incorrect. Marginal is not a type of tax system but a type of tax rate. The marginal tax rate is the tax rate paid on incremental income. Answer (D) is incorrect. Under a proportional income tax system, the average tax rate is the same for all levels of income. The average tax rate of this individual falls as income rises.

15. Which of the following designations refers to taxes that will **not** necessarily take a larger absolute amount of income as income rises?

A. Progressive.

B. Proportional.

C. Regressive.

D. Regenerative.

Answer (C) is correct. *(CIA, adapted)*
  REQUIRED: The taxes that will not necessarily take a larger absolute amount of income as income rises.
  DISCUSSION: Regressive taxes are those for which the average tax rate falls as income rises. They take a smaller percentage of income as income rises, so they will not necessarily take a larger absolute amount of income as income rises.
  Answer (A) is incorrect. Progressive taxes, for which the average tax rate rises as income rises, take both a larger percentage of income and a larger absolute amount of income as income rises. Answer (B) is incorrect. Proportional taxes, for which the average tax rate is constant for all income levels, always take a larger absolute amount of income as income rises. Answer (D) is incorrect. Regenerative is not a term used to designate types of taxes.

16. On what basis is value-added tax collected?

A. The difference between the value of an entity's sales and the value of its purchases from other domestic entities.

B. The difference between the selling price of a real estate property and the amount the entity originally paid for the property.

C. The value of an entity's sales to related companies.

D. The profit earned on an entity's sales.

Answer (A) is correct. *(CIA, adapted)*
  REQUIRED: The basis for collecting a value-added tax.
  DISCUSSION: A value-added tax (VAT) is collected on the basis of the value created by the entity. This tax is measured by the difference between the value of the entity's sales and the value of its purchases. A VAT is in effect a retail sales tax. Because a consumer can avoid the tax by not purchasing, a VAT encourages saving and discourages consumption.
  Answer (B) is incorrect. The difference between the selling price of a real estate property and the amount the entity originally paid for the property is a capital gain. Answer (C) is incorrect. The value of an entity's sales to related companies is the internal transfer price. Answer (D) is incorrect. The profit earned on an entity's sales is subject to the income tax.

17. In most countries <List A> taxes tend to be <List B> with respect to income.

	List A	List B
A.	General sales	Proportional
B.	Property	Regressive
C.	Personal income	Proportional
D.	Personal income	Regressive

Answer (B) is correct. *(CIA, adapted)*
REQUIRED: The correct match of a tax and its proportion of a taxpayer's income.
DISCUSSION: Property taxes tend to be regressive. Taxpayers with lower incomes must pay a higher portion of their incomes for necessities, such as housing.
Answer (A) is incorrect. General sales taxes tend to be regressive. The lower the taxpayer's income, the higher the proportion that is usually paid in sales taxes, which are collected at a flat rate per dollar. Low-income taxpayers are unable to save as high a portion of their income as high-income taxpayers. Thus, the latter are less exposed to general sales taxes because they avoid the tax on the amount saved. Answer (C) is incorrect. Personal income taxes tend to be progressive. Higher tax rates are charged on higher incomes. Answer (D) is incorrect. Personal income taxes tend to be progressive. Higher tax rates are charged on higher incomes.

7.5 Economic Indicators

18. Which of the following may provide a leading indicator of a future increase in gross domestic product?

A. A reduction in the money supply.

B. A decrease in the issuance of building permits.

C. An increase in the timeliness of delivery by vendors.

D. An increase in the average hours worked per week of production workers.

Answer (D) is correct. *(CIA, adapted)*
REQUIRED: The leading indicator.
DISCUSSION: An economic indicator is highly correlated with changes in aggregate economic activity. A leading indicator changes prior to a change in the direction of the business cycle. The leading indicators included in the Conference Board's index are average weekly hours worked by manufacturing workers, unemployment claims, consumer goods orders, share prices, orders for fixed assets, building permits, timeliness of deliveries, money supply, consumer confidence, and the spread between the yield on 10-year Treasury bonds and the federal funds rate. An increase in weekly hours worked by production workers is favorable for economic growth.
Answer (A) is incorrect. A falling money supply is associated with falling GDP. Answer (B) is incorrect. A decline in the issuance of building permits signals lower expected building activity and a falling GDP. Answer (C) is incorrect. An increase in the timeliness of delivery by vendors indicates reduced demand and potentially falling GDP.

19. The two main variables that contribute to increases in real gross domestic product (GDP) derived from labor inputs are labor productivity and

A. The potential labor force.

B. The inflation rate.

C. Quality of output.

D. Total worker hours.

Answer (D) is correct. *(CIA, adapted)*
REQUIRED: The other main variable contributing to increased real GDP derived from labor inputs.
DISCUSSION: Real GDP increases when resource inputs and their productivity increase. Thus, to the extent that real GDP depends on labor inputs, real GDP equals total worker hours (labor input) times labor productivity (real output per worker per hour).
Answer (A) is incorrect. The potential labor force is not a factor in the calculation. Rather, real GDP is determined by actual inputs and their productivity. Answer (B) is incorrect. Real GDP is adjusted for inflation. Answer (C) is incorrect. National income accounting does not address the quality of output.

20. Net domestic product is composed of the total market value of all

A. Final goods and services produced in the economy in 1 year.

B. Goods and services produced in the economy in 1 year.

C. Final goods and services produced in the economy in 1 year minus the capital consumption allowance.

D. Goods and services produced in the economy in 1 year minus the capital consumption allowance.

Answer (C) is correct. *(CIA, adapted)*
REQUIRED: The composition of net domestic product.
DISCUSSION: Net domestic product is the market value of all final goods and services produced within the boundaries of a country within 1 year minus the capital consumption allowance.
Answer (A) is incorrect. Net domestic product is calculated net of the capital consumption allowance. Answer (B) is incorrect. Net domestic product includes only final goods. The inclusion of intermediate goods would involve double counting. Also, net domestic product is calculated net of the capital consumption allowance. Answer (D) is incorrect. Net domestic product does not include intermediate goods. The inclusion of intermediate goods would involve double counting.

7.6 Legal Rules of Evidence

21. A contract dispute has arisen between an organization and a major supplier. To resolve the dispute, the most reliable evidence is

   A. Oral testimony of contracting parties.

   B. The original contract.

   C. Actions by parties to the contract.

   D. A letter from the supplier's attorney.

Answer (B) is correct. *(CIA, adapted)*
   REQUIRED: The most reliable evidence to resolve a contract dispute between an entity and a major supplier.
   DISCUSSION: The best (primary) evidence is the most persuasive evidence. Reliability and the best evidence rule are closely related. The best evidence rule is ordinarily applied only to documentary evidence, especially to proof of the content of a writing. If the original writing is available, the best evidence rule prohibits a party from proving the content of a writing through oral testimony. Thus, the original writing is the most reliable evidence.
   Answer (A) is incorrect. If the original writing is available, oral testimony cannot contradict the content of the writing.
Answer (C) is incorrect. The contract itself is the best evidence.
Answer (D) is incorrect. The contract itself is the best evidence.

22. During interviews with the inventory management personnel, an internal auditor learned that salespersons often order inventory for stock without receiving the approval of the vice president of sales. Also, detail testing showed that there are no written approvals on purchase orders for replacement parts. The detail testing is a good example of

   A. Indirect evidence.

   B. Circumstantial evidence.

   C. Corroborative evidence.

   D. Subjective evidence.

Answer (C) is correct. *(CIA, adapted)*
   REQUIRED: The evidence of which detail testing is a good example.
   DISCUSSION: Corroborative evidence is evidence from a different source that supplements and confirms other evidence. For example, oral testimony that a certain procedure was not performed may be corroborated by the absence of documentation.
   Answer (A) is incorrect. Detail testing provides direct evidence that the approvals were not received. Indirect evidence establishes immediately collateral facts from which the main fact may be inferred. Answer (B) is incorrect. Circumstantial evidence tends to prove a fact by proving other events or circumstances that afford a basis for a reasonable inference of the occurrence of the fact. Thus, it is also indirect evidence. Answer (D) is incorrect. Subjective evidence is opinion-oriented and is not dependable for reaching engagement conclusions. No subjective evidence is present in this situation.

23. Much of the internal auditor's work involves accumulation of engagement information. A duplicate of a contract rather than the original is an example of what kind of evidence?

   A. Secondary.

   B. Circumstantial.

   C. Hearsay.

   D. Opinion.

Answer (A) is correct. *(CIA, adapted)*
   REQUIRED: The type of evidence exemplified by the duplicate of a contract.
   DISCUSSION: Secondary evidence according to the legal view is acceptable if primary evidence (the strongest evidence, e.g., original documents) has been destroyed or is not reasonably procurable. Secondary evidence must be a proper representation of primary evidence, e.g., copies of a contract.
   Answer (B) is incorrect. Circumstantial evidence inferentially establishes one fact by proving another collateral fact. Answer (C) is incorrect. Hearsay is an out-of-court statement offered in evidence to prove the truth of the matter asserted. Answer (D) is incorrect. Except for testimony by experts, witnesses may normally testify as to facts only.

7.7 Contracts

24. Which of the following is **not** a required element of a contract?

   A. Legality.

   B. Consideration.

   C. Legal capacity.

   D. A writing.

Answer (D) is correct. *(Publisher, adapted)*
   REQUIRED: The element not required in a contract.
   DISCUSSION: The four essential elements of a contract are an agreement (offer and acceptance), consideration, legal capacity of the parties to contract, and a legal objective or purpose. A writing is not required to enter into a contract. However, some contracts are not enforceable unless a writing evidences the contract.
   Answer (A) is incorrect. Legality is a required element of a contract. Answer (B) is incorrect. Consideration is a required element of a contract. Answer (C) is incorrect. Legal capacity is a required element of a contract.

25. The necessary elements of a contract include

A. Some form of writing, equal consideration, and legal capacity.

B. Formal execution, definite terms, and a valid offer and acceptance.

C. Offer and acceptance, consideration, legal capacity, and mutual assent.

D. Bilateral promises, legal capacity, and legality of purpose.

Answer (C) is correct.   *(Publisher, adapted)*
REQUIRED: Elements of a contract that are necessary.
DISCUSSION: Contracts require each of the following:

1. Offer and acceptance
2. Mutual assent (meeting of the minds)
3. Consideration (bargained-for exchange)
4. Legality (legal purpose)
5. Capacity of parties (legal ability)

Answer (A) is incorrect. An oral contract is usually enforceable. Consideration must be legally sufficient and must be bargained for but need not have equal market value. Answer (B) is incorrect. Most contracts are informal (simple), and if a term is missing, it can be implied by the court, with the exception of a quantity term. Answer (D) is incorrect. Promises can be unilateral or divisible.

26. Consideration consists of

A. Something with monetary value.

B. Each party's receiving an actual benefit only.

C. Two promises.

D. Legal sufficiency and bargained-for exchange.

Answer (D) is correct.   *(Publisher, adapted)*
REQUIRED: The elements of consideration.
DISCUSSION: Consideration must be legally sufficient and intended as a bargained-for exchange. A promisee has provided legally sufficient consideration if (s)he incurs a legal detriment or if the promisor receives a legal benefit. An essential aspect of consideration is that it be bargained for, and given in exchange for, the consideration provided by the other party. That is, consideration is mutual.

Answer (A) is incorrect. Monetary value is relatively unimportant. For example, a mere promise satisfies the element of legal sufficiency. Answer (B) is incorrect. Consideration is an exchange of legal benefit that may not have actual benefit. Answer (C) is incorrect. Contracts can be unilateral, which involves only one promise.

27. Lamar became homeless at a very young age and was taken in by Aunt and Uncle. Many years later, Lamar became a detective in the city police department. When Aunt disappeared and was not heard from for a month, the case was assigned to Lamar. Uncle also came to Lamar and asked him to promise to find Aunt in return for the years of support. Lamar agreed to Uncle's request. Which of the following is true?

A. Lamar's contractual duty to find Aunt is based on past consideration.

B. Lamar has no contractual duty to find Aunt.

C. If Uncle had also promised Lamar US $1,000 for finding Aunt, he would be liable when Lamar found her.

D. Lamar will be liable for breach of contract if he does not find Aunt.

Answer (B) is correct.   *(Publisher, adapted)*
REQUIRED: The true statement regarding contractual duty.
DISCUSSION: Lamar has a pre-existing legal duty to find Aunt. Consideration does not exist if an existing duty was imposed by law or a person is already under a contractual agreement to render a specified performance. Lamar will suffer no new legal detriment by promising to find Aunt. Thus, no contractual obligation exists.

Answer (A) is incorrect. Past consideration does not satisfy the consideration requirement for the formation of a contract. Answer (C) is incorrect. Lamar has a pre-existing legal duty to find Aunt. Answer (D) is incorrect. Lamar has not made a valid contract with Uncle.

Use the additional questions in Gleim *CIA Test Prep* Software to create Test Sessions that emulate Pearson VUE!

STUDY UNIT EIGHT
IT CONTROLS, NETWORKS, AND BUSINESS APPLICATIONS

(22 pages of outline)

This study unit addresses the control frameworks commonly used in designing internal control systems over IT, the nature and modes of computer processing, and basic IT control concepts. It continues with a treatment of computer communications and concludes with discussions of electronic funds transfer, electronic commerce, and electronic data interchange.

8.1 CONTROL FRAMEWORKS

The increasing integration of controls over automated systems with the organization's overall system of internal control is most clearly displayed in the eSAC and COBIT frameworks. These documents discuss at some length the role played by automated systems in pursuing the organization's mission, safeguarding assets, etc. Candidates for the CIA exam must be aware not just of detailed controls such as field checks, but also the role that control over IT plays in the organization's strategy implementation.

1. **Control Framework**

   a. A control framework is a model for establishing a system of internal control.

      1) The framework does not prescribe the actual controls themselves, but it does force management to focus on risk areas and design controls accordingly.

      2) Often, a control framework describes "families" of controls, that is, conceptual groupings of controls that attempt to address a particular type of risk exposure.

2. **COSO**

   a. Probably the most well-known control framework in the U.S. is Internal Control – Integrated Framework, published in 1992 by the Committee of Sponsoring Organizations of the Treadway Commission (COSO). The document is commonly referred to as "the COSO Framework."

   b. The COSO Framework defines internal control as

   A process, effected by an organization's board of directors, management, and other personnel, designed to provide reasonable assurance regarding the achievement of objectives in the following categories:

   - *Effectiveness and efficiency of operations*
   - *Reliability of financial reporting*
   - *Compliance with applicable laws and regulations*

      1) COSO's simple and straightforward definition has proved extremely useful. Also, these principles are as applicable to an organization's IT function as they are to any other.

c.   COSO further describes five components of an internal control system:

1) Control environment
2) Risk assessment
3) Control activities
4) Information and communication
5) Monitoring

a) This part of the model also can easily be used in an IT context.

d.   The importance and durability of the COSO Framework was reinforced when the U.S. Securities and Exchange Commission acknowledged it as an appropriate model for designing internal controls under the requirements of the Sarbanes-Oxley Act of 2002.

3.   **eSAC**

a.   *Electronic Systems Assurance and Control (eSAC)* is a publication of The IIA. In the eSAC model, the organization's internal processes accept inputs and produce outputs.

1) Inputs: Mission, values, strategies, and objectives
2) Outputs: Results, reputation, and learning

b.   The eSAC model's broad control objectives are influenced by those in the COSO Framework:

1) Operating effectiveness and efficiency
2) Reporting of financial and other management information
3) Compliance with laws and regulations
4) Safeguarding of assets

c.   eSAC's IT business assurance objectives fall into five categories:

1) Availability. The organization must assure that information, processes, and services are available at all times.
2) Capability. The organization must assure reliable and timely completion of transactions.
3) Functionality. The organization must assure that systems are designed to user specifications to fulfill business requirements.
4) Protectability. The organization must assure that a combination of physical and logical controls prevents unauthorized access to system data.
5) Accountability. The organization must assure that transactions are processed under firm principles of data ownership, identification, and authentication.

4.   **COBIT**

a.   Specifically for IT controls, the best-known framework is *Control Objectives for Information and Related Technology (COBIT)*. Version 4.1 of this document was published in 2007 by the IT Governance Institute.

b.   Automated information systems have been woven into every function of the modern organization, making IT governance an integral part of overall organizational governance. The COBIT model for IT governance contains five focus areas:

1) Strategic alignment
2) Value delivery
3) Resource management
4) Risk management
5) Performance measurement

   c.   The COBIT framework embodies four characteristics:

      1) Business-focused
      2) Process-oriented
      3) Controls-based
      4) Measurement-driven

   d.   Each characteristic contains multiple components.

      1) Business-focused

         a) This characteristic lists seven distinct but overlapping information criteria: effectiveness, efficiency, confidentiality, integrity, availability, compliance, and reliability.

         b) Business goals must feed IT goals, which in turn allow the organization to design the appropriate enterprise architecture for IT.

         c) IT resources include applications, information, infrastructure, and people.

      2) Process-oriented. This part of the model contains four domains:

         a) Plan and organize
         b) Acquire and implement
         c) Deliver and support
         d) Monitor and evaluate

      3) Controls-based. "An IT control objective is a statement of the desired result or purpose to be achieved by implementing control procedures in a particular IT activity." COBIT describes controls in three areas:

         a) Process controls. "Operational management uses processes to organize and manage ongoing IT activities."

         b) Business controls. These impact IT at three levels: the executive management level, the business process level, and the IT support level.

         c) IT general controls and application controls. This dichotomy for IT controls is of very long standing.

            i) "General controls are those controls embedded in IT processes and services ... Controls embedded in business process applications are commonly referred to as application controls."

      4) Measurement-driven

         a) The centerpiece of the COBIT framework in this area is the maturity model.

            i) "The organization must rate how well managed its IT processes are. The suggested scale employs the rankings of non-existent, initial, repeatable, defined, managed, and optimized."

         b) Performance measurement

         Goals and metrics are defined in COBIT at three levels:

- *IT goals and metrics that define what the business expects from IT*
- *Process goals and metrics that define what the IT processes must deliver to support IT's objectives*
- *Process performance metrics*

5.   **GTAG**

a.   Beginning in 2005, The IIA replaced its Practice Advisories on IT topics with an extremely detailed series of documents known collectively as the *Global Technology Audit Guide (GTAG)*.

b.   The control model discussed in GTAG 1, *Information Technology Controls*, is very useful for this discussion.

c.   GTAG 1 recognizes three "families" of controls:

1)   General and application controls, described in the COBIT framework in item 4.d.3)c) on the previous page

2)   Preventive, detective, and corrective controls

a)   Preventive controls "prevent errors, omissions, or security incidents from occurring."

b)   Detective controls "detect errors or incidents that elude preventive controls."

c)   Corrective controls "correct errors, omissions, or incidents once they have been detected."

3)   Governance, management, and technical controls

a)   "Governance controls ... are linked with the concepts of corporate governance, which are driven both by organizational goals and strategies and by outside bodies such as regulators."

b)   Management controls "are deployed as a result of deliberate actions by management to recognize risks to the organization, its processes, and assets; and enact mechanisms and processes to mitigate and manage risks."

c)   Technical controls "are specific to the technologies in use within the organization's IT infrastructures."

Stop and review! You have completed the outline for this subunit. Study multiple-choice questions 1 through 3 on page 349.

8.2 ASPECTS OF AUTOMATED INFORMATION PROCESSING

1.   **Characteristics of Automated Processing**

a.   The use of computers in business information systems has fundamental effects on the nature of business transacted, the procedures followed, the risks incurred, and the methods of mitigating those risks. These effects flow from the characteristics that distinguish computer-based from manual processing.

1)   Transaction trails. A complete trail useful for audit and other purposes might exist for only a short time or only in computer-readable form. The nature of the trail is often dependent on the transaction processing mode, for example, whether transactions are batched prior to processing or whether they are processed immediately as they happen.

2)   Uniform processing of transactions. Computer processing uniformly subjects like transactions to the same processing instructions and thus virtually eliminates clerical error, but programming errors (or other similar systematic errors in either the hardware or software) will result in all like transactions being processed incorrectly when they are processed under the same conditions.

3)   Segregation of functions. Many controls once performed by separate individuals may be concentrated in computer systems. Hence, an individual who has access to the computer may perform incompatible functions. As a result, other controls may be necessary to achieve the control objectives ordinarily accomplished by segregation of functions.

4)   Potential for errors and fraud. The potential for individuals, including those performing control procedures, to gain unauthorized access to data, to alter data without visible evidence, or to gain access (direct or indirect) to assets may be greater in computer systems. Decreased human involvement in handling transactions can reduce the potential for observing errors and fraud. Errors or fraud in the design or changing of application programs can remain undetected for a long time.

5)   Potential for increased management supervision. Computer systems offer management many analytical tools for review and supervision of operations. These additional controls may enhance internal control. For example, traditional comparisons of actual and budgeted operating ratios and reconciliations of accounts are often available for review on a more timely basis. Furthermore, some programmed applications provide statistics regarding computer operations that may be used to monitor actual processing.

6)   Initiation or subsequent execution of transactions by computer. Certain transactions may be automatically initiated or certain procedures required to execute a transaction may be automatically performed by a computer system. The authorization of these transactions or procedures may not be documented in the same way as those in a manual system, and management's authorization may be implicit in its acceptance of the design of the system.

7)   Dependence of controls in other areas on controls over computer processing. Computer processing may produce reports and other output that are used in performing manual control procedures. The effectiveness of these controls can be dependent on the effectiveness of controls over the completeness and accuracy of computer processing. For example, the effectiveness of a manual review of a computer-produced exception listing is dependent on the controls over the production of the listing.

2.   **Processing Modes**

a.   Batch processing. In this mode, transactions are accumulated and submitted to the computer as a single "batch." In the early days of computers, this was the only way a job could be processed.

1)   In batch processing, the user cannot influence the process once the job has begun (except to ask that it be aborted completely). (S)he must wait until the job is finished running to see if any transactions in the batch were rejected and failed to post.

2)   Despite huge advances in computer technology, this accumulation of transactions for processing on a delayed basis is still widely used. It is very efficient for such applications as payroll, where large numbers of routine transactions must be processed on a regular schedule.

b.   Online, real-time processing. In some systems, having the latest information available at all times is crucial to the proper functioning of the system. An airline reservation system is a common example.

1)   In an online, real-time system, the database is updated immediately upon entry of the transaction by the operator. Such systems are referred to as online transaction processing, or OLTP, systems.

Stop and review! You have completed the outline for this subunit. Study multiple-choice questions 4 through 9 beginning on page 350.

8.3 IT CONTROLS

1. **Classification of Controls**

    a. The COBIT framework provides the following discussion about the business controls mentioned on page 329:

        At the executive management level, business objectives are set, policies are established and decisions are made on how to deploy and manage the resources of the enterprise to execute the enterprise strategy.

        At the business process level, controls are applied to specific business activities. Most business processes are automated and integrated with IT application systems, resulting in many of the controls at this level being automated as well. These controls are known as application controls.

        To support the business processes, IT provides IT services, usually in a shared service to many business processes, as many of the development and operational IT processes are provided to the whole enterprise, and much of the IT infrastructure is provided as a common service (e.g., networks, databases, operating systems and storage). The controls applied to all IT service activities are known as IT general controls.

    b. The organization must implement appropriate controls at each of the three levels described in the COBIT model.

        1) For example, at the executive level, an IT steering committee should be established, composed of senior managers from both the IT function and the end-user functions. The committee approves development projects, assigns resources, and reviews their progress.

        2) The steering committee also ensures that requests for new systems are aligned with the overall strategic plan of the organization.

    c. The interaction between the last two types of controls described above (general and application) is crucial in an audit context. As COBIT goes on to specifically state:

        The reliable operation of these general controls is necessary for reliance to be placed on application controls.

        1) In other words, because general controls affect the organization's entire processing environment, the auditor must achieve satisfaction about their proper operation before relying on application controls.

    d. The COBIT model divides general controls into four basic areas: systems development, change management, security, and computer operations. These general controls are discussed in Study Unit 9, Subunits 7 and 8; Study Unit 10, Subunit 3; and Study Unit 9, Subunit 1, respectively.

    e. The COBIT model gives the following as examples of types of application controls: completeness, accuracy, validity, authorization, and segregation of duties.

        1) Note the similarity between these controls and the management assertions about financial statements in the standard audit model.

        2) This similarity highlights the fact that a computer application is merely the automation of a business process and the objectives of internal control are the same.

2. **Application Controls**

   a. Application controls relate to the business tasks performed by a particular system. They should provide reasonable assurance that the recording, processing, and reporting of data are properly performed.

   b. The most economical point for correcting input errors in an application is the time at which the data are entered into the system.

      1) For these reasons, input controls are the focus of an internal auditor's activity. Each of the two major types of processing modes has its own controls.

   c. Batch Input Controls

      1) Financial totals summarize dollar amounts in an information field in a group of records. The total produced by the system after the batch has been processed is compared to the total produced manually beforehand.

      2) Record counts track the number of records processed by the system for comparison to the number that the user expected to be processed.

      3) Hash totals are control totals without a defined meaning, such as the total of vendor numbers or invoice numbers, that are used to verify the completeness of the data.

   d. Online Input Controls

      1) Preformatting of data entry screens, i.e., to make them imitate the layout of a printed form, can aid the operator in keying to the correct fields.

      2) Field checks are tests of the characters in a field to verify that they are of an appropriate type for that field. For example, the system is programmed to reject alphabetic characters entered in the field for Social Security number.

      3) Validity checks compare the data entered in a given field with a table of valid values for that field. For example, the vendor number on a request to cut a check must match the table of current vendors, and the invoice number must match the approved invoice table.

      4) Limit and range checks are based on known limits for given information. For example, hours worked per week must be between 0 and 100, with anything outside that range requiring management authorization.

      5) Self-checking digits are used to detect incorrect identification numbers. The digit is generated by applying an algorithm to the ID number. During the input process, the check digit is recomputed by applying the same algorithm to the code actually entered.

   e. An important detective control is user review of output. Users should be able to determine when output is incomplete or not reasonable, particularly when the user prepared the input. Thus, users as well as computer personnel have a quality assurance function.

Stop and review! You have completed the outline for this subunit. Study multiple-choice questions 10 through 14 beginning on page 351.

8.4 DATA COMMUNICATIONS, NETWORKS, AND CLIENT-SERVER SYSTEMS

1. **Background to Networking**

    a. Large mainframe computers dominated the electronic data processing field in its first decades.

        1) Mainframes were arranged so that all processing and data storage were done in a single, central location.

        2) Communication with the mainframe was accomplished with the use of dumb terminals, simple keyboard-and-monitor combinations with no processing power (i.e., no CPU) of their own.

    b. The next stage in the evolution of networking was to connect computers not in different rooms of a building, but in separate buildings and eventually separate countries.

        1) This required converting the digital signal used internally by the computer into an analog signal suitable for transmission over ordinary telephone lines.

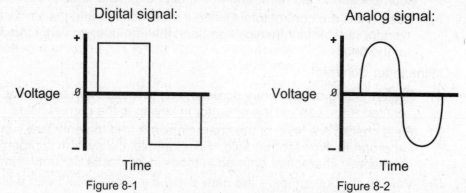

Figure 8-1   Figure 8-2

        a) This conversion is necessary because when a digital signal travels more than about 10 feet, it starts to lose its shape and eventually resembles an analog signal. By that point it has become completely unusable.

        2) In all-digital networks, such as LANs (see item 2. beginning on the next page) and connections between dumb terminals and mainframes, repeaters are placed every so often to revive the digital signal and return it to its full square-wave shape.

            a) This is obviously not an option with the existing telephone network and its hundreds of thousands of miles of wire.

            b) The solution is simply to convert the computer's digital signal into an analog signal (modulation), send it over the phone line, then reconvert it to a digital signal at the other end (demodulation).

            c) The device that performs these conversion and reconversion functions is a modem (short for modulator-demodulator).

        3) The introduction of the modem allowed organizations to begin moving information between locations in purely electronic format, eliminating the need for the passage of physical documents. The potential for cost savings in this technology was obvious.

    c. Improvements in technology have led to increasing decentralization of information processing.

        1) The mainframe-style computer was the only arrangement available in the early days of data processing. International Business Machines (now called IBM) dominated the marketplace.

        a)   Mainframes are still in use at large institutions, such as governments, banks, insurance companies, and universities.

            i)   However, remote connections to them are usually through desktop computers rather than through dumb terminals. This is known as terminal emulation.

        b)   In the 1980s, the minicomputer gave organizations the ability to perform data processing without the high cost and large dedicated facilities of a mainframe. Digital Equipment Corporation (DEC) and Hewlett-Packard (HP) dominated this market.

        c)   As minicomputers evolved, the concept of distributed processing arose.

            i)   Distributed processing involves the decentralization of processing tasks and data storage and assigning these functions to multiple computers, often in separate locations.

            ii)   This allowed for a drastic reduction in the amount of communications traffic because data that were needed locally could reside locally.

        d)   In 1981, IBM introduced the Personal Computer (PC). This designation quickly lost its status as a brand name and became a generic term for almost any computer smaller than a minicomputer.

    2)   During the 1980s, desktop computers, and the knowledge needed to build information systems, became widespread throughout the organization.

        a)   In the early part of this period, the only means of moving data from one computer to another was the laborious process of copying the data to a diskette and physically carrying it to the destination computer. This method of connecting computers was called sneakernet, after the footwear involved.

        b)   It was clear that a reliable way of wiring office computers together would lead to tremendous gains in productivity.

2.   LANs and Client-Server

    a.   This need led to the development of the local area network (LAN). A LAN is any interconnection between devices in a single office or building.

        1)   Very small networks with few devices can be connected using a peer-to-peer arrangement, where every device is directly connected to every other.

        2)   Peer-to-peer networks become increasingly difficult to administer with each added device.

    b.   The most cost-effective and easy-to-administer arrangement for LANs uses the client-server model.

        1)   Client-server networks differ from peer-to-peer networks in that the devices play more specialized roles. Client processes (initiated by the individual user) request services from server processes (maintained centrally).

        2)   In a client-server arrangement, servers are centrally located and devoted to the functions that are needed by all network users.

            a)   Examples include mail servers (to handle electronic mail), application servers (to run application programs), file servers (to store databases and make user inquiries more efficient), Internet servers (to manage access to the Internet), and web servers (to host websites).

            b)   Whether a device is classified as a server is not determined by its hardware configuration but rather by the function it performs. A simple desktop computer can be a server.

3) Technically, a client is any object that uses the resources of another object. Thus, a client can be either a device or a software program.

    a) In common usage, however, "client" refers to a device that requests services from a server. This understanding of the term encompasses anything from a powerful graphics workstation to a smartphone.

    b) A client device normally displays the user interface and enables data entry, queries, and the receipt of reports. Moreover, many applications, e.g., word processing and spreadsheet software, run on the client computer.

4) The key to the client-server model is that it runs processes on the platform most appropriate to that process while attempting to minimize traffic over the network.

5) Security for client-server systems may be more difficult than in a highly centralized system because of the numerous access points.

3. **OSI 7-Layer Model**

a. The Open Systems Interconnection (OSI) Reference Model provides a perspective for categorizing the functions that must be performed by any computer network.

b. Originally, it was devised by the International Organization for Standardization (ISO) as the basis for an actual family of protocols. Many nations and companies in Europe and Asia began adopting these protocols as they became standardized.

1) However, the OSI protocols were eventually overwhelmed worldwide by the spread of the Internet and its accompanying TCP/IP set of protocols [see item 6.d.2)a) on page 342].

2) Although the protocols did not survive, the reference model portion of the overall OSI project has proven useful for the study of networks.

c. The OSI reference model depicts any computer network as required to perform certain functions. The functions are grouped in seven layers.

1) Each layer provides "services" to the next higher layer. This can be depicted by the diagram below:

OSI 7-Layer Network Reference Model

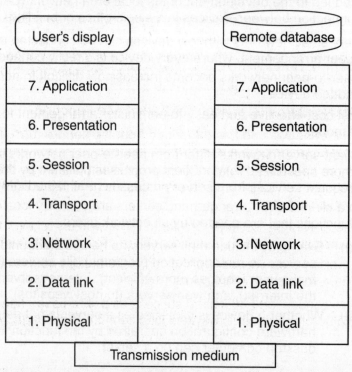

Figure 8-3

    d.   The functions performed by the layers can be summarized as follows:

        1)   The physical layer (layer 1) describes how the bits must be organized to flow over the medium being used (copper wire, fiber optic, microwave, etc.).

        2)   The data link layer (layer 2) ensures that errors in the stream of data are detected and corrected.

        3)   The network layer (layer 3) ensures the "packets" of data on the network move to the correct destination.

        4)   The transport layer (layer 4) establishes a "class of service" between the two communicating parties (such as batch or interactive) and ensures that sufficient resources are available to maintain it.

        5)   The session layer (layer 5) ensures a continuous session between the two communicating parties, such that the users experience no interruptions taking place on the transport layer beneath.

        6)   The presentation layer (layer 6) negotiates "syntax" differences between the two communicating parties. This refers to the various ways digital bits are arranged to represent letters and numbers (ASCII and EBCDIC are the best known).

        7)   The application layer (layer 7) interacts with the user's hardware, operating system, and application to make data entry and display possible.

    e.   The following analogy can be useful for understanding how the OSI reference model depicts the management of a data stream:

        1)   At the highest layer, a person writes a letter. The person then proceeds to fold the letter, insert it in an envelope, seal the envelope, address it, apply a stamp, and place it in the custody of the Postal Service.

            a)   The process just described corresponds to the movement of a data packet down the layers. The Postal Service is the transmission medium.

            b)   At each layer, some information is added to the packet, wrapping it in more and more extra data to perform the necessary functions.

        2)   The recipient of the envelope receives it, opens it, pulls out the letter, unfolds it, and reads it.

            a)   This corresponds to the movement of the data packet up the layers on the destination computer.

            b)   At each layer, the network strips away the extra data applied at that layer by the sender, eventually getting the message into a form understandable by the recipient.

4. Classifying Networks by Geographical Extent and Function

    a.   The range of networking has expanded from the earliest form (two computers in the same room) to the global reach of the Internet.

    b.   A local area network (LAN) connects devices within a single office or home or among buildings in an office park. The key aspect here is that a LAN is owned entirely by a single organization.

        1)   The LAN is the network familiar to office workers all over the world. In its simplest conception, it can consist of a few desktop computers and a printer.

    c.   A metropolitan area network (MAN) connects devices across an urban area, for instance, two or more office parks.

        1)   This conception had limited success as a wire-based network but may make a comeback using microwaves [see item 6.e.3) on page 343].

d. A wide area network (WAN) consists of a conglomerate of LANs over widely separated locations. The key aspect here is that a WAN can be either publicly or privately owned.

1) WANs come in many configurations. In its simplest conception, a WAN can consist of a lone desktop computer using a slow dial-up line to connect to an Internet service provider.

2) Publicly owned WANs, such as the public telephone system and the Internet, are available to any user with a compatible device. The assets of these networks are paid for by means other than individually imposed user fees.

a) Public-switched networks use public telephone lines to carry data. This arrangement is economical, but the quality of data transmission cannot be guaranteed and security is highly questionable.

3) Privately owned WANs are profit-making enterprises. They offer fast, secure data communication services to organizations that do not wish to make their own large investments in the necessary infrastructure.

a) Value-added networks (VANs) are private networks that provide their customers with reliable high-speed, secure transmission of data.

i) To compete with the Internet, these third-party networks add value by providing their customers with error detection and correction services, electronic mailbox facilities for EDI purposes, EDI translation, and security for email and data transmissions.

b) Virtual private networks (VPNs) emerged as a relatively inexpensive way to solve the problem of the high cost of leased lines.

i) A company connects each office or LAN to a local Internet service provider and routes data through the shared, low-cost public Internet.

ii) The success of VPNs depends on the development of secure encryption products that protect data while in transit.

c) A private branch exchange (PBX) is a specialized computer used to handle both voice and data traffic.

i) A PBX can switch digital data among computers and office equipment, e.g., printers, copiers, and fax machines. A PBX uses telephone lines, so its data transmission capacity is limited.

5. **Network Equipment**

a. Networks consist of (1) the hardware devices being connected and (2) the medium through which the connection is made.

b. Client devices. Devices of all sizes and functions (mainframes, laptop computers, personal digital assistants, MP3 players, printers, scanners, cash registers, ATMs, etc.) can be connected to networks.

1) Connecting a device to a network requires a network interface card (NIC). The NIC allows the device to speak that particular network's "language," that is, its protocol (see item 6. on page 341).

2) A development in the late 1990s called the thin client explicitly mimics the old mainframe-and-terminal model.

a) A typical thin client consists merely of a monitor, a keyboard, and a small amount of embedded memory. The key is that it has no local hard drive.

b) Essentially all processing and data storage is done on the servers. Just enough of an application is downloaded to the client to run it.

    c) An advantage of this architecture is the large amount of IT staff time and effort saved that formerly went to configuring and troubleshooting desktop machines. A disadvantage is that there must be 100% server availability for any work to be done by users.

    d) The thin client architecture has not met with widespread use because the cost of hard drives has continued to steadily decrease, defying predictions.

c. Types of media. The medium that connects the devices on a network can take many forms.

    1) Bandwidth is the signal-carrying capacity of a transmission medium. It is a rough indication of the highest "speed" that data can attain when traveling through it.

        a) A medium that can carry only one signal is called baseband. A medium that can carry multiple signals is called broadband.

    2) On a wired LAN, the choice of cabling depends on speed requirements.

        a) Twisted pair wiring is graded into categories, each of which denotes a different bandwidth. Twisted pair is fundamentally a baseband medium.

            i) Twisted pair takes its name from the continuous weaving of the strands of wire around each other within the cable.

                • A magnetic field is produced around any wire through which current is passed. These fields can disrupt the transmission of electrical signals, a phenomenon known as electromagnetic interference.

                • Twisting the strands of copper around each other within a cable has the effect of canceling the magnetic fields.

                • Twisted pair comes in shielded (STP) and unshielded (UTP) varieties. Shielded twisted pair carries extra protection against electromagnetic interference.

            ii) Category 1 twisted pair is unshielded. It is usually referred to as regular telephone wire.

            iii) Category 3 comes in both shielded and unshielded varieties and can support a higher bandwidth than Category 1.

            iv) Category 5 also comes in both shielded and unshielded varieties and can support a higher bandwidth than Category 3.

        b) Coaxial cable is a commonly used medium for LANs. Coax (pronounced *COE*-ax), as it is called, is also the familiar transmission medium of cable TV.

            i) Generally, coax is necessary when broadband transmission is desired.

            ii) This cable design is named coaxial because one signal conductor surrounds the other, giving them a common "axis."

    3) Wired LANs depend on two basic types of networking devices to connect the cabling:

        a) Hubs are, in computing terms, very simple ("dumb") and serve only to broadcast messages to every other device on the network.

            i) The device for which the message is intended will keep it and process it. The other devices will discard it.

b) Bridges improve traffic flow by dividing LANs into segments. Bridges are more "intelligent" than hubs.

i) Instead of simply broadcasting messages as hubs do, bridges read the destination address and isolate the message to the segment where the destination device is located, greatly reducing unnecessary traffic on the network.

c) Separate LANs are connected by either specialized bridges, called remote bridges, or by gateways.

4) On a wireless LAN, the NIC uses an antenna instead of a cable to connect to the hub or router through the air. The differences in wireless networks are best discussed in item 6.e on page 343.

5) WANs, with their greater traffic requirements, need higher-capacity media.

a) Fiber-optic cable consists of extremely fine threads of glass or plastic.

i) The electrical signal is converted to pulses of light, which are sent through the optical medium at much higher speeds than electrical signals can travel through copper wire.

ii) The light pulses do not travel straight down the fiber. They are deliberately aimed into the fiber at an angle with respect to the cable's insulation (called cladding).

- This angling causes the light pulses to continuously bounce from one side of the fiber to the other as they travel down the length of the cable.

- This bouncing phenomenon is an aid in separating the various signals when they arrive at the other end.

iii) Fiber optics has two major advantages over wire in addition to drastically greater bandwidth:

- The light pulses used in fiber optics are not subject to electromagnetic interference.

- Interception by unauthorized parties is impossible because the light pulses cannot be "tapped" as electrical signals can. Also, the cut end of an optical fiber becomes a mirror, immediately alerting the administrator that there is a problem with the cable.

b) Microwave transmission involves propagating electrical signals through air and space instead of through metal wire or optical fiber.

i) Satellite relay involves transmitting the microwave signal to a satellite in orbit, which retransmits the signal to the destination back on Earth. This medium offers very high speeds and wide geographic coverage.

ii) LOS (line-of-sight) microwave transmission is an older technology still in use in some places. It consists of beaming the signals from one tower to another from horizon to horizon.

- Almost all long-distance voice telephone calls in the United States were transmitted by LOS microwave between the 1960s and the advent of fiber-optic cable in the 1980s.

iii) Both satellite relay and LOS microwave systems have the advantage of not having to secure rights-of-way for the laying of physical cable over long distances.

6. **Classifying Networks by Protocol**

    a. A protocol is a set of standards for message transmission among the devices on the network.

    b. LAN Protocols

        1) Ethernet has been the most successful protocol for LAN transmission. The Ethernet (capitalized because it is a trademark) design breaks up the flow of data between devices into discrete groups of data bits called "frames."

            a) Ethernet is described as following the "polite conversation" method of communicating.

                i) Each device "listens" to the network to determine whether another conversation is taking place, that is, whether the network is busy moving another device's message.

                ii) Once the network is determined to be free of traffic, the device sends its message.

            b) Inevitably, frames collide on Ethernet networks constantly. When this happens, the two contending devices wait a random (and extremely brief) length of time, then transmit again. Eventually, both messages will hit the network at a moment when it is free.

            c) This design, while seemingly inefficient in accepting such a high number of collisions and retransmissions, has been extraordinarily successful. Over the years, Ethernet has proven to be secure, adaptable, and expandable.

        2) The token ring protocol originally had a much higher speed than Ethernet.

            a) Each device is directly connected to the next device in a ring configuration. A special frame called the token is passed continuously around the ring from one device to the next.

            b) When a device wishes to send a message, it attaches the message to the token. The token drops off the message when it arrives at the destination device.

            c) Token ring, though heavily promoted by IBM, is expensive and difficult to expand, and its early speed advantage has been eclipsed by advances in Ethernet.

    c. Switched Networks

        1) As described in item 4.b. on page 337, in a LAN, all the devices and all the transmission media belong to one organization.

            a) This single ownership of infrastructure assets plus the ability to unify all communication on a single protocol make for great efficiency and security.

        2) When communication must cross organizational boundaries or travel beyond a limited geographical range, this single ownership principle no longer applies. A WAN is the applicable model.

            a) A WAN, with its hundreds of users and much greater distances, could never function using the collision-detection-and-retransmission method of Ethernet. To overcome this, the technique called switching is used.

3) Switching takes two basic forms:

a) In circuit switching, a single physical pathway is established in the public telephone system, and that pathway is reserved for the full and exclusive use of the two parties for the duration of their communication.

i) An example is an ordinary landline telephone call or a dial-up connection from a modem. This is obviously a slow and insecure alternative for data transmission.

b) In packet switching, the data bits making up a message are broken up into "packets" of predefined length. Each packet has a header containing the electronic address of the device for which the message is intended.

4) Switches are the networking devices that read the address on each packet and send it along the appropriate path to its destination.

a) A convenient analogy is a group of 18-wheelers loaded with new machinery destined for a remote plant site. The trucks leave the machinery vendor's factory headed to the destination.

i) As each truck arrives at a traffic light, it stops while vehicles going in other directions pass through the intersection.

ii) As the trucks arrive at the plant site, they are unloaded and the machinery is installed.

5) By allowing message flow from many different organizations to pass through common points, switches spread the cost of the WAN infrastructure.

a) Frame relay and ATM (asynchronous transfer mode) are examples of fast packet switched network protocols.

d. Routed Networks

1) Routers have more intelligence than hubs, bridges, or switches.

a) Routers have tables stored in memory that tell them the most efficient path along which each packet should be sent.

b) The analogy is the trucks leaving the machinery vendor's factory with the same destination.

i) As the trucks stop at each intersection, traffic cops redirect them down different routes depending on traffic conditions.

ii) As the trucks arrive in unknown sequence at the plant site, they are held until the machinery can be unloaded in the correct order.

2) Routing is what makes the Internet possible.

a) Transmission Control Protocol/Internet Protocol (TCP/IP) is the suite of routing protocols that makes it possible to interconnect many thousands of devices from dozens of manufacturers all over the world through the Internet.

i) TCP/IP operates on layers 4 and 3 of the OSI reference model.

b) IP addressing (also called dotted decimal addressing) is the heart of Internet routing. It allows any device anywhere in the world to be recognized on the Internet through the use of a standard-format IP address.

   i) Each of the four decimal-separated elements of the IP address is a numeral between 0 and 255, for example: 128.67.111.25

   ii) The system just described is IPv4, that is, the fourth revision of the Internet addressing standard. As the Internet approaches the limit of the number of addresses IPv4 can handle, the Internet Engineering Task Force (IETF) is working on a system known as IPv6 with a different format that will support many more addresses.

c) Dynamic host configuration protocol (DHCP) allows tremendous flexibility on the Internet by enabling the constant reuse of IP addresses.

   i) Routers generally have their IP addresses hardcoded when they are first installed. However, the individual client devices on most organizational networks are assigned an IP address by DHCP from a pool of available addresses every time they boot up.

e. Wireless Networks

1) The Wi-Fi family of protocols supports client devices within a radius of about 300 feet around a wireless router. This usable area is called a hotspot.

   a) Wi-Fi avoids the collisions inherent in Ethernet by constantly searching for the best frequency within its assigned range to use.

   b) Security was a problem in early incarnations of Wi-Fi. Later versions alleviated some of these concerns with encryption.

2) The Bluetooth standard operates over a much smaller radius than Wi-Fi, about 30 feet. This distance permits the creation of what has come to be called the personal area network or PAN (i.e., a network of devices for a single user).

   a) A prominent example is the in-ear device that allows the wearer to make telephone calls hands-free or to listen to a personal music player in wireless mode. Wireless keyboards and mice also employ the Bluetooth standard.

   b) Bluetooth is considerably slower than Wi-Fi.

3) The WiMax standard uses microwaves to turn an entire city into a hotspot, reviving the old MAN model. The radius is about 10 miles and the speed is quite fast.

   a) Providers of wired networks can bill individual customers for use of the network. However, since anyone with the right device could access a WiMax network, the initial investment in infrastructure would have to be financed through a means other than user fees, making WiMax's widespread deployment unlikely in the near future.

4) Radio-frequency identification (RFID) technology involves the use of a combined microchip with antenna to store data about a product, pet, vehicle, etc. Common applications include

   a) Inventory tracking
   b) Lost pet identification
   c) Tollbooth collection

Stop and review! You have completed the outline for this subunit. Study multiple-choice questions 15 through 18 beginning on page 353.

8.5 ELECTRONIC FUNDS TRANSFER (EFT)

1. **Electronic Funds Transfer (EFT)**

    a. EFT is a service provided by financial institutions worldwide that is based on electronic data interchange (EDI) technology.

    b. EFT transaction costs are lower than for manual systems because documents and human intervention are eliminated from the transaction process. Moreover, transfer customarily requires less than a day.

    c. A typical consumer application of EFT is the direct deposit of payroll checks in employees' accounts or the automatic withdrawal of payments for cable and telephone bills, mortgages, etc.

2. **Check Collection**

    a. The most important application of EFT is check collection.

    b. To reduce the enormous volume of paper, the check-collection process has been computerized. The result has been to reduce the significance of paper checks because EFT provides means to make payments and deposit funds without manual transfer of negotiable instruments. Thus, wholesale EFTs among financial institutions and businesses (commercial transfers) are measured in the trillions of dollars.

        1) The two major systems for these "wire" or nonconsumer transfers are Fedwire (Federal Reserve wire transfer network) and CHIPS (New York Clearing House Interbank Payment System). Private systems also are operated by large banks.

Stop and review! You have completed the outline for this subunit. Study multiple-choice questions 19 and 20 on page 354.

8.6 E-COMMERCE

1. **Electronic Commerce (E-Commerce)**

    a. E-commerce is the purchase and sale of goods and services by electronic means. E-business is a more comprehensive term defined as all methods of conducting business electronically.

    b. E-commerce may occur via online transactions on public networks, electronic data interchange (EDI), and email.

2. **Security Issues**

    a. The correct identification of the transacting parties (authentication)

    b. Determination of who may rightfully make decisions, such as entering into contracts or setting prices (authorization)

    c. Methods for protecting the confidentiality and integrity of information, providing evidence of the transmission and receipt of documents, and guarding against repudiation by the sender or recipient

    d. The trustworthiness of listed prices and the confidentiality of discounts

    e. The confidentiality and integrity of orders, payments, delivery addresses, and confirmations

    f. The proper extent of verification of payment data

    g. The best method of payment to avoid wrongdoing or disagreements

    h. Lost or duplicated transactions

    i. Determining who bears the risk of fraud

3. **Responses to Security Issues**

   a. Encryption and the associated authentication methods

   b. Adherence to legal requirements, such as privacy statutes

   c. Documenting trading agreements, especially the terms of trade and methods of authorization and authentication

   d. Agreements for end-to-end security and availability with providers of information services and VANs

   e. Disclosure by public trading systems of their terms of business

   f. The capacity of the host computer to avoid downtime and repel attacks

4. **IIA Guidance**

   a. The IIA's former Practice Advisory 2100-6, *Control and Audit Implications of E-commerce Activities*, contains much useful information concerning engagements to audit electronic commerce activities.

   b. Electronic commerce (e-commerce) means "conducting commercial activities over the Internet." These activities can be business-to-business (B2B), business-to-consumer (B2C), and business to employee (B2E). Technology not only supports these e-commerce strategies but also is an integral part. Web-based and other technology changes have had a pervasive impact. Such changes and the dramatic growth of e-commerce create significant control and management challenges.

   c. In understanding and planning an e-commerce engagement, the auditor should understand the changes in business and information systems, the related risks, and the alignment of strategies with design and market requirements. The auditor reviews strategic planning and risk assessment and management's decisions about risks, controls, and monitoring.

   d. The auditor (1) assesses control and whether there is reasonable assurance that objectives are achievable, (2) determines risk acceptability, (3) understands information flow, (4) reviews interfaces, and (5) evaluates disaster recovery plans.

   e. The auditor considers many factors during the risk assessment, such as (1) the existence of a business plan; (2) its coverage of the integration of the planning, design, and implementation of the e-commerce system with the strategies of the organization; (3) the effect on the system; (4) whether users' needs will be met; (5) consideration of regulatory issues; (6) the security of hardware and software and whether they prevent or detect harmful effects and losses; (7) transaction processing integrity and accuracy; (8) strength of the control environment; (9) completeness of the risk assessment; (10) inherent risks associated with the Internet and Internet provider; (11) implications of dealing with outside vendors, e.g., whether a going concern evaluation has been conducted by a trusted, qualified third party, and if vendors provide hosting services, whether they have a tested business contingency plan; and (12) legal matters, e.g., issues involving taxes, contract enforcement in other countries, privacy, intellectual property, defamation, copyrights, trademarks, fraud, and electronic signatures.

f. Risk is the uncertainty of an event's occurrence that could adversely affect the achievement of objectives. Risk is inherent. Opportunity risks assumed by management are drivers of activities. Beyond them may be threats and other dangers not clearly understood and fully evaluated and too easily accepted. Managing risk requires an understanding of risk elements and an awareness of new threats and changes in technology affecting information security. Seven key questions identify organizational risk and possible ways of controlling or mitigating the exposures. The following are the questions and the related risk elements: (1) What adverse events could happen (threat events), (2) what will be the financial effect (single loss exposure value), (3) how often (frequency), (4) how probable are the preceding answers (uncertainty), (5) what can be done by way of risk management (safeguards and controls), (6) what is the cost (cost of safeguards and controls), and (7) how efficient is risk management (cost/benefit or ROI analysis).

g. The auditor should address the critical risk and control issues, such as (1) general project management, (2) specific security threats, (3) transaction integrity in a complex network, (4) website content changes, (5) technology change, (6) legal concerns, and (7) changes in business processes and structures.

h. The overall audit objective is effective control. Management of e-commerce should be documented in an approved strategic plan. Specific audit objectives for an e-commerce engagement should be defined, for example, (1) evidence of transactions, (2) availability and reliability of security, (3) effective interface with financial systems, (4) security of monetary transactions, (5) effectiveness of customer authentication, (6) adequacy of business continuity processes, (7) compliance with security standards, (8) use and control of digital signatures, (9) adequacy of control of public key certificates, (10) adequacy and timeliness of operating data, and (11) documentation of effective control.

i. The e-commerce audit program will vary with the organization. The following are the components of a general e-commerce audit protocol for key areas: (1) e-commerce organization, (2) fraud conditions (red flags), (3) authentication of transactions and evaluation of controls, (4) evaluation of controls over data integrity, (5) review of the continuity plan for coping with business interruptions, and (6) evaluation of how well business units are managing e-commerce.

Stop and review! You have completed the outline for this subunit. Study multiple-choice questions 21 through 24 beginning on page 354.

8.7 ELECTRONIC DATA INTERCHANGE (EDI)

1. **Electronic Data Interchange (EDI)**

   a. EDI is the communication of electronic documents directly from a computer in one entity to a computer in another entity, for example, to order goods from a supplier or to transfer funds. EDI was the first step in the evolution of e-business.

   b. EDI was developed to enhance JIT (just-in-time) inventory management.

   c. Advantages of EDI include reduction of clerical errors, speed of transactions, and elimination of repetitive clerical tasks. EDI also eliminates document preparation, processing, and mailing costs.

   d. Risks of EDI include

      1) Security of information

         a) End-to-end data encryption is a security procedure that protects data during transmission.

      2) Loss of data

   e. An extension of EDI is computer-stored records, which can be less expensive than traditional physical file storage.

2. **EDI Terms and Components**

   a. Standards concern procedures to convert written documents into a standard electronic document-messaging format to facilitate EDI.

      1) In the U.S., the American National Standards Institute's Accredited Standards Committee X12 provides standards.

      2) Many international entities use UN/EDIFACT (United Nations EDI for Administration, Commerce, and Transport).

   b. Conventions are the procedures for arranging data elements in specified formats for various accounting transactions, e.g., invoices, materials releases, and advance shipment notices.

   c. A data dictionary prescribes the meaning of data elements, including specification of each transaction structure.

   d. Transmission protocols are rules to determine how each electronic envelope is structured and processed by the communications devices.

      1) Normally, a group of transactions is combined in an electronic envelope and transmitted into a communications network.

      2) Rules are required for transmission and the separation of envelopes.

   e. Because EDI formats and elements vary, a large entity may gain a competitive advantage by forcing trading partners to adopt its standards. Other entities will need to negotiate EDI standards.

3. **Methods of EDI Communication**

   a. Originally, point-to-point connections were used in which both parties had fixed, dedicated computer connections.

   b. Third-party value-added networks (VANs) are private mailbox-type services in which the sender's and receiver's computers are never directly connected to each other. Instead, both parties to the EDI arrangement subscribe to a third-party VAN provider.

      1) Because of the third-party buffer, the VAN users are not required to conform to the same standards, conventions, and protocols. Also, VANs can store messages (in a mailbox), so the parties can batch outgoing and incoming messages.

      2) Encryption, preferably by physically secure hardware rather than software, is a critical control.

   c. Cost advantages are leading to increased use of the Internet as a means of conducting business directly with a trading partner. It can be used in a more open environment in which one firm transmits documents to another.

      1) This approach is based on less formal agreements between the trading partners than in EDI and requires the sending firm to format the documents into the format of the receiving firm.

4. **Implications for Internal Auditors**

   a. EDI eliminates the paper documents, both internal and external, that are the traditional basis for many procedures performed in substantive testing and in tests of controls.

   b. An organization that has reengineered its procedures and processes to take full advantage of EDI may have eliminated even the electronic equivalents of paper documents.

      1) For example, the buyer's point-of-sale (POS) system may directly transmit information to the seller, which delivers on a JIT basis. Purchase orders, invoices, and receiving reports are eliminated and replaced with

         a) A long-term contract establishing quantities, prices, and delivery schedules;

b)   Production schedules;

c)   Advance ship notices;

d)   Evaluated receipts settlements (periodic payment authorizations transmitted to the trading partner with no need for matching purchase orders, invoices, and receiving reports); and

e)   Payments by EFT.

2)   Internal auditors must seek new forms of evidence to support assertions about EDI transactions, whether the evidence exists at the client organization, the trading partner, or a third party, such as a VAN. Examples of such evidence are

a)   The authorized paper purchase contract,

b)   An electronic completed production schedule image, and

c)   Internal and external evidence of evaluated receipts settlements sent to the trading partner.

3)   Internal auditors must evaluate digital signatures and reviews when testing controls.

4)   Internal auditors may need to consider other subsystems when testing a particular subsystem. For example, production cycle evidence may be needed to test the expenditure cycle.

c.   EDI controls will vary with the organization's objectives and applications.

1)   Authorized users with independent access may include

a)   The people initiating transactions

b)   The people authorizing transactions

c)   Other authorizing parties

d)   Senders for exceptional transactions

2)   Message authentication may be accomplished using smart cards and other hardware and software techniques. Protection of message integrity by authentication is especially important for such EDI applications as EFT and ordering.

3)   Messages also must be protected from interception or tampering while in transit. Controls include

a)   Encryption

b)   Numerical sequencing to identify missing or false messages

c)   Nonrepudiation methods

i)   Digital certificates are used to prove origination and delivery so that parties cannot disclaim responsibility for sending or receiving a message.

ii)   E-commerce sellers and buyers routinely provide acknowledgments and confirmations, respectively, in a website dialogue to avoid later disputes.

iii)   In an EDI application, control over nonrepudiation is achieved by sequencing, encryption, and authentication.

Stop and review! You have completed the outline for this subunit. Study multiple-choice questions 25 through 29 beginning on page 355.

QUESTIONS

8.1 Control Frameworks

1. Control objectives regarding effectiveness and efficiency, reliability, and compliance are the basis of which control framework?

A. GTAG.

B. eSAC.

C. COBIT.

D. COSO.

Answer (D) is correct. *(Publisher, adapted)*
REQUIRED: The appropriate control framework.
DISCUSSION: Probably the most well-known control framework in the U.S. is *Internal Control – Integrated Framework*, published in 1992 by the Committee of Sponsoring Organizations of the Treadway Commission (COSO). The document is commonly referred to as "the COSO Framework." The COSO Framework defines internal control as

A process, effected by an organization's board of directors, management, and other personnel, designed to provide reasonable assurance regarding the achievement of objectives in the following categories:

- *Effectiveness and efficiency of operations*
- *Reliability of financial reporting*
- *Compliance with applicable laws and regulations*

Answer (A) is incorrect. GTAG, The IIA's *Global Technology Audit Guide*, is not the source of these three control objectives. Answer (B) is incorrect. The IIA's *Electronic Systems Assurance and Control*, eSAC, is not the source of these three control objectives. Answer (C) is incorrect. COBIT, the ITGI's *Control Objectives for Information and Related Technology*, is not the source of these three control objectives.

2. Which of the following control frameworks groups IT business assurance objectives into the five categories of availability, capability, functionality, protectability, and accountability?

A. COBIT.

B. COSO.

C. eSAC.

D. GTAG.

Answer (C) is correct. *(Publisher, adapted)*
REQUIRED: The control framework to which five business assurance objectives apply.
DISCUSSION: eSAC's IT business assurance objectives fall into these five categories: availability, capability, functionality, protectability, and accountability.
Answer (A) is incorrect. These five control objectives are not put forth by COBIT. Answer (B) is incorrect. These five control objectives are not put forth by COSO. Answer (D) is incorrect. These five control objectives are not put forth by GTAG.

3. Which of the following types of controls is not described in the IT Governance Institute's *Control Objectives for Information and Related Technology* (COBIT)?

A. General controls.

B. Exchange controls.

C. Business controls.

D. Process controls.

Answer (B) is correct. *(Publisher, adapted)*
REQUIRED: The type of control not described in COBIT.
DISCUSSION: COBIT describes controls in three areas: process controls, business controls, and IT general and application controls.

8.2 Aspects of Automated Information Processing

4. Which of the following statements accurately describes the impact that automation has on the controls normally present in a manual system?

A. Transaction trails are more extensive in a computer-based system than in a manual system because there is always a one-for-one correspondence between data entry and output.

B. Responsibility for custody of information assets is more concentrated in user departments in a computer-based system than it is in a manual system.

C. Controls must be more explicit in a computer-based system because many processing points that present opportunities for human judgment in a manual system are eliminated.

D. The quality of documentation becomes less critical in a computer-based system than it is in a manual system because data records are stored in machine-readable files.

Answer (C) is correct. *(CIA, adapted)*
REQUIRED: The impact that automation has on the controls normally present in a manual system.
DISCUSSION: Using a computer does not change the basic concepts and objectives of control. However, the use of computers may modify the control techniques used. The processing of transactions may be combined with control activities previously performed separately, or control function may be combined within the information system activity.
Answer (A) is incorrect. The "paper trail" is less extensive in an automated system. Combining processing and controls within the system reduces documentary evidence. Answer (B) is incorrect. Information assets are more likely to be under the control of the information system function. Answer (D) is incorrect. Documentation is more important in an information system. This is because information is more likely to be stored in machine-readable form than in hard copy, requiring specialized knowledge for retrieval.

5. A firm has recently converted its purchasing cycle from a manual process to an online computer system. Which of the following is a probable result associated with conversion to the new automatic system?

A. Processing errors are increased.

B. The firm's risk exposures are reduced.

C. Processing time is increased.

D. Traditional duties are less segregated.

Answer (D) is correct. *(CIA, adapted)*
REQUIRED: The probable result associated with conversion to the new automatic system.
DISCUSSION: In a manual system with appropriate internal control, separate individuals are responsible for authorizing transactions, recording transactions, and custody of assets. These checks and balances prevent fraud and detect inaccurate or incomplete transactions. In a computer environment, however, this segregation of duties is not always feasible. For example, a computer may print checks, record disbursements, and generate information for reconciling the account balance.
Answer (A) is incorrect. A computer system decreases processing errors. Answer (B) is incorrect. The conversion to a new system does not reduce the number of risk exposures. Answer (C) is incorrect. Processing time is decreased.

6. A small client recently put its cash disbursements system on a server. About which of the following internal control features would an auditor most likely be concerned?

A. Programming of the applications are in Visual Basic rather than Java.

B. The server is operated by employees who have cash custody responsibilities.

C. Only one employee has the password to gain access to the cash disbursement system.

D. There are restrictions on the amount of data that can be stored and on the length of time that data can be stored.

Answer (B) is correct. *(CPA, adapted)*
REQUIRED: The control feature of most concern to an auditor.
DISCUSSION: Segregation of duties is a basic category of control activities (AU 319). Functions are incompatible if a person is in a position both to perpetrate and conceal fraud or errors. Hence, the duties of authorizing transactions, recording transactions, and custody of assets should be assigned to different people. Those employees that operate the server may be able to override the controls to change records to conceal a theft of cash.
Answer (A) is incorrect. The choice of language would have little effect on internal control. Answer (C) is incorrect. The limitation on access would be considered a strength. Answer (D) is incorrect. Restrictions on the amount of data that can be stored and on the length of time that data can be stored do not constitute a control weakness.

7. A small company has changed from a system of recording time worked on clock cards to a computerized payroll system in which employees record time in and out with magnetic cards. The computer system automatically updates all payroll records. Because of this change,

A. A generalized computer audit program must be used.

B. Part of the audit trail is altered.

C. The potential for payroll-related fraud is diminished.

D. Transactions must be processed in batches.

Answer (B) is correct. *(CPA, adapted)*

REQUIRED: The effect of computerization of a payroll system.

DISCUSSION: In a manual payroll system, a paper trail of documents is created to provide audit evidence that controls over each step in processing are in place and functioning. One element of a computer system that differentiates it from a manual system is that a transaction trail useful for auditing purposes might exist only for a brief time or only in computer-readable form.

Answer (A) is incorrect. Use of generalized audit software is only one of many ways of auditing a computer-based system. Answer (C) is incorrect. Conversion to a computer system may actually increase the chance of fraud by eliminating segregation of incompatible functions and other controls. Answer (D) is incorrect. Automatic updating indicates that processing is not in batch mode.

8. Batch processing

A. Is not used by most businesses because it reduces the audit trail.

B. Allows users to inquire about groups of information contained in the system.

C. Accumulates transaction records into groups for processing against the master file on a delayed basis.

D. Can only be performed on a centralized basis.

Answer (C) is correct. *(CMA, adapted)*

REQUIRED: The true statement about batch processing.

DISCUSSION: Batch processing is the accumulation and grouping of transactions for processing on a delayed basis. The batch approach is suitable for applications that can be processed against the master file at intervals and involve large volumes of similar items, such as payroll, sales, inventory, and billing.

Answer (A) is incorrect. Batch processing provides as much of an audit trail as any computerized operation. Answer (B) is incorrect. Batch processing refers to the input of data, not inquiry. Answer (D) is incorrect. Batch processing can also be performed on a decentralized basis.

9. What type of computer processing system is characterized by data that are assembled from more than one location and records that are updated immediately?

A. Personal computer systems.

B. Data compression systems.

C. Batch processing systems.

D. Online, real-time systems.

Answer (D) is correct. *(CPA, adapted)*

REQUIRED: The system allowing data entry from multiple locations and immediate updating.

DISCUSSION: Real-time processing involves processing an input record and receiving the output soon enough to affect a current decision-making process. In a real-time system, the user interacts with the system to control an ongoing activity. Online indicates that the decision maker is in direct communication with the computer. Online, real-time systems usually permit access to the main computer from multiple remote terminals.

Answer (A) is incorrect. Access from multiple locations is more typical of larger computer systems than of personal computer systems. Answer (B) is incorrect. Data compression systems encode data to take up less storage space. Answer (C) is incorrect. Batching of transactions requires assembly of data at one place and a delay in updating.

8.3 IT Controls

10. When assessing application controls, which one of the following input controls or edit checks is most likely to be used to detect a data input error in the customer account number field?

A. Limit check.

B. Validity check.

C. Control total.

D. Hash total.

Answer (B) is correct. *(CIA, adapted)*

REQUIRED: The input control or edit check most likely to be used to detect a data input error in the customer account number field.

DISCUSSION: Validity checks are tests of identification numbers or transaction codes for validity by comparison with items already known to be correct or authorized. For example, Social Security numbers on payroll input records can be compared with Social Security numbers authorized by the personnel department.

Answer (A) is incorrect. Reasonableness, limit, and range checks are based upon known limits for given information. For example, the hours worked per week is not likely to be greater than 45. Answer (C) is incorrect. A record count is a control total of the number of records processed during the operation of a program. Financial totals summarize dollar amounts in an information field in a group of records. Answer (D) is incorrect. A hash total is the number obtained from totaling the same field value for each transaction in a batch. The total has no meaning or value other than as a comparison with another hash total.

11. The two broad groupings of information systems control activities are general controls and application controls. General controls include controls

A. Relating to the correction and resubmission of faulty data.

B. For developing, modifying, and maintaining computer programs.

C. Designed to ensure that only authorized users receive output from processing.

D. Designed to ensure that all data submitted for processing have been properly authorized.

Answer (B) is correct. *(Publisher, adapted)*

REQUIRED: The characteristics of general controls in relation to information systems control activities.

DISCUSSION: General controls are policies and procedures that relate to many information systems application and support the effective functioning of application controls by helping to ensure the continued proper operation of information systems. General controls include controls over (1) data center and network operations; (2) systems software acquisition and maintenance; (3) access security; and (4) application systems acquisition, development, and maintenance (AU 319).

---

12. The purpose of input controls is to ensure the

A. Authorization of access to data files.

B. Authorization of access to program files.

C. Completeness, accuracy, and validity of updating.

D. Completeness, accuracy, and validity of input.

Answer (D) is correct. *(CIA, adapted)*

REQUIRED: The purpose of input controls.

DISCUSSION: Input controls provide reasonable assurance that data received for computer processing have been properly authorized and are in a form suitable for processing, i.e., complete, accurate, and valid. Input controls also relate to rejection, correction, and resubmission of data that were initially incorrect.

Answer (A) is incorrect. Access controls authorize access to data files. Answer (B) is incorrect. Access controls authorize access to program files. Answer (C) is incorrect. Processing controls ensure the completeness, accuracy, and validity of updating.

---

13. Which of the following computerized control procedures would be most effective in ensuring that data uploaded from desktop computers to a server are complete and that no additional data are added?

A. Self-checking digits to ensure that only authorized part numbers are added to the database.

B. Batch control totals, including control totals and hash totals.

C. Passwords that effectively limit access to only those authorized to upload the data to the mainframe computer.

D. Field-level edit controls that test each field for alphanumerical integrity.

Answer (B) is correct. *(CIA, adapted)*

REQUIRED: The control over completeness of data uploaded from personal computers.

DISCUSSION: Batch control totals for the data transferred can be reconciled with the batch control totals in the existing file. This comparison provides information on the completion of the data transfer. Batch totals may include record counts, totals of certain critical amounts, or hash totals. A hash total is a control total without a defined meaning, such as the total of employee numbers or invoice numbers, that is used to verify the completeness of data. Thus, the hash total for the employee listing by the personnel department could be compared with the total generated during the payroll run.

Answer (A) is incorrect. Self-checking digits detect inaccurate identification numbers. They are an effective control to ensure that the appropriate part has been identified. However, the control objective is to ensure that data transfer is complete. Answer (C) is incorrect. Passwords help ensure that only authorized personnel make the transfer, not that data transfer is complete. Answer (D) is incorrect. Field checks are effective input controls, but they do not ensure completeness of data transfer.

---

14. The online data entry control called preformatting is

A. A program initiated prior to regular input to discover errors in data before entry so that the errors can be corrected.

B. A check to determine if all data items for a transaction have been entered by the person entering the data.

C. A series of requests for required input data that requires an acceptable response to each request before a subsequent request is made.

D. The display of a document with blanks for data items to be entered by the person entering the data.

Answer (D) is correct. *(CMA, adapted)*

REQUIRED: The definition of preformatting.

DISCUSSION: To avoid data entry errors in online systems, a preformatted screen approach may be used. It is a screen prompting approach that involves the display on a monitor of a set of boxes for entry of specified data items. The format may even be in the form of a copy of a transaction document. This technique is best suited to conversion of data from a source document.

Answer (A) is incorrect. An edit routine is a program initiated prior to regular input to discover errors in data before entry so that the errors can be corrected. Answer (B) is incorrect. A completeness check tests whether all data items for a transaction have been entered by the person entering the data. Answer (C) is incorrect. The dialogue approach is another screen prompting method for data entry. It is most appropriate when information is received orally, e.g., by phone.

8.4 Data Communications, Networks, and Client-Server Systems

15. When two devices in a data communications system are communicating, there must be agreement as to how both data and control information are to be packaged and interpreted. Which of the following terms is commonly used to describe this type of agreement?

A. Asynchronous communication.

B. Synchronous communication.

C. Communication channel.

D. Communication protocol.

Answer (D) is correct. *(CIA, adapted)*
REQUIRED: The agreement as to how both data and control information are to be packaged and interpreted.
DISCUSSION: A protocol is a set of formal rules or conventions governing communication between a sending and a receiving device. It prescribes the manner by which data are transmitted between these communications devices. In essence, a protocol is the envelope within which each message is transmitted throughout a data communications network.
Answer (A) is incorrect. Asynchronous communication is a mode of transmission. Communication is in disjointed segments, typically character by character, preceded by a start code and ended by a stop code. Answer (B) is incorrect. Synchronous communication is a mode of transmission in which a continuous stream of blocks of characters result in faster communications. Answer (C) is incorrect. A communication channel is a transmission link between devices in a network. The term is also used for a small processor that controls input-output devices.

16. Large organizations often have their own telecommunications networks for transmitting and receiving voice, data, and images. Very small organizations, however, are unlikely to be able to make the investment required for their own networks and are more likely to use

A. Public switched lines.

B. Fast-packet switches.

C. Standard electronic mail systems.

D. A WAN.

Answer (A) is correct. *(CIA, adapted)*
REQUIRED: The telecommunications networks likely to be used by small organizations.
DISCUSSION: Companies can use public switched lines (phone lines) on a per-transmission basis. This option is the most cost-effective way for low-volume users to conduct telecommunications.
Answer (B) is incorrect. Fast-packet switches receive transmissions from various devices, break the data into packets, and route them over a network to their destination. They are typically installed by telecommunication utility companies and other large companies that have their own networks. Answer (C) is incorrect. Electronic mail systems do not allow for voice transmissions. Answer (D) is incorrect. Large organizations would use a wide area network.

17. Using a telecommunications provider affects in-house networks. To prepare for changes resulting from enhanced external network services, management should

A. Optimize in-house networks to avoid bottlenecks that would limit the benefits offered by the telecommunications provider.

B. Plan for rapid implementation of new capabilities in anticipation of ready acceptance of the new technology.

C. Downsize the company's disaster recovery plan to recognize the increasing role of the telecommunications provider.

D. Enhance the in-house network management to minimize dependence on the telecommunications provider for network management.

Answer (A) is correct. *(CIA, adapted)*
REQUIRED: The appropriate action to prepare for changes resulting from enhanced external network services.
DISCUSSION: To prepare the company for changes resulting from the enhanced external network services, management should take appropriate action. A number of bottlenecks may limit the benefits that can be derived from the external network. For example, conversion from analog to digital technology is necessary to achieve rapid improvements in bandwidth and speed and to improve access to telecommunications services. Furthermore, applications, systems software, and communications protocols must be able to process information in a format and in a manner acceptable to end users. Communications security also has heightened importance as greater amounts of data are transmitted from remote sites.
Answer (B) is incorrect. Resistance to change, inflexible organizational structures, and skepticism about the technology should be expected and must be successfully managed if the company is to reap the benefits. Answer (C) is incorrect. A company's disaster recovery plan should be enhanced to ensure the reliability of the network. Answer (D) is incorrect. Network management may now be primarily a function, yet it will become more of a partnership arrangement with the communications carrier.

18. A local area network (LAN) is best described as a(n)

A. Computer system that connects computers of all sizes, workstations, terminals, and other devices within a limited proximity.

B. System to allow computer users to meet and share ideas and information.

C. Electronic library containing millions of items of data that can be reviewed, retrieved, and analyzed.

D. Method to offer specialized software, hardware, and data-handling techniques that improve effectiveness and reduce costs.

Answer (A) is correct.   *(CMA, adapted)*
REQUIRED: The best description of a local area network (LAN).
DISCUSSION: A LAN is a local distributed computer system, often housed within a single building. Computers, communication devices, and other equipment are linked by cable. Special software facilitates efficient data communication among the hardware devices.
Answer (B) is incorrect. A LAN is more than a system to allow computer users to share information; i.e., it is an interconnection of a computer system. Answer (C) is incorrect. A LAN is not a library. Answer (D) is incorrect. A LAN does not require specialized hardware.

8.5 Electronic Funds Transfer (EFT)

19. Which of the following risks is **not** greater in an electronic funds transfer (EFT) environment than in a manual system using paper transactions?

A. Unauthorized access and activity.

B. Duplicate transaction processing.

C. Higher cost per transaction.

D. Inadequate backup and recovery capabilities.

Answer (C) is correct.   *(CIA, adapted)*
REQUIRED: The risk not greater in an EFT environment than in a manual system using paper transactions.
DISCUSSION: EFT is a service provided by financial institutions worldwide that is based on EDI technology. EFT transaction costs are lower than for manual systems because documents and human intervention are eliminated from the transactions process.
Answer (A) is incorrect. Unauthorized access and activity is a risk specific to EFT. Answer (B) is incorrect. Inaccurate transaction processing (including duplication) is a risk specific to EFT. Answer (D) is incorrect. Inadequate backup and recovery capabilities is a risk specific to EFT.

20. Which of the following is usually a benefit of using electronic funds transfer (EFT) for international cash transactions?

A. Improvement of the audit trail for cash receipts and disbursements.

B. Creation of self-monitoring access controls.

C. Reduction of the frequency of data entry errors.

D. Off-site storage of source documents for cash transactions.

Answer (C) is correct.   *(CPA, adapted)*
REQUIRED: The benefit of using EFT for international cash transactions.
DISCUSSION: The processing and transmission of electronic transactions, such as EFTs, virtually eliminates human interaction. This process not only helps eliminate errors but also allows for the rapid detection and recovery from errors when they do occur.
Answer (A) is incorrect. The audit trail is typically less apparent in an electronic environment than in a manual environment. Answer (B) is incorrect. A key control is management's establishment and monitoring of access controls. Answer (D) is incorrect. Source documents are often eliminated in EFT transactions.

8.6 E-Commerce

21. All of the following are potential security issues for e-commerce **except**

A. Correct identification of transacting parties.

B. Proliferation of computer viruses.

C. Determining who may rightfully make transaction decisions.

D. Verification of payment data.

Answer (B) is correct.   *(Publisher, adapted)*
REQUIRED: The process that is not a potential security issue for e-commerce.
DISCUSSION: E-commerce is the purchase and sale of goods and services by electronic means. E-commerce may occur via online transactions on public networks, electronic data interchange (EDI), and email. E-commerce security issues include the correct identification of transacting parties (authentication), determining who may rightfully make decisions (authorization), and verification of payment data. While proliferation of computer viruses is a general security issue with regard to information systems, it is not a specific risk associated with e-commerce.
Answer (A) is incorrect. Authentication is a security issue related to e-commerce. Answer (C) is incorrect. Authorization is a security issue related to e-commerce. Answer (D) is incorrect. Verification of payment data is a security issue related to e-commerce.

22. Which of the following is **not** a major component of an audit of e-commerce activities?

    A. Make certain that goals and objectives can be achieved.

    B. Assess the internal control structure.

    C. Review the interface issues.

    D. Evaluate the business continuity and disaster recovery plans.

Answer (A) is correct. *(Publisher, adapted)*

    REQUIRED: The item that is not a major component of an audit of e-commerce activities.

    DISCUSSION: Auditing e-commerce activities should provide reasonable assurance – not ensure or make certain – that goals and objectives can be achieved. An auditor cannot be absolutely certain that goals and objectives will be achieved. The following are other major components of an audit of e-commerce activities:

- Assess the internal control structure, including the tone set by senior management,
- Determine whether the risks are acceptable,
- Understand the information flow,
- Review the interface issues (such as hardware to hardware, software to software, and hardware to software), and
- Evaluate the business continuity and disaster recovery plans.

23. Which type of risks assumed by management are often drivers of organizational activities?

    A. Opportunity risks.

    B. Inherent risks.

    C. General project management risks.

    D. Control risks.

Answer (A) is correct. *(Publisher, adapted)*

    REQUIRED: The type of risks assumed by management that are often drivers of organizational activities.

    DISCUSSION: Risk can be defined as the uncertainty of an event occurring that could have a negative impact on the achievement of objectives. Risk is inherent to every business or government entity. Opportunity risks assumed by management are often drivers of organizational activities. Beyond these opportunities may be threats and other dangers that are not clearly understood or fully evaluated and are too easily accepted as part of doing business.

24. What is the overall audit objective when auditing an e-commerce activity?

    A. To ensure that all e-commerce processes have efficient internal controls.

    B. To ensure that all e-commerce processes have effective internal controls.

    C. To ensure that all e-commerce processes are adequate to fulfill their intended objectives.

    D. To ensure that all e-commerce processes meet the functionality requirements of the end users.

Answer (B) is correct. *(Publisher, adapted)*

    REQUIRED: The overall audit objective when auditing an e-commerce activity.

    DISCUSSION: According to PA 2100-6, when auditing e-commerce activities, the overall audit objective should be to ensure that all e-commerce processes have effective internal controls.

    Answer (A) is incorrect. The overall audit objective is not about ensuring the efficiency of internal controls. It is about ensuring the effectiveness of internal controls. Answer (C) is incorrect. Adequacy of processes should be considered during the internal auditor's risk assessment. Answer (D) is incorrect. Meeting functional requirements should be considered during the internal auditor's risk assessment.

8.7 Electronic Data Interchange (EDI)

25. Companies now can use electronic transfers to conduct regular business transactions. Which of the following terms best describes a system in which an agreement is made between two or more parties to electronically transfer purchase orders, sales orders, invoices, and/or other financial documents?

    A. Electronic mail (email).

    B. Electronic funds transfer (EFT).

    C. Electronic data interchange (EDI).

    D. Electronic data processing (EDP).

Answer (C) is correct. *(CIA, adapted)*

    REQUIRED: The term best describing electronic transfer of documents.

    DISCUSSION: Electronic data interchange is the electronic transfer of documents between businesses. EDI was developed to enhance just-in-time (JIT) inventory management. Advantages include speed, reduction of clerical errors, and elimination of repetitive clerical tasks and their costs.

    Answer (A) is incorrect. Email can send text or document files, but the term encompasses a wide range of transfers. EDI specifically applies to the system described in the question. Answer (B) is incorrect. Electronic funds transfer (EFT) refers to the transfer of money. Answer (D) is incorrect. Electronic data processing (EDP) is a generic term for computerized processing of transaction data within organizations.

26. Which of the following is usually a benefit of transmitting transactions in an electronic data interchange (EDI) environment?

A. A compressed business cycle with lower year-end receivables balances.

B. A reduced need to test computer controls related to sales and collections transactions.

C. An increased opportunity to apply statistical sampling techniques to account balances.

D. No need to rely on third-party service providers to ensure security.

Answer (A) is correct.   *(CPA, adapted)*
REQUIRED: The benefit of EDI.
DISCUSSION: EDI transactions are typically transmitted and processed in real time. Thus, EDI compresses the business cycle by eliminating delays. The time required to receive and process an order, ship goods, and receive payment is greatly reduced compared with that of a typical manual system. Accordingly, more rapid receipt of payment minimizes receivables and improves cash flow.
Answer (B) is incorrect. Use of a sophisticated processing system would increase the need to test computer controls. Answer (C) is incorrect. Computer technology allows all transactions to be tested rather than just a sample. Answer (D) is incorrect. EDI often uses a VAN (value-added network) as a third-party service provider, and reliance on controls provided by the VAN may be critical.

27. The emergence of electronic data interchange (EDI) as standard operating practice increases the risk of

A. Unauthorized third-party access to systems.

B. Systematic programming errors.

C. Inadequate knowledge bases.

D. Unsuccessful system use.

Answer (A) is correct.   *(CIA, adapted)*
REQUIRED: The risk increased by the emergence of EDI as standard operating practice.
DISCUSSION: EDI is the communication of electronic documents directly from a computer in one entity to a computer in another entity. EDI for business documents between unrelated parties has the potential to increase the risk of unauthorized third-party access to systems because more outsiders will have access to internal systems.
Answer (B) is incorrect. Systematic programming errors are the result of misspecification of requirements or lack of correspondence between specifications and programs. Answer (C) is incorrect. Inadequate knowledge bases are a function of lack of care in building them. Answer (D) is incorrect. A benefit of EDI is to improve the efficiency and effectiveness of system use.

28. Which of the following are essential elements of the audit trail in an electronic data interchange (EDI) system?

A. Network and sender/recipient acknowledgments.

B. Message directories and header segments.

C. Contingency and disaster recovery plans.

D. Trading partner security and mailbox codes.

Answer (A) is correct.   *(CPA, adapted)*
REQUIRED: The essential element in an EDI audit trail.
DISCUSSION: An audit trail allows for the tracing of a transaction from initiation to conclusion. Network and sender/recipient acknowledgments relate to the transaction flow and provide for the tracking of transactions.
Answer (B) is incorrect. Message directories and header segments provide information controlling the message, such as originating and destination stations, message type and priority level, which are part of the message and not the audit trail. Answer (C) is incorrect. Although contingency and disaster recovery plans are important controls, they do not relate to the audit trail. Answer (D) is incorrect. Although maintaining control over security and mailbox codes is an important control, it does not relate to the audit trail.

29. Which of the following statements is true concerning internal control in an electronic data interchange (EDI) system?

A. Preventive controls generally are more important than detective controls in EDI systems.

B. Control objectives for EDI systems generally are different from the objectives for other information systems.

C. Internal controls in EDI systems rarely permit control risk to be assessed at below the maximum.

D. Internal controls related to the segregation of duties generally are the most important controls in EDI systems.

Answer (A) is correct.   *(CPA, adapted)*
REQUIRED: The true statement about EDI controls.
DISCUSSION: In general, preventive controls are more important than detective controls because the benefits typically outweigh the costs. In electronic processing, once a transaction is accepted, there is often little opportunity to apply detective controls. Thus, it is important to prevent errors or frauds before they happen.
Answer (B) is incorrect. The basic control objectives are the same regardless of the nature of the processing: to ensure the integrity of the information and to safeguard the assets. Answer (C) is incorrect. To gather sufficient evidence in a sophisticated computer system, it is often necessary to rely on the controls. Control risk may be assessed at below the maximum if relevant controls are identified and tested and if the resulting evidential matter provides the degree of assurance necessary to support the assessed level of control risk. Answer (D) is incorrect. The level of segregation of duties achieved in a manual system is usually not feasible in a computer system.

STUDY UNIT NINE
IT ROLES, SOFTWARE,
AND APPLICATION DEVELOPMENT

(23 pages of outline)

This study unit addresses the roles of IT personnel, the use of encryption to increase the security of data transmission, the protection of data from viruses and other threats, and an organization's investment in IT. It continues with a treatment of enterprise-wide resource planning and concludes with discussions of systems software (operating systems and utility programs), application development, program change control, and end-user computing.

9.1 FUNCTIONAL AREAS OF IT OPERATIONS

In the early days of computing, maintaining a rigid segregation of duties was a simple matter because the roles surrounding a mainframe computer were so specialized. As IT became more and more decentralized over the years, clear lines that once separated jobs such as systems analyst and programmer became blurred and then disappeared. Candidates for the CIA exam must be aware of the evolving roles of IT personnel.

1. **Segregation of Duties**

   a. Controls should ensure the efficiency and effectiveness of IT operations. They include proper segregation of the duties within the IT environment. Thus, the responsibilities of systems analysts, programmers, operators, file librarians, the control group, and others should be assigned to different individuals, and proper supervision should be provided.

   b. Segregation of duties is vital because a traditional segregation of responsibilities for authorization, recording, and access to assets may not be feasible in an IT environment.

      1) For example, a computer may print checks, record disbursements, and generate information for reconciling the account balance, which are activities customarily segregated in a manual system.

         a) If the same person provides the input and receives the output for this process, a significant control weakness exists. Accordingly, certain tasks should not be combined.

2. **Responsibilities of IT Personnel**

    a.   Systems analysts are specifically qualified to analyze and design computer information systems. They survey the existing system, analyze the organization's information requirements, and design new systems to meet those needs. The design specifications will guide the preparation of specific programs by computer programmers.

        1)   Systems analysts should not have access to the computer operations center, production programs, or data files.

    b.   The database administrator (DBA) is the individual who has overall responsibility for developing and maintaining the database and for establishing controls to protect its integrity.

        1)   Thus, only the DBA should be able to update data dictionaries.

        2)   In small systems, the DBA may perform some functions of a database management system (DBMS) (see Study Unit 10, Subunit 4). In larger applications, the DBA uses a DBMS as a primary tool.

    c.   Programmers design, write, test, and document the specific programs according to specifications developed by the analysts.

        1)   Programmers as well as analysts may be able to modify programs, data files, and controls. Thus, they should have no access to the computer operations center or to production programs or data.

    d.   The webmaster is responsible for the content of the organization's website. (S)he works closely with programmers and network technicians to ensure that the appropriate content is displayed and that the site is reliably available to users.

    e.   Operators are responsible for the day-to-day functioning of the computer center, whether the organization runs a mainframe, servers, or anything in between.

        1)   Operators load data, mount storage devices, and operate the equipment. Operators should not be assigned programming duties or responsibility for systems design. Accordingly, they also should have no opportunity to make changes in programs and systems as they operate the equipment.

            a)   Ideally, computer operators should not have programming knowledge or access to documentation not strictly necessary for their work.

    f.   Help desks are usually a responsibility of computer operations because of the operational nature of their functions. Help desk personnel log reported problems, resolve minor problems, and forward more difficult problems to the appropriate information systems resources, such as a technical support unit or vendor assistance.

    g.   Network technicians maintain the bridges, hubs, routers, switches, cabling, and other devices that interconnect the organization's computers. They are also responsible for maintaining the organization's connection to other networks such as the Internet.

    h.   End users must be able to change production data, but not programs.

Stop and review! You have completed the outline for this subunit. Study multiple-choice questions 1 through 5 beginning on page 380.

9.2 ENCRYPTION

1. **Overview**

   a. Encryption technology converts data into a code. A program codes data prior to transmission. Another program decodes it after transmission. Unauthorized users may still be able to access the data, but, without the encryption key, they will be unable to decode the information.

   b. Encryption software uses a fixed algorithm to manipulate plaintext and an encryption key to introduce variation. The information is sent in its manipulated form (cyphertext), and the receiver translates the information back into plaintext. Although data may be accessed by tapping into the transmission line, the encryption key is necessary to understand the data being sent.

      1) The machine instructions necessary to code and decode data can constitute a 20-to-30% increase in system overhead.

      2) Encryption technology may be either hardware- or software-based. Two major types of encryption software exist.

2. **Public-Key Encryption**

   a. Public-key (asymmetric) encryption requires two keys, one public and one private.

   b. These pairs of keys are issued by a trusted third party called a certificate authority (e.g., VeriSign, Thawte, GoDaddy).

      1) Every recipient's public key is available in the certificate authority's directory, but the associated private key is known only to the recipient.

      2) Any party who wishes to send a secure message encrypts it using the intended recipient's public key. The recipient then decrypts the message using the private key.

   c. This arrangement is more secure than a single-key system, in which the parties must agree on and transmit the single key that could be intercepted.

   d. RSA, named for its developers (Rivest, Shamir, and Adelman), is the most commonly used public-key method.

   e. A public-key system is used to create digital signatures (fingerprints).

      1) A digital signature is a means of authentication of an electronic document, for example, of the validity of a purchase order, acceptance of a contract, or financial information.

         a) The sender uses its private key to encode all or part of the message, and the recipient uses the sender's public key to decode it. Hence, if that key decodes the message, the sender must have written it.

         b) One variation is to send the message in both plaintext and cyphertext. If the decoded version matches the plaintext version, no alteration has occurred.

      2) A digital certificate is another means of authentication used in e-business. The certificate authority issues a coded electronic certificate that contains the holder's name, a copy of its public key, a serial number, and an expiration date. The certificate verifies the holder's identity.

         a) The recipient of a coded message uses the certificate authority's public key (available on the Internet) to decode the certificate included in the message. The recipient then determines that the certificate was issued by the certificate authority. Moreover, the recipient can use the sender's public key and identification data to send a coded response.

            i) Such methods might be used for transactions between sellers and buyers using credit cards.

    b)   A certificate also may be used to provide assurance to customers that a website is genuine.

    c)   The public key infrastructure permits secure monetary and information exchange over the Internet. Thus, it facilitates e-business.

    d)   The two main cryptographic protocols for secure communications over the Internet are SSL (Secure Sockets Layer) and TLS (Transport Layer Security).

       i)   When HTTP (Hypertext Transfer Protocol, a higher-level protocol that makes the graphics-intensive World Wide Web possible), is used in conjunction with SSL and/or TLS, it is called HTTPS (HTTP Secure).

       ii)   The URLs of secure web pages where shoppers enter their credit card numbers most often change from http:// to https://.

    e)   Digital time stamping services verify the time (and possibly the place) of a transaction. For example, a document may be sent to a service, which applies its digital stamp and then forwards the document.

3.   **Private-Key Encryption**

    a.   Private-key (symmetric) encryption requires only a single key for each pair of parties that want to send each other coded messages. This arrangement is less secure than public-key encryption.

    b.   Data Encryption Standard (DES), a shared private-key method developed by the U.S. government, is the most prevalent secret-key method. It is based on numbers with 56 binary digits.

    c.   The Advanced Encryption Standard (AES) is a recently adopted cryptographic algorithm for use by U.S. government organizations to protect sensitive information. The AES will be widely used on a voluntary basis by organizations, institutions, and individuals as well as by the U.S. government.

Stop and review! You have completed the outline for this subunit. Study multiple-choice questions 6 through 9 beginning on page 381.

9.3 INFORMATION PROTECTION

1.   **Business Objective**

    a.   The business assurance objective in the SAC model that is most concerned with malicious software (malware) is protectability. Thus, IT assets should be protected from "unauthorized access, use, or harm."

      1)   Control, e.g., over access and change management, should be in place to achieve the objective of protectability.

      2)   Moreover, security awareness by all concerned should be heightened. Consequently, the business assurance objective of accountability is also pertinent. The roles, actions, and responsibilities for security should be defined.

2.   **Malicious Software (Malware)**

    a.   Malicious software may exploit a known hole or weakness in an application or operating system program to evade security measures.

      1)   Such a vulnerability may have been caused by a programming error. It also may have been intentionally (but not maliciously) created to permit a programmer simple access (a back door) for correcting the code.

        2)   Having bypassed security controls, the intruder can do immediate damage to the system or install malicious software. In some cases, malware infection may have few or no effects noticeable by users.

    b.   A Trojan horse is an apparently innocent program (e.g., a spreadsheet) that includes a hidden function that may do damage when activated.

        1)   For example, it may contain a virus, which is a program code that copies itself from file to file. The virus may destroy data or programs. A common way of spreading a virus is by email attachments and downloads.

    c.   A worm copies itself not from file to file but from computer to computer, often very rapidly. Repeated replication overloads a system by depleting memory or disk space.

    d.   A logic bomb is much like a Trojan horse except it activates only upon some occurrence, e.g., on a certain date.

    e.   A maliciously created back door can be used for subsequent high-level access to data, computers, and networks.

    f.   Malware may create a denial of service by overwhelming a system or website with more traffic than it can handle.

3.   **Controls Against Malware**

    a.   Controls to prevent or detect infection by malware are particularly significant for file servers in large networks. The following are broad control objectives:

        1)   A policy should require use only of authorized software.

        2)   A policy should require adherence to licensing agreements.

        3)   A policy should create accountability for the persons authorized to maintain software.

        4)   A policy should require safeguards when data or programs are obtained by means of external media.

        5)   Antivirus software should continuously monitor the system for viruses (or worms) and eradicate them. It should also be immediately upgraded as soon as information about new threats becomes available.

        6)   Software and data for critical systems should be regularly reviewed.

        7)   Investigation of unauthorized files or amendments should be routine.

        8)   Email attachments and downloads (and files on unauthorized media or from networks that are not secure) should be checked.

        9)   Procedures should be established and responsibility assigned for coping with malware.

            a)   Procedures should reflect an understanding that another organization that has transmitted malware-infected material may have done so unwittingly and may need assistance. If such events occur repeatedly, however, termination of agreements or contracts may be indicated.

            b)   Procedures and policies should be documented, and employees must understand the reasons for them.

      10)   Business continuity (recovery) plans should be drafted, e.g., data and software backup.

      11)   Information about malware should be verified and appropriate alerts given.

      12)   Responsible personnel should be aware of the possibility of hoaxes, which are false messages intending to create fear of a malware attack. For example, a spurious email message may be received instructing users to delete supposedly compromised files.

      13)   Qualified personnel should be relied upon to distinguish hoaxes from malware.

b.   The following are specific controls:

1)   All computer media (incoming or outgoing) may be scanned by sheep dip (dedicated) computers.

2)   Nonscreened media should not be allowed on the organization's computers.

3)   Scanning may be done of standalone computers or those on networks as another line of defense if media control fails.

4)   Software may reside in memory to scan for malware communicated through a network.

5)   Email gateways may have software to scan attachments.

6)   Network servers may have software to detect and erase or store malware.

7)   Scanning software on a standalone device should be upgraded when it is networked.

c.   Use of external rather than internal expertise for coping with malware problems may be more costly and time consuming but less risky.

1)   External service providers should be subject to the terms of a contract, and access and other controls should be in place.

d.   Off-site computers and media of employees should be subject to malware controls, such as screening.

e.   Response to threats via covert channels and Trojan horse programs include the following:

1)   Purchases should be of evaluated products from trusted suppliers.

2)   Purchases should be in source code so that it is verifiable. This code should be inspected and tested prior to use.

3)   Access to and changes in code should be restricted after it is put in use.

4)   The availability of security patches for bugs in programs should be monitored constantly, especially regarding such items as network operating systems, email servers, routers, and firewalls. Patches should be tested and installed promptly.

5)   Trusted employees should be assigned to key systems.

6)   Known Trojan horses can be detected by scanning.

7)   Reviewing data outflows, for example, through the firewall, may detect suspicious activity meriting investigation.

f.   Hosts are the most common targets in a network because they furnish services to other requesting hosts.

1)   Protective measures include promptly installing the most recent patches, fixes, and updates.

a)   How they affect other elements of the system should be considered.
b)   Updates should be tested before installation.

4. Types of Attacks

a. Password Attacks

1) A number of methods may be used.

   a) A brute-force attack uses password-cracking software to try large numbers of letter and number combinations to access a network.

      i) A simple variation is the use of password-cracking software that tries all the words in a dictionary.

   b) Passwords (and user accounts) also may be discovered by Trojan horses, IP spoofing, and packet sniffers.

      i) Spoofing is identity misrepresentation in cyberspace, for example, by using a false website to obtain information about visitors.

      ii) Sniffing is use of software to eavesdrop on information sent by a user to the host computer of a website.

2) Once an attacker has access, (s)he may do anything the rightful user could have done.

   a) If that user has privileged access, the attacker may create a back door to facilitate future entry despite password and status changes.

   b) The attacker also may be able to leverage the initial access to obtain greater privileges than the rightful user.

3) If a user has the same password for multiple hosts, cracking that password for one compromises all.

4) Expressive methods of thwarting password attacks are one-time password and cryptographic authentication.

5) Optimal passwords are randomly generated, eight-character or longer combinations of numbers, uppercase and lowercase letters, and special symbols.

   a) A disadvantage is that users often write down passwords that are hard to remember. However, software has been developed that encrypts passwords to be kept on a handheld computer. Thus, the user only needs to know one password.

b. A man-in-the-middle attack takes advantage of networking packet sniffing and routing and transport protocols.

1) These attacks may be used to

   a) Steal data
   b) Obtain access to the network during a rightful user's active session
   c) Analyze the traffic on the network to learn about its operations and users
   d) Insert new data or modify the data being transmitted
   e) Deny service

2) Cryptography is the effective response to man-in-the-middle attacks. The encrypted data will be useless to the attacker unless it can be decrypted.

c. A denial-of-service (DOS) attack is an attempt to overload a system (e.g., a network or Web server) with false messages so that it cannot function (a system crash).

1) A distributed DOS (DDOS) attack comes from multiple sources, for example, the machines of innocent parties infected by Trojan horses. When activated, these programs send messages to the target and leave the connection open.

2) A DOS may establish as many network connections as possible to exclude other users, overloading primary memory, or corrupting file systems.

3) Responses

a) Firewalls should not permit use of Internet relay chat channels or other TCP/IP ports unless for business purposes. Thus, the organization should determine what relay kits have been installed, e.g., by employees connected to virtual private networks via cable or DSL.

i) These methods, intrusion detection systems, and penetration testing may prevent a system from being used to make a DOS attack.

b) The best protection by the target is the Internet service provider (ISP). The ISP can establish rate limits on transmissions to the target's website.

i) Thus, only a defined amount of message packets with certain characteristics are allowed to reach the site.

5. **Countermeasures -- Intrusion Detection Systems (IDS)**

a. If an organization's computer system has external connections, an IDS is needed to respond to security breaches.

1) The IDS complements the computer system's firewalls. It responds to attacks on

a) The network infrastructure (protected by the network IDS component)

i) Routers
ii) Switches
iii) Bandwidth

b) Servers (protected by the host IDS component)

i) Operating systems
ii) Applications

2) An IDS responds to an attack by

a) Taking action itself
b) Alerting the management system

b. A host IDS provides maximum protection only when the software is installed on each computer. It may operate in the following ways:

1) The aggressive response is to monitor every call on the operating system and application as it occurs.

2) A less effective method of preventing attacks is analysis of access log files.

3) A host IDS may also identify questionable processes and verify the security of system files.

c. A network IDS works by using sensors to examine packets traveling on the network. Each sensor monitors only the segment of the network to which it is attached. A packet is examined if it matches a signature.

1) String signatures (certain strings of text) are potential signs of an attack.

2) Port signatures alert the IDS that a point subject to frequent intrusion attempts may be under attack.

a) A port in this sense (as opposed to the physical serial and parallel ports on a personal computer) is a logical connection to the system.

i) A port number included in the message header stipulates how the message will be handled. Because many port numbers are widely known, an attacker may be able to send messages to determine whether ports are open and therefore vulnerable.

3) A header signature is a suspicious combination in a packet header.

    d.   The preferable IDS combines host IDS and network IDS components.

        1)   A host IDS has greater potential for preventing a specific attack, but the network IDS provides a necessary overall perspective. Thus, a host IDS should be in place for each host, with a network IDS for the whole system.

    e.   Knowledge-based detection is based on information about the system's weaknesses and searches for intrusions that take advantage of them.

        1)   This type of IDS depends on frequent and costly updating of information about intrusion methods. It is also specialized with respect to those methods and operating system methods.

            a)   Problems are compounded when different versions of the operating system (or different operating systems) are in place.

    f.   Behavior-based detection presumes that an attack will cause an observable anomaly. Actual and normal system behavior (a model of expected operations) are compared. A discrepancy results in an alert.

        1)   This approach is more complete than the knowledge-based approach because every attack should be detected. However, the level of accuracy is lower. False alarms may be generated, so the model must be updated whenever operational changes are made.

        2)   The advantages of behavior-based detection are that

            a)   Knowledge of specific new intrusion techniques is not necessary.
            b)   It is less specific to particular operating systems.

    g.   Responses to detection of an intrusion normally include an automatic component. Continuous monitoring and response by individuals may not be feasible or sufficiently rapid.

        1)   An automatically acting IDS provides continuous security. It responds without the presence of humans. Responses may include

            a)   Disconnecting the entire network from outside access
            b)   Locking access to all or part of the system
            c)   Slowing the system's activity to reduce injury
            d)   Validating the external user
            e)   Sending console, email, pager, or phone messages to appropriate personnel

        2)   Alarmed systems resources are dummy files or accounts, for example, a default administrator account with a default password set. They are traps for an intruder.

            a)   Access to a dummy resource results in automatic action or notice to appropriate employees.
            b)   The advantage of this method is that it is uncomplicated and inexpensive.
            c)   The disadvantage is that authorized persons may inadvertently cause an alarm.

Stop and review! You have completed the outline for this subunit. Study multiple-choice questions 10 through 13 on page 383.

9.4 INVESTMENT IN IT

1. **Overview**

    a. Hardware and software are significant assets that require careful management. Among the decisions to be made are resource requirements, evaluation of the full costs of the investment, and choosing whether to own or lease the technology.

        1) The growth of e-business means that greater resources are needed for transactions within the organization and with outside parties, for example, as a result of hosting websites with many users.

    b. Capacity planning should be undertaken by management and IT specialists. It determines whether the organization's current and future hardware resources relative to its priorities are, and will continue to be, sufficient. Among the issues are

        1) The maximum volume of transactions that can be simultaneously processed by the system
        2) The effect of software developments
        3) Performance measures, e.g., response time
        4) Changes in capacity needs resulting from business combinations, increased demand for the organization's products and services, and new applications

    c. Scalability is the characteristic of a system that permits its capacity to be increased to meet greater demands without a system failure.

        1) For example, a website should be supported by adequate processing, storage, and network assets to cope with peak demand.

2. **Costs of Ownership**

    a. The costs of ownership of IT assets include indirect as well as direct costs. Thus, rational economic decisions about hardware and software acquisition require an analysis of the true or full costs of all factors involved. Failing to consider total long-term costs may seriously underestimate the economic effects of IT decisions.

    b. The total cost of ownership (TCO) model will vary with the organization's unique needs. The following are typical factors to be considered:

        1) Capital costs of hardware, such as computers, terminals, storage devices, printers, and upgrades
        2) Capital costs of software, including purchase price or licensing cost per user, with upgrades
        3) Installation costs of hardware and software
        4) Training costs for IT specialists and end users
        5) Support costs incurred for help desks, other technical support labor, documentation, R&D, development of configuration standards, and review
        6) Maintenance costs for hardware and software upgrades
        7) Infrastructure costs of obtaining, supporting, and maintaining networks, back-up storage, etc.
        8) Costs of unproductive time (downtime) resulting from hardware or software failure
        9) Utility and real property costs of computer installations
        10) Costs of nonstandard personal computer configurations

            a) A standard configuration scheme for a given category of end users reduces costs by facilitating upgrades and support. However, new applications and updates of hardware may cause a loss of standardization.

       11) Costs of transferring end users

          a)   An end user is customarily restricted to a given personal computer with needed applications and access. Hence, transfer of an end user results in incurrence of costs for reinstallation and testing.

  c.   Managed systems are less costly to maintain and administer because hidden (indirect) costs are understood and minimized.

      1)   A centralized mainframe may be cheaper than a client-server architecture despite higher initial costs because of lower network administration and support costs.

      2)   In large entities, centralized acquisition policies save costs because organizational subunits are not allowed to purchase incompatible or redundant hardware and software. Standardized IT resources improve operations and decrease costs of administration.

      3)   Management of systems should include tracking IT resources and configuration changes. Tracking permits measurement of the cost of a configuration change in terms of personnel, money, time, and other resources. The cost can then be compared with the benefit.

  d.   The Systems Assurance and Control (SAC) model provides the following framework for determining TCO for an IT installation:

      1)   Cost of the standard configuration times the number of workstations

      2)   Sum of the technical infrastructure costs (hardware and software costs of servers, printers, routers, bridges, cables, supplier support, utility software, help desks, taxes, shipping, and upgrades over the productive life cycle of the configuration and infrastructure)

      3)   Sum of staff costs for full-time equivalent positions directly involved during the productive life cycle, plus administrative costs (e.g., for developing procedures and standards, capacity planning, and change control)

      4)   A percentage of the foregoing costs to reflect hidden costs, including such intangibles as end-user help provided by coworkers rather than the help desk

      5)   Costs of facilities, turnover, travel, and transportation

Stop and review! You have completed the outline for this subunit. Study multiple-choice questions 14 and 15 on page 384.

9.5 ENTERPRISE-WIDE RESOURCE PLANNING (ERP)

  1.   **Overview**

    a.   Enterprise-wide resource planning (ERP) is the latest phase in the development of computerized systems for managing organizational resources. ERP is intended to integrate enterprise-wide information systems across the organization by creating one database linked to all of the entity's applications.

    b.   ERP connects all functional subsystems (human resources, the financial accounting system, production, marketing, distribution, purchasing, receiving, order processing, shipping, etc.) and also connects the organization with its suppliers and customers.

      1)   Thus, ERP facilitates demand analysis and materials requirements planning.

      2)   By decreasing lead times, it improves just-in-time inventory management.

      3)   Even more importantly, ERP's coordination of all operating activities permits flexible responses to shifts in supply and demand.

    c.   The disadvantages of ERP are its extent and complexity, which make customization of the software difficult and costly.

d. The leading products in the field are R/3, distributed by SAP, and JD Edwards EnterpriseOne and PeopleSoft Enterprise, both distributed by Oracle.

e. Because ERP software is costly and complex, it is usually installed only by the largest enterprises. However, mid-size organizations are increasingly likely to buy ERP software.

f. The benefits of ERP may significantly derive from the required business process reengineering.

1) Using ERP software that reflects the best practices forces the linked subunits in the organization not only to redesign and improve their processes but also to conform to one standard.

2) An organization may wish to undertake a reengineering project before choosing ERP software. The project should indicate what best practices already exist in the organization's processes. This approach may be preferable for a unique enterprise in a highly differentiated industry.

a) Carrying out a reengineering project before installing an ERP system defines what process changes are needed and which vendor software should be used.

b) If the organization is not especially unique, vendor software probably is already based on industry best practices. In these circumstances, a preliminary reengineering project may not be needed. Thus, the organization should simply conform its processes to the software.

3) The processes reflected in the ERP software may differ from the organization's. In this case, the better policy is usually to change the organization's processes. Customizing the ERP software is expensive and difficult, and it may result in bugs and awkwardness in adopting upgrades.

a) Implementing an ERP system is likely to encounter significant resistance because of its comprehensiveness. Most employees will have to change ingrained habits and learn to use new technology. Hence, successful implementation requires effective change management.

2. Evolution

a. Materials requirements planning (MRP) was an early attempt to create an integrated computer-based information system. It was designed to plan and control materials used in a production setting.

1) MRP was a push system. It assumed that the demand for materials is typically dependent upon some other factor, which can be programmed. Thus, the timing of deliveries is vital to avoid production delays.

2) For example, an auto manufacturer need only tell the system how many autos of each type are to be manufactured. The MRP system then generates a complete list of every part and component needed. MRP, in effect, creates schedules of when items on inventory will be needed in the production departments.

a) If parts are not in stock, the system will automatically generate a purchase order on the proper date (considering lead times) so that deliveries will arrive on time. Hence, effective application of MRP necessitates the generation of accurate data about costs and amounts of inventory, setup costs, and costs of downtime.

b. Manufacturing resource planning (MRP II) continued the evolution begun with MRP. It is a closed-loop manufacturing system that integrates all facets of a manufacturing business, including production, sales, inventories, schedules, and cash flows. The same system is used for the accounting, finance, and directing functions, which use the same transactions and numbers.

1) MRP II includes forecasting and planning capacities for generating cash and other budgets.

2) MRP II uses an MPS (master production schedule), which is a statement of the anticipated manufacturing schedule for selected items for selected periods. MRP also uses the MPS. Thus, MRP is a component of an MRP II system.

c. The traditional ERP system is one in which subsystems share data and coordinate their activities.

1) Thus, if marketing receives an order, it can quickly verify that inventory is sufficient to notify shipping to process the order.

    a) Otherwise, production is notified to manufacture more of the product, with a consequent automatic adjustment of output schedules.

    b) If materials are inadequate for this purpose, the system will issue a purchase order.

    c) If more labor is needed, human resources will be instructed to reassign or hire employees.

    d) The foregoing business processes (and others) should interact seamlessly in an ERP system. Moreover, the current generation of ERP software also provides the capability for smooth (and instant) interaction with the business processes of external parties.

2) The subsystems in a traditional ERP system are internal to the organization. Hence, they are often called back-office functions. The information produced is principally (but not exclusively) intended for internal use by the organization's managers.

3. **Current Generation**

a. The current generation of ERP software (ERP II) has added front-office functions. These connect the organization with customers, suppliers, shareholders or other owners, creditors, and strategic allies (e.g., the members of a trading community or other business association). Accordingly, an ERP II system has the following interfaces with its back-office functions:

1) Supply-chain management applications for an organization focus on relationships extending from its suppliers to its final customers. Issues addressed include distribution channels, warehousing and other logistical matters, routing of shipments, and sales forecasting.

    a) In turn, one organization's supply chain is part of a linked chain of multiple organizations. This chain stretches from the producers of raw materials, to processors of those materials, to entities that make intermediate goods, to assemblers of final products, to wholesalers, to retailers, and lastly, to ultimate consumers.

    b) Supply chain management involves a two-way exchange of information. For example, a customer may be able to track the progress of its order, and the supplier may be able to monitor the customer's inventory. Thus, the customer has better information about order availability, and the supplier knows when the customer's inventory needs replenishment.

    c) An advanced planning and scheduling system may be an element of a supply chain management application for a manufacturer. It controls the flow of material and components within the chain. Schedules are created given projected costs, lead times, and inventories.

2) Customer relationship management applications extend to customer service, finance-related matters, sales, and database creation and maintenance.

   a) Integrated data is helpful in better understanding customer needs, such as product preference or location of retail outlets. Thus, the organization may be able to optimize its sales forecasts, product line, and inventory levels.

      i) Business intelligence software is used to analyze customer data.

3) Partner relationship management applications connect the organization not only with such partners as customers and suppliers but also with owners, creditors, and strategic allies (for example, other members of a joint venture).

   a) Collaborative business partnerships may arise between competitors or arise between different types of organizations, such as a manufacturer partnering with an environmental group. Special software may be helpful to the partners in sharing information, developing a common strategy, and measuring performance.

4. **Configuration**

   a. The following are the main elements of the architecture of an ERP:

      1) Current ERP systems have a client-server configuration with possibly scores or hundreds of client (user) computers.

         a) So-called thin clients have little processing ability, but fat clients may have substantial processing power.

         b) The system may have multiple servers to run applications and contain databases.

         c) The network architecture may be in the form of a local area network or wide-area network, or users may connect with the server(s) via the Internet.

         d) An ERP system may use almost any of the available operating systems and database management systems.

   b. An advantage of an ERP system is the elimination of data redundancy through the use of a central database. In principle, information about an item of data is stored once, and all functions have access to it.

      1) Thus, when the item (such as a price) is updated, the change is effectively made for all functions. The result is reliability (data integrity).

         a) If an organization has separate systems for its different functions, the item would have to be updated whenever it was stored. Failure of even one function to update the item would cause loss of data integrity. For example, considerable inefficiency may arise when different organizational subunits (IT, production, marketing, accounting, etc.) have different data about prices and inventory availability.

   c. An organization may not have the resources, desire, or need for an ERP system with the greatest degree of integration (e.g., SAP R/3).

      1) An alternative to a comprehensive system is a best-of-breed approach. Thus, an organization might install a traditional ERP system from one vendor and add e-commerce and other extended applications from separate niche vendors.

         a) An organization that adopts this approach needs to use middleware, that is, software that permits different applications to communicate and exchange data. This type of middleware is called an extended application interface.

      d.   An ERP system that extends to customers, suppliers, and others uses Internet portals. In this case, a portal is a website through which authorized external users may gain access to the organization's ERP.

           1)   Portals provide links to related websites and services (e.g., newsletters, email, and e-commerce capabilities).

5. Implementation

      a.   Implementation of ERP may take years and cost millions. Moreover, a poor implementation may cause the project to fail regardless of the quality of the software.

           1)   However, more rapid and less costly implementation may be possible if no customization is done.

      b.   The initial step is to do strategic planning and to organize a project team that is representative of affected employee groups.

      c.   The second step is to choose ERP software and a consulting firm.

           1)   One possibility is to choose the software before the consultants because the first decision may affect the second.

           2)   Another option is to hire consultants to help with the selection of the software.

                a)   The organization may then hire other consultants to help with implementation.

      d.   The third and longest step is preimplementation.

           1)   The length of the process design phase is a function of the extent of

                a)   Reengineering
                b)   Customization of the software

           2)   Data conversion may be delayed because all departments must agree on the meaning of every data field, i.e., what values will be considered valid for that field.

           3)   The ERP system and its interfaces must be tested.

      e.   Implementation ("going live") is not the final step. Follow-up is necessary to monitor the activities of the numerous employees who have had to change their routines. For example, a mistake caused by reverting to the old method of entering a sales order may have pervasive consequences in a new integrated system: a credit check, rescheduling of production, and ordering of materials.

      f.   Training should be provided during implementation not only regarding technical matters but also to help employees understand the reasons for process changes. For example, the employees who enter sales orders should know what the effects will be throughout the system.

           1)   Other change management techniques include effective communication to allay employee fears and the creation of user-friendly documents and interfaces.

6. Costs

      a.   The costs of an ERP system include

           1)   Losses from an unsuccessful implementation, e.g., sales declines
           2)   Purchasing hardware, software, and services
           3)   Data conversion from legacy systems to the new integrated system (but conversion software may help)
           4)   Training
           5)   Design of interfaces and customization
           6)   Software maintenance and upgrades
           7)   Salaries of employees working on the implementation

7.   **Benefits**

a.   The benefits of an ERP system may be hard to quantify. They include

1)   Lower inventory costs
2)   Better management of liquid assets
3)   Reduced labor costs and greater productivity
4)   Enhanced decision making
5)   Elimination of data redundancy and protection of data integrity
6)   Avoidance of the costs of other means of addressing needed IT changes
7)   Increased customer satisfaction
8)   More rapid and flexible responses to changed circumstances
9)   More effective supply chain management
10)   Integration of global operations

Stop and review! You have completed the outline for this subunit. Study multiple-choice questions 16 and 17 on page 385.

9.6 SYSTEMS SOFTWARE

1.   **Operating Systems**

a.   Systems software performs the fundamental tasks needed to manage computer resources. The most basic piece of systems software is the operating system.

1)   An operating system acts as an interface between users, application software, and the computer's hardware (CPU, disk drives, printers, communications devices, etc.).

a)   z/OS is the most recent operating system for the very successful IBM mainframe.

b)   Server operating systems include Unix, Linux, Microsoft Windows Server, and Apple MacOS X Server. Inherent networking capabilities are an important part of server operating systems.

c)   Microsoft Windows, Apple MacOS, and Linux are operating systems for desktop computers.

2.   **Utility Programs**

a.   Utility programs are another important type of systems software.

1)   Utilities perform basic data maintenance tasks, such as

a)   Sorting, e.g., arranging all the records in a file by invoice number
b)   Merging, meaning combining the data from two files into one
c)   Copying and deleting entire files

2)   Utilities are extremely powerful. Their use should be restricted to appropriate personnel, and each occurrence should be logged.

3.   **Databases**

a.   Databases are a third category of systems software. Databases are areas of storage in which data elements are mutually linked.

1)   Widely used database software packages include IBM's DB2, Software AG's Adabas, Oracle's Database, and Microsoft's SQL Server.

2)   The internal workings of databases are discussed in detail in Study Unit 10, Subunit 4.

Stop and review! You have completed the outline for this subunit. Study multiple-choice questions 18 and 19 beginning on page 385.

9.7 APPLICATION DEVELOPMENT

> The development of new systems is another IT area that has undergone profound change from its early days. New, high-productivity software tools have dissolved the lines separating the old rigid steps in the process. Internal auditors must remain focused on the ultimate goal of implementing stable, maintainable systems.

1. **Build or Buy**

   a. When an organization acquires a new system by purchasing from an outside vendor, contract management personnel oversee the process. The future end users of the system as well as IT personnel are also involved, drawing up specifications and requirements.

      1) However, when a new system is to be created in-house, planning and managing the development process is one of the IT function's most important tasks.

         a) The needs of the end users must be balanced with budget and time constraints; the decision to use existing hardware vs. the purchase of new platforms must be weighed.

      2) Because so much time and so many resources are devoted to the creation of a new application (and because, generally, the more important the business function being automated, the more complex the application is), having a well-governed methodology for overseeing the development process is vital.

      3) Both the end users who specified the new system's functionality and IT management who are overseeing the development process must approve progress toward the completion of the system at the end of each of the stages described below and on the following two pages. This requirement for ongoing review and approval of the project is a type of implementation control.

2. **Systems Development Life Cycle (SDLC)**

   a. The systems development life-cycle approach is the traditional methodology applied to the development of large, highly structured application systems.

      1) A major advantage of the life-cycle approach is enhanced management and control of the development process.

      2) Once the need for a new system has been recognized, the five phases (each with multiple steps) of the SDLC proceed as depicted in the diagram below (portions of the phases can overlap).

Systems Development Life Cycle

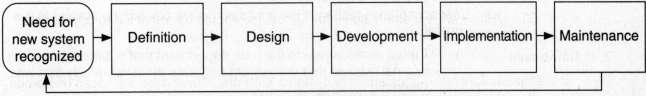

Figure 9-1

      3) Note that the feedback gathered during the maintenance of a system provides information for developing the next generation of systems, hence the name life cycle.

b.   The phases and component steps of the traditional SDLC can be described as follows:

1)   Definition

a)   A proposal for a new system is submitted to the IT steering committee describing the need for the application and the business function(s) that it will affect.

b)   Feasibility studies are conducted to determine

i)   What technology the new system will require
ii)   What economic resources must be committed to the new system
iii)   How the new system will affect current operations

c)   The steering committee gives its go-ahead for the project.

2)   Design

a)   Logical design consists of mapping the flow and storage of the data elements that will be used by the new system and the new program modules that will constitute the new system.

i)   Data flow diagrams (DFDs) and structured flowcharts are commonly used in this step.

ii)   Some data elements may already be stored in existing databases. Good logical design ensures that they are not duplicated.

b)   Physical design involves planning the specific interactions of the new program code and data elements with the hardware platform (existing or planned for purchase) on which the new system will operate.

i)   Systems analysts are heavily involved in these two steps.

3)   Development

a)   The actual program code and database structures that will be used in the new system are written.

b)   Testing is the most crucial step of the process.

i)   The programmers thoroughly test each new program module of the system, both alone and in concert with other modules.

●   The data used in testing new programs is never the organization's actual production data; such testing would be far too risky to the organization's business.

●   Instead, a carefully designed test database is filled with both good and bad data to test how well the new system deals with bad input.

c)   User acceptance testing is the final step before placing the system in live operation.

i)   IT must demonstrate to the user department that submitted the original request that the system performs the functionality that was desired.

ii)   Once the user department is satisfied with the new system, it acknowledges formal acceptance, and implementation begins.

    4)   Implementation

        a)   Four strategies for converting to the new system can be used:

            i)   With parallel operation, the old and new systems both are run at full capacity for a given period.

- This strategy is the safest since the old system is still producing output (in case there are major problems with the new system), but it is also the most expensive and time-consuming.

            ii)   With cutover conversion, the old system is shut down, and the new one takes over processing at once.

- This is the least expensive and least time-consuming strategy, but it is also the riskiest.

            iii)   Under pilot conversion, one branch, department, or division at a time is fully converted to the new system.

- Experience gained from each installation is used to benefit the next one. One disadvantage of this strategy is the extension of the conversion time.

            iv)   In some cases, phased conversion is possible. Under this strategy, one function of the new system at a time is placed in operation.

- For instance, if the new system is an integrated accounting application, accounts receivable could be installed, then accounts payable, cash management, materials handling, etc.
- The advantage of this strategy is allowing the users to learn one part of the system at a time.

        b)   Training and documentation are critical.

            i)   The users must be made to feel comfortable with the new system and have plenty of guidance available, either as a hard copy or online.

            ii)   Documentation consists of more than just operations manuals for the users. Layouts of the program code and database structures must also be available for the programmers who must modify and maintain the system.

        c)   Systems follow-up or post-audit evaluation is a subsequent review of the efficiency and effectiveness of the system after it has operated for a substantial time (e.g., 1 year).

    5)   Maintenance, the final phase of the SDLC, is discussed in Subunit 9.8.

3. Prototyping

    a.   Prototyping is an alternative approach to application development that involves creating a working model of the system requested, demonstrating it for the user, obtaining feedback, and making changes to the underlying code.

        1)   This process repeats through several iterations until the user is satisfied with the system's functionality.

    b.   Formerly, this approach was derided as being wasteful of resources and tending to produce unstable systems, but with vastly increased processing power and high-productivity development tools, prototyping can, in some cases, be an efficient means of systems development.

4.   **Application Authentication**

    a.   Application authentication is a means of taking a user's identity from the operating system on which the user is working and passing it to an authentication server for verification. This can be designed into an application from its inception.

5.   **Application Development Tools**

    a.   Computer-aided software engineering (CASE) applies the computer to software design and development.

        1)   It provides the capacity to maintain on the computer all of the system documentation, e.g., data flow diagrams, data dictionaries, and pseudocode (structured English); to develop executable input and output screens; and to generate program code in at least skeletal form.

        2)   Thus, CASE facilitates the creation, organization, and maintenance of documentation and permits some automation of the coding process.

    b.   Object-oriented programming (OOP) combines data and the related procedures into an object. Thus, an object's data can be operated on only within the object.

        1)   If the procedures (called methods) for manipulating the data in an object are changed, no other parts of the program are affected. The idea of limiting code that operates on an object to its own source code unit is called encapsulation.

            a)   The basic concepts of OOP are class and inheritance. Programs are written by describing the creation and interaction of objects. One class of objects can inherit the characteristics of a more general class. Thus, a basic advantage of OOP is that the code is reusable.

            b)   In OOP, every object has attached to it two sets of characteristics, called attributes and methods.

EXAMPLE

A company's programmers have created an object named "order."

"order" has the following attributes: order_number, order_date, customer_number, part_number, qty_ordered, unit_price, bin_number.

"order" is given the following methods:

- extended_price (qty_ordered × unit_price)
- three_month_history (every order with the same customer_number and order_date less than 3 months old is retrieved)
- quantity_remaining (uses bin_number to determine current quantity on hand and subtracts qty_ordered)

The object "order" can now be reused by the programmers without all of its attributes and methods having to be recreated in every application that uses it.

---

    c.   Rapid application development (RAD) is a software development process involving iterative development, the construction of prototypes, and the use of CASE tools.

        1)   The RAD process usually involves compromises in usability, features, and/or execution speed; increased speed of development occurs through rapid prototyping, virtualization of system related routines, and other techniques. However, there is usually decreased end-user utility.

> 2) RAD tools include requirements-gathering tools, data-modeling tools, and code-generation tools.
>
>> a) Requirements-gathering tools. All stages of the RAD methodology, particularly the requirements planning stage, specify that requirements should be captured in a tool rather than an unstructured document.
>>
>>> i) For this reason, and because the unified modeling language (UML) is the only language for this task, tools that support writing in the UML support RAD. Among the numerous tools that support UML notation is Microsoft Visio.
>>
>> b) Code-generation tools. RAD was designed in large part to take advantage of CASE technology, which involves aspects of requirements gathering and data modeling, but most especially of code generation.
>>
>>> i) Code generation involves taking some input and transforming it to the source code that a developer might otherwise have to write according to templates.

Stop and review! You have completed the outline for this subunit. Study multiple-choice questions 20 through 23 beginning on page 386.

9.8 PROGRAM CHANGE CONTROL

1. **Overview**

   a. Over the life of an application, users are constantly asking for changes. The process of managing these changes is referred to as systems maintenance, and the relevant controls are called program change controls.

2. **Program Change Control Process**

   a. Once a change to a system has been approved, the programmer should save a copy of the production program in a test area of the computer, sometimes called a "sandbox."

      1) Except in emergencies, and then only under close supervision, should a change be made directly to the production version of a computer program.

      2) The IT function must be able to revert immediately to the prior version of the program if unexpected results are encountered during an emergency change.

   b. The programmer makes the necessary changes to this copy of the program.

      1) The program appears on the programmer's screen, not as digital bits and bytes, but as English-like statements and commands. A computer program in this form, i.e., readable by humans, is called source code.

   c. The programmer transforms the changed program into a form that the computer can execute. The resulting production-ready program is referred to as executable code.

      1) Programming languages that are transformed from source code into executable code at run time by a specialized converter program are said to be interpreted.

      2) Programming languages that are transformed in one step, before run time, and then executed directly on the computer are said to be compiled.

   d. Once the executable version of the changed program is ready, the programmer tests it to see if it performs the new task as expected.

      1) This testing process must absolutely not be run against production data. A special set of test data must be available for running test programs against.

    e.   The programmer demonstrates the new functionality for the user who made the request.

         1)   The user either accepts the new program, or the programmer can go back and make further changes.

    f.   Once the program is in a form acceptable to the user, the programmer moves it to a holding area.

         1)   Programmers (except in emergencies) should never be able to put programs directly into production.

    g.   The programmer's supervisor reviews the new program, approves it, and authorizes its move into production, generally carried out by operations personnel.

         1)   The compensating control is that operators generally lack the programming knowledge to put fraudulent code into production.

Stop and review! You have completed the outline for this subunit. Study multiple-choice questions 24 through 26 beginning on page 387.

9.9 END-USER COMPUTING (EUC)

    1.   **End-User vs. Centralized Computing**

        a.   End-user computing involves user-created or user-acquired systems that are maintained and operated outside of traditional information systems controls.

        b.   Environmental control risks that are more likely in an EUC environment include copyright violations that occur when unauthorized copies of software are made or when software is installed on multiple computers.

        c.   Access to application programs and related data by unauthorized persons is another concern because of lack of physical access controls, application-level controls, and other controls found in mainframe or networked environments.

        d.   Moreover, an EUC environment may be characterized by inadequate backup, recovery, and contingency planning that may result in an inability to re-create the system or its data.

        e.   Program development, documentation, and maintenance may also suffer from the lack of centralized control found in larger systems.

            1)   The risk of allowing end users to develop their own applications is decentralization of control. End-user-developed applications may not be subject to an independent outside review by systems analysts and are not created in the context of a formal development methodology. These applications may lack appropriate standards, controls, and quality assurance procedures.

            2)   Moreover, when end users create their own applications and files, private information systems may proliferate in which data are largely uncontrolled. Systems may contain the same information, but end-user applications may update and define the data in different ways. Thus, determining the location of data and ensuring data consistency become more difficult.

            3)   The auditors should determine that the EUC applications contain controls that allow users to rely on the information produced. Identification of applications is more difficult than in a traditional centralized computing environment because few people know about and use them. The auditor's first concern is to discover their existence and their intended functions. One approach is to take an organization-wide inventory of major EUC applications. An alternative is to review major EUC applications in concert with the function or department that is the major user.

a)   The next step is risk assessment. The EUC applications that represent high-risk exposures are chosen for audit, for example, because they support critical decisions or are used to control cash or physical assets.

b)   The third step is to review the controls included in the applications chosen in the second phase.

f.   In a personal computer setting, the user is often the programmer and operator. Thus, the protections afforded by segregation of duties are eliminated.

g.   The audit trail is diminished because of the lack of history files, incomplete printed output, etc.

h.   In general, available security features for stand-alone machines are limited compared with those in a network configuration.

2.   **Three Types of End-User Computing Environments**

a.   Client-server model. A client-server system divides processing of an application between a client machine on a network and a server. This division depends on which tasks each is best suited to perform.

1)   However, user interaction is ordinarily restricted to the client part of the application. This portion normally consists of the user interface, data entry, queries, and receipt of reports.

2)   The server customarily manages peripheral hardware and controls access to shared databases. Thus, a client-server application must be designed as separate software components that run on different machines but appear to be one application.

3)   Security for client-server systems may be more difficult than in a mainframe-based system because of the numerous access points. They also use distributed processing methods that result in heightened risk of unauthorized access to data and processing. New methods of accessing data and processing, such as remote procedure calls, are also available.

b.   Dummy terminal model. In this architecture, desktop machines that lack stand-alone processing power have access to remote computers in a network.

1)   Applications run on the remote network computers. The terminal simply displays output from the application and sends input from the user back to the application.

2)   These machines are relatively inexpensive because they have no disk drives.

c.   The application server model involves a three-tiered or distributed network application. The middle (application) tier translates data between the database (back-end) server and the user's (front-end) server. The application server also performs business logic functions, transaction management, and load balancing.

1)   Business logic functions interpret transactions and determine how they will be processed, e.g., applicable discounts, shipping methods, etc. Mainly performed by the application server in contrast to the presentation logic performed by the user's front-end server.

2)   Transaction management keeps track of all of the steps in transaction processing to ensure completion, editing, and/or deletion.

3)   Load balancing is a process to distribute data and data processing among available servers, e.g., evenly to all servers or to the next available server.

Stop and review! You have completed the outline for this subunit. Study multiple-choice questions 27 through 30 beginning on page 388.

QUESTIONS

9.1 Functional Areas of IT Operations

1. The practice of maintaining a test program library separate from the production program library is an example of

A. An organizational control.

B. Physical security.

C. An input control.

D. A concurrency control.

Answer (A) is correct. *(CIA, adapted)*
  REQUIRED: The type of control represented by separating the test and production program libraries.
  DISCUSSION: This separation is an organizational control. Organizational controls concern the proper segregation of duties and responsibilities within the information systems department. Although proper segregation is desirable, functions that would be considered incompatible if performed by a single individual in a manual activity are often performed through the use of an information systems program or series of programs. Thus, compensating controls may be necessary, such as library controls, effective supervision, and rotation of personnel. Segregating test programs makes concealment of unauthorized changes in production programs more difficult.
  Answer (B) is incorrect. Physical security (e.g., climate control and restrictions on physical access) is another aspect of organizational control. Answer (C) is incorrect. Input controls validate the completeness, accuracy, and appropriateness of input. Answer (D) is incorrect. Concurrency controls manage situations in which two or more programs attempt to use a file or database at the same time.

2. An organization's computer help-desk function is usually a responsibility of the

A. Applications development unit.

B. Systems programming unit.

C. Computer operations unit.

D. User departments.

Answer (C) is correct. *(CIA, adapted)*
  REQUIRED: The entity in charge of a computer help desk.
  DISCUSSION: Help desks are usually a responsibility of computer operations because of the operational nature of their functions. A help desk logs reported problems, resolves minor problems, and forwards more difficult problems to the appropriate information systems resources, such as a technical support unit or vendor assistance.
  Answer (A) is incorrect. Applications development is responsible for developing systems, not providing help to end users. Answer (B) is incorrect. The responsibility of systems programming is to implement and maintain system-level software, such as operating systems, access control software, and database systems software. Answer (D) is incorrect. User departments usually lack the expertise to solve computer problems.

3. When a new application is being created for widespread use in a large organization, the principal liaison between the IT function and the rest of an organization is normally a(n)

A. End user.

B. Application programmer.

C. Maintenance programmer.

D. Systems analyst.

Answer (D) is correct. *(CIA, adapted)*
  REQUIRED: The principal liaison between the information technology (IT) department and the rest of the organization.
  DISCUSSION: Systems analysts are specifically qualified to analyze and design computer information systems. They survey the existing system, analyze the organization's information requirements, and design new systems to meet those needs. Systems analysts communicate with the entire organization and act as a liaison between the organization and the IT function.
  Answer (A) is incorrect. End users make up the rest of the organization. Answer (B) is incorrect. Programmers design, write, test, and document the specific programs developed by systems analysts. It is not the responsibility of an application programmer to act as a liaison between the IT department and the rest of the organization. Answer (C) is incorrect. Programmers design, write, test, and document the specific programs developed by systems analysts. It is not the responsibility of a maintenance programmer to act as a liaison between the IT department and the rest of the organization.

4. In the organization of the IT function, the most important separation of duties is

    A. Not allowing the data librarian to assist in data processing operations.

    B. Ensuring that those responsible for programming the system do not have access to data processing operations.

    C. Having a separate information officer at the top level of the organization outside of the accounting function.

    D. Using different programming personnel to maintain utility programs from those who maintain the application programs.

Answer (B) is correct. *(CMA, adapted)*
    REQUIRED: The most important separation of duties in the IT function.
    DISCUSSION: Separation of duties is a general control that is vital in a computerized environment. Some separation of duties common in noncomputerized environments may not be feasible in a computer environment. However, certain tasks should not be combined. Systems analysts and programmers should be separate from computer operators. Both programmers and analysts may be able to modify programs, files, and controls and should therefore have no access to those programs nor to computer equipment. Operators should not be assigned programming duties or responsibility for systems design and should have no opportunity to make changes in programs and systems.
    Answer (A) is incorrect. Librarians maintain control over documentation, programs, and data files; they should have no access to equipment, but they can assist in data processing operations. Answer (C) is incorrect. A separate information officer outside of the accounting function would not be as critical a separation of duties as that between programmers and processors. Answer (D) is incorrect. Programmers usually handle all types of programs.

5. The duties properly assigned to an information security officer could include all of the following **except**

    A. Developing an information security policy for the organization.

    B. Maintaining and updating the list of user passwords.

    C. Commenting on security controls in new applications.

    D. Monitoring and investigating unsuccessful access attempts.

Answer (B) is correct. *(CIA, adapted)*
    REQUIRED: The duty not properly assigned to an information security office.
    DISCUSSION: The information security officer should not know user passwords. They are normally stored on a computer in encrypted format, and users change them directly.
    Answer (A) is incorrect. Developing an information security policy for the organization is an appropriate duty of the information security officer. Answer (C) is incorrect. Commenting on security controls in new applications is an appropriate duty of the information security officer. Answer (D) is incorrect. Monitoring and investigating unsuccessful access attempts is an appropriate duty of the information security officer.

9.2 Encryption

6. A controller became aware that a competitor appeared to have access to the company's pricing information. The internal auditor determined that the leak of information was occurring during the electronic transmission of data from branch offices to the head office. Which of the following controls would be most effective in preventing the leak of information?

    A. Asynchronous transmission.

    B. Encryption.

    C. Use of fiber-optic transmission lines.

    D. Use of passwords.

Answer (B) is correct. *(CIA, adapted)*
    REQUIRED: The most effective control over electronic transmission of data.
    DISCUSSION: Encryption software uses a fixed algorithm to manipulate plain text and an encryption key (a set of random data bits used as a starting point for application of the algorithm) to introduce variation. Although data may be accessed by tapping into the transmission line, the encryption key is necessary to understand the data being sent.
    Answer (A) is incorrect. Asynchronous transmission is a method of data transmission, not a means of safeguarding data. It is used for slow, irregular transmissions, such as from a keyboard terminal. Each character is marked by a start and stop code. Answer (C) is incorrect. Although fiber-optic transmission lines are difficult to tap, their use will not prevent theft of unencrypted data by someone who has access to them. Answer (D) is incorrect. The use of passwords will control access at the sending location and the head-office computer. However, passwords will not prevent someone from tapping the transmission line.

7. The use of message encryption software

- A. Guarantees the secrecy of data.
- B. Requires manual distribution of keys.
- C. Increases system overhead.
- D. Reduces the need for periodic password changes.

Answer (C) is correct.   *(CIA, adapted)*

REQUIRED: The effect of message encryption software.

DISCUSSION: Encryption software uses a fixed algorithm to manipulate plain text and an encryption key (a set of random data bits used as a starting point for application of the algorithm) to introduce variation. The machine instructions necessary to encrypt and decrypt data constitute system overhead. As a result, processing speed may be slowed.

Answer (A) is incorrect. No encryption approach absolutely guarantees the secrecy of data. Answer (B) is incorrect. Keys may also be distributed electronically via secure key transporters. Answer (D) is incorrect. Periodic password changes are needed. Passwords are the typical means of validating users' access to unencrypted data.

8. Which of the following is an encryption feature that can be used to authenticate the originator of a document and ensure that the message is intact and has not been tampered with?

- A. Heuristic terminal.
- B. Perimeter switch.
- C. Default settings.
- D. Digital signatures.

Answer (D) is correct.   *(CPA, adapted)*

REQUIRED: The encryption feature used to authenticate the originator of a document and ensure that the original message is intact.

DISCUSSION: Businesses and others require that documents sent over the Internet be authentic. To authenticate a document, a company or other user may transmit a complete plaintext document along with an encrypted portion of the same document or another standard text that serves as a digital signature. If the plaintext document is tampered with, the two will not match.

Answer (A) is incorrect. The term "heuristic terminal" is not meaningful in this context. Answer (B) is incorrect. The term "perimeter switch" is not meaningful in this context. Answer (C) is incorrect. In a computer program, a default setting is a value that a parameter will automatically assume unless specifically overridden.

9. The encryption technique that requires two keys, a public key that is available to anyone for encrypting messages and a private key that is known only to the recipient for decrypting messages, is

- A. Rivest, Shamir, and Adelman (RSA).
- B. Data encryption standard (DES).
- C. Modulator-demodulator.
- D. A cypher lock.

Answer (A) is correct.   *(CIA, adapted)*

REQUIRED: The encryption technique requiring two keys.

DISCUSSION: RSA is an encryption standard licensed to hardware and software vendors. Public-key encryption requires management of fewer keys for a given client-server environment than does private-key encryption. However, compared with DES, RSA entails more complex computations and therefore has a higher processing overhead. RSA requires two keys: The public key for encrypting messages is widely known, but the private key for decrypting messages is kept secret by the recipient.

Answer (B) is incorrect. DES is a shared private-key method developed by the U.S. government. It encrypts data into 64-bit blocks using a 56-bit key. DES requires only a single key for each pair of parties that want to send each other encrypted messages. DES is being replaced by AES, Advanced Encryption Standard, as the method of choice by the U.S. government. Answer (C) is incorrect. A modem is used for telecommunications. Answer (D) is incorrect. A cypher lock is a physical device.

9.3 Information Protection

10. Which of the following is a computer program that appears to be legitimate but performs some illicit activity when it is run?

- A. Hoax virus.
- B. Web crawler.
- C. Trojan horse.
- D. Killer application.

Answer (C) is correct. *(CPA, adapted)*
REQUIRED: The apparently legitimate computer program that performs an illicit activity.
DISCUSSION: A Trojan horse is a computer program that appears friendly, for example, a game, but that actually contains an application destructive to the computer system.
Answer (A) is incorrect. A hoax virus is a false notice about the existence of a computer virus. It is usually disseminated through use of distribution lists and is sent by email or via an internal network. Answer (B) is incorrect. A web crawler (a spider or bot) is a computer program created to access and read information on websites. The results are included as entries in the index of a search engine. Answer (D) is incorrect. A killer application is one that is so useful that it may justify widespread adoption of a new technology.

11. The best preventive measure against a computer virus is to

- A. Compare software in use with authorized versions of the software.
- B. Execute virus exterminator programs periodically on the system.
- C. Allow only authorized software from known sources to be used on the system.
- D. Prepare and test a plan for recovering from the incidence of a virus.

Answer (C) is correct. *(CIA, adapted)*
REQUIRED: The best preventive measure against a computer virus.
DISCUSSION: Preventive controls are designed to prevent errors before they occur. Detective and corrective controls attempt to identify and correct errors. Preventive controls are usually more cost beneficial than detective or corrective controls. Allowing only authorized software from known sources to be used on the system is a preventive measure. The authorized software from known sources is expected to be free of viruses.
Answer (A) is incorrect. Comparing software with authorized versions is a detective control used to determine whether only authorized versions of the software are being used on the system. Answer (B) is incorrect. Executing virus exterminator programs is a corrective control against a computer virus. Answer (D) is incorrect. Preparing and testing a plan for virus recovery is a corrective control against a computer virus.

12. Which of the following is an indication that a computer virus is present?

- A. Frequent power surges that harm computer equipment.
- B. Unexplainable losses of or changes to data.
- C. Inadequate backup, recovery, and contingency plans.
- D. Numerous copyright violations due to unauthorized use of purchased software.

Answer (B) is correct. *(CIA, adapted)*
REQUIRED: The indicator of a computer virus.
DISCUSSION: The effects of computer viruses range from harmless messages to complete destruction of all data within the system. A symptom of a virus would be the unexplained loss of or change to data.
Answer (A) is incorrect. Power surges are caused by hardware or power supply problems. Answer (C) is incorrect. Inadequate backup, recovery, and contingency plans are operating policy weaknesses. Answer (D) is incorrect. Copyright violations represent policy or compliance problems.

13. Which of the following operating procedures increases an organization's exposure to computer viruses?

- A. Encryption of data files.
- B. Frequent backup of files.
- C. Downloading public-domain software from websites.
- D. Installing original copies of purchased software on hard disk drives.

Answer (C) is correct. *(CIA, adapted)*
REQUIRED: The procedure that increases exposure to viruses.
DISCUSSION: Viruses are spread through shared data. Downloading public-domain software carries a risk that contaminated data may enter the computer.
Answer (A) is incorrect. Viruses are spread through the distribution of contaminated programs. Answer (B) is incorrect. Backing up files does not increase the chances of a virus entering the computer system. Answer (D) is incorrect. Original copies of purchased software on hard disk drives should be free of viruses.

9.4 Investment in IT

14. Inefficient use of excess computer equipment can be controlled by

- A. Contingency planning.
- B. System feasibility studies.
- C. Capacity planning.
- D. Exception reporting.

Answer (C) is correct.   *(CIA, adapted)*
REQUIRED: The control over inefficient use of excess computer equipment.
DISCUSSION: Planning is as important for the information systems function as for any other part of the organization. The master plan for this function should be consistent with the strategic plan for the organization and include goals and objectives, an inventory of current capacity, and a forecast of future needs. The plan is the basis for determining hardware needs.
Answer (A) is incorrect. Contingency planning concerns the arrangements for alternative processing facilities in the event of equipment failure. Answer (B) is incorrect. A feasibility study is one of the phases in the systems development life cycle. Answer (D) is incorrect. Exception reports are meant to list errata and bring them to the attention of management.

15. An automobile and personal property insurer has decentralized its information processing to the extent that headquarters has less processing capacity than any of its regional processing centers. These centers are responsible for initiating policies, communicating with policyholders, and adjusting claims. The company uses leased lines from a national telecommunications company. Initially, the company thought there would be little need for interregion communication, but that has not been the case. The company underestimated the number of customers that would move between regions and the number of customers with claims arising from accidents outside their regions. The company has a regional center in an earthquake-prone area and is planning how to continue processing if that center, or any other single center, were unable to perform its processing.

The company considered mirroring the data stored at each regional center at another center. A disadvantage of such an arrangement is

- A. Lack of awareness at headquarters of the state of processing.
- B. Increased cost and complexity of network traffic.
- .C. Interference of the mirrored data with original source data.
- D. Confusion on the part of insurance agents about where customer data are stored.

Answer (B) is correct.   *(CIA, adapted)*
REQUIRED: The disadvantage of mirroring data across centers.
DISCUSSION: If data stored at one regional center is to mirror the data stored at another center, the most efficient method to ensure each center has the most current data is to transfer data across a network. Consequently, the cost of network traffic would increase dramatically. The complexity of the network would also increase as the network would need to provide a great deal of security when transferring data.
Answer (A) is incorrect. Headquarters could monitor the network on a real-time basis and have complete awareness of the state of processing. Answer (C) is incorrect. Adequate controls will ensure that the mirrored data will not affect the source data. Answer (D) is incorrect. The location of the data is not relevant to the insurance agents. The agents will retrieve customer data through the network.

9.5 Enterprise-Wide Resource Planning (ERP)

16. An enterprise-wide resource planning (ERP) system integrates the organization's computerized subsystems and may also provide links to external parties. An advantage of ERP is that

A. The reengineering needed for its implementation should improve business processes.

B. Customizing the software to suit the unique needs of the organization will facilitate upgrades.

C. It can be installed by organizations of all sizes.

D. The comprehensiveness of the system reduces resistance to change.

Answer (A) is correct. *(Publisher, adapted)*
REQUIRED: The advantage of ERP.
DISCUSSION: The benefits of ERP may significantly derive from the business process reengineering that is needed for its implementation. Using ERP software that reflects the best practices forces the linked subunits in the organization not only to redesign and improve their processes but also to conform to one standard.
Answer (B) is incorrect. The disadvantages of ERP are its extent and complexity, which make customization of the software difficult and costly. Answer (C) is incorrect. ERP software is costly and complex. It is usually installed only by the largest enterprises. Answer (D) is incorrect. Implementing an ERP system is likely to encounter significant resistance because of its comprehensiveness.

17. A manufacturing resource planning (MRP II) system

A. Performs the same back-office functions for a manufacturer as an ERP system.

B. Uses a master production schedule.

C. Lacks the forecasting and budgeting capabilities typical of an ERP system.

D. Performs the same front-office functions for a manufacturer as an ERP system.

Answer (B) is correct. *(Publisher, adapted)*
REQUIRED: The true statement about MRP II.
DISCUSSION: Manufacturing resource planning (MRP II) continued the evolution begun with MRP. It is a closed-loop manufacturing system that integrates all facets of manufacturing, including production, sales, inventories, schedules, and cash flows. The same system is used for accounting and finance functions, which use the same transactions and numbers. MRP II uses an MPS (master production schedule), a statement of the anticipated manufacturing schedule for selected items for selected periods. MRP also uses the MPS. Thus, MRP is a component of an MRP II system.
Answer (A) is incorrect. An MRP II system does not integrate all the subsystems internal to the organization (back-office functions), such as human resources and customer service. Answer (C) is incorrect. MRP II includes forecasting and planning capacities for generating cash and other budgets. Answer (D) is incorrect. MRP, MRP II, and traditional ERP do not provide for front-office functions, that is, connections with customers, suppliers, owners, creditors, and strategic allies.

9.6 Systems Software

18. Auditors often make use of computer programs that perform routine processing functions, such as sorting and merging. These programs are made available by computer companies and others and are specifically referred to as

A. Compiler programs.

B. Supervisory programs.

C. Utility programs.

D. User programs.

Answer (C) is correct. *(CPA, adapted)*
REQUIRED: The term for programs used to perform routine functions.
DISCUSSION: Utility programs are provided by manufacturers of equipment to perform routine processing tasks required by both clients and auditors, such as extracting data, sorting, merging, and copying. Utility programs are pretested, are independent of the client's own programming efforts, and furnish useful information without the trouble of writing special programs for the engagement.
Answer (A) is incorrect. Compiler programs convert source programs written in a higher-level language into computer-readable object programs, i.e., into machine language. Answer (B) is incorrect. Supervisory programs, also termed operating systems, are master programs responsible for controlling operations within a computer system. Answer (D) is incorrect. User programs are those prepared for a particular application.

19. In general, mainframe or server production programs and data are adequately protected against unauthorized access. Certain utility software may, however, have privileged access to software and data. To compensate for the risk of unauthorized use of privileged software, IT management can

A. Prevent privileged software from being installed on the mainframe.

B. Restrict privileged access to test versions of applications.

C. Limit the use of privileged software.

D. Keep sensitive programs and data on an isolated machine.

Answer (C) is correct.   *(CIA, adapted)*

REQUIRED: The best alternative information systems management can take to minimize unauthorized use of privileged software.

DISCUSSION: Since certain utility software may have privileged access to software and data stored on the mainframe or server, management must control the use of this utility software. Management should limit the use of this software to only those individuals with appropriate authority.

Answer (A) is incorrect. Privileged software may be needed to modify programs and data. Answer (B) is incorrect. Privileged access may be necessary to modify the final versions of applications. Answer (D) is incorrect. Authorized users must access sensitive programs and data through their workstations that are connected to the mainframe or server.

9.7 Application Development

20. Effective internal control for application development should provide for which of the following?

I. A project steering committee to initiate and oversee the system

II. A technical systems programmer to evaluate systems software

III. Feasibility studies to evaluate existing systems

IV. The establishment of standards for systems design and programming

A. I and III only.

B. I, II, and IV only.

C. I, III, and IV only.

D. II, III, and IV only.

Answer (C) is correct.   *(CISA, adapted)*

REQUIRED: The components of effective internal control for application development.

DISCUSSION: Effective systems development requires participation by top management. This can be achieved through a steering committee composed of higher-level representatives of system users. The committee approves or recommends projects and reviews their progress. Studies of the economic, operational, and technical feasibility of new applications necessarily entail evaluations of existing systems. Another necessary control is the establishment of standards for system design and programming. Standards represent user and system requirements determined during systems analysis.

Answer (A) is incorrect. Standards must be established. Answer (B) is incorrect. A technical systems programmer has a role in the development and modification of the operating system but not necessarily in applications development. The technical support in this area would be provided by systems analysts rather than programmers. Answer (D) is incorrect. A technical systems programmer has a role in the development and modification of the operating system but not necessarily in applications development.

21. A benefit of using computer-aided software engineering (CASE) technology is that it can ensure that

A. No obsolete data fields occur in files.

B. Users become committed to new systems.

C. All programs are optimized for efficiency.

D. Data integrity rules are applied consistently.

Answer (D) is correct.   *(CIA, adapted)*

REQUIRED: The benefit of CASE.

DISCUSSION: CASE is an automated technology (at least in part) for developing and maintaining software and managing projects. A benefit of using CASE technology is that it can ensure that data integrity rules, including those for validation and access, are applied consistently across all files.

Answer (A) is incorrect. Obsolete data fields must be recognized by developers or users. Once recognized, obsolete data fields can be treated consistently in CASE procedures. Answer (B) is incorrect. Using CASE will not ensure user commitment to new systems if they are poorly designed or otherwise do not meet users' needs. Answer (C) is incorrect. Although it has the potential to accelerate system development, CASE cannot ensure that all programs are optimized for efficiency. In fact, some CASE-developed modules may need to be optimized by hand to achieve acceptable performance.

22. User acceptance testing is more important in an object-oriented development process than in a traditional environment because of the implications of the

A. Absence of traditional design documents.

B. Lack of a tracking system for changes.

C. Potential for continuous monitoring.

D. Inheritance of properties in hierarchies.

Answer (D) is correct. *(CIA, adapted)*
REQUIRED: The reason user acceptance testing is more important in an object-oriented development process.
DISCUSSION: In object-oriented development, all objects in a class inherit the properties of higher classes in the hierarchy. Thus, changes in one object may affect many other objects, and the extent and effects of errors significantly increase. Testing one object provides no assurance that the objects are properly coordinated. Accordingly, user acceptance testing to verify correct functioning of the whole system becomes more important.
Answer (A) is incorrect. Instead of traditional design documents, items such as the business model, narratives of process functions, iterative development screens, computer processes and reports, and product descriptions guides are produced in object-oriented development. Answer (B) is incorrect. In general, object-oriented development systems include tracking systems for changes made in objects and hierarchies. Answer (C) is incorrect. Object-oriented systems are usually developed in client-server environments, so the potential exists for continuous monitoring of system use. However, continuous monitoring typically occurs during system operation, not during development.

23. A systems development approach used to quickly produce a model of user interfaces, user interactions with the system, and process logic is called

A. Neural networking.

B. Prototyping.

C. Reengineering.

D. Application generation.

Answer (B) is correct. *(CIA, adapted)*
REQUIRED: The approach used to produce a model of user interfaces, user interactions with the system, and process logic.
DISCUSSION: Prototyping produces the first model(s) of a new system. This technique usually employs a software tool for quick development of a model of the user interface (such as by report or screen), interaction of users with the system (for example, a menu-screen approach or data entry), and processing logic (the executable module). Prototyping stimulates user participation because the model allows quick exploration of concepts and development of solutions with quick results.
Answer (A) is incorrect. Neural networking involves hardware or software that imitates the processing activities of the human brain. Answer (C) is incorrect. Reengineering salvages reusable components of existing systems and restructures them to develop new systems or to improve the old systems.
Answer (D) is incorrect. An application generator is software that can be used to develop an application simply by describing its requirements to the computer rather than by writing a procedural program.

9.8 Program Change Control

24. The process of monitoring, evaluating, and modifying a system as needed is referred to as systems

A. Analysis.

B. Feasibility study.

C. Maintenance.

D. Implementation.

Answer (C) is correct. *(CMA, adapted)*
REQUIRED: The term for the process of monitoring, evaluating, and modifying a system.
DISCUSSION: Systems maintenance must be undertaken by systems analysts and applications programmers continually throughout the life of a system. Maintenance is the redesign of the system and programs to meet new needs or to correct design flaws. These changes should be part of a regular program of preventive maintenance.
Answer (A) is incorrect. Systems analysis is the process of determining user problems and needs, surveying the organization's present system, and analyzing the facts.
Answer (B) is incorrect. A feasibility study determines whether a proposed system is technically, operationally, and economically feasible. Answer (D) is incorrect. Implementation involves training and educating users, testing, conversion, and follow-up.

25. Change control typically includes procedures for separate libraries for production programs and for test versions of programs. The reason for this practice is to

A. Promote efficiency of system development.

B. Segregate incompatible duties.

C. Facilitate user input on proposed changes.

D. Permit unrestricted access to programs.

Answer (B) is correct. *(CIA, adapted)*
REQUIRED: The reason for having separate libraries for production programs and for test versions of programs.
DISCUSSION: Separating production and test versions of programs facilitates restricting access to production programs to the individuals, such as computer operators, who need access. The effect is to separate the incompatible functions of operators and programmers.
Answer (A) is incorrect. Production and test programs can be separated only if a specific procedure exists for placing programs in production libraries. Thus, maintaining the separation requires its own procedure, which may decrease development efficiency. Answer (C) is incorrect. Separating production and test versions of programs is independent of facilitating user input on proposed changes. Answer (D) is incorrect. Separating production and test versions of programs restricts access to programs.

26. A company often revises its production processes. The changes may entail revisions to processing programs. Ensuring that changes have a minimal impact on processing and result in minimal risk to the system is a function of

A. Security administration.

B. Change control.

C. Problem tracking.

D. Problem-escalation procedures.

Answer (B) is correct. *(CIA, adapted)*
REQUIRED: The approach to ensure changes have a minimal impact on processing.
DISCUSSION: Change control is the process of authorizing, developing, testing, and installing coded changes so as to minimize the impact on processing and the risk to the system.
Answer (A) is incorrect. Security administration is concerned with access to data. Answer (C) is incorrect. Problem tracking is concerned with collecting data to be analyzed for corrective action. Answer (D) is incorrect. Problem escalation-procedures are a means of categorizing problems so that the least skilled person can address them.

9.9 End-User Computing (EUC)

27. Traditional information systems development procedures that ensure proper consideration of controls may not be followed by users developing end-user computing (EUC) applications. Which of the following is a prevalent risk in the development of EUC applications?

A. Management decision making may be impaired due to diminished responsiveness to management's requests for computerized information.

B. Management may be less capable of reacting quickly to competitive pressures due to increased application development time.

C. Management may place the same degree of reliance on reports produced by EUC applications as it does on reports produced under traditional systems development procedures.

D. Management may incur increased application development and maintenance costs for EUC systems, compared with traditional (mainframe) systems.

Answer (C) is correct. *(CIA, adapted)*
REQUIRED: The risk in development of EUC applications.
DISCUSSION: End-user-developed applications may not be subject to an independent outside review by systems analysts and are not created in the context of a formal development methodology. These applications may lack appropriate standards, controls, quality assurance procedures, and documentation. A risk of end-user applications is that management may rely on them as much as traditional applications.
Answer (A) is incorrect. EUC systems typically increase flexibility and responsiveness to management's information requests. Such systems are more easily modified. Answer (B) is incorrect. EUC systems typically reduce application development cycle time. Answer (D) is incorrect. EUC systems typically result in reduced application development and maintenance costs.

28. The marketing department's proposal was finally accepted, and the marketing employees attended a class in using the report writer. Soon, the marketing analysts found that it was easier to download the data and manipulate it on their own desktop computers in spreadsheets than to perform all the data manipulation on the server. One analyst became highly skilled at downloading and wrote downloading command sequences for the other employees. When the analyst left the company for a better job, the department had problems making modifications to these command sequences. The department's problems are most likely due to inadequate

A. Documentation.

B. Data backup.

C. Program testing.

D. Antivirus software.

Answer (A) is correct. *(CIA, adapted)*
REQUIRED: The reason for difficulties in modifying the command sequences.
DISCUSSION: One risk of end-user computing is that documentation may be poor and that important knowledge may be limited to one person. The command sequences should have been documented so that other analysts could use and modify them readily.
Answer (B) is incorrect. The inability of other analysts to understand the command sequences is not a function of inadequate data backup procedures. Answer (C) is incorrect. The inability of other analysts to understand the command sequences is not a function of inadequate testing. Answer (D) is incorrect. The inability of other analysts to understand the command sequences is not a function of inadequate use of antivirus software.

29. Traditional information systems development and operational procedures typically involve four functional areas. The systems analysis function focuses on identifying and designing systems to satisfy organizational requirements. The programming function is responsible for the design, coding, testing, and debugging of computer programs necessary to implement the systems designed by the analysis function. The computer operations function is responsible for data preparation, program/job execution, and system maintenance. The user function provides the input and receives the output of the system. Which of these four functions is often poorly implemented or improperly omitted in the development of a new end-user computing (EUC) application?

A. Systems analysis function.

B. Programming function.

C. Computer operations function.

D. User function.

Answer (A) is correct. *(CIA, adapted)*
REQUIRED: The function often omitted in development of a new EUC application.
DISCUSSION: Systems analysis is one step that is not absolutely required in the development of a system. The desire to produce a system quickly may result in this step being eliminated or poorly implemented. A system is often produced and then analyzed to see if it will satisfy the needs of the organization. In an EUC application, the systems analysis is often incomplete or omitted.
Answer (B) is incorrect. Without programming, there would be no system. Answer (C) is incorrect. Without computer operations, the system would not be able to do anything. Answer (D) is incorrect. Without users, there would be no need for the system.

30. Responsibility for the control of end-user computing (EUC) exists at the organizational, departmental, and individual user level. Which of the following should be a direct responsibility of the individual users?

A. Acquisition of hardware and software.

B. Taking equipment inventories.

C. Strategic planning of end-user computing.

D. Physical security of equipment.

Answer (D) is correct. *(CIA, adapted)*
REQUIRED: The direct responsibility of an individual user.
DISCUSSION: EUC involves user-created or user-acquired systems that are maintained and operated outside of traditional information systems controls. In this environment, an individual user is ordinarily responsible for the physical security of the equipment (s)he uses.
Answer (A) is incorrect. The acquisition of hardware and software is an organizational- and departmental-level responsibility. Answer (B) is incorrect. Taking equipment inventories is an organizational-level responsibility. Answer (C) is incorrect. Strategic planning is an organizational- and departmental-level responsibility.

Use the additional questions in Gleim *CIA Test Prep* Software to create Test Sessions that emulate Pearson VUE!

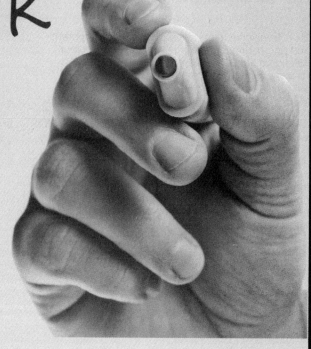

STUDY UNIT TEN
IT CONTINGENCY PLANNING,
SYSTEMS SECURITY, AND DATABASES

(15 pages of outline)

This study unit addresses voice communications, planning for contingencies (i.e., interruptions of normal processing), and systems security. It continues with a treatment of databases and concludes with discussions of software licensing and web infrastructure.

10.1 VOICE COMMUNICATIONS

1. **Channels**

   a. Voice communications channels differ from the data channels connecting the CPU and peripheral equipment. They are the communications media for transmitting voice signals and are classified according to their capacity.

      1) An example of a voiceband channel is a telephone line.

      2) Internet telephony, known as voice over IP (VoIP), is any transmission of two-way voice communication that uses the Internet for all or part of its path. This can be performed with traditional telephone devices, desktop computers equipped with a sound card, microphone, and speakers, or terminals dedicated to this function.

2. **Devices**

   a. Voice recognition input devices are still another alternative to keyboard input. These systems compare the speaker's voice patterns with prerecorded patterns. Advanced systems now have large vocabularies and shorter training periods. They allow for dictation and are not limited to simple commands. A voice output device converts digital data into speech using prerecorded sounds.

   b. Pagers have long been used to alert the recipient of a message, but newer systems permit transmission of text messages.

   c. A cell phone uses radio waves to transmit voice and data through antennas in a succession of cells or defined geographic areas.

   d. Personal communications services (PCS) is a cellular technology based on lower-power, higher-frequency radio waves. Cells must be smaller and more numerous, but the phones should be smaller and less expensive and be able to operate where other such devices cannot.

Stop and review! You have completed the outline for this subunit. Study multiple-choice question 1 on page 406.

10.2 CONTINGENCY PLANNING

1. **Overview**

    a. The information security goal of data availability is primarily the responsibility of the IT function.

        1) Contingency planning is the name commonly given to this activity.

            a) Disaster recovery is the process of resuming normal information processing operations after the occurrence of a major interruption.

            b) Business continuity is the continuation of business by other means during the period in which computer processing is unavailable or less than normal.

        2) Two major types of contingencies must be planned for: those in which the data center is physically available and those in which it is not.

            a) Examples of the first type of contingency are power failure, random intrusions such as viruses, and deliberate intrusions such as hacking incidents. The organization's physical facilities are sound, but immediate action is required to keep normal processing going.

            b) The second type of contingency is much more serious. This type is caused by disasters such as floods, fires, hurricanes, earthquakes, etc. An occurrence of this type necessitates the existence of an alternate processing facility (see item 4.b. on the next page).

2. **Backup and Rotation**

    a. Periodic backup and offsite rotation of computer files is the most basic part of any disaster recovery/business continuity plan.

        1) It is a truth seldom grasped by those who are not computer professionals that an organization's data is more valuable than its hardware. Hardware can be replaced for a price, but each organization's data bundle is unique and is indispensable to carrying on business. If it is ever destroyed, it cannot be replaced. For this reason, periodic backup and rotation are essential.

        2) A typical backup routine involves duplicating all data files and application programs once a month. Incremental changes are then backed up and taken to the offsite location once a week. (Application files must be backed up in addition to data since programs change too.)

        3) The offsite location must be temperature- and humidity-controlled and guarded against physical intrusion. Just as important, it must be geographically remote enough from the site of the organization's main operations that it would not be affected by the same natural disaster. It does the organization no good to have adequate backup files if the files are not accessible or have been destroyed.

        4) In case of an interruption of normal processing, the organization's systems can be restored such that, at most, 7 days of business information is lost. This is not an ideal situation, but it is a far cry from a complete loss of a company's files, which could essentially put it out of business.

3. **Risk Assessment Steps**

    a. Identify and prioritize the organization's critical applications.

        1) Not all of an organization's systems are equally important. The firm must decide which vital applications it simply cannot do business without and in what order they should be brought back into operation.

b. Determine the minimum recovery time frames and minimum hardware requirements.

1) How long will it take to reinstall each critical application, and what platform is required? If the interruption has been caused by an attack, such as a virus or hacker, how long will it take to isolate the problem and eliminate it from the system?

c. Develop a recovery plan.

1) Each type of contingency requires its own specific recovery procedures (see item 4. below and on the next page).

4. **Contingencies**

a. Data Center Available

1) Power failures can be guarded against by the purchase of backup electrical generators. These can be programmed to automatically begin running as soon as a dip in the level of electric current is detected. This is a widespread practice in settings such as hospitals where 24-hour system availability is crucial.

2) Attacks such as viruses and denial-of-service call for a completely different response. The system must be brought down "gracefully" to halt the spread of the infection. The IT staff must be well trained in the nature of the latest virus threats to know how to isolate the damage and bring the system back to full operation.

b. The most extreme contingency is when the organization's main facility is rendered uninhabitable by flood, fire, earthquake, etc. It is to prepare for these cases that organizations contract for alternate processing facilities.

1) An alternate processing facility is a physical location maintained by an outside contractor for the express purpose of providing processing facilities for customers in case of disaster.

a) The recovery center, like the offsite storage location for backup files, must be far enough away that it will likely be unaffected by the same natural disaster that forced the abandonment of the main facility. Usually, companies contract for backup facilities in another city.

b) Once the determination is made that processing is no longer possible at the principal site, the backup files are retrieved from the secure storage location and taken to the recovery center.

2) Recovery centers take two basic forms. Organizations determine which facility is best by calculating the tradeoff between the cost of the contract and the cost of downtime.

a) A hot site is a fully operational processing facility that is immediately available. Usually, the organization enters into a contract with a service provider.

i) For a set fee, the service provider agrees to have a hardware platform and communication lines substantially identical to the organization's ready for use 24 hours a day, 365 days a year.

ii) This is the least risky and most expensive solution.

b) A cold site is simply a shell facility with sufficient electrical power, environmental controls, and communication lines to permit the organization to install its own newly acquired equipment.

i) On an ongoing basis, this is a much less expensive solution.

ii) However, the time to procure replacement equipment can be weeks or months. Also, emergency procurements from equipment vendors can be very expensive.

3) Any contract for a hot site must include a provision for annual testing.

a) The service provider agrees to a window of time in which the organization can declare a fake disaster, load its backup files onto the equipment at the hot site, and determine how long it takes to resume normal processing.

5. **Other Technologies for Continuity of Processing**

a. Fault-tolerant computer systems (formerly called fail-soft systems) have additional hardware and software as well as a backup power supply. A fault-tolerant computer has additional chips and disk storage. This technology is used for mission-critical applications that cannot afford to suffer downtime.

1) The enabling technology for fault-tolerance is the redundant array of inexpensive discs, or RAID. It is a grouping of multiple hard drives with special software that allows for data delivery along multiple paths. If one drive fails, the other discs can compensate for the loss.

b. High-availability computing is used for less-critical applications because it provides for a short recovery time rather than the elimination of recovery time.

Stop and review! You have completed the outline for this subunit. Study multiple-choice questions 2 through 6 beginning on page 406.

10.3 SYSTEMS SECURITY

 Broadly conceived, "security" can extend to almost any aspect of automated systems. An internal auditor's awareness of information security should encompass three general types: logical, physical, and communication.

1. **Data Integrity**

a. The difficulty of maintaining the integrity of the data is the most significant limitation of computer-based audit tools.

1) Electronic evidence is difficult to authenticate and easy to fabricate.

2) Internal auditors must be careful not to treat computer printouts as traditional paper evidence. The data security factors pertaining to electronic evidence must be considered.

3) The degree of reliance on electronic evidence by the auditor depends on the effectiveness of the controls over the system from which such evidence is taken.

4) The most important control is to enact an organization-wide network security policy. This policy should promote the following objectives:

a) Availability. The intended and authorized users should be able to access data to meet organizational goals.

b) Security, privacy, and confidentiality. The secrecy of information that could adversely affect the organization if revealed to the public or competitors should be ensured.

c) Integrity. Unauthorized or accidental modification of data should be prevented.

b.   Many controls once performed by separate individuals may be concentrated in computer systems. Hence, an individual who has access to the computer may perform incompatible functions. As a result, other control procedures may be necessary to achieve the control objectives ordinarily accomplished by segregation of functions.

1)   These controls can be classified as one of two broad types, physical controls and logical controls. Physical controls are further divided into two subcategories.

2.   **Physical Controls**

a.   Physical access controls limit who can physically enter the data center.

1)   Keypad devices allow entry of a password or code to gain entry to a physical location or computer system.

2)   Card reader controls are based on reading information from a magnetic strip on a credit, debit, or other access card. Controls can then be applied to information about the cardholder contained on the magnetic strip.

3)   Biometric technologies. These are automated methods of establishing an individual's identity using physiological or behavioral traits. These characteristics include fingerprints, retina patterns, hand geometry, signature dynamics, speech, and keystroke dynamics.

b.   Environmental controls are also designed to protect the organization's physical information assets. The most important are

1)   Temperature and humidity control
2)   Gaseous fire-suppression system (not water)
3)   Data center not located on an outside wall
4)   Building housing data center not located in a flood plain

3.   **Logical Controls**

a.   Logical security controls are needed because of the use of communications networks and connections to external systems. User identification and authentication, restriction of access, and the generation of audit trails are required in this environment. Thus, access controls have been developed to prevent improper use or manipulation of data files and programs. They ensure that only those persons with a bona fide purpose and authorization have access to computer systems.

1)   Access control software (a) protects files, programs, data dictionaries, processing, etc., from unauthorized access; (b) restricts use of certain devices (e.g., terminals); and (c) may provide an audit trail for both successful and unsuccessful access attempts. For example, a firewall separates internal from external networks.

2)   Passwords and ID numbers. The use of passwords and identification numbers is an effective control in an online system to prevent unauthorized access to computer files. Lists of authorized persons are maintained in the computer. The entry of passwords or identification numbers; a prearranged set of personal questions; and the use of badges, magnetic cards, or optically scanned cards may be combined to avoid unauthorized access.

a)   A security card may be used with a personal computer so that users must sign on with an ID and a password. The card controls the machine's operating system and records access data (date, time, duration, etc.).

b)   Proper user authentication by means of a password requires password-generating procedures to ensure that valid passwords are known only by the proper individuals. Thus, a password should not be displayed when entered at a keyboard.

        c)   Password security may also be compromised in other ways. For example, log-on procedures may be cumbersome and tedious. Thus, users often store log-on sequences on their personal computers and invoke them when they want to use mainframe facilities. A risk of this practice is that anyone with access to the personal computers could log on to the mainframe.

        d)   To be more effective, passwords should consist of random letters, symbols, and numbers. They should not contain words or phrases.

    3)   File attributes can be assigned to control access to and the use of files. Examples are read/write, read only, archive, and hidden.

    4)   A device authorization table restricts file access to those physical devices that should logically need access. For example, because it is illogical for anyone to access the accounts receivable file from a manufacturing terminal, the device authorization table will deny access even when a valid password is used.

        a)   Such tests are often called compatibility tests because they ascertain whether a code number is compatible with the use to be made of the information. Thus, a user may be authorized to enter only certain kinds of data, have access only to certain information, have access but not updating authority, or use the system only at certain times. The lists or tables of authorized users or devices are sometimes called access control matrices.

    5)   A system access log records all attempts to use the system. The date and time, codes used, mode of access, data involved, and operator interventions are recorded.

    6)   Encryption involves using a fixed algorithm to manipulate plaintext.

    7)   Controlled disposal of documents. One method of enforcing access restrictions is to destroy data when they are no longer in use. Thus, paper documents may be shredded and magnetic media may be erased.

    8)   Automatic log-off (disconnection) of inactive data terminals may prevent the viewing of sensitive data on an unattended data terminal.

    9)   Security personnel. An organization may need to hire security specialists. For example, developing an information security policy for the organization, commenting on security controls in new applications, and monitoring and investigating unsuccessful access attempts are appropriate duties of the information security officer.

  4. **Internet Security**

    a.   Connection to the Internet presents security issues.

    1)   Thus, the organization-wide network security policy should at the very least include

        a)   A user account management system

        b)   Installation of an Internet firewall

        c)   Methods such as encryption to ensure that only the intended user receives the information and that the information is complete and accurate

    2)   User account management involves installing a system to ensure that

        a)   New accounts are added correctly and assigned only to authorized users

        b)   Old and unused accounts are removed promptly

        c)   Passwords are changed periodically, and employees are educated on how to choose a password that cannot be easily guessed (e.g., a password of at least six diverse characters that do not form a word)

        3) A firewall separates an internal network from an external network (e.g., the Internet) and prevents passage of specific types of traffic. It identifies names, Internet Protocol (IP) addresses, applications, etc., and compares them with programmed access rules.

          a) A firewall may have any of the following features:

            i) A packet filtering system examines each incoming network packet and drops (does not pass on) unauthorized packets.

            ii) A proxy server maintains copies of web pages to be accessed by specified users. Outsiders are directed there, and more important information is not available from this access point.

            iii) An application gateway limits traffic to specific applications.

            iv) A circuit-level gateway connects an internal device, e.g., a network printer, with an outside TCP/IP port. It can identify a valid TCP session.

            v) Stateful inspection stores information about the state of a transmission and uses it as background for evaluating messages from similar sources.

          b) Firewall systems ordinarily produce reports on organization-wide Internet use, unusual usage patterns, and system penetration attempts. These reports are very helpful to the internal auditor as a method of continuous monitoring, or logging, of the system.

            i) Firewalls do not provide adequate protection against computer viruses. Thus, an organization should include one or more antivirus measures in its network security policy.

        4) Data traveling across the network can be encoded so that it is indecipherable to anyone except the intended recipient.

        5) Other Controls

          a) Authentication measures verify the identity of the user, thus ensuring that only the intended and authorized users gain access to the system.

            i) Most firewall systems provide authentication procedures.
            ii) Access controls are the most common authentication procedures.

          b) Checksums help ensure the integrity of data by checking whether the file has been changed. The system computes a value for a file and then proceeds to check whether this value equals the last known value for this file. If the numbers are the same, the file has likely remained unchanged.

5. Data Storage

    a. Storing all related data on one storage device creates security problems.

        1) If hardware or software malfunctions occur, or unauthorized access is achieved, the results could be disastrous.

        2) Greater emphasis on security is required to provide backup and restrict access to the database.

          a) For example, the system may employ dual logging, that is, use of two transaction logs written simultaneously on separate storage media. It may also use a snapshot technique to capture data values before and after transaction processing. The files that store these values can be used to reconstruct the database in the event of data loss or corruption.

        3) The responsibility for creating, maintaining, securing, and restricting access to the database belongs to the database administrator (DBA).

4)   A database management system (DBMS) includes security features. Thus, a specified user's access may be limited to certain data fields or logical views depending on the individual's assigned duties.

Stop and review! You have completed the outline for this subunit. Study multiple-choice questions 7 through 12 beginning on page 408.

10.4 DATABASES

1.   **Overview**

a.   A database is a series of related files combined to eliminate redundancy of data items. A single integrated system allows for improved data accessibility.

b.   When systems within the organization are not integrated, they not only may contain different data but also may define and update data in inconsistent ways. Thus, determining the location of data and ensuring their consistency are more difficult.

EXAMPLE of Data Redundancy

The various files related to human resources in the conventional record systems of most organizations include payroll, work history, and permanent personnel data.

An employee's name must appear in each of these files when they are stored and processed separately. The result is redundancy. When data are combined in a database, each data item is usually stored only once.

---

c.   The data are stored physically on direct-access storage devices (e.g., magnetic disks). They are also stored for efficient access.

1)   The most frequently accessed items are placed in the physical locations permitting the fastest access.

2)   When these items were stored in separate files under older file-oriented systems, the physical locations were usually similar to the logical structure of the data. Items that logically belonged together were stored in physical proximity to one another.

3)   A logical data model is a user view. It is the way a user describes the data and defines their interrelationships based on the user's needs, without regard to how the data are physically stored.

2.   **Database Structures**

a.   To understand the vast improvement in performance brought about by database technology, it is helpful to review the development of file structures.

1)   The early mainframe computers used flat files, meaning that all the records and all the data elements within each record followed one behind the other. Much early mainframe storage was on magnetic tape, which naturally stored data in this fashion.

EXAMPLE of a Flat File

Here are two records excerpted from a tape file:

Record	Customer	Street	City	Order_Nbr	Part_Nbr_1	Qty_1	Price_1	Ext_1	Part_Nbr_2	Qty_2	Price_2	Ext_2
116385	Zeno's Paradox Hardware	10515 Prince Avenue	Athens, GA	19742133	A316	3	$0.35	$1.05	G457	12	$1.15	$13.80

——————————— (Many intervening records) ———————————

Record	Customer	Street	City	Order_Nbr	Part_Nbr_1	Qty_1	Price_1	Ext_1
122406	Zeno's Paradox Hardware	10515 Prince Avenue	Athens, GA	19742259	A316	4	$0.35	$1.40

Figure 10-1

---

2) Two inefficiencies are apparent at once in this method of accessing data:

   a) The customer's address has to be stored with every order the customer places, taking up much unnecessary storage.

   b) All intervening records must be read and skipped over in order to find both records pertaining to this customer.

b. Database technology overcame these two difficulties. There are three main ways of organizing a database:

   1) A tree or hierarchical structure arranges data in a one-to-many relationship in which each record has one antecedent but may have an unlimited number of subsequent records.

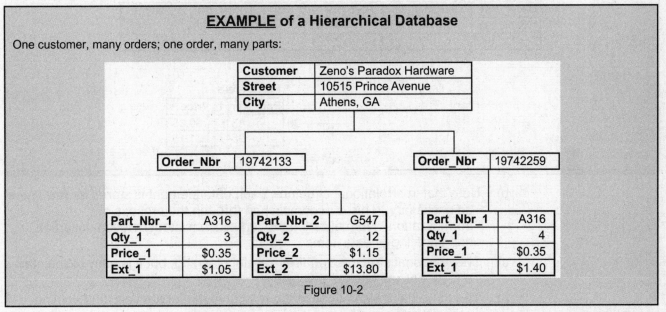

EXAMPLE of a Hierarchical Database

One customer, many orders; one order, many parts:

Customer	Zeno's Paradox Hardware
Street	10515 Prince Avenue
City	Athens, GA

Order_Nbr	19742133

Order_Nbr	19742259

Part_Nbr_1	A316
Qty_1	3
Price_1	$0.35
Ext_1	$1.05

Part_Nbr_2	G547
Qty_2	12
Price_2	$1.15
Ext_2	$13.80

Part_Nbr_1	A316
Qty_1	4
Price_1	$0.35
Ext_1	$1.40

Figure 10-2

   a) Because the records are not stored one after the other, a tree database structure stores a pointer with each record. The pointer is the storage address of the next record.

   b) The tree structure cuts down on data redundancy but retains the necessity of searching every record to fulfill a query. Thus, like the flat file, adding new records is awkward and ad hoc queries are inefficient.

2) The network structure connects every record in the database with every other record.

   a) This was an attempt to make queries more efficient. However, the huge number of cross-references inherent in this structure makes maintenance far too complex.

3) A relational structure organizes data in a conceptual arrangement.

   a) An individual data item is called a field or column (e.g., name, date, amount).

      i) Related fields are brought together in a record or row (e.g., for a single sales transaction).

      ii) Multiple records make up a file or table (e.g., sales).

      iii) Tables can be joined or linked based on common fields rather than on high-overhead pointers or linked lists as in other database structures.

      iv) Every record in a table has a field (or group of fields) designated as the key. The value (or combination of values) in the key uniquely identifies each record.

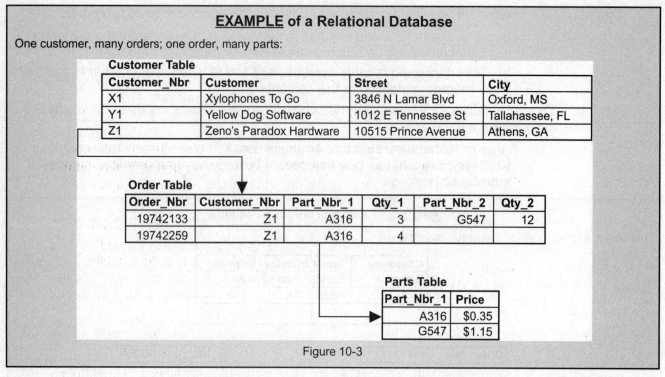

EXAMPLE of a Relational Database

One customer, many orders; one order, many parts:

Customer Table

Customer_Nbr	Customer	Street	City
X1	Xylophones To Go	3846 N Lamar Blvd	Oxford, MS
Y1	Yellow Dog Software	1012 E Tennessee St	Tallahassee, FL
Z1	Zeno's Paradox Hardware	10515 Prince Avenue	Athens, GA

Order Table

Order_Nbr	Customer_Nbr	Part_Nbr_1	Qty_1	Part_Nbr_2	Qty_2
19742133	Z1	A316	3	G547	12
19742259	Z1	A316	4		

Parts Table

Part_Nbr_1	Price
A316	$0.35
G547	$1.15

Figure 10-3

b) Note that in a relational structure, each data element is stored as few times as necessary. This is accomplished through the process of normalization. Normalization prevents inconsistent deletion, insertion, and updating of data items.

c) The relational structure requires careful planning, but it is easy to maintain and processes queries efficiently.

d) The three basic operations in the relational model are selecting, joining, and projecting.

   i) Selecting creates a subset of records that meet certain criteria.

   ii) Joining is the combining of relational tables based on a common field or combination of fields.

   iii) Projecting results in the requested subset of columns from the table. This operation creates a new table containing only the required information.

e) Cardinality expresses the bounds (a minimum and a maximum) of the association between related entities. For example, a college class must have a minimum of three students and can have a maximum of 59. The student-class relationship has a cardinality limit expressed as (3, 59).

4) The data in a database are subject to the constraint of referential integrity. This means that if data are collected about something, e.g., a payment voucher, all reference conditions regarding it must be met; thus, for a voucher to exist, a vendor must also exist.

5) A distributed database is stored in two or more physical sites using either replication or partitioning.

   a) The replication or snapshot technique makes duplicates to be stored at multiple locations.

      i) Changes are periodically copied and sent to each location. If a database is small, storing multiple copies may be cheaper than retrieving records from a central site.

         b)   Fragmentation or partitioning stores specific records where they are most needed.

              i)   For example, a financial institution may store a particular customer's data at the branch where (s)he usually transacts his/her business. If the customer executes a transaction at another branch, the pertinent data are retrieved via communication lines.

              ii)   One variation is the central index. A query to this index obtains the location in a remote database where the complete record is to be found.

              iii) Still another variation is the ask-the-network distributed database. In this system, no central index exists. Instead, the remote databases are polled to locate the desired record.

         c)   Updating data in a distributed system may require special protocols.

              i)   Thus, a two-phase commit disk-writing protocol is used. If data are to be updated in two places, databases in both locations are cleared for updating before either one performs (commits) the update.

              ii)   In the first phase, both locations agree to the update. In the second phase, both perform the update.

     6)   A deadly embrace (deadlock) occurs when each of two transactions has a lock on a single data resource.

         a)   When deadly embraces occur, the DBMS must have an algorithm for undoing the effects of one of the transactions and releasing the data resources it controls so that the other transaction can run to completion. Then, the other transaction is restarted and permitted to run to completion.

         b)   If deadly embraces are not resolved, response time worsens or the system eventually fails.

3.   **Database Terminology**

    a.   A database management system (DBMS) is an integrated set of computer programs that create the database, maintain the elements, safeguard the data from loss or destruction, and make the data available to applications programs and inquiries.

       1)   The DBMS allows programmers and designers to work independently of the technical structure of the database.

         a)   Before the development of DBMSs, designing and coding programs that used databases was extremely time-consuming (and therefore expensive) because programmers had to know the exact contents and characteristics of the data in every database.

         b)   DBMSs provide a common language for referencing databases, easing the design and coding of application programs.

    b.   The schema is a description of the overall logical structure of the database using data-definition language, which is the connection between the logical and physical structures of the database.

       1)   A subschema describes a particular user's (application's) view of a part of the database using data definition language.

    c.   A fundamental characteristic of databases is that applications are independent of the database structure; when writing programs or designing applications to use the database, only the name of the desired item is necessary.

    d.   A data item is identified using the data manipulation language, after which the DBMS locates and retrieves the desired item(s).

       1)   The data manipulation language is used to add, delete, retrieve, or modify data or relationships.

e. The physical structure of the database can be completely altered without having to change any of the programs using the data items. Thus, different users may define different views of the data (subschemas).

f. The database administrator (DBA) is the individual who has overall responsibility for developing and maintaining the database and for establishing controls to protect its integrity.

   1) Thus, only the DBA should be able to update data dictionaries. In small systems, the DBA may perform some functions of a DBMS. In larger applications, the DBA uses a DBMS as a primary tool.

g. The data dictionary is a file, either computer or manual, that describes both the physical and logical characteristics of every data element in a database.

   1) The data dictionary includes, for example, the name of the data element (e.g., employee name, part number), the amount of disk space required to store the data element (in bytes), and what kind of data is allowed in the data element (e.g., alphabetic, numeric).

   2) Thus, the data dictionary contains the size, format, usage, meaning, and ownership of every data element. This greatly simplifies the programming process.

h. The database mapping facility is software that is used to evaluate and document the structure of the database.

i. The data control language specifies the privileges and security rules governing database users.

j. Data command interpreter languages are symbolic character strings used to control the current state of DBMS operations.

k. Storing all related data on one storage device creates security problems.

   1) Should hardware or software malfunctions occur, or unauthorized access be achieved, the results could be disastrous.

   2) Greater emphasis on security is required to provide backup and restrict access to the database.

      a) For example, the system may employ dual logging, that is, use of two transaction logs written simultaneously on separate storage media.

      b) It may also use a snapshot technique to capture data values before and after transaction processing.

      c) The files that store these values can be used to reconstruct the database in the event of data loss or corruption.

   3) The responsibility for creating, maintaining, securing, and restricting access to the database belongs to the database administrator.

   4) A DBMS includes security features. Thus, a specified user's access may be limited to certain data fields or logical views depending on the individual's assigned duties.

l. Databases and the associated DBMS permit efficient storage and retrieval of data for formal system applications.

   1) They also permit increased ad hoc accessing of data (e.g., to answer inquiries for data not contained in formal system outputs) as well as updating of files by transaction processing.

   2) These increased capabilities, however, result in increased cost because they require

      a) The use of sophisticated hardware (direct-access devices)
      b) Sophisticated software (the DBMS)
      c) Highly trained technical personnel (database administrator, staff)
      d) Increased security controls

    m. An object-oriented database is a response to the need to store not only numbers and characters but also graphics and multimedia applications.

        1) Translating these data into tables and rows is difficult. However, in an object-oriented database, they can be stored, along with the procedures acting on them, within an object.

    n. In a hypermedia database, blocks of data are organized into nodes that are linked in a pattern determined by the user so that an information search need not be restricted to the predefined organizational scheme. A node may contain text, graphics, audio, video, or programs.

        1) Hybrid systems containing object-oriented and relational database capabilities have also been developed.

    o. Advanced database systems provide for online analytical processing (OLAP), also called multidimensional data analysis, which is the ability to analyze large amounts of data from numerous perspectives.

        1) OLAP is an integral part of the data warehouse concept.

    p. A data warehouse contains not only current operating data but also historical information from throughout the organization. Thus, data from all operational systems is integrated, consolidated, and standardized into an organization-wide database into which data is copied periodically. This data is maintained on one platform and can be read but not changed. Graphics and query software and analytical tools assist users. Accordingly, data mining is facilitated by a data warehouse.

Stop and review! You have completed the outline for this subunit. Study multiple-choice questions 13 through 18 beginning on page 409.

10.5 SOFTWARE LICENSING

1. **Rights Pertaining to Software**

    a. Software is copyrightable, but a substantial amount is in the public domain. Networks of computer users may share such software.

        1) Shareware is software made available for a fee (usually with an initial free trial period) by the owners to users through a distributor (or websites or electronic bulletin board services).

    b. Software piracy is a problem for vendors. The best way to detect an illegal copy of application software is to compare the serial number on the screen with the vendor's serial number.

        1) Use of unlicensed software increases the risk of introducing computer viruses into the organization. Such software is less likely to have been carefully tested.

        2) To avoid legal liability, controls also should be implemented to prevent use of unlicensed software that is not in the public domain. A software licensing agreement permits a user to employ either a specified or an unlimited number of copies of a software product at given locations, at particular machines, or throughout the organization. The agreement may restrict reproduction or resale, and it may provide subsequent customer support and product improvements.

        3) Software piracy can expose an organization's people to both civil and criminal penalties. The Business Software Alliance (BSA) is a worldwide trade group that coordinates software vendors' efforts to prosecute the illegal duplication of software.

c.   Diskless workstations increase security by preventing the copying of software to a flash drive from a workstation. This control not only protects the company's interests in its data and proprietary programs but also guards against theft of licensed third-party software.

d.   To shorten the installation time for revised software in a network, an organization may implement electronic software distribution (ESD), which is the computer-to-computer installation of software on workstations. Instead of weeks, software distribution can be accomplished in hours or days and can be controlled centrally. Another advantage of ESD is that it permits the tracking of PC program licenses.

Stop and review! You have completed the outline for this subunit. Study multiple-choice questions 19 and 20 on page 411.

10.6 WEB INFRASTRUCTURE

1.   **Overview**

a.   The Internet is a network of networks all over the world. The Internet is descended from the original ARPANet, a product of the Defense Department's Advanced Research Projects Agency (ARPA), introduced in 1969.

1)   The idea was to have a network that could not be brought down during an enemy attack by bombing a single central location. ARPANet connected computers at universities, corporations, and government. In view of the growing success of the Internet, ARPANet was retired in 1990.

b.   The Internet facilitates inexpensive communication and information transfer among computers, with gateways allowing mainframe computers to interface with personal computers.

1)   Very high-speed Internet backbones carry signals around the world and meet at network access points.

c.   Most Internet users obtain connections through Internet service providers (ISPs) that in turn connect either directly to a backbone or to a larger ISP with a connection to a backbone.

1)   The topology of the backbone and its interconnections may once have resembled a spine with ribs connected along its length but is now almost certainly more like a fishing net wrapped around the world with many circular paths.

d.   The three main parts of the Internet are the servers that hold information, clients that view the information, and the Transmission Control Protocol/Internet Protocol (TCP/IP) suite of protocols that connect the two.

2.   **Languages and Protocols**

a.   The Internet was initially restricted to email and text-only documents.

1)   In the 1980s, English computer scientist Tim Berners-Lee conceived the idea of allowing users to click on a word or phrase (a hyperlink) on their screens and having another document automatically be displayed.

2)   Berners-Lee created a simple coding mechanism called Hypertext Markup Language (HTML) to perform this function. He also created a set of rules called Hypertext Transfer Protocol (HTTP) to allow hyperlinking across the Internet rather than on just a single computer. He then created a piece of software, called a browser, that allowed users to read HTML from any brand of computer. The result was the World Wide Web (often simply called the Web).

3)   As the use of HTML and its successor languages spread, it became possible to display rich graphics and streaming audio and video in addition to text.

    b.   Extensible Markup Language (XML) was developed by an international consortium and released in 1998 as an open standard usable with many programs and platforms. XML is a variation of HTML (hypertext markup language), which uses fixed codes (tags) to describe how web pages and other hypermedia documents should be presented.

        1)   XML codes all information in such a way that a user can determine not only how it should be presented but also what it is; i.e., all computerized data may be tagged with identifiers.

        2)   Unlike HTML, XML uses codes that are extensible, not fixed. Thus, if an industry can agree on a set of codes, software for that industry can be written that incorporates those codes.

        3)   For example, XML allows the user to label the Uniform Product Code (UPC), price, color, size, etc., of goods so that other systems will know exactly what the tag references mean. In contrast, HTML tags would only describe how items are placed on a page and provide links to other pages and objects.

        4)   Standard setters and other entities are attempting to find ways to incorporate XML with EDI.

    c.   Extensible Business Reporting Language (XBRL) for financial statements is the specification developed by an AICPA-led consortium for commercial and industrial entities that report in accordance with U.S. GAAP. It is a variation of XML that is expected to decrease the costs of generating financial reports, reformulating information for different uses, and sharing business information using electronic media.

3.   **Uses**

    a.   With the explosive growth of the World Wide Web in the 1990s, whole new distribution channels opened up for businesses. Consumers can browse a vendor's catalog using the rich graphics of the Web, initiate an order, and remit payment, all from the comfort of their homes.

        1)   An organization's presence on the Web is constituted in its website. The website consists of a home page, the first screen encountered by users, and subsidiary web pages (screens constructed using HTML or a similar language).

        2)   Every page on the World Wide Web has a unique address, recognizable by any web-enabled device, called a Uniform Resource Locator (URL). However, just because the address is recognizable does not mean it is accessible to every user -- security is a major feature of any organization's website.

    b.   An intranet permits sharing of information throughout an organization by applying Internet connectivity standards and web software (e.g., browsers) to the organization's internal network.

        1)   An intranet addresses the connectivity problems of an organization with many types of computers. It is ordinarily restricted to those within the organization and to outsiders after appropriate identification.

        2)   An extranet consists of the linked intranets of two or more organizations, for example, of a supplier and its customers. It typically uses the public Internet as its transmission medium but requires a password for access.

Stop and review! You have completed the outline for this subunit. Study multiple-choice questions 21 through 23 on page 412.

QUESTIONS

10.1 Voice Communications

1. An electronic meeting conducted between several parties at remote sites is referred to as

    A. Teleprocessing.

    B. Interactive processing.

    C. Telecommuting.

    D. Teleconferencing.

Answer (D) is correct. *(CMA, adapted)*
    REQUIRED: The process of holding an electronic meeting between several parties at remote sites.
    DISCUSSION: Conducting an electronic meeting among several parties at remote sites is teleconferencing. It can be accomplished by telephone or electronic mail group communication software. Videoconferencing permits the conferees to see each other on video screens. The practice has grown in recent years as companies have attempted to cut their travel costs.
    Answer (A) is incorrect. Teleprocessing refers to connections in an online system. Answer (B) is incorrect. Interactive processing allows users to converse directly with the system. It requires online processing and direct access to stored information. Answer (C) is incorrect. Telecommuting refers to the practice of individuals working out of their homes by communicating with their office via the computer.

10.2 Contingency Planning

2. Contingency plans for information systems should include appropriate backup agreements. Which of the following arrangements would be considered too vendor-dependent when vital operations require almost immediate availability of computer resources?

    A. A "hot site" arrangement.

    B. A "cold site" arrangement.

    C. A "cold and hot site" combination arrangement.

    D. Using excess capacity at another data center within the organization.

Answer (B) is correct. *(CIA, adapted)*
    REQUIRED: The contingency plan that is too vendor-dependent.
    DISCUSSION: Organizations should maintain contingency plans for operations in the case of a disaster. These plans usually include off-site storage of important backup data and an arrangement for the continuation of operations at another location. A "cold site" has all needed assets in place except the needed computer equipment and is vendor-dependent for timely delivery of equipment.
    Answer (A) is incorrect. A "hot site" has all needed assets in place and is not vendor-dependent. Answer (C) is incorrect. A "cold and hot site" combination allows the "hot site" to be used until the "cold site" is prepared and is thus not too vendor-dependent. Answer (D) is incorrect. Excess capacity would ensure that needed assets are available and would not be vendor-dependent.

3. Each day, after all processing is finished, a bank performs a backup of its online deposit files and retains it for 7 days. Copies of each day's transaction files are not retained. This approach is

    A. Valid, in that having a week's worth of backups permits recovery even if one backup is unreadable.

    B. Risky, in that restoring from the most recent backup file would omit subsequent transactions.

    C. Valid, in that it minimizes the complexity of backup/recovery procedures if the online file has to be restored.

    D. Risky, in that no checkpoint/restart information is kept with the backup files.

Answer (B) is correct. *(CIA, adapted)*
    REQUIRED: The true statement about retention of backup files but not each day's transaction files.
    DISCUSSION: At appropriate intervals, the disk files should be copied on magnetic tape so that restart procedures can begin at those points if data are lost or destroyed. However, not retaining each day's transaction files is risky because information processed since the last backup file was created will be lost.
    Answer (A) is incorrect. The practice of not retaining daily transaction data is unsound in that the bank loses a day's transactions for each backup that is unreadable. Answer (C) is incorrect. The practice of not retaining daily transaction data certainly minimizes complexity but at the expense of losing transaction data if the online file must be restored from the backup. Answer (D) is incorrect. Checkpoint/restart information is not needed. The backups are created after all processing is finished for the day.

4. A company updates its accounts receivable master file weekly and retains the master files and corresponding update transactions for the most recent 2-week period. The purpose of this practice is to

A. Verify run-to-run control totals for receivables.

B. Match internal labels to avoid writing on the wrong volume.

C. Permit reconstruction of the master file if needed.

D. Validate groups of update transactions for each version.

Answer (C) is correct. *(CIA, adapted)*
REQUIRED: The purpose of periodic retention of master files and transaction data.
DISCUSSION: The grandfather-father-son approach normally employs magnetic tapes to furnish backup in a batch processing system. The procedure involves creation and retention of three generations of master files so that lost or destroyed data may be regenerated from the remaining master files and transaction data. In this case, a master file (the grandfather) and the first week's transactions are used to generate a second master file (the father). This file and the second week's transactions are the basis for the current master file (the son). Online systems employ rollback and recovery procedures; i.e., the master file is periodically dumped onto a storage medium. Reconstruction is then possible using the backup copy and the transactions log.
Answer (A) is incorrect. Comparison of batch totals is a control over the completeness of processing, not a recovery procedure. Answer (B) is incorrect. Internal labels may avoid destruction of data but do not aid in recovery. Answer (D) is incorrect. Validation may avoid destruction of data but does not aid in recovery.

5. Good planning will help an organization restore computer operations after a processing outage. Good recovery planning should ensure that

A. Backup/restart procedures have been built into job streams and programs.

B. Change control procedures cannot be bypassed by operating personnel.

C. Planned changes in equipment capacities are compatible with projected workloads.

D. Service level agreements with owners of applications are documented.

Answer (A) is correct. *(CIA, adapted)*
REQUIRED: The condition ensured by good recovery planning.
DISCUSSION: The disaster plan should embrace data center recovery, critical application recovery, and network recovery. It should be updated and current with regard to recent test results and new applications, equipment, and network configurations. The plan should also ensure that backup facilities are still able to process critical applications and that end-user responsibility is established. Another essential component of a disaster recovery plan is that backup/restart procedures have been anticipated and provided for in the application systems.
Answer (B) is incorrect. Whether change control procedures can be bypassed is not usually a consideration in disaster recovery planning. Answer (C) is incorrect. Planned rather than actual changes in equipment capacities are not relevant in disaster recovery planning. Answer (D) is incorrect. Ensuring that service level agreements with owners of critical applications are adequate is not a function of disaster recovery planning.

6. In an online, real-time system, which of the following is most likely to be used as backup for an application's master file maintained on magnetic disk?

A. At specified periods, the disk files are dumped to (copied on) magnetic tape; a transaction log is maintained as inputs are received and processed.

B. A duplicate disk file is maintained and all activity is copied on magnetic tape continuously.

C. The grandfather-father-son technique is employed to retain disk files.

D. All source documents for transactions are retained.

Answer (A) is correct. *(CMA, adapted)*
REQUIRED: The backup procedure most likely to be used in an online, real-time system.
DISCUSSION: When an application's master file is maintained on magnetic disk in an online, real-time system, the backup procedure most likely to be used is the rollback and recovery method. This method involves the dumping of the master file's contents and associated data structures onto a backup file. In the event of a loss of data, the dump is used together with the transaction log or file to reconstruct the master file.
Answer (B) is incorrect. It describes dual logging.
Answer (C) is incorrect. The grandfather-father-son technique is used as a backup procedure in batch-processing systems.
Answer (D) is incorrect. It is not a sufficient backup procedure for an online, real-time system. Often, tangible source documents do not exist in an online system.

10.3 Systems Security

7. Which of the following would **not** be appropriate to consider in the physical design of a data center?

A. Evaluation of potential risks from railroad lines and highways.

B. Use of biometric access systems.

C. Design of authorization tables for operating system access.

D. Inclusion of an uninterruptible power supply system and surge protection.

Answer (C) is correct.   *(CIA, adapted)*
REQUIRED: The inappropriate consideration in the physical design of a data center.
DISCUSSION: Authorization tables for operating system access address logical controls, not physical controls.
Answer (A) is incorrect. External risks should be evaluated to determine the center's location. Answer (B) is incorrect. Biometric access systems control physical access to the data center. These devices identify such unique physical qualities as fingerprints, voice patterns, and retinal patterns. Answer (D) is incorrect. Power supply systems and surge protection are included in data center design. Thus, two separate power lines, line conditioning equipment, and backup power are typical elements in the design.

8. Application control objectives do **not** normally include assurance that

A. Authorized transactions are completely processed once and only once.

B. Transaction data are complete and accurate.

C. Review and approval procedures for new systems are set by policy and adhered to.

D. Processing results are received by the intended user.

Answer (C) is correct.   *(CISA, adapted)*
REQUIRED: The assurance not provided by an application control.
DISCUSSION: Application controls provide reasonable assurance that the recording, processing, and reporting of data are properly performed. Review and approval procedures for new systems are among the general controls known as system software acquisition and maintenance controls.
Answer (A) is incorrect. An objective of application controls is that authorized transactions are completely processed once and only once. Answer (B) is incorrect. An objective of application controls is that transaction data is complete and accurate. Answer (D) is incorrect. An objective of application controls is that processing results are received by the intended user.

9. Authentication is the process by which the

A. System verifies that the user is entitled to enter the transaction requested.

B. System verifies the identity of the user.

C. User identifies him/herself to the system.

D. User indicates to the system that the transaction was processed correctly.

Answer (B) is correct.   *(CISA, adapted)*
REQUIRED: The definition of authentication.
DISCUSSION: Identification is the process of uniquely distinguishing one user from all others. Authentication is the process of determining that individuals are who they say they are. For example, a password may identify but not authenticate its user if it is known by more than one individual.
Answer (A) is incorrect. Authentication involves verifying the identity of the user. This process does not necessarily confirm the functions the user is authorized to perform. Answer (C) is incorrect. User identification to the system does not imply that the system has verified the identity of the user. Answer (D) is incorrect. This procedure is an application control for accuracy of the transaction.

10. Which of the following issues would be of most concern to an auditor relating to an organization's Internet security policy?

A. Auditor documentation.

B. System efficiency.

C. Data integrity.

D. Rejected and suspense item controls.

Answer (C) is correct.   *(Publisher, adapted)*
REQUIRED: The item of most concern to the auditor relating to Internet security.
DISCUSSION: Controls are intended to ensure the integrity, confidentiality, and availability of information. An auditor relies on the integrity of the system's data and programs in making critical decisions throughout the audit process.
Answer (A) is incorrect. Auditor documentation is not as crucial as data integrity. Answer (B) is incorrect. Efficiency does not affect the basis for critical auditor decisions using information provided by the system. Answer (D) is incorrect. Rejected and suspense item controls represent a portion of the techniques used to ensure data integrity.

11. Passwords for personal computer software programs are designed to prevent

    A. Inaccurate processing of data.

    B. Unauthorized access to the computer.

    C. Incomplete updating of data files.

    D. Unauthorized use of the software.

Answer (D) is correct. *(CIA, adapted)*
    REQUIRED: The function of passwords.
    DISCUSSION: The use of passwords is an effective control in an online system to prevent unauthorized access to computer files. Lists of authorized users are maintained in the computer. The entry of passwords or ID numbers; a prearranged act of personal questions; and use of badges, magnetic cards, or optically scanned cards may be combined to avoid unauthorized access.
    Answer (A) is incorrect. Passwords concern authorization, not accuracy of data. Answer (B) is incorrect. Passwords do not prevent physical access to the computer. Answer (C) is incorrect. Passwords concern authorization, not completeness of data.

12. As organizations become more computer integrated, management is becoming increasingly concerned with the quality of access controls to the computer system. Which of the following provides the most accountability?

	Option I	Option II	Option III	Option IV
Restrict access by:	Individuals	Groups	Individuals	Departments
Identify computer data at:	Field level	Workstation	Workstation	Individual record level
Restrict access:	Need to know	Right to know	Normal processing by employee type	Items identified as processed by department
Identify users by:	Password	Password	Key access to workstation, or password on workstation	Departmental password
Limit ability to:	Delete, add, or modify data	Add or delete files	Add, delete, or modify data stored at workstation	Add, delete, or modify data normally processed by department

    A. Option I.

    B. Option II.

    C. Option III.

    D. Option IV.

Answer (A) is correct. *(CIA, adapted)*
    REQUIRED: The access control option providing the most accountability.
    DISCUSSION: Access should be limited to those whose activities necessitate access to the computer system. Moreover, the degree of access allowed should be consistent with an individual's responsibilities. Restricting access to particular individuals rather than groups or departments clearly establishes specific accountability. Not everyone in a group will need access or the same degree of access. Thus, passwords assigned to individuals should be required for identification of users by the system. Furthermore, data should be restricted at the field level, not the workstation level. It may be possible to limit access to a workstation, but most workstations are connected to larger mainframe or network databases. Thus, the security at the workstation level only would be insufficient.

10.4 Databases

13. Of the following, the greatest advantage of a database (server) architecture is

    A. Data redundancy can be reduced.

    B. Conversion to a database system is inexpensive and can be accomplished quickly.

    C. Multiple occurrences of data items are useful for consistency checking.

    D. Backup and recovery procedures are minimized.

Answer (A) is correct. *(CIA, adapted)*
    REQUIRED: The greatest advantage of a database architecture.
    DISCUSSION: Data organized in files and used by the organization's various applications programs are collectively known as a database. In a database system, storage structures are created that render the applications programs independent of the physical or logical arrangement of the data. Each data item has a standard definition, name, and format, and related items are linked by a system of pointers. The programs therefore need only to specify data items by name, not by location. A database management system handles retrieval and storage. Because separate files for different applications programs are unnecessary, data redundancy can be substantially reduced.
    Answer (B) is incorrect. Conversion to a database is often costly and time consuming. Answer (C) is incorrect. A traditional flat-file system, not a database, has multiple occurrences of data items. Answer (D) is incorrect. Given the absence of data redundancy and the quick propagation of data errors throughout applications, backup and recovery procedures are just as critical in a database as in a flat-file system.

14. In an inventory system on a database management system (DBMS), one stored record contains part number, part name, part color, and part weight. These individual items are called

A. Fields.

B. Stored files.

C. Bytes.

D. Occurrences.

Answer (A) is correct. *(CIA, adapted)*
REQUIRED: The term for the data elements in a record.
DISCUSSION: A record is a collection of related data items (fields). A field (data item) is a group of characters representing one unit of information.
Answer (B) is incorrect. A file is a group or set of related records ordered to facilitate processing. Answer (C) is incorrect. A byte is a group of bits (binary digits). It represents one character. Answer (D) is incorrect. Occurrences is not a meaningful term in this context.

15. An inventory clerk, using a computer terminal, views the following on screen: part number, part description, quantity on hand, quantity on order, order quantity, and reorder point for a particular inventory item. Collectively, these data make up a

A. Field.

B. File.

C. Database.

D. Record.

Answer (D) is correct. *(CIA, adapted)*
REQUIRED: The term for the collection of data described.
DISCUSSION: A record is a collection of related data items (fields). A field (data item) is a group of characters representing one unit of information. The part number, part description, etc., are represented by fields.
Answer (A) is incorrect. Field refers to a single data item. Answer (B) is incorrect. File refers to multiple records. Answer (C) is incorrect. Database refers to multiple files.

16. Which of the following is the elementary unit of data storage used to represent individual attributes of an entity?

A. Database.

B. Data field.

C. File.

D. Record.

Answer (B) is correct. *(CIA, adapted)*
REQUIRED: The elementary unit of data storage that is used to represent individual attributes of an entity.
DISCUSSION: A data item (or field) is a group of characters. It is used to represent individual attributes of an entity, such as an employee's address. A field is an item in a record.
Answer (A) is incorrect. A database is an organized collection of files. Answer (C) is incorrect. A file is a collection of records. Answer (D) is incorrect. A record is a collection of data items.

17. A file-oriented approach to data storage requires a primary record key for each file. Which of the following is a primary record key?

A. The vendor number in an accounts payable master file.

B. The vendor number in a closed purchase order transaction file.

C. The vendor number in an open purchase order master file.

D. All of the answers are correct.

Answer (A) is correct. *(CIA, adapted)*
REQUIRED: The item(s) used as a primary record key.
DISCUSSION: The primary record key uniquely identifies each record in a file. Because there is only one record for each vendor in an accounts payable master file, the vendor number would be the appropriate key.
Answer (B) is incorrect. Purchase order files can have multiple purchase orders made out to the same vendor. The primary key in purchase order files would be the purchase order number because it is the only unique identifier for the record. Answer (C) is incorrect. Purchase order files can have multiple purchase orders made out to the same vendor. The primary key in purchase order files would be the purchase order number because it is the only unique identifier for the record. Answer (D) is incorrect. Not all of the answer choices are correct.

18. A business is designing its storage for accounts receivable information. What data file concepts should be used to provide the ability to answer customer inquiries as they are received?

- A. Sequential storage and chains.

- B. Sequential storage and indexes.

- C. Record keys, indexes, and pointers.

- D. Inverted file structure, indexes, and internal labels.

Answer (C) is correct. *(CIA, adapted)*
REQUIRED: The data file concepts needed to answer customer inquiries as they are received.
DISCUSSION: A record key is an attribute that uniquely identifies or distinguishes each record from the others. An index is a table listing storage locations for attributes, often including those other than the unique record key attribute. A pointer is a data item that indicates the physical address of the next logically related record.
Answer (A) is incorrect. The ability to respond immediately to customers requires direct access. Answer (B) is incorrect. The ability to respond immediately to customers requires direct access. Answer (D) is incorrect. Internal labels are used to indicate various things to the computer, such as the contents of various types of data storage media, the beginning of each file (with identification information), and the end of each file. However, they do not provide information for locating specific records in a file. An inverted file structure (inverted list) is an index based on a secondary key, for example, years of experience rather than an employee number (the primary key).

10.5 Software Licensing

19. Which of the following would be the most appropriate starting point for a compliance evaluation of software licensing requirements for an organization with more than 15,000 computer workstations?

- A. Determine if software installation is controlled centrally or distributed throughout the organization.

- B. Determine what software packages have been installed on the organization's computers and the number of each package installed.

- C. Determine how many copies of each software package have been purchased by the organization.

- D. Determine what mechanisms have been installed for monitoring software usage.

Answer (A) is correct. *(CIA, adapted)*
REQUIRED: The most appropriate starting point for a compliance evaluation of software licensing requirements in a large entity.
DISCUSSION: The logical starting point is to determine the point(s) of control. Evidence of license compliance can then be assessed. For example, to shorten the installation time for revised software in a network, an organization may implement electronic software distribution (ESD), which is the computer-to-computer installation of software on workstations. Instead of weeks, software distribution can be accomplished in hours or days and can be controlled centrally. Another advantage of ESD is that it permits tracking or metering of PC program licenses.
Answer (B) is incorrect. Before taking this step, an auditor should first determine whether installation is controlled centrally. This determination affects how the auditor will gather information about the installed software. Answer (C) is incorrect. This procedure helps an auditor determine whether software was legitimately purchased. However, a better starting point is determining where the software is installed. Answer (D) is incorrect. Monitoring usage is not as important as determining installation procedures when evaluating licensing compliance.

20. Use of unlicensed software in an organization

- I. Increases the risk of introducing viruses into the organization

- II. Is not a serious exposure if only low-cost software is involved

- III. Can be detected by software checking routines that run from a network server

- A. I only.

- B. I and II only.

- C. I, II, and III.

- D. I and III only.

Answer (D) is correct. *(CIA, adapted)*
REQUIRED: The true statement(s) about unlicensed software.
DISCUSSION: Antivirus measures should include strict adherence to software acquisition policies. Unlicensed software is less likely to have come from reputable vendors and to have been carefully tested. Special software is available to test software in use to determine whether it has been authorized.

10.6 Web Infrastructure

21. The Internet consists of a series of networks that include

    A. Gateways to allow personal computers to connect to mainframe computers.

    B. Bridges to direct messages through the optimum data path.

    C. Repeaters to physically connect separate local area networks (LANs).

    D. Routers to strengthen data signals between distant computers.

Answer (A) is correct. *(CIA, adapted)*
    REQUIRED: The composition of the Internet.
    DISCUSSION: The Internet facilitates information transfer between computers. Gateways are hardware or software products that allow translation between two different protocol families. For example, a gateway can be used to exchange messages between different email systems.
    Answer (B) is incorrect. Routers are used to determine the best path for data. Answer (C) is incorrect. Bridges connect LANs. Answer (D) is incorrect. Repeaters strengthen signals.

22. Which of the following is true concerning HTML?

    A. The acronym stands for HyperText Material Listing.

    B. The language is among the most difficult to learn.

    C. The language is independent of hardware and software.

    D. HTML is the only language that can be used for Internet documents.

Answer (C) is correct. *(Publisher, adapted)*
    REQUIRED: The true statement concerning HTML.
    DISCUSSION: HTML is the most popular language for authoring web pages. It is hardware and software independent, which means that it can be read by several different applications and on many different kinds of computer operating systems. HTML uses tags to mark information for proper display on web pages.
    Answer (A) is incorrect. HTML is the acronym for Hypertext Markup Language. Answer (B) is incorrect. The language is relatively easy to learn. Almost anyone can learn and use HTML, not just computer programmers. Answer (D) is incorrect. A number of other languages can be used for Internet transmissions, including JAVA and XML.

23. Which of the following is a **false** statement about XBRL?

    A. XBRL is freely licensed.

    B. XBRL facilitates the automatic exchange of information.

    C. XBRL is used primarily in the U.S.

    D. XBRL is designed to work with a variety of software applications.

Answer (C) is correct. *(Publisher, adapted)*
    REQUIRED: The false statement about XBRL.
    DISCUSSION: XBRL stands for eXtensible Business Reporting Language. It is being developed for business and accounting applications. It is an XML-based application used to create, exchange, and analyze financial reporting information and is being developed for worldwide use.
    Answer (A) is incorrect. The AICPA-led consortium that developed XBRL has promoted the application as a freely licensed product. Answer (B) is incorrect. XBRL will facilitate the exchange of information. Answer (D) is incorrect. XBRL will allow exchange of data across many platforms and will soon be integrated into accounting software applications and products.

Use the additional questions in Gleim *CIA Test Prep* Software to create Test Sessions that emulate Pearson VUE!

APPENDIX A
IIA EXAM CONTENT OUTLINES
AND CROSS-REFERENCES

For your convenience, we have reproduced verbatim The IIA's exam content outlines for this CIA exam part from its website (www.globaliia.org/certification/cia-certification/pages/exam-syllabus.aspx). Note that those levels labeled "proficiency level" mean the candidate should have a thorough understanding and the ability to apply concepts in the topics listed. Those levels labeled "awareness level" mean the candidate must have a grasp of the terminology and fundamentals of the concepts listed. We also have provided cross-references to the study units and subunits in this book that correspond to The IIA's more detailed coverage. If one entry appears above a list, it applies to all items. Please visit The IIA's website for updates and more information about the exam. Rely on the Gleim materials to pass each part of the exam. We have researched and studied The IIA's content outlines as well as questions from prior exams to provide you with an excellent review program.

PART 3 – BUSINESS ANALYSIS AND INFORMATION TECHNOLOGY

A. **BUSINESS PROCESSES (15 - 25%)**

1. Quality management (e.g., TQM) (awareness level) (1.1-1.4)
2. The International Organization for Standardization (ISO) framework (awareness level) (1.5)
3. Forecasting (awareness level) (1.6-1.9)
4. Project management techniques (proficiency level) (1.10)
5. Business process analysis (e.g., workflow analysis and bottleneck management, theory of constraints) (proficiency level) (1.11-1.13)
6. Inventory management techniques and concepts (proficiency level) (2.1, 2.2)
7. Marketing -- pricing objectives and policies (awareness level) (2.3)
8. Marketing -- supply chain management (awareness level) (2.4)
9. Human Resources (Individual performance management and measurement, supervision, environmental factors that affect performance, facilitation technique, personnel sourcing/staffing, training and development, safety) (proficiency level) (2.5)
10. Balanced scorecard (awareness level) (2.6)

B. **FINANCIAL ACCOUNTING AND FINANCE (15 - 25%)**

1. Basic concepts and underlying principles of financial accounting (e.g., statements, terminology, relationships) (proficiency level) (3.1-3.4, 3.10, 3.11)
2. Intermediate concepts of financial accounting (e.g., bonds, leases, pensions, intangible assets, R&D) (awareness level) (3.5-3.9, 3.12-3.15, 4.1-4.9)
3. Advanced concepts of financial accounting (e.g., consolidation, partnerships, foreign currency transactions) (awareness level) (4.10-4.13)
4. Financial statement analysis (proficiency level) (5.1-5.6)
5. Cost of capital evaluation (awareness level) (5.11)
6. Types of debt and equity (awareness level) (5.9, 5.10)
7. Financial instruments (e.g., derivatives) (awareness level) (5.7, 5.8)
8. Cash management (treasury functions) (awareness level) (5.12)

9. Valuation models (awareness level)

    a. Inventory valuation (3.8-3.9)
    b. Business valuation (5.5)

10. Business development life cycles (awareness level) (5.13)

C. MANAGERIAL ACCOUNTING (10 - 20%)

1. Cost concepts (e.g., absorption, variable, fixed) (proficiency level) (6.1-6.3)
2. Capital budgeting (awareness level) (6.4)
3. Operating budget (proficiency level) (6.5, 6.6)
4. Transfer pricing (awareness level) (6.7)
5. Cost-volume-profit analysis (awareness level) (6.8)
6. Relevant cost (awareness level) (6.9)
7. Costing systems (e.g., activity-based, standard) (awareness level) (6.10-6.12)
8. Responsibility accounting (awareness level) (6.13)

D. REGULATORY, LEGAL, AND ECONOMICS (5 - 15%) (awareness level)

1. Impact of government legislation and regulation on business (7.1)
2. Trade legislation and regulations (7.2)
3. Taxation schemes (7.4)
4. Contracts (7.7)
5. Nature and rules of legal evidence (7.6)
6. Key economic indicators (7.3, 7.5)

E. INFORMATION TECHNOLOGY – IT (30 - 40%) (awareness level)

1. Control frameworks (e.g., COBIT) (8.1)
2. Data and network communications/connections (e.g., LAN, VAN, and WAN) (8.4)
3. Electronic funds transfer (EFT) (8.5)
4. e-Commerce (8.6)
5. Electronic data interchange (EDI) (8.7)
6. Functional areas of IT operations (e.g., data center operations) (9.1)
7. Encryption (9.2)
8. Information protection (e.g., viruses, privacy) (9.3)
9. Evaluate investment in IT (cost of ownership) (9.4)
10. Enterprise-wide resource planning (ERP) software (e.g., SAP R/3) (9.5)
11. Operating systems (9.6)
12. Application development (9.7-9.9)
13. Voice communications (10.1)
14. Contingency planning (10.2)
15. Systems security (e.g., firewalls, access control) (10.3)
16. Databases (10.4)
17. Software licensing (10.5)
18. Web infrastructure (10.6)

APPENDIX B
IIA EXAMINATION BIBLIOGRAPHY

The Institute has prepared a listing of references for the CIA exam, reproduced below. These publications have been chosen by the Professional Certifications Department as reasonably representative of the common body of knowledge for internal auditors. However, all of the information in these texts will not be tested. When possible, questions will be written based on the information contained in the suggested reference list. This bibliography for Part 3 is listed to give you an overview of the scope of the exam. The IIA also indicates that the examination scope includes

1. Articles from *Internal Auditor* (The IIA periodical)
2. IIA research reports
3. IIA pronouncements, e.g., The IIA Code of Ethics and SIASs
4. Past published CIA examinations

The IIA bibliography is reproduced for your information only. The texts you will need to acquire (use) to prepare for the CIA exam will depend on many factors, including

1. Innate ability
2. Length of time out of school
3. Thoroughness of your undergraduate education
4. Familiarity with internal auditing due to relevant experience

SUGGESTED REFERENCES FOR PART 3 OF THE CIA EXAM

Part 3: Business Analysis and Information Technology

Practice Guides of *International Professional Practices Framework (IPPF)*, including Global Technology Audit Guide (GTAG) and Guides to the Assessment of IT Risk (GAIT) series, 2009, The Institute of Internal Auditors, Inc., www.globaliia.org/standards-guidance/pages/standards-and-guidance-ippf.aspx.

Sawyer's Internal Auditing, 5th Ed., L.B. Sawyer, et al., 2003, The Institute of Internal Auditors, Inc., www.globaliia.org/knowledge/pages/bookstore.aspx.

Internal Auditing Manual, 2004 Ed., Stephen Head, WG&L Financial Reporting & Management, ria.thomsonreuters.com/estore/.

Management, 10th Ed., Robert Kreitner, 2008, Houghton Mifflin Co., www.cengage.com/southwestern/.

Accounting Principles, with CD, 9th Ed., Jerry J. Weygandt, Donald E. Kieso, Paul D. Kimmel, 2008, John Wiley & Sons, www.wiley.com.

International Financial Reporting Standards (IFRS), 2008, International Accounting Standards Board (IASB), www.iasb.org.

Information Systems Control and Audit, Ron A. Weber, 1998, Prentice Hall, www.mypearsonstore.com.

Internal Auditing: An Integrated Approach, 2nd Ed., Richard Cascarino and Sandy van Esch, 2006, Juta and Co. Ltd., www.globaliia.org/knowledge/pages/bookstore.aspx.

AVAILABILITY OF PUBLICATIONS

The listing above presents only some of the current technical literature available, and The IIA does not carry all of the reference books. Quantity discounts are provided by The IIA. Request a current catalog by mail, call, or visit www.globaliia.org/knowledge/pages/bookstore.aspx.

The IIARF Bookstore
1650 Bluegrass Lakes Pkwy
Alpharetta, GA 30004-7714
iiapubs@pbd.com
(877) 867-4957 (toll-free in U.S. and Canada) or (770) 280-4183

Contact the publisher directly if you cannot obtain the desired texts from The IIA or your local bookstore. Begin your study program with the Gleim CIA Review, which most candidates find sufficient. If you need additional reference material, borrow books from colleagues, professors, or a library.

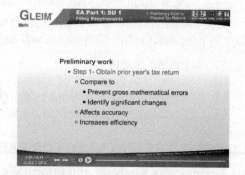
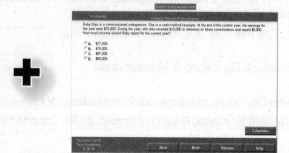
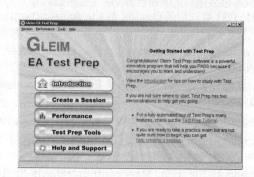

APPENDIX C
SAMPLE FINANCIAL STATEMENTS

We have annotated these audited financial statements to show how the various elements interrelate. For instance, (a) is the year-end balance of cash and equivalents; this annotation is found on both the balance sheet and the statement of cash flows. (See Subunits 10 and 11 in Study Unit 3 for detailed explanations of financial statement elements.)

Consolidated Statement of Operations

FORD MOTOR COMPANY AND SUBSIDIARIES
For the Years Ended December 31, 2011, 2010, and 2009
(in millions, except per share amounts)

	2011	2010	2009
Revenues			
Automotive	US $128,168	US $119,280	US $103,868
Financial Services	8,096	9,674	12,415
Total revenues	136,264	128,954	116,283
Costs and expenses			
Automotive cost of sales	113,345	104,451	98,866
Selling, administrative and other expenses	11,578	11,909	13,029
Interest expense	4,431	6,152	6,790
Financial Services provision for credit and insurance losses	(33)	(216)	1,030
Total costs and expenses	129,321	122,296	119,715
Automotive interest income and other non-operating income/(expense), net	825	(362)	5,284
Financial Services other income/(loss), net	413	315	552
Equity in net income/(loss) of affiliated companies	500	538	195
Income/(Loss) before income taxes	8,681	7,149	2,599
Provision for/(Benefit from) income taxes	(11,541)	592	(113)
Income/(Loss) from continuing operations	20,222	6,557	2,712
Income/(Loss) from discontinued operations	–	–	5
Net income/(loss)	20,222	6,557	2,717
Less: Income/(Loss) attributable to noncontrolling interests	9	(4)	–
Net income/(loss) attributable to Ford Motor Company	US $ 20,213	US $ 6,561	US $ 2,717
NET INCOME/(LOSS) ATTRIBUTABLE TO FORD MOTOR COMPANY			
Income/(Loss) from continuing operations	US $ 20,213	US $ 6,561	US $ 2,712
Income/(Loss) from discontinued operations	–	–	5
Net income/(loss) attributable to Ford Motor Company	US $ 20,213 (m)	US $ 6,561 (n)	US $ 2,717 (o)
AMOUNTS PER SHARE ATTRIBUTABLE TO FORD MOTOR COMPANY COMMON AND CLASS B STOCK			
Basic income/(loss)			
Income/(Loss) from continuing operations	US $ 5.33	US $ 1.90	US $ 0.91
Income/(Loss) from discontinued operations	–	–	–
Net income/(loss)	US $ 5.33	US $ 1.90	US $ 0.91
Diluted income/(loss)			
Income/(Loss) from continuing operations	US $ 4.94	US $ 1.66	US $ 0.86
Income/(Loss) from discontinued operations	–	–	–
Net income/(loss)	US $ 4.94	US $ 1.66	US $ 0.86
Cash dividends declared	US $ 0.05	US $ –	US $ –

Consolidated Balance Sheet

FORD MOTOR COMPANY AND SUBSIDIARIES
(in millions)

	December 31,	
	2011	2010
Assets		
Cash and cash equivalents	US $ 17,148 (a)	US $ 14,805 (b)
Marketable securities	18,618	20,765
Finance receivables, net	69,976	70,070
Other receivables, net	8,565	8,381
Net investment in operating leases	12,838	11,675
Inventories	5,901	5,917
Equity in net assets of affiliated companies	2,936	2,569
Net property	22,371	23,179
Deferred income taxes	15,125	2,003
Net intangible assets	100	102
Other assets	4,770	5,221
Total assets	US $178,348	US $164,687
Liabilities		
Payables	US $ 17,724	US $ 16,362
Accrued liabilities and deferred revenue	45,369	43,844
Debt	99,488	103,988
Deferred income taxes	696	1,135
Total liabilities	163,277	165,329
Equity		
Capital stock		
Common Stock, par value US $0.01 per share (3,745 million shares issued)	37 (c)	37 (d)
Class B Stock, par value US $0.01 per share (71 million shares issued)	1 (c)	1 (d)
Capital in excess of par value of stock	20,905 (e)	20,803 (f)
Retained earnings/(Accumulated deficit)	12,985 (g)	(7,038)(h)
Accumulated other comprehensive income/(loss)	(18,734) (i)	(14,313) (j)
Treasury stock	(166) (k)	(163) (l)
Total equity/(deficit) attributable to Ford Motor Company	15,028	(673)
Equity/(Deficit) attributable to noncontrolling interests	43	31
Total equity/(deficit)	15,071	(642)
Total liabilities and equity	US $178,348	US $164,687

Consolidated Statement of Cash Flows

FORD MOTOR COMPANY AND SUBSIDIARIES
For the Years Ended December 31, 2011, 2010, and 2009
(in millions)

	2011	2010	2009
Cash flows from operating activities of continuing operations			
Net Income/(loss) attributable to Ford Motor Company	US $ 20,213 (m)	US $ 6,561 (n)	US $ 2,717 (o)
(Income)/Loss of discontinued operations	–	–	(5)
Depreciation and special tools amortization	5,376	5,900	7,667
Other amortization	(1,120)	(316)	(1,087)
Impairment charges	–	–	311
Held-for-sale impairment	–	–	650
Provision for credit and insurance losses	(33)	(216)	1,030
Net (gain)/loss on extinguishment of debt	128	983	(4,737)
Net (gain)/loss on investment securities	82	(83)	(410)
Net (gain)/loss on pension and OPEB curtailment	–	(29)	(4)
Net (gain)/loss on settlement of U.S. hourly retiree health care obligation	–	–	248
Net losses/(earnings) from equity investments in excess of dividends received	(169)	(198)	(45)
Foreign currency adjustments	(37)	(348)	92
Net (gain)/loss on sale of businesses	(421)	18	33
Stock compensation	171	34	29
Cash changes in operating assets and liabilities were as follows:			
Provision for deferred income taxes	11,071	34	(746)
Decrease/(Increase) in equity method investments	–	–	74
Decrease/(Increase) in accounts receivable and other assets	(927)	781	8,283
Decrease/(Increase) in inventory	(367)	(903)	2,201
Increase/(Decrease) in accounts payable and accrued and other liabilities	(680)	(704)	(2,832)
Reclassification from investing to operating cash flows:			
Wholesale receivables	(2,010)	–	–
Finance receivables	21	–	–
Other	628	(37)	2,008
Net cash (used in)/provided by operating activities	9,784	11,477	15,477
Cash flows from investing activities of continuing operations			
Capital expenditures	(4,293)	(4,092)	(4,059)
Acquisitions of retail and other finance receivables and operating leases	(35,866)	(28,873)	(26,392)
Collections of retail and other finance receivables and operating leases	33,964	37,757	39,884
Purchases of securities	(68,723)	(100,150)	(78,200)
Sales and maturities of securities	70,795	101,077	74,344
Proceeds from sales of retail and other finance receivables and operating leases	–	–	911
Proceeds from sale of businesses	333	1,318	382
Settlements of derivatives	353	(37)	478
Elimination of cash balances upon disposition of discontinued/held-for-sale operations	(69)	(456)	–
Receipt of cash from purchase of Bordeaux	–	94	–
Cash change due to deconsolidation of joint ventures	–	–	(343)
Other	465	270	(386)
Net cash (used in)/provided by investing activities	(3,041)	6,908	6,619
Cash flows from financing activities of continuing operations			
Sales of Common Stock	–	1,339	2,450
Changes in short-term debt	2,841	(1,754)	(5,881)
Proceeds from issuance of other debt	35,921	30,821	45,993
Principle payments on other debt	(43,095)	(47,625)	(61,822)
Payments on notes/transfer of cash equivalents to the UAW Voluntary Employee Benefit Association ("VEBA") Trust	–	(7,302)	(2,574)
Other	92	100	(996)
Net cash (used in)/provided by financing activities	(4,241)	(24,421)	(22,830)
Effect of exchange rate changes on cash	(159)	(53)	454
Cumulative correction of Financial Services prior-period error	–	–	(630)
Net increase/(decrease) in cash and cash equivalents	US $ 2,343	US $ (6,089)	US $ (910)
Cash and cash equivalents at January 1	US $ 14,805	US $ 20,894	US $ 21,804
Net increase/(decrease) in cash and cash equivalents	2,343	(6,089)	(910)
Cash and cash equivalents at December 31	US $ 17,148 (a)	US $ 14,805 (b)	US $ 20,894

Consolidated Statement of Equity

FORD MOTOR COMPANY AND SUBSIDIARIES
For the Years Ended December 31, 2011, 2010, and 2009
(in millions)

	Capital Stock	Cap. in Excess of Par Value of Stock	Retained Earnings/ (Accumulated Deficit)	Accumulated Other Comprehensive Income/(Loss)	Treasury Stock	Total	Equity/ (Deficit) Attributable to Non-controlling Interests	Total Equity/ (Deficit)
YEAR ENDED DECEMBER 31, 2009								
Balance at beginning of year	US $24	US $10,875	US $(16,316)	US $(10,123)	US $(181)	US $(15,721)	US $ 350	US $(15,371)
Comprehensive income/(loss)								
Net income/(loss)	–	–	2,717 (o)	–	–	2,717	–	2,717
Foreign curr. translation (net of US $65 of tax)	–	–	–	2,235	–	2,235	–	2,235
Net gain/(loss) on derivative instruments (net of US $0 of tax)	–	–	–	(127)	–	(127)		(127)
Employee benefit related (net of US $302 of tax benefit & other)	–	–	–	(2,851)	–	(2,851)		(2,851)
Net holding gain/(loss) (net of US $0 of tax)	–	–	–	2	–	2	–	2
Comprehensive income/(loss)						1,976		1,976
Common Stock issued	10	5,911	–	–	–	5,921	–	5,921
Impact of deconsolidation of AutoAlliance International, Inc.	–	–	–	–	–	–	(269)	(269)
Treasury stock/other	–	–	–	–	4	4	(40)	(36)
Cash dividends declared	–	–	–	–	–	–	(3)	(3)
Balance at end of year	US $34	US $16,786	US $(13,599)	US $(10,864)	US $(177)	US $ (7,820)	US $ 38	US $ (7,782)
YEAR ENDED DECEMBER 31, 2010								
Balance at beginning of year	US $34	US $16,786	US $(13,599)	US $(10,864)	US $(177)	US $ (7,820)	US $ 38	US $ (7,782)
Comprehensive income/(loss)								
Net income/(loss)	–	–	6,561 (n)	–	–	6,561	(4)	6,557
Foreign curr. translation (net of US $2 of tax benefit)	–	–	–	(2,233)	–	(2,233)	(1)	(2,234)
Net gain/(loss) on derivative instruments (net of US $0 of tax)	–	–	–	(24)	–	(24)		(24)
Employee benefit related (net of US $222 of tax benefit & other)	–	–	–	(1,190)	–	(1,190)	–	(1,190)
Net holding gain/(loss) (net of US $0 of tax)	–	–	–	(2)	–	(2)	–	(2)
Comprehensive income/(loss)						3,112	(5)	3,107
Common Stock issued	4	4,017	–	–	–	4,021	–	4,021
Treasury stock/other	–	–	–	–	14	14	–	14
Cash dividends declared	–	–	–	–	–	–	(2)	(2)
Balance at end of year	US $38 (d)	US $20,803 (f)	US $ (7,038) (h)	US $(14,313) (j)	US $(163) (l)	US $ (673)	US $ 31	US $ (642)
YEAR ENDED DECEMBER 31, 2011								
Balance at beginning of year	US $38	US $20,803	US $ (7,038)	US $(14,313)	US $(163)	US $ (673)	US $ 31	US $ (642)
Comprehensive income/(loss)								
Net income/(loss)	–	–	20,213 (m)	–	–	20,213	9	20,222
Foreign curr. translation (net of US $2 of tax benefit)	–	–	–	(718)	–	(718)	(2)	(720)
Net gain/(loss) on derivative instruments (net of US $67 of tax benefit)	–	–	–	(152)	–	(152)	–	(152)
Employee benefit related (net of US $1,560 of tax benefit & other)	–	–	–	(3,553)	–	(3,553)		(3,553)
Net holding gain/(loss) (net of US $0 of tax)	–	–	–	2	–	2	–	2
Comprehensive income/(loss)						15,792	7	15,799
Common Stock issued	–	102	–	–	–	102	–	102
Treasury stock/other	–	–	–	–	(3)	(3)	5	2
Cash dividends declared	–	–	(190)	–	–	(190)		(190)
Balance at end of year	US $38 (c)	US $20,905 (e)	US $ 12,985 (g)	US $(18,734) (i)	US $(166) (k)	US $ 15,028	US $ 43	US $ 15,071

INDEX

GLEIM CPA REVIEW SYSTEM

All 4 sections, including Gleim Online, Review Books, *Test Prep Software Download*, *Simulation Wizard*, Audio Review, *CPA Review: A System for Success* Booklet, plus bonus Book Bag.

$989.95 x _____ = $_____

Also available by exam section (does not include Book Bag).

GLEIM CMA REVIEW SYSTEM

Includes: Gleim Online, Review Books, *Test Prep Software Download*, Audio Review, *Essay Wizard*, *CMA Review: A System for Success* Booklet, plus bonus Book Bag.

$739.95 x _____ = $_____

Also available by exam part (does not include Book Bag).

GLEIM CIA REVIEW SYSTEM

Includes: Gleim Online, Review Books, *Test Prep Software Download*, Audio Review, *CIA Review: A System for Success* Booklet, plus bonus Book Bag.

$824.95 x _____ = $_____

Also available by exam part (does not include Book Bag).

GLEIM EA REVIEW SYSTEM

Includes: Gleim Online, Review Books, *Test Prep Software Download*, Audio Review, *EA Review: A System for Success* Booklet, plus bonus Book Bag.

$629.95 x _____ = $_____

Also available by exam part (does not include Book Bag).

"THE GLEIM REVIEW SERIES" EXAM QUESTIONS AND EXPLANATIONS

Includes: 5 Books and *Test Prep Software Download*.

$112.25 x _____ = $_____

Also available by part.

GLEIM ONLINE CPE

Try a FREE 4-hour course at gleim.com/cpe
- Easy-to-Complete
- Informative
- Effective

Contact
GLEIM PUBLICATIONS
for further assistance:

gleim.com
800.874.5346
sales@gleim.com

SUBTOTAL $_____

Complete your
order on the
next page

GLEIM® PUBLICATIONS, INC.

P. O. Box 12848   Gainesville, FL 32604

TOLL FREE:	800.874.5346	Customer service is available (Eastern Time):
LOCAL:	352.375.0772	8:00 a.m. - 7:00 p.m., Mon. - Fri.
FAX:	352.375.6940	9:00 a.m. - 2:00 p.m., Saturday
INTERNET:	gleim.com	Please have your credit card ready,
EMAIL:	sales@gleim.com	or save time by ordering online!

SUBTOTAL (from previous page) $_____

Add applicable sales tax for shipments within Florida. _____

Shipping (nonrefundable)   14.00

TOTAL $_____

Email us for prices/instructions on shipments outside the 48 contiguous states, or simply order online.

NAME (please print) _____

ADDRESS _____ Apt. _____
(street address required for UPS/Federal Express)

CITY_____ STATE_____ ZIP_____

_____ MC/VISA/DISC/AMEX _____ Check/M.O. Daytime Telephone (_____)_____

Credit Card No. _____ - _____ - _____ - _____

Exp. ____/____ Signature _____
Month / Year

Email address _____

1. We process and ship orders daily, within one business day over 98.8% of the time. Call by 3:00 pm for same day service.

2. Gleim Publications, Inc. guarantees the immediate refund of all resalable texts, unopened and un-downloaded Test Prep Software, and unopened and un-downloaded audios returned within 30 days. Accounting and Academic Test Prep online courses may be canceled within 30 days if no more than the first study unit or lesson has been accessed. In addition, Online CPE courses may be canceled within 30 days if no more than the Introductory Study Questions have been accessed. Accounting Practice Exams may be canceled within 30 days of purchase if the Practice Exam has not been started. Aviation online courses may be canceled within 30 days if no more than two study units have been accessed. This policy applies only to products that are purchased directly from Gleim Publications, Inc. No refunds will be provided on opened or downloaded Test Prep Software or audios, partial returns of package sets, or shipping and handling charges. Any freight charges incurred for returned or refused packages will be the purchaser's responsibility.

3. Please PHOTOCOPY this order form for others.

4. No CODs. Orders from individuals must be prepaid.

Subject to change without notice. 02/12

For updates and other important information, visit our website.

GLEIM
KNOWLEDGE
TRANSFER
SYSTEMS®

gleim.com